JOHN WILLIS'

THEATRE WORLD

1978–1979 SEASON

VOLUME 35

CROWN PUBLISHERS, INC.
ONE PARK AVENUE
NEW YORK, NEW YORK 10016

PHILIP ANGLIM and CAROLE SHELLEY
in "The Elephant Man"
1979 winner of Drama Critics Circle Award, and "Tony" for Best Play

CONTENTS

EDITOR: JOHN WILLIS

Assistant Editor: Stanley Reeves

Staff: Alberto Cabrera, Maltier Hagan, Don Nute, William Schelble

Staff Photographers: Joseph Abeles, Bert Andrews, Van Williams

THE SEASON IN REVIEW
June 1, 1978–May 31, 1979

For the sixth consecutive year, both Broadway and the road enjoyed a record-breaking season. In spite of continuing inflation and the soaring prices of tickets ($25 top), attendance showed a healthy increase. The New York League of Theatres reported that during the last six years attendance has risen 81%. *Variety's* tabulations show that there were more "playing weeks" this season than in any other from their over 40 years of records. The touring companies, mostly musicals with major stars, surpassed Broadway in boxoffice receipts and in cultivation of new audiences. The 13 hold-overs from previous seasons caused a theatre shortage that may have frustrated prospective new productions but pleased both theatre owners and working actors. Fortunately, the prolonged newspaper strike of 88 days (August–October 1978) had little effect on the theatre boxoffices. TV and radio advertising helped keep the public well informed. National and international television advertising also increased attendance during the entire season. Because of mounting production costs, there was a tendency toward an increased number of New York previews in preference to more expensive out-of-town try-outs. Film companies became more interested in legitimate productions as future properties and invested more heavily on Broadway than in the past.

Of this season's 50 productions (only 5 revivals), 29 were straight plays, 17 were musicals, 2 were revues, and 2 were solo performances. The quality was generally mediocre, but, as always, there were several meritorious productions, primarily British imports. "The Elephant Man" (transplanted from Off-Broadway) received the New York Drama Critics Circle citation and 3 "Tony" Awards: Best Play, Outstanding Direction, Outstanding Actress (Carole Shelley tied with Constance Cummings of "Wings," another acclaimed play). Philip Anglim also gave a memorable performance in the title role. Other praise-worthy plays were "Whose Life Is It Anyway?" for which Tom Conti received a "Tony" for Outstanding Actor of the season; "Bedroom Farce" with a delightful English cast, two of whom (Joan Hickson, Michael Gough) won "Tonys" for outstanding featured performances. Limited, but successful runs were enjoyed by Jack Lemmon in "Tribute," Henry Fonda and Jane Alexander in "The First Monday in October," Alec McCowen in "St. Mark's Gospel," Rex Harrison and Claudette Colbert in "The Kingfisher." However, this season, stars in inferior vehicles did not guarantee a hit. Among those unfortunates were Julie Harris, Liv Ullmann, James Mason, Joel Grey, Alexis Smith, Bruce Dern, and Sammy Davis, Jr. Additional performers worth noting were Frances Sternhagen, Joseph Maher, Edward James Olmos, Laurie Kennedy, George Grizzard, Susan Littler, Mary-Joan Negro, Max Wright, Michael Moriarty, Fred Gwynne, and Michael Jeter.

Perhaps exorbitant production costs were responsible for the dearth of musicals this season. There were fewer musicals and more failures of musical productions than in many previous years. Several, however, might have had lengthier runs if they had had more intensive promotional campaigns. The uniquely enjoyable and overwhelming "Sweeney Todd" was the recipient of 8 "Tonys," as well as the NY Drama Critics Circle and Drama Desk awards. It was cited as Best Musical, and its stars, Angela Lansbury and Len Cariou, won "Tonys" for outstanding performers in a musical. It also had impressive performances by Victor Garber, Sarah Rice, and Ken Jennings. Outstanding Featured Performer "Tonys" went to Carlin Glynn and Henderson Forsythe in the highly entertaining "The Best Little Whorehouse in Texas." Dorothy Loudon was excellent in the beautifully nostalgic and "Tony" Award-winning choreography of Michael Bennett's "Ballroom." Another memorable performance was given by Charles Repole in "Whoopee!" Joel Grey received critical applause in "The Grand Tour," as did Lucie Arnaz and Robert Klein in "They're Playing Our Song," Gregory Hines in "Eubie!," and Maxine Sullivan in "My Old Friends." Other outstanding musical performers were Ron Holgate, Florence Lacey, Millicent Martin, Don Scardino, and Richard Cox.

Off-Broadway had a greater number of productions this season than last. Although there were fewer hits, there were several artistic successes, and several transfers to Broadway. Once again the Pulitzer Prize went to an Off-Broadway play: Sam Shepard's "Buried Child." The only musical hit was Gretchen Cryer in "I'm Getting My Act Together . . ." that was transferred from the Public Theater for an open-end run. Other New York Shakespeare Festival productions did not fare as well this season. Its new company of black and Hispanic actors to perform the classics was a great disappointment. However, the Public's production of "Taken in Marriage" had excellent performances by Colleen Dewhurst, Dixie Carter, Kathleen Quinlan, Meryl Streep, and Elizabeth Wilson. For other nonprofit organizations it was an equally uninspired and uninspiring season. Among the more commendable productions were "Talley's Folley" with Judd Hirsch and Trish Hawkins, "Getting Out" with a notable performance by Susan Kingsley, "On Golden Pond," "The Price" with Fritz Weaver and an exemplary supporting cast, "Strider" with beautiful ensemble work, "Tip-Toes," "Chincilla," "The Diary of Anne Frank" with Eli Wallach and Anne Jackson never better, "Spring Awakening," "Are You Now or Have You Ever Been," "Piano Bar," "Rear Column," "An Evening with Quentin Crisp," and Comedie Francaise productions of "The Misanthrope" and "A Flea in Her Ear." Other Off-Broadway performers who should be acknowledged are Christine Lahti, Dan Lauria, Gordon Chater, William Hurt, Sharon Madden, John Monteith, Suzanne Rand, Russ Thacker, Kelly Bishop, John Shea, Boyd Gaines, Tom Aldredge, Jose Ferrer, Morgan Freeman, Shirley Knight, Patricia Elliott, Pamela Burrell, Hector Mercado, Lorna Johnson, and Michael Cristofer.

Other notable events during the season that should be reported are: Actors Equity's continuing fight with agents and also with the Off-Off-Broadway Alliance. TKTS (Broadway's cut-rate ticket booth) accounted for 8% of this season's revenue. Sunday matinees became more profitable so Monday nights became dark for many houses. The Apollo, after 40 years as a 42nd Street movie house, was reconverted to a legitimate theatre, and two more such conversions were promised. The Billy Rose Theatre changed ownership, was refurbished, named the Trafalgar, and opened with the English import "Whose Life Is It Anyway?" The old Latin Quarter nightclub became the legit 22 Steps Theatre. On upper Broadway, the Beacon Theatre was redecorated and became a home for cultural events. Radio City Music Hall was saved, at least temporarily, as an entertainment center. Sunday, April 22, 1979, was "V.I.P. Night on Broadway" at the Shubert Theatre where stars entertained to pay for bulletproof vests for NYC policemen. On May 3, 1979, "The Fantasticks" began its incredible 20th year. At the Winter Garden on Monday, May 14, there was a star-studded tribute to Alan Jay Lerner and Frederick Loewe—two of Broadway's musical geniuses. Monday, May 21, 1979, on the stage of the Vivian Beaumont Theater, Lincoln Center celebrated its 20th year, and announced a contract to reopen the Beaumont in 1980. On Sunday, June 3, 1979, Alexander H. Cohen televised the "Tony" Awards, once again proving his superiority in producing such entertaining television spectaculars.

"Sweeney Todd"

"The Elephant Man"

BROADWAY CALENDAR
June 1, 1978 through May 31, 1979

"Wings"

"The Best Little Whorehouse
in Texas"

"The Kingfisher"

"Ballroom"

BROADWAY PRODUCTIONS THAT OPENED JUNE 1, 1978 THROUGH MAY 31, 1979

BROOKS ATKINSON THEATRE
Opened Thursday, June 1, 1978.*
Morton Gottlieb presents:

TRIBUTE

By Bernard Slade; Director, Arthur Storch; Scenery, William Ritman; Costumes, Lowell Detweiler; Lighting, Tharon Musser; Associate Producers, Ben Rosenberg, Warren Crane; Wardrobe, Penny Davis; Hairstyles, Angela Gari

CAST

Lou Daniels	A. Larry Haines
Dr. Gladys Petrelli	Tresa Hughes
Scottie Templeton	Jack Lemmon
Sally Haines	Catherine Hicks
Maggie Stratton	Rosemary Prinz
Jud Templeton	Robert Picardo
Hilary	Joan Welles
Mrs. Everhardt	Anne Dodge

STANDBYS: John Carpenter (Scottie/Lou), Tom Capps (Jud), Anita Keal (Gladys/Maggie/Hilary/Mrs. Everhardt), Laura Beattie (Sally)

A comedy in two acts and seven scenes. The action takes place at the present time in the living room of a New York townhouse and on the stage of a New York theatre.

General Manager: Ben Rosenberg
Company Manager: Martin Cohen
Press: Solters & Roskin, Milly Schoenbaum, Fred Nathan
Stage Managers: Warren Crane Tom Capps, Laura Beattie

* Closed Dec. 2, 1978 after 212 performances and 4 previews.

Martha Swope Photos

**Right: Jack Lemmon, Rosemary Prinz
Top: Jack Lemmon, A. Larry Haines**

Jack Lemmon, Rosemary Prinz

Robert Picardo, Jack Lemmon

CIRCLE IN THE SQUARE
Opened Thursday, June 15, 1978.*
Circle in the Square (Theodore Mann, Artistic Director; Paul Libin, Managing Director) present:

ONCE IN A LIFETIME

By Moss Hart and George S. Kaufman; Director, Tom Moore; Scenery, Karl Eigsti; Costumes, Carol Luiken; Lighting, F. Mitchell Dana; Wigs and Hairstyles, Paul Huntley; Wardrobe Supervisor, Virginia Merkel

CAST

Jolsons	Michael Jeter, Richard Peterson, Jim Shankman
George Lewis.	John Lithgow
May Daniels.	Deborah May
Jerry Hyland	Treat Williams
Helen Hobart.	Jayne Meadows Allen
Susan Walker.	Julia Duffy
First Couple.	Jill P. Rose, Michael Brindisi
Second Couple.	Elizabeth Kemp, Eric Uhler
Cigarette Girl/Bridesmaid	Ellen March
Coat Check Girl/Bridesmaid.	Alma Cuervo
Porter/Chauffeur/Fulton/Painter	Bob Harper
Chauffeur/Sullivan/Truckman/Reporter	Lance Davis
Maid/Secretary	Jill P. Rose
Maid/Woman/Script Girl	Elizabeth Kemp
Phyllis Fontaine	Sydney Blake
Florabel Leigh.	Lee Meredith
Bellboys	Jim Shankman, Michael Jeter
Mrs. Walker	Beverly May
Ernest/Cameraman/Necktie Man.	Keith Perry
Norton/Flick/Boom Man	Peter Bosche
Meterstein.	Peter J. Saputo
Weisskopf.	Jerry Zaks
Policeman/Bishop/Reporter	Jack Straw
Miss Chasen	Phyllis Somerville
Herman Glogauer	George S. Irving
Miss Leighton	Bella Jarrett
Lawrence Vail	Max Wright
Pages	Michael Jeter, Jim Shankman
Moulton/Leading Man	Richard Peterson
Rudolph Kammerling.	MacIntyre Dixon
Electricians	Michael Brindisi, Eric Uhler
Biographer	Michael Brindisi

A comedy in 3 acts and 7 scenes. The action takes place in a theatre dressing room, a pullman car, the Gold and Red Room of the Hotel Stilton in Hollywood, the reception room of the Glogauer Studio, and on the set of "Gingham and Orchids."

Company Manager: William Conn
Press: Merle Debuskey, David Roggensack, William Schelble
Stage Managers: Randall Brooks, Rick Ralston

* Closed Aug. 27, 1978 after 85 performances and 23 previews. Original production opened Sept. 24, 1930 and ran for 406 performances with Hugh O'Connell, Jean Dixon, George S. Kaufman, and Spring Byington.

Marianne Barcellona Photos

Top Right: John Lithgow, Deborah May, Treat Williams, (seated) George S. Irving, Max Wright Below: Treat Williams, John Lithgow, Deborah May

John Lithgow, Deborah May, Jayne Meadows Allen

John Lithgow, Max Wright

FORTY-SIXTH STREET THEATRE
Opened Monday, June 19, 1979.*
Universal Pictures presents:

THE BEST LITTLE WHOREHOUSE IN TEXAS

Book, Larry L. King, Peter Masterson; Music and Lyrics, Carol Hall; Direction, Peter Masterson, Tommy Tune; Musical Numbers Staged by Tommy Tune; Sets, Marjorie Kellogg; Costumes, Ann Roth; Lighting, Dennis Parichy; Musical Supervision, Direction and Vocal Arrangements, Robert Billig; Hairstylist, Michael Gottfried; Associate Choreographer, Thommie Walsh; Wardrobe Mistress, Karen L. Eifert; Original Cast Album by MCA Records

CAST

Rio Grande Band	Craig Chambers, Ben Brogdon, Lynn Frazier, Jim Haber, Michael Holleman, Ernie Reed
Girls	Lisa Brown, Carol Chambers, Donna King, Susan Mansur, Louise Quick-Bowen, Debra Zalkind
Cowboys	Robin Haynes†1, Michael Scott, Paul Ukena, Jr.†2
Farmer/Melvin P. Thorpe	Clint Allmon
Shy Kid	Gerry Burkhardt
Miss Wulla Jean	Edna Milton†3
Traveling Salesman/C.J. Scruggs /Chip Brewster/Governor	Jay Garner
Governor's Aide	Jay Bursky
Slick Dude/Soundman	K. C. Kelly
Choir	Jay Bursky, Becky Gelke, Edwina Lewis, Jan Merchant, James Rich, Marta Sanders
Amber	Pamela Blair†4
Shy	Joan Ellis†5
Jewel	Delores Hall
Mona Strangley	Carlin Glynn†6

Her Girls:

Linda Lou	Donna King
Dawn	Lisa Brown†7
Ginger	Louise Quick-Bowen
Beatrice	Jan Merchant
Taddy Jo	Carol Chambers†8
Ruby Rae	Becky Gelke
Eloise	Marta Sanders†9
Durla	Debra Zalkind
Leroy Sliney	Clayton King†2
The Dogettes	Gerry Burkhardt, Jay Bursky, Michael Scott, Paul Ukena, Jr.
Stage Manager/Cameraman/Specialty Dancer	Tom Cashin
Mayor Poindexter/Senator Wingwoah	J. Frank Lucas
Sheriff Ed Earl Dodd	Henderson Forsythe†10
Melvin Thorpe Singers	Becky Gelke, Robin Haynes, Carol Chambers, Jan Merchant, James Rich, Marta Sanders
Edsel Mackey	Don Crabtree
Doatsey Mae	Susan Mansur
Townspeople	Carol Chambers, Robin Haynes, Debra Zalkind, James Rich, Marta Sanders
TV Announcer	Larry L. King
Angelette Imogene Charlene	Lisa Brown†7
Angelettes	Becky Gelke, Carol Chambers, Donna King, Debra Zalkind, Jan Merchant
Aggies	Paul Ukena, Jr. (21), Michael Scott (71), Jay Bursky (11), K. C. Kelly (1), James Rich (17), Gerry Burkhardt (7), Tom Cashin (12), Robin Haynes (77)
Photographers	Michael Scott, Paul Ukena, Jr., James Rich, Jay Birsky
Reporters	Susan Mansur, Paul Ukena, Jr., Michael Scott
Alternate Dancers	Laura Ackerman, Jerry Yoder

UNDERSTUDIES: Susan Mansur (Miss Mona), Lisa Brown (Shy), Jan Merchant (Doatsey Mae), Don Crabtree (Sheriff/Mayor/-Senator/Scruggs), Gerry Burkhardt (Governor/Melvin P. Thorpe), Becky Gelke (Ginger), Monica Tiller (Dance Alternate/Amber/-Dawn), Edwina Lewis (Jewel), Paul Ukena, Jr. (Edsel/Bandleader)

MUSICAL NUMBERS: "Prologue," "20 Fans," "A Lil Ole Bitty Pissant Country Place," "Girl You're a Woman," "Watch Dog Theme," "Texas Has a Whorehouse in It," "24 Hours of Lovin'," "Doatsey Mae," "Angelette March," "Aggie Song," "Bus from Amarillo," "The Sidestep," "No Lies," "Good Old Girl," "Hard Candy Christmas," Finale

A musical comedy in two acts. The action takes place in the State of Texas.

General Management: Jack Schlissel/Jay Kingwill
Company Manager: Alan Wasser
Press: Jeffrey Richards, Warren Knowlton, Karen Gromis
Stage Managers: Paul J. Phillips, Jay Schlossberg-Cohen, Nancy Lynch

* Still playing May 31, 1979. Opened originally Apr. 17, 1978 Off-Broadway at the Entermedia Theatre where it played 85 performances before closing June 1, 1978 to move to Broadway. Miss Glynn and Mr. Forsythe received "Tonys" for their "Outstanding Performances in a Musical."

†1 Succeeded by: 1. Stephen McNaughton, 2. Gene O'Neill, 3. Debra Zalkind, 4. Gena Ramsel, 5. Cheryl Ebarb, 6. Carol Hall during vacation, 7. Monica Tiller, 8. Jill Cook, 9. Diana Broderick, 10. Larry L. King during vacation

Ilene Jones Photos

Top Right: Henderson Forsythe, Susan Mansur, Don Crabtree Below: Jay Garner, Clint Allmon, J. Frank Lucas

Above: Carlin Glynn, Henderson Forsythe

LYCEUM THEATRE

Opened Wednesday, September 6, 1978.*
The Kennedy Center and Eddie Kulukundis present:

PLAYERS

By David Williamson; Director, Michael Blakemore; Scenery and
Costumes, Hayden Griffin; Production Supervisor, Charles Vaughan
III; Lighting, Martin Aronstein; Wardrobe Supervisor, Dorothy
Brousseau

CAST

Gerry Cooper	Gene Rupert
Ted Parker	Thomas A. Carlin
Laurie Holden	Rex Robbins
Danny Rowe	Tom Flagg
Jock Riley	Fred Gwynne
Geoff Hayward	Michael O'Hare

UNDERSTUDIES AND STANDBYS: Joseph Warren (Ted/-
Jock), Peter Lombard (Gerry/Laurie), J. Gilpin (Geoff/Danny)

A drama in two acts. The action takes place at the present time
in the board room of a top professional football club in Australia.

General Manager: Ralph Roseman
Press: Jeffrey Richards,
Warren Knowlton, Jeanna Gallo
Stage Managers: Wayne Carson, Peter Lombard

* Closed Sept. 24, 1978 after 23 performances and 10 previews.

Richard Braaten Photos

**Seated: Michael O'Hare, Thomas A. Carlin, Tom Flagg, Standing: Rex Robbins,
Fred Gwynne, Gene Rupert Top Right: Fred Gwynne**

11

AMBASSADOR THEATRE
Opened Wednesday, September 20, 1978.*
Ashton Springer in association with Frank C. Pierson and Jay
J. Cohen presents:

EUBIE!

Music by Eubie Blake; Conceived and Directed by Julianne Boyd;
Choreographer and Musical Staging, Billy Wilson; Choreographer
and Tap Choreography, Henry LeTang; Musical Supervision and
Arrangements, Danny Holgate; Set, Karl Eigsti; Costumes, Bernard
Johnson; Lighting, William Mintzer; Sound, Lou Gonzalez; Choral
Arrangements, Chapman Roberts; Musical Direction, Vicki Carter;
Production Supervisor, Ron Abbott; Associate Producer, John N.
Hart, Jr.; Orchestrations, Neal Tate; Wardrobe, Olga Anderson,
Ellen Lee; Makeup, Michael Craig Robinson; Production Asso-
ciates, James Holyfield, Sean Cunningham; Original Cast Album by
Warner Brothers Records.

CAST

Ethel Beatty†1	Mel Johnson, Jr.
Terry Burrell	Lonnie McNeil†4
Leslie Dockery	Janet Powell
Lynnie Godfrey	Marion Ramsey†3
Gregory Hines	Alaina Reed
Maurice Hines†2	Jeffery V. Thompson

UNDERSTUDIES: Skip Cunningham, David Jackson, Nathan Jennings, Bernard J. Marsh, Deborah Burrell, Leslie Dockery, Jenifer
Lewis, Carol Lynn Maillard, Gail Nelson.

MUSICAL NUMBERS: "Goodnight Angeline," "Charleston
Rag," "Shuffle Along," "In Honeysuckle Time," "I'm Just Wild
about Harry," "Baltimore Buzz," "Daddy," "There's a Million Little Cupids in the Sky," "I'm a Great Big Baby," "My Handyman
Ain't Handy No More," "Low Down Blues," "Gee, I Wish I Had
Someone to Rock Me in the Cradle of Love," "I'm Just Simply Full
of Jazz," "High Steppin' Days," "Dixie Moon," "Weary," "Roll
Jordan," "Memories of You," "If You've Never Been Vamped by
a Brownskin, You've Never Been Vamped at All," "You Got to Git
the Gittin While the Gittin's Good," "Oriental Blues," "I'm Craving
for That Kind of Love," "Hot Feet," Finale

A musical in two acts.
General Management: Theatre Management Associates
Company Manager: Robert Ossenfort
Press: Max Eisen, Irene Gandy, Francine Trevens
Stage Managers: Clinton Turner Davis, Kellie Williams, Kimako,
Terry Burrell. David Jackson

* Closed Oct. 7, 1979 after 439 performances and 7 previews.
†1 Succeeded by: 1. Gail Nelson, 2. Winston DeWitt Hemsley, 3.
Jenifer Lewis, 4. David Jackson

Bert Andrews Photos

**Gregory Hines, Maurice Hines, Ethel Beatty,
Lonnie McNeil Above: Gregory Hines, Ethel Beatty**

**Top Left: Lonnie McNeil, Janet Powell, Ethel
Beatty, Mel Johnson, Jr. Below: Lonnie
McNeil, Jeffery V. Thompson, Maurice
Hines, Mel Johnson, Gregory Hines**

CIRCLE IN THE SQUARE THEATRE
Opened Thursday, September 21, 1979.*
Circle in the Square (Theodore Mann, Artistic Director; Paul Libin, Managing Director) presents:

THE INSPECTOR GENERAL

By Nikolai Gogol; Translated by Betsy Hulick; Director, Liviu Ciulei; Scenery, Karen Schulz; Costumes, William Ivey Long; Lighting, F. Mitchell Dana; Hairstylist, Michael Wasula; Wardrobe Supervisor, Virginia Merkel; Assistant to Mr. Ciulei, Caitlin Buchman

CAST

Luka Lukitch Khlopov	Arnold Soboloff
Fyodr Andreyevich Lyulykov/Priest/Merchant	Keith Perry
Ivan Lazarevich Rastakovsky/ Dyershimorda/Merchant	Bob Harper
Korobkin/Mishka/Merchant	Timothy Farmer
Amos Fyodorovich Lyapkin-Tyapkin	Thomas Toner
Stepan Illyich Ukhovyortov/Merchant	Peter Van Norden
Artemii Filipovich Zemlyanika	Bill Nunnery
Svistunov/Waiter	Jon DeVries
Avdotya	Renee Lippin
Christian Ivanovich Giebner/Merchant	Warren Pincus
Mayor Anton Antonovich Skvoznik-Dmukhanovsky	Theodore Bikel
Pyotr Ivanovich Dobchinsky	Bill McIntyre
Pyotr Ivanovich Bobchinsky	William Duell
Ivan Kusmich Shpyokin	Kenneth Welsh
Anna Andreyevna	Helen Burns
Marya Antonovna	Christine Estabrook
Ossip	Bob Balaban
Ivan Alexandrovich Khlestakov	Max Wright
Rastokovsky's wife	Lynne Charnay
Pevronya Petrovna Poshlyopkina/ Khlopov's wife	Mary Lou Rosato
Sergeant's widow/Chief of Police's wife	Jean Barker

UNDERSTUDIES: Lynne Charnay (Anna), Jon DeVries (Mayor), Kenneth Welsh (Khlestakov), Timothy Farmer (Ossip/Giebner), Bob Harper (Judge/Chief of Police), Keith Perry (Khlopov/Postmaster), Warren Pincus (Dobchinsky/Bobchinsky), Peter Van Norden (Zemlyanika)

A drama in two acts and four scenes. The action takes place in the Mayor's house and in a room at the inn.

Company Manager: William Conn
Press: Merle Debuskey, David Roggensack, William Schelble
Stage Managers: Randall Brooks, Rick Ralston

* Closed Nov. 19, 1978 after 69 performances and 23 previews.

Martha Swope Photos

Right: Helen Burns, Theodore Bikel, Christine Estabrook Top: Bob Balaban, Theodore Bikel

Max Wright, Theodore Bikel, Christine Estabrook, Helen Burns

Max Wright, Theodore Bikel

HELEN HAYES THEATRE
Opened Thursday, September 28, 1978.*
Lester Osterman, Richard Horner, Terry Allen Kramer, John Wulp present:

THE CRUCIFER OF BLOOD

Written and Directed by Paul Giovanni; Based on characters created by Conan Doyle; Scenery, John Wulp; Supervised by Lynn Pecktal; Costumes, Ann Roth; Lighting Design, Roger Morgan; Makeup, Joseph Cranzano; Wigs and Hairstyles, Paul Huntley; Assistant to Director, David Edgeli; Technical Adviser, Mitch Miller; Wardrobe, Florence Aubert; Sound created by Leonard Will; Special Effects, Bran Ferrin; Dialect Coach, Elizabeth Smith

CAST

Major Alistair Ross	Dwight Schultz
Captain Neville St. Claire	Nicolas Surovy
Jonathan Small	Christopher Curry
Durga Dass/Inspector Lestrade	Edward Zang
Wali Dad/Birdy Johnson	Tuck Milligan
Mohammed Singh/Mordecai Smith	Andrew Davis
Sherlock Holmes	Paxton Whitehead
John Watson, M.D.	Timothy Landfield
Irene St. Claire	Glenn Close
Tonga	Roumel Reaux
Fung Tching	Melvin Lum
Hopkins	Martin LePlatney

UNDERSTUDIES: Jeffrey Jones (Holmes), Martin LaPlatney (Watson/Smith/St. Claire), Andrew Davis (Small/Johnson/Wali Dad), Cynthia Carle (Irene), Richard Fancy (Ross/Lestrade/Durga). Mark Hoyt (Singh/Hopkins), Tobee Roberts (Tonga)

A melodrama in three acts and six scenes. The action takes place at the Red Fort in Agra, India in 1857; and thirty years later in 221-B Baker Street in London, Pondicherry Lodge at Maidenhead, the Gate of a Hundred Sorrows, and on the River Thames.

Company Manager: Malcolm Allen
Press: Seymour Krawitz, Louise Weiner Ment, Patricia McLean Krawitz
Stage Managers: Robert L. Borod, Robert Charles, Mark Hoyt

* Closed April 22, 1979 after 236 performances and 16 previews. Roger Morgan received a "Tony" for his lighting design.

Martha Swope Photos

Right: Nicolas Surovy, Christopher Curry, Dwight Schultz Top: Timothy Landfield, Glenn Close, Paxton Whitehead

Glenn Close, Paxton Whitehead

Timothy Landfield, Paxton Whitehead

14

MAJESTIC THEATRE

Opened Tuesday, October 3, 1978.*

The Kennedy Center and Plumstead Theatre Society (Martha Scott, Joel Spector, Bernard Wiesen) present:

FIRST MONDAY IN OCTOBER

By Jerome Lawrence and Robert E. Lee; Director, Edwin Sherin; Settings, Oliver Smith; Lighting, Roger Morgan; Costumes, Ann Roth; Production Assistant, Bill Becker; Wardrobe, Agnes Farrell

CAST

Custodians	John Stewart, P. Jay Sidney
Chief Justice James Jefferson Crawford	Larry Gates
Associate Justice Josiah Clewes	Earl Sydnor
Associate Justice Waldo Thompson	Maurice Copeland
Associate Justice Daniel Snow	Henry Fonda
Associate Justice Harold Webb	John Wardwell
The Marshall	John Newton
Judge Ruth Loomis	Jane Alexander
Mason Woods	Tom Stechschulte
Associate Justice Ambrose Quincy	Alexander Reed
Associate Justice Richard Carey	Eugene Stuckmann
Associate Justice Christopher Halloran	Patrick McCullough
Miss Birnbaum	Carol Mayo Jenkins
Photographer	John Stewart
Blake	Ron Faber

STANDBYS AND UNDERSTUDIES: John Newton (Snow), Carol Mayo Jenkins (Loomis), Maurice Copeland (Crawford), P. Jay Sidney (Clewes/Nightwatchman), Alexander Reed (Webb/-Blake), John Stewart (Woods), Eugene Stuckmann (Marshall)

A drama in two acts. The action takes place backstage at the United States Supreme Court during "the imaginary now."

General Manager: Theatre Now, Inc.
Press: John Springer, Louis Sica,
Suzanne Salter, Ann Todaro, Barbara Ball
Stage Managers: Frederic de Wilde, Robert Crawley, John Stewart, Eugene Stuckmann

* Closed Dec. 10, 1978 after a limited engagement of 79 performances and 17 previews.

Richard Braaten Photos

Top: Alexander Reed, Earl Sydnor, Patrick McCullough, Jane Alexander (standing), Maurice Copeland, Henry Fonda, Larry Gates, John Wardwell, Eugene Stuckmann

Henry Fonda, Jane Alexander

MINSKOFF THEATRE
Opened Sunday, October 22, 1978.*
Joseph Kipness and Patty Grubman in association with Jerome Minskoff present:

KING OF HEARTS

Book, Joseph Stein; Based on screenplay by Philippe de Broca, Maurice Bessy and Daniel Boulanger; Music, Peter Link; Lyrics, Jacob Brackman; Direction andChoreography, Ron Field; Settings, Santo Loquasto; Costumes, Patricia Zipprodt; Lighting, Pat Collins; Musical Director, Karen Gustafson; Dance Arrangements, Dorothea Freitag; Orchestrations, Bill Brohn; Sound, Jack Shearing; Assistant to Director, John Calvert; Assistant to Choreographer, Marianne Selbert; Hairstylist and Makeup, Patrik D. Moreton; Production Associate, Nan Pearlman; Associate Producers, Lee Minskoff, Charlotte Dicker; Production Assistant, Edward Isser; Wardrobe, Clarence Sims; Animals from Animal Actors, Inc.

CAST

INMATES:

Demosthenes (Le Muet)	Gary Morgan
Madeleine (La Madame)	Millicent Morgan
Genevieve (La Courtisane)	Mitzi Hamilton
Simone (La Ballerine)	Marilyn D'Honau
Dahlia (La Servante)	Isabelle Farrell
Raoul (Le Patron du Cirque)	Bob Gunton
Jeunefille (La Jeune Fille)	Pamela Blair
Valerie (La Flutiste)	Neva Rae Powers
Jacques (Le Fermier)	Rex David Hays
DuBac (Le Monseigneur)	Michael McCarty
Therese (La Maman)	Maria Guida
Isolde (La Chanteuse d'Opera)	Gerianne Raphael
Claude (Le Coiffeur)	Gordon J. Weiss
Guy-Louis (Le Petit Garcon)	Timothy Scott
M. Clichy (Le Photographe)	David Thomas
Philippe (Le Maitre d'Hotel)	Bryan Nicholas
Marie-Claire (La Duchesse)	Julia Shelley
Henri (Le Duc)	Will Roy
Monsieur Cochon (Le Porc)	Wilbur

AMERICAN SOLDIERS:

Private Johnny Perkins	Donald Scardino
Lieutenant McNeill	Jay Devlin
Frank	Robert Brubach
Steve	Harry Fawcett
Joe	John Scoullar
Tom	Jamie Haskins
Phillip	Richard Christopher

GERMAN SOLDIERS:

Hans	Scott Allen
Kapitan Kost	Alexander Orfaly
Siegfried	Scott Barnes
Fritz	Roger Berdahl
Karl	Timothy Wallace
Willie	Karl Heist

UNDERSTUDIES: Harry Fawcett (Johnny), Gerrianne Raphael (Madeleine), Neva Rae Powers (Jeunefille), Timothy Scott (Demosthenes/Claude), Rex David Hays (Raoul), Richard Christopher (McNeill), Timothy Wallace (DuBac/Kost/Clichy/Jacques), Bryan Nicholas (Henri), Marilyn D'Honau (Marie-Claire), Spence Ford (Genevieve/Isolde/Simone/Valerie/Dahlia/Theresa), Navarre Matlovsky (Guy-Louis/Philippe/American and German soldiers)

MUSICAL NUMBERS: "A Stain on the Name," "Deja Vu," "Promenade," "Turn Around," "Nothing, Only Love," "King of Hearts," "Close Upon the Hour," "A Brand New Day," "Le Grand Cirque de Provence," "Hey, Look at Me, Mrs. Draba," "Going Home Tomorrow," "Somewhere Is Here," "March, March, March"

A musical in 2 acts and .4 scenes. The action takes place during one day in September of 1918 toward the end of World War I, in the French town of DuTemps, and the trenches that surround it.

General Managers: Marvin A. Krauss, Gary Gunas
Company Manager: Bob Skerry
Press: Merlin Group, Patt Dale, Beatrice DaSilva, Glen Gary
Stage Managers: Janet Beroza, Clint Jakeman, Robert Schear

* Closed Dec. 3, 1978 after 48 performances and 6 previews.

Brent Nicholson Photos

Top Left: Pamela Blair, Donald Scardino Below: Gary Morgan, Millicent Martin, Donald Scardino, Michael McCarty

Gordon J. Weiss, Donald Scardino

BOOTH THEATRE
Opened Monday, October 30, 1978.*
Terry Allen Kramer, Harry Rigby, Hale Matthews and John Wulp present:

GOREY STORIES

Written and Designed by Edward Gorey; Director, Tony Tanner; Adaptation, Stephen Currens; Music, David Aldrich; Scenery Supervision, Lynn Pecktal; Costumes, David Murin; Lighting, Roger Morgan; Musical Director, Martin Silvestri; Furs, Ben Kahn; Production Associate, Joanne Schwartz; Assistant Conductor, Jeffrey Waxman; Wardrobe, Bill Campbell

CAST

Mona (a maid)	Gemze de Lappe
Harold (a butler)	Sel Vitella
Lady Celia (the hostess)	Julie Kurnitz
Mary Rosemarch (a spinster)	June Squibb
C. F. Earbrass (an author)	Leon Shaw
Hamish (a beautiful young man)	John Michalski
Little Henry (a child)	Tobias Haller
Jasper Ankle (an opera freak)	Dennis McGovern
Ortenzia Caviglia (a singer)	Susan Marchand

UNDERSTUDIES: Meg Bussert (Ortenzia/Mona), C. A. Hutton (Earbrass/Hamish/Harold), Rose Roffman (Celia/Mary), Bill Stratton (Henry/Jasper)
STORIES: The Hapless Child, The Wuggly Ump, The Curious Sofa, The Sinking Spell, The Gilded Bat, The Insect God, The Willowdale Handcar, The Doubtful Guest, The Blue Aspic, The Unstrung Harp, The Pious Infant, The Osbick Bird, The Deranged Cousins, The Lost Lions, The Loathsome Couple, The Gashlycrumb Tinies, and limericks from The Listing Attic

"An entertainment with music" in two acts. The action takes place in Lady Celia's drawing room, and in the summer house.

General Management: Jack Schlissel/Jay Kingwill
Company Manager: Alan Wasser
Press: Henry Luhrman, Anne Obert Weinberg, Terry M. Lilly
Stage Managers: Franklin Keysar, Beth Prevor

* Closed Oct. 30, 1978 after one performance and 16 previews.

Martha Swope Photos

John Michalski, June Squibb, Leon Shaw, Julie Kurnitz (back), Susan Marchand (front), Edward Gorey (author), Gemze de Lappe, Sel Vitella, Tobias Haller, Dennis McGovern

MARK HELLINGER THEATRE
Opened Sunday, November 12, 1978.*
Gladys Rackmil, Fritz Holt, Barry M. Brown present:

PLATINUM

Book, Will Holt, Bruce Vilanch; Music, Gary William Friedman; Lyrics, Will Holt; Based on an original idea by Will Holt; Directed and Choreographed by Joe Layton; Scenery, David Hays; Lighting, John Gleason; Costumes, Bob Mackie; Orchestrations, Fred Thaler, Jimmie Haskell; Arrangements, Fred Thaler, Jimmie Haskell, Gary William Friedman; Musical Director, Fred Thaler; Sound, Paramount Sound, Steve Wooley; Multi-Media Design, Sheppard Kerman; Hairstylist, Joe Tubens; Assistant Choreographer, Damita Jo Freeman; Producers Associate/Casting, Amos Abrams; Assistant Conductor, Mark Hummel; Wardrobe, Sydney Smith; Assistant to Mr. Layton, Rhoda Dreskenoff; Management Assistants, Eric Angelson, Robin Plevener, Elizabeth Mangle

CAST

Shultz	Tony Shultz
Lila Halliday	Alexis Smith
Snake	Ronnie B. Baker
Minsky	Jonathan Freeman
Boris	John Hammil
Damita	Damita Jo Freeman
Robin	Robin Frean
Avery	Avery Sommers
Jeff Leff	Stanley Kamel
Crystal Mason	Lisa Mordente
Dan Danger	Richard Cox
Christine	Christine Faith
Wenndy	Wenndy Leigh MacKenzie
Alan Fairmont	Jonathan Freeman

The Sidemen ... Fred Thaler (Conductor/Piano), Gregory Block (Violin), Dick Frank (Guitar), Steve Mack (Bass), Roy Markowitz (Drums)

"Wings of Destiny" film sequence cast:

War Bride	Lila Halliday
Mack	Alan Fairmont

UNDERSTUDIES: Tony Shultz (Dan), Wenndy Leigh MacKenzie (Crystal/Damita/Robin/Avery), Jonathan Freeman (Shultz), Ronnie B. Baker (Jeff Leff)

MUSICAL NUMBERS: "Back with a Beat/Nothing But," "Sunset," "Ride, Baby, Ride," "Destiny," "Disco Destiny," "I Am the Light," "Movie Star Mansion," "Platinum Dreams," "Trials and Tribulations/I Like You," "1945," "Too Many Mirrors," "Old Times, Good Times"

A musical in two acts. The action takes place at the present time in the newest environmental recording studio in Hollywood.

General Manager: Marvin A. Krauss
Company Manager: Sam Pagliaro
Press: Shirley Herz, Jan Greenberg
Stage Managers: Frank Hartenstein,
Charles Collins, Bonnie Walker

* Closed Dec. 10, 1978 after 33 performances and 12 previews.

Martha Swope Photos

Top: Lisa Mordente, Richard Cox Right: Robin Grean, Alexis Smith, Avery Sommers, Damita Jo Freeman Below: Stanley Kamel, Alexis Smith

Jonathan Freeman, Alexis Smith

Sunday, December 3, 1978.*
The Playhouse Repertory Company presents:

THE NEIGHBORHOOD PLAYHOUSE AT 50: A CELEBRATION

Producers, Michael Gennaro, Karl Allison; Conceived and Supervised by Kent Paul; Staged by Peter Gennaro; Written by David Mamet and John Weidman; Musical Direction and Arrangements, David Krane; Lighting, Richard Winkler; Production Consultant, Barry Andrew Kearsley; Costume Coordinators, Pat Britton, Michelle Nezwarsky; Production Assistants, Alice Mary Honeycutt, Jennifer Kirk; Pianists, David Krane, David Baker; Co-chairpersons, Allen Grossman, Mary Susan Miller

APPEARANCES BY: Stella Adler, Barbara Baxley, James Broderick, Zoe Caldwell, Harold Clurman, Keir Dullea, Sandy Faison, Julie Garfield, Peter Gennaro, Martha Graham, Tammy Grimes, Anne Jackson, Diane Keaton, Louise Lasser, Peter Link, David Mamet, Sanford Meisner, Kathleen Nolan, Sydney Pollack, Tony Randall, Mark Rydell, Marian Seldes, Maureen Stapleton, Brenda Vaccaro, Jon Voight, Eli Wallach, John Weidman, Robert Whitehead, Elizabeth Wilson, Joanne Woodward and others

General Managers: Marvin A. Krauss, Gary Gunas
Press: Susan Bloch & Associates
Stage Managers: Donnis Honeycutt, Marjorie Horne, Carol Horne

* One performance only

Donna Svennevik Photos

Right: Mary Jane Houdina, Peter Gennaro
Below: Diane Keaton introduces Sanford Meisner (4th from left)

Zoe Caldwell, Maureen Stapleton
Above: Louise Lasser

Tony Randall, Sandy Faison

BILTMORE THEATRE
Opened Wednesday, December 6, 1978.*
Elliot Martin with Hinks Shimberg in association with John
Gale presents:

THE KINGFISHER

By William Douglas Home; Director, Lindsay Anderson; Setting,
Alan Tagg; Costumes, Jane Greenwood; Lighting, Thomas Skelton;
Assistant to Director, Louis Pulvino; Wardrobe Supervisor, Cindy
Chock; Assistant to the Producer, Ann R. Waite; Wigs, Paul Huntley

CAST

Hawkins	George Rose
Cecil	Rex Harrison
Evelyn	Claudette Colbert

STANDBYS AND UNDERSTUDIES: Michael Evans (Cecil/-Hawkins), Betty Low (Evelyn), Wally Peterson (Hawkins)

A comedy in two acts and four scenes. The action takes place at
the present time in Cecil's garden over 24 hours.

General Manager: Victor Samrock
Company Manager: Robert H. Wallner
Press: Seymour Krawitz, Louise Weiner Ment, Patricia McLean
Krawitz
Stage Managers: Bill Weaver, Wally Peterson

* Closed May 13, 1979 after 181 performances and 9 previews.

**Left: George Rose, Claudette Colbert,
Rex Harrison**

Rex Harrison, Claudette Colbert

Opened Thursday, December 14, 1978.*
Michael Bennett presents:

BALLROOM

Book, Jerome Kass; Music, Billy Goldenberg; Lyrics, Alan and Marilyn Bergman; Direction and Choreography, Michael Bennett; Co-Choreographer, Bob Avian; Assistant to Choreographers, T. Michael Reed; Scenery, Robin Wagner; Costume Design, Theoni V. Aldredge; Lighting, Tharon Musser; Orchestrations, Jonathan Tunich; Sound, Otts Munderloh; Musical Direction, Don Jennings; Hairstylist, Ted Azar; Co-Producers, Bob Avian, Bernard Gersten, Susan MacNair; Technical Coordinator, Arthur Siccardi; Wardrobe, Alyce Gilbert; Production Assistant, Michael LaPoff; Assistant Conductor, Les Scott; Original Cast Recording by Columbia Records

CAST

Bea Asher	Dorothy Loudon
Helen (her sister-in-law)	Sally-Jane Heit
Jack (her brother-in-law)	John Hallow
Diane (her daughter)	Dorothy Danner
David (her son)	Peter Alzando

AT THE STARDUST BALLROOM:

Alfred Rossi	Vincent Gardenia
Marlene	Lynn Roberts
Nathan Bricker	Bernie Knee
Angie	Patricia Drylie
Johnny "Lightfeet"	Howard Parker
Martha	Barbara Erwin
Petey	Gene Kelton
Shirley	Liz Sheridan
Paul	Michael Vita
"Scooter"	Danny Carroll
Eleanor	Jayne Turner
Pauline Krim	Janet Stewart White
Faye	Roberta Haze
Harry "The Noodle"	Victor Griffin
Marie	Adriana Keathley
Emily	Mary Ann Niles
Mario	Terry Violino
Anitra	Svetlana McLee Grody
Carl	David Evans
Margaret	Mavis Ray
Thomas	Peter Gladke
Bill	Rudy Tronto

and Marilyn Cooper, Dick Corrigan, Bud Fleming, Carol Flemming, Mickey Gunnersen, Alfred Karl, Dorothy D. Lister, John J. Martin, Joe Milan, Frank Pietri

CUSTOMER'S AT BEA'S STORE:

Natalie	Marilyn Cooper
Estelle	Roberta Haze
Kathy	Carol Flemming

UNDERSTUDIES: Liz Sheridan (Bea), John J. Martin(Rossi), Joe Milan (Jack), Rudy Tronto (Scooter), Mary Ann Niles (Angie), Adriana Keathley (Martha/Emily/Shirley), Carol Flemming (Diane), Marilyn Cooper (Helen/Marlene), Gene Kelton (Lightfeet), Roberta Haze (Eleanor), Jayne Turner (Pauline), Alfred Karl (David), Michael Vita (Bricker), Swings: Kathie Dalton, Ken Urmston

MUSICAL NUMBERS: "A Terrific Band and a Real Nice Crowd," "A Song for Dancing," "One by One," "The Dance Montage," "Dreams," "Somebody Did Alright for Herself," "Tango Contest," "Goodnight Is Not Goodbye," "I've Been Waiting All My Life," "I Love to Dance," "More of the Same," "Fifty Percent," "The Stardust Waltz," "I Wish You a Waltz"

A musical performed without intermission. The action takes place at the present time in The Bronx in Bea's Shop, Bea's apartment, and The Stardust Ballroom.

General Manager: Maurice Schaded
Company Managers: Sally Campbell, Linda Cohen
Press: Merle Debuskey, Leo Stern, William Schelbe
Stage Managers: Jeff Hamlin, David Taylor, Pat Trott

* Closed March 24, 1979 after 116 performances and 11 previews. Michael Bennett and Bob Avian received a 1979 "Tony" for "Outstanding Choreography."

Martha Swope Photos

Top Right: Stardust Ballroom Gala Below: Dorothy Loudon, Vincent Gardenia

Dorothy Loudon, Vincent Gardenia Above: Sally-Jane Heit, Dorothy Loudon, Dorothy Danner, Peter Alzado

CIRCLE IN THE SQUARE

Opened Thursday, December 14, 1978.*

Circle in the Square (Theodore Mann, Artistic Director; Paul Libin, Managing Director) presents:

MAN AND SUPERMAN

By George Bernard Shaw; Director, Stephen Porter; Scenery and Costumes, Zach Brown; Lighting, F. Mitchell Dana; Wigs and Hair-styles, Paul Huntley; Wardrobe, Rachele Bussanich

CAST

Roebuck Ramsden	Richard Woods
Parlourmaid	Barbara Lester
Octavious Robinson	Mark Lamos
John Tanner	George Grizzard
Ann Whitefield	Ann Sachs
Mrs. Whitefield	Kate Wilkinson
Susan Ramsden	Bette Henritze
Violet Robinson	Laurie Kennedy
Henry Straker	Nicholas Woodeson
Hector Malone, Jr.	Michael O'Hare
Mendoza	Philip Bosco
Anarchist	George Hall
Sulky Social Democrat	John Carroll
Rowdy Social Democrat	James Storm
Goathered	David Berman
The Officer	David Berman
Hector Malone, Sr	Robert Nichols

STANDBYS: Jerry ver Dorn (Tanner), Deanna Donegan (Violet/-Parlourmaid)

A comedy in 3 acts and 4 scenes. The action takes place in Roebuck Ramsden's study, a carriage drive of a country house near Richmond, an evening in the Sierra Nevada, and in a garden of a villa in Granada.

Company Manager: Janet Spencer
Press: Merle Debuskey, David Roggensack, William Schelble
Stage Managers: James Bernardi, Rick Ralston

* Closed Feb. 18, 1979 after 77 performances and 23 previews.

Martha Swope Photos

Top: George Grizzard, Ann Sachs Right: Laurie Kennedy, Michael O'Hare Below: Philip Bosco, Ann Sachs, Richard Woods, George Grizzard

Kate Wilkinson, Mark Lamos

LUNT-FONTANNE THEATRE
Opened Thursday, December 21, 1978.*
Norman Kean and Garth H. Drabinsky present:

A BROADWAY MUSICAL

Book, William F. Brown; Music, Charles Strouse; Lyrics, Lee Adams; Production Supervised by Gower Champion; Sets, Peter Wexler; Costumes, Randy Barcelo; Lighting, John DeSantis; Musical Conductor, Kevin Farrell; Orchestrations, Robert M. Freedman; Musical Supervision and Vocal Arrangements, Donald Pippin; Dance Arrangements, Donald Johnston; Co-choreographer, George Bunt; Sound, Abe Jacob; Production Coordinator, Barbara-Mae Phillips; Associate Producer, Maria Di Dia; Assistant to Producer, Connie Dash; Production Associate, Jacob Weisbarth; Dance Assistant, Calvin McRae; Production Assistants, David Thalenberg, Robert G. Adams; Assistant Conductor, Tim Stella; Wardrobe, Toni Baer; Associate to Producer, Arnold Gottlieb; Hairstylist, Ronald DeMann; Assistant to Director, Barry Moss; Associate Scenic Designer, Hal Tine

CAST

Policeman/Nathaniel	Nate Barnett
James Lincoln	Irving Allen Lee
Eddie Bell	Warren Berlinger
Lonnie Paul	Larry Riley
Melinda Bernard	Jackee Harry
Stan Howard	Alan Weeks
Maggie Simpson	Patti Karr
Stephanie Bell	Gwyda DonHowe
Kumi-Kumi	Christina Kumi-Kimball
Smoke & Fire Back-Up Singers	Maris Clement, Loretta Devine, Jackee Harry
Richie Taylor's Lawyers	Sydney Anderson, Michael Gallagher
Rehearsal Pianist	Gwen Arment
Richie Taylor	Larry Marshall
Richie's Secretary	Jo Ann Ogawa
Shirley Wolfe	Anne Francine
Theatre Party Associates	Sydney Anderson, Maris Clement, Loretta Devine
Male Dancers	Albert Stephenson, Robert Melvin, Martin Rabbett
Sylvester Lee	Tiger Haynes
Louie	Reggie Jackson
Jake	Martin Rabbett
Big Jake	Albert Stephenson
Junior	Robert Melvin

ENSEMBLE: Sydney Anderson, Gwen Arment, Nate Barnett, Maris Clement, Prudence Darby, Don Edward Detrick, Loretta Devine, Sharon Ferrol, Michael Gallagher, Scott Geralds, Maggy Gorrill, Jackee Harry, Leon Jackson, Reggie Jackson, Carleton Jones, Christina Kumi-Kimball, Michael Kubala, Robert Melvin, Jo Ann Ogawa, Karen Paskow, Martin Rabbett, Albert Stephenson, Marilynn Winbush, Brad Witsger

SWING DANCERS: Valarie Pettiford, Calvin McRae

MUSICAL NUMBERS: "Broadway, Broadway," "A Broadway Musical," "I Hurry Home to You," "Smoke and Fire," "Lawyers," "Yenta Power," "Let Me Sing My Song," "The 1934 Hot Chocolate Jazz Babies Revue," "It's Time for a Cheer-Up Song," "You Gotta Have Dancing," "What You Go Through," "Don't Tell Me," "Together"

"A musical about a Broadway musical" in two acts and nine scenes.

General Manager: Marilyn S. Miller
Press: Jeffrey Richards, Warren Knowlton, Mark Arnold
Stage Managers: David Rubinstein, Judy Binus, Sherry Cohen

* Closed Dec. 21, 1978 after one performance and 14 previews.

Martha Swope Photos

**Top Right: Gwyda DonHowe, Warren Berlinger
Below: Larry Riley, Patti Karr, Irving Allen Lee, Warren Berlinger, Jackee Henry, Alan Weeks**

Larry Marshall, Patti Karr, Anne Francine

MINSKOFF THEATRE
Opened Tuesday, December 19, 1978.*
Charlotte Kirk, David Singer and Cubby Downe in association
with Peter Wiese present:

ICEDANCING

Choreographed by Jean-Pierre Bonnefous, Robert Cohan, John
Curry, Norman Maen, Kenneth MacMillan, Peter Martins, Douglas
Norwick, Donald Saddler, Twyla Tharp; Settings, Tony Straiges;
Costumes Supervision, Florence Klotz; Lighting, Marilyn Rennagel;
Costume Designs, Nadine Baylis, Sara Brook, Norberto Chiesa, Joe
Eula, Florence Klotz, Santo Loquasto, D. D. Ryan; Sound, Jack
Mann; Entire Production Supervised by Ruth Mitchell; Technical
Supervisor, Mitche Miller; Wardrobe, Elonzo Dann

CAST

John Curry	JoJo Starbuck
Angela Adney	Patricia Dodd
Ron Alexander	Cathy Foulkes
Yvonne Brink	Brian Grant
Lorna Brown	Deborah Page
Jack Courtney	Paul Toomey

PROGRAM: "Palais de Glace," "Scoop," "Feux Follets," "Moon
Dances," "Tango-Tango," "Anything Goes," "Afternoon of a
Faun," "Night and Day pas de deux from Myth," "Icemoves"

Presented in two acts.

General Management: Theatre Now, Inc., Charlotte W. Wilcox
Company Manager: Norman E. Rothstein
Press: Tom Kerrigan
Stage Managers: Joe Lorden, Jack Gianino

* Closed Dec. 31, 1978 after limited engagement of 16 performances. Had given 21 performances at Felt Forum from Nov. 21
through Dec. 3, 1978.

**Left: Patricia Dodd, Brian Grant in "Palais
du Glace" Top: Jack Courtney, JoJo Starbuck
in "Myth"** *Kenn Duncan, Nathaniel Tileston Photos*

24

**John Curry, Cathy Foulkes
in "Afternoon of a Faun"**

**John Curry
in "Afternoon of a Faun"**

BOOTH THEATRE
  Opened Tuesday, January 2, 1979.*
  James Lipton Productions presents:

MONTEITH AND RAND

  Assisted by bill-boy russel; Lighting, Gilbert V. Hemsley, Jr., Costumes, Donald Brooks; Assistant to Producer, Rosemary Winckley; Production Consultant, Arthur Siccardi

CAST

John Monteith
Suzanne Rand

Presented in two acts.

  General Manager: Max Allentuck
  Assistants: Bruce Birkenhead, Jane Robisen
  Press: Bill Evans, Howard Atlee, Claudia McAllister, Greg Kilarjian
  Stage Managers: Charles Gray, bill-boy russell

* Closed March 10, 1979 after limited engagement of 79 performances and 8 previews.

  Martha Swope Photos

Top: John Monteith, Suzanne Rand

John Monteith, Suzanne Rand

PALACE THEATRE

Opened Thursday, January 11, 1979.*

James M. Nederlander, Diana Shumlin, Jack Schlissel in association with Carole J. Shorenstein and Stewart F. Lane present:

THE GRAND TOUR

Music and Lyrics, Jerry Herman; Book, Michael Stewart and Mark Bramble; Based on play "Jacobowsky and the Colonel" by Franz Werfel and the American play based on the same by S. N. Behrman; Director, Gerald Freedman; Choreography, Donald Saddler; Sets, Ming Cho Lee; Costumes, Theoni V. Aldredge; Lighting, Martin Aronstein; Musical Direction, Wally Harper; Orchestrations, Philp J. Lang; Dance Music Arranged by Peter Howard; Vocal Arrangements, Donald Pippin; Assistant Choreographer, Mercedes Ellington; Hair Designs and Makeup, Vincenzo Prestia; Sound, Jack Mann; Wardrobe, Adelaide Laurino; Assistant Conductor, Rod Derefinko; Original Cast Album by Columbia Records

CAST

S. L. Jacobowsky	Joel Grey
Mme. Bouffier/Peasant/Bride's Mother	Grace Keagy†
Cziesno	Jack Karcher
Jeannot/Groom	Mark Waldrop
Colonel Tadeusz Boleslav Stjerbinsky	Ron Holgate
Szabuniewicz	Stephen Vinovich
Chauffeur/Peddler	Stan Page
Captain Meuller	George Reinholt
Mme. Vauclain/Mme. Manzoni Bride's Aunt	Chevi Colton
Marianne	Florence Lacey
Conductor/Bride's Father	Gene Varrone
Mme. Marville/Mother Madeleine	Travis Hudson
Hugo/Bargeman	Kenneth Kantor
Stiltwalker/Papa Clairon	Jay Pierce
Man with flower in lapel	Jay Stuart
Claudine	Jo Speros
Bride	Michelle Marshall
Commissaire of Police	Bob Morrisey
Swing Dancers	Bronna Lipton, Jeff Richards

REFUGEES, SOLDIERS, GUESTS, SISTERS, ETC.: Bjarne Buchtrup, Carol Dorian, Kenneth Kantor, Jack Karcher, Debra Lyman, Michelle Marshall, Bob Morrisey, Stan Page, Tina Paul, Jay Pierce, Linda Poser, Theresa Rakov, Paul Solen, Jo Speros, Mark Waldrop, Jeff Veazey, Bonnie Young

UNDERSTUDIES AND STANDBYS: Charles Abbott (Jacobowsky), Jay Stuart (Colonel), Linda Poser (Marianne/Vauclain/Mother Madeleine), Kenneth Kantor (Szabuniewcz), Jack Karcher (Capt.), Bob Morrisey (Man with flower), Bronna Lipton (Bride's Aunt), Theresa Rakov (Mmes. Marville and Manzoni)

MUSICAL NUMBERS: "I'll Be Here Tomorrow," "For Poland," "I Belong Here," "Marianne," "We're Almost There," "More and More/Less and Less," "One Extraordinary Thing," "Mrs. S. L. Jacobowsky," "Wedding Conversation," "Mazeltov," "I Think, I Think," "You I Like"

A musical in 2 acts and 13 scenes, with a prologue. The action takes place from June 13 to June 18, 1940, between Paris and the Atlantic Coast of France.

General Management: Jack Schlissel/Jay Kingwill
Associate Manager: Charles Willard
Press: Betty Lee Hunt, Maria Cristina Pucci
Stage Managers: Mary Porter Hall, Richard Elkow, Marc Schlackman, Debra Lyman

* Closed March 4, 1979 after 61 performances and 18 previews to tour.

†Succeeded by Lynne Charnay

Roger Greenawalt Photos

Top Left: Ron Holgate, Stephen Vinovich, Joel Grey
Below: Stephen Vinovich, Joel Grey, Florence Lacey
Ron Holgate

Florence Lacey, Ron Holgate
Above: Grace Keagy, Joel Grey

LYCEUM THEATRE

Opened Sunday, January 28, 1979.*
The Kennedy Center in association with Claus Von Bulow presents:

WINGS

By Arthur Kopit; Director, John Madden; Scenery, Andrew Jackness; Costumes, Jeanne Button; Lighting, Tom Schraeder; Sound, Tom Voegeli; Wardrobe Supervisor, Dorothy Brousseau; Wigs and Hairstyles, Steve Atha

CAST

Emily Stilson	Constance Cummings
Amy	Mary-Joan Negro
Doctors	Roy Steinberg, Ross Petty
Nurses	Gina Franz, Mary Michelle Rutherfurd
Billy	James Tolkan
Mr. Brownstein	Carl Don
Mrs. Timmins	Betty Felzer

STANDBYS: Jane Hoffman (Emily), Leah Chandler (Amy/Nurses/Mrs. Timmins), Brian Meister (Doctors/Billy/Brownstein)

A drama performed without intermissions.

General Management: Theatre Now, Inc.
Company Manager: Michael Lonergan
Press: Jeffrey Richards, Helen Stern, Warren Knowlton, Anne Obert Weinberg, Ken Sherber
Stage Managers: Patrick Horrigan, Brian Meister

* Closed May 5, 1979 after 113 performances and 6 previews. It had previously played 16 performances at the Public/Newman Theatre from June 21 through July 2, 1978. Miss Cummings received a 1979 "Tony" for outstanding performance by an actress in a play, in an unusual tie with Carole Shelley of "The Elephant Man."

William L. Smith Photos

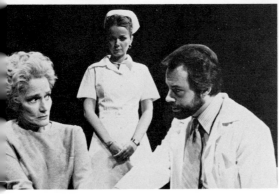

Constance Cummings, Mary Michelle Rutherfurd, Ross Petty Above: Gina Franz, Constance Cummings (also top)

Constance Cummings, Carl Don Above: Mary-Joan Negro, Constance Cummings

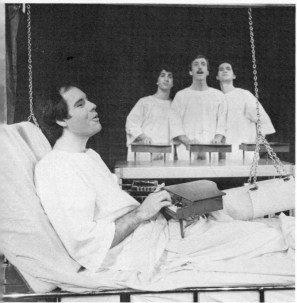

IMPERIAL THEATRE
Opened Sunday, February 11, 1979.*
Emanuel Azenberg presents:

THEY'RE PLAYING OUR SONG

Book by Neil Simon; Music, Marvin Hamlisch; Lyrics, Carole Bayer Sager; Director, Robert Moore; Musical Numbers Staged by Patricia Birch; Scenery and Projections, Douglas W. Schmidt; Costumes, Ann Roth; Lighting, Tharon Musser; Music Direction, Larry Blank; Orchestrations, Ralph Burns, Richard Hazard, Gene Page; Assistant to Mr. Moore, George Rondo; Sound, Tom Morse; Associate Conductor, Fran Liebergall; Wardrobe, Michael Dennison; Hairstylist, John Qualgia, Assistant to Producer, Leslie Butler; Hair and Wig Designs, Kathryn Blondell; Original Cast Album by Casablanca Records

CAST

Vernon . . . . Robert Klein
Sonia Walsk . . . . Lucie Arnaz
Voices of Vernon Gersch . . . . Wayne Mattson, Andy Roth, Greg Zadikov
Voices of Sonia Walsk . . . . Helen Castillo, Celia Celnik Matthau, Debbie Shapiro
Voice of Phil the Engineer . . . . Philip Cusack

STANDBYS AND UNDERSTUDIES: John Getz (Vernon), Debbie Shapiro (Sonia), Max Stone (Swing Singer-Dancer), Lani Sundsten (Swing Singer-Dancer/Dance Captain)

MUSICAL NUMBERS: "Fallin'," "Workin' It Out," "If He Really Knew Me," "They're Playing Our Song," "Right," "Just for Tonight," "When You're in My Arms," "I Still Believe in Love" (reprise sung by Johnny Mathis), "Fill in the Words"

A comedy with music in 2 acts and 13 scenes. The action takes place at the present time in Vernon's New York City apartment, in Le Club, Sonia's apartment, on the street, on the road, in a beach house in Quogue, Long Island, in a recording studio, in a Los Angeles hospital room.

General Manager: Jose Vega
Company Managers: Susan Bell, Maria Anderson
Press: Bill Evans, Howard Atlee, Claudia McAllister
Stage Managers: Robert D. Currie, Philip Cusack, Bernard Pollock

* Still playing May 31, 1979.

Jay Thompson Photos

Top: Robert Klein, Greg Zadikov, Wayne Mattson, Andy Roth Right: Debbie Shapiro, Helen Castillo, Celia Celnik Matthau, Lucie Arnaz (seated)

Lucie Arnaz, Robert Klein

ANTA THEATRE
    Opened Wednesday, February 14, 1979.*
    Ashton Springer, Frank C. Pierson, Michael P. Price present:

WHOOPEE!

Book, William Anthony McGuire; Based on "The Nervous Wreck" by Owen Davis; Music, Walter Donaldson; Lyrics, Gus Kahn; Director, Frank Corsaro; Choreography and Musical Staging, Dan Siretta; Musical Direction, Lynn Crigler; Scenery, John Lee Beatty; Costumes, David Toser; Lighting, Peter M. Ehrhardt; Sound, Warren E. Jenkins; Music Research Consultant, Alfred Simon; Hairstylist, Masarone; Production Supervisor, Ron Abbott; Production Consultant, G. William Oakley; Orchestrations and Dance Arrangements, Russell Warner; Associate Producers, Martin Markinson, Joseph Harris, Donald Tick; Assistant Choreographer, Larry McMillan; Wardrobe, Olga Anderson, Linda Lee; Production Assistants, Martha Gonsalves, June Archibald, Michael Kerley

CAST

Sheriff Bob	J. Kevin Scannell†1
Mary Custer	Carol Swarbrick†2
Judson Morgan	Bob Allen
Sally Morgan	Beth Austin
Henry Williams	Charles Repole
Wanenis	Franc Luz
Black Eagle	Leonard Drum
Chester Underwood	Garrett M. Brown†3
Harriet Underwood	Catherine Cox
Jerome Underwood	Peter Boyden
Mort	Vic Polizos†4
Andy McNab	Bill Rowley
Jim	Al Micacchion
Slim	Steven Gelfer
Jack	Rick Pessagno
Pete	Paul M. Elkin
Red Buffalo	Brent Saunders
Matape	Candy Darling
Leslie	Susan Stroman
Becky	Robin Black
Tilly	Diane Epstein
Olive	Teri Corcoran
Ensemble Alternates	Jo-Ann Cifala, Jonathan Aronson

STANDBYS AND UNDERSTUDIES: Al Micacchion (Bob), Candy Darling (Mary), Robin Black (Sally), Paul M. Elkin (Wanenis), Brent Saunders (Black Eagle/Mort), Rick Pessagno (Chester/Andy), Susan Stroman (Harriet), Bill Rowley (Judson/Jerome), Steven Gelfer (Henry)

MUSICAL NUMBERS: "Let's All Make Whoopee Tonight," "Makin' Whoopee," "I'm Bringing a Red, Red Rose," "Go Get 'Im," "Until You Get Somebody Else," "Love Me or Leave Me," "My Baby Just Cares for Me," "Out of the Dawn," "The Tapahoe Tap," "Reaching for Someone," "You," "Yes, Sir, That's My Baby"

A musical comedy in 2 acts and 12 scenes. The action takes place in Mission Rest, Arizona, in Black Top Canyon, Bar "M" Ranch, Indian Reservation, in the desert.

General Management: Theatre Management Associates, Trudy Brown
Company Manager: Alexander Holt
Press: Max Eisen, Irene Gandy, Francine L. Trevens
Stage Managers: John J. Bonanni, John Beven, Joann Cifala

* Closed Aug. 12, 1979 after 204 performances and 8 previews.
† Succeeded by: 1. Nicholas Wyman, 2. Bonnie Leaders, 3. John Sloman, 4. John Ahlin

Bert Andrews Photos

**Top Right: Charles Repole, Beth Austin
Below: Peter Boyden, Garrett M. Brown,
Catherine Cox, J. Kevin Scannell**

Bob Allen, Charles Repole, J. Kevin Scannell

MARK HELLINGER THEATRE
Opened Friday, February 23, 1979.*
(Moved to Broadway Theatre Thursday, March 1, 1979)
Eugene V. Wolsk presents:

SARAVA

Book and Lyrics, N. Richard Nash; Music, Mitch Leigh; Based on "Dona Flor and Her Two Husbands" by Jorge Amado; Directed and Choreographed by Rick Atwell; Sets and Costumes, Santo Loquasto; Lighting, David F. Segal; Musical Direction and Vocal Arrangements, David Friedman; Orchestrations, Daniel Troob; Dance Arrangements, Dom Salvador; Sound, Robert Kerzman; Hairstylist, Vincent Tucker; Assistant to Producer, Cheryl Raab; Wardrobe, Grayson L. Wideman; Assistant Choreographer, Joseph Pugliese; Production Assistant, Mark Eichorn; Production Manager, Nicholas Russiyan

CAST

Vadinho . . . . P. J. Benjamin
Flor . . . . Tovah Feldshuh
Arigof . . . . Roderick Spencer Sibert
Costas . . . . Doncharles Manning
Manuel . . . . Wilfredo Suarez
Dealer . . . . Jack Neubeck
Dionisia . . . . Carol Jean Lewis
Policemen . . . . Loyd Sannes, Gaetan Young
Dona Paiva . . . . Betty Walker
Rosalia . . . . Randy Graff
Antonio . . . . Alan Abrams
Priest . . . . Ken Waller
Teo . . . . Michael Ingram
Senhor Baldez . . . . Jack Neubeck
Pinho . . . . David Kottke

PEOPLE OF BAHIA: Steve J. Ace, Frank Cruz, Donna Cyrus, Marlene Danielle, Adrienne Frimet, Brenda Garratt, Trudie Green, Jane Judge, David Kottke, Daniel Lorenzo, Doncharles Manning, Jack Nuebeck, Thelma Anne Nevitt, Ivson Polk, Wynonna Smith, Michelle Stubbs, Wilfredo Suarez, Ken Waller, Freida Ann Williams, John Leslie Wolfe, Gaetan Young

UNDERSTUDIES: Donna Cyrus (Flor/Rosalia), Jack Neubeck (Vadinho/Antonio), Ken Waller (Teo), Jane Judge (Dona Paiva), Freida Ann Williams (Dionisia), Doncharles Manning (Arigof), Gaetan Young (Costas), Daniel Lorenzo (Priest), Frank Cruz (Policeman/Manuel), John Brigleb (Dealer/Baldez/Pinho)

MUSICAL NUMBERS: "Sarava," "Makulele," "Vadinho Is Gone," "Hosanna," "Nothing's Missing," "I'm Looking for a Man," "A Simple Man," "Viva a Vida," "Muito Bom," "Play the Queen," "Which Way Do I Go?," "Remember," "You Do," "A Single Life," Finale

A musical in 2 acts and 17 scenes. The action takes place in Bahia, Brazil from Carnival to Carnival.

General Management: GRQ Productions, Manny Kladitis
Press: John A. Prescott, M. J. Boyer
Stage Managers: Douglas F. Goodman, John Brigleb

* Closed June 17, 1979 after 140 performances and 37 previews.

Bert Andrews Photos

Top Left: Tovah Feldshuh

Tovah Feldshuh, Michael Ingram

Center: P. J. Benjamin, Tovah Feldshuh, Michael Ingram

NEW APOLLO THEATRE
Opened Wednesday, February 28, 1979.*
Arthur Cantor and Greer Garson present:

ON GOLDEN POND

By Ernest Thompson; Director, Craig Anderson; Set Design and Costumes, Steven Rubin; Lighting, Craig Miller; Assistant to Director, Matthew Laurance; Production Coordinator, Louis D. Pietig; Sound, David S. Rapkin; Wardrobe, Bruce A. H. Horowitz; Production Assistants, Doug Hughes, Thomas C. Madigan, Loretta Robertson, Christopher S. Rosen; A Hudson Guild Theatre Production (Craig Anderson, Producing Director)

CAST

Norman Thayer, Jr.	Tom Aldredge
Ethel Thayer	Frances Sternhagen
Charlie Martin	Ronn Carroll
Chelsea Thayer Wayne	Barbara Andres
Billy Ray	Mark Bendo
Bill Ray	Stan Lachow

UNDERSTUDIES AND STANDBYS: Helen Harrelson (Ethel), Bryan E. Clark (Norman/Charlie/Bill), Eric Brown (Billy), Judith Elizabeth Lowry (Chelsea)

A comedy in two acts and five scenes. The action takes place at the present time in the living room of the Thayers' summer home on Golden Pond in Maine.

Manager: Harvey Elliott
Company Manager: Jim Fiore
Press: C. George Willard, Kevin Patterson
Stage Managers: Daniel Morris, Judith Elizabeth Lowry

* Closed June 16, 1979 after 126 performances and 5 previews. It had played a limited engagement of 36 performances at the Hudson Guild Theatre from Sept. 15 through Oct. 22, 1978.

Ronn Carroll, Frances Sternhagen, Barbara Andres
Above: Frances Sternhagen, Mark Bendo,
Tom Aldredge

Top: Tom Aldredge, Frances Sternhagen

URIS THEATRE
Opened Thursday, March 1, 1979.*
Richard Barr, Charles Woodward, Robert Fryer, Mary Lea Johnson, Martin Richards in association with Dean and Judy Manos present:

SWEENEY TODD
The Demon Barber of Fleet Street

Music and Lyrics, Stephen Sondheim; Book, Hugh Wheeler; Based on a version of "Sweeney Todd" by Christopher Bond; Director, Harold Prince; Dance and Movement, Larry Fuller; Production Design, Eugene Lee; Costumes, Franne Lee; Lighting, Ken Billington; Orchestrations, Jonathan Tunick; Musical Director, Paul Gemignani; Associate Producer, Marc Howard; Assistant to Mr. Prince, Ruth Mitchell; Assistants to the Producers, Jerry Sirchia, Sam Crothers; Sound, Jack Mann; Wigs, Lynn Quiyou; Makeup, Barbara Kelly; Technical Director, Arthur Siccardi; Wardrobe, Adelaide Laurino; Hairstylist, Vincenzo Prestia; Production Assistants, Fran Soeder, Toby Beckwith; Original Cast Album by RCA Records

CAST

Anthony Hope	Victor Garber
Sweeney Todd	Len Cariou
Beggar Woman	Merle Louise
Mrs. Lovett	Angela Lansbury
Judge Turpin	Edmund Lyndeck
The Beadle	Jack Eric Williams
Johanna	Sarah Rice
Tobias Ragg	Ken Jennings
Pirelli	Joaquin Romaguera
Jonas Fogg	Robert Ousley

THE COMPANY: Duane Bodin, Walter Charles, Carole Doscher, Nancy Eaton, Mary-Pat Green, Cris Groenendaal, Skip Harris, Marthe Ihde, Betsy Joslyn, Nancy Killmer, Frank Kopyc, Spain Logue, Robert Ousley, Richard Warren Pugh, Maggie Task, and Swings: Heather B. Withers, Robert Hendersen

UNDERSTUDIES: Maggie Task (Mrs. Lovett), Walter Charles (Sweeney), Cris Groenendaal (Anthony), Betsy Joslyn (Johanna), Richard Warren Pugh (Beadle), Robert Ousley (Judge), Skip Harris (Tobias), Frank Lopyc (Pirelli), Pamela McLernon (Beggar Woman)

MUSICAL NUMBERS: "The Ballad of Sweeney Todd," "No Place Like London," "The Barber and His Wife," "The Worst Pies in London," "Poor Thing," "My Friends," "Green Finch and Linnet Bird," "Ah, Miss," "Johanna," "Pirelli's Miracle Elixir," "The Contest," "Wait," "Kiss Me," "Ladies in Their Sensitivities," "Quartet," "Pretty Women," "Epiphany," "A Little Priest," "God, That's Good!," "By the Sea," "Not While I'm Around," "Parlor Songs," "City on Fire!," Finale

A musical in two acts. The action takes place during the 19th Century in London on Fleet Street and environs.

General Management: Gatchell & Neufeld Ltd.
Company Manager: Drew Murphy
Press: Mary Bryant, Ruth V. Pivirotto
Stage Managers: Alan Hall, Ruth E. Rinklin, Arthur Masella

* Still playing May 31, 1979. Winner of 1979 "Tonys" for Best Book, Best Score, Best Scenic Design, Best Costume Designs, Best Actress (Angela Lansbury), Best Actor (Len Cariou), Best Direction, and Best Musical. It also received the Drama Critics Circle Award.

Van Williams, Martha Swope Photos

**Top Left: Angela Lansbury, Len Cariou
(also below)**

Angela Lansbury, Len Cariou

Ken Jennings, Angela Lansbury Above: Jack Eric Williams, Len Cariou, Angela Lansbury

Sarah Rice Above: Ken Jennings (L), Joaquin Romaguera (R) Top: Angela Lansbury

GOLDEN THEATRE
Opened Sunday, March 4, 1979.*
Mike Merrick and Bill Wilson in association with Peter Owens
present:

STRANGERS

By Sherman Yellen; Director, Arvin Brown; Settings, David Jenkins; Costumes, Ann Roth; Lighting, Ronald Wallace; Business Manager, Peter T. Kulok; Wardrobe, Anthony Karniewich; Hairstylists, J. Roy Helland, Christopher Calabrese; Assistant to Producers, Linda Clark; Makeup, Joseph Cranzano

CAST

Sinclair "Hal" Lewis . . . . Bruce Dern
Dorothy Thompson . . . . Lois Nettleton
German Guest/Waiter/Russian Commissar/
  Hotel Manager/Swedish Reporter/
  American Reporter/Psychiatrist . . . . William Newman
German Guest/Dancer/Russian Commissar/
  Moira/Crista/American Reporter/Corinna . . . . . . Ellen Parker
German Guest/Dancer/German Pilot/
  Russian Commissar/Josef/S.S. Man . . . . . . Jean-Pierre Stewart

STANDBYS AND UNDERSTUDIES: Jacqueline Coslow (Miss Nettleton), William Newman (Mr. Dern), Jean-Pierre Stewart (Mr. Newman), Dan Hild (Mr. Stewart)

A drama in two acts. The action takes place in Europe and the United States between the years 1927–1948.

General Managers: Joseph Harris, Ira Bernstein, Nancy Simmons
Press: Seymour Krawitz, Louise Weiner Ment, Patricia McLean
Krawitz
Stage Managers: Franklin Keysar, Dan Hild
* Closed March 11, 1978 after 9 performances and 12 previews.

Sy Friedman Photos

Lois Nettleton, Bruce Dern
(also at top)

CIRCLE IN THE SQUARE
Opened Thursday, March 15, 1979.*
Circle in the Square (Theodore Mann, Artistic Director; Paul
Libin, Managing Director) and Long Wharf Theatre (Arvin
Brown, Artistic Director; M. Edgar Rosenblum, Executive Director) present:

SPOKESONG
or The Common Wheel

By Stewart Parker; Music, Jimmy Kennedy; Lyrics, Stewart
Parker; Director, Kenneth Frankel; Set, Marjorie Kellogg; Costumes, Bill Walker; Lighting, John McLain; Wigs and Hairstyles,
Paul Huntley; Musical Director and Pianist, Thomas Fay; Cycle
Coach, John Jenack; Wardrobe, Rachele Bussanich; Vocal Coach,
Elizabeth Smith

CAST

The Trick Cyclist	Joseph Maher
Frank	John Lithgow
Daisy	Virginia Vestoff
Francis, Frank's grandfather	Josef Sommer
Kitty, Francis' wife	Maria Tucci
Julian, Frank's brother	John Horton

A drama in two acts. The action takes place in the 1970's and the
80 years preceding in a bicycle shop in Belfast, Northern Ireland.

Company Manager: William Conn
Press: Merle Debuskey, Leo Stern, William Schelble
Stage Managers: Anne Keefe, James Bernardi

* Closed May 20, 1979 after 77 performances and 21 previews.

W. B. Carter Photos

**Right: John Lithgow, Virginia Vestoff
Top: Virginia Vestoff, John Lithgow,
John Horton**

Joseph Maher

Maria Tucci, Josef Sommer

Cast and playwright (C)

WINTER GARDEN THEATRE

Opened Sunday, March 25, 1979.*

The Shubert Organization (Gerald Schoenfeld, Chairman; Bernard B. Jacobs, President), Center Theatre Group of Los Angeles/Mark Taper Forum (Gordon Davidson, Artistic Director; William Wingate, General Manager), and Gordon Davidson present the Mark Taper Forum Production of:

ZOOT SUIT

Written and Directed by Luis Valdez; Choreographic Sequences, Patricia Birch; Musical Sequences and Production, Daniel Valdez; Setting, Thomas A. Walsh (Concept by Roberto Morales, Thomas A. Walsh); Costumes, Peter J. Hall; Lighting, Dawn Chiang; Sound, Abe Jacob; Production Associate, Kenneth S. Brecher; Assistant Director, Jack Bender; Presented in association with Lou Adler; Wardrobe, Thomas Gautier. Margaret Floyd; Music Coordinator, Earl Shendell; Technical Director, Robert Routolo; Production Assistant, Trisha Whitehurst; Hairstylist, Ronald DeMann; Original Arrangements. Dan Kuramoto, Daniel Valdez; Additional Orchestrations, Dan Kuramoto; Theme by Daniel Valdez

CAST

El Pachuco	Edward James Olmos
Henry Reyna	Daniel Valdez

His Family:

Enrique Reyna	Abel Franco
Dolores Reyna	Lupe Ontiveros
Lupe Reyna	Roberta Delgado Esparza
Rudy Reyna	Tony Plana

His Friends:

George Shearer	Charles Aidman
Alice Bloomfield	Karen Hensel

His Gang:

Della Barrios	Rose Portillo
Smiley Torres	Geno Silva
Joey Castro	Mike Gomez
Tommy Roberts	Paul Mace
Elena Torres	Laura Leyva
Bertha Villareal	Angela Moya
Cholo	Luis Manuel

Los Angelinos:

Swabbie	Dennis Stewart
Manchuka	Kim Miyori
Zooter	Lewis Whitlock
Little Blue	Darlene Bryan

The Downey Gang:

Rafas	Miguel Delgado
Ragman	Lee Mathis
Hobo	Richard Jay-Alexander
Guera	Gela Jacobson
Blondie	Helena Andreyko
Hoba	Michele Mais
Lt. Edwards/Judge Charles/Guard	Vincent Duke Milana
Sgt. Smith/Bailiff/Sailor	Raymond Barry
Press	Arthur Hammer
Cub Reporter/Sailor	Dennis Stewart
Newsboy/Sailor	Lee Mathis
Marine	Richard Jay-Alexander

UNDERSTUDIES: Raymond Barry (Lt./Judge/Guard/Press), Laura Leyva (Della/Lupe), Gela Jacobson (Alice), Richard Jay-Alexander (Smiley/Rudy/Rafas/Cub Reporter), Michele Mais (Bertha/Elena), Lee Mathis (Sgt./Bailiff), Vincent Duke Milana (George), Luis Manuel (Joey/Marine/Swabbie/Sailors), Angela Moya (Dolores), Tony Plana (Henry), Dennis Stewart (Tommy), Geno Silva (El Pachuco/Enrique), Lewis Whitlock (Newsboy)

A drama with music in two acts. The action takes place between the fall of 1942 and the fall of 1944 in the barrios of Los Angeles, San Quentin Prison, and the mind of Henry Reyna, and loosely based on actual events.

General Manager: Max Allentuck
Company Manager: Leo K. Cohen
Press: Merle Debuskey, Owen Levy
Stage Managers: Milt Commons, Bethe Ward, Miguel Delgado

* Closed April 29, 1979 after 41 performances and 17 previews.

Martha Swope Photos

Top Left: Edward James Olmos (C), Daniel Valdez (R) Below: Charles Aidman

BROOKS ATKINSON THEATRE

Opened Thursday, March 29, 1979.*

Whitehead-Stevens, George W. George, Frank Milton present the National Theatre Company of Great Britain in:

BEDROOM FARCE

By Alan Ayckbourn; Directed by Alan Ayckbourn, Peter Hall; Designed by Timothy O'Brien, Tazeena Firth; Lighting, Peter Radmore; Scenery and Lighting Supervised by Marc B. Weiss; Production Assistant, Bill Becker; Wardrobe, Arlene Konowitz; Hairstylist, Andre Verna

CAST

Ernest	Michael Gough†1
Delia	Joan Hickson†2
Nick	Michael Stroud†3
Jan	Polly Adams†4
Malcolm	Derek Newark†5
Kate	Susan Littler†6
Trevor	Stephen Moore†7
Susannah	Delia Lindsay†8

STANDBYS: Richard Bey (Nick), Wayne Carson (Nick/Malcolm), Judith Ivey (Kate), Marion Lines (Jan/Kate), Ellen Tobie (Jan), Jane House (Susannah), Joan White (Delia), Barry Cullison (Trevor)

A comedy in two acts. The action takes place at the present time on one long Saturday night.

General Manager: Oscar E. Olesen
Company Manager: Marshall Young
Press: Jeffrey Richards, Warren Knowlton, Helen Stern
Stage Managers: Frederic De Wilde, Wayne Carson, Barry Cullison

* Still playing May 31, 1979. Michael Gough and Joan Hickson received 1979 "Tonys" for oustanding performances by featured actress and actor in a play.
† Succeeded by: 1. Robert Coote, 2. Mildred Natwick, 3. John Horton, 4. Lynn Milgrim, 5. David Schramm, 6. Judith Ivey, 7. John Lithgow, 8. Alma Cuervo

*Anthony Crickmay, John Haynes,
Richard Braaten Photos
Sy Friedman Photos*

Top Left: Stephen Moore, Susan Littler, Derek Newark Below: Michael Gough, Joan Hickson

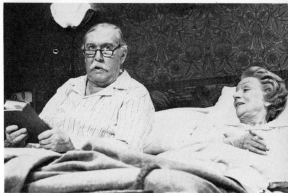

Stephen Moore, Delia Lindsay
Above: Michael Stroud, Polly Adams

Robert Coote, Mildred Natwick
Above: Alma Cuervo, John Lithgow

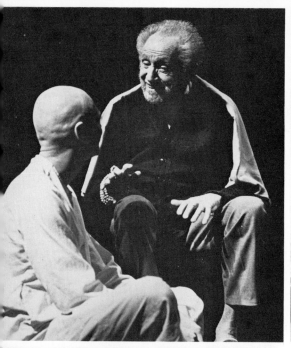

PALACE THEATRE
 Opened Wednesday, March 28, 1979.*
 Terry Allen Kramer and Harry Rigby present:

A MEETING BY THE RIVER

By Christopher Isherwood and Don Bachardy; Director, Albert Marre; Scenery, Robert Mitchell; Lighting, Clarke W. Thornton; Costumes, Marianne Custer; Incidental Music, Glen Roven; Associate Producer, Jack Schlissel; Assistant to Director, Ed Kerrigan; Production Assistants, Adam Marre, Cathy Caster; Hairstylists, Wayne Herndon, Jennifer Berman; Wardrobe, Patricia Lang

CAST

Margaret	Siobhan McKenna
Oliver	Simon Ward
Patrick	Keith Baxter
Penelope	Meg Wynn-Owen
Asim	Gilbert Cole
Passport Official	Jonathan Epstein
Rafferty	Paul Collins
Head Swami	Ronald Bishop
Second Swami	Faizul Khan
Third Swami	Arjun Sajnani
Tarun Maharaj	Sam Jaffe
Fourth Swami	Leslie Goldstein
Swami Vegananda	Ed Kerrigan
Photographer	Harsh Nayyar
Tom	Keith McDermott

UNDERSTUDIES: Paul Collins (Oliver/Patrick), Bettye Ackerman (Margaret/Penelope), Gilbert Cole (Tom), Arjun Sajnani (Head Swami), Jonathan Epstein (Rafferty), Faizul Khan (Tarun Maharaj)

A play in three acts. The major action takes place at the present time in and about the grounds of a monastery outside Calcutta on the banks of the Ganges. Other locales include the Calcutta airport, a country house in England, a hotel room in Japan, and an apartment in Los Angeles.

General Management: Jack Schlissel/Jay Kingwill
Press: Henry Luhrman, Bill Miller, Terry M. Lilly, Kevin P. McAnarney
Stage Managers: Susie Cordon, Andy Bew, Ron Durbian

* Closed March 28, 1979 after one performance and 10 previews.

Bill Nation Photos

Keith Baxter, Simon Ward Above: Faizul Khan, Keith Baxter, Ronald Bishop

**Top: Siobhan McKenna, Meg Wynn-Owen
Left: Simon Ward, Sam Jaffe**

LONGACRE THEATRE
Opened Thursday, April 5, 1979.*
Morton Gottlieb presents:

FAITH HEALER

By Brian Friel; Director, Jose Quintero; Scenery, John Lee Beatty; Costumes, Jane Greenwood; Lighting, Marilyn Rennagel; Associate Producers, Ben Rosenberg, Warren Crane; Production Assistant, John McManus; Wardrobe, Penny Davis; Assistant to Director, John Handy

CAST

Frank	James Mason
Grace	Clarissa Kaye
Teddy	Donal Donnelly

STANDBYS: William Myers (Frank/Teddy), Barbara Lester (Grace)

A drama in two acts and four scenes.

General Manager: Ben Rosenberg
Company Manager: Martin Cohen
Press: Solters & Roskin, Milly Schoenbaum, Rima Corben, David LeShay
Stage Managers: Warren Crane, John Handy

* Closed April 21, 1979 after 20 performances and 7 previews.

Martha Swope Photos

(No production photos)

Jose Quintero (director), Clarissa Kaye, James Mason
Top Right: Donal Donnelly

ST. JAMES THEATRE
Opened Sunday, April 8, 1979.*
Roger L. Stevens, J. W. Fisher, Joan Cullman and Jujamcyn
Productions present:

CARMELINA

Book, Alan Jay Lerner. Joseph Stein; Based on the film "Buona Sera, Mrs. Campbell"; Music, Burton Lane; Lyrics, Alan Jay Lerner; Director, Jose Ferrer; Choreography. Peter Gennaro; Sets, Oliver Smith; Costumes, Donald Brooks; Lighting, Feder; Sound, John McClure; Orchestrations, Hershy Kay; Musical Direction, Don Jennings; Vocal Arrangements, Maurice Levine; Dance Music Arrangements, David Krane; A Whitehead-Stevens Production; Production Assistant, William Becker; Assistant to Director, P. J. Laurel; Assistant to Choreographer, Marybeth Kurdock; Wardrobe, Toni Baer; Hairstylist, Masarone; Assistant Conductor, Fred Manzella

CAST

Bellini	Marc Jordan
Mayor Nunzio Manzoni	Gonzalo Madurga
Vittorio Bruno	Cesare Siepi
Rosa	Grace Keagy
Salvatore	Ian Towers
Signora Carmelina Campbell	Georgia Brown
Signora Bernardi	Judy Sabo
Roberto Bonafaccio	Joseph d'Angerio
Father Tommaso	Frank Bouley
Gia Campbell	Jossie de Guzman
Walter Braddock	Gordon Ramsey
Steve Karzinski	Howard Ross
Carlton Smith	John Michael King
Flo Braddock	Virginia Martin
Mildred Karzinski	Kita Bouroff
Katherine Smith	Caryl Tenney
Father Federico	David E. Thomas

ENSEMBLE: Frank Bouley, Kita Bouroff, Kathryn Carter, Karen DiBianco, Spence Ford, Ramon Galindo, Liza Gennaro, Laura Klein, Michael Lane, Morgan Richardson, Judy Sabo, Charles Spoerri, Caryl Tenney, David E. Thomas, Ian Michael Towers, Kevin Wilson, Lee Winston, and Swing Dancers: Debra Mathews, Michael Rivera

UNDERSTUDIES: Lorraine Serabian (Carmelina), Howard Ross (Vittorio), Frank Bouley (Braddock/Smith), Judy Sabo (Rosa/Mildred/Katherine), Debra Matthews (Gia), Michael Rivera (Roberto), Marc Jordan (Manzoni), Charles Spoerri (Karzinski/Bellini), Kita Bouroff (Flo)

MUSICAL NUMBERS: "It's Time for a Love Song," "Why Him?," "I Must Have Her," "Someone in April," "Signora Campbell," "Love Before Breakfast," "Yankee Doodles Are Coming to Town," "One More Walk Around the Garden," "All That He'd Want Me to Be," "Carmelina," "The Image of Me," "I'm a Woman"

A musical in 2 acts and 12 scenes. The action takes place in 1961 somewhere in Italy.

General Manager: Oscar E. Olesen
Company Manager: David Hedges
Press: Jeffrey Richards, Warren Knowlton, Avivah Simon, Ken Sherber
Stage Managers: William Dodds, Jay Adler, Donnis Honeycutt

* Closed April 21, 1979 after 17 performances and 11 previews.

Martha Swope Photos

Georgia Brown, Cesare Siepi Above: Howard Ross, Jossie de Guzman, John Michael King, Gordon Ramsey

**The Ensemble
Top Left: Grace Keagy, Georgia Brown**

TRAFALGAR THEATRE
Opened Tuesday, April 17, 1979.*
Emanuel Azenberg, James M. Nederlander and Ray Cooney present:

WHOSE LIFE IS IT ANYWAY?

By Brian Clark; Director, Michael Lindsay-Hogg; Scenery, Alan Tagg; Costumes, Pearl Somner; Lighting, Tharon Musser; Presented by arrangement with Mermaid Theatre Trust; Technical Supervisor, Arthur Siccardi; Wardrobe, Reet Pell; Production Assistant, Gary Zabinski; Hairstylist, Patrik D. Moreton

CAST

Ken Harrison	Tom Conti
Sister Anderson	Beverly May
Kay Sadler	Pippa Pearthree
John	Damien Leake
Dr. Scott	Jean Marsh
Dr. Emerson	Philip Bosco
Mrs. Boyle	Veronica Castang
Philip Hill	Kenneth Welsh
Dr. Paul Travers	Peter McRobbie
Peter Kershaw	Russell Leib
Dr. Barr	Edward Genest
Andrew Eden	Richard DeFabees
Mr. Justice Millhouse	James Higgins

UNDERSTUDIES: Richard DeFabees (Ken), Catherine Gaffigan (Dr. Scott/Mrs. Boyle/Sister Anderson), Dianne Trulock (Kay), James Higgins (Dr. Emerson), Russell Leib (Dr. Barr)

A comedy in two acts. The action takes place in a hospital in England.

General Manager: Jose Vega
Company Manager: Laurel Ann Wilson
Press: Bill Evans, Howard Atlee, Claudia McAllister, James Baldassare
Stage Managers: Martin Herzer, Cathy B. Blaser, Dianne Trulock

* Still playing May 31, 1979. Mr. Conti received a 1979 "Tony" for outstanding performance by an actor in a play.

Martha Swope Photos

Left: Pippa Pearthree, Damien Leake Above: Beverly May, Tom Conti, Pippa Pearthree Top: Jean Marsh, Tom Conti

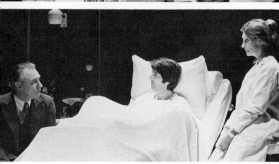

Philip Bosco, Tom Conti, Jean Marsh

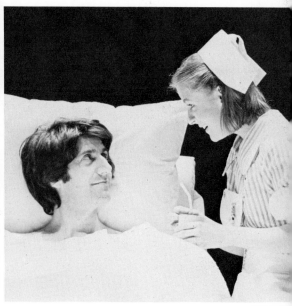

Tom Conti, Pippa Pearthree

BOOTH THEATRE
Opened Thursday, April 19, 1979.*
Richmond Crinkley, Elizabeth I. McCann, Nelle Nugent present the American National Theatre and Academy Production of:

THE ELEPHANT MAN

By Bernard Pomerance; Director, Jack Hofsiss; Setting, David Jenkins; Costumes, Julie Weiss; Lighting, Beverly Emmons; Associate Producers, Ray Larsen, Ted Snowdon; Production Supervisor, Brent Peek; Wardrobe, Lillias Norel; Hairstylist, Frank A. Melon; Wigs, Paul Huntley; Production Coordinator, Scott Steele; Assistant to Director, Eugene Draper; Projections, Wendall Harrington; Music by Bach, Sammartini, Saint-Saens, Faure, Elgar, Heiss

CAST

Belgian Policeman/Dr. Frederick Treves	Kevin Conway†1
Carr Gomm/Conductor	Richard Clarke
Ross/Bishop How/Snork	I. M. Hobson
John Merrick	Philip Anglim
Pinhead Manager/Policeman/Will/Earl/ Lord John	John Neville-Andrews
Pinhead/Miss Sandwich/Countess/ Princess Alexandra	Cordis Heard
Pinhead/Mrs. Kendal	Carole Shelley†2
Orderly	Dennis Creaghan
Cellist	David Heiss

UNDERSTUDIES: John Neville-Andrews (Belgian Policeman/Treves), Cordis Heard (Mrs. Kendal), Jack Weatherall (Merrick), Dennis Creaghan (Manager/Policeman/Will/Earl/Lord John), JoAnne Belanger (Miss Sandwich/Pinhead/Countess/Princess/Orderly), Michael Goldschlager (Cellist)

A drama in 2 acts and 21 scenes. John Merrick was a real person who spent the years 1886 to his death in 1890 in the London Hospital, Whitechapel.

Company Manager: Susan Gustafson
Press: Solters & Roskin, Joshua Ellis, Craig Macdonald, David LeShay
† Succeeded by: 1. Donal Donnelly, 2. Patricia Elliott

* Still playing May 31, 1979. Recipient of the NY Drama Critics Circle Award, and 1979 "Tonys" for Best Play, Best Direction, and Carole Shelley tied with Constance Cummings of "Wings" for outstanding actress in a play.

Left: I. M. Hobson, Kevin Conway

Philip Anglim, Kevin Conway

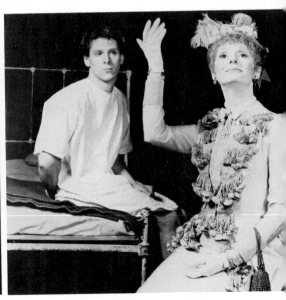

Philip Anglim, Carole Shelley

Philip Anglim, Carole Shelley, also
Top with Kevin Conway

Jack Wetherall, Donal Donnelly,
Patricia Elliott

SHUBERT THEATRE

Sunday, April 22, 1979.*
Kenneth Waissman and Maxine Fox present:

V.I.P. NIGHT ON BROADWAY

Conceived by Phyllis Newman as a star-studded evening of entertainment to buy bulletproof vests for New York City policemen; Sponsored by Burger King Restaurants of New York; Production Supervised by Patricia Birch; Music Direction, Larry Blank; Sets, Douglas W. Schmidt; Special Material, Jerome Alden; Lighting, Marilyn Rennegal; Production Coordinator, Bill Siegler; Assistant to Producers, Linda Schulz, Donna Donaldson; Assistant to Miss Birch, Peggy Peterson; Production Assistant, Laura Lawler Toole; Talent Coordinator, Ernie Angstadt; Music Coordinator, Earl Shendell; Musical Preparation, Matilde Pincus, Al Miller

Chita Rivera

Robin Williams

Marlo Thomas

PROGRAM

ACT I: Overture; Emerald Society Band; Chaplin Film Clip; Brooke Shields introducing New York's Finest; Marlo Thomas introducing Mayor Koch; American Dance Machine performing "I Love a Cop" and "Gee, Officer Krupke" featuring Liza Gennaro; Ken Page with a medley from "Ain't Misbehavin'"; Tovah Feldshuh and Charles Repole performing "Just an Honest Mistake" from "Let It Ride"; Geraldine Fitzgerald in "Street Songs"; Andy Kaufman; Sarah Jessica Parker, Alfred Toigo and Sandy from "Annie" performing "Tomorrow"; Bill Butler's Roller Disco.

ACT II: "Theatre Cops" read by Lauren Bacall, Barnard Hughes. Tovah Feldshuh, Kevin Kline and Maureen Stapleton; Chita Rivera, Victor Borge, James Mason introduction of Angela Lansbury who sang "Not While I'm Around" from "Sweeney Todd"; Lucie Arnaz, Millicent Martin, Janie Sell and Bill Boggs performing "Little Old New York" from "Tenderloin"; Robin Williams; Phyllis Newman; Steve Karmen performing his "I Love New York"

General Manager: Theatre Now/Edward H. Davis
Press: Pete Sanders, Tony Origlio, Robert DeVito

* Presented for one performance only.

Victor Borge

Maureen Stapleton

Andy Kaufman

Sam DeMillia, Kevin Kline, Ken Waissman, Tovah Feldshuh, Burger King, Ken Page, Adolph Green, Maxine Fox *(Doug Young Photo)*

PALACE THEATRE
Opened Sunday, April 29, 1979.*
Stephen R. Friedman, Irwin Meyer and Kenneth D. Laub in association with Arthur Mogull, Jerold H. Rubinstein and Warner Plays, Inc. present:

David Margulies (foreground), Patricia O'Connell, Jack Weston, Michael Connolly, Julie Harris, Joseph Leon, Rene Auberjonois, James Cahill, Timothy Lewis

BREAK A LEG

By Ira Levin; Director, Charles Nelson Reilly; Scenery, Peter Larkin; Costumes, Theoni V. Aldredge; Lighting, Marc B. Weiss; Production Associate, Claire Nichtern; Hairstylist, Ray Iagnocco; Assistant Director, Timothy Helgeson; Producers Assistants, Ellen Segal, Wendy Harris; Production Assistant, Chip Neufeld; Technical Coordinator, Arthur Siccardi; Wardrobe, Warren Morrill

CAST

Dietrich Merkenschrift, a theatrical manager	Jack Weston
Freitag, his assistant	Joseph Leon
Pepi Lubauer, a scenic designer	Michael Connolly
Imre Laszlo, a playwright	David Margulies
Gertie Kessel, an actress	Julie Harris
Johann Schiml, a critic	Rene Auberjonois
Mitzi Karlowe, a singing sweetheart	Patricia O'Connell
Carlo Mizzi, a singing sweetheart	James Cahill
Cleaning Woman/Wardrobe Mistress/ Usher/Actress	Patricia O'Connell
Coachman/Usher/Actor/Painter	James Cahill
Stagehand/Actors	Timothy Lewis
Actresses	Natalie Norwick

STANDBYS AND UNDERSTUDIES: Natalie Norwick (Gertie), Joseph Leon (Dietrich), Michael Connolly (Johann/Imre), Carlo Mizzi (Pepi), Timothy Lewis (Freitag), Fred Chalfy (Coachman/Usher/Actors/Painter)

A comedy in two acts and ten scenes. The action takes place "long ago in Vienna or Berlin, or Prague or Buda-Pesth. Anyway it's not New York and not now."

General Management: Gatchell & Neufeld
Company Manager: James G. Mennen
Press: Solters & Roskin, Milly Schoenbaum, Rima Corben, David LeShay
Stage Managers: Peter Lawrence, Fred Chalfy, James Woolley

* Closed April 29, 1979 after 1 performance and 12 previews.

Martha Swope Photos

Rene Auberjonois, Julie Harris

BELASCO THEATRE
   Opened Monday, April 30, 1979.*
Joseph Kipness and Maurice Rosenfield present:

THE GOODBYE PEOPLE

By Herb Gardner; Director, Jeff Bleckner; Setting, Santo Loquasto; Lighting, Jennifer Tipton; Costumes, Elizabeth Palmer; Associate Producers, Charlotte Dicker, Jamie Rosenfield

CAST

Arthur Korman	Ron Rifkin
Max Silverman	Herschel Bernardi
Nancy Scott	Melanie Mayron
Eddie Bergson	Marvin Lichterman
Michael Silverman	Michael Tucker
Marcus Soloway	Sammy Smith

A comedy in two acts. The action takes place on the beach at Coney Island in February of the present time.

Press: The Merlin Group
Production Supervisor/Stage Manager: Fritz Holt

* Closed April 30, 1979 after one performance and 16 previews. Original production opened Dec. 3, 1968 at the Ethel Barrymore Theatre and ran for 7 performances with Milton Berle, Brenda Vaccaro, Jess Osuna, Tony LoBianco, Sammy Smith.

Arne Lewis Photos

**Herschel Bernardi, also top with
Ron Rifkin, Melanie Mayron**

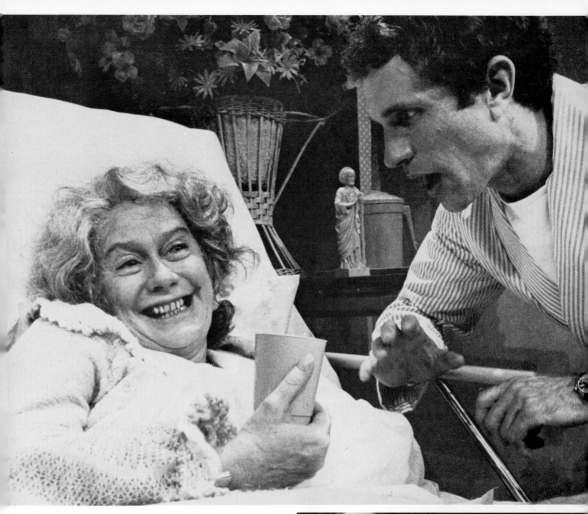

LONGACRE THEATRE
Opened Thursday, May 3, 1979.*
Bernard Gersten and John Wulp present:

BOSOMS AND NEGLECT

By John Guare; Director, Mel Shapiro; Scenery, John Wulp; Supervised by Lynn Pecktal; Costumes, Willa Kim; Lighting, Jennifer Tipton; Technical Coordinator, Arthur Siccardi; Wardrobe, Kate Gaudio

CAST

Scooper.................................... Paul Rudd
Henny...................................... Kate Reid
Deirdre................................. Marian Mercer

A comedy with a prologue and two acts. The action takes place at the present time in Henny's apartment, Deirdre's apartment, and Henny's hospital room.

General Manager: Max Allentuck
Press: Merle Debuskey, Leo Stern, William Schelble
Stage Managers: Zane Weiner, Peter Von Mayhauser

* Closed May 5, 1979 after 4 performances and 7 previews.

Thomas England Photos

Top: Kate Reid, Paul Rudd

Marian Mercer, Paul Rudd

47

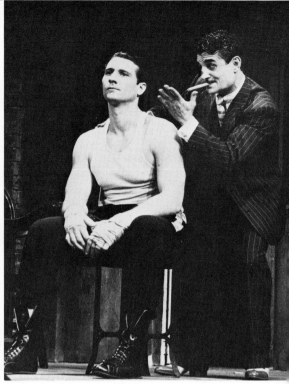

HELEN HAYES THEATRE
Opened Sunday, May 6, 1979.*
Bill Sargent presents:

KNOCKOUT

By Louis LaRusso II; Director, Frank Corsaro; Set, Karl Eigsti; Costumes, Jane Greenwood; Lighting, Neil Peter Jampolis; Technical Consultant, Jose Torres; Hairstylist, Phyllis Della; Executive Producer, Norman Maibaum; A SEE Theatre Network Presentation; Karen Rosetti, Executive in Charge of Production in association with Edward B. Rood, Sr.; Wardrobe, Bill Campbell

CAST

Damie Ruffino	Danny Aiello
Mac	David Patrick Kelly
Sonny Vincent	Michael Aronin
Gracie	Janet Sarno
Champ Sella	Frank Bongiorno
Paddy Klonski	Edward O'Neill
Kay	Margaret Warncke†

UNDERSTUDIES: Lou Tiano (Damie), Brad Gordon (Mac), Edward Horre, Jr. (Sonny), Erik Sonne (Paddy), Jeanne Napoli (Gracie), Carolyn Lenz (Kay), Eddie Miller (Champ)

A "romantic comedy" in 2 acts and 9 scenes. The action takes place in the Winter-Spring of 1948 in the River Street Recreation Center in Hoboken, NJ.

General Manager: M Square Management
Company Manager: David Lawlor
Press: Seymour Krawitz, Louise Weiner Ment, Patricia McLean Krawitz
Stage Managers: Jack Gianino, Brad Gordon, Shyler Nepveux

* Closed Sept. 16, 1979 after 154 performances and 10 previews.
† Succeeded by Judith McGilligan

Sy Friedman Photos

Danny Aiello, Janet Sarno, Michael Aronin
Above: Edward O'Neill, Judith McGilligan, Aiello

Top: Edward O'Neill, Frank Bongiorno
Left: David Patrick Kelly, Danny Aiello

MARK HELLINGER THEATRE
Opened Sunday, May 13, 1979.*
Arthur Whitelaw, Albert W. Selden, H. Ridgely Bullock in
association with Marc Howard present:

THE UTTER GLORY OF MORRISSEY HALL

Book, Clark Gesner, Nagle Jackson; Music and Lyrics, Clark
Gesner; Director, Nagle Jackson; Musical Numbers and Dances
Staged by Buddy Schwab; Sets and Lighting, Howard Bay; Costumes, David Graden; Hairstylist, Vincent of Enrico Caruso; Musical Director, John Lesko; Orchestrations, Jay Blackton, Russell
Warner; Dance Music Arrangements, Allen Cohen; Associate Producer, Sandy Stern; Production Assistant, Tom Carroll; Wardrobe,
Remigia Marmo; Sound, Charles Bellin; Producers Assistant, Howard P. Lev; Associate Conductor, Woody Kessler

CAST

Julia Faysle, Headmistress	Celeste Holm
Elizabeth Wilkins, Secretary	Marilyn Caskey
Foresta Studley	Patricia Falkenhain
Teresa Winkle	Laurie Franks
Mrs. Delmonde	Taina Elg
Miss Newton	Karen Gibson
Mr. Weyburn, Groundskeeper	John Wardwell
Carswell	Mary Saunders
Vickers	Gina Franz
Boody	Adrienne Alexander
Dale	Jill P. Rose
Dickerson	Kate Kelly
Haverfield	Polly Pen
Alice	Cynthia Parva
Helen	Becky McSpadden
Frances	Dawn Jeffory
Angela	Bonnie Hellman
Marjorie	Anne Kaye
Mary	Lauren Shub
Richard Tidewell	Willard Beckham
Charles Hill	John Gallogly
Mr. Osgood	Robert Lanchester

UNDERSTUDIES: Patricia Falkenhain (Headmistress), Willi
Burke (Studley/Newton), Karen Gibson (Winkle/Delmon-
de/Elizabeth). Polly Pen (Sixth Form Students), Mary Garripoli
(Fifth Form Students), Jonathan Arterton (Richard/Charles/-
Weyburn/Osgood)

MUSICAL NUMBERS: Overture, "Promenade," "Proud, Erst-
while, Upright, Fair," "Elizabeth's Song," "Way Back When,"
"Lost," "Morning," "The Letter," "Oh Sun," "Give Me That Key,"
"Duet," "Interlude and Gallop," "You Will Know When the Time
Has Arrived," "You Would Say," "See the Blue," "Dance of Resig-
nation," "Reflection," "The War," "The Ending"

A musical in two acts. The action takes place at the present time
in the Morrissey Hall School for Girls in England.

General Managers: Jack Schlissel/Jay Kingwill
Press: Betty Lee Hunt, Maria Cristina Pucci
Stage Managers: Mark S. Krause, Bryan Young, Gail Pearson

* Closed May 13, 1979 after one performance and seven previews.

Top Right: Celeste Holm

JOHN GOLDEN THEATRE
Opened Thursday, May 17, 1979.*
Lee Guber and Shelly Gross present:

MURDER AT THE HOWARD JOHNSON'S

By Ron Clark and Sam Bobrick; Director, Marshall W. Mason; Scenery, Karl Eigsti; Costumes, Sara Brook; Lighting, Richard Nelson; Associate Producers, David S. Newman, Fred Walker; Assistant to Director, John Manulis; Technical Supervisor, Mitch Miller; Wardrobe, Randy Beth; Producers Assistant, Connie Simmons; Production Assistant, Sherry Lambert; Creative Consultant, Bob Dishy.

CAST

Arlene Miller...........................Joyce Van Patten
Mitchell Lavell...........................Tony Roberts
Paul Miller...................................Bob Dishy

STANDBYS: Dorothy Emmerson, Harvey Siegel

A comedy in two acts and three scenes. The action takes place at the present time in Room 514 a week before Christmas, Room 907 on the Fourth of July, and Room 1015 on New Year's Eve.

General Managers: Theatre Now, Inc.
Company Manager: Stephen H. Arnold
Press: Solters & Roskin, Joshua Ellis, Rima Corben, David LeShay
Stage Managers: Mortimer Halpern, Conwell Worthington

* Closed May 19, 1979 after four performances and ten previews.

Martha Swope Photos

Left: Joyce Van Patten

Tony Roberts

Bob Dishy

BILTMORE THEATRE
Opened Wednesday, May 23, 1979.*
Ron Delsener presents the Dee Anthony Production of:

PETER ALLEN
"UP IN ONE"
with
Lenora Nemetz

Conceived by Peter Allen and Craig Zadan; Director, Craig Zadan; Choreography, Betsy Haug; Songs and Additional Musical Material Written by Peter Allen with Adrienne Anderson, Jeff Barry, Marvin Hamlisch, Marsha Malamet, Dean Pitchford, Carole Bayer Sager; Additional Material, Bruce Vilanch; Scenery, Douglas W. Schmidt; Lighting, Marilyn Rennagel; Costumes, Charles Suppon; Projections, Douglas W. Schmidt, Wendall K. Harrington; Sound, Thomas Morse; Production Coordinator, Gregory Connell; Production Supervisor, Janet Beroza; Musical Direction and Arrangements, Marc Shaiman; Special Arrangements, Marvin Hamlisch; Assistant Director, Neil Meron; Producer, Dee Anthony; Executive Producer, Vince Mauro; Wardrobe, Warren Morrill; Hairstylist and Makeup, James Barron

MUSICAL NUMBERS: "Dixie," "Don't Cry Out Loud," "Don't Wish Too Hard," "Everything Old Is New Again," "Fly Away," "Harlem on My Mind," "I Could Have Been a Sailor," "I Could Really Show You Around," "You," "Impatient Heart," "I Never Thought I'd Break," "Just a Gigolo," "Love Crazy," "Make 'Em Pay," "More Than I Like You," "Only Wounded," "Paris at 21," "Planes," "Puttin' Out Roots Again," "6:30 Sunday Morning," "Tenterfield Saddler," "Two Boys," "We've Come to an Understanding," "What Am I Doing Here," "You Oughta Hear Me Sing"

Performed without intermission.

General Managers: Marvin A. Krauss. Gary Gunas
Company Manager: Sam Pagliaro
Press: Betty Lee Hunt, Maria Cristina Pucci, Fred Hoot

* Closed June 30, 1979 after 46 performances and 5 previews.

Top: Peter Allen, Lenora Nemetz　　　　　**Lenora Nemetz, Peter Allen**

MAJESTIC THEATRE
Opened Thursday, May 31, 1979.*
Alexander H. Cohen and Hildy Parks present:

I REMEMBER MAMA

Music, Richard Rodgers; Lyrics, Martin Charnin; Book, Thomas Meehan; Additional Lyrics, Raymond Jessel; Based on play of same title by John Van Druten, and stories by Kathryn Forbes; Director, Cy Feuer; Musical Numbers Staged by Danny Daniels; Scenery, David Mitchell; Costumes, Theoni V. Aldredge; Lighting, Roger Morgan; Sound, Otts Munderloh; Orchestrations, Philip J. Lang; Musical Direction and Vocal Arrangements, Jay Blackton; Hairstylist, J. Roy Helland; Co-Producer, Roy A. Somlyo; Production Supervisor, Jerry Adler, Technical Coordinator, Arthur Siccardi; Wardrobe, Elonzo Dann; Assistant Conductor, Robert Stanley

CAST

Katrine	Maureen Silliman
Christine	Carrie Horner
Dagmar	Tara Kennedy
Johanne	Kristen Vigard†1
Nils	Ian Ziering
Papa	George Hearn
Mama	Liv Ullmann
Mr. McGuire	Dick Ensslen
Aunt Trina	Elizabeth Hubbard
Aunt Jenny	Dolores Wilson†2
Aunt Sigrid	Betty Ann Grove
Mr. Petersen	John Dorrin
Mr. Thorkelson	Armin Shimerman
Uncle Chris	George S. Irving
Lucie	Janet McCall
Nurse	Sigrid Heath
Dr. Anderson	Stan Page
Dame Sybil Fitzgibbons	Myvanwy Jenn

STEINER STREET NEIGHBORS: Angela App, Austin Colyer, John Dorrin, Mickey Gunnersen, Daniel Harnett, Danny Joel, Jan Kasni, Kevin Marcum, Richard Maxon, Marisa Morell, Frank Pietri, Elissa Wolfe

UNDERSTUDIES: Dick Ensslen (Uncle Chris), Stan Page (Papa), Janet McCall (Aunt Trina/Dame Sybil), Myvanwy Jenn (Aunt Jenny), Sigrid Heath (Aunt Sigrid), Kristen Vigard (Katrine), Elissa Wolfe (Johanne/Christine), Daniel Harnett (Nils), Marisa Morell (Dagmar), Austin Colyer (McGuire), Arthur Whitfield (Thorkelson), Elizabeth Hubbard (Mama), Alternate Performers: Cathy Rice, Arthur Whitfield

MUSICAL NUMBERS: "I Remember Mama," "A Little Bit More," "A Writer Writes at Night," "Ev'ry Day Comes Something Beautiful," "The Hardangerfjord," "You Could Not Please Me More," "Uncle Chris," "Easy Come, Easy Go," "It Is Not the End of the World," "Mama Always Makes It Better," "Lars, Lars," "Fair Trade," "It's Going to Be Good to Be Gone," "Time," Finale

A musical in two acts. The action takes place in San Francisco during the summer and fall of 1910 and the spring of 1911.

Company Managers: Charles Willard, David Hedges
Press: David Powers, Barbara Carroll, Martha Mason
Stage Managers: Robert Bennett, Christopher Cohen

* Closed Sept. 2, 1979 after 108 performances and 40 previews.

†Succeeded by: 1. Elissa Wolfe, 2. Grace Keagy

Martha Swope Photos

Top Left: Carrie Horner, George Hearn, Tara Kennedy (on lap), Kristen Vigard, Ian Ziering, Liv Ullmann, Maureen Silliman Below: Elizabeth Hubbard, Armin Shimerman, Betty Ann Grove, George S. Irving, Dolores Wilson

Liv Ullmann, Tara Kennedy

LONGACRE THEATRE
Opened Tuesday, May 8, 1978.*
(Moved Jan. 29, 1979 to Plymouth Theatre)
Emanuel Azenberg, Dasha Epstein, the Shubert Organization, Jane Gaynor and Ron Dante present:

AIN'T MISBEHAVIN'

Conceived and Directed by Richard Maltby, Jr.; Based on an idea by Murray Horwitz and Richard Maltby, Jr.; Musical Numbers Staged by Arthur Faria; Music Supervision, Luther Henderson; Associate Director, Murray Horwitz; Orchestrations and Arrangements, Luther Henderson; Vocal Arrangements, William Elliott, Jeffrey Gutcheon; Sets, John Lee Beatty; Costumes, Randy Barcelo; Lighting, Pat Collins; Sound, Otts Munderloh; Hairstylist, Paul Lopez; Wardrobe, Warren S. Morrill; Technical Coordinator, Arthur Siccardi; Assistant to Producers, Leslie Butler; Production Assistants, Jane Robison, Lisa Denton, Claudia McAllister, Evan Ross; Originally produced by Manhattan Theatre Club; Production Supervisor, Clint Spencer; Manager, Jose Vega

CAST

Neill Carter†1	Ken Page†6
Andre De Shields†2	Charlaine Woodard†3
Armelia McQueen†5	Luther Henderson (Pianist)†4

STANDBYS: Yolanda Graves (Debbie Allen), Vivian Jett (Armelia McQueen), Irving Allen Lee (Ken Page), Zoe Walker (Avery Sommers), Eric Riley (Alan Weeks)

MUSICAL NUMBERS: Ain't Misbehavin', Lookin' Good But Feelin' Bad, 'Tain't Nobody's Biz-ness If I Do, Honeysuckle Rose, Squeeze Me, Handful of Keys, I've Got a Feelin' I'm Fallin', How Ya Baby, The Jitterbug Waltz, The Ladies Who Sing with the Band, Yacht Club Swing, When the Nylons Bloom Again, Cash for Your Trash, Off-Time, The Joint Is Jumpin', Spreadin' Rhythm Around, Lounging at the Waldorf, The Viper's Drag, Mean to Me, Your Feet's Too Big, That Ain't Right, Keepin' Out of Mischief Now, Find Out What They Like, Fat and Greasy, Black and Blue, Finale

A musical entertainment based on the music of Thomas "Fats" Waller, performed in two acts.

Company Manager: John M. Kirby
Press: Bill Evans, Howard Altee, Claudia McAllister, Jim Baldassare
Stage Managers: Lani Ball, D. W. Koehler

Martha Swope Photos

* Still playing May 31, 1979. For original production, see THEATRE WORLD, Vol. 34. Received 1978 "Tonys" for Best Musical, Featured Actress (Nell Carter), Director; Voted Best Musical by NY Drama Critics, Drama Desk, and Outer Crictics Circle.
† Succeeded by: 1. Avery Sommers, 2. Alan Weeks, 3. Debbie Allen, Adriane Lenox, 4. Frank Owens, 5. Yvette Freeman, 6. Ken Prymus

Top Right: Andre DeShields, Armelia McQueen, Nell Carter, Charlaine Woodard, Ken Page, Luther Henderson Below: Ken Page, Hank Jones

Debbie Allen, Alan Weeks

Reid Shelton, Sandy, Shelley Bruce

ALVIN THEATRE
Opened Thursday, April 21, 1977.*
Mike Nichols presents:

ANNIE

Book, Thomas Meehan; Based on "Little Orphan Annie" comic strip; Music, Charles Strouse; Lyrics, Martin Charnin; Choreography, Peter Gennaro; Director, Martin Charnin; Producers, Irwin Meyer, Stephen R. Friedman, Lewis Allen; Settings, David Mitchell; Costumes, Theoni V. Aldredge; Lighting, Judy Rasmuson; Musical Direction and Dance Music Arrangements, Peter Howard; Orchestrations, Philip J. Lang; Produced by Alvin Nederlander Associates-Icarus Productions; Produced in association with Peter Crane; Assistant Conductor, Robert Billig, Paul Cianci; Technical Coordinator, Arthur Siccardi; Wardrobe, Adelaide Laurino; Production Assistants, Sylvia Pancotti, Stephen Graham; Assistant Choreographer, Mary Jane Houdina; Hairstylist, Ted Azar; Original Cast Album by Columbia Records.

CAST

Molly	Danielle Briseboist†1
Pepper	Robyn Finn†2
Duggy	Donna Graham†3
July	Janine Ruane†4
Tessie	Diana Barrows$15
Kate	Shelley Bruce†6
Annie	Andrea McArdle†7
Miss Hannigan	Dorothy Loudon†8
Bundles McCloskey/Ickes/ Sound Effects	James Hosbein
Dog Catcher/Jimmy Johnson/Honor Guard	Steven Boockvor†9
Dog Catcher/Bert Healy/Hull	Donald Craig
Sandy	Himself
Lt. Ward/Morganthau	Richard Ensslen
Harry/FDR	Raymond Thorne†15
Sophia/Cecile/Bonnie Boylan/Perkins	Laurie Beechman†10
Grace Farrell	Sandy Faison†11
Drake	Edwin Bordo
Mrs. Pugh/Connie Boylan	Edie Cowan
Annette/Ronnie Boylan	Penny Worth†12
Oliver Warbucks	Reid Shelton†13
Rooster Hannigan	Robert Fitch
Lily	Barbara Erwin†14
Fred McCracken/Howe	Bob Freschi†16
NBC Page	Mari McMinn

MUSICAL NUMBERS: Maybe, It's the Hard-Knock Life, Tomorrow, We'd Like to Thank You, Little Girls, I Think I'm Gonna Like It Here, N.Y.C., Easy Street, You Won't Be an Orphan for Long, You're Never Fully Dressed without a Smile, Something Was Missing, I Don't Need Anything But You, Annie, A New Deal for Christmas

A musical in 2 acts and 13 scenes. The action takes place December 11–25, 1933 in New York City.

General Management: Gatchell & Neufeld
Company Manager: Douglas C. Baker
Press: David Powers, Barbara Carroll
Stage Managers: Jack Timmers, Patrick O'Leary
* Still playing May 31, 1979. For original production see THEATRE WORLD, Vol. 33. Received 1977 NY Drama Critics Circle and "Tony" Awards for Best musical.
Succeeded by: 1. Jennine Babo, 2, Penny Marie Chaney, Jenn Thompson, 3. Randall Ann Brooks, 4. Kathy Jo Kelly, Sarah Jessica Parker, Jodi Ford, 5, Kimm Fedena, 6. Kim Fedena, Karen Schleifer, 7. Shelley Bruce, Sarah Jessica Parker, 8. Alice Ghostley, Dolores Wilson, 9. Gary Gendell, 10. Chris Jamison, 11. Lynn Kearney, Mary Bracken Phillips, 12. Jane Robertson, Ann Ungar, 13. Keene Curtis, John Schuck during vacation, 14. Annie McGreevey, 15. Alfred Toigo, 16. John Deyle,

Martha Swope Photos

Left Center: Alice Ghostley, Shelley Bruce, Sandy Faison Above: Alice Ghostley (C) and Jenn Thompson, Kim Fedena, Karen Schleifer, Sarah Jessica Parker, and (sitting) Randall Anne Brooks, Jennine Babo Top: Sandy and Shelley Bruce (C)

WINTER GARDEN THEATRE

Opened Wednesday, June 1, 1977.*
(Moved to Lunt-Fontanne Theatre, Thursday, March 1, 1979.)
David Krebs and Steven Leber present:

BEATLEMANIA

Songs written by John Lennon, Paul McCartney, George Harrison; Editorial Content, Robert Rabinowitz, Bob Gill, Lynda Obst; Visuals Director, Charles E. Hoefler; Multi-Media Images, Robert Rabinowitz, Bob Gill, Shep Kerman, Kathleen Rabinowitz; Original Concept, Steve Leber, David Krebs, Jules Fisher; Sound, Abe Jacob; Scenery, Robert D. Mitchell; Lighting Production Supervision, Jules Fisher; Musical Supervision, Sandy Yagudo; Hairstylist, Phyllis Della

CAST

Joe Pecorino	Leslie Fradkin
Mitch Weissman	Justin McNeill

A musical entertainment in two acts and nine scenes, celebrating the 1960's.

General Management: Marvin A. Krauss Associates
Company Managers: David Lawlor, Gary Gunas
Press: Solters & Roskin, Fred Nathan, David LeShay
Stage Managers: Robert V. Straus, John Actman, Robert I. Cohen, Sammy Knox

* Still playing May 31, 1979, without an official opening. For original production, see THEATRE WORLD, Vol. 34.

Mitch Weissman, Leslie Fradkin, Justin McNeill, Joe Pecorino
Top Left: Justin McNeill, Mitch Weissman, Leslie Fradkin

IMPERIAL THEATRE
    Opened Sunday, December 4, 1977.*
    (Moved to Eugene O'Neill Theatre, Tuesday, January 16, 1979)
    Emanuel Azenberg presents:

CHAPTER TWO

By Neil Simon; Director, Herbert Ross; Scenery, William Ritman; Costumes, Noel Taylor; Lighting, Tharon Musser; Wardrobe Supervisor, Frances LoDrini; Production Assistant, Jane Robinson; Assistant to Producer, Leslie Butler; Assistant to Director, Tony Elmaleh

CAST

George Schneider	Judd Hirsch[1]
Leo Schneider	Cliff Gorman[2]
Jennie Malone	Anita Gillette[3]
Faye Medwick	Ann Wedgeworth[4]

STANDBYS: Donald Gantry (George/Leo), Beverly Ballard (Jennie/Faye), Debra Mooney (Faye/Jennie), George Guidall (George/Leo)

A comedy in two acts. The action takes place from late February to mid-spring of the present time in Jennifer Malone's upper East Side apartment and George Schneider's lower Central Park West apartment in Manhattan.

Manager: Jose Vega
Company Manager: Leo Cohen
Press: Bill Evans, Claudia McAllister
Stage Managers: Martin Herzer, Beverly Randolph

* Still playing May 31, 1979. For original production, see THEATRE WORLD, Vol. 34.
  Succeeded by: 1. David Groh, Laurence Luckinbill, 2. Dick Latessa, Richard Zavaglia, 3. Robin Strasser, 4. Delphi Harrington, Jean DeBaer

Martha Swope Photos

Top: Jean DeBaer, Richard Zavaglia (also below)
Right and Below: Laurence Luckinbill, Robin Strasser

Anita Gillette, David Groh

SHUBERT THEATRE
Opened Sunday, October 19, 1975.*
Joseph Papp presents a New York Shakespeare Festival production in association with Plum Productions:

A CHORUS LINE

Conceived, Choreographed and Directed by Michael Bennett; Book, James Kirkwood, Nicholas Dante; Music, Marvin Hamlisch; Lyrics, Edward Kleban; Co-Choreographer, Bob Avian; Musical Direction/Vocal Arrangements, Don Pippin; Associate Producer, Bernard Gersten; Setting, Robin Wagner; Costumes, Theoni V. Aldredge; Lighting, Tharon Musser; Sound, Abe Jacob; Music Coordinator, Robert Thomas; Orchestrations, Bill Byers, Hershy Kay, Jonathan Tunick; Assistant to Choreographers/Dance Captain, Baayork Lee; Wardrobe, Alyce Gilbert; Production Supervisor, Jason Steven Cohen; Original Cast Album by Columbia Records.

CAST

Roy	Danny Ruvolo†1
Kristine	Deborah Geffner†2
Sheila	Kathrynann Wright
Val	Mitzi Hamilton†3
Mike	Jim Litten†4
Butch	Larry G. Bailey†5
Larry	Adam Grammis†6
Maggie	Donna Drake†7
Richie	Edward Love†8
Tricia	Cynthia Carrillo Onrubia
Tom	Cameron Mason†9
Zach	Kurt Johnson†10
Mark	Paul Charles†11
Cassie	Vicki Frederick†12
Judy	Sandahl Bergman†13
Lois	Patti D'Beck†14
Don	David Thome
Bebe†	Gillian Scalici†15
Connie	Janet Wong
Diana	Loida Iglesias†16
Al	Ben Lokey†17
Frank	Tim Cassidy†18
Greg	Justin Ross†19
Bobby	Christopher Chadman†20
Paul	Danny Ruvolo†21
Vicki	Crissy Wilzak†22
Barbara	Patti D'Beck
Ed	Mark Fotopoulos†23
Sam	Steve Riley
Jenny	Candace Tovar
Jarad	Troy Garza
Ralph	Dennis Parlato
Linda	Diane Fratantoni
Agnes	Betty Lynd

UNDERSTUDIES: Dean Badolato (Mike/Al), James Beaumont (Paul/Mark/Larry), Jim Corti (Paul), Patti D'Beck (Diana/Bebe/-Cassie), Michael Dean (Richie), Gail Mae Ferguson (Cassie/Sheila), Diane Fratantoni (Diana/Val/Connie/Maggie/Bebe), Troy Garza (Mike/Mark/Paul/Larry/Al), Angelique Ilo (Kristine), Betty Lynd (Val/Kristine/Maggie/Connie), Jon Michael Richardson (Greg), Claude Tessier (Bobby/Greg/Don/Al), David Thome (Zach), Timothy Wahrer (Paul), Marcia Lynn Watkins (Sheila)

MUSICAL NUMBERS: "I Hope I Get It," "I Can Do That," "And . . .," "At the Ballet," "Sing!," "Hello Twelve, Hello Thirteen, Hello Love," "Nothing," "Dance: Ten, Looks: Three," "Music and the Mirror," "One," "The Tap Combination," "What I Did for Love," Finale

A musical performed without intermission. The action takes place at the present time during an audition in this theatre.

General Manager: Robert Kamlot
Company Manager: Harris Goldman, Bob MacDonald
Press: Merle Debuskey, Bob Ullman, Richard Kornberg, Leo Stern
Stage Managers: Tom Porter, Wendy Mansfield, Jon Michael Richardson, James Beaumont

Top Right: Cheryl Clark, Scott Pearson

* Still playing May 31, 1979. Cited as Best Musical by NY Drama Critics Circle, Winner of Pulitzer Prize, 1976 "Tonys" for Best Musical, Best Book, Best Score, Best Director, Best Lighting, Best Choreography. A Special Theatre World Award was presented to every member of the creative staff and original cast. See THEATRE WORLD Vol. 31.

† Succeeded by: 1. Dean Badolato, 2. Christine Barker, 3. Gail Mae Ferguson, Lois Englund, 4. Jeff Hyslop, Don Correia, 5. Ken Rogers, Michael Dean, 6. Paul Charles, R. J. Peters, 7. Christina Saffran, Marcia Lynn Watkins, 8. A. William Perkins, Larry G. Bailey, 9. Anthony Inneo, Jon Michael Richardson, 10. Eivind Harum, Scott Pearson, 11. R. J. Peters, Timothy Wahrer, 12. Pamela Sousa, Cheryl Clark, 13. Murphy Cross, Victoria Tabaka, Joanna Zercher, 14. Julie Pars, Gail Mae Ferguson, 15. Karen Meister, 16. Chris Bocchino, 17. Don Percassi, Jim Corti, 18. Claude Tessier, 19. Danny Weathers, 20. Ron Kurowski, Ronald Stafford, 21. Rene Clemente, 22. Carol Marik, Angelique Ilo, 23. Jon Michael Richardson

Martha Swope Photos

MOROSCO THEATRE
Opened Monday, May 1, 1978.*
Lester Osterman, Marilyn Strauss, Marc Howard present the
Hudson Guild Theatre (Craig Anderson, Producer) Production
of:

DA

By Hugh Leonard; Director, Melvin Bernhardt; Set, Marjorie
Kellogg; Costumes, Jennifer von Mayrhauser; Lighting, Arden Fingerhut; Technical Adviser, Mitch Miller; Wardrobe Mistress, Margot Moore; Assistant to Director, Christine Banas

CAST

Charlie Now	Brian Murray†1
Oliver	Ralph Williams
Da	Barnard Hughes†2
Mother	Sylvia O'Brien†3
Young Charlie	Richard Seer†4
Drumm	Lester Rawlins
Mary Tate	Mia Dillon
Mrs. Prynne	Lois de Banzie

UNDERSTUDIES AND STANDBYS: Hansford Rowe (Da/
Drumm), Edwin McDonough (Charlie/Oliver), Faith Catlin
(Mary), Tim Choate (Young Charlie)

A comedy in two acts. The action takes place in a kitchen and
places remembered in May 1968 and in times remembered.

General Manager: Richard Horner
Company Manager: Allan Francis
Press: Howard Atlee, Bill Evans, Claudia McAllister, James
Baldassare
Stage Managers: Edward R. Fitzgerald, Georgory Johnson

* Still playing May 31, 1979. Winner of 1978 "Tonys" for Best Play,
Director, Actor (Barnard Hughes), and Featured Actor (Lester
Rawlins), and voted Best Play by NY Drama Critics Circle,
Drama Desk, Outer Critics Circle. For original production, see
THEATRE WORLD, Vol 34.
Succeeded by: 1. David Leary, 2. Brian Keith, 3. Ruby Holbrook,
Helen Stenborg for vacation, 4. Charley Lang

Martha Swope Photos

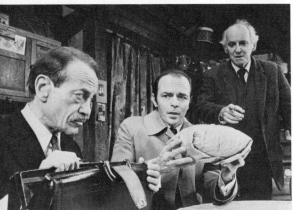

**Brian Keith, Ruby Holbrook Above: Lester
Rawlins, David Leary, Barnard Hughes**

**Top: Ralph Williams, Charley Lang, David
Leary, Barnard Hughes, Sylvia O'Brien**

BROADHURST THEATRE
Opened Monday, March 27, 1978.*
Jules Fisher, The Shubert Organization (Gerald Schoenfeld, Chairman; Bernard B. Jocobs, President), Columbia Pictures present:

DANCIN'

Conceived, Directed and Choreographed by Bob Fosse; Scenery, Peter Larkin; Costumes, Willa Kim; Lighting, Jules Fisher; Music and Lyrics, Johann Sebastian Bach, Ralph Burns, George M. Cohan, Neil Diamond, Bob Haggart, Ray Bauduc, Gil Rodin, Bob Crosby, Jerry Leiber, Mike Stoller, Johnny Mercer, Harry Warren, Louis Prima, John Philip Sousa, Carole Bayer Sager, Melissa Manchester, Barry Mann, Cynthia Weil, Felix Powell, George Asaf, Sigmund Romberg, Oscar Hammerstein II, Cat Stevens, Edgard Varese, Jerry Jeff Walker; Producer, Jules Fisher; Associate Producer, Patty Grubman; Music Arranged and Conducted by Gordon Lowry Harrell; Orchestrations, Ralph Burns; Hairstylist, Romaine Greene; Sound, Abe Jacob; Wardrobe, Joseph Busheme; Production Assistant, Vicki Stein; Assistant to Mr. Fisher, Robin Ullman; Assistants to Mr. Fosse, Kathryn Doby, Christopher Chadman, Gwen Verdon.

CAST

Gail Benedict	Vicki Frederick †6
Sandahl Bergman †1	Linda Haberman
Karen G. Burke †2	Richard Korthaze
Rene Ceballos	Edward Love †7
Christopher Chadman †3	John Mineo
Wayne Cilento	Ann Reinking †8
Jill Cook †4	Blane Savage †9
Gregory B. Drotar †5	Charles Ward †10

ALTERNATES: Christine Colby †11, William Whitener †12, Zelda Pulliam, Eugene Little, Anita Ehrler, Chet Walker, Shanna Reed, Michael Kubala, Deborah Phelan.

MUSICAL NUMBERS: Prologue (Hot August Night), Crunchy Granola Suite, Mr. Bojangles, Chaconne, Percussion, Ionisation, I Wanna Be a Dancin' Man, Big Noise from Winnetka, If It Feels Good, Let It Ride, Easy, I've Got Them Feelin' Too Good Today Blues, Was Dog a Doughnut, Sing Sing Sing, Here You Come Again, Yankee Doodle Dandy, Gary Owen, Stouthearted Men, Under the Double Eagle, Dixie, When Johnny Comes Marching Home, Rally Round the Flag, Pack Up Your Troubles in Your Old Kit Bag, Stars and Stripes Forever, Yankee Doodle Disco, Dancin'.

A "musical entertainment" in 3 acts and 13 scenes.

General Manager: Marvin A. Krauss
Company Manager: G. Warren McClane
Press: Merle Debuskey, William Schelble
Stage Managers: Perry Cline, Patrick Ballard, Richard Korthaze

* Still playing May 31, 1979. For original production, see THEATRE WORLD, Vol. 34. Received 1978 "Tonys" for Best Choreography and Lighting.
† Succeeded by: 1. P. J. Mann, 2. Wendy Edmead, 3. Gary Flannery, Christopher Chadman, 4. Eileen Casey, 5. Ross Miles, Gregory B. Drotar, 6. Christine Colby, 7. Bruce Anthony Davis, 8. Vicki Frederick, Ann Reinking, 9. David Warren-Gibson, 10. James Dunne, 11. Valerie-Jean Miller, 12. David Warren-Gibson

Martha Swope Photos

**Top Right: Ann Reinking on shoulders of Clif de Raita in opening number
Below: Wendy Edmead, Bruce Anthony Davis**

Ann Reinking, Christopher Chadman, Christine Colby in "Dancin' Man" 59

THE MUSIC BOX
Opened Sunday, February 26, 1978.*
Alfred de Liagre, Jr. and Roger L. Stevens present:

DEATHTRAP

By Ira Levin; Director, Robert Moore; Set William Ritman; Costumes, Ruth Morley; Lighting, Marc B. Weiss; Wardrobe Supervision, Mariana Torres; Assistant to Director, George Rondo; Assistants to Producers, Dorothy Spellman, Jean Bankier

CAST

Sidney Bruhl	John Wood †1
Myra Bruhl	Marian Seldes
Clifford Anderson	Victor Garber †2
Helga ten Dorp	Marian Winters †3
Porter Milgrim	Richard Woods †4

Standby: Ernest Townsend

A "thriller" in two acts and six scenes. The action takes place at the present time in Sidney Bruhl's study in the Bruhl home in Westport, Connecticut.

General Manager: C. Edwin Knill
Press: Jeffrey Richards, Warren Knowlton
Stage Managers: Ben Strobach, Robert St. Clair

* Still playing May 31, 1979. For original production, see THEATRE WORLD, Vol. 34.
† Succeeded by: 1. Patrick Horgan, Stacy Keach, John Cullum, 2. Daren Kelly, 3. Elizabeth Parrish, 4. William LeMassena

Sy Friedman Photos

Marian Seldes, Daren Kelly, William LeMassena, Elizabeth Parrish, and Stacy Keach (seated) Top Right: John Cullum

MARTIN BECK THEATRE
Opened Thursday, October 20, 1977.*
Jujamcyn Theaters, Elizabeth Ireland McCann, John Wulp, Victor Lurie, Nelle Nugent, Max Weitzenhoffer present:

DRACULA

By Hamilton Deane, John L. Balderston; From the novel "Dracula" by Bram Stoker; Director, Dennis Rosa; Scenery and Costumes, Edward Gorey; Scenery Supervision, Lynn Pecktal; Costume Supervision, John David Ridge; Lighting, Roger Morgan; Wardrobe, Rosalie Lahm; Special Effects, Chic Silber; Bat Handler, Timothy Abel; Assistant to Director, Howard Marren; Hairstylist, Tommy de Maio; Wigs, Paul Huntley

CAST

Lucy Seward	Ann Sachs †1
Miss Wells, a maid	Gretchen Oehler
Jonathan Harker	Alan Coates
Dr. Seward	Dillon Evans
Abraham Van Helsing	Jerome Dempsey
R. M. Renfield	Richard Kavanaugh †2
Butterworth	Baxter Harris †3
Count Dracula	Frank Langella †4

UNDERSTUDIES AND STANDBYS: Johanna Leister (Lucy/Miss Wells), Dalton Cathey (Harker/Butterworth), Jack Betts (Seward), Alan Coates (Dracula), Stephen Scott (Van Helsing)

A melodrama in 3 acts and 4 scenes. The action takes place in the 1920's in the library of Dr. Seward's sanatorium in Purley, England, in Lucy's boudoir, and in a vault.

Company Manager: Susan Gustafson
Press: Solters & Roskin, Joshua Ellis, Sophie McBride-Pope, David LeShay
Stage Managers: Marnel Sumner, Charles Kindl, Dalton Cathey

* Still playing May 31, 1979. Received 1978 "Tonys" for Most Innovative Production of a Revival, and Best Costume Design. For original production, see THEATRE WORLD, Vol. 34.
† Succeeded by: 1. Valerie Mahaffey, 2. Richard S. Levine, Sam Tsoutsouvas, 3. Everett McGill, 4. Raul Julia, David Dukes, Jean LeClerc

Martha Swope, Kenn Duncan Photos

Top: Jean LeClerc   **Jean LeClerc, Lauren Thompson**

THE LITTLE THEATRE
Opened Saturday, May 21, 1977.*
Jerry Arrow by arrangement with Circle Repertory Company
and PAF Playhouse presents:

GEMINI

By Albert Innaurato; Director, Peter March Schifter; Supervised
by Marshall W. Mason; Setting, Christopher Nowak; Costumes,
Ernest Allen Smith; Lighting, Larry Crimmins; Sound, Leslie A.
DeWeerdt, Jr.; Production Assistant, Thomas Bain; Wardrobe, Arthur Curtis; Hairstylist, Peter Brett

CAST

Francis Geminiani	Dennis Bailey †1
Bunny Weinberger	Jessica James
Randy Hastings	Reed Birney †2
Judith Hastings	Stephanie Musnick †3
Herschel Weinberger	Warren Pincus †4
Fran Geminiani	Danny Aiello †5
Lucille Pompi	Anne DeSalvo †6

UNDERSTUDIES: Jennie Ventriss (Lucille/Bunny), Phillip Cates
(Francis/Randy), Lisa Sloan (Judith)

A comedy in 2 acts and 4 scenes. The action takes place June 1
& 2, 1973 in the Geminiani-Weinberger backyard in South Philadelphia, Pa.

General Manager; R. Robert Lussier
Press: Max Eisen, Robert Ganshaw
Stage Managers: James Arnemann, Thom Shovestull

* Still playing May 31, 1979. For original production, see THE-
ATRE WORLD, Vol. 33.
† Succeeded by: 1. Phillip Cates, 2. Bill Randolph, 3. Lisa Sloan, 4.
Wayne Knight, 5. Dick Boccelli, 6. Barbara Coggin, Jennie Ven-
triss

**Top: Richard Boccelli, Barbara Coggin, Dennis Bailey,
Stephanie Musnick, Wayne Knight, William Randolph**

**Dennis Bailey, Stephanie Musnick,
Jessica James**

EDENS THEATRE

Opened Monday, February 14, 1972.*
(Moved June 7, 1972 to Broadhurst Theatre, and November 21, 1972 to Royale Theatre) Kenneth Waissman and Maxine Fox in association with Anthony D'Amoto present:

GREASE

Book, Music and Lyrics, Jim Jacobs, Warren Casey; Director, Tom Moore; Musical Numbers and Dances Staged by Patricia Birch; Orchestrations, Michael Leonard; Musical Supervision, Vocal and Dance Arrangements, Louis St. Louis; Scenery, Douglas W. Schmidt; Costumes, Carrie F. Robbins; Lighting, Karl Eigsti; Musical Direction, Jeremy Stone; Sound, Jack Shearing; Hairstylist, John DeLaat; Assistant to Director, Nancy Robbins; Wardrobe, Doris Boyhan; General Management, Theatre Now, Inc.; Original Cast Album by MGM Records

CAST

Miss Lynch .... Dorothy Leon †1
Patty Simcox .... Ilene Kristen †2
Eugene Florczyk .... Tom Harris †3
Jan .... Garn Stephens †4
Marty .... Katie Hanley †5
Betty Rizzo .... Adrienne Barbeau †6
Doody .... James Canning †7
Roger .... Walter Bobbie †8
Kenickie .... Timothy Meyers †9
Sonny LaTierri .... Jim Borelli †0
Frenchy .... Marya Small †1
Sandy Dumbrowski .... Carole Demas †2
Danny Zuko .... Barry Bostwick †3
Vince Fontaine .... Don Billett †4
Johnny Casino/Teen Angel .... Alan Paul †5
Cha-Cha DeGregorio .... Kathi Moss †6

UNDERSTUDIES: Lori Ada Jaroslow, Linda Nenno (Female Roles), Scott Holmes, Bob Reynolds (Male Roles), Frank Piegaro (Danny Zuko)

MUSICAL NUMBERS: Alma Mater, Summer Night, Those Magic Changes, Freddy My Love, Greased Lightning, Mooning, Look at Me I'm Sandra Dee, We Go Together, Shakin' at the High School Hop, Born to Hand-Jive, Beauty School Drop-Out, Alone at a Drive-In Movie, Rock 'n' Roll Party Queen, There Were Worse Things I Could Do, All Choked Up, Finale

A rock musical in 2 acts and 12 scenes. The action takes place in the late 1950's.

General Manager; Edward H. Davis
Press: Betty Lee Hunt, Maria Cristina Pucci
Stage Managers: Lynne Guerra, Steve Beckler, Scott Holmes

* Still playing May 31, 1979. For original production, see THEATRE WORLD, Vol. 28.
† Succeeded by: 1. Sudie Bond, Ruth Russell, 2. Joy Rinaldi, Carol Culver, Katherine Meloche, Forbesy Russell, Jo Ela Flood, 3. Barrey Smith, Lloyd Alann, Randy Powell, Stephen Van Benschoten, 4. Jamie Donnelly, Randee Heller, Rebecca Gilchrist, Mimi Kennedy, Pippa Pearthree, Cynthia Darlow, 5. Meg Bennett, Denise Nettleton, Marilyn Henner, Char Fontane, Diane Stilwell, Sandra Zeeman, 6. Elaine Petricoff, Randee Heller, Livia Genise, Judy Kaye, Lorelle Brina, Marcia Mitzman, 7. Barry J. Tarallo, Bill Vitelli, 8. Richard Quarry, John Driver, Michael Tucci, Ray DeMattis, Dan Woodard, 9. John Fennessy, Jerry Zaks, Michael Tucci, Danny Jacobson, 10. Matt Landers, Albert Insinnia, David Paymer, 11. Ellen March, Joy Rinaldi, Jill P. Rose, Forbesy Russell, Peggy Lee Brennan, Duffi, 12. Ilene Graff, Candice Earley, Robin Lamont, Shannon Fanning, 13. Jeff Conaway, John Lansing, Lloyd Alann, Treat Williams, Peter Gallagher, 14. Jim Weston, John Holly, Walter Charles, Stephen M. Groff, Stan Birnbaum, 15. Bob Garrett, Philip Casnoff, Joe Rifici, Frank Piegaro, 16. Robin Vogel

ETHEL BARRYMORE THEATRE
Opened Sunday, April 17, 1977.*
By arrangement with Joseph Kipness, Terry Allen Kramer and
Harry Rigby present:

I LOVE MY WIFE

Book and Lyrics, Michael Stewart; From a play by Luis Rego;
Music Composed and Arranged by Cy Coleman; Director, Gene
Saks; Scenery, David Mitchell; Lighting, Gilbert V. Hemsley, Jr.;
Costumes, Ron Talsky; Musical Numbers Staged by Onna White;
Musical Direction, John Miller; Sound, Lou Gonzalez; Associate
Producer, Frank Montalvo; Technical Supervisor, Mitch Miller;
Production Assistant, Jon Puleo, Hank Flacks; Wardrobe, Terence
Kotch; Original Cast Album by Atlantic Records.

CAST

Cleo	Ilene Graff †1
Monica	Joanna Gleason †2
Wally	James Naughton †3
Stanley	Michael Mark
Quentin	Joseph Saulter
Harvey	John Miller
Norman	Ken Bichel †4
Alvin	Lenny Baker †5

MUSICAL NUMBERS: We're Still Friends, Monica, By Threes, A
Mover's Life, Love Revolution, Someone Wonderful I Missed, Sexu-
ally Free, Hey There Good Times, Lovers on Christmas Eve,
Scream, Everybody Today Is Turning On, Married Couple Seeks
Married Couple, I Love My Wife

A musical in two acts. The action takes place at the present time
in Trenton, NJ.

General Management: Jack Schlissel, Jay Kingwill
Press: Henry Luhrman, Anne Obert Weinberg, Terry M. Lilly
Stage Managers: Bob Vandergriff, Tony Manzi

* Closed May 20, 1979 after 857 performances and 7 previews. For
original production, see THEATRE WORLD, Vol. 33.
† Succeeded by: 1. Barbara Sharma, Maureen Moore, Hattie Winston, 2. Virginia Sandifur, Janie Sell, Marjorie Barnes, 3. James
Seymour, Brad Blaisdell, Tom Wopat, Tom Smothers, Larry Riley, 4. Mark Franklin, 5. James Brennan, Lawrence John Moss,
Dick Smothers, Lawrence-Hilton Jacobs

Sy Friedman Photos

**Left: (seated) Tom Smothers, Barbara Sharma,
Janie Sell, Dick Smothers Top: Dick Smothers,
Barbara Sharma, Tom Smothers**

**Dick Smothers, Barbara Sharma,
Janie Sell, Tom Smothers**

**Lawrence-Hilton Jacobs, Marjorie Barnes,
Hattie Winston, Larry Riley**

EDISON THEATRE
Opened Friday, September 24, 1976.*
Hillard Elkins, Norman Kean, Robert S. Fishko present:

OH! CALCUTTA!

Devised by Kenneth Tynan; Contributors, Jules Feiffer, Dan Greenburg, Lenore Kandel, John Lennon, Jacques Levy, Leonard Melfi, David Newman and Robert Benton, Sam Shepard, Clovis Trouille, Kenneth Tynan, Sherman Yellen; Music and Lyrics, Robert Dennis, Peter Shcickele, Stanley Walden; Additional Music and Lyrics, Stanley Walden Jacques Levy; Choreography, Margo Sappington; Musical Director, Stanley Walden; Conceived and Directed by Jacques Levy; Scenery, James Tilton; Lighting, Harry Silverglat; Costumes, Kenneth M. Yount, supervised by James Tilton; Musical Conductor, Norman Bergen; Sound, Sander Hacker; Assistant to Director, Nancy Tribush; Projected Media Design, Gardner Compton; Assistant Musical Conductor, Dan Carter; Technical Directors, Thomas Healy, Charles Moran; Wardrobe, Gordon Needham

CAST

Jacqueline Carol	Tom Lantzy
Cheryl Hartley	Katherine Liepe
Mary Hendrickson	Gary Meitrott
Barra Kahn	James K. Reiley †2
William Knight †1	September Thorp

ACT I: Taking Off the Robe, Will Answer all Sincere Replies, Rock Garden, Delicious Indignities, The Paintings of Clovis Trouille, Suite for Five Letters, One on One
ACT II: Jack and Jill, Spread Your Love Around, Was It Good for You Too?, Coming Together Going Together

An erotic musical in two acts.

Company Managers: Maria Di Dia, Doris J. Buberl
Press: Les Schecter
Stage Managers: Bruce Kagel, Maria Di Dia

* Still playing May 31, 1979. For original production, see THEATRE WORLD. Vol. 33.
† Succeeded by: 1. William Mesnik, 2. Jerry Clark

Martha Swope Photos

Top: Tom Lantzy, September Thorp
Right: James K. Reiley, Barra Kahn

Jacqueline Carol

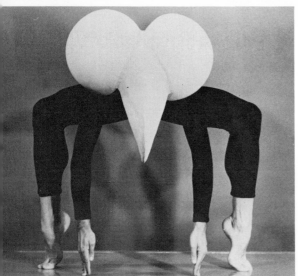

BIJOU THEATRE
Opened Wednesday, March 30, 1977.*
Arthur Shafman International, Ltd. presents:

MUMMENSCHANZ

Created by Andres Bossard, Floriana Frassetto, Bernie Schurch; Production Adviser, Richard G. Miller; Production Associates, Evelyn Gross, Susan Balsam

CAST

Andres Bossard†
Floriana Frassetto
Bernie Schurch

A program of mime in two parts with the use of masks, flexible body wrappings, props and costumes.

General Manager: Christopher Dunlop
Company Manager: John Scott
Press: Jeffrey Richards, Warren Knowlton
Stage Manager: Nancy T. Finn

* Still playing May 31, 1979. For original production, see THEATRE WORLD, Vol. 33,
†Original cast was succeeded by Louis Gilbert, James Greiner, Dominique Weibel, Roger Reed, Donald VanHorn

BROADWAY PRODUCTIONS FROM PAST SEASONS THAT CLOSED THIS SEASON

Title	Opened	Closed	Performances
The Act	10/29/77	7/1/78	233
For Colored Girls Who Have Considered Suicide When The Rainbow Is Enuf	9/10/76	7/16/78	747
The Gin Game	10/6/77	12/31/78	528
Hello, Dolly!	3/5/78	7/9/78	152
I Love My Wife	4/17/77	5/20/79	864
The King and I	5/2/77	12/30/78	719
The Magic Show	5/28/74	12/31/78	1859
On the 20th Century	2/19/78	3/18/79	460
Runaways	5/13/78	12/31/78	199
Same Time, Next Year	3/13/75	9/3/78	1444
Timbuktu!	4/1/78	9/10/78	243
The Wiz!	1/5/75	1/28/79	1672

OFF-BROADWAY PRODUCTIONS THAT OPENED JUNE 1, 1978 THROUGH MAY 31, 1979

WESTSIDE THEATRE
Opened Thursday, June 8, 1978.*
Lantern Productions presents:

PIANO BAR

Music, Rob Fremont; Lyrics, Doris Willens; Story, Doris Willens, Rob Fremont; Staged and Directed by Albert Takazauckas; Set and Costumes, Michael Massee; Lighting, Gary Porto; Arrangements, Philip J. Lang; Musical Director, Joel Silberman; Associate Producer, Charles W. Gould; Choreography, Nora Peterson; Production Assistant, Reisa Sperlin.

CAST

Bartender	Jim McMahon
Julie	Kelly Bishop
Prince	Joel Silberman
Walt	Richard Ryder
Ned	Steve Elmore
Debbie	Karen DeVito

Understudy: Sylvia Ippolito

MUSICAL NUMBERS: "Intro," "Sweet Sue's," "Today," "Pigeon-Hole Time," "Congratulations," "Believe Me," "Tango," "Everywhere I Go," "Dinner at the Mirklines," "Scenes from Some Marriages," "Personals," "Nobody's Perfect," "One Two Three," "Greenspons," "Moms and Dads," "Meanwhile Back in Yonkers," "Walt's Truth," "New York Cliche," "It's Coming Back to Me," "Tomorrow Night," "Closing"

A musical in two acts. The action takes place at the present time in a New York City bar.

General Management: Dorothy Olim Associates
Company Manager: Gail Bell
Press: Shirley Herz
Stage Managers: Mark Hare, Sylvia Ippolito

*Closed Oct. 1, 1978 after 133 performances and 8 previews.

Ken Howard Photos

Steve Elmore, Kelly Bishop, Joel Silberman, Karen DeVito, Jim McMahon, Richard Ryder in "Piano Bar"

Virginia Martin (R)

18th STREET PLAYHOUSE
Tuesday, June 13–26, 1978. (12 performances)
Swen Swenson presents:

SING MELANCHOLY BABY

A comedy in two acts by Michael Devereaux; Directed by Mr. Devereaux; Associate Producer, Francine Trevens; Sets, Peter Grimes; Costumes, Reve Richards; Art Director, Marc Greene; Lighting, Richard Clausen; Stage Managers, Robin McCarty, Mark Dennis; Press, Max Eisen, Irene Gandy

CAST

Chuck Karel (Sam), Eric Schurenberg (Nick DeWitt), Margery Beddow (Kelly Long), Maggie Task (Grace Francs), Terry Eno (Brian), John Stratton (Charlie Pellot), Jackie Cornin (Leslie Taylor) Dallas Johann (Sailor), Virginia Martin (Rene)

Michael Uffer Photo

Don Johanson, Patti Mariano

CENTURY THEATRE
Opened Wednesday, June 14, 1978.*
Lee Theodore and Louis K. and Gloria Sher present:

THE AMERICAN DANCE MACHINE
Alpha Company

Founder-Director, Lee Theodore; Entire Production Supervised and Directed by Lee Theodore; Costumes, John David Ridge; Lighting, Jeremy Johnson; Musical Direction, David Baker, David Krane; Associate Director, David Baker; Special Arrangements, Danny Hurd; Wardrobe, Steven Burdick; Production Assistant, Lynn Peterson

COMPANY

Steven Gelfer, Don Johanson, Patti Mariano, Joseph Pugliese, Nancy Chismar, Liza Gennaro, Louise Hickey, Amy Lester, Kristine Koebel, Gina Martin, Greg Minahan, Candice Prior, Morgan Richardson, Kevin Ryan, Donald Young, and GUEST ARTISTS Janet Eilber, Harold Cromer, Denny Shearer

PROGRAM

"Terrific Rainbow" from "Pal Joey,""Popularity" from "George Me.""June is Bustin' Out All Over" from "Carousel,""Whip Dance" from "Destry Rides Again," "All Aboard for Broadway" from "George M,""Charleston" from "The Boy Friend," "Rich Kid's Rag" from "Little Me,""If the Rain's Gotta Fall" from "Half a Sixpence," "Satin Doll" from television, "Monte Carlo Crossover" and "Up Where the People Are" from the "The Unsinkable Molly Brown,""Come To Me, Bend To Me" and "Funeral Dance" from "Brigadoon,""Quadrille" from "Can-Can,""You Can Dance with Any Girl at All" from "No, No, Nanette,""Clog Dance" from "Walking Happy." Intermission material narrated and danced by Harold Cromer.

General Manager: James Walsh
Press: Michael Alpert, Marilynn LeVine, Randi Cone
Stage Managers: Murray Gitlin, Audrey Frankowski

*Closed December 3, 1978 after 198 performances.

Sy Friedman Photos

**Top: Steven Gelfer, Liza Gennaro,
Helena Andreyko, Denny Shearer**

CITY CENTER DOWNSTAIRS
Thursday, June 22–July 9, 1978 (21 performances and 8 previews)
A. Arthur Altman, Joseph H. Lillis, Jr. and Jean Altman present:

THE COOLEST CAT IN TOWN

A musical comedy in two acts; Music, Diane Leslie; Book and Lyrics, William Gleason; Director, Frank Carucci; Choreography, Mary Lou Crivello; Musical Direction, Bob Goldstone; Costumes, Faded Glory; A Pendragon Production; Assistant Director, Mary Ann Vlattas; Assistant Choreographer, Joni Masella; Production Assistant, Mane Pujals; Hairstylist, Patrik D. Moreton; Scenery, Ark Associates; General Manager, Joseph H. Lillis; Press, Gary Stevens; Stage Managers, Pat DeRousie, J. Gordon Matthews

CAST

Michael Hayward-Jones (Leon Bumpers), Christopher Callan (Martha Bumpers), Lennie Del Duca, Jr. (Junior Bumpers), William Parry (Billy Dee Bumpers), Maura Silverman (Melinda), Rowena Rollins (Ida), Joey Faye (Marvin), Bill Britten (Dr. Henrich), Jerry Sroka (Igor), J. Gordon Matthews (Electrician), Mary Lou Crivello (Sue), Joni Masella (Gail), Pamela Ann Wilson (Terri), Adrienne Del Monte (Jane), Mark Morales (Leonard), Steven Jack (Joe), Danny Rounds (Bob), Bradley Jones (Ed)

MUSICAL NUMBERS: Disco Rag, Born to Rock and Roll, Don't Say Shoo-Be-DoBop, Melinda Schecker, Superstar, One Kiss, Suspended Animation, Lost My Cool, Rock Back the Clock, The Bop Will Never Die, Let's Live It Over Again, You're My Last Chance, Hula Hoop, The Coolest Cat in Town, Mr. Know It All, So What?, Finale

Right: Joey Faye, Rowena Rollins

Cast of "Crimes Against Nature"

ACTORS PLAYHOUSE
Thursday, June 22–August 6, 1978 (54 performances and 9 previews)
Howard Solomon and Stickdance present Gay Men's Theater Collective in:

CRIMES AGAINST NATURE

Written, Directed and Performed by the Collective; Lighting, Greg Kollenborn; General Manager, Albert Poland; Press, Betty Lee Hunt, Maria Cristina Pucci, Fred Hoot

CAST

The Collective: David Baker, Anthony Eschbach, Greg Kollenborn, Richard La Rose, Timo Lupine-Child, Tommy Pace, John Sokoloff, Charles Solomon, Martin Worman, General Understudy: John Albano

Frank Kolleogy Photo

Lucie Arnaz

JONES BEACH THEATRE
Thursday, June 29–September 4, 1978.
Lee Guber and Shelly Gross in association with the Jones Beach State Parkway Authority present:

ANNIE GET YOUR GUN

Music and Lyrics, Irving Berlin; Book, Herbert Fields, Dorothy Fields; Staged and Directed by Richard Barstow; Choreography, Bert Michaels; Musical Director, Jay Blackton; Scenery, Karl Eigsti; Lighting, Richard Nelson; Costumes, Sara Brook; Production Supervisor, Mortimer Halpern; Wardrobe, Agnes Farrell, Lee Decker; Sound, Daniel O'Brien; Assistant to Director, Sherry Lambert; Production Assistant, Michael Grant; Assistant Conductor, Robert Stanley

CAST

Little Boy	Robert Rizzo
Little Girl	Danielle Susan Carter
Charlie Davenport	Don Potter
Dolly Tate	Travis Hudson
Mac	Harry Fawcett
Foster Wilson/Waiter	Ralph Vucci
Frank Butler	Harve Presnell
Annie Oakley	Lucie Arnaz
Nellie, Annie's sister	Tamara Jones
Minnie, Annie's sister	Susie Davis
Little Jake, Annie's brother	Johnny Morgal
Col. Wm. F. Cody/Buffalo Bill	Jack Dabdoub
Conductor	Clint Clifford
Porter	Donald H. Coleman
Pawnee Bill	Sherman Lloyd
Chief Sitting Bull	Alan North
Footman	Dan Entriken
Sylvia Potter Porter	Dixie Stewart

ENSEMBLE: Dru Alexandrine, Danielle Susan Carter, Helen Castillo, Michel DeSilva, Mona Elgh, Debbie Gornay, Ginny King, Sherry Lambert, Lora Jeanne Martens, Patricia Michaels, Donna Monroe, Vicki Patik, Darci Phifer, Rochelle Seldin, Cynthia Stewart, Dixie Stewart, Caroline Thompson, Laurie Scandurra, Anthony Balcena, Clint Clifford, Donald H. Coleman, Joel Dzarlinsky, John Dorrin, Dan Entriken, Harry Fawcett, Alan Gilbert, D. Michael Heath, Navarre Matlofsky, G. Eugene Moose, Stan Page, Ernest Tagnano, Richard Parman, Robert Rizzo, Ralph Vucci, Steve Ward, David Mallard

UNDERSTUDIES: Donna Monroe (Annie), Stan Page (Frank), John Dorrin (Buffalo Bill), Richard Parman (Sitting Bull), Dan Entriken (Charlie), Cynthai Stewart (Dolly), G. Eugene Moose (Pawnee), Danielle Susan Carter (Nellie/Minnie), Robert Rizzo (Little Jake)

MUSICAL NUMBERS: Overture, "Buffalo Bill,""I'm a Bad, Bad Man,""Doin' What Comes Natur'ly,""The Girl That I Marry,"-"You Can't Get a Man with a Gun,""Show Business," "They Say It's Wonderful,""Moonshine Lullaby,""Wild West Pitch Dance,'-"My Defenses Are Down,""Ceremonial Dance,""I'm an Indian Too,""Adoption Dance,""Lost in His Arms,""I Got the Sun in the Morning,""Anything You Can Do," Finale

A musical in two acts.

Managing Director: Stephen Arnold
Press: Saul Richman, Rosemary Carey
Stage Managers: Bob Bernard, Ralph Vucci, Sherry Lambert

Top Left: Travis Hudson, Harve Presnell, Don Potter Below: Harve Presnell, Jack Dabdoub, Lucie Arnaz

INTAR THEATRE
July 7 – 18, 1978 (12 performances)
Maria Norman/Duo Theatre presents:

THE DISPOSAL

By William Inge; Director, Ann Raychel; Lighting, Jenny Ball; Music and Sound, John Broeck; Production Coordinator, Sandra Barreras; Costumes, Maria Marrero; Stage Managers, Richard Lenchner, Jack Lane, Robert McMillan; Press, Marian Graham

CAST

Michael Beckett, Paul Carpinelli, Octavio Ciano, Robert Denis, Hubert Edwards, Mallory Hoover, Robert Louis Jackson, Robert McMillan, Bradley Smith, Richard White

Gerry Goodstein Photo

Michael Beckett, Octavio Ciano, Bradley Smith

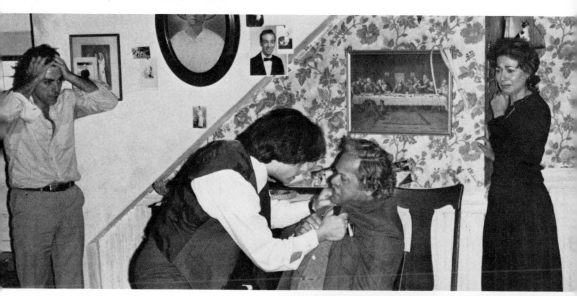

QUAIGH THEATRE
Opened Wednesday, July 19, 1978.*
Bill Sargent in association with Tony Conforti presents:

MOMMA'S LITTLE ANGELS

By Louis LaRusso II; Director, Ernest Martin; Set and Costumes, Frank J. Boros; Lighting, Marcia Madeira; Assistant to Producer, Diane Matthews; Assistant to Director, Dan Grimaldi; Coordinator, Michael Hajek

CAST

Aunt Tillie................................. Mimi Cecchini
Dr. Carillo............................... Raymond Serra
Tony Mastice............................ Matt Landers
Patsie Mastice, his sister .... Janet Sarno
Larry Mastice, their brother .... David Proval

A drama in two acts and six scenes. The action takes place during the summer of 1969 in a small row house in Hoboken, NJ.

General and Company Manager: Rick Richardson
Press: Max Eisen, Francine L. Trevens
Stage Manager: Joseph Capone

* Closed Oct. 21, 1978 after 112 performances and 12 previews.

Ron Reagan Photos

**Center: David Proval, Matt Landers,
Raymond Serra, Janet Sarno**

David Proval

NEW YORK STATE THEATER
Opened Monday, July 17, 1978.*
James and Joseph Nederlander in association with City Center
of Music and Drama, Inc., and in association with the D'Oyly
Carte Opera Trust Limited and Dame Bridget D'Oyly Carte by
arrangement with Barclays Bank International Present:

D'OYLY CARTE OPERA COMPANY
GILBERT & SULLIVAN

Musical Director, Royston Nash; Production Director, Leonard
Osborn; Technical Consultant, Rouben Ter-Arutunian; Executive
Producer, Lillian Libman; Production Supervisor, Robert Crawley;
Production Assistant, Susan Lichtman; Technical and Stage Direc-
tor, Peter Riley; Assistant Stage Director, Ken Robertson; Associate
Conductor/Chorus Master, David Mackie; Producer, Leonard Os-
born; Assistant Producer, James Marsland; Wardrobe, Veronica
Carnegie, John Carnegie, Stephanie Cheretun; Production Assis-
tants, Claire Calkins, Michael Marshall

COMPANY

John Reed, John Ayldon, Meston Reid, Julia Goss, Jane Metcalfe,
James Conroy-Ward, Kenneth Sanford, Michael Rayner, Geoffrey
Shovelton, Patricia Leonard, Barbara Lilley
Richard Brabrooke, Michael Buchan, Barry Clark, Malcolm Coy,
Jon Ellison, Michael Farran-Lee, Gareth Jones, Guy Matthews,
Richard Mitchell, Edwin Rolles, Thomas Scholey, Bryan Secombe,
Alan Spencer, William Strachan, Kevin West, Patrick Wilkes
Patricia Anne Bennett, Susan Cochrane, Linda D'Arcy, Lorraine
Dulcie Daniels, Elizabeth Denham, Madeleine Hudson, Beti Lloyd-
Jones, Roberta Morrell, Suzanne O'Keeffe, Andrea Phillips, Patricia
Rea, Suzanne Sloane, Gillian Swankie, Viven Tierney, Alison West,
Helen Witcombe

PRODUCTIONS

"Iolanthe or the Peer and the Peri," "H. M. S. Pinafore," "The
Mikado or the Town of Titipu," "The Pirates of Penzance," and
"Princess Ida"

General Manager: Arthur Rubin, McCann & Nugent
Company Manager: James Kimo Gerald
Press: Sheila Porter, Alpert-LeVine, Randi Cone

* Closed July 25, 1978 after a limited engagement of 10 performances.

**Top Right: Patricia Anne Bennett, Lorraine
Dulcie Daniels, Patricia Leonard, John
Reed, Suzanne O'Keefe in "Iolanthe"
Below: "H.M.S. Pinafore"**

**Roberta Morrell, Julia Goss, Jane Metcalfe
in "The Mikado"**

John Reed in "H.M.S. Pinafore"

THEATRE EAST

Thursday, July 27 through Saturday, August 19, 1978 (31 performances)

David Silberg presents:

JOHN MONTEITH & SUZANNE RAND

An evening of comedy routines and improvisation that was transferred to Broadway. See Broadway Calendar, page 25.

Press: Jeffrey Richards, Maurice Turet, Jeanna Gallo, Gordon Edelstein
Stage Manager: Bill Russell

Right: Suzanne Rand, John Monteith

NEW YORK STATE THEATER

Opened Thursday, August 3, 1978.*

James and Joseph Nederlander in association with City Center of Music and Drama, Inc. present the Hillard Elkins production of:

STOP THE WORLD I WANT TO GET OFF

Book, Music and Lyrics by Leslie Bricusse and Anthony Newley; Director, Mel Shapiro; Choreography and Musical Staging, Billy Wilson; Sets and Costumes, Santo Loquasto; Lighting, Pat Collins; Music Supervised and Arranged by Ian Fraser; Musical Direction, George Rhodes; Orchestrations, Bill Byers, Joseph Lipman; Associate Producers, Barbara Platoff, William Ross; Sound, Thomas W. Morse; Assistant to Director, John Elkins; Wardrobe, Pixie Esmond; Production Supervisor, Robert Crawley; Production Assistant, Susan Lichtman; Original Cast Album by Warner/Curb Records

CAST

Littlechap	Sammy Davis, Jr.
Baton Twirler/Death/Country Club M.C.	Dennis Daniels
Schoolgirl/Newscaster	Donna Lowe
Evie/Anya/Ilse/Lorene	Marian Mercer
First Girl in Crow's Nest	Debora Masterson
Second Girl in Crow's Nest/Hadassah M.C./ Solo Singer in Sunvale	Joyce Nolen
Susan	Wendy Edmead
Guitar Player/M.C. Spanish Group	Patrick Kinser-Lau
Jane	Shelly Burch
The Boy	Charles Willis, Jr.
M.C. Black Group/Speaker of the House	Edwetta Little

ENSEMBLE: Marcus B. F. Brown, Dennis Daniels, Karen Giombetti, Linda Griffin, Patrick Kinser-Lau, Edwetta Little, Donna Lowe, Debora Masterson, Billy Newton-Davis, Joyce Nolen, Robert Yori-Tanna

UNDERSTUDIES: Joyce Nolen (Evie/Anya/Ilse/Lorene), Edwetta Little (Susan), Debora Masterson (Jane), Allison McKibbon (The Boy)

MUSICAL NUMBERS: "I Wanna Be Rich," "Typically English," "Lumbered," "Welcome to Sludgeville," "Gonna Build a Mountain," "Glorious Russian," "Meilinki Meilchick," "Family Fugue," "Typische Deutsche," "Life Is a Woman," "All-American," "Once in a Lifetime," "Mumbo Jumbo," "Welcome to Sunvale," "Someone Nice Like You," "What Kind of Fool Am I?"

A musical in two acts.

General Managers: Max Allentuck, Arthur Rubin
Company Manager: Leo Cohen
Press: Sheila Porter, Solters & Roskin, Fred Nathan, Sophronia McBride-Pope, Tim Schoch
Stage Managers: Robert D. Currie, Bernard Pollack, Jon R. Hand

* Closed Aug. 27, 1978 after limited engagement of 29 performances and 1 preview. Original production opened Oct. 3, 1962 and played 555 performances with Anthony Newly and Anna Quayle

Sammy Davis, Jr., Marian Mercer

ONE SHERIDAN SQUARE
Friday, August 11 through Saturday, October 14, 1978 (21 performances)
Virago Productions present:

HOLLYWOOD CONFIDENTIAL

Written and Performed by Charles Busch; Director, Patrick Brafford; Production Supervisor, Edward Taussig; Production Assistant, Andy Cohen; Management, New Arts, Cathy Smith.

Jeremy Sundgaard Photo

**Charles Busch
in "Hollywood Confidential"**

CIRCLE REPERTORY THEATRE
Monday, August 14 through August 31, 1978. (14 performances)
Circle Repertory Company The Late Show presents:

PUSHING THIRTY

A One-Man Show concocted and performed by Jonathan Hadary; Lighting, Gary Seltzer; Stage Manager, Michael Herzfeld; Press, Richard Kornberg

Susan Cook Photo

Left: Jonathan Hadary

MARYMOUNT MANHATTAN THEATRE
Opened Thursday, September 7, 1978.*
Arthur Cantor and Greer Garson present:

ST. MARK'S GOSPEL

A solo performance devised by Alec McCowen; Lighting, Robert Spitzer; Production Manager, Larry Bussard; Production Assistant, Thomas C. Madigan.

Performed by
ALEC McCOWEN

Company Manager: Arthur Cantor
Press: C. George Willard

* Closed Sept. 24, 1978 after limited engagement of 18 performances and 2 previews. Returned Oct. 24 – Nov. 12, 1978 for 18 additional performances at the Playhouse Theatre. Lighting was by Leo B. Meyer, and Keith Waggoner was Production Manager.

Donald Cooper Photo

Alec McCowen

THEATRE FOUR

Thursday, September 14 through Sunday, September 24, 1978
(16 performances)

Basil Bova presents:

GAME PLAN

By Dan Lauria; Scenic Design, Joseph W. Long; Lighting, Gary S. Seltzer; Director, Vincent Gugleotti; Art Director, Gary Gaccione; Technical Director, Billy Dave Woods; Company Manager, James O'Neill; Press, Judy Jacksina, Glenna Freedman; Stage Managers, Ed M. Colcord, R. Bruce Connelly

CAST

Fred J. Scollay (Fred Ryan), Dan Lauria (John Ryan), Wally Salisbury (Lou Ryan), Sam Locante (Father Burke), Bili Marcus (Ray D'Orio), Ralph Oliva (Coach Delfano)

A drama in 5 acts and 6 scenes performed with one intermission. The action takes place at the close of the Viet Nam War in Bakersville, U.S.A.

Bert Andrews Photo

Right: Fred J. Scollay, Dan Lauria
Below: Bill Marcus, Fred J. Scollay
Right Center: Dan Lauria, Wally Salisbury

GALLERY THEATRE

Friday, September 15 through Sunday, October 1, 1978. (12 performances)

Swen Swenson presents:

JUST LOOKING

Written and Directed by Michael Devereaux; Associate Producer, Francine L. Trevens; Setting, Tom Warren; Lighting, William J. Plachy, Robert Johansen; Art Director, Marc Greene; Press, Max Eisen; Stage Managers, Robin McCarty, Mark J. Dennis

CAST

John Stratton (Sam), Bonner Parker (Leslie), Eric Schurenberg (Nick), Maggie Task (Grace), Margery Beddow (Kelly), Terry Eno (Brian), Michael Rafkin (Charlie), Frank Dent (Sailor), Casey Wayne (Rene)

A comedy in two acts. The action takes place at the present time on Christmas afternoon in a bar on New York's Upper West Side.

Bonner Parker Photo

Terry Eno, Margery Beddow, Maggie Task,
Eric Schurenberg, John Stratton 75

PROMENADE THEATRE
Opened Sunday, October 15, 1978.*
(Moved Thursday, January 25, 1979 to Century Theatre)
Frank Gero and Budd Block present the Rutgers Theater Company production of:

ARE YOU NOW OR HAVE YOU EVER BEEN

By Eric Bentley; Director, John Bettenbender; Set, Joseph F. Miklojcik, Jr.; Costumes, Vicki Rita McLaughlin; Lighting, Kathryn M. Pinner

CAST

Committee Members. .	Tom Brennan, Robert Nichols, Jim Haley
The Investigator	Jerry ver Dorn
The Narrators	Gene Terruso, Mary Beth Fisher
Sam G. Wood	Jim Haley
Edward Dymtryk/Martin Berkeley	Joseph Rose
Ring Lardner, Jr./Tony Kraber	Benjamin Bettenbender
Larry Parks	W. T. Martin
Abe Burrows	Frank Gero
Sterling Hayden/Elliott Sullivan	Raymond Baker
Elia Kazan/Marc Lawrence	David Francis Barker
Jerome Robbins	Kevin Motley
Lillian Hellman	Colleen Dewhurst†1
Lionel Stander	Tom Brennan†2
Paul Robeson	Avery Brooks

A play in two acts. The action takes place during the hearings before the Un-American Activities Committee (1947–1956).

General Managers: Soloway & Francis
Press: Betty Lee Hunt/Maria Cristina Pucci, Fred Hoot
Stage Managers: Donald E. Peterson, Kevin Motley

* Closed March 4, 1979 after 149 performances.
† Succeeded by: 1. Rosemary Murphy, Frances Sternhagen, Tammy Grimes, Barbara Baxley, Peggy Cass, Joan Copeland, Viveca Lindfors, Marcella Markham, Liza Minnelli, Louise Lasser, Dina Merrill, 2. Mike Kellin

Top Right: Tom Brennan, Jerry ver Dorn, Gene Terruso

Peggy Cass   **Joan Copeland**

Louise Lasser   **Rosemary Murphy**

Jose Ferrer, Morgan Freeman

THEATRE DE LYS
Thursday, October 19 through Sunday, October 29, 1978. (14 performances and 18 previews)
Jose Ferrer presents:

WHITE PELICANS

Written and Directed by Jay Broad; Setting, David Chapman; Costumes, Carol Oditz; Lighting, Marshall S. Spiller; Associate Producer, Paul B. Berkowsky; Assistant to Producer, Michael Adkins; Assistant to Director, Jayne Shaw; Technical Director, Eric Marantz; Wardrobe, Robin Walker

CAST

Harry	Jose Ferrer
Winston	Morgan Freeman

Standby: Peter Jason

A drama in two acts. The action takes place at the present time in a cabin in an Arctic wasteland.

John Chang McCurdy Photo

HAROLD CLURMAN THEATRE

Wednesday, October 18 through Saturday, December 9, 1978 (59 performances)
Jack Garfein and Harold Clurman, Artistic Directors of the Harold Clurman Theatre, present:

THE LESSON

By Eugene Ionesco; Translated by Donald M. Allen; Director, Jack Garfein; Costumes, Ruth Morley; Sets, Ralph Alswang; Lighting, Ralph Alswang, Michael White; Technical Director, Michael White; Assistants to the Director, June E. Moore, Philip Hohenlohe; General Manager, Ron Comenzo; Company Manager, Dione Lewis; Stage Manager, Jerry Bihm; Press, Max Eisen

CAST

Sandra Seacat (The Maid), Didi Conn (The Young Pupil), Joseph Wiseman (The Professor)
This performance was preceded by a film, "The California Reich" by Walter F. Parkes and Keith F. Critchlow.

Gerry Goodstein Photo

Joseph Wiseman, Sandra Seacat, Didi Conn in "The Lesson"

ALL SOULS UNITARIAN CHURCH

Friday, October 20 through Thursday, November 30, 1978. (10 performances)
The All Souls Players present:

ONE FOR MY BABY: JOHNNY MERCER

Narration and Direction, Tran William Rhodes; Choreography and Musical Staging, Randy Fields; Costumes, Hank Laurencelle; Musical Direction, Joyce Hitchcock; Vocal Orchestrations, Tran William Rhodes; Producers, Peter Sauerbrey, Howard Van der Meulen; Pianos, Joyce Hitchcock, David Lahm, Michael Edelstein; Guitar, Jon Harris; Stage Manager, Michael Shisko

CAST

Larry Hansen, Michael Irwin, Ronald Owen, Susan Phillips, Richard Pohlers, Cliff Roberts, Melanie Helton, Tom Keiser, Charlotte Patton, Tacey Phillips, Jennifer Pritchett, Monona Rossol

A 90 song salute to the Broadway, Hollywood and Tin Pan Alley lyricist, Johnny Mercer.

Geoff Rosengarten Photo

Right: Ronald Owen, Tom Keiser, Larry Hansen

Shoshana Ron, Shimon Dzigan, Mina Bern, Ben Bonus, Herschel Fox

NORMAN THOMAS THEATRE

Sunday, October 22, through Sunday, December 3, 1978. (20 performances)
The Lively and Yiddish Company presents:

LAUGH A LIFETIME

A satirical musical revue with music by Hanoch Cohen, I. Lustig, and Sol Berezowsky; Written by J. Tunkeler, J. Bratt, M. Nudelman, I. Heyblum, A. Shulman and E. Kishon; Director, Shimon Dzigan; Musical Director, William Gunther

CAST

Shimon Dzigan, Ben Bonus, Mina Bern, Herschel Fox, Shoshana Ron

PROGRAM: "A Face to Face Meeting," "How to Prevent a Nuclear Explosion," "A Star? No, A Bomb," "Tel-Aviv Construction Worker," "Let's Make Up," "In the Theatre Mirror," "Cave of the Patriachs," "The Hitch-Hiker," "A Fortunate Father," "There Were Times," Finale

STAGE 73
Tuesday, October 24 through Sunday, November 5, 1978. (12 performances)

BRASS BIRDS DON'T SING

By Samm-Art Williams; Director, Michael Jameson; Set, George Creczylo; Costumes, Abby McFadden; Lighting, Debbie Wieser; Production Coordinator, Suzanne Caton; Music, Donna Cribari; Assistant to Director/Stage Manager, Terria Joseph; Press, Howard Atlee

CAST

Eliza DeCroes (Anna Withers/Donia Danzinger), Darrie Lawrence (Janet Withers/Frieda Danzinger), Richard Young (Pete Barrington), Dennis Black (Lenny DeMarco/S.S. Officer), Steve Lincoln (Josh Withers)

The action takes place in New York City during the early fall of 1961.

Susan Olup Photo

Top Right: Dennis Black, Steve Lincoln

LION THEATRE
Tuesday, October 26 through Sunday, November 12, 1978. (19 performances)
Lion Theatre Company (Gene Nye, Producing Director; Larry Carpenter, Managing Director) presents:

MUSIC-HALL SIDELIGHTS

By Jack Heifner; Director, Garland Wright; Music, John McKinney; Lyrics, Jack Heifner; Choreography, Randolyn Zinn; Setting, John Arnone; Costumes, David James; Lighting, Francis Aronson; Technical Coordinator, David Harnish; Technical Director, Henry Millman; Sound, Sarah Lambert; Stage Managers, Susana Myer, John Lyons; Wardrobe, Cathy Meils, Stephen Williams; Press, Ellen Levene

CAST

Kim Ameen (La Tou Tou/Little Jady), Kathy Bates (Colette), Wanda Bimson (Lise Damoiseau/ Giseal), Tony Campisi (Dog Trainer/Sultan), Janice Fuller (Ida/Gribiche's mother), Jane Galloway (Bastienne/Gitanette), John Guerrasio (Marcel/Starvling), Jennifer Jestin (Misfit/Rita), Barbara LeBrun (Carmen Brasero), James McLure (Brague/Pierrot), Susan Merson (La Rousalika/Gribiche), Gene Nye (Compere)

A Theatrical Scrapbook drawn from Collette's "L'Envers du Music-hall," in two acts.

Nathaniel Tileston Photos

James McLure, Kathy Bates
in "Music Hall Sidelights"

THREE MUSES THEATRE
Friday, November 3 through Sunday, November 19, 1978. (17 performances)
Lohmann/Taylor presents:

BOSOM BUDDIES

By Sharon Tipsword; Director, Shan Willson; Set, John Jackson; Lighting, Paul Everett; Costume Coordinator, Glenda Price; Art Director, Paul Plumadore; Stage Managers, Gordon Kupperstein, Barrie Moss; Press, Ellen Levene

CAST

Act I: "Bonzo Doesn't Count": Clyde Burton (Frank), Jeffrey Horowitz (Harry), Act II: "A Long Story": Susan Genis (Emily), James Rebhorn (Ed), Act III: "Second Verse": Rebecca Taylor (Viv), Nancy McCall (Helen), Standbys: Gordon Kupperstein, Barrie Moss

Susan Genis, James Rebhorn, Jeffrey Horowitz,
Clyde Burton, Rebecca Taylor, Nancy McCall

FOLKSBIENE PLAYHOUSE
Saturday, November 4, 1978 through Saturday, March 31, 1979. (260 performances)
Folksbeine Playhouse (Morris Adler, Ben Schechter, Managers) presents:

THE INHERITORS

By Sholem Aleichem; Adapted and Directed by Jakub Rotbaum; Set and Costumes Design, Jadwiga Przeradzka; Lighting, Rick Shannin; Hairstylist, Nick DiLeo; Stage Managers, Marvin Schwartz, Harry Grape, Betty Glaser; Press, Max Eisen, Francine L. Trevens

CAST

Mina Kern (Miriam Blank), Joyce Smoleroff Riggs (Klara), Moishe Rosenfeld (Chaim), I. W. Firestone (Marcus), Betty Glaser (Lisotchka), Sandy Levitt (Froike), Leon Liebgold (Sender Blank), Jacob Gostinsky (Ziamke Gingold), Pearl Eisenbaum (Zelde), Ruth Selman (Sonia), Shmuel Goldstein (Reb Meir), Morris Adler (Reb Kalmen), Sol Migdal (Reb Zalmen), Jack Rechtzeit (Osip), Marilyn Gold (Reveka), Zypora Spaisman (Dobrish), Joshua Zeldis (Dr. Kluger)

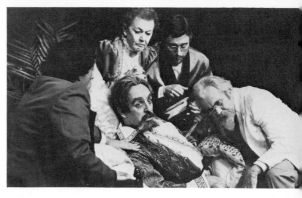

Leon Liebgold, Mina Kern, Moishe Rosenfeld, Joshua Zeldis

AVERY FISHER HALL
Sunday, November 12, 1978.*
Cy Feuer and Ernest H. Martin present:

SING HAPPY!

The work of John Kander and Fred Ebb; Directed and Staged by Tony Stevens; Musical Director, Paul Gemignani; Continuity, Stuart Hample; Lighting, David F. Segal; Sound, T. Richard Fitzgerald; Associate Producers, David and Jan Martin; Stage Managers, Ed Aldridge, Craig Jacobs, James Lockhart; Costume Coordinator, Greg Fauss; Press, Susan L. Schulman

CAST

Cy Coleman, Jack Gilford, Anita Gillette, Joel Grey, Jerry Herman, Henrietta Jacobson, Larry Kert, Lotte Lenya, Liza Minnelli, John Raitt, Chita Rivera, Charles Strouse, Gwen Verdon assisted by Obba Babatunda, Trudie Carson, Kathie Dalton, Susan Danielle, Mary Sue Finnerty, Connie Gould, Brenda Holmes, Randy Hugill, Angelique Llo, Lesley Kingsley, Frank Mastracola, Meredith McIver, Roger Minami, Denise Pence, Gena Ramsel, Michael Serrecchia, Freda Soiffer
MUSICAL NUMBERS: Willkommen, The Life of the Party, Married, Mr. Cellophane, Meeskite, Sing Happy, I Don't Remember You, My Own Space, Me and My Baby, How Lucky Can You Get, All That Jazz, Liza with a Z, Yes, Maybe This Time, Lucky Lady, A Quiet Thing, City Lights, Cabaret, I Don't Care Much, Isn't This Better?, Sara Lee, Go Visit Your Grandmother, My Coloring Book, Coffee in a Cardboard Cup, Nowadays, Keep It Hot, Pain, Razzle Dazzle, Walking Among My Yesterdays, That's a Beginning, I Am Free, Life Is, So What?, It Couldn't Please Me More, New York New York

* A special benefit performance for the American Musical and Dramatic Academy and the George Junior Republic

Andrew Ian Rubenoff Photos

Chita Rivera, Liza Minnelli, Jack Gilford, John Kander, Fred Ebb Above: Rivera, Minnelli with Gwen Verdon Top: Anita Gillette

Above: Lotte Lenya, Jack Gilford

79

PLAYHOUSE THEATRE
Opened Thursday, November, 16, 1978.*
Arthur Cantor and Greer Garson present:

THE PLAYBOY OF THE WEEKEND WORLD

A solo entertainment devised by Emlyn Williams from the stories of Saki (H. H. Munro); Director, Peter Woodthorpe; Lighting, Leo B. Meyer; Assistant to Producers, Harvey Elliott; Production Assistant, Thomas C. Madigan

CAST

EMLYN WILLIAMS

PROGRAM (performed in two parts): Introducing Saki, On House-parties, The Secret Sin of Septimus Brope, The Lost Soul, The Disappearance of Crispina Umberleigh, Gabriel-Ernest, Where's Louise?, The Lumber Room, On Presents, The Open Window, Laura, Sredni Vashtar, A Mild Attack of Poetry, An Improper Story, Birds on the Western Front

Company Manager: Arthur Cantor
Press: C. George Willard

* Closed Dec. 10, 1978 after limited engagement of 29 performances and 3 previews.

Top Left: Emlyn Williams

THEATER OF THE OPEN EYE
November 16, – December 3, 1978 (14 performances)*

THE COACH WITH THE 6 INSIDES

Written and Staged by Jean Erdman; Inspired by James Joyce's "Finnegan's Wake"; Music, Teiji Ito; Costumes, Gail Ryan; Lighting, William Morrison; Decor, Dan Butt; Projections, Milton Howarth; Costume Revisions, Melissa Adzima; Props, Perry Arthur Kroeger; Stage Manager, Patricia Saphier; Presented by The Theater of the Open Eye (Jean Erdman, Artistic Director; Elizabeth Rudolf, Administrative Director); Press, Ellen Levene, Tom Trenkle

CAST: Caryll Coan, Jean Erdman, Howard Schechter, Leslie Dillingham, Trueman Kelley, Lola-Belle Smith, Teiji Ito, Guy Klucevsek, Rumiko Wellington

Left: Trueman Kelly, Leslie Dillingham, Caryll Coan

COURTYARD THEATRE
Tuesday, November 28, 1978 through Sunday, January 21, 1979. (66 performances)
Chester Fox and Martin J. Ain present:

PORNO STARS AT HOME

By Leonard Melfi; Director, Ken Eulo; Setting, Robert Anthony; Costumes, Andy Navarre; Lighting, Sam Buccio; Set Coordinator, Anthony Rizzo; Incidental Music composed and played by Philip Adelman; Assistant to Producers, Ingrid Lakin; Press, David Lipsky, Lisa Lipsky

CAST

Tara Tyson (Georgia Lloyd Bernhardt), Philip Adelman (Musician), Justin Deas (Barry Olivier), Jody Catlin (Norma Jean Brando), Alan Brooks (Montgomery McQueen), Meg Wittner (Uta Bergman-Hayes)

A comedy-drama in two acts. The action takes place at the present time in the New York apartment of Georgia Lloyd Bernhardt

Stephanie Saia Photo

Alan Brooks, Meg Wittner, Tara Tyson, Justin Deas, Jody Catlin

THEATRE DE LYS

Opened Friday, December 1, 1978.*

William Donnell, Burry Fredrik, Richard Humphrey, Rosita Sarnoff present the Theatre for the New City production of:

BURIED CHILD

By Sam Shepard; Director, Robert Woodruff; Set, Jonathan Putnam; Costumes, Jess Goldstein; Lighting, John P. Dodd; Presented by special arrangement with Lucille Lortel Productions; Assistant Director, Denise Sherman; Technical Director, James Carhart; Wardrobe, Pan Riley

CAST

Dodge	Richard Hamilton
Halie	Jacqueline Brookes†1
Tilden	Tom Noonan
Bradley	Jay Sanders†2
Shelly	Mary McDonnell
Vince	Christopher McCann
Father Dewis	Bill Wiley

UNDERSTUDIES: Edward Seamon (Dodge/Tilden/Bradley/Father Dewis), Jonathan Putnam (Vince), Victoria Ezer (Halie/Shelly)

A comedy-drama in three acts. The action takes place at the present time in the home of Dodge and Halie.

General Manager: David Lawlor
Press: Shirley Herz, Jan Greenberg, Bruce Cohen
Stage Managers: Ruth Kreshka, James Sprague, Jonathan Putnam

* Closed April 15, 1979 after 152 performances and 5 previews. It was the recipient of the 1979 Pulitzer Prize.
† Succeeded by: 1. Mary Louise Wilson, 2. William Russ

Richard Hamilton, Mary Louise Wilson, Mary McDonnell, Tom Noonan, Bill Wiley, Christopher McCann, William Russ Top Right: Bill Wiley, Jacqueline Brookes

Anthony Whitehouse, Arlena Rolant
in "Cartoons for a Lunch Hour"

PERRY STREET THEATRE
Tuesday, November 28 through Sunday, December 3, 1978. (12 performances)
Seven Ages Performances Ltd. presents:

CARTOONS FOR A LUNCH HOUR

Book and Lyrics, Loften Mitchell; Music and Additional Lyrics, Rudy Stevenson; Director, Akin Babatunde; Choreography and Musical Staging, Frank Hatchett; Costumes, Bernard Johnson; Setting, Phillip Graneto; Lighting, Terry Chandler; Production Coordinator, Percival Borde; Assistant to Director, Arlena Rolant; Assistant Choreographer, Rick Odums; Production Assistants, Bennie Williams, Charles Hargrave, McKinley Johnson; Technical Director, Grant Orenstein; Stage Manager, Mark R. Paquette; Press, Max Eisen

CAST

Johnny Barracuda (Labor Leader), Rosita Broadous (Noire), Don Butler (Vice President), Nora M. Cole (Mayda), Denise DeMirjian (Blanche), Clinton Derricks-Carroll (Jay), Charlene Harris (Carmella), Amy E. Hennessy (Dancer), Stephanie Madden (Ann), Brenda Mitchell (Heavenly Choir), Linda Morton (Heavenly Choir), Rick Odums (Gabriel), Geisha Otero (Satan), Claudia Peluso (Dina), Roy Rogers (Heavenly Choir), Arlena Rolant (Peter's Angel), Stephen J. Smith (Dancer/Herald), Grant Stewart (Business Executive), Nancy-Suzanne (Dancer), Anthony Whitehouse (Peter), Christopher Wynkoop (President), Linda E. Young (Heavenly Choir)

MUSICAL NUMBERS: Come On in This House, This Angel's Arrivin', I Thought, Why Me?, Wanna Go to Heaven, Hail to Peter, Ain't You Ashamed?, Heaven Come and Help Us Out, I Am the President, Stay Ahead of the People, I'll Demonstrate, I'm Here, Heaven in Your Eyes, Stories, Just a Little Italian Girl, Smile Little Irish Girl, There's a New Place, Latin Girl, A Place Somewhere, A Party at Peter's Place, Finale

AMDA STUDIO ONE THEATRE
Friday, December 1, through Sunday, December 17, 1978. (12 performances)
i & i productions present:

ALBERT/LOOSE END

By James Pashalides; Director, Dan Plucinski; Set, William Marshall; Lighting, Charles S. Bullock; Costumes, Jane Trapnell; Production Assistant, Al Rivera; Stage Manager, Sally Hopkinson; Press, Ellen Levene

CAST

"Albert": Dan Plucinski (Albert), Steven Hiott (Edward), Wilma Smart (Lillian), Al Rivera (Delivery Man), Linda Deming (Miss Symbol), Elizabeth Girling (Pleure), "Loose Ends": Wilma Smart (Marilyn Monroe), Dan Plucinski (James Dean)

Right: Wilma Smart, Dan Plucinski

PARK ROYAL THEATRE
Tuesday, December 5 through Sunday, December 10, 1978. (7 performances, 5 previews)
R. Tyler Gatchell, Jr., Peter Neufeld in cooperation with T.O.M.I. Inc. present:

NIGHT GAMES

Three one-act plays by Richard Broadhurst; Director, Jill Andre; Scenery, Dan Leigh; Lighting, Martin Tudor; Production Associate, James B. Slemmons; Costume Coordinator, Kathy Grayson; Stage Managers, Dean Vallas, Chip Neufeld; Press, Judy Jacksina, Glenna Freedman

CAST

"Media": In Poughkeepsie, N.Y., at 9:30 P.M.: Kimberly Vaughn (Miriam Watson), Paul Avery (Ray Watson), "Night Games": An Upper West Side studio apartment in New York City at 8:30 P.M.: September Thorp (April Dawn), John Cirigliano (Jimmy DeFuri), "Hand Man": In a New York City Mid-Town hotel at 2:30 A.M.: Paul Avery (Lester Thompson), Kimberly Vaughn (A Woman)

**Kimberly Vaughn, Paul Avery
in "Night Games"**

Barbara Coggin, Norb Joerder, Edna Manilow, Edward Penn, Joan Kobin, Lou Corato, Joan Susswein, Maitland Peters, Lisa M. Steinman, Jim Jeffrey, Lynne Stuart

PLAYERS THEATRE
Opened Wednesday, December 20, 1978.*
Hillard Elkins and Bill Sargent present:

AN EVENING WITH QUENTIN CRISP
The Naked Civil Servant

Devised by Richard Gollner; Associate Producers, Marcelle Garfield, Barbara Platoff
General Manager: Theatre Now, Inc.
Press: Jeffrey Richards, Warren Knowlton, Helen Stern, Mark Arnold
Stage Manager: Larry Forde

* Closed March 4, 1979 after 83 performances.

Right: Quentin Crisp

THEATRE FOUR
Opened Thursday, December 28, 1978.*
Richard Seader and Don Saxon present:

THE DIARY OF ANNE FRANK

By Frances Goodrich and Albert Hackett; Based on book "Anne Frank: The Diary of a Young Girl;" Director, Martin Fried; Setting, Karl Eigsti; Costumes, Ruth Morley; Lighting, William Mintzer; Associate Producers, Donald Checki, Diana McDonell, Steve Salvatore; Assistant to Producers, Howard Rogut; Production Assistant, Michael Pappalardo

CAST

Mr. Frank	Eli Wallach
Miel	Judith Egor
Mrs. Van Daan	Rose Gregorio
Mr. Van Daan	Tom Brennan
Peter Van Daan	Robert Joy
Mrs. Frank	Anne Jackson
Margot Frank	Katherine Wallach
Anne Frank	Roberta Wallach
Mr. Kraler	Ken Costigan
Mr. Dussell	Anthony Holland

UNDERSTUDIES: Elise Warner (Mrs. Frank/Mrs. Van Daan), Mary Shortkroff (Anne/Margot), Kathy Flanagan (Miep/Mrs. Frank), Brian Zoldessy (Peter)

A drama in 2 acts and 10 scenes. The action takes place on the top floors of a warehouse in Amsterdam, Holland, during the years of World War II and immediately thereafter.
Press: Faith Geer
Stage Managers: Bob D. Bernard, Elise Warner

*Closed March 4, 1979 after 77 performances.

BRUNO WALTER AUDITORIUM
Monday, Tuesday, Wednesday, December 18, 19, 20, 1978. (3 performances)
Stage Directors and Choreographers Workshop Foundation presents:

TUNE THE GRAND UP!

Words and Music by Jerry Herman; Created and Staged by Jeffrey K. Neill; Musical Adaptation and Direction, Wendell Kindberg; Set, Roger Benischek; Costumes, Charles W. Roeder; Lighting, Chris Peabody; Additional Dialogue, Mary McCartney; Producers, Sally E. Parry, Peter M. Paulino; At the piano, Wendell Kindberg; Stage Managers, John Vought, Ruth E. Kramer

CAST

Barbara Coggin, Lou Corato, Jim Jeffrey, Norb Joerder, Joan Kobin, Edna Manilow, Ed Penn, Maitland Peters, Lisa M. Steinman, Lynne Stuart, Joan Susswein

David Wasson Photo

Eli Wallach, Roberta Wallach, Anne Jackson

CENTURY THEATRE

Thursday, December 28 through Sunday, December 31, 1978.
(6 performances, 7 previews)
Joe Regan presents:

TAXI TALES

By Leonard Melfi; Director, Edward Berkeley; Scenery, Hugh Landwehr; Costumes, Hilary Rosenfeld; Lighting, Arden Fingerhut; Sound, Gary Harris; Original Song "Taxi" by Jonathan Hogan; General Manager, Leonard A. Mulhern; Company Manager, Paul Matwiow; Press, Ellen Levene, Tina Clarke, Victoria Heslin; Stage Managers, Ellen Raphael, Paul Diaz, Barbara Abel

CAST

Paula Christopher	Dolly Jonah
Al Corley	Ken Olin
Julie DeLaurier	Michael Strong

Understudies: Barbara Marchant, Paul Diaz

A comedy that takes place at the present time inside and outside of five Manhattan taxi cabs: Taffy's Taxi, Tripper's Taxi, Toddy's Taxi, Teaser's Taxi, Mr. Tucker's Taxi

Nathaniel Tileston Photos

**Right: Al Corley, Dolly Jonah, Michael
Strong, Paula Christopher Top: Dolly
Jonah, Ken Olin, Julie DeLaurier,
Michael Strong**

ORPHEUM THEATRE

Opened Friday, January 12, 1979.*
Larry Abrams presents:

MY OLD FRIENDS

Book, Lyrics and Music by Mel Mandel and Norman Sachs; Director, Philip Rose; Musical Staging, Bob Tucker; Sets and Lighting, Leon Munier; Costumes, George Drew; Wardrobe, Sylvia Myrvold; Piano, Norman Sachs, Larry Hochman; Bass, Thom Janusz

CAST

Catlan	Allen Swift
Fineberg	Leslie Barrett
Slocum	Robert Weil
Arias	Norberto Kerner
Mrs. Polianoffsky	Grace Carney
Mrs. Cooper	Maxine Sullivan
Heloise Michaud	Sylvia Davis
Peter Schermann	Peter Walker
Mrs. Stone	Brenda Gardner
A Carpenter/Gettlinger	Fred Morsell

MUSICAL NUMBERS: "Thank God I'm Not Old,""My Old Friends,""For Two Minutes," "What We Need Around Here,""Oh, My Rose,""I Bought a Bicycle,""Battle at Eagle Rock,""The Only Place for Me,""I Work with Wood,""A Little Starch Left," "Mambo '52,""Our Time Together,""You've Got to Keep Building"

A musical performed without intermission. The action takes place at the present time in the Golden Days Retirement Hotel.

General Managers: Helen Richards, Karen Gromis
Press: Bruce Cohen, Jan Greenberg, Shirley Herz
Stage Managers: Arturo E. Porazzi, Brenda Gardner

*Closed April 8, 1979 after 100 performances, and re-opened April 12, 1979 at 22 Steps where it gave 54 additional performances before closing there May 27, 1979. Opened originally November 23, 1978 at La Mama.

Carol Rosegg Photos

**Norberto Kerner, Leslie Barrett, Grace Carney,
Allen Swift, Maxine Sullivan, Robert Weil**

PLAYHOUSE THEATRE

Sunday, February 4 through Sunday, February 11, 1979. (9 performances, 19 previews)
Joshus Logan presents:

TRICK

Written and Directed by Larry Cohen; Setting, Raymond C. Recht; Lighting, Marshall S. Spiller; Costumes, Judy Dearing; Hairstylist, Patrik D. Moreton; Associate Producers, Paul B. Berkowsky, Sheila Tronn Cooper; Wardrobe, Linda Martin; Executive Assistant, Elisa Septee; General Manager, Paul B. Berkowsky; Stage Managers, Tom Kelly, John Barrett; Sound, Gary Harris; Press, Merlin Group, Becky Flora, Beatrice DaSilva, Glen Gary

CAST

Paula Cramer . . . . Tammy Grimes
Wallace Barrows . . . . Donald Madden
Andrew Creed . . . . Lee Richardson

Understudies: Gwyn Gilliss, John Barrett

A "comedy thriller" in 2 acts and 5 scenes. The action takes place at the present time in Wallace Barrows' duplex flat in London.

Top Right: Lee Richardson, Tammy Grimes

WOLLMAN AUDITORIUM/COLUMBIA UNIVERSITY

February 6–18, 1979 (17 performances)
Columbia University Theatre Arts and Mark Hall Amitin present:

ALBEE DIRECTS ALBEE

Eight one-act plays of Edward Albee, directed by the author; Settings, Karl Eigsti; Lighting, Stephen Pollock; Managers, Lindsay Gambini, Gary Hotvedt; Masks, Ralph Lee; Assistants to Director, Glyn O'Malley, Michael Kovaka; Assistant to Producer, Stephen Dym; Technical Director, Joseph Lenihan, Jr.; Press, Becky Flora

CAST

Sudie Bond, Eileen Burns, Steven Holmes, Patricia Kilgarrif, Wyman Pendleton, Stephen Rowe

Understudies: Catherine Bruno, Eileen Burns, Steven Holms, Patricia Kilgarriff
PLAYS: The American Dream, The Zoo Story, Fam and Yam, The Sandbox, Box, Quotations from Chairman Mao Tse-Tsung, County the Ways, Listening

Gerry Goodstein Photos

Patricia Kilgariff, Eileen Burns, Wyman Pendleton in "The American Dream" Above: "Box/Quotations"

BEACON THEATRE

February 6–18, 1979. (16 performances)
Concert Arts Society, Inc., (Kazuko Hillyer, Director) presents:

THE GRAND KABUKI
National Theatre of Japan

Artistic Director, Kanzaburo Nakamura XVII; Stage Director, Tokutaro Takeshiba; Executive Producer, Takeomi Hagayama

COMPANY

Tomijurp Nakamura V. Gato-O Kataoka V, Tojuro Sawamura II, Kankuro Nakamura V. Yoshigoro Ichimura II, Kosanza Nakamura, Shirogoro Nakamira, Sukegoro Nakamura, Kitsusaburo Arashi, Nakasude Nakamura, Nakaichiro Nakamura, Nakaji Nakamura, Nakasahuro Nakamura, Tomishiro Nakamura, Senjiro Kataoka, Kinosuke Kataoka

PROGRAM: Shunkan, Renjishi

Tomijuro Nakamura in "Renjishi"

ST. BART'S PLAYHOUSE
February 8 through March 3, 1979. (28 performances)
Harve Bronsten presents:

TELECAST

Book and Lyrics, Barry Harman; Music, Martin Silvestri; Direction, Barry Harman, Wayne Cilento; Scenery, Franco Colavecchia; Lighting, Jane Reisman, Neil Peter Jampolis; Costumes, Kristine Haugen; Musical Director, John Kroner; Assistant Musical Director, Grant Sturiale, Choreography, Wayne Cilento; Stage Manager, Roger Shea.

CAST

Jill Corey, Matt Landers, J. J. Lewis, Doug Andros, Valerie Leigh Bixler, C. A. Hutton, Mary Jay, Carolyn Kirsch, Laura McCarthy, Linda Ravinsky, Carles Ryan, Jana Schneider, Janice Solia, Robert Tananis, Terpsie Toon, Tony Turco, Wendy Wolfe, Christopher Wynkeep

Right: Matt Landers, Mary Jay, Jana Schneider, Wendy Wolfe, Robert Tananis

COLUMBIA UNIVERSITY/CASA ITALIANA
February 9–23, 1979 (10 performances)
The Classic Theatre (Maurice Edwards, Artistic Director) in association with The Contexts Company present:

PYGMALION

By George Bernard Shaw; Director, Michael Bergmann; Producer, Nicholas John Stathis; Production Supervisor, Lawrence Gilligan; Costumes, Sheila Horowitz; Original Music, Daniel Werts; Sets, Susan Webster, Alan Abramowitz; Stage Manager, Andrea Grober; Technical Staff, Joe Enright, Robert Whittemore, Alan Abramowitz, Robert Winston, Brian Walls, Stuart Schoener; Press, Patricia Miller, Margaret Underwood

CAST: Brian Allen, Richard Caliban, Victoria Berditchevskaya, Michael Cashman, Michael Dorsey, Bob Fitzsimmons, Frances Ford, Susan Herl, Susan Jaffe, Melanie Mansour, Martha Meade, Boris Ouspenskaya, Cip Pemberton, Nicole Potter, Ruth E. Sherman, Lillian Silverstone, George Villiers, Larry Victor

Lisa Anderson Photo

Left Center: Martha Meade, Richard Caliban

FELLOWSHIP HALL
February 16–26, 1979. (11 performances)
The All Souls Players present:

THE CONSTANT WIFE

By Somerset Maugham; Director, Jeffery K. Neill; Sets and Costumes, Charles W. Roeder; Producers, Marie Landa, Disbrow Hadley; Lighting, Helen Gatling, Peter Sauerbrey; Wardrobe, Doris Kennedy, Jean Turney; Stage Managers, Ruth E. Kramer, John Vought

CAST

Geraldine Hanning (Mrs. Culver), Andrew Alloy (Bentley), Ann McLoughlin (Martha Culver), Mary Rocco (Barbara Fawcett), Jillian Lindig (Constance Middleton), Leslie Blake (Marie-Louise Durham), William Wright (John Middleton), Edward Penn (Bernard Kersal), Richard Voigts (Mortimer Durham), Valerie Adami, Elizabeth Chambers, Jane Heyman, Doris Pratt (Maids)

A comedy in three acts. The action takes place in John and Constance Middleton's house in Harley Street, London.

Richard Voights, Mary Rocco, Ann McLoughlin, Gerald Hanning, Jillian Lindig, William Wright, Edward Penn Andrew Alloy, Leslie Blake

PUERTO RICAN TRAVELING THEATRE
February 20–April 8, 1979 (55 performances)

SIMPSON STREET

World Premiere by Edward Gallardo; Producer-Director, Miriam Colon; Translated by Miriam Colon, Tony Diaz; Set, Carl A. Baldasso; Lighting, Larry Johnson; Costumes, Maria Contessa; Assistant Director, Jose Machado; Production Manager, Ron Cappa; Administrator, Gary S. Levine; Title Song by Miriam Colon (lyrics), Pepe Castillo and Edgardo Miranda (music); Stage Manager, Sheldon Rieke; Wardrobe & Props, Mary Ann Terrell; Community Coordinator, Margarita Morales; Press, David Lipsky

CAST

Antonia Rey (Lucy), Iraida Polanco (Rosa), Maria Norman (Angela), Martha de la Cruz (Elva), Freddy Valle (Michael), Jeannette Collazo (Sonia)

Ken Howard Photos

Jeannette Collazo, Martha de la Cruz, Antonia Rey, Freddy Valle, Iraida Polanco, Maria Norman in "Simpson Street"

"Coquelico"

22 STEPS
February 22, through April 1, 1979. (45 performances)
Olivier Coquelin presents:

COQUELICO

Created, Written and Directed by Joseph Svoboda; Film Written and Directed by Evald Schorm; Choreography, Karel Vrtiska; General Manager, Ralph Lee; Starring the National Theatre of Prague; Press, The Merlin Group. Cheryl Sue Dolby

SOUTH STREET THEATRE
February 22–April 1, 1979 (40 performances)

JOE ORTON'S FUNERAL GAMES

Two one-act plays by Joe Orton; Director, John J. D. Sheehan; Producers, Jean Sullivan, Michael Fischetti; Setting, Gerald Allen; Lighting, J. Mallary Perry; Costumes, Jess Goldstein; Production Associate, Robert Freedman; Design Coordinator, Paul Hellerman; Stage Managers, John Pantozzi, Wendy Chapin, Cindy S. Tennenbaum, Linda Voorhis; Assistant to Director, Audrey H. Kallman; Production Consultant, Bob McDonald; Production Assistants, Lucy Cavallo, Bob Thompson; Props, June Moore; Press, Bob Ullman

CAST

FUNERAL GAMES: Kenneth Meseroll, Louis Turenne, Joan Pape, Leo Creed

THE RUFFIAN ON THE STAIR: Betty Burrows, Eddie Jones, Matt Carlson

Susan Cook Photos

Leo Creed, Kenneth Meseroll in "Funeral Games"

Danny Watkins, Steve Vesce

February 27, through March 3, 1979. (5 performances, 3 previews)
The Eyes Smiling Co. presents:

THE WAIT

By Barry Anbinder; Director, Donald Biehn; Scenery, Eugene Warner; Lighting, Richard Belzer; Costumes, Fred Marchese; Sound, Howard Schwartz; Stage Managers, Marc Elliott Field, David Stuart Thalenberg; Press, Robert Pontarelli

CAST

Sara Croft (Nurse), Steve Vesce (Gus), Norman Rose (Phil), Danny Watkins (Seth), Louise Rizzo (Joany), Maggie Flanigan (Fran), Jody Price (Shelly)

A play in two acts. The action takes place at the present time in a Brooklyn hospital from 5 P.M. to 3 A.M.

Gerry Goodstein Photo

THE VILLAGE GATE
March 1–11, 1979. (7 performances)
David Silberg presents:

STERLING SILVER

Music and Lyrics by Frederick Silver; Director. Sue Lawless; Choreography, Bick Goss; Sets, Kenneth Foy; Costumes, David Toser; Lighting, Michael J. Hotopp; Musical Director and Arranger, Elman R. Anderson; Assistant to Director, Myra Turley; Technical Supervisor, Andrea Wilson; Wardrobe, Kyria Krezel; Associate Producer, Neil Greenberg; General Manager, Helen Richards; Press, Jeffrey Richards, Warren Knowlton, Ted Goldsmith, Ken Sherber; Stage Managers, Robert Neu, Allan Gruet

CAST

Roger Berdahl, Alan Brasington, Karen Jablons, Cynthia Meryl, Lee Roy Reams

MUSICAL NUMBERS: Age of Elegance, Rainbow, Twelve Days after Christmas, Visiting Hours, Wooing in the Woods, Freddy Like to Fugue, A Simple Song, Waiting in the Wings, Very New York, I Do Like London, When You Are on the Coast, Mr. Ravel, A Matter of Position, Plain Song, Blues, Someone in My Life, Closing Time, Days of the Dancing

A "musical entertainment" in two acts.

Martha Holmes Photo

Roger Berdahl, Karen Jablons, Alan Brasington, Cynthia Meryl, Lee Roy Reams in "Sterling Silver"

Edward Morehouse, Joan Matthiessen

WESTBETH STUDIO THEATRE
March 6–18, 1979 (12 performances)
The Guardians Theatre Company presents:

THE COCKTAIL PARTY

By T. S. Eliot; Director, Christopher Cade; Scenery, Michael Massee; Costumes, John Whitmore; Lighting, Tom Schraeder; Music, George David Weiss; Arranged by Robert Stecko; Hairstylist, Jerry Masarone; Stage Managers, Ching Gonzalez, Richard Lockwood; Press, Ellen Levene, Susan Dudley-Allen, Victoria Heslin

CAST

Jay Bond (Peter), Elizabeth Brigulio (Miss Barraway), Kathryn Callaghan (Lavinia), Richard Lockwood (Caterer), Joan Matthiessen (Celia), Tom McGreevey (Sir Henry Harcourt Reilly), Edward Morehouse (Edward), Naomi Riordan (Julia), James Umphlett (Alex)

Nathaniel Tileston Photo

NAMELESS THEATRE
March 8–25, 1979 (12 performances)
Hilary James presents:

SOUNDS OF A TRIANGLE

Three Fables by Jean Reavey; Director, Gordon Heath; Technical Director, Sandra Cottone; Stage Manager, Alain Woisson; Sculptures, Carol Parker

CAST

"Klingo's Glove": Castulo Guerra (The Actor), "Madame De Mosque-Kee-Toe": Gordon Heath (The Actor), "Adora": Castulo Guerra (Musket), Gordon Heath (Cannon)

Gilles Vauclair Photo

**Gordon Heath, Castulo Guerra
in "Adora"**

ALL-CRAFT COMMUNITY THEATRE
March 15–April 8, 1979 (16 performances)
The Labor Theater presents:

JACK LONDON: THE MAN FROM EDEN'S GROVE

A solo performance conceived, written and performed by C. R. Portz; Based on the life and writings of Jack London; Advisers, Philp S. Foner, Robert Barltrop

Ed Snider Photo

C. R. Portz as Jack London

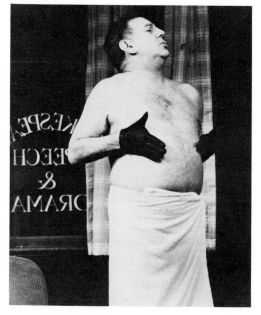

Gordon Chater

THEATRE FOUR
Opened Tuesday, March 20, 1979.*
Arthur Shafman and Andrea Shapiro present the Nimrod Theatre of Australia production of:

THE ELOCUTION OF BENJAMIN

By Steve J. Spears; Director, Richard Wherrett; Designed by Larry Eastwood; Produced by arrangement with George W. George, Frank Milton and Mrs. Oscar Hammerstein; Wardrobe, Epp Kotkas; Production Associates, Evelyn Gross, Beth Veranes

a solo performance by
GORDON CHATER

General Manager: Carl Sawyer
Press: Jeffrey Richards, Warren Knowlton, Ted Goldsmith
Stage Managers: Jack Welles, Tom Boyd

* Closed April 8, 1979 after 24 performances.

James Armstrong Photo

Seth Allen   **Janet Dowd**

GENE FRANKEL THEATRE
March 23, through April 8, 1979. (12 performances)
The Gene Frankel Theatre and Vassilis Voglis present:

JARDIE'S ROOMMATE

By John Cromwell; Director, David Mills; Sets and Lighting, David Loveless; Costumes, Robert Anton; Music Composed by Lee Pockriss; Lighting Coordinator, Randy Dunn; Technical Director, Paul Feldman; Stage Manager, Margi Rountree; Press, Howard Atlee, James Baldassare

CAST

Seth Allen (Jared Stark "Jardie"), Jeff Hayenga (Jake), Roger Serbagi (Dr. Brewster/Dad), Billie Lou Watt (Bernice/Baronessa/Miss Longfellow/Mother), Janet Dowd (Coral/Pale Lady), Sylvia Averbach (Marylou), H. C. Peterson, Allyn McCourt, Tessa George (Tourists, Playgoers, Patients)

CHELSEA THEATER CENTER
Opened Thursday, April 5, 1979.*
Chelsea Theater Center (Robert Kalfin, Producing Director) presents:

BIOGRAPHY: A GAME

By Max Fisch; Translated by Michael Bullock; Director, Arne Zaslove; Sets, Robert Ellsworth; Costumes, Elizabeth P. Palmer; Lighting, Robert Graham Small; Technical Director, Sander Gossard; Props, Dennis E. Schwartz, Betty Martin; Sound, David Rapkin; Assistant to Director, Mark Reiff; Production Assistant, Evan Handler

CAST

Claudia Albetta (Helen/Pina/Ballet Student), Charles Berendt (Hornacher/Henrik/Pastor), Katherine Mary Brown (Frau Henrik/Nurse), Roger Alan Brown (Cpl./Ambulance Man), Pamela Burrell (Antoinette), James Carruthers (Ballet Master/Rector/Schneider/Guest), Roger DeKoven (Krolevsky/Father-in-law), Igors Gavon (Father/Detective/Guest), Bonnie Gould (Frau Stahel/- Refugee/Ballet Student), Elaine Grollman (Frau Hubalek/Mother), Evan Handler (Thomas), Jeannine Khoutieff (Ballet Student/Marlis/Guest), Jeanne Koren (Nurse), Skip Lawing (Egon/Academic), Chris Limber (Waiter/Refugee/Funk/Ambulance Man), Rose Mackey (Mother-in-law/Frau Schneider/Guest/Ballet Student), George Morfogen (Kurmann), Paul Sparer (Recorder), Frederic Walters (Old Snot/Detective/Academic Guest), Charles White (Doctor)

A play in two acts.

Martha Swope Photos
*Closed May 6, 1979 after 48 performances.

**Paul Sparer, Pamela Burrell,
George Morfogen**

FASHION INSTITUTE AUDITORIUM
April 3, through April 14, 1979. (11 performances)
The Rubenstein Theater Foundation presents:

AM I ASKING TOO MUCH

Written and Directed by Ken Rubenstein; Assistant Director, Lois Weaver; Musical Director, Lamar Alford, Tap Dancing, Charles "Cookie" Cook; Costumes, Carola Polakov; Lighting, Sets, Lenny Cowles, Ken Rubenstein; Assistant Musical Director, Eric Stern; Nightclub Costumes, Carola Polakov, Liberato Miranda; Pianist, Eric Stern; Stage Manager, Jack Mashel; Press, Susan Bloch, Sally Christiansen, Bill Rudkin

CAST

Judith Jamison (Jaj), Bernard Lias (Bernie), Kristy Vant (Kristy), Cristobal Carambo (Cuba), Fae Rubenstein (Favolosa), Charles "Cookie" Cook (Cookie)

A musical in three acts.

Martha Swope Photos

Charles "Cookie" Cook, Fae Rubenstein

ENTERMEDIA THEATRE
April 9, through May 12, 1979. (41 performances)
George Braun, Richard Torrence and Marshall Yaeger in association with Entermedia (David Sector, Creative Director) present the Phe Zulu Company of Africa in:

UMABATHA
The Zulu Macbeth

Created by Welcome Msomi; Director, Phillip Msomi; Choreographers, Daisy Dumakude, Maqhude Nyawose, Madoda Mbambo; Lighting, John H. Paull, III; Technical Director, Preston Yarber; Stage Managers, Mishack Nhlapho, Michael Zulu, John Watts; Wardrobe, Cyril Msomi, Jabu Msomi; Assistant to Producers, Robert Fry; Production Assistant, Linda Fox; Executive Director, Joseph Asaro; Stage Manager, John Watts; Press, Valerie Warner

CAST

Lorraine Nyathikazi, Veronica Hlatshwayo, Gertrude Khanyile (Three Witches), Sleby Kunene, Sipho Ndlovu (King), Sipho Ndlovu (King's son), Cyril Msomi. Michael Xulu, Ned Shongwe (Chief Warriors), Reginald Msomi, Lawrence Msomi (Princes of Royal Family), Bukisisa Phakathi (Lady Macbeth), Mishack Nhlapho (Macbeth's attendant), Mboya Sibiya, Mishack Nhlapho (Guards), Musa Dludla, Ned Shongwe, Cyril Msomi (Murderers), Barbara Soni (Mafudu's wife), Welcome Msomi, Jr., Daphne Dumakude (Mafudu's children), Gloria Mkhize, Silindile (Kamakhawulane's friends), Mboya Sibiya (Messenger), Silindile Sokutu (Old Nurse), Ned Shongwe (Doctor), Lorraine Naythikazi, Gertrude Khanyile, Veronica Hlatshwayo, Silindile Sokutu, Barbara Soni, Daphne Dumakude, Lorraine Mahlangu, Gloria Mkhize (Dancers and Attendants), Patridk Sefolosha, Selby Kunene (Congo Drummers), Maqhude Nyawose, Madoda Mbambo (Dance Leaders), Mziwemvunge Mtshali, Buzubani Mchunu, Mbonwa Mthembu, Falakhe Vyawose, Petros Shange, Milton Nyawose, Zwelonke Vezi, Zakufa Qwathubane, Mpiyezwe Mthembu, Dingumkhonto Makhathini, Patrick Maluleka, Bukisisaq Phakathi, Mbusiseni Mnyandu (Warriors and Dancers), Mboya Sibiya, Zalana Shange (Drummers)

Top Right: The Three Witches

PLAYHOUSE THEATRE
Opened Monday, April 16, 1979.*
Robert S. Fishko, Rick Hobard, Donald Warfield present:

G. R. POINT

By David Berry; Director, William Devane; Lighting, Neil Peter Jampolis, Jane Reisman; Scenery, Peter Larkin; Sound, Kirk Nurock; Technical Supervisor, Joe Golden; Wardrobe, Dolores Gamba; Assistant to Producers, Susan Dorsey; Costumes Coordinated by Laura J. Castro

CAST

Tito	Lazaro Perez
Deacon	Howard E. Rollins, Jr.
Straw	Michael Jeter
Micah	Michael Moriarty
Zan	Mark Jenkins
Johnston	Paul Espel
Shoulders	Mansoor Najee-Ullah
K. P.	Brent Jennings
Mama-San	Lori Tan Chinn

STANDBYS AND UNDERSTUDIES: Elliot Berk (Johnston/Tito/Zan), Robert Schenkkan (Micah/Straw), Arlene Quiyou (Mama-San), Johnny "Sugar Bear" Willis (K.P./Deacon/Shoulders)

A drama in two acts. The action takes place in the Republic of South Vietnam from April through November of 1969.

General Manager: Robert S. Fishko
Company Manager: Harris Goldman
Press: Solters & Roskin, Milly Schoenbaum, Rima Corben, David LeShay
Stage Managers: Michael J. Frank, Johnny Willis

* Closed May 13, 1979 after 32 performances and 24 previews.

Right Center: Michael Moriarty, Lori Tan Chinn

Michael Moriarty, Michael Jeter, Howard E. Rollins, Jr., Lazaro Perez

CITY CENTER DOWNSTAIRS
April 12, through April 15, 1979. (6 performances)
Harry Eggart, Jeffrey B. Moss, John A. Viola present:

SHINDIG

Conceived and Directed by Anthony J. Ingrassia; Choreography, Liz Williamson; Musical Direction, Jimmy Wynbrandt, Tommy Wynbrandt; Lighting, David Kissel; Musical Supervision, Martin Silvestri; Costumes, George Bergeron; Media Consultant, Charles S. Gerber; Sound, Joel Nuss; Title Song, Louis St. Louis; Associate Producer, Marsha Wagner; Wardrobe, Veronica Crawford; Hairstylist, Henri Chevrier; Company Manager, Peninah Serrill; Stage Manager, Daniel Dragon; Press, Ken Sherber, Jeffrey Richards, Warren Knowlton

CAST

Paul Binotto, Leigh Henry, Donna Matthews, Mona Stolfi, Pat Tortorici, Ivy Jo Naistadt, Kevin Sessums, Bobby Blain, Chris Cioe, Mark Kaufman, Jon Gerber, Jimmy Wynbrandt, Tommy Wynbrandt

Sonya Moskowitz Photo

Cast of "Shindig"

CENTURY THEATRE
April 18 through May 13, 1979. (31 performances, 5 previews)
Robert R. Blume, Tony Conforti, Manny Taustine present:

MANNY

By Raymond Serra; Director, Harold J. Kennedy; Set, John Kasarda; Lighting, Rick Belzer; Costumes, Bob Graham; Art Director, Sam Harte; Multi-Media, Nanzi Productions, John Annunziato; Associate Producers, Michael E. Bash, Howard Effron; Production Associate, Joseph Peck; Production Assistants, Elizabeth Ottilie Preim, Toomas Rohtia, Lisa Sommerfeld; Wardrobe, Bob Graham; Hairstylist, Marylou Conforti; Management, Theatre Works; Press, Max Eisen, Robert Ganshaw; Stage Managers, Gary Stein, Paul Guskin

CAST

Raymond Serra (Manny), Pierre Epstein who was succeeded by Fredrick Sirasky (Sam), Frances Helm (Gladys), Paul Guskin (Thalberg), Hy Anzell (Harry), Maxine Taylor-Morris (Margarita), Loren Haynes (Eddie, Jr.), Myra Chason (Debbie), Suni Castrilli (Understudy)

A drama in 2 acts and 11 scenes. The action takes place from October of 1927 through January of 1973.

HAROLD CLURMAN THEATRE
Opened Thursday, April 19, 1979.*
Jack Garfein in association with Jack Clark presents:

THE PRICE

By Arthur Miller; Director, John Stix; Setting, David Mitchell; Costumes, Bob Wojewodski; Lighting, Todd Elmer; Assistant to Director, Katherine Perry

CAST

Victor Franz .... Mitchell Ryan
Esther Franz .... Scotty Bloch
Gregory Solomon .... Joseph Buloff
Walter Franz.............................. Fritz Weaver

A drama in two acts. The action takes place in 1958 on the attic floor of a Manhattan Brownstone.

General Manager: Albert Poland
Press: Bruce Cohen
Stage Manager: Patricia Hannigan

* Closed May 19, 1979 after 33 performances and 14 previews, and then played 12 performances at the Spoleto Festival, U.S.A. in Charleston, S.C.

Inge Morath Photos

**Left: Joseph Buloff, Mitchell Ryan,
Scotty Bloch, Fritz Weaver**

Raymond Serra, Frances Helm

THEATER AT HOLY NAME HOUSE

April 19 through May 13, 1979. (16 performances)
American Folk Theater (Dick Gaffield, Artistic Director)
presents:

BUY THE BI AND BYE

By Felton Perry; Director, Dick Gaffield; Sets, Patrick Mann;
Lighting, Sandra Ross; Costumes, Del Sheard; Associate Director,
Jewelle Gomez; Program Coordinator, Donald Griffith; Stage Manager, Eric McGill

CAST

David Gale (WD), Carol Case (A3), Erma Campbell (A1), Hugh L.
Hurd (A2), Joyce Griffen (A4), E. Frantz Turner (A5)

A play in two acts. The action takes place during the spring of
1979.

Taylor Oliver Photo

Top Right: Scene from "Buy the Bi and Bye"

ST. JEAN BAPTISTE HIGH SCHOOL AUDITORIUM

April 19–29, 1979 (9 performances)
The New Eymard Players present:

ANYTHING GOES

Music and Lyrics, Cole Porter; Book, Guy Bolton, P. G. Wodehouse, Howard Lindsay, Russell Crouse; Direction and Choreography, Jeffery K. Neill; Musical Director, Bill Hindin; Settings, Roger Benischek; Lighting, Chris Peabody; Costumes, Joseph Harding; Assistant Choreographer, Suzanne Kaszynski; Stage Manager, Ruth E. Kramer; Producers, Sally Parry, Peter Paulino; Production Managers, Richard C. Snider, Barbara Connell, Ann McLoughlin, J. Kevin Reilly; Props, Tom DiGiovanni, Diane Ceribelli; Press, Barbara Connell, Ann McLoughlin

CAST

Andrew Alloy (Steward), Neil Applebaum (Ching/Sailor), Denis Bellocq (Purser), Russell Bond (Sailor), Mary Boyer (Bonnie), DeeGee Brandemour (Virtue), Thomas Brooks (Moonface), John Dennehy, Jr. (Photographer/Sailor), Larry Frenock (Sailor), Helene Galek (Charity), Kristie K. Hannum (Chastity), Geraldine Hanning (Mrs. Wadsworth T. Harcourt), J. Douglas James (Sailor), Frank Mangiaracina (Billy Crocker), John Mayer (Elisha J. Whitney), Joseph A. McCarthy (Bishop/Captain), Kathee Morris (Purity), Diane Piro (Girl), Magda Pyrek (Reporter/Girl), Rob Richardson (Sir Evelyn Oakleigh), Billie Roe (Reno Sweeney), Larry Ward (Ling-/Sailor), Mary E. P. Young (Hope Harcourt)

Cast of "Anything Goes"

ORPHEUM THEATRE

May 2 through May 6, 1979 (7 performances, 9 previews)
Hamilton Richardson and John Cullum in association with
Steven Suskin present:

PEOPLE IN SHOW BUSINESS MAKE LONG GOODBYES

By H. Jean Schaeffer; Director, John Cullum; Scenery and Costumes, John Falabella; Lighting, Ken Billington; Music, Russell Warner; General Manager, Steven Suskin; Stage Managers, Dean Vallas, James E. Ryan; Press, Susan L. Schulman

CAST

Sylvie .... Karen Jablons
Theresa................................. Emily Frankel
Mario............................. Hector Jaime Mercado
Waiter .... James E. Ryan

A play in two acts. The action takes place at the present time in
Theresa's apartment, Mario's apartment, and the Blue Lake Hotel
in the mountains.

Gustavo Gonzalez Photo

**Emily Frankel, Hector Mercado,
Karen Jablons**

93

BLACK THEATRE FESTIVAL U.S.A.

Mical Whitaker, Director
Hazel J. Bryant, Producer
May 1–June 3, 1979

Presented by the Richard Allen Center for Culture and Art; Set Designer, Edward Burbridge; Lighting Consultant, Shirley Prendergast in association with Mitch Dana; Technical Director, Patricia Golden; Stage Manager, Ron McIntyre; Assistant to Producer, Ty Collins; Assistant to Director, Cheryl Francis; Press, Les Schecter, Barbara Schwei, Rosemary Carey

MITZI E. NEWHOUSE THEATER

May 1 & 2, 1979

WHEN HELL FREEZES OVER I'LL SKATE the Urban Arts Corps production; Conceived and Directed by Vinette Carroll; Musical Direction, Cleavant Derricks; Stage Manager, Gerard Campbell. CAST: Lynne Clifton-Allen, Brenda Braxton, Clinton Derricks-Carroll, Cleavant Derricks, Jeffrey Anderson-Gunter, Alde Lewis, Jr., Marilynn Winbush

May 5 & 6, 1979

LANGSTON the Karamu House production; Conceived, Directed and Choreographed by Mike Malone; Set, John Conley; Stage Manager, Dana Perry-Cooper; Prose, Poetry and Lyrics by Langston Hughes; Original Music, H. G. Thompson. CAST: Willie Gibson, Marvin Wright, Gwen Frost, Joe Jefferson, Yvette Lockett, Margaret Ford-Taylor, Michael Holiday, Marsha Taylor

May 11, 12, 13, 1979

SECOND THOUGHTS the Richard Allen Center for Culture and Art production; Book, Lyrics, Music by Lamar Alford; Producer, Hazel J. Bryant; Director, Helaine Head; Choreography, Siri Sat Nam Singh; Arranger-Conductor, Jerry Jemmott; Set, Felix E. Cochren; Lighting, Gerry Klug. CAST: Reyno, Sarallen, Paul McCarren, Terria Joseph, S. Epatha Merkerson. Jackee Harry, Brian Keeler, Lynn Oliver, Zaida Coles, Mary Alice, Franklin Robinson, Bob Molock, Al Thomas, Cookie Holt

May 15 & 16, 1979

INADCENT BLACK AND THE FIVE BROTHERS by A. Marcus Hemphill; The Billie Holiday Theatre production; Director, Mikell Pinkney; Executive Producer, Marjorie Moon; Set, Felix E. Cochren; Lighting, Tim Phillips; Stage Manager, Lisa Watson. CAST: Maurice Carlton, Valerie Drummond, Earl Fields, Jr., Elaine Graham, Sam Jackson, Avan Littles, Gregory Miller, Ebony JoAnn Pinkney, Joyce Sylvester, Carol Woods

May 19 & 20, 1979

PUTTIN' ON THE MASK a production by the Workshops for Careers in the Arts Living Library Company; Producer, Michael Jackson; Director, Mike Malone; Executive Director, Marilyn C. Greene; Set, Ron Truitt; Costumes, Quay Barnes-Truitt; Choreography, Mike Malone; Music Director, Sam Wilkens; Technical Director, Ron Anderston, Assistant Director, Kenneth Daugherty. CAST: Matthew Dicken, Ralph Glenmore, Maria Gordon, Willie Jackson, Reginald Kelly, Lydia Kellogg, Arnold Kingsbury, Tracey Legion, Chuck Lewis, James McBryde, Tawanna Mickles, Lamont Prince, Angelina Reed, Valerie Scott, Kathy Smith, Jocelyn Taylor, Edii Williams, Julie McGirt

May 22 & 23, 1979

FIVE ON THE BLACK HAND SIDE by Charles Russell; A production by Repertory Inc. of Washington, D.C.; Director, Jaye T. Stewart; Set, Costumes, Lighting, Moto Jicho; Stage Manager, Edward Mayes; Producers, Carolyn Smith, Carl Anderson, Lynn Dyson. CAST: Robert Hatcher, Deborah Chavis, Arthur Dailey, Jr., Jamaal Huggins, Luzern Washington, Ed deShae, Mustafa Muhammed, Sadiqa Pettaway, Patsy Washington, Caren Clark Taylor, Edward Mays, Mike Morris, Tabia Thomas, Kent Jackman

Right Center: Pamela Polk, Patricia McGuire Hill, Barbara Tasker, Carol Sutton in "The Fabulous Miss Marie" *(Ted Gilliam Photo)* **Above: Kuumba Workshop's "The Amen Corner" Top: "Five on the Black Hand Side" by Repertory Inc.**

MITZI E. NEWHOUSE THEATER

May 25 & 26, 1979

THE AMEN CORNER by James Baldwin; Director, Mical Whitaker; A Kuumba Workshop production; Stage Manager, Akintola Ward. CAST: Val Gray Ward, Gwethalyn Bronner, Maria Mitchell, Candace Hunter Lee. Adisa Jayhmu, Donald Franklin, Ernest Rayford, Cynthia Hardy, Erelah Ajao, Paula Russell, Rhonda Ward

May 29 & 30, 1979

THE FABULOUS MISS MARIE by Ed Bullins; A Dashiki Project Theatre production; Director, Ted Gilliam; Set and Lighting, Arthur C. Essex, Jr.; Costumes. Warren Kenner. CAST: Patricia McGuire Hill, Percy Ewell, Pamela Polk, Frank Foster, Mark Taylor, Carol Sutton, Barbara Tasker, Charles Pitts, Chauncey Gilbert, Eddie Bolds

June 2 & 3, 1979

IAGO by C. Bernard Jackson; An Inner City Repertory production; Director, C. Bernard Jackson; Stage Manager, Tony Allen. CAST: Sab Shimono, Gloria Calomee, Cheryl Smith, J. D. Hall, Gralin Jerald, Rita Browne, Lucia Hwong

ST. MALACHY'S THEATER

May 3–26, 1979. (16 performances)
National Musical Theater (Paulette Attie, Executive Director)
presents:

ENCORE

Book, Ronald Rogers, Bob Sonderskov; Director/Choreographer, Denny Shearer; Music Director, Stan Free; Set, Alan Kimmel; Lighting, Michael Newton-Brown; Costumes, Mariann Verheyen; Production Coordinator, Luther Goins, Assistant to Director, Ann Crowley; Stage Manager, Robert L. Anderson; Production Assistant, Jeff Sorg; Press, Howard Atlee, Lark Gilmer, James Baldassare

CAST

Joe Silver (Host), Malita Barron (Leading Lady), Michael Hayward (Leading Man), Bob Morrisey (Juvenile), Sally Ann Swarm (Ingenue), Stan Free (Piano), Frank G. Martenez (Bass)

A musical performed without intermission.

Peter Folonia Photo

**Bob Morrisey, Sally Ann Swarm, Joe Silver,
Michael Hayward, Malita Barron
in "Encore"**

ACTORS PLAYHOUSE

May 7 through June 3, 1979 (5 performances)
Vakasha, Peter Rodis and Elliot Blair present:

SAINTS ALIVE

By Charles Carmello; Director, Frank Leary; Costumes, Phyllis Craig; Set and Audio Design, Robert Layne; Hairstyles and Makeup, Jay Cannistraci.

CAST

Maryellen Badger (Annie), Bruce Strickland (Satan), Louis Consentino (St. Anthony), Stanley Sayer (Father O'Brien/Voice of God), George Pollock (St. Christopher), Joseph Montalbo (Jesus), Robert Carnegie (Jailer)

A play in three acts. The action takes place in a small chapel and in Hades.

(No photos available)

WESTBETH THEATRE CENTER

May 9 through May 26, 1979. (16 performances)
Public Players, Inc. presents:

BEA'S PLACE

Music and Lyrics, John Goodwin; Book, Daniel O'Connor, John Goodwin; Scenic and Costumes Design, Jack McGroder; Lighting, Gail Dahl; Props, Tony Reitano; Orchestrations and Musical Direction, Michael Holmes, Conceived and Directed by Daniel O'Connor; Assistant to Directors, Chris Smithbaker; General Manager, Ricki Klein; Stage Manager, J. Gordon Mathews; Musicians, Michael Holmes, Jonathan Helfand, John Kumnick, George Andoniadis

CAST

Jonathan Bricklin (Tommy), Al Franz (Willy), Howard Hagan (Floyd), Janey Kelley (Bea), Shyrl Rynharrt (Dot), Scott Stevensen (Mitch), Gail Titunik (Evie), Barbara Trunz (Martha Ann)

A musical play performed without intermission. The action takes place at the present time in a bar just outside Las Vegas.

**Right Center: Howard Hagan, Shyrl Ryanharrt
Jonathan Bricklin, Janie Kelly, Al Franz (rear),
Barbara Trunz, Scott Stevensen, Gail Titunik**

**Scott Stevensen, Barbara Trunz,
Jonathan Bricklin, Shyrl Ryanharrt**   95

DRAMA COMMITTEE

May 15 through June 10, 1979. (16 performances)
The Drama Committee Repertory Theatre (Arthur Real, Artistic Director) presents:

MISS STANWYCK IS STILL IN HIDING

By Larry Puchall and Reigh Hagen; Director, William E. Hunt; Set and Lighting, The Committee; Costumes, Bob Graham; Production Manager, Julienne Fisher; Stage Manager, Patrick Flanagan; Press, Laura Darious

CAST

Mike Bradford (Everett), Carleton Carpenter (Brian), Mary Cooper (Eleanor), Lee H. Doyle (Henry), Peter Flint (Tony), Trent Jones (Don), Elaine Swann (Doris), David Vogel (Barney)

A comedy in two acts and six scenes. The action takes place at the present time in the New York City apartment of Brian.

Richard Berger Photo

Carleton Carpenter, Elaine Swann

CITY CENTER DOWNSTAIRS

May 16 through May 20, 1979. (7 performances, 6 previews)
Roger Berlind, Franklin R. Levy and Mike Wise in association with Kep Richard Krones and Leslie Moonves present:

FESTIVAL

Book and Lyrics, Stephen Downs, Randal Martin; Music, Stephen Downs; Additional Book and Special Material, Bruce Vilanch; Based on the chantefable "Aucassin & Nicolette"; Scenery and Lighting, George Gizienski; Costumes, Madeline Ann Graneto; Musical and Vocal Arrangements, Tony Berg; Musical Direction, David Spear; Choreography, Stan Mazin; Director, Wayne Bryan; Stage Managers, Mark Goldman, Wayne Bryan; Production Coordinator, Matthew Rushton; Assistant Musical Director, Jay Leslie; General Managers, Theatre Now, Inc.; Press, Susan L. Schulman, Carol Broad

CAST

Michael Rupert (The Troubador), Bill Hutton (Aucassin), Maureen McNamara (Nicolette), Tina Johnson (Shepherdess), Michael Magnusen (Beaucaire), Lindy Nisbet (Queen of the Gypsies), Roxann Parker (Viscountess), Leon Stewart (Oxherd), Robin Taylor (Shepherdess), John Windsor (Valence)

Musical Numbers: Our Song, Ballad of Oh and For the Love, Beata Biax, Prelude to War and War, Just Like You, Special Day, The Time is Come, Roger the Ox, When the Lady Passes, Gifts to You, The Escape, Pirates Song, I Can't Remember, One Step Further, Let Him Love You, The Ceremony, Unfinished Song, Finale

A musical performed without intermission.

Richard Braaten Photo

Michael Rupert, Leon Stewart, Maureen McNamara, Michael Magnusen, Lindy Nisbet, Bill Hutton, Tina Johnson, John Windsor, Roxann Parker

THEATRE FOUR

May 16 through June 3, 1979. (22 performances)
Seymour Vall and Dean Kyburz in association with Ruth Adler present the MetroRep production of:

LAST DAYS AT THE DIXIE GIRL CAFE

By Robin Swicord; Director, Lynn M. Thomson; Set, Don Jensen; Lighting, Gregory Chabay; Production Assistant, James Bohr; Costume Coordinator, Kathryn Dinos; General Management, Dorothy Olim Associates; Management Associate, Thelma Cooper; Company Manager, Gail Bell; Stage Manager, Suzanne Prystup; Press, Jeffrey Richards, Warren Knowlton, Ben Morse, Avivah Simon

CAST

Lisa Brown (Little Lanette Blossom), Lorna Johnson (Jeri Lee), Ronald Johnson (Wayne Blossom, Sr.), Julie Nesbitt (Joy Knight Blossom), Robert Schenkkan (Wayne Blossom, Jr.)

A drama in two acts. The action takes place at the present time in Bainbridge, Georgia, during September.

Robin Swicord Photos

Lorna Johnson, Robert Schenkkan

TRINITY LUTHERAN CHURCH
May 24–June 25, 1979 (16 performances)
The Trinity Players present:

THE CORN IS GREEN

By Emlyn Williams; Director, Jody Hiatt; Lighting, Linda McNeilly; Stage Manager, Betty Howe; Set, Elizabeth Morgan; Costumes, Ann Sehrt; Props, Elizabeth Howe; Musical Director, Carl Johnson; Producer, John Backe; Press, Marguerite Wolfe; General Manager, Kevin McMahon

CAST

John Goronwy Jones	Ray Paolino
Miss Ronberry	Shami Jones
Idwal	Ted Geislinger
Sarah Pugh	Ibbits Warriner
The Squire	David McConeghey
Mrs. Watty	Anne Barclay
Bessie Watty	Martha Hodge
Miss Moffat	Penelope Morgan
Robbart Robbatch	James Baird
Morgan Evans	Kristofer Batho
John Owen	Jared Seide
Will Hughes	Stephen Fisher

Top Right: Kristofer Batho, Penelope Morgan

CHELSEA THEATER CENTER
Opened Thursday, May 31, 1979.
The Chelsea Theater Center (Robert Kalfin, Producing Director) presents the American Premiere of:

STRIDER: THE STORY OF A HORSE

By Mark Rozovsky; Adapted from a story by Leo Tolstoy; English stage version by Robert Kalfin, Steve Brown; Based on a translation by Tamara Bering Sunguroff; Music, M. Rozovsky, S. Vetkin; Adapted and additional music composed by Norman L. Berman; Vocal and Instrumental Arrangements, Norman L. Berman; Original Russian Lyrics, Uri Riashentsev; New English Lyrics, Steve Brown; Directed and Staged by Robert Kalfin, Lynne Gannaway; Musical Director, Norman L. Berman; Set, Wolfgang Roth; Costumes, Andrew Marley; Lighting, Robby Monk; Sound, Gary Harris; Production Manager, Robert Graham Small; Wardrobe, Jim Lower; Assistant to Director, Lois Alexander; Associate Director, Robert Graham Small

CAST

Vaska/Mr. Willingstone	Roger DeKoven
Actor/Prince Serpuhofsky	Gordon Gould
Actor/General/Announcer	Ronnie Newman
Actor/Viazapurikha/Mathieu/Marie	Pamela Burrell
Actor/Strider	Gerald Hiken
Actor	Katherine Mary Brown
Actor	Jeannine Khoutieff
Actor/Groom	Skip Lawing
Actor/Gypsy	Nina Dova
Actor/Count Bobrinsky/Darling/Lt.	Benjamin Hendrickson
Actor/Feofan/Fritz	Igors Gavon
Actor/Vendor	Charles Walker
Actor	John Brownlee
Actor	Nancy Kawalek
Actor/Gypsy	Karen Trott
Actor	Tad Ingram
Actor/Bet Taker	Evan Handler
Actor/Gypsy	Steven Blane

A drama in two acts.

General Manager: Michael Kinter
Press: Susan Bloch, Sally Christiansen, Bill Rudman
Stage Managers: Zoya Wyeth, Tad Ingram, Laurie Stone, Vincent Ferraudo

Peter Krupenye Photos

Right Center: Cast of "Strider"
Above: Gerald Hiken, John Brownlee, Skip Lawing, Igors Gavon, Gordon Gould

Nina Dova, Karen Trott, Pamela Burrell (reclining), Gordon Gould, Steven Blane

THE ACTORS STUDIO
Lee Strasberg, Artistic Director
Carl Schaeffer, Executive Producer

ACTORS STUDIO
February 16 - March 14, 1979 (15 performances)

HILLBILLY WOMEN

Boy Elizabeth Stearns; Director, Peter Bennett; Music and Lyrics, Clint Ballard, Jr.; Choreography, Robert Fitch; Producer, Marilyn Fried; Set, Hugh Landwehr; Lighting, Leslie Spohn; Costume Coordination, Penny Davis; Associate Producer, Lee Pucklis; Administrative Associate, Marlene Butler; Stage Managers, Bill Hare, Ellen Friedman, Reisa Sperling, Jeff Zinn; Technical Director, Kim Novick; Assistant to Choreographer, Terry Rieser; Musical and Choreographic Coordinator, Pauline Fitch; Studio Coordinator, Janet Merry Doeden; Press, George Culver

CAST

Jacqueline Knapp (Della), Katherine Squire (Siddy), Sharon Goldman (Sharleen), Janet Ward (Jewel), Susan Peretz (Sue Ellen), Lois Smith (Denise), Robin Howard (Ada), Standbys: Susan Burns, Wendy Girard

MUSICAL NUMBERS: Lay a Little Love on Me, Which Side Are You On, Hillbilly Hambone, Amazing Grace, Crocadile Lounge, Hillbilly Woman Go Home, Damned If You Do, Jubilee, Livin'. Performed without intermission. The action takes place here and now.

Catherine Squire, Susan Peretz, Jacqueline Knapp, Janet Ward, Sharon Goldman, Lois Smith, Robin How

ACTORS STUDIO
May 6 - 21, 1979 (15 performances)

SECOND ANNUAL NEW PLAYS FESTIVAL
Israel Horovitz, Artistic Director

THE BREAKERS by Herbert Liebman; Director, Ray Whelan; Stage Managers, Harry Boda, Debbie Renee; CAST: M. Patrick Hughes, Mark Kaplan, Mallory Jones

ROCKET AND SNOOD by Peter Parnell; Director, Sheldon Larry; Stage Manager, Forrest Lee Wallace; CAST: Michael Margotta, Ben Masters, Mary Joan Negro, Parker McCormick, Joel Sorkin, Kathy McKenna, Jack Hallet, Richard Reiner

THE GOOD PARTS by Israel Horovitz; Director, Ray Whelan; Stage Managers, Ernie Townsend, Brett Knobel; CAST: Robert Fields, Sabin Bernstein, Ellen Barber, Teri Garr, Elaine Rinehart, David Scholar

VALENTINE by Linda Segal; Director, Richard E. Hughes; Stage Manager, Debbe Renee; CAST: Kitty Troll, Joe Tobin, Gloria Szymkowicz, Candy Trabucco, Tom Badal, Wendy Girard, Candace Derra, J. J. Quinn, Jean Alexander, Gayle Greene, Mari Coates, Harry Boda, Mary Lee Kellerman, Julia Curry

THE CITY AT 4 A.M. by Bruce Serlen; Director, Sylvia Tucker; Stage Manager, Sara F. Bunn; CAST: Katherine Cortez, Jacqueline Jacobus, J. J. Quinn, Barry Miller

ROCKAWAY BOULEVARD by Richard Vetere; Director, Stephen Zuckerman; Stage Manager, Cindy Russell; CAST: Suzannah Knight, Frank Piazza, J. J. Quinn

SURVIVORS by Herbert Liebman; Director, Ernest Martin; Stage Manager, Peter Sapienza; CAST: Julie Ariola, Robert Carnegie, Dan Hedaya, Eric Loeb, Elaine Rinehart, Joe Tobin

THE CONSOLING VIRGIN by Bruce Serlen; Director, Barbara Covington; Stage Manager, Connie McDonnell; CAST: Katherine Cortez, James Hayden, Scott Kuba, Barry Schaeffer

THE WIDOW'S BLIND DATE by Israel Horovitz; Director, Sheldon Larry; Stage Manager, Kim Novick; CAST: Jill Eikenberry, Robert Fields, Ebbe Roe Smith

Gregory Abels

Trish Van Devere

Jane Cronin

Paul Gleason

ACTORS STUDIO
May 29 - June 9, 1979 (12 performances)

THE VIOLANO-VIRTUOSO

By Betty Suyker; Director, John Desmond; Set, Richard B. Williams; Costumes, Karen M. Hummel; Lighting, Andrea Wilson; Sound, David Rapkin; Producers, Linda Lehman, Michael Wright; Stage Managers, John Pantozzi, Christine Child; Technical Director, Matthew Ellison; Props, Marvi Haynes; Production Assistants, Dana Cooper, Leslie Linn

CAST

Gregory Abels (Thomas Jefferson Hadley III), Trish Van Devere (Sarah Woodhouse), Jane Cronin (Constance Merritt), Paul Gleason (Richard Rowan), Geoffrey Horne (Harrison Bell)

A play in three acts. The action takes place at the present time in Sarah Woodhouse's apartment in Greenwich Village.

AMAS REPERTORY THEATRE

Rosetta LeNoire, Artistic Director

AMAS REPERTORY THEATRE
November 2, - 19, 1978 (12 performances)

SPARROW IN FLIGHT

A musical based on the life of Ethel Waters; By Charles Fuller; Based on a concept by Rosetta LeNoire; Director, Dean Irby; Choreography and Costumes, Bernard Johnson; Music and Vocal Director-Arranger-Conductor, Larry Garner; Vocal and Choral Supervisor-Assistant Conductor, William "Gregg" Hunter; Set, Michael Meadows; Lighting, Paul Sullivan; Stage Managers, William Michael Maher, Carolyn Greer

CAST

Ethel Ayler, Charles Brown, Charles "CB" Murray, John Martin Green, Don Paul, Amy Pivar, Kevin John Gee, Troi C. Jackson, Michelle Beteta, Cathy Orum, Pauletta Pearson, Robert Ray, James Moody, Fran Salisbury, Sandra Phillips, Lillette Harris-Jekins, William "Gregg" Hunter, Mary Louise, Pauletta Pearson

November 30, - December 17, 1978 (12 performances)

Ambur Hiken Photo

HELEN

A musical based on Helen of Troy; Lyrics and Music, Johnny Brandon; Book and Direction, Lucia Victor; Musical Direction and Arrangements, Danny Holgate; Vocal Arrangements and Assistant Musical Direction, Carl Maultsby; Set, Michael Meadows; Lighting, Paul Sullivan; Choreography and Costumes, Bernard Johnson; Stage Managers, William Michael Maher, Carolyn Greer

CAST

Jean Dushon, Chuck Patterson, Fran Salisbury, Newton Winters, Rob Barnes, Jamil K. Garland, Gerri Griffin, Pauletta Pearson, Kevin John Gee, James Moody, Paul Dinotto, Charlie J. Rodriguez, Amy Piva, Joella Breedlove, Trudy Miller, Diane Wilson, Darnell Williams, Charles 'CB' Murray, Carol Jean Lewis, John Russell

MUSICAL NUMBERS: Nothing Ever Happens in Greece, Come on and Dance, Somethin's Doin', Bring It on Home, Bite Your Tongue, There Are Ways of Gettin' Things Done, Diplomacy, You've Got It, Do Us a Favor, Dance of the Golden Apple, Helen, Hold on Tight, Do What You Must, Somebody Touched Me, You Never Know the Mind of a Woman, Good or Bad, Finale

February 22, - March 11, 1979 (12 performances)

IT'S SO NICE TO BE CIVILIZED

A musical Written and Composed by Micki Grant; Director, Jeffrey Dunn; Choreography, Fred Benjamin; Musical Supervision and Arrangements, Danny Holgate; Choral Arrangements and Direction, Chapman Roberts; Conductor, William "Gregg" Hunter; Set, Patrick Mann; Lighting, Paul Sullivan; Costumes, Bill Baldwin; Stage Managers, Carolyn Greer, Gwendolyn M. Gilliam

COMPANY

Charles Berry, Karen G. Burke, David Cahn, Claudine Cassan, Jean Cheek, Kevin DeVoe, Eugene Edwards, Joey Ginza, Dwayne Grayman, Paul Harman, Sundy Leake, Carol Lynn Maillard, Brenda Mitchell, Ennis Smith, Cassie Stein, Diane Wilson

MUSICAL NUMBERS: Step into My World, Wake Up Sun, Subway Rider, God Help Us, Who's Gonna Teach the Children, Out on the Street, Welcome Anderson, Why Can't Me and You, When I Rise, Up Front Behind, Walkin' the Dog, I Want to Be Your Congressman, Everybody's Got a Pitch, Terrible Tuesday, Come Back Baby, Alice, It's So Nice to Be Civilized, The World Keeps Going Round, Talking to People, Old Things, I've Still Got My Bite, Look at Us, Jun-Jub, Bright Lights, Like a Lady, Me and Jesus, Pass a Little Love Around

Don Paul Photo

**Top Right: Kevin John Gee, Charles "CB" Murray,
Robert Ray, Mary Louise in "Sparrow in Flight"
Below: "It's So Nice to Be Civilized" Right
Center: Mary Louise (C) and company
in "Suddenly the Music Starts"**

AMAS REPERTORY THEATRE
May 3, - May 20, 1979 (12 performances)

SUDDENLY THE MUSIC STARTS

A revue written and composed by Johnny Brandon; Musical Direction and Arrangements, Neal Tate; Choreography, Henry Le Tang; Musical Staging, Henry Le Tang, Lucia Victor; Associate Choreographer, Eleanor Le Tang; Choral Arrangements and Direction, Carl Maultsby; Musical Coordination and Dance Arrangements, Danny Holgate; Set, Patrick Mann; Costumes, Virginia Johnson; Lighting, Paul Sullivan; Stage Managers, Carolyn Greer, Gwendolyn M. Gilliam; Technical Director, Sam Gonsalez

CAST

Mary Ellen Ashley, Jean Cheek, Debbi Dee, Kevin John Gee, George Hillman, William "Gregg" Hunter, Kelli Kahn, Mable M. Lee, Mary Louise, Wayne McCarthy, Rozlyn Sorrell, Andy Torres

MUSICAL NUMBERS: Suddenly the Music Starts, My Home Town, Faces in a Crowd, Funky People, Super Bad, I'll Scratch Your Back, Goodnight, Boogie Woogie Ball, Talk Your Feelings, Your Love Is My Love, Dancing Dan, Dance! Dance! Dance!, Whole Lotta Real Good Feeling, Remember Someone, Everybody's Doing the Disco, Guides, Stuff, Syncopatin', Kansas City Blues, Manhattan Lullaby, One Day at a Time, You, It's My Turn Now, Strolling down Broadway, Finale

Larry Neilson Photo

AMERICAN MIME THEATRE

Paul J. Curtis, Director
Jean Barbour, Administrator
Joel S. Charleston, Counsel
New York, N.Y.

COMPANY

Jean Barbour
Charles Barney
Paul J. Curtis
Dale Fuller

Jean Gennis
Kevin Kaloostian
Erica Sarzin
Mr. Bones

REPERTORY: The Lovers, The Scarecrow, Dreams, Hurly-Burly, Evolution, Sludge, Six, Abstraction

David Eng Photo

Charles Barney, Paul Curtis, Arthur Yorinks in "Hurly-Burly"

AMERICAN MUSICAL & DRAMATIC ACADEMY

David Martin, Artistic Director
Jan Martin, Executive Director

AMDA STUDIO ONE
July 26, - August 4, 1978 (5 performances)

LADIES AT THE ALAMO by Paul Zindel; Director, David Martin; Set, Andrew Ian Rubenoff; Costumes, Elaine R. Mason; Lighting, Joseph P. Tilford; Production Manager, Jonathan Field; Technical Director, Ron Daley; Stage Manager, Brett Cochrane; Production Assistant, Joe Abate. CAST: Carol Kastendieck, Shelli Leon, Carole Round, Sandy Spurney, Dorothy Whylling

July 29, - August 6, 1978 (6 performances)

HENRY IV by Luigi Pirandello; Director, David Martin; Stage Manager, Rick Dallago CAST: Emilio Del Pozo, Fern Radov, Zita-Ann Geoffroy, Lee Welch, Marty Hoffman, James A. Kroll, Louis Schwartz, Joseph Bloom, Larry Hornick, Jon Ostrow, Francis Barnard, Tony Corrente

August 8, - 13, 1978 (6 performances)

THE RUNNER STUMBLES by Milan Stitt; Director, Carol Kastendieck; Lighting, Lisa Grossman; Costumes, Steven L. Birnbaum; Music, Richard Beck-Meyer; Stage Manager, Brett Cochrane CAST: Jon Ostrow, Scott Allen, Dorothy Whylling, Lee Brockman Welch, Lydia Allyn Mahan, Fern Radov, Marty Hoffman, Jonathan Field, Margie Sloven

August 16, - 20, 1978 (6 performances)

THE CONTRAST by Royall Tyler; Direction and Choreography, Carol Kastendieck; Musical Direction, New Material and Arrangements, Francis Barnard; Set and Lighting, Marc Surver; Costumes, Elaine R. Mason; Stage Manager, Jonathan Field CAST: Ronald A. Hester, Larry Hornick, Fern Radov, Sandy Spurney, Regina Alexander, Zita-Ann Geoffroy, Marty Hoffman, Lee Brockman Welch, T. Edward Thayer, James A. Kroll

Jerry Gelb Photo

September 29, - October 16, 1978 (12 performances)

RICHARD II by William Shakespeare; Director, Ron Daley; Lighting, Toby Mailman; Fights, Dennis Divito; Music, Francis Barnard; Set, Bridget Thorne; Stage Manager, G. Warren Steele
CAST: Stephen Novelli, Ward Asquith, Tim Flanagan, Hugo Napier, Charles Fontana, Bernie Mantell, Michael Dryansky, Shelli Leon, Barbara D. Flatt, Cathy Hews, Leslie Barrett, Richard Abernethy, Tom Sminkey, Paul Welsh, Helen Breed, Dennis Divito, Lee Owens, John Rosene, Craig Purinton, Marie Virag

Pictures of People Photo

May 11, - 20, 1979

THE PRISONERS OF QUAI DONG by Harold Willis; Director, David Martin; Coordinating Producer, James T. Ahlberg
CAST: Lee Brockman Welch, Chas Glaser, Richard Hughes, Glenn Cabrera, Harry Rudolph, Jerry Rago, John DiBenedetto, Ten Boonthanakit, G. Warren Steele

Susan Cook Photo

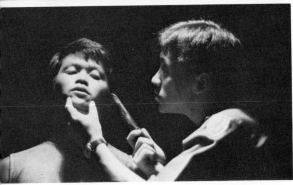

Ted Boonthanakit, Richard Hughes in "Prisoners of Quai Dong" Above: "Richard II"

Top Left: Sandy Spurney, James A. Kroll in "The Contrast"

AMERICAN PLACE THEATRE

Wynn Handman, Director
Julia Miles, Associate Director
Fifteenth Season

AMERICAN PLACE THEATRE
Sunday, October 15 through Sunday, November 5, 1978. (25 performances)
The American Place Theatre presents:

THE GRINDING MACHINE

By Annalita Marsili Alexander; Director, Frederick Rolf; Design, Wolfgang Roth; Costumes, Willa Kim; Lighting, Edward M. Greenberg; Technical Director, Craig Evans; Wardrobe, Kathleen Fredericks; Stage Managers, Nancy Harrington, Jeffrey Rowland; Press, Jeffrey Richards, Sy Sandler, Karen Gromis

CAST

Thomas Barbour (Gordon Wilson), Joanna Merlin (Anna Colonna), Ronald Hunter (Georgi Valmas), Loren Brown (Krista Karitonova), William Lyman (Ian Campbell, Ron Randell (Yury Fiodorovich Kyrkov), Andrew Jarkowsky (Andrei Bulatov), Josephine Nichols (Vera Campbell), Rebecca Schull (Understudy)

A play in two acts and three scenes. The action takes place on a summer morning at the present time in a dacha outside of Moscow.

Martha Holmes Photo

AMERICAN PLACE THEATRE
Sunday December 10 through Sunday, December 31, 1978. (24 performances)
The American Place Theatre (Wynn Handman, Director; Julia Miles, Associate Director) presents:

TOUCHING BOTTOM

Three one-act plays by Steve Tesich; Director, Robert Brink; Sets, Henry Milligan; Lighting, Craig Evans; Costumes, Mimi Maxmen; Wardrobe, Kathleen L. Fredericks; Technicians, Lee Copenhaver, Phillip Kerzner, Ray Kline; Sound, Jeffrey Rowland; Flute Music, Didi Charney; Press, Jeffrey Richards, Sy Sandler, Mark Arnold

CAST

Harold Gould
Lois Smith

The Plays: (performed with two intermissions) "The Road," "A Life," "Baptismal"

Martha Holmes Photos

AMERICAN PLACE THEATRE
April 21 through May 13, 1979. (32 performances)

TUNNEL FEVER
or
The Sheep Is Out

By Jonathan Reynolds; Director, Marshall Oglesby; Sets and Costumes, Donato Moreno; Lighting, Dennis Parichy; Choreography, Dalienne Majors; Technical Director, Billings LaPierre; Stage Managers, Nancy Harrington, W. Scott Allison; Press, Jeffrey Richards, Anne Obert Weinberg

CAST

Fumio . . . . Ron Randell
Dr. Paulie . . . . Richard Dow
Morosini . . . . Marcus Smythe
Grunion . . . . Martin Marinaro
Carvalho . . . . Ron Faber
Lucy . . . . Jill Haworth
Standbys: Ron Faber, Marcus Smythe, Martin Marinaro

A play in two acts.

Martha Holmes Photo

Top Right: William Lyman, Joanna Merlin, Ron Randell in "The Grinding Machine" Below: Ron Randell, Richard Dow in "Tunnel Fever"

AMERICAN PLACE THEATRE
Thursday, February 1, through Sunday, February 25, 1979. (43 performances)
The American Place Theatre presents:

SEDUCED

By Sam Shepard; Director, Jack Gelber; Sets, Henry Millman; Costumes, Whitney Blausen; Lighting, Edward M. Greenberg; Furs, Ben Kahn; Stage Managers, Nancy Harrington, W. Scott Allison; Technical Director, Billings Lapierre; Wardrobe, Kathleen L. Fredericks; Press, Jeffrey Richards, Sy Sandler, Ken Sherber

CAST: Rip Torn (Henry Hackamore), Richard Bright (Raul), Pamela Reed (Luna), Carla Borelli (Miami), Understudies: Tracey Loggia, Ed Setrakian

A drama in two acts. The action takes place on the top floor of a Caribbean luxury hotel.

Martha Holmes Photo

Carla Borelli, Rip Torn, Pamela Reed in "Seduced"

BAM/BROOKLYN ACADEMY OF MUSIC

Harvey Lichtenstein, President/Chief Executive Officer
Judith E. Daykin, Executive Vice President/General Manager

LEPERCQ SPACE
Opened Tuesday, December 5, 1978.*
Dodger Theater (Associate Directors: Michael David, Des McAnuff, Edward Strong, Sherman Warner) presents:

GIMME SHELTER

A trilogy by Barrie Keeffe; Director, Des McAnuff; Scenery, Stuart Wurtzel; Costumes, Carol Oditz; Lighting, Dennis Parichy; Electronic Orchestrations/Sound, Pril Smiley; Dialect Coach, Elizabeth Smith; Production Assistant, Tina Turturro; Production Manager, Malcolm J. Waters

CAST

"Gem": by a cricket pitch on an August Bank Holiday

Kev	Richard Backus
Gary	Philip Casnoff
Janet	Randy Danson
Bill	Brad O'Hare

"Gotcha": in a school stockroom at end of spring term.

Ton	Maury Chaykin
Lynne	Judith Calder
Kid	Keith Gordon
Head	Kensyn Crouch

"Getaway": by a cricket pitch a year later.

Kev	Richard Backus
Janet	Randy Danson
Gary	Philip Casnoff
Kid	Keith Gordon

Press: John Howlett, Philip Rinaldi
Stage Managers: Peter Dowling, Karen Gerst, Richard Goodwin

* Closed Dec. 23, 1978 after limited engagement of 19 performances.

Paul Kolnik Photos

**Philip Casnoff, Richard Backus
Above: Judith Calder, Maury Chaykin,
Keith Gordon, Kensyn Crouch Top: Brad
O'Hare, Richard Backus, Philip Casnoff,
Randy Danson**

LEPERCQ SPACE
January 9–19, 1979. (12 performances)
Dodger Theater presents:

BREAD AND PUPPET JOAN OF ARC

Part I: Legend of Joan of Arc, Part II: Story of Her Horse

Paul Kolnik Photo

"Joan of Arc"

BAM/HELEN CAREY PLAYHOUSE
Opened Wednesday, March 21, 1979.*
The Brooklyn Academy of Music presents the Goodspeed Opera House production (Michael P. Price, Executive Producer) of:

TIP-TOES

Music, George Gershwin; Lyrics, Ira Gershwin; Book, Guy Bolton, Fred Thompson; Director, Sue Lawless; Choreography and Musical Staging, Dan Siretta; Musical Director, William Cox; Costumes, David Toser; Lighting, Peter M. Ehrhardt; Music Research, Alfred Simon; Assistant Musical Director, Gregory Dlugos; Assistant Choreographer, Larry McMillian; Producer, Warren Pincus; Stage Managers, Alan Coleridge, Ric Barrett; Hairstylist, Michael Lanza; Press, John Howlett, Philip Rinaldi

CAST

Georgia Engel (Tip-Toes Kaye), Russ Thacker (Steve Burton), Bob Gunton (Rollo), Jana Robbins (Sylvia), Haskell Gordon (Hen Kaye), Michael Hirsch (Al Kaye), Nicole Barth (Denise), Jon Engstrom (Attendant), Erik Geier (Sam), Dawn Le Ann Herbert (Miss Mitchell), Ronn Robinson (Hodge/Detective), Susan Danielle (Miss Wright), Gwen Hillier Lowe (Peggy), David Monzione (Steward), Rodney Pridgen (Quinn), Brad Witsger (Otto), Sally O'Donnell (Miss Jones), Jill Owens (Miss Hart), Bobby Longbottom (Shay)

MUSICAL NUMBERS: Waiting for the Train, Nice Baby, Looking for a Boy, Lady Luck, When Do We Dance?, These Charming People, That Certain Feeling, Sweet and Low-Down, Our Little Captain, It's a Great Little World, Why Do I Love You?, Nightie-Night, Tip-Toes, Finale

A musical comedy in 2 acts and 5 scenes.

* Closed Apr. 8, 1979 after limited engagement of 24 performances.

Paul Kolnik Photos

**Right: Jana Robbins, Bob Gunton
Above: Georgia Engel (C) and company
Top: Russ Thacker, Georgia Engel
in "Tip-Toes"**

BAM/OPERA HOUSE
March 27 through April 8, 1979. (16 performances)
The Brooklyn Academy of Music with the National Youth Theatre of Great Briatain presents:

GOOD LADS AT HEART

By Peter Terson; Director, Michael Croft; Wardrobe, Rosemary Clayton; Company Manager, Fergus Logan; Stage Manager, Roderick Potter; Press, John Howlett, Philip Rinaldi, Rex Hearn

CAST

Sean Aita (Closey), Philip Beckwith (Hodgkinson), Paul Blackman (Dukes), Richard Burge (Drama Teacher), Ashley Burns (Bates), Tim Coombs (Garvey), Colin Cox (Caldwell), Jonathon Dunn (Fletcher), Patrick Field (Scott), Tony Gouveia (Charkham), Douglas Hodge (Naylor), Antony Howes (Doug), Stephen Jacobs (Butler), Benedict Kenney (Arlott), Glen Kinch (Smith), Peter Lennon (P. T. Teacher), Ann Miller (Assistant Drama Teacher), Rod Potter (Mavison), David Taggart (Headmaster), Tom Vavrecka (Chammy), Owen Whittaker (Horricks)

A play in two acts. The action takes place in the gymnasium of a reform school in the 1970's

Nobby Clark Photos

Scene from "Good Lads at Heart"

"La Puce a L'Oreille" (A Flea in Her Ear)
Top: "Le Misanthrope"

BAM/OPERA HOUSE

May 1–13, 1979. (16 performances)
The Brooklyn Academy of Music by arrangement with the John F. Kennedy Center for the Performing Arts under the auspices of the Association Francaise d'Action Artistique presents Comedie Francaise in:

LE MISANTHROPE

By Moliere; Director, Pierre Dux; Assistant Director, Gerard Giroudon; Scenery and Costumes, Jacques Marillier; Music, Alain Margoni

CAST

Oronte	Bernard Dheran
Philinte	Michael Duchaussoy
Dubois	Alain Pralon
Alceste	Francois Beaulieu
Basque	Jean-Francois Remi
Le Garde	Georges Riquier
Clitandre	Philippe Rondest
Acaste	Guy Michel
Arsinoe	Berengere Dautun
Celimene	Beatrice Agenin
Eliante	Fanny Delbrice

A comedy in five acts.

LA PUCE A L'OREILLE

By Georges Feydau; Director, Jean-Laurent Cochet; Scenery, Georges Wakhevitch; Costumes, Rosine Delamare

CAST

Carlos Homenides de Histangua	Georges Descrieres
Augustin Ferraillon	Michel Aumont
Docteur Finache	Bernard Dheran
Camille Chandebise	Michel Duchaussoy
Romain Tournel	Alain Pralon
Rugby	Jean-Francois Remi
Baptistin	Jean-Paul Moulinot
Etienne	Guy Michel
Chandebise and Poche	Jean Le Poulain
Olympe Ferraillon	Denise Gence
Raymond Chandebise	Paule Noelle
Eugenie	Berengere Dautun
Antoinette	Claire Vernet
Lucienne Homenides de Histangua	Alberte Aveline

A comedy in three acts.

Agence de Presse Bernard Photos

Jacqueline Brookes, Rebecca Schull,
Brad O'Hare

BAM/SIXTH FLOOR

May 16–26, 1979. (12 performances)
Dodger Theater (Michael David, Des McAnuff, Edward Strong, Sherman Warner, Associate Directors) present:

ON MOUNT CHIMBORAZO

By Tankred Dorst in collaboration with Ursula Ehler; English version by Peter Sander; Director, John Palmer; Scenery, Christopher Nowak; Costumes, Nancy Thun; Lighting, Victor En Yu Tan; Stage Managers, Karen Gerst, James Furlong; Press, Philip Rinaldi

CAST

Janni Brenn (Irene), Jacqueline Brookes (Dorothea), Dan Desmond (Tilman), Brad O'Hare (Henrich), Rebecca Schull (Clara)

A comedy performed without intermission. The action takes place in the summer of 1970 on a mountain standing alone by the East German border woods from sunset to night.

Paul Kolnik Photo

CIRCLE REPERTORY THEATRE

Marshall W. Mason, Artistic Director
Tenth Season

General Manager, Earl R. Hughes; Press, Rima Corben, Glenna Clay; Technical Director, Robert Yanez; Assistant to Mr. Mason, Carol Patella; Art Director, Daniel Irvine; Business Manager, William Waters; Late Show Director, Daniel Irvine; Stage Managers, Fred Reinglas, Amy Schecter

CIRCLE REPERTORY THEATRE

June 8–30, 1978 (15 performances)
The Late Show presents:

MY CUP RANNETH OVER

By Robert Patrick; Director, Marlyn Baum; Set, Linda Hacker; Costumes, David Menkes; Lights, Gary Seltzer; Lyrics, Robert Patrick; Music, Henry Krieger; Sound, Chuck London; Stage Managers, Michael Herzfeld, David Csontos; Assistant Director, Elliot Kreloff; Musical Coordinator, Andrew Mishkind
CAST: Amy Wright (Yucca), Nancy Snyder (Paula)

CIRCLE REPERTORY THEATRE

October 18–November 19, 1978 (35 performances) *World Premiere*

GLORIOUS MORNING

Patrick Meyers; Director; Terry Schreiber; Set, Hal Tine; Costumes, Laura Crow; Lighting, Dennis Parichy; Stage Manager, Michael Herzfeld.

CAST

Tanya Berezin (Sally), Jonathan Hogan (Robbie), Nancy Snyder (Alicia), Douglass Watson (Frank), James Ray Weeks (Harvey)

November 2–17, 1978 (12 performances)
The Late Show presents:

STARGAZING

By Tom Cone; Director, Daniel Irvine; Setting, Nina Friedman; Costumes, Joan E. Weiss; Lighting, Gary Seltzer; Sound, Chuck London; Stage Managers, Michael Herzfeld, Liz Rothberg.

CAST

Debra Mooney (Jan), Nancy Snyder (Eleanore), Timothy Shelton (Henry), Michael Ayr (Edward)

November 29–December 31, 1978 (35 performances) *World Premiere*

IN THE RECOVERY LOUNGE

By James Farrell; Director, Marshall W. Mason; Setting, Tom Lynch; Costumes, Laura Crow; Lighting, Dennis Parichy; Sound, Charles London; Stage Manger, Fred Reinglas

CAST

Jack Davidson (Mr. Hauck), Sharon Madden (Alice), Burke Pearson (Zacks), Helen Stenborg (Mrs. McGinn), Danton Stone (Jack)

December 19–29, 1978 (7 performances)
The Late Show presents:

TOTAL RECALL

By Martin Halpern; Director, Ronald Roston; Lighting, Gary Seltzer; Costumes, Joan E. Weiss; Stage Managers, Fred Reinglas, Susan Bushard

CAST

Bruce Gray (Wilfrid Porter), Lindsay Crouse (Eleanor Manning)

The action takes place at the present time in Porter's one room studio on the lower East Side of NYC.

Ken Howard, Michael Goldstein Photos

Top Right: Tanya Berezin, Jonathan Hogan in "Glorious Morning" Below: Nancy Snyder, Debra Mooney, Michael Ayr in "Stargazing" Right Center: Sharon Madden, Burke Pearson in "In the Recovery Lounge"

Lindsay Crouse, Bruce Gray in "Total Recall"

CIRCLE REPERTORY THEATRE
January 12–February 18, 1979 (40 performances)

THE RUNNER STUMBLES

By Milan Stitt; Director, B. Rodney Marriott; Setting, David Potts; Costumes, Kenneth M. Yount; Lighting, Dennis Parichy; Music, Tom Spivey; Sound, Charles London; Production Manager, David Bradford; Technical Director, Robert Yanez; Stage Managers, Fred Reinglas, Michael Herzfeld, Gary Seltzer; Wardrobe, Joan E. Weiss; Props, Liz Rothberg

CAST

Jack Davidson (Amos), William Hurt (Father Rivard), Bobo Lewis (Mrs. Shandig), Burke Pearson (Monsignor Nicholson), Joyce Reehling (Sister Rita), Timothy Shelton (Prosecutor), June Stein (Louise), Elizabeth Sturges (Erna Prindle), James Ray Weeks (Toby Felker)

A drama in two acts. The action takes place during April 1911 in a cell and courtroom in Solon, Michigan.

Ken Howard Photo

January 14–18, 1979 (5 special benefit performances)
The Late Show presents:

THE HUMAN VOICE

By Jean Cocteau; Translated by Paulette Robinstein; Director, Jose Quintero; Setting, Eric Head; Costumes, Theoni V. Aldredge; Lighting, Dennis Parichy; Production Manager, David Bradford; Technical Director, Robert Yanez; Stage Managers, Fred Reinglas, Michael Herzfeld; Press, Rima Corben, Glenna Clay

CAST

Liv Ullmann

**Liv Ullmann in "The Human Voice"
Top: Joyce Reehling, William Hurt
in "The Runner Stumbles"**

January 23–February 8, 1979 (12 performances)
The Late Show presents:

MINNESOTA MOON

By John Olive; Director, Carole Rothman; Set, Nina Friedman; Costumes, Joan E. Weiss; Lighting, Gary Seltzer; Stage Manager, Fred Reinglas

CAST

Gary Berner
Jeff Daniels

Michael Goldstein Photo

February 28–April 1, 1979 (35 performances)
Circle Repertory presents:

WINTER SIGNS

By John Bishop; Director, Marshall W. Mason; Setting, David Potts; Costumes, Laura Crow; Lighting, Dennis Parichy; Sound, Chuck London; Production Manager, David Bradford; Technical Director, Robert Yanez; Stage Managers, Fred Reinglas, Michael Herzfeld, Wendy Weinstein; Props, Peter Bogyo

CAST

Jack Davidson (Leslie Finley), Bruce Gray (Ken Timmons), Stephanie Gordon (Judith Finley)

A play in two acts and four scenes. The action takes place at the present time in a house in a small college town in Minnesota.

Ken Howard Photo

**Bruce Gray, Jack Davidson, Stephanie
Gordon in "Winter Signs"**

**Left Center: Jeff Daniels, Gary Berner
in "Minnesota Moon"**

CIRCLE REPERTORY THEATRE
March 15–30, 1979 (10 performances)
The Late Show presents:

THE DESERTER

By Norman Beim; Director, John Bard Manulis; Lighting, Gary Seltzer; Costumes, Joan E. Weiss; Stage Managers, Fred Reinglas, Gary Berner; Sound, Chuck London, Peter Bogyo; Props, Kate McCamy; Press, Richard Frankel, Glenna Clay

CAST

Michael Ayr (The Soldier), Timothy Shelton (The Sergeant), James Ray Weeks (A Priest)

A drama in one act. the action takes place in a deserted chateau behind the front lines in France just before dawn on a winter morning in 1945.

Michael Goldstein Photo

April 18–June 3, 1979 (50 performances)
Circle Repertory Company presents:

TALLEY'S FOLLY

By Lanford Wilson; Director, Marshall W. Mason; Setting, John Lee Beatty; Lighting, Dennis Parichy; Costumes, Jennifer von Mayrhauser; Sound, Chuck London; Production Manager, David Bradford; Technical Director, Robert Yanez; Stage Managers, Fred Reinglas, Michael Herzfeld, Liz Rothberg; Props, Stewart Schneck; Press, Richard Frankel, Glenna Clay

CAST

Matt Friedman .... Judd Hirsch
Sally Talley .... Trish Hawkins

A drama performed without intermission. The action takes place on a July evening in 1944 in an old boathouse on the Talley Place, a farm near Lebanon, Missouri.

Gerry Goodstein Photo

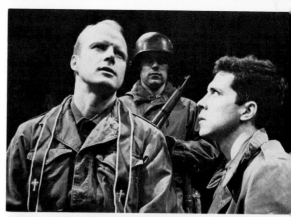

Trish Hawkins, Judd Hirsch in "Talley's Folly" Top: James Ray Weeks, Timothy Shelton, Michael Ayr in "The Deserter"

CIRCLE REPERTORY THEATRE
May 15–June 1, 1979 (11 performances)
The Late Show presents:

LIFE AND/OR DEATH

Three one-act plays by Herb Gardner; Director, Porter Van Zandt; Setting, Andrew Ian Rubenoff; Lighting, Gary Seltzer; Costumes, Joan E. Weiss; Sound, Chuck London; Stage Managers, Fred Reinglas, Michael Herzfeld, Peter Bogyo; Technical Director, Robert Yanez; Assistant to Director, Penny Gebhard; Artistic Coordinator, Daniel Irvine; Press, Richard Frankel, Glenna Clay

CAST

"HOW I CROSSED THE STREET FOR THE FIRST TIME ALL BY MYSELF" with Judd Hirsch. The action takes place in 1945 in a Brooklyn classroom.
"THE FOREVER GAME" with Johann Carlo (Amanda) and Joyce Reehling (Annie). The action takes place at the present time on a Sunday afternoon in a teen-aged girl's room in a Central Park West apartment in NYC.
"I'M WITH YA DUKE" with Judd Hirsch (Samuel Margolis) and James Ray Weeks (Dr. MacIntyre). The action takes place at the present time at 8 P.M. in a semi-private room in St. Vincent's Hospital in NYC.

Michael Goldstein Photo

Friday, Saturday. Sunday, April 6, 7, 8, 1979 (3 performances)

AN EVENING WITH RITA GARDNER
"A Woman's Life in the Theatre"
with Jim Litt at the piano

Rita Gardner Above: James Ray Weeks, Judd Hirsch in "Life and/or Death"

COLONNADES THEATRE LAB

Michael Lessac, Artistic Director
Robert N. Lear, Executive Producer
Associate Artistic Director, Tom V. V. Tammi; Chairman of the Board, Derek Hornby; General Manager, Mary T. Nealon; Administrative Assistant, Mary Ann Dent; Production Manager, Randy Becker; Technical Director, Terry Noble; Stage Managers, Arthur J. Schwartz, Rebecca Kreinen; Wardrobe, Dolores Gamba; Sound, Garry Rindfuss; Sets, Maura Smolover, Robert U. Taylor; Costumes, Rebecca Kreinen, Tere Eglar, Hilary A. Sherred

COMPANY

Nesbitt Blaisdell, Stephen Casko, Jacqueline Cassel, Edward Edwards, Louis Giambalvo, Tom Gustin, Marcia Hyde, Carol Mayo Jenkins, Peter Kingsley, Berwit Lagerwall, Debra Monk, Bill Noone, Brady Rifkin, Peter Scolari, Karen Shallo, Tony Simotes, Charlie Stavola, Tom V. V. Tammi, Michael Jay, David Morgan, Louis Phillips, Hilary A. Sherred, Maura Smolover, Robert U. Taylor, Michael Lessac, Robert N. Lear

PRODUCTIONS: "The Ballroom in St. Patrick's Cathedral" by Louis Phillips, "Moliere in spite of Himself" conceived and directed by Michael Lessac; Adapted from Mikhail Bulgakov's "A Cabal of Hypocrites" by David Morgan, with music by Michael Jay.

Gerry Goodstein Photo

Top Right: Peter Kingsley (top), Marcia Hyde, Tom V. V. Tammi in "Moliere in spite of Himself"

COUNTERPOINT THEATRE COMPANY

Howard Green, Artistic Director
Paulene Reynolds, Managing Director
Terry Walker, Associate Artistic Director
Fifth Season

COUNTERPOINT THEATRE
October 6–23, 1978 (12 performances)

A DOLL'S HOUSE by Henrik Ibsen; Translated by Rolf Fjelde; Director, Don Marlette; Scenery, Milad Ishak; Lights, Jesse Ira Berger; Costumes, Deborah Shaw; Stage Managers, Cindy Russell, Connie L. McDonnell; Technical Director, W. Scott Allison. CAST: Elaine Kilden (Nora), Pat Lawler (Helene), Mark Spergel (Delivery Boy), Peter DeMaio (Torvald), Carol Morley (Kristine), Joseph Daly (Nils), Howard Green (Dr. Rank), Hope Cameron (Anne Marie), Jason Gladstone, Jonathan Margulies, Micaela Elizabeth Walker (Helmer Children)

November 17–December 4, 1978 (12 performances)

WAITING FOR GODOT by Samuel Beckett; Director, Terry Walker; Set, Randi Frank; Lights. Jesse Ira Berger; Costumes, Karen M. Hummel; Assistant to Director, Lynn Polan; Stage Manager, Connie L. McDonnell; Technical Director, Milad Ishak. CAST: Paul Ladenheim (Estragon), Dimo Condos (Vladimir), Cola Pinto (Pozzo), John Copley-Quinn (Lucky), Dylan Schaffer (Boy)

March 9–26, 1979 (12 performances)

DIVERSIONS with Set by Randi Frank; Lights, Jesse Ira Berger; Costumes, Karen M. Hummel; WOOED AND VIEWED by Georges Feydeau, translated by Norman Shapiro; Director, Lynn Polan; Stage Manager, Cindy Russell. CAST: Christine Jansen, Tom Leo, THE PLEASURE OF PARTING by Jules Renard, translated by Stanley Hochman; CAST: Carol Case, Rick Friesen; CONVERSATION-SINFONIETTA BY Jean Tardieu, translated by Colin Duckworth; Director, Howard Green; Stage Manager, Gary Marks. CAST: Tom Leo, Jack Barry, Sam Gray, Hope Cameron, Carol Grant, Tanny McDonald, Michael Mantel, Rick Friesen, Ed Crowley

April 27, May 14, 1979 (12 performances)

A TASTE OF HONEY by Shelagh Delaney; Director, Terry Walker; Set, Milad Ishak; Lights, Jesse Ira Berger; Costumes, Karen Barbano; Technical Director, Jason G. Kantrowitz; Music Consultant, Suzanne George; Pianist/Composer, Lee Calhoun; Stage Managers, Gary Marks, Bill Thorne. CAST: Carol Rosenfeld, Linda Kampley, Howard Green, Dino Shorte, William McEnaney

Left Center: Peter De Maio, Elaine Kilden in "A Doll's House"

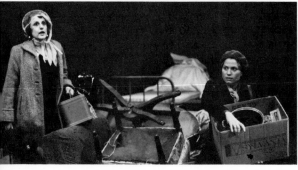

Carol Rosenfeld, Linda Kampley in "A Taste of Honey"

ENSEMBLE STUDIO THEATRE

Curt Dempster, Artistic Director
Marian Godfrey, Associate Director

ENSEMBLE STUDIO THEATRE

October 4–29, 1978 (20 performances)
THE END OF THE WAR by Vincent Canby; Director, David Margulies; Set, David Mitchell; Lighting, Richard Nelson; Costumes, Madeline Cohen; Stage Managers, Michael S. Mantel, Lynn Foss; Press, Faith Geer CAST: Matthew Cowles, Bruce McGill, Paul Austin, John Ellerbrock, Richard Minchenberg, Dominic Chianese, Hy Anzel, John Seitz, David Givens, David Rasche

December 7–23, 1978 (18 performances)
THREE: Directors, Ellen Sandler, Jerry Zaks; Producer, Anthony McKay; Set, Christopher Nowak; Lighting, Geoffrey Dunbar; Costumes, Madeline Cohen, Marcia L. Whitney; Technical Director, Randy Hartwig; Stage Managers, Dwight R. B. Cook, Marianne Regan, John Clinton, Jan Bromberg; Sound, Robert Saidenberg; Production Supervisor, Dennis Drew; Assistant to Artistic Director, Risa Bramon Abromovitch; Press, Faith Geer CAST: BICYCLE BOYS by Peter Maloney, with Kevin Scannell, Dann Florek, Cathleen McKiernan, George Bamford; PLAYING DOLLS by Susan Nanus, with Gina Savage, Caitlin Dulany, Kathy Galvin; BUDDY PALS by Neil Cuthbert, with Alan Bruun, Chris Lutkin, Willie Reale, Cathleen McKiernan

February 21–March 11, 1979 (18 performances)
A SPECIAL EVENING: Two one act plays directed by David Shookhoff; Set, Brian Martin; Lighting, Cal Vornberger; Costumes, Madeline Cohen; Stage Manager, David S. Rosenak THE MAN WITH THE FLOWER IN HIS MOUTH by Luigi Pirandello, with David Margulies, Stefan Gierasch, Schellie Archibold; THE OLD TUNE by Robert Pinget; English text by Samuel Beckett; with David Margulies and Stefan Gierasch

April 15–22, 1979 (8 performances)
NEW VOICES: Concert Readings of Plays by New American Playwrights; Set, Brian Martin; Costumes, Madeline Cohen, Kim Dennis, Karen Miller; Lighting, Marie Louise Moretto; Stage Managers, Don Buschmann, J. E. Andrews, Ralph Edwards, John Clinton NESTING by Christopher Ceraso, directed by Bill Cwikowski; with Gina Barnett, Joseph Carberry, Kathy Danzer, Sylvia Gassell, Robert Haufrecht, Reuben Schaffer. THE ICE FARM by Peter Maeck, directed by Thomas Bullard; with Jarlath Conroy, Sylvia Gassell, Eddie Jones, Ben Masters, Tom McKitterick, Susan Merson. WHAT'S SO BEAUTIFUL ABOUT A SUNSET OVER PRAIRIE AVENUE? by Edward Allan Baker; Director, Paul Austin; with Jack Caputo, Ian Cohen, Lelia Gastil, Marcia Haufrecht, Lisa Maurer, Michael McCleery, Jack McClure, John McComb, Don Marino, John Nesci, Marilyn Rockafellow, Michael Santoro, Ed Setrakian, Ann Spettell, Jennie Ventriss, Joe White. NEW MEXICAN RAINBOW FISHING by Jerry Stubblefield; Director, Curt Dempster; with Bill Cwikowski, Don Plumley, Lori Putnam

May 2–27, 1979 (20 performances)
WELFARE by Marcia Haufrecht; Director, Anthony McKay; Set, Brian Martin; Lighting. Cal Vornberger; Stage Manager, Spence Halperin; Costumes, Madeline Cohen; Assistant Director, Laurie Sayet CAST: Mariann Aalda, David Connell, Essene R., Carol Simmons, Robert Judd, William McKinney, Jack R. Marks, Sam McMurray, Rochelle Parker, Paul Ricci, Rosalba Rolon, Socorro Santiago, Laurie Sayet, Thurman Scott, Wende Dasteel Sherman, John Tufino, Rosemarie Tufino, Juanita Valree, Yvonne Warden

Gerry Goodstein Photos

Top Right: Gina Savage, Caitlin Dulany in "Three / Playing Dolls"
Below: "Eulogy for a Small Time Thief"

Stefan Gierasch, David Margulies in "A Special Evening"

Gretchen Van Aken, David Hart, Tom Wopat
in "Oklahoma!"

MASTER THEATRE
September 14–October 8, 1978 (30 performances)
Equity Library Theatre presents:

OKLAHOMA!

Music, Richard Rodgers; Book and Lyrics, Oscar Hammerstein II; Based on "Green Grow the Lilacs" by Lynn Riggs; Director, Russell Treyz; Musical Director, Eric Stern; Choreography, John Montgomery; Sets, John Falabella; Costumes, Kenneth M. Yount; Lighting, Victor En Yu Tan; Stage Managers, James Pentecost, Les Cockayne, Hannah Cohen, Peter Alexis; Wardrobe, Dolores Gamba

CAST

Kathryn Cordes, Clayton Davis, David Eric, Lynne Gannaway, Kenneth Gildin, David Hart, Mary Jane Joffman, Stephen Joseph, Robert Nersesian, Caroline Nova, Elyssa Paternoster, Donna Pelc, Ginny Reinas, Joe Romagnoli, Justin Ross, Rebecca Ann Seay, Gretchen Van Aken, Martin Van Treuren, Lee Winston, Sally Woodson, Tom Wopat

Gary Wheeler Photo

Mark Hofmaier, Jan Granger, Nicholas
Guest, Kendall March in
"A Midsummer Night's Dream"

October 19–November 5, 1978 (22 performances)

A MIDSUMMER NIGHT'S DREAM

By William Shakespeare; Director, Bolen High; Choreography, Dennis Grimaldi; Music, Elizabeth Myers; Set, Linda Skipper; Costumes, A. Christina Giannini; Lighting, Robby Monk; Sound, Gary Harris; Stage Managers, Shari Genser, William Paster, Gayle Palmieri; Wardrobe, Mary Lou Rios

CAST

Bennett Cooperman, Ken Costigan, Dann Florek, John Goodman, Jan Granger, Nicholas Guest, Mark Hofmaier, Ted Houck, Arlene Kaplan, Nathan Lane, Jacob Laufer, Kendall March, Ellen Newman, Danny Redmon, Bill Roulet, Mary Key Simpson, Michaelan Sisti, Jacalyn Switzer, Charles Tachovsky, Sturgis Warner, Kevin Winkler

Gary Wheeler Photo

Mary Lynne Metternich, William McCauley
in "Can-Can"

November 16–December 10, 1978 (30 performances)

CAN-CAN

Music and Lyrics, Cole Porter; Book, Abe Burrows; Director, Charles Kondek; Musical Director/Arrangements, Evans Haile; Sets, Dennis Bradford; Costumes, Tom McKinley; Lighting, David H. Murdock; Choreography, David Holdgreiwe; Stage Managers, Sally Hassenfelt, Belle Baxter, Brian Donnell, Becky Wold; Props, Philip Bond; Wardrobe, Michael Fields; Press, Lewis Harmon, Sol Jacobson; Keyboards, Evans Haile, Ethyl Wil, Eric Stern

CAST

Eric Aaron, Lee Chew, Lou Corato, Michael P. Estes, Leslie Feagan, Lisa Guignard, Andrea Green, Tonda Hannum, Larry Hansen, James Horvath, Terry Iten, Peter Kapetan, Jonathan Kestly, Lesley Kingley, Steve Liebman, William McCauley, Mary Lynne Metternich, Michael Neville, James Newell, Carlo Pellegrini, Michele Pigliavento, Chris Reisner, Joe Romagnoli, Kara Stannard, Lisa M. Steinman, Bill Tynes

Gary Wheeler Photo

MASTER THEATRE
January 4–21, 1979 (22 performances)

THE MIRACLE WORKER

By William Gibson; Director, Ted Weiant; Scenery, Gibbs Murray; Lighting, Richard Dorfman; Costumes, Deborah Shaw; Original Music, David McHugh; Fight Coach/Assistant to Director, Tony Melchior; Stage Managers, Candace Baer, John Retif, Allison Sommers; Props, Nette Reynolds, Steve Shereff; Sound, Larry Collen; Hairstylist, Stephen Campanella; Wardrobe, Barbara Burroughs Johnson; Press, Lewis Harmon, Sol Jacobson

CAST

Toni L. Agard, Kathy Bernard, Patty Burtt, Chandra, John Henry Cox, Paul Craggs, Carrie Dunn, Gussie Harris, Mary Hayden, Patrick Hazelwood, Rod Houts, Marla Johnson, Edith Larkin, Tom McDermott, Anna Minot, Amy Nathan, Richard Rizzo, Cristine Rose, Jo Lynn Sciarro, Laurie Thorp

Gary Wheeler Photo

**Cristine Rose, Kathy Bernard
in "The Miracle Worker"**

February 1–21, 1979 (24 performances)

LA RONDE

By Arthur Schnitzler; Adapted by Eric Bentley; Director, Warren Kliewer; Sets, Sally Locke; Costumes, Gina Taulane; Lighting, Craig Kennedy; Stage Managers, Nidal Mahayni, Barbara Schneider, Kathy Uhler; Production Assistant, Laura Spitzer; Props, Nette Reynolds, Allison Sommers; Wardrobe, Mary Lou Rios

CAST

Donald Ainsworth, Alan Clement, Mary Donnet, Ellen Fiske, Jodv Hingle, J. C. Hoyt, Deborah B. MacHale, Michael Morin, Maeen Rockafellow, Richard Sabellico

Gary Wheeler Photo

**J. C. Hoyt, Ellen Fiske
in "La Ronde"**

March 1–25, 1979 (30 performances)

MARY

By Otto Harbach, Louis Hirsch, Frank Mandel; Director, Clinton Atkinson; Musical Direction, Donald Chan; Choreography, Dennis Dennehy; Musical Staging, Clinton Atkinson, Dennis Dennehy; Sets, Wade Giampa; Costumes, Jack McGroder; Lighting, Ruth Roberts; Assistant Choreographer, J. H. Clark; Assistant Conductor, Paul Ford; Animal Trainer, Ron Bock; Stage Managers, M. R. Jacobs, Mark Schorr, Stephen Shereff, Kathleen Marsters; Wardrobe, Christina L. Ringelstein; Pianists, Donald Chan, Paul Ford

CAST

Eric Alderfer, Jay Barney, Betsy Beard, Rustin Billingsly, Cathy Brewer-Moore, Rick DeFilipps, Michael Estes, Fiona Hale, John High, W. M. Hunt, Mary Ellen Landon, Mark Manley, Debbie McLeod, Nancy Meadows, Vince Rhomberg, Bonni Simmons, Robin Stone, Kay Walbye, Michael Waldron, Peggy Ann Zitko

Gary Wheeler Photo

**Betsey Beard, Michael Waldron
in "Mary"**

THE IMPORTANCE OF BEING EARNEST

By Oscar Wilde; Director, Alfred Gingold; Set, Ursula Belden; Lighting, Cynthia J. Hawkins; Costumes, Mary Brownlow; Stage Managers, Victoria Bradshaw, Shauna Vey, Rebecca Guy; Assistant to Director, Nadja Tesich; Press, Lewis Harmon, Sol Jacobson

CAST

Gerard A. Burke, Dorothy Kobs, Harris Laskawy, Sally Mercer, Martha Miller, Marc Murray, Ellen Newman, Wesley Stevens, Ralph David Westfall

Gary Wheeler Photo

May 3–27, 1979 (30 performances)

ON A CLEAR DAY YOU CAN SEE FOREVER

Book and Lyrics, Alan Jay Lerner; Music, Burton Lane; Director, Richard Mogavero; Musical Direction, Paul Ford; Choreography, Ed Brazo; Scenery, Richard Harmon; Lighting, Norman Coates; Costumes, Kenneth M. Yount, Jack Peyron; Stage Managers, Susan K. Butcher, Mark Keller, Mary O'Leary; Props, Kate Doyle; Pianists, Paul Ford, Mary McBride; Percussion, Margaret Capossela

CAST

Maggie Anderson, Mary Lou Belli, Ralph Bruneau, Clint Clifford, Byron Conner, Julie Ann Fogt, Lenore Fuerstman, Dale Furry, Kenneth Gildin, Stephen Gleason, Kristie Hannum, Lois Diane Hicks, Diana-Jeanne LeBlanc, Ele Logan, Craig Mason, Vance Mizelle, Ginny Reinas, Yolanda Rubio, Michael Schilke, Jay Schneider, Chuck Voight, Mark Zimmerman

Gary Wheeler Photo

Ginny Reinas, Mark Zimmerman in "On a Clear Day...."

EQUITY LIBRARY THEATRE INFORMALS

George Wojtasik, Managing Director
Ann B. Grassilli, Bridget Ragan, Co-Producers

LINCOLN CENTER LIBRARY & MUSEUM
September 11, 12, 13, 1978 (3 performances)
Equity Library Theatre Informals series presents:

LORELI, PLEASE! DON'T SIT THAT WAY by Jeanne Michels, Neal Thompson; Director, Neal Thompson; Stage Manager, Gary Dyer. CAST: Jeanne Michels, Virgil Roberson

October 16, 17, 18, 1978 (3 performances)

WE'LL BE RIGHT BACK!! by John O'Creagh; Director, Michael Burke; Set and Lighting, Stephen Edelstein; Costumes, Edmond Felix; Technical Director, David Kaye. CAST: Linda Bernhard, Michele Mais, Maralyn Nell, James Niesen, Charlie Serrano, M. Jonathan Steele

November 27, 28, 29, 1978 (3 performances)

MANHATTAN BREAKDOWN by James Pentecost and Robert McNamara; Music, Andy Bloor; Lyrics, Robert McNamara; Sets, Paul Kelly; Costumes, Gayland Spaulding; Lighting, David H. Murdock; Music arrangements, James Stenborg, Andy Bloor; Musical Direction, James Stenborg; Musical Numbers Staged by Randy Hugill, James Pentecost; Choreography, Randy Hugill; Director, James Pentecost; Stage Managers, Les Cockayne, Hannah Cohen, Arthur Barsamian; Wardrobe, Sylvia Myrvold. CAST: Elly Barbour, Kathryn McAteer, Maureen McNamara, Steven Memel, Kim Morgan, Richard Sabellico, Lenny Wolpe

December 11, 12, 13, 1978 (3 performances)

MUSICAL BRITANNIA presented by Cameo Productions Ltd; A celebration of British theatre music with Jacqueline Kroschell, Michael Sedgewick, Karen Sund, Shirley Ann Sequin, Savario Barbieri, Sean Barker, Ron Forsmo, Jeannette Gardner, Dominic Guastaferro

February 5, 6, 7, 1979 (3 performances)

NESTING by Christopher Ceraso; Director, Mitchell Engelmeyer; Stage Manager, The Ninos; Technical Director, David E. Kaye. CAST: Joseph Carberry, David Chandler, Kathy Danzer, David Kerman, Rusti Moon, Lisa Sloane

March 5, 6, 7, 1979 (3 performances)

A NEW ENGLAND LEGEND by Estelle Ritchie; Suggested by Nathaniel Hawthorne's "The Scarlet Letter"; Director, Warren Kliewer; Set, Gregory Buch; Lighting, Philip Lippel; Costumes, Florence L. Rutherford; Stage Managers, Robert Stevenson, Sandy Crimins, Manuel Norat

April 16, 17, 18, 1979 (3 performances)

QUADRILLE by Gregory Peterson; Director, Rodney Griffin; Set and Lighting, William Marshall; Costumes, Bud Santora; Stage Manager, Randy Hartwig; Sound, Tom Whalen; Props, Susan Caputo; Original Music, Jeffrey Kresky; Technical Director, Bruce Farnworth

May 14, 15, 16, 1979 (3 performances)

LIFESONGS with Music and Lyrics by Robert Mitchell; Director, Lou Rodgers; Musical Direction, John Klingberg; Choreography, Joel Czarlinsky; Lighting, Stephen Ross; Costumes, Rene Gladstein; Stage Manager, Stephanie Brown. CAST: Cayce Blanchard, Michael Calkins, Cindy Cobitt, Hylan Kunerth, Bob Morrissey, Sally Ann Swarm, John Klingberg, Robert Mitchel

(No photos)

Top Left: Sally Mercer, Ellen Newman, Wesley Stevens, Harris Laskawy in "The Importance of Being Earnest"

FANTASY FACTORY
Bill Vitale, Director
BRUNO WALTER AUDITORIUM/DONNELL LIBRARY
November 13–25, 1978 (12 performances)

LIKE THE SONG SAYS
By Ed Kuczewski; Director, Jamie Brown; Music, Richard Foltz; Lighting, Richard Dorfman

CAST

Richard Foltz, Joyce Griffen, Parker McCormick, Cheryl Lesley Royce, Beatrice Winde

THE TROUPE THEATRE
December 22, 1978–January 7, 1979 (12 performances)

HOT VOODOO MASSAGE
Book, Ed Kuczewski; Music and Lyrics, Bill Vitale; Musical Direction, Michael Lee Stockler, Laura Florman; Staged and Directed by Bill Vitale; Costumes, Milly Russell; Lighting, Daniel Charles Abrahamsen; Stage Managers, Laura Stuart, Bruce Bell, John Tarone, Bruce MacCartney

CAST

Rabin Adras, Donna Lee Betz, Marc Castle, Joseph Garran, Joan Neuman, Barbara Sandek, Raymond Shelton, Ted Sod, Valerie Swift, Ross G. Tatum, DeeAnn Devnie, LizaGrace Vachon-Coco, Louis Zippin, Martina Maniculata

THE TROUPE THEATRE
May 11–June 3, 1979 (12 performances)

INDULGENCES
Book, Ed Kuczewski; Music and Lyrics, Bill Vitale, Richard Foltz; Musical Direction, Bruce MacCartney; Arrangements, Sergio Garcia-Marruz; Lighting, Alex Palacios; Costumes, Milly Russell; Puppets, Spike Kleinman; Stage Managers, Tom Tippett, David Weymouth; Director, Bill Vitale

CAST

Donna Lee Betz, Kevin Canterna, Marc Conrad, Maria Ferrari, Steve Fifield, Richard Foltz, Jerome Foster, Stephen Foster, Vincent Gangi, Joyce Griffen, Earl Arthur Imbert, Arthur Kearney, Angel Martin, James Margolin, Joan Neuman, Louis Zippin

Cast of "Indulgences" *(Jon Phillips Photo)*
Top Left: Barbara Sandek, Louis Zippin in "Hot Voodoo Massage" *(Mary Bloom Photo)*

113

FESTIVAL THEATRE FOUNDATION

Robert O'Rourke, Artistic Director
Douglas Gester, Managing Dierctor

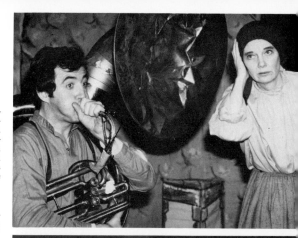

FESTIVAL THEATRE

December 1–17, 1978 (12 performances)
THE SUICIDE by Nikolai Erdman; Translated by Eileen Thalenberg, Alan Richardson; (American Premiere) Director, Robert O'Rourke; Set, Jeffery Pavelka; Costumes, Cheryl Blalock; Lighting, John Hastings; Stage Managers, Jay Gorstein, Joy Hooper; Production Manager, Bruce Kaiden CAST: Colman DeKay, Kathleen Forbes, Reily Hendrickson, Bonnie Kaiden, Richard Kendall, John Little, Sally Parrish, Howard Renensland, Andy Schefman, Marcus Smythe, Richard Spore, Brad Stoddard, Jim Swanson, Florence Winston

December 6–17, 1978 (10 performances)

THE PLEASURE OF PARTING by Jules Renard; American Premiere; Translated by Stanley Hochman; Director, Bruce Kaiden; with Patricia Mertens, John Gray. THE FOURTEEN LOVERS OF UGLY MARY-ANN by Andrei Amalrik; American Premiere; Director, Fredric Stone; Set, Jeffery Pavelka; Costumes, Maggie Delgado; Stage Manager, Sally Jane Gellert; with Amy Gootenberg, Michael Bahr, Michael Arabian, Jerry Beal, Vanessa Hollingshead

December 13–17, 1978 (4 performances)

STRANGLE ME by Frank Shiras; Director, Robert O'Rourke; Lighting, Joy Hooper; Set and Costumes, Jeffery Pavelka; CAST: Anne Louise Hoffmann, Louise Turner, Russell Duffy, Jane Crawley, Michael Arabian, Kevin O'Malley

February 23–March 11, 1979 (12 performances)

ONE HUSBAND TOO MANY by Barnett Shaw; Based on Georges Feydeau's "Champignol Malgre Lui"; Stage Managers, Joy Hooper, Tori Beauclaire. CAST: Michael Arabian, Doug Baldwin, Jane Crawley, Bill Britten, Colman DeKay, Richard Kendall, Nancy LeBrun, Sheri Myers, Tony Natarella, Katie Ortleib, Sally Parrish, Dan Plucinski, Veryle Rupp, Andre Schefman, Ronald Sopyla, James Stolper, Jim Swanson, Ronald Willoughby

February 28–March 10, 1979

WOOED AND VIEWED by Georges Feydeau; Translated by Norman Shapiro; Director, Gene Santarelli; Stage Manager, Carol D. Smith. CAST: Bruce Kaiden, Bonnie Kaiden

March 5–8, 1979 (4 performances)
May 4–20, 1979 (12 performances)

THE EDOUARD CASE by Georges Feydeau; Adaptation by Barnett Shaw; Director, Robert O'Rourke; Assistant Director/Stage Manager, Trevor Drake. CAST: Alan Brooks, Sharon Pierson, Ronald Sopyla, William March, Brian McEleney, Joel Stevens, John Gray, Evelyn Seubert, Collin Leslie Fox

March 2–10, 1979 (4 performances)

MIDNIGHT SNACKS written and performed by Anne Louise Hoffmann, Paul Lawrence, Brian McEleney, Barry M. Press, Louise Turner

May 8–18, 1979 (8 performances)

PASSION, POISON AND PETRIFICATION by George Bernard Shaw; Director, Craig Macdonald; Stage Manager, Marty Kovach. CAST: Nancy Boykin, Katie Ortleib, Veryle Rupp, Paul Bonner, John Kaye, David Bickford, David Willis

May 11–19, 1979 (8 performances)
TOOTH & CONSEQUENCE by Norman R. Shapiro; Adapted from Georges Feydeau's "Hortense A Dit'Je M' En Fous!" with Timothy Hall, Ronald Sopyla, Carla Charny, Nancy LeBrun, Paul Bonner, Dan Plucinski, Florence Winston, Merrill Vaughn, Veryle Rupp

SELF TORTURE AND STRENOUS EXERCISE by Harry Kondoleon; Director, Trevor Drake; Set, Jeffery Pavelka; Lighting, Joy Hooper; with Timothy Hall, Fred Sanders, Colby Willis, Louise Turner

Kevin O'Rourke Photos

Top Right: Howard Renensland, Sally Parrish in "The Suicide" Below: Dan Plucinski, Bill Britten in "One Husband Too Many" Center: Sharon Pierson, Alan Brooks in "The Edouard Case"

Katie Ortlieb, Jim Swanson, James Stolper, Sally Parrish in "One Husband Too Many"

HENRY STREET SETTLEMENT'S
New Federal Theatre
Woddie King, Jr., Producer

HARRY DeJUR PLAYHOUSE
October 19–29, 1978 (12 performances)
HOT DISHES! with book, music and lyrics by Maurice Peterson; Direction and Choreography, Irving Lee; Set, Robert Edmonds; Lighting, George Grecyzlo; Costumes, Rene Lavergneau, Wia Carpenter; Assistant to Director, Gary Easterling; Musical Direction, Arrangements, Adaptation, Original Dance Music by Grenoldo Frazier; Production Assistants, Ernestine Collins, Ngoma; Press, Howard Atlee, Newton Lamson; Wardrobe, Vivianne Jones; Props, Gwen Gilliams. CAST: Ernestine Jackson, Gia Galeano, Berniece Hall, Matthew Inge, Harold Jurkiewicz, Suzanne Klewan, James Moody, Sandra Phillips, James Patterson, Eric Riley, Besseye Ruth Scott, Andrea Suter

November 16–December 3, 1978 (13 performances)
THE GOD OF VENGEANCE by Sholem Asch; Music, Jonathan Firstenberg; Director, Stanley Brechner; Set and Lighting, Bart Healy, Costumes, A. Christina Giannini; Stage Manager, Sharon Brown Levy. CAST: Jerry Alan Cole, Barry Golditch, Virginia Hut, Laura Julian, Joseph S. King, Joan Lowell, Ken Metiver, Gabrielle Olejniczak, Jo Ann Schmidler, Ruth Selnick, Ann Spettell, Leonard Sragow, Allan Wasserman

December 8–17, 1978 (12 performances)
BLACK MEDEA by Ernest Ferlita; Director, Glenda Dickerson; Set, Michael Fish; Lights, Pat Stern; Costumes, Ellen Lee; Stage Manager, Kimako Baraka. CAST: Vinie Burrows, Rose Marie Guiraud, Patricia Hayling, Roger Hill, Leon Morenzie, Shirley Peacock, Carol Pennyfeather, Warrington Winters

January 18–28, 1979 (12 performances)
TAKE IT FROM THE TOP by Ruby Dee; Director, Ossie Davis, Musical Director, Guy Davis; Choreography, Kimee Joyce; Set, Michael Fish; Lighting, Shirley Prendergast, Costumes, Judy Dearing; Stage Manager, Dwight R.B. Cook. CAST: Ruby Dee, Ossie Davis, Jariann Aalda, Robert Burr, Laurie Carlos, Maurice Carlton, Rony Clanton, Pamela Poitier, Chiquita Jackson, Kimee Joyce, Jack Landron, Tom McCleister, Lou Myers, Robert Townsend, David Van Fleet

February 22–March 4, 1979 (12 performances)
FLAMINGO FLOMONGO by Lucky Cienfuego; Director-Choreographer, Erick Santamaria; Set, Bob Edmonds; Lighting, Faith Baum; Costumes, Joaquin LaHabana; Stage Manager, Richard Johnson; Music and Musical Direction, Steve Tarshis. CAST: Nelia Bacmeister, Alex Bernardo, David Borres, Tere Chaviano, Juan DeJesus, Hector Frias, Rebecca Holm, Joaquin LaHabana, Frank Martinez, Orlando Penn, Essene R, Larry Ramos, Craig Robinson, Sloan Robinson, Fran Salisbury, Deryck Smuth

November 10–20, 1978 (12 performances)
ANNA LUCASTA by Philip Yordan; Director, Ernestine M. Johnston; Lighting, Shirley Prendergast; Costumes, Edna Watson; Stage Manager, Phillip Shawn King; Set, C. Richard Mills; Press, Howard Atlee. CAST: Debbie Allen, Thomas Anderson, Rony Clanton, Miriam Burton, Juanita Clark, Sam Singleton, Charles Grant Green, Neil Harris, Marcella Lowery, Carles Cleveland, Carl Drudup, Maxwell Glanville, Neville Richen, Elizabeth Van Dyke

Right Center: Joseph King in "God of Vengeance."

Sara Herrnstadt, D. M. Levine, Gwynne Press in "Green Fields"

PILGRIM THEATRE
November 30–December 10, 1978 (12 performances)
TAKE A GIANT STEP by Louis Peterson; Director, Oz Scott; Lights, Victor En Yu Tan; Costumes, Judy Dearing; Set, C. Richard Mills; Stage Manager, Gail Dahl; Assistant Director, Jerry Cleveland. CAST: Rony Clanton, Juanita Clark, Paco Coleman, Starletta DuPois, Flloyd Ennis, Minnie Gentry, Joyce Griffen, Neil Harris, Terria Joseph, David Phillips, Michael Nobel, Ted Sod, Louise Stubbs, Richard Thorne, Elizabeth Van Dyke

December 14–24, 1978 (12 performances)
IN SPLENDID ERROR by William Branch; Director, Charles Turner; Lighting, Shirley Prendergast. CAST: Arthur Anderson, Dan Barbaro, Carles Cleveland, Charles Grant-Greene, Neil Harris, Wanda Hines, Bette Howard, Gilbert Lewis, Carl Moebus, Dennis Tate, George Taylor

January 4–14, 1979 (12 performances)
TROUBLE IN MIND by Alice Childress; Director, Shauneille Perry; Stage Manager, Jerry Cleveland. CAST: Don Butler, Carl Crudup, Carol Foster Sidney, Walter Jones, Terria Joseph, Donald Keyes, Hy Mencher, Theresa Merritt, William Parry

January 19–28, 1979 (11 performances)
RAISIN IN THE SUN by Lorraine Hansberry; Director, Ernie McClintock; Stage Manager, Phillip Shawn King; Costumes, Edna Watson; Set, C. Richard Mills; Lighting, Victor En Yu Tan; Press, Howard Atlee. CAST: Glynn Turman, Carles Cleveland, Starletta DuPois, Lou Ferguson, Minnie Gentry, Charles Harley, Eric Brown, Claude Jones, Cortez Nance, Sam Singleton, Elizabeth Van Dyke, Dan Strickler

HUDSON GUILD THEATRE

Craig Anderson, Producing Director
David Kerry Heefner, Associate Director
Harold Sogard, Managing Director

HUDSON GUILD THEATRE
Friday, July 7 through Sunday, August 13, 1978 (42 performances)
A. L. Productions present:

JUST THE IMMEDIATE FAMILY

By Grace Kimmins; Director, Richard Russell Ramos; Sets, Tony Straiges; Lighting, Ian Calderon; Costumes, Hilary Rosenfeld; Sound, David S. Rapkin; Dances Staged by Jay Fox; General Management, Prism Productions; Press, Clarence Allsopp; Stage Managers, Ellen Zalk, Elizabeth Torgersen; Production Supervisors, Daniel Koetting, Gary Olson; Wardrobe, Judy Fauvell; Production Assistant, Eloida G. Hulbert

CAST

Sheila Coonan (Florie Dugan), Eugenia Rawls (Charlotte Keller), James Ray Weeks (George Dugan), William Wise (Eddie Keller), Elizabeth Torgersen (Barbara Beal), Timothy Near (Lorraine Dugan), Michael Storm (Ron Dugan), Thomas Callaway (Chet Keller)

A drama in three acts. The action takes place at the present time in late spring in a large Victorian house in upstate New York.

Clifford Lipson Photos

Elizabeth Torgersen, Eugenia Rawls, William Wise in "Just the Immediate Family"

Wednesday, September 13 through Sunday, October 22, 1978.* (36 performances)
Hudson Guild Theatre presents:

ON GOLDEN POND

By Ernest Thompson; Director, Craig Anderson; Set Design and Costumes, Steven Rubin; Lighting, Craig Miller; Assistant to the Director, Matthew Lawrence; Technical Director, Patricia Moeser; Sound, David Rapkin

CAST

Tom Aldredge (Norman Thayer, Jr.), Frances Sternhagen (Ethel Thayer), Ronn Carroll (Charlie Martin), Zina Jasper (Chelsea Thayer Wayne), Mark Bendo (Billy Ray), Stan Lachow (Bill Ray)

A comedy in 3 acts and 5 scenes. The action takes place at the present time in the living room of the Thayer summer home on Golden Pond in Maine.

Martha Swope Photo

See Broadway Calendar page 31.

Ronn Carrol, Tom Aldredge, Frances Sternhagen in "On Golden Pond"

HUDSON GUILD THEATRE
Opened Sunday, November 26, 1978.*
Hudson Guild Theatre (Craig Anderson, Producing Director) presents:

WINNING ISN'T EVERYTHING

By Lee Kalcheim; Director, George Abbott; Set and Costume Design, Fred Voelpel; Lighting, Annie Wrightson; Assistant to Director, Judy Abbott; Technical Director, Patricia Moeser; Sound, Robert L. Etter II; Production Assistant, Douglas Hughes; Production Manager, Louis D. Pietig; Stage Manager, Daniel Morris; Press, Howard Atlee

CAST

Bryan E. Clark (Sam Duffy), Forbesy Russel (Kathy Myer), Marshall Purdy (P. J. Whittlsie), Steven Ryan (Mason Sternwell), Tom Everett (Reese Mandel), Mara Landi (Sarah), Ralph Farquhar (Bellboy), Jim Lovelett (Harvey), Bobo Lewis (Mrs. Florence Wheeler), Richard Kuss (Congressman Davis), Television Voices: John Peter Barrett, Sam Tsoutsouvas

A comedy in two acts and three scenes. The action takes place at the present time in a room in a second-class hotel in a medium-sized American city.

* Closed Dec. 10, 1978 after limited engagement of 30 performances.

Cast of "Winning Isn't Everything" with Director George Abbott (C)

HUDSON GUILD THEATRE
January 10–February 18, 1979. (36 performances)
Hudson Guild Theatre (Craig Anderson, Producing Director)
presents:

A LOVELY SUNDAY FOR CREVE COEUR

By Tennessee Williams; Director, Keith Hack; Set, John Conklin; Lighting, Craig Miller; Costumes, Linda Fisher; Production Manager, Louis D. Pietig; Associate Production Supervisor, David Caines; Technical Director, Richard Singer; Scenic Artist, John E. Bolger

CAST

Dorothea .... Shirley Knight
Bodey .... Peg Murray
Helena .... Charlotte Moore
Miss Gluck .... Jane Lowry

A drama in two acts. The action takes place in a St. Louis apartment, late on a Sunday morning in June of 1935.

Press: Howard Atlee
Stage Manager: James W. Pentecost

Martha Swope Photo

Shirley Knight in "A Lovely Sunday for Creve Coeur"

HUDSON GUILD THEATRE
March 7–April 3, 1979 (29 performances)
Hudson Guild Theatre (Craig Anderson. Producing Director)
presents the American Premiere of:

RIDE A COCK HORSE

By David Mercer; Director, Geoffrey Sherman; Set, Philipp Jung; Lighting, Toni Goldin; Costumes, Julie Weiss; Production Supervisor, Les Cockayne; Assistant to Director, Alex Dmitriev; Technical Director, Patricia Moeser; Wardrobe, Holly Coleman; Production Associates, Mary O'Leary, Leo Lewkowitz

CAST

Peter .... Kenneth Welsh
Nan .... Megan Cole
Myra .... Barbara Caruso
Fanny .... Veronica Castang

A drama in two acts. The action takes place at the present time in Peter and Nan's flat in Hampstead, Mura's flat in St. John's Wood, and Fanny's flat in Camden Town.

Production Manager: Louis D. Pietig
Press: Howard Atlee, James Baldassare
Stage Manager: James W. Pentecost

Martha Swope Photo

Megan Cole, Kenneth Welsh, Veronica Castang, Barbara Caruso in "Ride a Cock Horse"

HUDSON GUILD THEATRE
May 2 through June 3, 1979. (30 performances)
Hudson Guild Theater (Craig Anderson, Producing Director; David Kerry Heefner, Associate Director; Harold Sogard, Managing Director) presents the New York premiere of:

DEVOUR THE SNOW

By Abe Polsky; Director, Terry Schreiber; Set, Steven Rubin; Lighting, Dennis Parichy; Costumes, David Murin; Production Manager, Louis D. Pietig; Technical Director, Richard Singer; Props, Debra Jefferson-Fedyk; Assistant to Director, Garry Semeniuk, Marsha Carlson; Production Assistants, Grey Schmidt, Dana Nau; Stage Managers, David Caine, Mark Prendergast; Press, Howard Atlee, James Baldassare

CAST

Jon DeVries (Lewis Keseberg), Laura Cullen (Georgia Donner), Berkeley Harris (James Reed), Robert Air (Sheriff McKinstry), Philip Oxnam (Ned Coffeemeyer), James Ray Weeks (William Eddy), Paul David Richard (John A. Sutter), Edward Seamon (Bill Foster), Berit Lagerwall (Phillipine Keseberg), Gloria Maddox (Margaret Reed), William Andrews (Capt. Fall, "Le Grow")

A drama in three acts. The action takes place in May of 1847 in a common hall serving as a courtroom in Sutter's Fort in Northern California.

Jon DeVries, Gloria Maddox, Berkeley Harris in "Devour the Snow"

IMPOSSIBLE RAGTIME THEATRE

Ted Story, Artistic Director
Laurice Firenze, Managing Director

IMPOSSIBLE RAGTIME THEATRE

September 22–October 16, 1978 (12 performances)
PERIL AT END HOUSE by Agatha Christie; Adapted by Arnold Ridley; Director, Jude Schanzer; Set, Edelmiro Olavarria; Lighting, James Chaleff; Costumes, James Corry; Sound, John North; Assistant Director, Darlene Kaplan; Production Manager, Jon Fraser; Stage Manager, Cathy Galon; Co-Producer/Press, Cynthia Crane. CAST: Tom Bade, Christopher Culkin, Margaret A. Flanagan, Suzanne Galliher, Roberta Goodman, Diane Kamp, Annette Kurek, Jerry McGee, Dennis Marino, Steve Massa, Babette New, William R. Riker, Virginia Stevens, Robert Toperzer, Michael Zuckerman

October 20–30, 1978 (12 performances)
ILLEGAL USE OF HANDS by Michael Zettler; From an idea by Joe Pasqualone; Director, Penelope Hirsch; Set, Larry Fulton; Lighting, Gary Seltzer; Costumes, Margo LaZaro; Assistant Director, Jamie Pelino; Production Manager, Richard Pagano; Stage Manager, Robert Sturgill; Props, David Sculnick; Production Assistants, Kathy Holme, Jean L. Hays, Ralph Alswang, Jr., Bob Hammond, Jeff Schoener; Wardrobe, Phil Saraceno. CAST: David Duhaime, Susan Greenhill, Brian Hartigan, Annette Hunt, Patrick McCord, Jennifer Sternberg

November 3–27, 1978 (12 performances)
THE UNICORN IN CAPTIVITY by Mel Arrighi; Director, Ted Story; Set, James Leonard Joy; Lighting, Curt Osterman; Costumes, Margo LaZaro; Assistant Director, Darlene Kaplan; Production Manager, John Page Fisher; Stage Manager, Judith Lewis; Props, Brenda Ratliff; Production Assistants, Christine Child, Cathy Holm; Wardrobe, Charley Reardon. CAST: Molly Adams, Paul Avery, Cynthia Crane, James Farkas, James Pritchett

November 10–27, 1978 (12 performances)
VICTORIA'S CLOSET by Laurence Carr; Director, Stephen Zuckerman; Set, Raymond C. Recht; Lighting, Richard Winkler; Costumes, Christina Weppner; Assistant Director, Bevya Rosten; Production Manager, Michael Bloom; Stage Manager, J. Rudolph Abate; Props, Nette Reynolds. CAST: Stephen Mellor, Cecelia Riddett, William R. Riker, Carlotta Sherwood, Mary Skinner, Peter Umbras, Michael Zuckerman

December 8–31, 1978 (12 performances)
WINDFALL APPLES by Roma Greth; Director, Anita Khanzadian; Music and Sound, Peter Kallish; Set and Lighting, Terry Bennett; Costumes, Sheryl R. Barenboim; Assistant Director, Christine Child; Production Manager, Bill Blackwell; Stage Managers, Penny Stegenga, E. Ashley Malmfeldt; Hairstylist, Morey Greenberg. CAST: John Del Regno, Patrick Desmond, Ron Jacobson, Lily Knight, Charmian Sorbello, Adrienne Wallace

January 5–22, 1979 (12 performances)
THE GLASS OF WATER by Eugene Scribe; Translated by DeWitt Bodeen; Director, Jon Fraser; Set, Roger Paradiso; Lighting, Charles Bullock; Costumes, Dolores Gamba; Production Manager, Paul Suchecki; Stage Managers, Robin Schuman, Tina S. Ringlestein; Sound, Brad Swift; Production Assistants, Diane Brown, Cynthia Cascante, Christine Child, Zan Dubin, Michele Haracz, Hollis Meltzer. CAST: Penelope Bodry, Terence Cartwright, Charley Cordts, Francois de la Giroday, Margaret A. Flanagan, Elizabeth Flynn-Jones, Robert Lempert, Ashley Malmfeldt, Peg Osborne, George Taylor

January 26–February 19, 1979 (12 performances)
BRAND by Henrik Ibsen; Translated by Michael Meyer; Director, Stephen Zuckerman; Lighting, Seltzer; Costumes, Margo LaZaro; Set, Stephen Zuckerman; Original Music, Nigel Rollings; Assistant Director, Darlene Kaplan; Production Manager, Richard Pagano; Stage Manager, Lawrence Berrick; Props, Shawn LaValle. CAST: Terry Bennett, Helen Lloyd Breed, David Cloud, Jay Devlin, Tim Flanagan, Joan Fogarty, Erik Fredricksen, Margo Martindale, Ann-Sara Matthews, Jamie Pelino, Jeff Schoener, Joan Shangold, Michael Zuckerman

March 9–April 2, 1979 (12 performances)
SUICIDE IN B FLAT by Sam Shepard; Director, Tom Story; Music Composed and performed by Mitchell Weiss; Set, Larry Fulton; Costumes, Amanda J. Klein; Lighting, Curt Osterman; Assistant Director, Christine Child; Production Manager, Michael Bloom; Stage Managers, Cynthia Cascante, Amarae Brockway; Production Assistants, David Anderson, Deborah Gable, Shawn LaVallee. CAST: Ann Crumb, Brian Hartigan, Stephen Mellor, Earl Miller, Thomas O'Rourke, Ilsebet Tebesli

**Ann-Sara Matthews, Erik Fredricksen in "Brand"
Above: Cecilia Riddett, Mary Skinner, Stephen
Mellor in "Victoria's Closet"**

April 27–May 14, 1979 (12 performances)
TAKE DEATH TO LUNCH Book and Lyrics, Thomas L. Faitos and Amielle Zemach; based on play by James H. Bierman; Music, Thomas L. Faitos; Director, Amielle Zemach; Choreography, Sally Edelstein; Set and Costumes, Loy Arcenas; Lighting, Lisa Grossman; Assistant Directors, Fred Gorman, Janis Leventhal; Stage Managers, John Brady, Derek Erb; Production Manager, Carol Sussman. CAST: Johnetta Alayne Alston, Robin Boudreau, Chester Clark, Gus Demos, Paul E. Hart, Bruce McCarty, Mary Liz McNamara, Aaron Morishia, Lonny Price, Caroline Ryburn, Jeff Severson, Claudia Shear, Karen Trott, Andy Yavelow

May 3–21, 1979 (12 performances)
THREE MEN ON A HORSE by John Cecil Holm, George Abbott; Director, John Pynchon Holms; Set, Tom Warren; Costumes, Steven L. Birnbaum; Lighting, Charles S. Bullock; Assistant Director, Helen Timblin; Stage Managers, Mark Schorr, Douglas Benjamin; Production Manager, Thom Yarnal; Props, Sean McGuire. CAST: Robert Barry, P.L. Carling, David Cloud, William Meisle, Sheri Myers, Colleen O'Neil, Robert Shrewsbury, T'Challa, Robert Trebor, Scott Wentworth, Karen Porter White, Ray Xifo

Michael Zettler Photos

**Top: James Pritchett, Hector Troy
in "The Unicorn in Captivity"**

INTERART THEATRE

Margot Lewitin, Artistic Director
Regina Hoover, Executive Director

Managing Director, Kirsten Beck; Technical Director, Chris Wright, Whitney Quesenbery; Stage Managers, Ray Hubener, Michael Bellino; Sound, Roy Carch; Props, Peggy I. Joyner; Wardrobe, Betsy Montrose, Bessie Ballantine; Press, Ellen Levene

INTERART THEATRE
June 16–July 9, 1978 (16 performances)

THE PRICE OF GENIUS

By Betty Neustat; Director, Susan Lehman; Set, Christina Weppner; Lighting, Pat Stern; Costumes, Mary Alice Orito; Wigs, Fredrick Holtz; Stage Manager, Ray Hubener CAST: Jeremy Brooks, Robert Conquest, Judith A. Greentree, Peggy I. Joyner, Patricia Mertens, Edward Morehouse, Patricia Newcastle, Gray Palmer, Richard W. Spore, Susan Stevens, Eloise Watt

October 6–29, 1978 (9 performances)

MAGIC AND LIONS

Conceived and Directed by Glenda Dickerson; Prose-Poetry by Ernestine Walker; Music, Janyse Singleton; Additional Music, E. L. James, Bruce Strickland; Set, Tyrone Mitchell; Lighting, Vantile E. Whitfield, Katie Fallon; Costumes, Ellen Lee; Stage Manager, Kenneth L. Johnson; Assistant to Director, Jennifer Nelson; Musical Director, Jimmy Foster CAST: Lee Dobson, E. L. James, Jacqueline Jones, David LeBron, Carol Pennyfeather, Freda Scott, Bruce Strickland

November 3–December 10, 1978 (14 performances)

DAUGHTERS

Written and Directed by Clare Coss, Sondra Segal, Roberta Sklar; Lighting, Annie Wrightson; Costumes, Sharon Romanski; Stage Manager, Francesca Zambello; Technical Assistant, Randy Hartwig; Press, Ellen Levene CAST: Mary Lum, Mary Lyon, Debbie Nitzberg, Sondra Segal. Performed in repertory with SISTER SISTER, same credits and cast.

November 30–December 24, 1978 (16 performances)

OLYMPIC PARK

By Myrna Lamb; Director, Georgia Fleenor; Scenery, Pat Woodbridge; Lighting, Paul Sullivan; Costumes, Mary Alice Orito; Sound, Nick Meyers; Stage Managers, Marion Z. Murphy, Nancy Ann Adler, Kathleen McHugh; Production Manager, Whitney Quesenbery; Press, Ellen Levene CAST: Joseph Bergmann, Michael Graves, Nancy Haffner, Molly McCarthy, Linda Manning, JoAnn Mariano, Ilsebet Tebesli, Janet Ward, Mary Stark

February 1–March 4, 1979 (20 performances)

SUNDAY

By Michel Deutsch; Director, Francoise Kourilsky; Translation by Francoise Kourilsky, Lynne Greenblatt; Scenery, Beth Kuhn; Costumes, Sydney Brooks; Lighting, Beverly Emmons; Music, Stephen Lockwood; Stage Managers, Judith Lewis, Bernadette Yeager; Props, Nanette Reynolds; Press, Ellen Levene, Victoria Heslin CAST: Marcella Andre, Louise Campbell, Gaynor Cote, Daniel Davin, Lynne Greenblatt, Saskia Noordhoek Hegt, Quincy Long, Babette McKee, Dennis Packan, Gale Pike, James Shearwood, Lise Speidel, Bob Liebowitz, Stephen Corak

April 20–May 13, 1979 (15 performances)

ANTONY AND CLEOPATRA

By William Shakespeare; Director, Estelle Parsons; Set, Christina Weppner; Lighting, Pat Stern; Costumes, Mary Alice Orito; Sound, Teiji Ito; Stage Managers, Francesca Zambello, Jeffrey Shandler, Bernadette Yeager; Assistant to Director, Nancy Weems; Props, Deedra X. Cooper, Christopher W. Wright; Wardrobe, Bessie Ballantine; Press, Ellen Levene, Victoria Heslin CAST: Juan Manuel Aguero, George Bass, Learie Peter Callender, Jeff Carpenter, Carlos Carrasco, David Courier, Tony Diaz, Lee Dobson, Kathleen Gaffney, Annibal O. Lleras, John Lordan, Jose Medina, Manquo, Maria Norman, Aurelio Padron, Francisco Prado, Joe Rosario, Irwin Sackowitz-Colon, Arnaldo Santana, Ahvi Spindell, Laura Summer, Nancy Weems, Emmanuel Yesckas

Photos by Nathaniel Tileston, Laura Pettibone, Gerry Goodstein

Top Right: "The Price of Genius"

Scene from "Magic and Lions"

"Olympic Park" Above: "Sunday"

119

Debra Somerville, Joel Craig, Natalie Priest,
Carole Monferdini in "At Her Age"

JOSEPH JEFFERSON THEATRE COMPANY

Cathy Roskam, Executive Director
John Henry Davis, Artistic Director
Marshall B. Purdy, Managing Director

October 18–November 4, 1978

THE ENTERTAINER by John Osborne; Music, John Addison; Director, John Henry Davis; Musical Director/Pianist, Jeffrey Fohnz; Musical Adviser, William Lester; Choreographer, Helen Butleroff; Set, Raymond C. Recht; Costumes, Jane Suttell; Lighting, Todd Lichtenstein; Sound, Sam Agar; Stage Managers, David Caine, Laura Lawler Toole, Renee Dykas; Press, Anne Einhorn; Production Manager, Will Maitland Weiss. CAST: Humbert Allen Astredo, P. L. Carling, Gwyllum Evans, Caroline Kava, William Mahone, Carol Teitel, Geoffrey Wade

November 29–December 16, 1978

TOO MUCH JOHNSON by William Gillette; Director, Jack Shannon; Scenery, Philip Graneto; Lighting, Dennis McHugh; Costumes, Kenneth M. Yount; Stage Managers, Laura Lawler Toole, Mary R. Lockhart; Assistant Director, Michael Kerley; Technical Director/Press, Anne Einhorn. CAST: Jonathan Alper, Thomas Bair, Marvin Einhorn, Joseph Jamrog, Craig Kuehl, Nita Novy, Marilyn Redfield, Diane Tarleton

GREENWICH NEWS THEATER

February 22–March 11, 1979

ONWARD VICTORIA! with Book and Lyrics by Charlotte Anker, Irene Rosenberg; Music, Keith Herrmann; Director, Julianne Boyd; Choreographer, Judith Haskell; Musical Director, John Mahoney; Set, Raymond C. Recht; Costumes, Kenneth M. Yount; Lighting, Boyd Masten; Stage Managers, David Rosenberg, Mary Lockhart, Renne F. Lutz; Technical Director, Philip Lippel. CAST: Susan Bigelow, Allan Carlsen, Louisa Flaningam, Karl Heist, Natalie Helms, Jim Jansen, Christina Putnam, Tom Rolfing, Sheldon Silver, Martha Jean Sterner, Evan Thompson, Lenny Wolpe, Michael Zaslow

April 27–May 12, 1979 (12 performances)

SIGHTLINES by Mark Eisman; Director, John Henry Davis; Set, Philipp Jung; Lighting, Gary Seltzer; Costumes, Ann Sehrt; Sound, Sandy McIntyre; Sound, David S. Rapkin; Stage Managers, Evan Canary, David Simpson. CAST: Marge Redmond, Douglass Watson

LITTLE CHURCH AROUND THE CORNER

April 23–May 8, 1979 (12 performances)

EXCELSIOR by Ted Pezzulo; Director, Bill Herndon; Set, Carl A. Baldasso; Lighting, Gary Seltzer; Costumes, Christina Giannini; Stage Managers, Linda Lichtman, Abby Saraf, Sherri Wisoff. CAST: Sal Carollo, Marilyn Cooper, George Dickerson, Dorothy Dorff, Julie Follansbee, Anthony Swords

May 17, 18, 19, 1979 (3 performances)

TALLULAH—A MEMORY conceived and performed by Eugenia Rawls

May 29–June 9, 1979

AT HER AGE by Eve Merriam; Music, William Lester; Director, John Henry Davis; Choreography, Terry Rieser; Set, Ursula Belden; Costumes, Carol Buele; Lighting, Joseph Gasiorowski; Stage Manager, Renee F. Lutz. CAST: Joel Craig, Norma Curley, Carol Monferdini, Natalie Priest, Debra Somerville

Cathy Blaivas Photos

Left Center: Douglass Watson, Marge Redmond in "Sightlines" Above: Julie Follansbee, Sal Carollo, Dorothy Dorff in "Excelsior" Top: Diane Tarleton, Joseph Jamrog, Nita Novy in "Too Much Johnson"

LIGHT OPERA OF MANHATTAN

William Mount-Burke, Producer-Director
June 7, 1978–May 31, 1979
Tenth Year

EASTSIDE PLAYHOUSE

Chairman of the Board, Dr. Milton Hopkins; Stage Director/Conductor, William Mount-Burke; Sets, Louise Krozek, William Schroder, Elouise Meyer, Michael Sharp; Costumes, George Stinson, James Nadeaux, William Schroder; Lighting, Peggy Clark; Choreographer/Stage Manager, Jerry Gotham; Press, Walter Cavalieri, Jean Dalrymple, Todd Pearthree; Associate Director, Raymond Allen; Assistant Conductor-Organist, J. Michael Bart; Assistant Musical Director-Pianist, Brian Molloy

COMPANY

Raymond Allen, Jeanne Beauvais, Robert Berlott, Brian Bonnar, Cathy Cosgrove, Hallie Frazer, Karen Hartman, Thomas Heath, Joanne Jamieson, George Kopp, Joan Lader, Catherine Lankford, Elizabeth Larson, Darrell Lormand, Georgia McEver, Jean Stroup Miller, James Nadeaux, Tom Olmstead, Todd Pearthree, Gary Ridley, Julio Rosario, Mary Lee Rubens, Cheryl Savitt, Donna Shanklin, Thomas J. Stone, Nancy Temple, Ronald L. Thomas, James Weber, Steven Wusinich

PRODUCTIONS

Mlle, Modiste, The Merry Widow, The Student Prince, Babes in Toyland, Trial by Jury, The Sorcerer, H. M. S. Pinafore, The Pirates of Penzance, Patience, Iolanthe, Princess Ida, The Mikado, Ruddigore, The Yeoman of the Guard, The Gondoliers, Utopia Ltd. The Grand Duke *World Premieres* of new versions of "The Grand Duke" (July 26, 1978), and "Babes in Toyland" (November 29, 1978)

James Jensen Photos

Julio Rosario, Robert Berlott, Jeanne Beauvais, Jack Washburn, Georgia McEver, Sharlee Stuart in "Babes in Toyland" Top: "The Merry Widow" Left: Raymond Allen, Eleanor Wold in "The Mikado"

LION THEATRE COMPANY

Producing Director, Gene Nye
Company Director, Garland Wright
Managing Director, Larry Carpenter

LION THEATRE

June 22–July 16, 1978 (30 performances)
MARY ROSE by J. M. Barrie; Director, Larry Carpenter; Scenery, Holmes Easley; Lighting, Frances Aronson; Costumes, Syndey Brooks; Incidental Music, Philip Campanella; Stage Managers, John Lyons, Mary Burns; Technical Director, Jeff Goodman; Wardrobe, Karen Staples; Hairstylist, Konnie Kittrell; Props, Ruth E. Kramer; Sound, Cathy Prager; Press, Ellen Levene, Tom Trenkle. CAST: David Anthony, Gwyllum Evans, Thomas MacGreevy, Julia MacKenzie, Lucille Patton, Robert Shrewsbury, Kate Wilkinson, Mark Winkworth

February 1–25, 1979 (24 performances)

THREE SISTERS by Anton Chekhov; Director, Gene Nye; Sets, Miguel Romero; Lights, John Gisondi; Costumes, Ken Yount; Translation, Sharon M. Carnicke; Sound, Phillip Campanella; Technical Director, Bruce Porter; Stage Managers, Kathy Arlt, Jeff Browne, Larry Kirchgaessner; Wardrobe, Dru-Ann Chuckran; Hairstylist, Esther Teller. CAST: Kim Ameen, David Anthony, Jeff Browne, Tony Campisi, Maria Cellario, Dru-Ann Chuckran, David Faulkner, David Gallagher, John Ingle, Larry Kirchgaessner, Sofia Landon, Julia MacKenzie, Fred Miller, Robert Shrewsbury, Virginia Stevens, Ron Van Lieu, Mark Windworth

April 4–29, 1979 (24 performances)
DUEL a romantic opera by Randal Wilson; Director, Larry Carpenter; Set, Ray Recht; Lighting, John Gisondi; Costumes, Kenneth M. Yount; Musical Direction, Jeffrey Olmsted; Stage Managers, Wendy Chapin, Gail Palmieri; Technical Director, Paul Moore; Press, Ellen Levene. CAST: Bertilla Baker, Holly Lipton, Barbara Niles, Tom Westerman, Stan Wilson, Thomas Young

Nathaniel Tileston Photos

Stan Wilson, Tom Westerman in "Duel"

MANHATTAN THEATRE CLUB

Lynne Meadow, Artistic Director
Barry Grove, Managing Director
Robert Pontarelli, Press

Stephen Pascal, Associate Artistic Director; Thomas Bullard, Associate Director; Robert Buckler, Technical Director; Connie L. Alexis, Business Manager; Ruby Lerner, Audience Development; Diane de Mailly, Administrative Assistant; Caryn Katkin, Lynda C. Kinney, Press Assistants; Andy Wolk, Casting/Literary Assistant; Betsy Tanner, Technical Assistant

MANHATTAN THEATRE CLUB

June 4–18, 1978 (24 performances)

STRAWBERRY FIELDS by Stephen Poliakoff; Director, Stephen Pascal; Set, Robert Yodice; Costumes, Judy Dearing; Lighting, Dennis Parichy; Sound, Gary Harris; Stage Manager, Paul Fitzmaurice. CAST: Nicholas Woodeson (Kevin), Susan Sharkey (Charlotte), Brad O'Hare (Nick), Geraldine Sherman (Mrs. Roberts/Cleaner), Ralph Seymour (Kid)

November 7–December 10, 1978 (40 performances)

THE REAR COLUMN by Simon Gray; Director, James Hammerstein; Setting, John Lee Beatty; Costumes, Judy Dearing; Lighting, Dennis Parichy; Sound, Gary Harris; Dialect Coach, Timothy Monich; Assistant to Director, Ann Egbert; Production Assistants, Virginia Hunter, Barbara Abel. CAST: Alvin Alexis (John Henry), Josh Clark (W. Bonny), Paul Collins (J. R. Troup), Louise H. Gorham (Native Woman), Benjamin Hendrickson (H. Ward), John Horton (J. S. Jameson), Remak Ramsay (Major E. M. Barttelot), Edward Seamon (H. M. Stanley).

A drama in 3 acts and 6 scenes with an epilogue. The action takes place in a large store room in the Yambuya Camp on the banks of the Arruimi River in the Congo from June 1886 to June of 1887

December 26, 1978–January 28, 1979. (40 performances)

GRAND MAGIC by Eduardo De Filippo; Translated by Carlo Ardito; Director, Michael Kahn; Setting, Ed Wittstein; Costumes, Andrew B. Marlay; Lighting, Dennis Parichy; Sound, Gary Harris; Assistant to Director, Granville Wyche Burgess; Hairstylist, Christine Cooper; Production Assistants, Eugene Greenberg, P'nenah Goldstein, Buzz Cohen, Virginia Hunter, Sheryl Barrenboim, Elizabeth M. Mascio; Technical Director, Robert Buckler; Production Manager, Paul Fitzmaurice; Stage Managers, Amy Pell, Kevin Mangan; Magician's Consultant, Munro Gabler.

CAST: Vera Lockwood (Mrs. Locascio), Janice Fuller (Mrs. Marino), Lynne Charnay (Mrs. Zampa), Lianne Kressin (Miss Zampa), Claudia Peluso (Marta De Spelta), Tony Musante (Calogero Di Spelta), Christopher Goutman (Mariano D'Albino), Humbert Allen Astredo (Gervasio Penna), R. T. Edelman (Arturo Recchia), Johann Carlo (Amelia Recchia), Phillip Piro (Waiter), Fred Gwynne (Professor Otto Marvuglia), Sasha Von Scherler (Zaira Marvuglia), Tom Mardirosian (Police Inspector), Gabor Morea (Robert Magliano/Gennarino Fucecchio), Christopher Goutman (Gregoria Di Spelta), Vera Lockwood (Matilde Di Spelta), Janice Fuller (Rosa Intrugli), Tom Mardirosian (Oreste Intrugli), Eugene Greenberg, Kevin Mangan (Porters), Lynne Charnay, Lianne Kressin (Otto's Neighbors).

A play in 3 acts. The action takes place at a seaside resort somewhere in Italy, at the Grand Hotel Metropole, in Professor's home, and in Calogero's apartment four years later.

Remak Ramsay, Josh Clark, Benjamin Hendrickson in "The Rear Column" Top: Susan Sharkey, Brad O'Hare in "Strawberry Fields"

November 15–December 10, 1978 (12 performances)

NONGOGO by Athol Fugard; Director, Oz Scott; Setting, David Potts; Costumes, Rachel Kurland; Lighting, Victor En Yu Tan; Sound, Robert Eckhart; Dialect Coach, Timothy Monich; Stage Managers, Jason LaPadura, Eugene Greenberg; Production Assistant, David Simpson; Sound, Sandy McIntyre. CAST: Terry Alexander, Mary Alice, Thomas Martell Brimm, Roger Lawson, John McCurry

November 15–December 10, 1978 (12 performances)

A LADY NEEDS A CHANGE: A tribute to Dorothy Fields; Compiled and directed by Bill Gile; Musical Direction and Vocal Arrangements, William Roy; Choreography, Graciela Daniele; Costumes, David Tosier; Stage Manager, Bonnie Sue Schloss; Musical Consultant; Press, Robert Pontarelli. CAST: Patti Allison, Kelly Bishop, Tyra Ferrell, Chip Garnett, Carolyn Mignini, Scott Robertson

January 3–February 3, 1979 (28 performances)

DANCING IN THE DARK: The Music of Arthur Schwartz with Lyrics by Howard Dietz; A revue devised by Mary O'Hagan; Direction and Choreography, Christopher Chadman; Musical-Direction and Arrangements, Paul Trueblood; Stage Manager, Shari Genser; Assistant Musical Director, James Stenborg. CAST: John Cunningham, Merilee Magnuson, Allyn Ann McLerie, Donn Simione

February 7–March 4, 1979

GIVE MY HEART AN EVEN BREAK: A Tribute to Music by George Quincy and Lyrics by Thayer Burch; Director, Jim Kramer; Musical Direction, George Quincy; Stage Manager, Charles Bari. CAST: Margery Cohen, James Congdon, Sally Cooke, Joseph Neal, Margaret Wright

March 28–April 22, 1979

SONGS FROM THE CITY STREETS by Jake Holmes; Director, Gui Andrisano; Musical Direction and Arrangements, John Lewis; Stage Manager, Penny Stegenga. CAST: Emily Bindiger, Mel Dowd, John Hammil, Larry Riley, Charlie Stavola

May 9–27, 1979

AT HOME WITH MARGERY COHEN directed by Josep Fernandez; Musical Director, Eric Stern; Stage Manager, Marla E. Spitzer

Gerry Goodstein Photos

**Fred Gwynne, Tony Musante
in "Grand Magic"**

MANHATTAN THEATRE CLUB

January 3–28, 1979. (20 performances)
BEETHOVEN/KARL by David Rush; Director, Paul Schneider; Costumes and Setting, Barry Robison; Lighting, Frances Aronson; Production Assistants, Stephen Schwartz, Sheila Spencer; Stage Managers, Amarae Brockway, John Clinton; Press, Robert Pontarelli.

CAST: Jean-Pierre Stewart (Anton Schindler), Paul Milikin (Ignaz Schuppanzigh), Josh Clark (Karl), Nicolas Mize (Franz Niemetz), Susan Willis (Frau Koch), George Voskovec (Beethoven), Pierre Epstein (Johann van Beethoven), Victoria Boothby (Countess Guilietta Gallenberg).

A play in 2 acts and 8 scenes. The action takes place during 1826–1827 in the apartment of Ludwig van Beethoven in Vienna.

February 7 through March 4, 1979 (20 performances)
STEVIE by Hugh Whitmore; Director, Brian Murray; Set and Costumes, Barry Robison; Lighting, Frances Aronson; Stage Managers, Elliott Woodruff, Michael S. Mantel; Production Assistant, Danna Doyle; Press, Robert Pontarelli CAST: James Higgins (Man), Margaret Hilton (Aunt), Roberta Maxwell (Stevie)
A play in two acts. The action takes place in the sitting room of Stevie's home at One Avondale Road, Palmers Green.

February 13–March 18, 1979. (20 performances)
ARTICHOKE by Joanne McClelland Glass; Director, Lynne Meadow; Setting, Fred Voelpel; Costumes, Patricia McGourty; Lighting, Jennifer Tipton; Assistant to Director, Douglas Hughes; Production Assistants, Virginia Hunter, David Simpson; Wardrobe, Susan Cox; Stage Managers, Jason LaPadura, Michael Wideben; Press, Robert Pontarelli CAST: Patricia Elliott (Margaret Morley) succeeded by Zina Jasper, James Greene (Archie), Michael Higgins (Gramps), Nicholas Hormann (Gibson McFarland), Daniel Keyes (Jake), Amanda Michael Plummer (Lily Agnes), Rex Robbins (Walter Morley)

A drama in two acts. The action takes place at the present time during the summer on the Saskatchewan Prairie.

March 28, through April 22, 1979 (20 performances)
LOSING TIME by John Hopkins; Director, Edwin Sherin; Set, Barry Robison; Lighting, Frances Aronson; Costumes, Donna Meyer; Stage Managers, Amy Pell, P'nenah Goldstein; Production Assistants, Danna Doyle, Helga Kopperl, Jane Persen, Gale Salus; Press, Robert Pontarelli, Lynda C. Kinney

CAST

Jane Alexander (Joanne), Shirley Knight (Ruth), Tom Mardirosian (Mike), Bernie McInerney (Wally), James Naughton (Tod)

A play in two acts. The action takes place at the present time in Joanne's New York City apartment.

April 3, through May 6, 1979. (20 performances)
DON JUAN COMES BACK FROM THE WAR by Odon von Horvath; Translated by Christopher Hampton; Director, Stephen Pascal; Set, Tony Straiges, Kate Edmunds; Costumes, Jess Goldstein; Lighting, Dennis Parichy; Sound, John McKinny; Assistant to Director, Rachel Lange; Production Assistants, James P. Cusack, Priscilla Gustavino, Michael L. Ravin, Maria E. Spitzer; Stage Managers, William Chance, Barbara Abel; Press, Robert Pontarelli, Lynda C. Kinney; Technical Director, Robert Buckler; Production Manager, Paul Fitzmaurice

CAST

Peter Evans (Don Juan), and the 35 women are played by Johann Carlo, Lynn Cohen, Patricia Cosgrove, Shaine Marinon, Tanny McDonald, Viveca Parker, Eleanor Phelps, Christine Rose, Ellen Tovatt, Rachel Lange, Janine Schachter, Heather Ann Steinmetz

Performed without intermission. The action takes place in Bavaria during late fall to winter of 1918.

Gerry Goodstein Photos

**Top Right: Patricia Elliott, Rex Robbins
in "Artichoke" Center: Shirley Knight,
Jane Alexander in "Losing Time"**

Peter Evans in "Don Juan Comes Back . . ."

MANHATTAN THEATRE CLUB
May 9 through June 3, 1979. (20 performances)
Manhattan Theatre Club presents:

JUST A LITTLE BIT LESS THAN NORMAL

By Nigel Baldwin; Director, Paul Schneider; Set, Barry Robison; Costumes, Judith Dolan; Lighting, Tom Schrader; Dialect Coach, Timothy Monich; Musical Director and Arranger, Richard Honoroff; Stage Managers, Kevin Mangan, Katharine Peyton, Bill McGrath; Assistant to Director, Anne Pratt; Press, Robert Pontarelli, Lynda C. Kinney
CAST: Mary Carney (Lin), Josh Clark (Danny), John Clarkson (Dad), Chris Noth (Jerv), Jamey Sheridan (Spud), Sylvia Short (Mum)

A musical performed without intermission

MANHATTAN THEATRE CLUB
May 22 through June 24, 1979. (25 performances)

THE ARBOR by Brother Jonathan; Director, Kenneth Frankel; Set, Fred Kolouch; Costumes, Barry Robison; Lighting, Jamie Gallagher; Composer, Thomas Fay; Assistant to Director; Elizabeth Bailey; Production Assistants, Donald G. Creech, Jr., Janet Friedman, Douglas Andrew Slobodien; Production Manager, Paul Fitzmaurice; Technical Director, Robert Buckler
CAST: Robert Burke (Chris), James Greene (Ben), George Hall (Finn), Rosemary Murphy (McGuire), Joe Ponazecki (Dave), William Schilling (Carlucci), Joseph Warren (Andy)
A play in two acts and six scenes. The action takes place during March of 1959 in St. Francis' Monastery, a Franciscan Monastery in Brooklyn, N.Y.

Gerry Goodstein Photos

Right: George Hall, Rosemary Murphy in "The Arbor" Top: Sylvia Short, John Clarkson in "Just a Little Bit Less Than Normal"

MANHATTAN PUNCH LINE

Faith Catlin/Mitch McGuire, Founding Directors
Steve Kaplan, Artistic Director

April 1–June 24, 1979
Designer, William Otterson; Technical Director, David Temple; Musical and Cabaret Director, Kathrin King Segal; Press, Doug Baldwin; Administrative Consultant, David Berry; Management Consultant, Howard Crampton-Smith

MANHATTAN PUNCH LINE
SLICE OF LIFE/FLAGSHIP by Donald Wollner; Director, Steve Kaplan; Assistant Director, Odie Snell; Lighting, Shari Teitelbaum; Props, Maggie Low; Costumes, Liz Bass; Choreographer, Cathryn Williams; Stage Manager, Steven D. Nash; Music, Ethan Fein; Lyrics, Donald Wollner. CAST: "Slice of Life:" George Bamford, Mary E. Baird, Kathrin King Segal, Royce Rich, Faith Catlin; "Flagship:" Mitch McGuire, Christopher Coddington, Joan Grant, Doug Baldwin, Joe White, David Berry, Linda Phillips, Mary E. Baird, Brad Bellamy, Royce Rich

THE JACK THE RIPPER REVUE written and directed by Peter Mattaliano; Music, Stephen Jankowski; Choreography, Janet Watson; Sets, Charles McCarry; Costumes, Liz Bass; Stage Managers, Charles Bari, Lucy Stovall; Musical Director, Laurence J. Esposito; Lighting, Philip Lippel; Props, Maggie Low; Technical Director, David Temple; Set, Neil Conboy. CAST: Brad Bellamy, Harold Shepard, Robin Grean, Joanna Seaton, Jean Elliott, Kathrin King Segal, Donna Trinkoff, Timothy Meyers, William Perley, Dan O'Connell, Ian Stuart, Julie J. Hafner, Christopher Coddington, John Spalla, Robert McCallum, Jim Siatkowski, Christopher Bondy, Mary E. Baird, Ruth Moore, Judy Soto

THE CAT AND THE CANARY by John Willard; Director, Roderick Cook; Set, David Temple, Costumes, Francis L. Sabino; Stage Manager, Herman Boykin; Lighting, Ron Daley; Sound, Nicki Stephens; Assistant Director, Sarah Nall. CAST: Julie J. Hafner, Lee Moore, Richard Stack, Alice Cannon, Gloria Rossi, Dalton Cathey, Brad Bellamy, Faith Catlin, Mitch McGuire, Ronald Willoughby, Marcia Hepps, William Perley

Jean Elliott, Donna Trinkoff, Kathrin King Segal in "Jack the Ripper Revue"

Left Center: Christopher Coddington, Mitch McGuire in "Flagship"

THE MEAT & POTATOES COMPANY

Neal Weaver, Artistic Director
Jane Dwyer, Administrative Director
September 14–October 8, 1978 (16 performances)
A SUMMER OF EDUCATION by Neal Weaver; Director, Mr. Weaver; Assistant Director, Ann Folke; Set, Neal Weaver; Lighting, Terry H. Wells; Stage Manager, Elliott Landen. CAST: Harris Laskawy, Frank South, Jack Wrangler, Helene Cameron, Ralph DeLia, Catherine Doray, Ann Folke, Ellen Friedman, Joanne Garahan, John Holt-Hall, Mary Jay, Mark Kaplan, Barbara Leto, Lium O'-Begley.

October 19–November 12, 1978 (16 performances)
WIDOWER'S HOUSES by George Bernard Shaw; Director, Robert Einenkal; Stage Managers, Richard Burke, Evan Turk. CAST: Andrew Winner, Paul Deboy, Richard Burke, Joel Kramer, Robert Einenkel, Barbara Leto, Matthew Lewis, Alan Huisman, Sona Vogel

November 24–December 17, 1978 (16 performances)
THE HOLLOW by Agatha Christie; Director, Neal Weaver; Stage Managers, Evan Turk, Victor Sarmiento. CAST: Ken Bush, Joan Conrad, Catherine Doray, Colin Leslie Fox, Ben Lemon, Alta McKay, Anastasia Nicole, Lynn Oliver, Joel Parsons, Janeice Scarbrough, Dickson Shaw, Frank South

January 11–February 4, 1979 (16 performances)
TWO BY STRINDBERG directed by Neal Weaver. CASTS: "Playing with Fire:" David Cooper-Wall, Barbara Knowles, Toni Brown, Vyvyan Pinches, Carol Aubrey, Alan Spitz. "Creditors:" Ben Lemon, Vyvyan Pinches, Sara Eldridge, Carol Aubrey, Barbara Knowles, Evan Turk, William Cutler

February 15–March 11, 1979
EDWARD II by Christopher Marlowe; Director, Neal Weaver; Set, Terry H. Wells, Stage Managers, Richard Burke, Evan Senreich, Beth Lincks, Joanna Malley; Lighting, Ann Folke, Production Assistant, Jane Dwyer; Combat Choreographer, Byam Stevens. CAST: Paul Borden, Richard Bourg, Richard Burke, Ken Bush, David Cooper-Wall, William Cutler, Paul E. Doniger, John Holt Hall, Arthur A. Hanket, William Herman, Ken Lansdowne, Beth Lincks, Lynn Oliver, J. Patrick O'Sullivan, Stephen Pershing, Vyvyan Pinches, Robert Sanders, Evan Senreich, Evan Turk, James Wright

March 22–April 15, 1979 (16 performances)
IN THE SUMMER HOUSE by Jane Bowles; Director, Neal Weaver; Stage Managers, Evan Senreich, Tom Starace; Press, Mary Jane Geiger. CAST: Judy Allen, Richard Bourg, Margarita Bracht, Ann Folke, Gloria Irizarry, Nicholas Irizarry, Lin Kosy, Anita Lobel, Beth Lincks, Heidi Mendez, J. Patrick O'Sullivan, Pat Pearce, Sandi Rios, Evan Senreich

April 26–May 20, 1979 (16 performances)
THE SEA GULL by Anton Chekhov; Directed and Designed by Neal Weaver; Stage Managers, Jim Curran, Pat Pearce. CAST: Grace Jackman, Ben Lemon, Clark Wiswell, Rebecca Sullivan, Edward Rutzisky, Elisabeth Corddry, Barbara Knowles, Robert Einenkel, Harry Spillman, Richard Bourg, Jim Curran, Pat Pearce

May 31–June 24, 1979
NOSOTROS by Roland Solis; Designed and Directed by Neal Weaver; Stage Manager, Ina Votolato. CAST: Carmen Maya, Emil Belasco, Shawn Elliott, Miriam Cruz, Richard Valladares, Millie Santiago

Herbert Fogelson Photos

Right Center: Ken Bush, Vyvyan Pinches, Arthur Hanket in "Edward II" Above: Joel Parsons, Joan Conrad in "The Hollow" Top: Paul DeBoy, Barbara Leto in "Widowers' Houses"

Ann Folke, Beth Lincks, J. Patrick O'Sullivan
in "In the Summer House"

LYRIC THEATER OF NEW YORK

Neal Newman, Artistic Director
EIGHTEENTH STREET PLAYHOUSE
September 12–20, 1978 (4 performances)

THE CRADLE WILL ROCK

By Marc Blitzstein; Director, Neal Newman; Musical Direction, Bruce W. Coyle; Set, Terrence B. Byrne; Costumes, Susan Cox; Lighting, Richard Clauson; Choreography, Colleen Heffernan; Stage Manager, G. Michael Trupiano CAST: Jane Milne, Tom Fitzmaurice, Michael Lopez, Dominic Adinolfi, Maximilliam St. James, Jon Arterton, Jay Aubrey Jones, Alvin Railey, John Dennehy, Jr. Charles Dietrich, Dominic Guastaferro, Marjorie Burren, Paul Canestro, Kathryn Morath, Dan Kirsch, Paul Christoforidis, Karen Siegel, Mel Black, Teresa Elwert

NAMELESS THEATRE
October 19–November 5, 1978 (12 performances)

ORPHEUS IN THE UNDERWORLD

By Jacques Offenbach; Libretto, Ludovic Halevy, Hector Cremieux; English book and lyrics, Karen Siegel, Neal Newman; Producer-Director, Neal Newman; Musical Direction, Bruce W. Coyle; Choreography, Andrea McCullough; Set, Terrence B. Byrne; Costumes, Susan Cox; Lighting, Richard Clauson; Stage Manager, Douglas Cox
CAST: Teresa Elwert, Jon Arterton, Karen Longwell, Lawrence Raiken, Larry Cahn, Debra Arch, Susan Van Zant, Thomas Brooks, Marjorie Burren, Mara Beckerman, Karen Siegel, Oliver Dixon, Dan Kirsch, Colleen Heffernan, Peter McDowell, John Vetere, Kathryn Morath

Terry Byrne Photos

WONDERHORSE THEATRE
April 19–29, 1979 (12 performances)

SAGA

World Premiere of an American Folk Opera with book, music and lyrics by Kelly Hamilton; Produceer-Director, Neal Newman; Musical Direction, Bruce W. Coyle; Choreography, Colleen Heffernan; Set, Terrence B. Byrne; Costumes, Susan Cox; Lighting, John Vetere; Assistant Producer, Maximilian St. James; Stage Manager, G. Michael Trupiano
CAST: Mara Beckerman, Stephen Bogardus, Tony Calabro, Paul Canestro, Ellyn Gale, Daryl Hunt, Scott Hunt, Jay Aubrey Jones, Karen Longwell, Deborah MacHale, Megan McPherson, Teresa Parente, Stacy Peppell, Barbara Porter, Angelena Reaux, Tianna Jo Schlittne, Sharon Talbot, David Sloan, Mark Wolff

"**Orpheus in the Underworld**"

NAT HORNE THEATRE

Albert B. Reyes, Executive Producer
Nat Horne, Artistic Director
Administrative Director, Virginia Brown; Resident Director, Edward Brown; Technical Director/Administrative Assistant, Brian Hollingsworth; Press, Jeffrey Brown, Mary Burns

September 15–November 5, 1978 (32 performances)

MISS TRUTH

Script, Music and Lyrics by Glory Van Scott; Directed and Choreographed by Louis Johnson; Associate Producer, Amy Bjornson; Settings, Don Warshaw; Lighting, Nina Votolato; Production Manager, Julie Behar; Costumes, Alice E. Carter; Stage Manager, Scott Groves CAST: Glory Van Scott, Lochandra Aarons, Loretta Abbott, Jamil Garland, Lloyd McNeill, Al Perryman, Dolores Vanison-Blakely, Christophe Pierre, Lezlie Romain, Ronell Seay, Tina Harrison, Gene Casey, Keith Loving, Babafumi Akunyun

September 25–October 19, 1978 (16 performances)

THE CHANCE AND THE CHALLENGE

Based on "The Black Crook" by Charles M. Barras; Producer-Director, George Zagoren. No other details submitted.

November 17–December 17, 1978 (20 performances)

THE FIGHT FOR BARBARA

By D. H. Lawrence; Director, David MacEnulty; Settings, Nidal Mihayni, Richard George; Costumes, Ron Tombaugh; Stage Managers, Charlie Benners, Judy Premus; Press, Robin-David Associates CAST: Michael Finnerty, Elizabeth Medina, George Vlachos, Dick Terry, Mimi Wedell, Marty Dowd

December 6–20, 1978 (3 performances)

CHARACTERS AND IMAGES

Pantomime by Simon Kudrov; Art Director, Natasha Kudrov

Marth 8–April 1, 1979 (16 performances)

PIGEON

By Leonard Kantor; Director, Barbara A. Forst; Presented by Tundra Productions and Gary F. Mottola; Set and Lighting, Daniel Charles Abrahamsen; Costumes, Danajean Cicerchi; Stage Manager, Sam Buccio; Technical Director, John McGree; Props, Neil Conboy CAST: Martin Donegan, Mindy Zepp, Robert Magnozzi

April 13–29, 1979 (12 performances)

BREEDERS

By Bob Ost; Director, Albert Reyes; Technical Director, John McGee; Lighting Design, Bill Higgins; Stage Manager, Tom Mangieri; Costumes, Richard Westby-Gibson; Press, Arthur Jay CAST: Tom Viola, Anne Simon, Justin Magnus, Howard McMaster, Rebecca Allard, Peg Osborne, Matt Sampson, Bill Elverman

May 10–27, 1979 (12 performances)

THE TOUCH DREAMED UP

By John Kendall Wilson; Director, David Wright; Presented by David Silberman in association with New Georgia; Set, Thomas M. Williams; Lighting, Helen Anne Gatling; Choreography, Nancy Hill; Production Manager, Carl Clifford; Costumes, Barbara J. Hause; Sound, Regina M. Mullen; Stage Manager, Marsha Gillette; Props, Terry Walker; Production Assistant, Helen Butler; Press, Mary Ann Smith, Brian Reddy CAST: Clee Burtonya, B. Lynne Jebens, Doff Meyer, Dolores Miller, David Wright
(No photos submitted)

NEGRO ENSEMBLE COMPANY
Douglas Turner Ward, Artistic Director
Eleventh Season
Managing Director, Gerald S. Krone; General Manager, Leon Denmark; Press, Howard Atlee, Jim Baldassare; Assistant General Manager, Asante Scott; Executive Assistant, Deborah McGee

ST. MARKS PLAYHOUSE
December 6–7, 1978, February 22–April 1, 1979 (61 performances)

NEVIS MOUNTAIN DEW by Steve Carter; Director, Horacena J. Taylor; Scenery, Wynn Thomas, Costumes, Alvin Perry; Lighting, Larry Johnson; Stage Managers, Horacena J. Taylor, Clinton Turner Davis; Technical Directors, Samuel Gonzalez, Marvin Watkins; Production Assistant, Amelia R. Haywood; Wardrobe, Herman Cortez; Sound, Maliki Oluwamti.

CAST
Ethel Ayler (Zepora), Charles Brown (Lud), Graham Brown (Jared), Frances Foster (Everelda), Arthur French (Ayton), Barbara Montgomery (Billie), Samm-Art Williams (Boise)

January 24–February 4, 1979 (15 performances)

A SEASON TO UNRAVEL by Alexis DeVeaux; Director, Lenda Dickerson; Scenery, Wynn Thomas; Costumes, Alvin Perry; Lighting, Larry Johnson. CAST: Olivia Williams, Barbara Montgomery, Michele Shay, L. Scott Caldwell, Graham Brown, Adolph Caesar, Charles Brown, Leon Morenzie, Chuck Patterson, Shirley Rushing

February 7–February 18, 1979 (15 performances)

OLD PHANTOMS by Gus Edwards; Director, Horacena J. Taylor; Scenery, Wynn Thomas; Costumes, Alvin Perry; Lighting, Larry Johnson. CAST: L. Scott Caldwell, Chuck Patterson, Samm-Art Williams, Douglas Turner Ward, Olivia Williams, Barbara Montgomery, Charles Brown, Leon Morenzie

Bert Andrews Photos

Left Center: L. Scott Caldwell, Douglas Turner Ward, Charles Brown in "Old Phantoms" Above: Charles Brown, Leon Morenzie in "Everyman" Top: Arthur French, Ethel Ayler, Frances Foster in "Nevis Mountain Dew"

Olivia Williams, Shirley Rushing, Barbara Montgomery in "A Season to Unravel"

Barbara Montgomery, Frances Foster, Olivia Williams, Michele Shay (front) in "Daughters of the Mock"

NEW YORK SHAKESPEARE FESTIVAL PUBLIC THEATER

Joseph Papp, Producer

PUBLIC/NEWMAN THEATER
Opened Friday, June 2, 1978.*
Joseph Papp presents the Yale Repertory Theatre Production
(Robert Brustein, Artistic Director) of:

SGANARELLE
An Evening of Moliere Farces

By Moliere; Translated by Albert Bermel; Director, Andrei Serban; Sets, Michael H. Yeargan; Costumes, Dunya Ramicova; Lighting, James H. Gage; Choral Direction. Patrizia Norcia; Technical Director, A. D. Carson; Assistant Director, Katherine Mendeloff; Production Supervisor, Jason Steven Cohen

CAST

"THE FLYING DOCTOR": Michael Gross (Gorgibus), Marianne Owen (Lucile), Elizabeth Norment (Sabine), David Marshall Grant (Valere), Mark Linn Baker (Sganarelle), Richard Grusin (Gros-Rene), Jonathan Marks (A Lawyer)

"THE FORCED MARRIAGE": Eugene Troobnick (Sganarelle), Richard Grusin (Geronimo), Joyce Fideor (Dorimene), Marianne Owen (Pancrace), Mark Linn Baker (Marphurius), William Converse-Roberts (Lycaste), David Marshall Grant (Alcidas), Jeremy Geidt (Alcantor), Gypsies: Norma Brustein, Patrizia Norcia, Elizabeth Norment, Marianne Owen

"SGANARELLE": Richard Grusin (Gorgibus), Joyce Fideor (Celie), William Converse-Roberts (Lelie), Jonathan Marks (Gros-Rene), Michael Gross (Sganarelle), Norma Brustein (Martine), Peter Crombie (Villebrequin), Patrizia Norcia (Lisette), Jeremy Geidt (Dorante), Mark Linn Baker (Valere)

"A DUMB SHOW" based on "The Doctor in spite of Himself" performed by Mark Linn Baker, William Converse-Roberts, Peter Crombie, Joyce Fideor, David Marshall Grant, Michael Gross, Richard Grusin, Jonathan Marks, Elizabeth Norment, Marianne Owen

Performed with two intermissions.

Company Manager: Richard Ostreicher
Press: Merle Debuskey, Bob Ullman, Richard Kornberg
Stage Manager: Frank S. Torok

* Closed June 18, 1978 after limited engagement of 15 performances.

Eugene Cook Photos

**Michael Gross, Mark Linn Baker in
"The Flying Doctor"** *(Eugene Cook Photo)*
Top: Michael Gross, Elizabeth Norment, Marianne O
Mark Linn Baker in "Sganarelle" *(Bruce Siddons Phot)*

PUBLIC/NEWMAN THEATER
Wednesday, June 21 through Sunday, July 2, 1978 (16 performances)
Joseph Papp presents the Yale Repertory Theatre Production of:

WINGS

A drama by Arthur Kopit without intermission; Director, John Madden; Setting, Andrew Jackness; Costumes, Jeanne Button; Lighting, Tom Schraeder; Sound, Tom Voegeli; Music, Herb Pilhofer; Technical Director, A. D. Carson; Assistant Director, Bill DeLuca; Sound, Marcus F. Dilliard; Production Supervisor, Jason Steven Cohen; General Manager, Robert Kamlot; Press, Merle Debuskey, Robert Ullman, Richard Kornberg; Stage Managers, James F. Ingalls, H. Lloyd Carbaugh; Company Manager, Brian R. Mann

Cast

Constance Cummings (Emily Stilson), Marianne Owen (Amy), Geoffrey Pierson, Roy Steinberg (Doctors), Caris Corfman, Carol Ostrow (Nurses), Richard Grusin (Billy), Eugene Troobnick (Mr. Brownstein), Betty Pelzer (Mrs. Timmins) UNDERSTUDIES: Norma Brustein (Emily/Mrs. Timmins), Caris Corfman (Amy), H. Loyd Carbaugh (Doctors), Deborah Van Drimmelen (Nurses), Roy Steinberg (Billy), Robert Brustein (Brownstein)

Eugene Cook Photo

**Marianne Owen, Constance Cummings
in "Wings"**

PUBLIC/ANSPACHER THEATER
Opened Wednesday, June 14, 1978*
(Moved to Circle in the Square December 16, 1978)
Joseph Papp presents:

I'M GETTING MY ACT TOGETHER AND TAKING IT ON THE ROAD

Book and Lyrics, Gretchen Cryer; Music, Nancy Ford; Director, Word Baker; Costumes, Pearl Somner; Lighting, Martin Tudor; Associate Producer, Bernard Gersten; Choreography Assistant, Tina Johnson; Assistant to Director, Thomas Burke; Wardrobe, Barbara Rosenthal, Cynthia Demand; Sound, Gary Massey, Todd McEwen; Production Supervisor, Jason Steven Cohen; Original Cast Records by CSP.

CAST

Heather	Gretchen Cryer†1
Joe	Joel Fabiani†2
Alice	Margot Rose†3
Cheryl	Betty Aberlin
Jake	Don Scardino†4
Piano	Scott Berry
Guitar	Lee Grayson
Drums	Bob George
Bass and Flute	Dean Swenson

UNDERSTUDIES: Nadine Connors (Alice/Cheryl), Gene Lindsey (Joe), Michael Ayr (Jake), Betty Aberlin (Heather)

MUSICAL NUMBERS: "Natural High,""Smile,""In a Simple Way I Love You,""Miss America,""Strong Woman Number,""Dear Tom,""Old Friend,""Put in a Package and Sold," "Feel the Love,""Lonely Lady,""Happy Birthday"

A musical performed without intermission.

General Manager: Robert Kamlot
Company Manager: Noel Gilmore
Press: Merle Debuskey, Bob Ullman, Richard Kornberg, William Schelble
Stage Managers: Marjorie Horne, Andy Lopata

* Still playing May 31, 1979, after 226 performances at Public/Anspacher Theater.
† Succeeded by: 1. Virginia Vestoff, 2. Steven Keats, 3. Jackee Harry, 4. Michael Ayr, Jake Turner, James Mellon, Mark Buchan

Sy Friedman Photos

Top Right: Lee Grayson, Dean Swenson, Gretchen Cryer Below: Betty Aberlin, Gretchen Cryer, Margot Rose, Joel Fabiani

Virginia Vestoff, Steven Keats

Gretchen Cryer, Joel Fabiani

PUBLIC/NEWMAN THEATER

Thursday, July 7 through Sunday, July 23, 1978 (12 performances)

Joseph Papp presents the Juilliard Theater Center Production of:

SPRING AWAKENING

By Frank Wedekind; New Adaptation by Edward Bond; Directed and Designed by Liviu Ciulei; Lighting, William Haviland; Costumes, Daniel Michaelson; Director Juilliard Theater Center, Alan Schneider; Associate Producer, Bernard Gersten; Production Supervisor, Jason Steven Cohen; General Manager, Robert Kamlot; Press, Merle Debuskey, Bob Ullman, Richard Kornberg; Stage Managers, Amy Pell, Janet DeMay; Assistant to Mr. Ciulei, Rachel Buchman; Wardrobe, Carol Clow; Production Manager, Andrew Mihok; Technical Director, Mervyn Haines, Jr.

CAST

Girls: Kathryn Dowling (Wendla), Janet DeMay (Martha), Laura Hicks (Thea), Sheila Dabney or Anne Kerry (Ilse), Boys: Boyd Gaines (Melchior Gabor), Richard Frank (Moritz Stiefel), William Deacutis (Hanschen Rilow), Miahcel Butler (Ernst Robel), James Curt Bergwall (Otto), Mitch Litrofsky (Georg), Charles Janasz (Robert), Boys in reformatory: Kevin Bergman (Dieter), James Curt Bergwall (Reinhold), Richard Howard (Rupert), Steve Bassett (Helmut), Steve Levitt (Gaston), Parents: Rebecca Guy (Frau Bergmann), Sarah Felder (Frau Bagor), Bob Lovitz (Herr Gabor), Barry Heins (Herr Stiefel), Teachers: Steve Levitt (Headmaster), Steve Bassett (Tonguetwister), Richard Howard (Flyswatter), Professors: Jessica Drake, Sheila Dabney, Katie Grant, Anne Kerry, Other Grown-Ups: Kevin Bergman (Fastcrawler), Barry Heins (Dr. Lemonade), Katie Grant (Ina), Denise Woods (Mother Schmidt), Stephen Destefano (Rev. Baldbelly), Keith Williams (Masked Man)

A drama in two acts. The action takes place in and around a provincial town in Germany from spring to winter in 1892.

Louisa Johnson Photos

Boyd Gaines, Kathryn Dowling Above: Reformatory Boys in "Spring Awakening"

PUBLIC/NEWMAN THEATER

Opened Tuesday, October 24, 1978.*

Joseph Papp presents:

DRINKS BEFORE DINNER

By E. L. Doctorow; Director, Mike Nichols; Designed by Tony Walton; Lighting, Jennifer Tipton; Makeup, Way Bandy; Production Supervisor, Jason Steven Cohen; Assistant to Director, Tony Cookson; Wardrobe, Melissa Adzima; Hairstylist, Marlies Vallant; Costume Coordination, Dona Granata; Technical Director, Mervyn Haines, Jr.

CAST

Edgar	Christopher Plummer
Joan	Zohra Lampert
Joel	Charles Kimbrough
Claudette	Barbara eda-Young
Michael	James Naughton
Andrea	Maria Tucci
Grace	Virginia Vestoff
Alan	Josef Sommer
Boy	John Kimbrough
Girl	Carrie Horner
Housekeeper	Fiona Hale

UNDERSTUDIES: Linda Selman (Andrea/Joan), Theodore Sorel (Edgar/Michael), Bill Moor (Alan/Joel), Daphne Youree (Girl), Mark Reiss (Boy)

A drama in two acts. The action takes place at the present time in Edgar's apartment.

General Manager: Robert Kamlot
Company Managers: Roger Gindi, Bert Ottley
Press: Merle Debuskey, Bob Ullman, Richard Kornberg
Stage Managers: Peter von Mayrhauser, Frank DiFilia

* Closed December 3, 1978 after a limited engagement of 48 performances.

Martha Swope Photos

Left Center: Charles Kimbrough, Barbara eda-Young, Christopher Plummer, Virginia Vestoff

Cast of "Drinks Before Dinner"

November 10,–December 3, 1978 (24 performances)

FATHERS AND SONS

By Thomas Babe; Director, Robert Allan Ackerman; Music, Brad Burg; Settings, Marjorie Kellogg; Costumes, Bob Wojewodski; Lighting, Arden Fingerhut; Stage Managers, Kitzi Becker, Michael Spellman; Assistant to Director, Caitlin Buckman; Props, Sharon Seymour; Wardrobe, George Potts; General Manager, Robert Camlot; Company Managers, Roger Gindi, Bert Ottley; Production Supervisor, Jason Steven Cohen; Press, Merle Debuskey, Bob Ullman, Richard Kornberg CAST: Robin Bartlett (Crooked-Eye), Graham Beckel (Garrison), Dixie Carter (Calamity Jane), Richard Chamberlain (Wild Bill Hickok), Brenda Currin (Lili), Stephen Daley (Pacific Pete), David Harris (Ivory Jaw), Emil Herrera (Horror Zeke), John G. Kellogg (California Joe), Matthew Lewis (Pinegrove), Jodi Long (Blossom), Tom McKitterick (McCall), Addison Powell (Colorado Charlie), J. C. Quinn (Carl), Eddie Rabin (Diamond Al), William Robertson (Amarillo Kid), Marie Santell (Ruby Redd), Joe Sharkey (Sammy)

(No photos available)

November 15,–December 3, 1978 (24 performances)

THE MASTER AND MARGARITA

By Mikhail Bulgakov; A project by Andrei Serban; Collaborator, Patrick Burke; Setting, Andrei Serban; Costumes, Dunya Ramicova; Lighting, Victor En Yu Tan; Assistant to the Director, Jeremy Blahnik; Stage Managers, Richard Jakiel, Bill McComb; Props, Pat Robertson; Wardrobe, Jean Hays, Philip Saraceno CAST: F. Murray Abraham, John Ahlburg, Gerry Bamman, Reed Birney, Jani Brenn, Roy Brocksmith, Patrick Burke, Laura Esterman, Marilyn Hamlin, Michael Jeter, Onni Johnson, Tom Klunis, Thom McCleister, Bill McComb, Patrizia Norcia, David Sabin, Sam Schacht, Wallace Shawn, John Shea, Jeremiah Sullivan, Jan Triska

Martha Swope Photo

Top Right: Director Andrei Serban (C) with cast of "The Master and Margarita"

Wednesday, December 27–Friday, December 29, 1978. (3 performances)
Joseph Papp presents:

WONDERLAND IN CONCERT

Based on Lewis Carroll's "Alice in Wonderland" and "Through the Looking Glass;" Music, additional lyrics, and direction by Elizabeth Swados; Production Supervisor, Jason Steven Cohen; Lighting, Jennifer Tipton; Sound, Bill Dreisbach; Stage Manager, Gregory Meeh; Press, Merle Debuskey, Bob Ullman, Richard Kornberg; A New York Shakespeare Festival Production

CAST

Meryl Streep (Alice), Karen Evans, Gloria Hodes, Rodney Hudson, Paul Kreppel, Joan MacIntosh, Jim McConaughty, William Parry, Joanna Peled as everybody else.

A musical in two acts.

Martha Swope Photos

Meryl Streep (C) and above in "Wonderland in Concert"

PUBLIC/ANSPACHER THEATER
Thursday, January 25 through April 1, 1979.*
Joseph Papp presents:

JULIUS CAESAR

By William Shakespeare; Director, Michael Langham; Music Composed by Stanley Silverman; Lighting, Jennifer Tipton; Fight Sequences, Erik Fredricksen; Military Consultant, Patrick Crean; Assistants to Director, Wilford Leach, Robbie McCauley, Shari Upbin; Textual Consultant, Ada Brown Mather; Wardrobe, Katherine Roberson; Hairstylist and Makeup, Marlies Termine-Vallant; Stage Managers, Louis Rackoff, Zane Weiner, Jacqueline Yancey, J. J. Johnson; General Manager, Robert Kamlot; Production Supervisor, Jason Steven Cohen; Press, Merle Debuskey, Bob Ullman, Richard Kornberg

CAST

Frank Adu (Soothsayer/Soldier), Mary Alice (Portia), Bimbo (Soldier/Pindarus), Christine Campbell (Citizen), Robert Christian (Metellus Cimbar/Cinna the Poet), Miriam Colon (Calpurnia) Keith Esau (Octavius' Officer/Soldier), Jay Fernandez (Trebonius/-Soldier), Clebert Ford (Caesar's servant/Citizen), Peter Francis-James (Octavius Caesar), Morgan Freeman (Casca), Arthur French (Flavius/Soldier/Lepidus), Sonny Jim Gaines (Julius Caesar), Ben Halley, Jr. (Cobbler/Citizen/Dardanius), Earle Hyman (Cicero/-Messala), J. J. Johnson (Augerer), Gylan Kain (Caius Cassius), Jose Maldonado (Antony's Officer/Citizen), Norman Matlock (Marullus/ Strato), Robbie McCauley (Lictor), Cynthia McPherson (Citizen), Clark Morgan (Publius/Lictor), Roscoe Orman (Marcus Brutus), Francisco Prado (Artemidorus/Citizen/Volumnis), Reyno (Lucius), Jaime Sanchez (Marc Anthony), Tucker Smallwood (Cinna/Titinius), Count Stovall (Decius Brutus/Lucilius), Reginald Vel Johnson (Soldier/Clitis), Maurice Woods (Soldier)

Bert Andrews Photo

*76 performances in repertory with "Coriolanus"

Jaime Sanchez (C) Top: Roscoe Orman, Sonny Jim Gaines, Gylan Kain in "Julius Caesar"

PUBLIC/OTHER STAGE
January 30,–February 25, 1979 (24 performances)

NEW JERUSALEM

By Len Jenkin; Director, Garland Wright; Scenery, John Arnone; Costumes, Patricia McGourty; Lighting, Frances Aronson; Stage Managers, Dorothy French, Bill McComb; Props, De Paskos; Production Supervisor, Jason Steven Cohen; Original Music/Vocals, Shelley Hirsch; Slide Show, Gerald Marks; General Manager, Robert Kamlot; Press, Merle Debuskey, Bob Ullman, Richard Kornberg CAST: Shawn Elliott, Christopher Hewett, Shelley Hirsch, James McClure, Nancy Mette, Jon Polito, William Sadler, Ebbe Roe Smith, Dale Soules, Jan Triska, Sigourney Weaver

PUBLIC/CABARET THEATER
Thursday, February 1 through Sunday, March 4, 1979. (78 performances)
Joseph Papp presents:

THE UMBRELLAS OF CHERBOURG

Book, Jacques Demy; English Translation, Sheldon Harnick in association with Charles Burr; Music, Michel Legrand; Director, Andrei Serban; Scenery, Michael Yeargan; Costumes, Jane Greenwood; Lighting, Ian Calderon; Orchestrations and Arrangements, Michel Legrand; Musical Direction and Adaptation of Orchestrations and Arrangements, Steven Margoshes; Assistant Director, Craig Zadan; Assistant To Director, Neil Meron; Dance Movement, Dorothy Danner; Sound, Otts Munderloh; Wardrobe, Melissa Adzima, Jean Hays; General Manager, Robert Kamlot; Production Supervisor, Jason Steven Cohen; Press, Merle Debuskey, Bob Ullman, Richard Kornberg; A New York Shakespeare Festival Production

CAST

Stuart Baker-Bergen (Pierre/Minister/Customer), Stephen Bogardus (Jean/Waiter), Shirley Chester (Mme. Germaine), Stefanianne Christopherson (Genevieve), Jennifer Governor (Francoise), Laurence Guittard (Cassard), Marc Jordan (Aubin), Joe Palmieri (Bernard/Postman), Michael Pearlman (Francois), Dean Pitchford (Guy), Lizabeth Pritchett (Aunt Elise), Judith Roberts (Mme. Emery), Maureen Silliman (Madeleine), Jeannine Taylor (Jenny), William Tost (Customer/ Dubourg/Care Owner)

Understudies: Stephen Bogardus (Guy), Joe Palmieri (Aubin), Brian Stuart (Cassard/Dubourg), Jeannine Taylor (Madeleine), Shirley Chester (Aunt Elise), Leila Martin (Mme. Emery/ Mme. Germaine)

A musical in three parts, performed with one intermission. The action takes place during 1957 through 1963.

Martha Swope Photos

Stefanianne Christopherson, Dean Pitchford in "Umbrellas of Cherbourg"

PUBLIC/NEWMAN THEATER
Opened Sunday, February 25, 1979.*
Joseph Papp presents:

TAKEN IN MARRIAGE

By Thomas Babe; Director, Robert Allan Ackerman; Scenery, Karen Schultz; Costumes, Bob Wojewodski; Lighting, Arden Fingerhut; Dance Sequences, Harry Streep III; A New York Shakespeare Festival Production; Production Supervisor, Jason Steven Cohen; Assistant to Director, Tom McKitterick; Production Assistant, Sally Greenhut; Wardrobe, Barbara Rosenthal; Hairstyles and Makeup, J. Roy Helland

CAST

Dixie Avalon	Dixie Carter
Annie	Kathleen Quinlan
Andrea	Meryl Streep
Ruth Chander	Colleen Dewhurst†
Aunt Helen	Elizabeth Wilson

UNDERSTUDIES: Scotty Bloch (Ruth/Helen), Ann-Sara Matthews (Annie/Andrea), Meg Myles (Dixie)

A drama in two acts. The action takes place at the present time in a small town in New Hampshire.

General Manager: Robert Kamlot
Company Manager: Roger Gindi
Press: Merle Debuskey, Bob Ullman, Richard Kornberg
Stage Managers: Haig Shepherd, Peter Glazer

* Closed April 1, 1979 after limited engagement of 55 performances.
† Succeeded by Nancy Marchand

Martha Swope Photos

Right: Colleen Dewhurst, Kathleen Quinlan, Dixie Carter Top: Kathleen Quinlan, Meryl Streep, Elizabeth Wilson, Colleen Dewhurst, Dixie Carter

Gloria Foster, Morgan Freeman (also above)

PUBLIC/ANSPACHER THEATER
Opened Wednesday, March 14, 1979.*
Joseph Papp presents the New York Shakespeare Festival production of:

CORIOLANUS

By William Shakespeare; Director, Michael Langham; Music, Stanley Silverman; Lighting, Jennifer Tipton; Fight Sequences, Erik Fredricksen; Stage Managers, Louis Rackoff, Jacqueline Yancey, J. J. Johnson; Assistants to the Director, Wilford Leach, Robbie McCauley, Shari Upbin; Wardrobe, Katherine Roberson; Hairstylist, Marlies Termine-Vallant; General Manager, Robert Kamlot; Company Manager, Roger Gindi; Production Supervisor, Jason Steven Cohen; Production Manager, Andrew Mihok; Technical Director, Mervyn Haines, Jr; Press, Merle Debuskey, Bob Ullman, Richard Kornberg

CAST

Maurice Woods (Menenius Agrippa), Earle Hyman (Cominius), Morgan Freeman (Caius Martius/Coriolanus), Jaime Sanchez (Titus Lartisu), Gloria Foster (Volumnia), Michele Shay (Virgilia), Khyyam Kain (Young Martius), C. C. H. Pounder (Valeria), Clebert Ford (Sicinius), Frank Adu (Junius Brutus), Count Stovall (First Citizen), Reginald Vel Johnson (Second Citizen), Roscoe Orman (Nicanor), Clark Morgan, Bimbo, J. J. Johnson, Jay Fernandez, Frankie Faison, William Jay, Christine Campbell, Peter Francis-James, Ben Halley, Jr., Jose Maldonado, Robbie McCauley, Cynthia McPherson, George Lee Miles, Francisco Prado, Catherine E. Slade, Tucker Smallwood, Gilbert Lewis (Adrian), Keith Esau (Lt.), Robert Christian (Tullus Aufidius)

Performed in two acts. The action takes place in Rome, and in the neighboring Volscian cities of Corioli and Antium.

* Closer Apr. 1, 1979 after 76 performances in repertory with "Julius Caesar."

Bert Andrews Photos

Gail Strickland, Mark Soper
in "Nasty Rumors"

PUBLIC/LuESTHER HALL

Wednesday, March 28, through April 1, 1979. (7 performances, 31 previews)
Joseph Papp presents:

SANCOCHO

Book, Ramiro (Ray) Ramirez; Music and Lyrics, Jimmy Justice, Ramiro (Ray) Ramirez; Director and Choreography, Miguel Godreau; Scenery and Costumes, Frank J. Boros; Lighting, Nananne Porcher; Musical Director, Jimmy Justice; Production Supervisor, Jason Steven Cohen; A New York Shakespeare Festival Production; Assistant Choreographer, Fred C. Mann III; Assistant Director, Alba Oms; Production Assistant, M. E. Hutchinson, Jr., Assistant Musical Director; Neal Tate; Wardrobe, Kate Rogers, Timothy Buckley, Marjorie Vanselow; Stage Managers, Elizabeth Holloway, M. W. Reid; Press, Merle Debuskey, Bob Ullman, Richard Kornberg

CAST

Haru Aki (Yemaya/Miss Conley), Ka-Ron Brown (Valerie/Chief's daughter), Cintia Cruz (Margarita), Stephen DeGhelder (Brown/-Flasher/Jerry/Priest/Orunla), Ramon Franco (Young Raul), Kenneth Frett (Guard/Announcer), Guillermo Gonzalez (Cabasa Player), Anthonio Iglesias (Junkie/Vendor/Eleggua), Marzetta Jones (Bible Lady), Terri Lombardozzi (Hooker/Late Student/O-shun), Fred C. Mann III (Slave Trader), Hector Jaime Mercado (Raul), Bryan Nicholas (Hippie/Hot Dog Man), Pamela Pilkenton (Bag Lady/Oggun/Miss Tucker/Nun), Ramiro (Ray) Ramirez (Saguita/Sanchez), M. W. Reid (Dude/Chango/Bubba/Witch Doctor), Beth Shorter (Obatala/Mrs. Mapp), Avery Sommers (Mattie/-Carrie), Dan Strayhorn (Don/Janitor/Rudolph Davis III), Ellis Williams (Drunk/Chief/Rev. McCook), Teresa Yenque (Mrs. Sanchez)

A musical in two acts. The action takes place in New York City from the mid 1960's to the present.

Bert Andrews Photo

PUBLIC/OTHER STAGE

March 29, throgh April 7, 1979. (15 performances)
Joseph Papp presents the New York Shakespeare Festival Workshop Production of:

LEAVE IT TO BEAVER IS DEAD

Written and Directed by Des McAnuff; Music, Larry David, Des McAnuff; Costumes, Jennifer von Mayrhauser; Scenery, Heidi Landesman; Lighting, Victor En Yu Tan; Musical Director, Larry Davis; Production Supervisor, Jason Steven Cohen; General Manager, Robert Kamlot; Assistant to Mr. McAnuff, James Furlong; Wardrobe, Sally Thomas; Props, David Harnish; Stage Managers, Peter Dowling, Sherman Warner; Press, Merle Debuskey, Bob Ullman, Richard Kornberg

CAST

Maury Chaykin (Bill Thompson), Mandy Patinkin (Saverin), Saul Rubinek (Dennis), Brent Spiner (Luke), Dianne Wiest (Lizzard)

A musical in two acts. The action takes place during the 1970's.

Susan Cook Photo

PUBLIC/OLD PROP SHOP

April 12, through April 15, 1979. (12 performances)
Joseph Papp presents a New York Shakespeare Festival Workshop Production of:

NASTY RUMORS AND FINAL REMARKS

By Susan Miller; Director, A. J. Antoon; Scenery and Costumes, Robert Yodice; Lighting, Arden Fingerhut; Music Composed by Ken Guilmartin; Wardrobe, Rebecca Blankenship, General Manager, Robert Kamlot; Production Supervisor, Jason Steven Cohen; Stage Managers, Mick Turque, Marge Pfleiderer; Press, Merle Debuskey, Bob Ullman, Richard Kornberg

CAST

Kathryn Grody (Fran), Kenneth Kimmins (Doctor), Karen Ludwig (Max), Sylvia Short (Woman), Mark Soper (T.K.), Bill Gerber (Nicholas), Gail Strickland (Raleigh)

A drama in two acts. The action takes place at the present time.

Gerry Goodstein Photo

Top Left: Ka-Ron Brown, Hector Jaime Mercado in "Sancocho" Below: Diane Wiest, Saul Rubinek, Mandy Patinkin in "Leave It to Beaver"

PUBLIC/CABARET THEATER

April 19, through June 10, 1979. (77 performances)
Joseph Papp presents a New York Shakespeare Festival production of:

DISPATCHES

Adapted, Composed and Directed by Elizabeth Swados; Based on book by Michael Herr; Scenery, Patricia Woodbridge; Costumes, Hilary Rosenfeld; Lighting, Jennifer Tipton; Sound, John K. Chester; Production Supervisor, Jason Steven Cohen; Production Assistant, Dinah Crosland; Wardrobe, Mark Niedzolkowski; General Manager, Robert Kamlot; Stage Managers, Gregory Meeh, Patricia Morinelli; Press, Merle Debuskey, Bob Ullman, Richard Kornberg

CAST

Penelope Bodry, Ray Contreras, Karen Evans, Tony Franklin, Rodney Hudson, Roger Lawson, Joan Macintosh, Paul McCrane, William Parry, David Schechter, Gedde Watanabe, and musicians Caroline Dutton, Dan Erkkila, Judith Fleisher, Leopoldo Fleming, Steve Peskoff, David Sawyer, John Schimmel

UNDERSTUDIES: Richard Dunne (Paul/Bill), Timm Fujii (Gedde), Tony Franklin (Rodney/Roger), Don Scotti (David/Ray), Martha Wingate (Penelope/Joan)

MUSICAL NUMBERS: "Crazy," "Thou Shalt Not Be Afraid," "Breathing In," "These Were the Faces," "The Ground Was Always in Play," "Song of the LURP," "Helicopter, Helicopter," "Stoned in Saigon," "Beautiful for Once," "Tiger Lady," "Prayers in the Delta," "Flip Religion," "Quakin' and Shakin'," "Six Fucking Shades of Green," "Bougainvillea," "The Mix," "I See a Road," "Take the Glamor Out of War," "This War Gets Old," "Back in the World Now," "Freezing and Burning"

A rock-war musical without intermission.

Martha Swope Photo

PUBLIC/OTHER STAGE

April 24,–May 13, 1979 (18 performances)

REMEMBRANCE

By Derek Walcott; Director, Charles Turner; Scenery, Wynn P. Thomas; Costumes, Judy Dearing; Lighting, Spencer Mosse; Production Supervisor, Jason Steven Cohen; Production Manager, Andrew Mihok; General Manager, Robert Kamlot; Press, Merle Debuskey, Bob Ullman, Richard Kornberg CAST: Cynthia Belgrave, Roscoe Lee Browne, Frankie R. Faison, Lou Ferguson, Earle Hyman, Laurie Kennedy, Gil Rogers

(No photos)

PUBLIC/LuESTHER THEATER

April 27 through June 10, 1979. (53 performances)
Joseph Papp presents the New York Shakespeare Festival Production of:

WAKE UP, IT'S TIME TO GO TO BED!

Conceived, Written and Directed by Carson Kievman; Scenery and Costumes, Robert Yodice; Lighting, Pat Collins, Musical Direction, David Arden; Production Supervisor, Jason Steven Cohen; Assistant to Mr. Kievman, Jeremy Blahnick; Wardrobe, Epp Kotkas, Ellise Garber; Hairstylist, Marlies Vallant; General Manager, Robert Kamlot; Production Manager, Andrew Mihok; Technical Director; Mervyn Haines, Jr.; Props, Joe Toland; Stage Managers, Michael Chambers, Greg Fauss; Press, Merle Debuskey, Bob Ullman, Richard Kornberg

CAST

Keith Carradine (Orpheus), Erika Nelson Boras, Elizabeth C. Brown, Sean Caposella, Sara Cutler, Ruth Ann DeMarco, Marty Ehrlich, Claudia Hafer, Ellen Greene, Susan Krongold, Joseph Kubera, Dennis Masuzzo, William N. Moersch, Steven Paysen, Renee Pearl, Michael Pearlman, Lawrence Raiken, Kurt Richards, Richard Sacks, David Van Tieghem, Michael Edwin Willson

The curtain raiser was "The Temporary and Tentative Extended Piano" with Joseph Kubera, Dennis Masuzzo, Lawrence Raiken, Michael Edwin Willson, Sara Cutler, Elizabeth C. Brown, Marty Ehrlich

Tom Victor Photo

Right Center: Chris Sarandon, Christine Lahti in "The Woods" Above: Keith Carradine, Ellen Greene in "Wake Up . . ."

PUBLIC/NEWMAN THEATER

April 29 through May 13, 1979. (32 performances)
Joseph Papp presents the New York Shakespeare Festival production of:

THE WOODS

By David Mamet; Director, Ulu Grosbard; Scenery, John Lee Beatty; Costumes, Bob Wojewodski; Lighting, Jennifer Tipton; Production Supervisor, Jason Steven Cohen; Assistant to Director, Sally Greenhut; Wardrobe, Barbara Rosenthal

CAST

Ruth . . . . Christine Lahti
Nich . . . . Chris Sarandon

A drama in two acts. The action takes place at the present time during early September on the porch of a summer house.

General Manager: Robert Kamlot
Press: Merle Debuskey, Bob Ullman, Richard Kornberg
Stage Managers: Kitzi Becker, Michael Spellman

Sy Friedman Photo

Top: "Dispatches"

THE PHOENIX THEATRE

T. Edward Hambleton, Norris Houghton, Founders
26th Season

MARYMOUNT MANHATTAN THEATRE

Thursday, October 19 through Sunday, November 5, 1978.* (22 performances)
The Phoenix Theatre (T. Edward Hambleton, Managing Director; Daniel Freudenberger, Artistic Director) present:

GETTING OUT

By Marsha Norman; Director, Jon Jory; Scenery and Lighting, James Tilton; Costumes, Kurt Wilhelm; Production Coordinator, Johnna Murray; Wardrobe, Marnie Powers; General Manager, Mitchell Kurtz; Press, Susan Bloch, Sally Christiansen; Stage Manager, Tom Aberger

CAST

Pamela Reed (Arlie), Susan Kingsley (Arlene), John C. Capodice (Guard 1), Barry Corbin (Bennie), David Berman (Guard 2), William Jay (Doctor), Madeleine Thornton-Sherwood (Mother), Anna Minot (School Principal), Kevin Bacon (Ronnie), Leo Burmester (Carl), Hansford Rowe (Warden), Joan Pape (Ruby)

A drama in two acts. The action takes place at the present time in an apartment in a rundown section of downtown Louisville.

Martha Swope Photo

*Re-opened Tuesday, May 15, 1979 at Theatre De Lys.

MARYMOUNT MANHATTAN THEATRE

January 11–January 28, 1979. (22 performances)
The Phoenix Theatre presents:

LATER

By Corinne Jacker; Director, Daniel Freudenberger; Scenery and Lighting, James Tilton; Costumes, Julie Weiss; General Manager, Mitchell Kurtz; Stage Managers, Tom Aberger, George Roger Abell; Sound, Eric Drosin; Wardrobe, Mary Giddons; Press, Susan Block

CAST

Molly . . . . Pauline Flanagan
Kate . . . . Louise Sorel
Laurie . . . . Dorothy Lyman

A drama in two acts and three scenes. The action takes place next summer at the Dowson summer home on the Rhode Island coast on the Labor Day weekend.

Karen Gilborn Photos

MARYMOUNT MANHATTAN THEATRE

February 19, through March 4, 1979. (22 performances)
The Phoenix Theatre presents:

SAYS I, SAYS HE

By Ron Hutchinson; Director, Steven Robman; Scenery, David Jenkins; Costumes, Dona Granata; Lighting, Spencer Mosse; Musical Director, Mick Maloney; Music by The Irish Tradition; Choreographer, Tom Cashin; Dialect Consultant, Timothy Monich; General Manager, Mitchell Kurtz; Stage Managers, Tom Aberger, George Roger Abell; Press, Susan Bloch, Sally Christiansen

CAST

Jeanne Ruskin (Bella Phelan), Brian Dennehy (Pete Hannafin), Joe Grifasi (Mick Phelan), Christine Baranski (Maeve Macpherson), Andrew Davis (Jigger Hannafin), Sylvia Short (Landlady/May/Bridie), George Taylor (Lodger/Carradine/Hughes/Sam), The Irish Tradition (The Band)

A drama in two acts. The action takes place in present-day Ulster and London.

Top Right: Pamela Reed, Susan Kingsley in "Getting Out" Below: Barbara Barrie in "Big and Little"

MARYMOUNT MANHATTAN THEATRE

March 29, through April 15, 1979. (22 performances)
The Phoenix Theatre (T. Edward Hambleton, Managing Director) presents:

BIG AND LITTLE

By Botho Strauss; Translated by Anne Cattaneo; Director, Daniel Freudenberger; Scenery and Lighting, James Tilton; Costumes, Julie Weiss; Drawings, Barbara Nessim; Music Composed by Paul Allen Levi; Film Sequences by John de Forest and Charles Peck; Choreography, Ara Fitzgerald; Production Coordinator, Donna Lieberman; Props, Buzz Cohen; Wardrobe, Mary Gibbons; Production Assistant, Margaret Brady; Sound, David Rapkin

CAST

Humbert Allen Astredo (Paul/Wilhelm/Schneider/Doctor), Barbara Barrie (Lotte), Janni Brenn (Fat Woman/Meggy), Randy Danson (Gudrun), Peter Friedman (Floyd/Jurgen/Albert/Bob Fechter), Peter Maloney (Soren/Bernard/Alf), Carol Teitel (Inge/Josephine), Daniel Charles Abrahamsen (Media Supervisor)

A play in two acts.

General Manager: Mitchell Kurtz
Press: Susan Bloch & Co.
Stage Managers: Tom Aberger, George Roger Abell

Martha Swope Photo

PLAYWRIGHTS HORIZONS
MANHATTAN/QUEENS

Robert Moss, Producing Director
Jane Moss, Managing Director
Andre Bishop, Artistic Director
Business Manager, Ira Schlosser; Production Manager, Dorothy J. Maffei; Press, Lucy Stille; Coordinator of Musical Workshop, Ira Weitzman; Technical Directors, Duane Taft, Robert Baldwin; Props, Karen McDuffee, Costumer, Antonette Giammarinaro

MANHATTAN/MAINSTAGE
December 5–17, 1978 (12 performances)

LIVING AT HOME by Anthony Giardina; Director, Thomas Gruenewald; Set, James Leonard Joy; Lighting, David K. H. Elliott; Costumes, Kenneth M. Yount; Stage Manager, Wendy Chapin. CAST: Victor Bevine, Joyce Cohen, Al Corley, David Garrison, Linda Kampley, Tania Myren, Gerald Richards, Lisa Sloan

January 18–28, 1979 (12 performances)

THE VIENNA NOTES by Richard Nelson; Director, Andre Ernotte; Set, Heidi Landesman; Lighting, Paul Gall; Costumes, William Ivey Long; Sound, David Rapkin; Special Effects, Jack Stewart; Stage Manager, Paul Lazarus. CAST: Richard Bey, Dan Desmond, Kate McGregor-Stewart, Marcell Rosenblatt

February 21–March 18, 1979 (24 performances)

IN TROUSERS with music and lyrics by William Finn; Director, William Finn; Choreography, Marta Renzi; Set, Donato Moreno; Lighting, Annie Wrightson; Costumes, Bob Wojewodski; Musical Direction and Orchestrations, Michael Starobin; Stage Manager, Larry Mengden. CAST: Alison Fraser, Joanna Green, Mary Testa, Chip Zien

April 19–May 6, 1979 (12 performances)

THE TERRORISTS by Dallas Murphy, Jr.; Director, Gary Pearle; Set, Judie Juracek; Lighting, Frances Aronson; Costumes, Kenneth M. Yount; Stage Manager, Michael S. Mantel. CAST: Cathy Baldwin, Thomas Barbour, Robert Dorfman, Barbara eda-Young, Wayne Elbert, Jon Polito, Michael M. Ryan

November 14–19, 1978 (10 performances)

SAY GOODNIGHT GRACIE by Ralph Pape; Director, Austin Pendleton; Set, Douglas E. Ball; Lighting, Cheryl Thacker; Costumes, Patricia A. Weigleb; Stage Manager, Ellen Zalk. CAST: Mark Blum, Carolyn Groves, Willard Morgan, Molly Regan, Danton Stone

December 8–18, 1979 (8 performances)

IN TROUSERS, music and lyrics by William Finn; Director, William Finn; Set, Donato Moreno; Lighting, Annie Wrightson; Stage Manager, Paul Lazarus. Cast: William Finn, Alison Fraser, Joanna Green, Mary Testa.

January 24–29, 1979 (8 performances)

BREAKING AND ENTERING by Neal Bell; Director, Barnett Kellman; Set, Bil Mikulewicz; Lighting, Annie Wrightson; Costumes, Bob Wojewodski; Stage Manager, Michael Spellman. Cast: Joel Brooks, Philip Casnoff, Bella Jarrett.

March 21–April 1, 1979 (12 performances)

TABLE SETTINGS by James Lapine; Director, James Lapine; Set, Richard Goodwin; Lighting, Annie Wrightson; Costumes, Bob Wojewodski; Sound, Michael Spellman; Stage Manager, Kevin Mangan. Cast: Clayton Berry, Frances Chaney, David Marshall Grant, Carolyn Hurlburt, Carlo Imperator, Marta D. Kobler, Cris Weatherhead.

April 3–5, 1979 (4 performances)

THE CAST OF JONATHAN TUNICK. Musical Director, Daniel Troob. Cast: Steve Elmore, Nancy Killmer, Karen Morrow.

April 22–30, 1979 (4 performances)

DON'T TELL ME EVERYTHING and other musical arrangements, lyrics by Josh Rubins, music by Peter Larson, John Lewis and Josh Rubins; Director, Caymichael Patten; Set, Barry Robison; Lighting, Annie Wrightson; Choreography, Dalienne Majors; Musical Direction, Peter Larson; Stage Manager, Greg McCaslin. Cast: Raymond Baker, Kimberley Farr, Jane Galloway, Harris Shore.

May 17–27, 1979 (10 performances)

SWEET MAIN STREET, based on the songs and poems of Carol Hall, with additional material and concept by Shirley Kaplan; Director, Shirley Kaplan; Set, Henry Millman; Lighting, Milton Duke; Costumes, Genii Charnin; Stage Manager, Michael Sweeney. Cast: Susannah Blinkoff, Alan Brasington, Andy Graham, Farley Granger, Carol Hall, Nina Hennessey, Paul Kreppel, Jennifer O'Horan, Pauletta Pearson.

Joanna Green, Alison Fraser, Chip Zien, Mary Testa in "In Trousers"

QUEENS:
October 14–November 5, 1978 (17 performances)

OH! WHAT A LOVELY WAR! by Joan Littlewood; Director, Philip Himberg; Musical Director, Eric W. Diamond; Dances and Musical Sequences, Dennis Grimaldi; Set, Heidi Landesman; Lighting, Paul Gallo; Costumes, A. Christina Giannini; Stage Manager, Frederic H. Orner. Cast: Charles Abbott, Ronald Bagden, Scott Bakula, Susie Duff, Frank Root, Jana Schneider, Virginia Seidel, James Seymour, Diane Tarleton, Robert Yacko.

November 25–December 17, 1978 (17 performances)

ECCENTRICITIES OF A NIGHTINGALE by Tennessee Williams. Director, Betsy Shevey; Set, Bob Phillips; Lighting, Candice Dunn; Costumes, Elizabeth P. Palmer; Sound, Bob Lepre; Stage Manager, Michael S. Mantel. Cast: Peter Bosche, Katherine Mary Brown, Edward Cannan, Jill Eikenberry, Jen Jones, Rusti Moon, Frances Peter, Ethan Phillips, Peter Phillips, David Wilborn.

March 3–25, 1979 (17 performances)

HEDDA GABLER by Henrik Ibsen, translated by John Osborne. Director, Philip Himberg; Set, Richard B. Williams; Lighting, Pat Stern; Costumes, Andrew Marlay; Sound, Bob Lepre; Stage Manager, Frederic H. Orner. Cast: John Bergstrom, Cynthia Dickason, Suzanne Granfield, Shaine Marinson, Josephine Nichols, Larry Pine, Michael M. Ryan.

March 31–April 22, 1979 (17 performances)

LADYHOUSE BLUES by Kevin O'Morrison. Director, Tony Giordano; Set, Hugh Landwehr; Lighting, Spencer Mosse; Costumes, David Murin; Sound, Philip Campanella; Stage Manager, David N. Feight. Cast: Christine Estabrook, Teri Garr, Jo Henderson, Diane Kagan, Lisa Sloan.

May 12–June 2, 1979 (17 performances)

PRIVATE LIVES by Noel Coward. Director, Garland Wright; Set, John Arnone; Lighting, Frances Aronson; Costumes, Lindsay W. Davis; Sound, Philip Campanella; Stage Manager, Amy F. Leveen. Cast: Jacqueline Barnett, Linda Carlson, Richard Council, Michael Gross, Carolyn Hurlburt.

June 9–July 1, 1979 (17 performances)

THE SHOW-OFF by George Kelly. Director, Bill Ludel, Set, Bil Mikulewicz; Lighting, Annie Wrightson; Costumes, Elizabeth P. Palmer; Sound, Billy Ahearn; Stage Manager, Larry Mengden. Cast: Arthur Brooks, Edward Cannan, Beth Dixon, Lisa Goodman, Peter Jolly, Conrad McLaren, Richard Pilcher, Sloan Shelton, Eric Tull.

Molly Regan, Danton Stone, Carolyn Groves in "Say Goodnight, Gracie"

QUAIGH THEATRE

William H. Lieberson, Artistic Director
Executive Director, Ted Mornel; Managing Director, Paul Matwiow; Artistic Consultant, Albert Brower; Production Corrdinator, Richard Young; Sound Technician, George Jacobs; Administrative Consultant, Susanne Braham

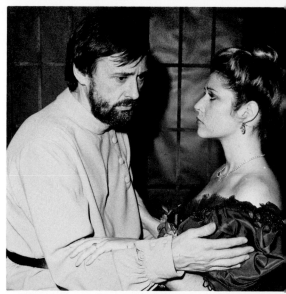

QUAIGH THEATRE
January 9–28, 1979 (18 performances)

LIGHT SHINES IN DARKNESS

(World Premiere) Adapted by George Styles from Tolstoy's autobiographical drama; Director, Will Lieberson; Setting, Bob Phillips; Lighting, Daniel Charles Abrahamsen; Costumes, Daniel Orlandi; Sound, George Jacobs; Production Coordinator, Ted Mornel; Stage Managers, Irene Klein, Ruby Payne, Tony Barbera; Wardrobe, Darcy Heller; Press, Max Eisen CAST: Warren Ball, Tony Barbera, Barbara Lynn Brodsky, Donna Dundon, Paul E. Hart, Darcy Heller Fred Ivory, Mel Jurdem, Joyce Renee Korbin, Amy Lieberson, Steve Lincoln, Meredith McComb, Terrence Markovich, Patricia Mertens, John Neary, Candace O'Heron, Gerald Oliver, Ruby Payne, Robert Resnikoff, Dickson Shaw, Richard Spoke, Michael Streich, Nancy Hubert Textor

February 20–March 4, 1979 (12 performances)

ON TRIAL

By Elmer Rice; Director, Ted Mornel; Lighting and Sets, Daniel Charles Abrahamsen; Costumes, Danajean Cicerchi; Stage Manager, Ruby Payne; Sound, George Jacobs; Wardrobe, Kevin Cuba CAST: Chuck Allen, Tony Barbera, Robert Berger, Kevin Cuba, Robert Carnegie, Richard Dahlia, Charles Gemmill, Burt Grosselfinger, Carolyn Lenz, Steve Lincoln, Desnader J. Mas, Meredith McComb, Frank Meyer, Richard Muller, Candace O'Heron, Ruby Payne, E. D. Phillips, Dickson Shaw, Glen Vincent, Allan Wikman

April 10–June 17, 1979 (48 performances)

VICTIM

By Mario Fratti; *(U.S. Premiere)* Director, Gino Giglio; Set and Lighting, John Kenny; Stage Managers, Irene Klein, Jef Palmer, Richard Mueller; Press, Hunt/Pucci, James Sapp CAST: Greta Thyssen, Dan Grimaldi, Michael Dorkin

QUAIGH THEATRE
LUNCHTIME SERIES
October 9–13, 1978: MIME WORLD I starring Moni Yakim with Maryln Galfin, Tony Lopresti, Lindanell Rivera, Joseph Zwerling. November 6–17, 1978: HEART MELODIES: POETRY OF LANGSTON HUGHES read by John S. Patterson. November 20–December 3, 1978: BIRDBATH by Leonard Melfi; Director, Bob McAndrew; with Danny Watkins and Jane Fuller. January 9–26, 1979: JUST A SONG AT TWILIGHT by Marcia Savin; Director, John Wolf; with Bill DaPrato, Naomi Riordan. January 30–February 16, 1979: LEMONADE by James Prideaux; Director, Linda Koevary; with Rusti Moon, Joyce Renee Korbin. March 13–23, 1979: FIT FOR CONSUMPTION by T. J. Camp III; Director, Granville Wyche Burgess; with Richard Patrick-Warner, David Graff, Michael Robertson. April 3–30, 1979: THE WITCH by Ferenc Molnar; Director, Peter Del Valle; with Noni Pratt, Martha Sherrill, Felicity Love. April 24–May 11, 1979: PASSING TIME by Thomas Cumella; Director, Spence Halperin; with B. Constance Barry, Joan Turetzky

Peter M. Lerman Photos

Top Right: Terry Markovich, Barbara Brodsky in "Light Shines in Darkness" Below: Carolyn Lenz, Robert Berger in "On Trial"

Dan Grimaldi, Greta Thyssen in "Victim"

ROUNDABOUT THEATRE

Gene Feist   Michael Fried
Producing Directors

Assistant to Producing Directors, Arthur Pearson; Press, Mark Arnold; Business Manager, Allison Burchell; Stage Managers, Holley Jack Horner, Paul Moser; Technical Director, Phillip Giller; Composer-Musical Director, Philip Campanella; Scenic Artists, Richard Harper, Mark McGurty, Stan Thomas; Costume Supervisor, Shelly Friedman

ROUNDABOUT/STAGE ONE

July 6, 1978–December 17, 1978 (226 performances)

PINS AND NEEDLES

By Harold Rome; Director, Milton Lyon; Choreography, Haila Strauss; Scenery and Lighting, Scott Johnson; Costumes, Donna Meyer; Lighting, Robert Strohmeier; Musical Director, Philip Campanella; Additional Material Staged by Stephen Rosenfeld; At twin pianos, Philip Campanella, Marc Segan; Technical Director, Philip Giller; Props, Nancy Ann Adler; Stage Manager, Holley Jack Horner

CAST: Trudy Bayne, David Berman, Richard Casper, Daniel Fortus, Mary Garripoli, Randy Graff, Robin Hoff, Christopher Nelson, Tom Offt, Dennis Perren, Elaine Petricoff, Kitty Preston, Corliss Taylor-Dunn

MUSICAL NUMBERS: Social Significance, Not Cricket to Picket, I've Got the Nerve to Be in Love, We're the Ads, Pappa Don't Love Mama Anymore, Room for One, F. D. R. Jones, I'm Just Nuts about You, What Good Is Love, Doing the Reactionary, Chain Store Daisy, Back to Work, Sunday in the Park, When I Grow Up, It's Better with a Union Man, One Big Union for Two, Nobody Makes a Pass at Me, Mene Mene Tekel, Call It Unamerican, Status Quo, We Sing America

ROUNDABOUT STAGE ONE

Opened Tuesday, January 2, 1979.*
Gene Feist and Michael Fried present:

GERALDINE FITZGERALD
in
"STREETSONGS"

Directed by Richard Maltby, Jr.; Musical Direction and Arrangement, Stanley Wietrzychowski; Vocal Director, Andy Thomas Anselmo; Lighting, Robert F. Strohmeier; Costumes, Bill Walker; Production Stage Manager, Holly Jack Horner; Technical Director, Philip Giller

*Closed April 1, 1979 after 96 performances.

ROUNDABOUT STAGE TWO

December 21, 1978–April 1, 1979 (115 performances)
Roundabout Theatre Company (Gene Feist, Michael Fried, Producing Directors) presents:

CANDIDA

By George Bernard Shaw; Director, Harold J. Kennedy; Scenery, Billy Puzo; Lighting Design, Robert Strohmeier; Costumes, Debra Stein; Stage Manager, Morton Milder; Technical Director, Philip Giller; Production Assistants, Linet Henry, Kathy Bird; Press, Susan Block, Bill Rudman, Adrian Bryan-Brown

CAST

Miss Proserpine Garnett	Elizabeth Owens
Rev. James Mavor Morell	Barry Boys
Rev. Alexander Mill	Lucien Douglas
Mr. Burgess	Ralph Clanton
Candida	Mary Denham
Eugene Marchbanks	Mark Soper

A drama in three acts. The action takes place during the early autumn of 1894 in St. Dominic's Parsonage, Hackney road, Victoria Park, London, England.

Right Center: "Awake and Sing" Above: "Candida" Top: "Pins and Needles"

ROUNDABOUT STAGE ONE

April 19,–May 27 1979 (45 performances)
Roundabout Theatre Company (Gene Feist, Michael Fried, Producing Directors) presents:

AWAKE AND SING!

By Clifford Odets; Director, Stephen Rosenfield; Scenery, Billy Puzo; Lighting, Robert Strohmeier; Costumes, Debra Stein; Sound, Philip Campanella; Stage Manager, Morton Milder; Press, Susan Bloch, Bill Rudman, Adrian Bryan-Brown

CAST

Ralph Berger	Hal Lehrman, Jr.
Myron Berger	Joey Faye
Hennie Berger	Patricia Mauceri
Jacob	King Donovan
Bessie Berger	Vera Lockwood
Schlosser	Ralph Farnworth
Moe Axelrod	Marco St. John
Uncle Morty	Herman O. Arbeit
Sam Feinschreiber	Peter Silbert

A drama in three acts and four scenes. The action takes place in 1935 in the Berger apartment in The Bronx, New York City.

Martha Swope, Peter Krupenye Photos

THEATRE OFF PARK

Executive Director, Patricia Flynn Peate
General Manager, Jeffrey Solis

October 11–28, 1978 (12 performances)
AIN'T DOIN' NOTHIN' BUT SINGIN' MY SONG with Lyrics and Music by Johnny Brandon; Director, Lucia Victor; Musical Direction/Vocal and Dance Arrangements, Carl Maultsby; Orchestrations, Neal Tate; Assistant Musical Director, Zane Mark, Scenery and Costumes, Don Jensen; Lighting, Jeff Davis; Choreography, Mabel Robinson; Stage Managers, Robert I. Cohen, Sherry Lambert. CAST: Pi Douglass, Pat Lundy, Ken Prescott, Judy Stevens, Marian Taylor

January 17–February 3, 1979 (14 performances)
THE MADMAN AND THE NUN by Stanislaw Ignacy Witkiewicz; Translated by Dan Gerould and C. S. Durer; Director, Paul Berman; Set, Bob Provenza; Lighting, Stephen Stawbridge; Costumes, Georgia Baker. CAST: Eddie Allen, Cordelia Biddle, Ann Crumb, Robert DeFrank, Michael Farace, Gordon Gray, Tobias Haller, Dennis O'Keefe

February 14–March 3, 1979 (8 performances)
THE CONFESSION STONE written and directed by Owen Dodson; Music, Bruce Strickland; Choreography, Mike Malone; Associate Director, Glenda Dickerson; Lighting, Larry Johnson; Costumes, Tamara Block; Stage Managers, Kimako, Chip Neufeld; Production Assistants, Candice Tarpley, Judy Thames. CAST: Ruth Attaway, Dan Barbaro, Marilyn Berry, Graham Brown, Erma Campbell, Lex Monson, Darryl Croxton, Charles Turner, Doug Cameron, LaMont Clark, Rickey Davenport, Kenneth Johnson

May 9–June 2, 1979 (14 performances)
A SEXUAL INCIDENT AT THE INSTITUTE OF ADVANCED LEARNING by H. N. Levitt; Director, Jay Stephens; Set, Bil Mikulewicz; Lighting, Julie Campbell; Stage Manager, Tamara Block; Costumes, James Delany Collum; Production Assistants, Marjorie Parkis, Heidi Spivak. CAST: Michael Beckett, Norma Fire, Stephen Gabis, John Leighton, Harsh Nayyar, R. Patrick Sullivan

Nathaniel Tileston Photos

Ann Crumb, Tobias Haller, Cordelia Biddle, Gordon Gray, Robert DeFrank in "The Madman and the Nun" Above: Pi Douglass, Ken Preston in "Ain't Doin' Nothin'"

Noreen Jeremiah, Kinley Scott in "A Month in the Country"

TRUNK MATERIAL

J. Perry McDonald, Director

CUBAN CENTRE
January 4–21, 1979 (12 performances)
CRAWLING ARNOLD by Jules Feiffer; Director, J. Perry McDonald. CAST: Richard Pierce, Randy Knolle, Barbara Gregg, Janet Cristenfeld, Paul DeBoy, Virginia Jackson.
THE DWARFS by Harold Pinter; Stage Manager, Fredd Gordon. CAST: Richard Pierce, Randy Knolle, Paul DeBoy

March 22–April 8, 1979 (12 performances)
A MONTH IN THE COUNTRY by Ivan Turgenev; Director, J. Perry McDonald; Music and Lyrics, John Sheehan; Music Director, Stephen Borsuk; Set, Bill Lehne; Lighting, Duane Taft; Production Coordinator, Lynn Marrapodi; Press, Dale Zeidman; Stage Managers, Nina Zirato, Cris Mire. CAST: Allyn Arden, Ed Brady, Randy Knolle, Bill Edwards. Letha Elliot, Bruce Goldstein, Mimi Weddell, Mary Jay, Noreen Jeremiah, Terry Markovich, Ivan Paslavsky, Kinley Scott, Ann Sheehy, Tom Thayer

May 10–27, 1979 (12 performances)
TRELAWNY OF THE WELLS by Arthur W. Pinero; Director, J. Perry McDonald; Lighting, Duane Taft; Stage Managers, Nina Zirato, Chris Mire. CAST: Don Auspitz, Neale Cahan, Richard Charles Hoh, Mary Jay, John Jamiel, Noreen Jeremiah, Robert Maitland, Lynn Marrapodi, Susan Micari, Mae Munroe, Ruth Neuman, Grady Parrish, Kinley Scott, John Sheehan, Ann Sheehy, Tom Thayer, Mimi Weddell

Bruce Shenton, Chip Goebert Photos

Left Center: Mary Jay, Tom Thayer, Noreen Jeremiah, Richard Charles Hoh in "Trelawny of the Wells"

WPA THEATRE

Howard Ashman, Artistic Director
Kyle Renick, Producing Director
Edward T. Gianfrancesco, Designer-Technical Director
Eleventh Season

WPA THEATRE

June 3–11, 1978 (12 performances)
FESTIVAL OF NEW ONE ACT PLAYS: "Ceremony" by Andrew
Corwin; Director, R. Stuart White; with Maureen MacDougall, Dan
Bonnell, Rod Houts. "Fits and Starts" by Grace McKeaney; Direc-
tor, Theodore Pappas; with Linda Daughtery, David Wohl, Estelle
Gettleman, Bill Karnovsky. "Ocean Cliff Drive" by Valcour
Lavizzo; Director, Bette Howard; Assisted by Terry Carpenter; with
Joy Moss, Anthony F. Chase, Louise Mike. "How Well I Know" by
Louis Phillips, Director, Robert Pesola; with Andrew Esterman,
Glenn Cabrera, Janice Kay Young, James Klawin. "Cabin Fever"
by John Schenkar; Director, Sande Shurin, Assisted by Bo Levy;
with Georgia Southcotte, William Robertson, Wyman Pendleton.
"Solitude Forty," by Percy Granger; Director, Ted Weiant, assisted
by John Retif; with Tom McDermott, Ed Herlihy.

October 19–November 5, 1978 (12 performances)
DAYS TO COME by Lillian Hellman; Director, R. Stuart White;
Setting, Edward T. Gianfrancesco; Press, Alan Eichler; Lighting,
Kathy Giebler; Costumes, Marcia Cox; Stage Managers, Frances
Smith, Mary Robinson; CAST: Carl Don, Patricia Guinan, J. R.
Horne, Ed Lally, Kaiulani Lee, Pirie MacDonald, Mark Margolis,
Mardi Philips, Kathleen Roland, Reno Roop, William Schilling

November 30–December 17, 1978 (12 performances)
JOSEPHINE THE MOUSE SINGER by Michael McClure; Direc-
tor, Gerry Woodard; Set and Lighting, Craig Evans; Costumes,
David Menkes; Stage Managers, Duane Fletcher, Joseph Coleman.
CAST: Dan Bonnell, Brian Carpenter, Larry Dilg, Mary Diveny,
Michael French, Gale Garnett, Davis Hall, Vicki Hirsch, Sanford
Morris, Nancy Parent, David Swatling, William Verderber, Janice
Kay Young

January 18–February 4, 1979 (12 performances)
ETHAN FROME by Edith Wharton; Adapted by Owen and Don-
ald Davis; Suggested by a dramatization by Lowell Barrington; Di-
rector, William Esper; Setting, Edward T. Gianfrancesco; Lighting,
Kathleen Giebler; Costumes, David Menkes; Music Composed by
H. Ross Levy; Stage Manager, Paul Mills Holmes, Assistant to
Director, Linda Romano. CAST: Henrietta Bagley, Bob Beuth,
Charles Eugene Denney, Bruce Fuller, Lisa Gwynn, Susan Hanley,
Jonathan Hogan, Dennis Logan Schneider, Jon Stevens, David Ta-
bor, Del Willard, Elizabeth Wingate

February 22–March 11, 1979 (12 performances)
MOTEL by Donna de Matteo; Director, Joel Harvey; Setting, Ed-
ward T. Gianfrancesco; Lighting, John Senter; Costumes, Susan
Denison; Stage Managers, Paul Mills Holmes, Sarah Whitman; As-
sistant to Director, Anne Phillips; with Richard Kurtzman, Edna
Dix. OPENING NIGHT by Bury St. Edmund; with Edna Dix,
James Hornbeck, Kit LeFever, Richard Kurtzman

April 14–April 29, 1979 (12 performances)
THE FREQUENCY by Larry Ketron; Director, William Martin;
Setting, James Stewart; Lighting, Kathleen Giebler; Costumes, Su-
san Denison; Stage Managers, Renee F. Lutz, Susan Kipp. CAST:
Elizabeth Perry, Kevin O'Connor, Dann Harvey Florek, Anthony
Call, Jane Cronin, Patricia Richardson

May 17–June 3, 1979 (12 performances)
GOD BLESS YOU, MR. ROSEWATER by Kurt Vonnegut;
Adapted and Directed by Howard Ashman; Music, Alan Menken;
Additional Lyrics, Dennis Green; Musical Staging, Dalienne Ma-
jors; Setting, Edward T. Gianfrancesco; Lighting, Craig Evans; Cos-
tumes, David Menkes; Stage Managers, Sarah Whitham, Beth
Prevor; Musical Direction and Arrangements, Alan Menken; Assis-
tant Director, Nancy Parent. CAST: Albert S. Bennett, Marvin A.
Chatinover, Frederick Coffin, Anne DeSalvo, Douglas Fisher, Jona-
than Hadary, Jim Jansen, David Little, Elizabeth Moore, Peter J.
Saputo, John Towey, Mimi Turque, Ed VanNuys, Holly Villaire

Ian Anderson, Chip Goebert Photos

**Top Right: Jonathan Hogan, Susan Hanley
in "Ethan Frome" Below: Richard Kurtzman,
James Hornbeck, Kit LeFever in "Opening
Night"**

**Kevin O'Connor, Anthony Call
in "The Frequency"**   **141**

ASTOR PLACE THEATRE
Opened Wednesday, April 12, 1978.*
Honey Waldman presents:

FAMILY BUSINESS

By Dick Goldbert; Director, John Stix; Scenery, Done Jensen; Lighting, Todd Elmer; Hairstylist, Michael Holland; Production Assistant, Marybeth Mann

CAST

Isaiah Stein	Harold Gary
Jerry Stein	Joel Polis †1
Norman Stein	David Garfield †2
Bobby Stein	Richard Greene
Phil Stein	David Rosenbaum
Young Man	Richard Levine †3

A drama in three acts. The action takes place in late autumn of 1974 in the main room of Isaiah Stein's home in Beverly, Mass.

General Manager: Lily Turner
Press: Betty Lee Hunt, Maria Cristina Pucci
Stage Manager: Richard Delahanty

* Moved May 29, 1979 to Roundabout Stage One, and closed there June 24, 1979 after a total of 470 performances. For original production, see THEATRE WORLD, Vol. 34.
† Succeeded by: 1. Charlie M. Adler, John Guerrasio, 2. David Kagen, 3. Albert Neal

Richard Greene, David Rosenbaum, Harold Gary
Top Right: Harold Gary, Joel Polis, David Garfield

SULLIVAN STREET PLAYHOUSE
Opened Tuesday, May 3, 1960.*
Lore Noto presents:

THE FANTASTICKS

Book and Lyrics, Tom Jones; Suggested by Edmond Rostand's "Les Romanesques"; Music, Harvey Schmidt; Director, Word Baker; Original Musical Direction and Arrangements, Julian Stein; Designed by Ed Wittstein; Associate Producers, Sheldon Baron, Dorothy Olim, Robert Alan Gold; Assistant Producers, Bill Mills, Thad Noto; Production Assistant, John Krug; Original Cast Album by MGM Records

CAST

The Narrator	Douglas Clark †1
The Girl	Anne S. Kaye †2
The Boy	Jeff Knight †3
The Boy's Father	Lore Noto
The Girl's Father	Sy Travers †4
The Actor	Elliott Levine †5
The Man Who Dies	Robert Oliver
The Mute	Robert Crest †6
At the piano	Penna Rose †7
At the harp	Barbara Weiger †8

UNDERSTUDIES: Glenn Davish (Narraator/Boy), Kathryn Morath (Girl), Jack Schmidt (Boy's Father)

MUSICAL NUMBERS: Overture, Try to Remember, Much More, Metaphor, Never Say No, It Depends on What You Pay, Soon It's Gonna Rain, Rape Ballet, Happy Ending, This Plum Is Too Ripe, I Can See It, Plant a Radish, Round and Round, They Were You

A musical in two acts.

Press: Anthony Noto
Stage Managers; Kathy J. Faul, Robert R. Oliver

* Still playing May 31, 1979. For original production, see THEATRE WORLD, Vol. 16.
† Succeeded by: 1. Joseph Galiano, 2. Debbie McLeod, 3. Christopher Seppe, 4. Jack Schmidt, 5. Robert Molnar, 6. Glenn Davish, 7. J. Anthony Strong, 8. Andre C. Tarantiles

Van Williams Photos

Cast of "The Fantasticks"
(Ralph Lewin Photo)

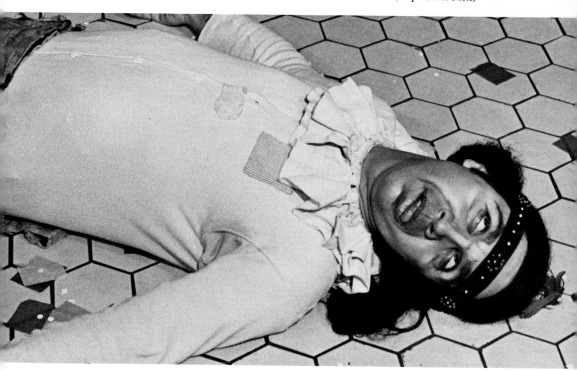

Robert Oliver

CHERRY LANE THEATRE
Opened Wednesday, September 27, 1977.*
The Dracula Theatrical Company presents:

THE PASSION OF DRACULA

By Bob Hall, David Richmond; Based on novel by Bram Stoker; Director, Peter Bennett; Sets, Bob Hall, Allen Cornell; Costumes, Jane Tschetter; Lighting and Special Effects, Allen Cornell, Frank Wolff; Executive Producer, Eric Krebs; Assistant to Producers, David Cleaver; Wardrobe, Gayle Palmieri; Vampire Consultant, Dr. Steven Kaplan; Production Assistant, Georganne Rogers

CAST

Jameson	Brian Bell †1
Dr. Cedric Seward	K. Lype O'Dell †2
Prof. Van Helsing	Michael Burg †3
Dr. Helga Van Zandt	Alice White †4
Lord Gordon Godalming	K. C. Wilson
Mr. Renfield	Elliott Vileen †5
Wilhelmina Murray	Gielia Pagano †6
Jonathan Harker	Samuel Maupin †7
Count Dracula	Christopher Bernau †8

UNDERSTUDIES: K. C. Wilson (Van Helsing), Mitchell Steven Tebo (Dracula/Godalming/Harker/ Seward), Paul Falzone (Renfield/Jameson), Maggie Hawthorne (Helga/Wilhelmina)

A "Gothic Entertainment" in three acts. The action takes place in England during the autumn of 1911 in the study of Dr. Seward's home.

General Manager: Linda Canavan
Press: Jeffrey Richards, Warren Knowlton
Stage Managers: Steven W. Login, Maggie Hawthorne, Paul Falzone

* Closed July 22, 1979 after 718 performances. For original production, see THEATRE WORLD Vol. 34.
† Succeeded by: 1. Martin LaPlatney, Alexander Woolff, Mitchell Steven Tebo, 2. Victor Raider-Wexler, Steve Meyer, Paul Meacham, 3. Stefan Schnabel, Andy Backer, 4. Karen Savage, Miss White returned, 5. Robert Schenkkan, Brian Kale, Paul Falzone, 6. Ann Twomey, Teresa Link, 7. Neal Mandell, Jim Stubbs, Barrett Nolan, 8. William Lyman, David Combs

Gerry Goodstein Photos

David Combs, Teresa Link
Top Left: Jim Stubbs, Teresa Link

CHELSEA WESTSIDE THEATER
Opened Monday, March 22, 1976.*
The Chelsea Theater Center presents the Lion Theatre Company/Playwrights Horizons production of:

VANITIES

By Jack Heifner; Director, Garland Wright; Scenery, John Arnone; Lighting, Patrika Brown; Costumes, David James; Wardrobe Mistress, Gertrude Sloan

CAST

Kathy	Jane Galloway †1
Mary	Susan Merson †2
Joanne	Kathy Bates †3

A comedy in three acts. The action takes place in 1963 in a gymnasium, in 1968 in a sorority house, and 1974 in the garden of an apartment.

Press: Betty Lee Hunt, Maria Cristina Pucci, Fred Hoot
Stage Manager: Dan Early

* Closed May 27, 1979 after 1313 performances. Re-opened Tuesday, June 19, 1979. For original production, see THEATRE WORLD. Vol. 32.
† Succeeded by: 1. Cordis Heard, Jane Dentinger, 2. Monica Merryman, Patricia Miller, 3. Sally Sockwell

Roger Greenawalt Photos

**Sally Sockwell, Jane Dentinger, Patricia Miller
Top: Jane Galloway, Sally Sockwell, Susan Merson**

OFF-BROADWAY PRODUCTIONS FROM PAST SEASONS THAT CLOSED THIS SEASON

Title	Opened	Closed	Performances
The Biko Inquest	5/17/78	6/11/78	37
Catsplay	5/30/78	7/16/78	53
5th of July	4/27/78	10/1/78	168
A Life in the Theatre	10/20/77	7/9/78	288
The Neon Woman	4/16/78	7/16/78	92
P.S. Your Cat Is Dead!	3/22/78	12/10/78	356
The Show-Off	4/25/78	7/16/78	104
Waiting for Godot	5/25/78	6/18/78	30

AIN'T MISBEHAVIN'

Based on an idea by Murray Horwitz and Richard Maltby, Jr.; Music of Fats Waller; Conceived and Directed by Richard Maltby, Jr.; Musical Numbers Staged by Arthur Faria; Music Supervision, Luther Henderson; Conductor and Pianist, J. Leonard Oxley; Associate Director, Murray Horwitz; Orchestrations and Arrangements, Luther Henderson; Musical Direction and Vocal Arrangements, William Elliott; Sets, John Lee Beatty; Costumes, Randy Barcelo; Lighting, Pat Collins; Presented by Emanual Azenberg, Dasha Epstein, The Shubert Organization (Gerald Schoenfeld, Chairman; Bernard B. Jacobs, President), Jane Gaynor and Ron Dante; General Managers, John M. Kirby, Jose Vega; Company Manager, Stephanie S. Hughley; Stage Managers, Clint Spencer, Scott Faris; Assistant Company Manager, Young T. Hughley, Jr.; Music Coordinator, Earl Shendell; Technical Coordinator, Arthur Siccardi; Press, Bill Evans, Patt Dale

CAST

Teresa Bowers
Yvette Freeman
Ben Harney
Adriane Lenox
Ken Prymus

STANDBYS: Debra Byrd, Denise Rogers, Tim Parker, Anthony White. For musical numbers, see Broadway Calendar, page 53.

Teresa Bowers, Ken Prymus, Adriane Lenox, Ben Harney, Yvette Freeman, J. Leonard Oxley

ANNIE

Book, Thomas Meehan; Based on "Little Orphan Annie" comic strip; Music, Charles Strouse; Lyrics, Martin Charnin; Director, Mr. Charnin; Choreography, Peter Gennaro; Sets, David Mitchell; Costumes, Theoni V. Aldredge; Lighting, Judy Rasmuson; Musical Direction, Glen Clugston; Dance Arrangements, Peter Howard; Orchestrations, Philip J. Lang; Production Supervisor, Janet Beroza; Assistant Conductor, Steve Hinnenkamp; Wardrobe, Linda Lee; Production Assistants, Mark Miller, Kathy Meehan; General Management, Gatchell & Neufeld; Hairstylists, Charles LaFrance, Ed de Orienzo; Producers, Irwin Meyer, Stephen R. Friedman, Lewis Allen, Peter Crane, Alvin Nederlander Associates, JFK Center for Performing Arts, Icarus Productions; Presented by Mike Nichols; Company Manager, Mark Andrews; Stage Managers, Martha Knight, Bethe Ward, B. J. Allen, Moose Peting; Press, David Powers, Barbara Carroll, Kevin Carroll O'Connor; Opened Thursday, March 23, 1979 at O'Keefe Center, Toronto, Canada, and still touring May 31, 1979.

CAST

Annie	Kathy-Jo Kelly
Oliver Warbucks	Norwood Smith
Miss Hannigan	Ruth Kobart
Grace Farrell	Kathryn Boulet†1
Rooster Hannigan	Gary Beach
FDR	Sam Stoneburner
Lily	Lisa Raggio
July	Dara Brown
Tessie	April Lerman
Pepper	Shelle Monahan
Duffy	Alyson Mord
Kate	Dana Tapper
Molly	Kristin Williams
Sandy	Himself
Bundles McCloskey/Ickes	Gordon Stanley
Dog Catcher/Bert Healy/Hull	Michael Shaw†2
Dog Catcher/Jimmy Johnson/Guard	Edmond Dante
Lt. Ward/Justice Brandeis	Charles Cagle
Sophie/Cecile/Ronnie Boylan	Linda Rios
Drake	Tom Avera†3
Mrs. Pugh/Connie Boylan	Linda Lauter
Mrs. Greer/Page/Perkins	Lynn Kearney
Annette/Bonnie Boylan	Penny Carroll
Fred McCracken/Howe	Michael Connolly

Alternates: Richard Flanders†4, Mimi Wallace

For musical numbers, see Broadway Calendar, page 54.

† Succeeded by: 1. Jan Pessano, 2. Stephen Everett, 3. John Anania, 4. G. Wayne Hoffman

Martha Swope Photos

Kathy-Jo Kelly, Sandy, Norwood Smith

Left Center: Lisa Raggio, Ruth Kobart, Gary Beach *(Ray Fisher Photo)*

ANNIE

Book, Thomas Meehan; Music, Charles Strouse; Lyrics, Martin Charnin; Based on "Little Orphan Annie" comic strip; Presented by Mike Nichols; Producers, Irwin Meyer, Stephen R. Friedman, Lewis Allen; Director, Martin Charnin; Choreography, Peter Gennaro; Settings, David Mitchell; Costumes, Theoni V. Aldredge; Lighting, Judy Rasmuson; Musical Direction, Milton Greene; Dance Arrangements, Peter Howard; Orchestrations, Philip J. Long; Production Supervisor, Janet Beroza; Produced by Alvin Nederlander Associates, JFK Center for Performing Arts, Icarus Productions, in association with Peter Crane; Stage Managers, Elizabeth Caldwell, Bryan Young, Ron Cummins, Lynda N. Lavin; Company Managers, John Corkill, Maria Anderson; Assistant to Director, Janice Steele; Associate Conductor, Arthur Greene; Wardrobe, Adelaide Laurino, Robert Daily; Hairstylists, Ted Azar, Jack Mei Ling, Lily Pon; General Management, Gatchell & Neufeld; Assistant Choreographer, Mary Jane Houdina; Press, David A. Powers, Kevin Carroll O'Connor, Barbara Carroll; Opened at the Curran Theatre, San Francisco, Ca., Thursday, June 22, 1978, and still touring May 31, 1979.

CAST

Molly	Michele De Cuir
Pepper	Jenny Cihi
Duffy	Paula Benedetti
July	Lori Kickliter
Tessie	Kristan Sauter
Kate	Molly Ringwald
Annie	Patricia Ann Patts
Miss Hannigan	Jane Connell
Bundles McCloskey/Ickes/ Sound Effects Man	David Green
Dog Catcher/Fred McCracken/Honor Guard	Chuck Bergman
Dog Catcher/Bert Healy/Hull	Frank O'Brien
Sandy	Himself
Lt. Ward/Morganthau/Brandeis	John J. Fox
Sophie/Mrs. Pugh/WEAF Producer/Perkins	Toni Lamond
Grace Farrell	Kathryn Boule
Drake	Jack Collins
Mrs. Greer/Connie Boylan	Lisa Robinson
Cecille/Star to Be/Bonnie Boylan	Carol Secretan
Annette/Ronnie Boylan	Frances Asher
Oliver Warbucks	Keene Curtis
Rooster Hannigan	Swen Swenson
Lily	Connie Danese
Jimmy Johnson/Howe	Walter Niehenke
FDR	Tom Hatten

Alternates: Barbara Brummel, Jon Rider, Ron Cummins

UNDERSTUDIES: Jack Collins (Warbucks), Toni Lamond (Miss Hannigan), Lisa Robinson (Grace), Frank O'Brien (Rooster), Michele Graham (Pepper/Duffy/July/Tessie/Kate), David Green (FDR), Frances Asher (Lily), Walter Niehenke (Healy), Buttercup (Sandy) For musical numbers, see Broadway Calendar, page 54.

Jay Thompson Photos

Right Center: Kristan Sauter, Molly Ringwald, Michele DeCuir, Patricia Ann Patts, Paula Benedetti, Jenny Cihi, Lori Kickliter Top: Keene Curtis, Dan, Patricia Ann Patts

Dara Brown, Kristin Williams, Alyson Mord, Dana Tapper, April Lerman, Shelle Monahan

Connie Danese, Swen Swenson, Jane Connell

CALIFORNIA SUITE

A comedy by Neil Simon; Director, Jerry Adler; Scenery, William Ritman; Costumes, Jane Greenwood; Lighting, Tharon Musser; Presented by Tom Mallow in association with James Janek; Production Associates, Jerry R. Moore, Richard Martini; Production Supervisor, Jack Welles; Company Manager, Donald Joslyn; Stage Managers, Ric Barrett, Aurelia DeFelice; Props, James Wearne; Wardrobe, Donna Peck; Hairdresser, Coral Carlson; Production Assistant, David Kerley; Tour Direction, American Theatre Productions; Opened Thursday, Aug. 31, 1978 in Norfolk, Va., and closed Dec. 3, 1978 in Memphis, Tn. For Original Broadway production, see THEATRE WORLD, Vol. 33.

CAST

"Visitor from New York"
Hannah Warren .... Carolyn Jones
William Warren .... James Drury
"Visitors from London"
Sidney Nichols......................... Peter Bailey-Britton
Diana Nichols .... Carolyn Jones
"Visitors from Philadelphia"
Marvin Michaels........................... James Drury
Bunny.................................. Aurelia DeFelice
Millie Michaels .... Carolyn Jones

Understudies: George Emch, Aurelia DeFelice

Martha Swope Photos

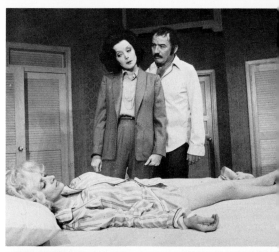

Peter Bailey-Britton, Carolyn Jones
Top: Aurelia DeFelice, Carolyn Jones,
James Drury

CHAPTER TWO

By Neil Simon; Original Direction, Herbert Ross; Restaged by Martin Herzer; Scenery, William Ritman; Costumes, Noel Taylor; Lighting, Tharon Musser; Presented by Emanuel Azenberg; General Manager, Jose Vega; Company Manager, L. Liberatore; Stage Managers, Jake Hamilton, Jon R. Hand; Wardrobe, Mary Beth Regan; Assistant to Producer, Leslie Butler; Production Assistant, Jane Robison; Press, Bill Evans, Claudia McAllister, Harry Davies. Opened Wednesday, December 27, 1978 in Symphony Hall, Atlanta, Ga., and still touring May 31, 1979. For original NY production, see THEATRE WORLD, Vol. 34.

CAST

George Schneider .... Jerry Orbach
Leo Schneider .... Herbert Edelman
Jennie Malone........................... Marilyn Redfield
Faye Medwick........................... Jane A. Johnston

Standbys: James Doerr, Elaine Cancilla

A comedy in two acts. The action takes place at the present time in Jennifer's apartment, and in George's apartment in New York City.

Charles Rafshoon, Martha Swope Photos

Marilyn Redfield, Jerry Orbach

Left Center: Jane A. Johnston, Herbert Edelman

A CHORUS LINE

Conceived, Directed and Choreographed by Michael Bennett; Book, James Kirkwood, Nicholas Dante; Music, Marvin Hamlisch; Lyrics, Edward Kleban; Set, Robin Wagner; Costumes, Theoni V. Aldredge; Lighting, Tharon Musser; Sound, Abe Jacob; Co-Choreographer, Bob Avian; Musical Direction, Tom Hancock; Music Coordinator, Robert Thomas; Associate Conductor, Nicholas Archer, Jr.; General Managers, Emanuel Azenberg, Robert Kamlot; Company Manager, Lilli Afan; Press, Merle Debuskey, Margie Korshak; Stage Managers, Jeff Hamlin, Tom Porter, Martin Gold, Carlos Gorbea; Opened Tuesday, May 11, 1975 at the Curran Theatre, San Francisco, Ca., and still touring May 31, 1979. For original NY production, see THEATRE WORLD, Vol.31.

CAST

Kristine	Cookie Vasquez
Val	Lois Englund
Roy	Noel Craig
Mark	James Beaumont
Maggie	Christina Saffron
Mike	William Mead
Richie	Larry G. Bailey
Judy	Victoria Garland
Greg	Andy Keyser
Don	Dennis Edenfield
Bebe	Rise Clemmer
Connie	Sachi Shimizu
Diana	Chris Bocchino
Zach	Anthony S. Teague
Cassie	Wanda Richert
Vicki	Denise Direnzo
Bobby	Michael Austin
Al	Jack Karcher
Sheila	Sally Benoit
Larry	Keith Keen
Butch	Dennis Birchall
Tom	Michael Lane
Frank	Jack Magradey
Paul	Stephen Crenshaw
Lois	Tina Paul
Tricia	Laura Klein

MUSICAL NUMBERS: see Broadway Calendar, page 57.

Martha Swope Photos

Deborah Henry, Scott Pearson

A CHORUS LINE

Conceived, Directed and Choreographed by Michael Bennett; Book, James Kirkwood, Nicholas Dante; Music, Marvin Hamlisch; Lyrics, Edward Kleban; Set, Robin Wagner; Costumes, Theoni V. Aldredge; Lighting, Tharon Musser; Sound, Abe Jacob; Co-Choreographer, Bob Avian; Musical Direction, Sherman Frank; Associate Producer, Bernard Gersten; Production Supervisor, Jason Steven Cohen; Assistant Conductor, Tony Geralis; Presented by Joseph Papp and the New York Shakespeare Festival in association with Plum Productions; General Managers, Jeff Hamlin, Frank Hartenstein, Kate M. Pollock, Scott Faris. Opened Monday, May 3, 1976 at the Royal Alexandra Theatre, Toronto, Can., and still touring May 31, 1979. For original NY production, see THEATRE WORLD, Vol. 31.

CAST

Paul	Guillermo Gonzalez
Jarad	Michael Austin
Kristine	P. J. Mann
Al	Frank Hooper
Vicki	Niki Harris
Tom	Steve Belin
Maggie	Betty Lynd
Frank	Robert Warner
Val	Patti Colombo
Zach	Buddy Vest
Mike	C. J. McCaffrey
Diana	Diane Fratantoni
Louis	Anthony Inneo
Greg	Larry Blum
Bobby	Ronald Stafford
Connie	Cherylene Lee
Lois	Bebe Neuwirth
Judy	Shanna Reed
Richie	Millard Hurley
Barbara	Michelle Stubbs
Larry	John Fogarty
Butch	Eric Riley
Cassie	Deborah Henry
Mark	Scott Geralds
Roy	Scott Faris
Sheila	Judy Burns
Bebe	Teresa Rossomando
Tricia	Janie Gleason
Don	Barry Thomas
Rosemary	Gail Mae Ferguson
Claude	Gary Sullivan
Doug	Sam Viverito

MUSICAL NUMBERS: see Broadway Calendar, page 57.

Martha Swope Photos

DANCIN'

A Musical Entertainment Conceived, Directed and Choreographed by Bob Fosse; Production Supervisor, Gwen Verdon; Choreography Recreated by Kathryn Doby and Christopher Chadman; Scenery, Peter Larkin; Costumes, Willa Kim; Lighting/Executive Producer, Jules Fisher; Orchestrations, Ralph Burns; Music Arranged and Conducted by Gordon Lowry Harrell; Sound, Abe Jacob; Hairstylist, Romaine Greene; Presented by Jules Fisher, The Shubert Organization (Gerald Schoenfeld, Chairman; Bernard B. Jacobs, President), and Columbia Pictures; General Manager, Marvin A. Krauss; Company Manager, Steven E. Goldstein; Wardrobe, Robert Strong Miller, Colleen Gieryn; Assistant Conductor, Don Rebic; Production Assistants, Vicki Stein, Robin Ullman, Steve Fahey; Stage Managers, Phil Friedman, Charles Collins, Karen De Francis; Press, Merle Debuskey, William Schelble, Margie Korshak. Opened Thursday, April 19, 1979 at the Shubert Theatre in Chicago, Il., and still playing May 31, 1979.

CAST

Hinton Battle, Sandahl Bergman, Stuart Carey, Gary Chapman, Anita Ehrler, Gary Flannery, Vicki Frederick, Bick Goss, Keith Keen, Frank Mastrocola, Valerie-Jean Miller, Cynthia Onrubia, Valarie Pettiford, Timothy Scott, Charles Ward, Allison Williams, Barbara Yeager

For musical numbers, see Broadway Calendar, page 59.

Martha Swope Photos

**Charles Ward (L) and company
Top: Timothy Scott, Hinton Battle,
Gary Flannery in "Dancin' "**

DEATHTRAP

By Ira Levin; Director, Robert Moore; Scenery, William Ritman; Costumes, Ruth Morley, Lighting, Marc B. Weiss; General Manager, C. Edwin Knill; Company Manager, Kim Sellon; Stage Managers, Murray Gitlin, Don Howard; Wardrobe, Frank Green; Presented by Alfred de Liagre, Jr. and Robert Stevens; Press, Jeffrey Richards, Gertrude Bromberg. Opened Monday, February 19, 1979 at the Lyric Theatre in Kansas City, Mo., and still touring May 31, 1979. For original Broadway production, see THEATRE WORLD, Volume 34.

CAST

Sidney Bruhl . . . . Brian Bedford
Myra Bruhl . . . . Betty Miller
Clifford Anderson . . . . Kevin Conroy
Helga ten Dorp . . . . Kathleen Freeman
Porter Milgrim . . . . George Ede

STANDBYS: William Kiehl (Sidney Bruhl), Marilyn Alex (Myra/Helga), Don Howard (Clifford Anderson)

A "comedy thriller" in two acts and six scenes. The action takes place at the present time in Sidney Bruhl's study in the Bruhl home in Westport, Connecticut.

Sy Friedman Photos

**Brian Bedford, Betty Miller, Kevin Conroy
Above: George Ede, Brian Bedford**

DRACULA

By Hamilton Deane and John L. Balderston from Bram Stoker's novel "Dracula"; Director, Dennis Rosa; Scenery and Costumes, Edward Gorey; Supervised by Lynn Pecktal, John David Ridge; Lighting, Roger Morgan; Presented by Jujamcyn Theaters, John Wulp, Elizabeth Ireland McCann, Nelle Nugent, Victor Lurie, Max Weitsenhoffer; Company Manager, Robert P. Bron; Stage Managers, Michael Maurer, John Weeks, Chaz Denny, Mary Dierson; Bat Handler, Dennis Randolph; Wardrobe, Byron Brice; Hairstylist, Tommy de Maio; Special Effects, Chic Silber; Assistant Director, Steven Deshler; Press, Solters & Roskin, Joshua Ellis, Milly Schoenbaum, Stan Brody. Opened Friday, May 19, 1978 at the Mechanic Theatre, Baltimore, Md., and still touring May 31, 1979.

CAST

Lucy Seward	Margaret Whitton
Miss Wells, a maid	Victoria Page
Jonathan Harker	Nick Stannard
Dr. Seward	Dalton Dearborn
Abraham Van Helsing	David Hurst
R. M. Renfield	John Long
Butterworth	Fritz Sperberg
Count Dracula	Raul Julia†

STANDBYS AND UNDERSTUDIES: Lee Corbett (Dracula), Mary Dierson (Lucy/Miss Wells), Chaz Denny (Harker/ Butterworth/Renfield), Fritz Sperberg (Harker)

A melodrama in 3 acts and 4 scenes. The action takes place in the 1920s in the library of Dr. Seward's sanatorium in Purley, England, in Lucy's boudoir, and in a vault.

† Succeeded by Jean LeClerc, Jeremy Brett. For original production, see THEATRE WORLD, Vol. 34

Kenn Duncan Photos

**Right Center: Jeremy Brett, Margaret Whitton
Top: Jeremy Brett, Margaret Whitton, Nick Stannard**

THE GIN GAME

The 1978 Pulitzer Prize Play by D. L. Coburn; Director, Mike Nichols; Setting, David Mitchell; Costumes, Bill Walker; Lighting, Ronald Wallace; Production Supervisor, Nina Seely; Producers, Hume Cronyn, Mike Nichols; Co-Produced by Icarus Productions and The Cronyn Company; Presented by the Shubert Organization (Gerald Schoenfeld, Chairman; Bernard B. Jacobs, President); General Managers, McCann & Nugent; Company Manager, James Kimo Gerald; Press, David A. Powers, Maurice Turet, Barbara Carroll; Stage Manager, Peter B. Mumford. Opened Thursday, Oct. 5, 1978 at the Wilbur Theatre in Boston, Ma., and closed June 10, 1979 at the Blackstone Theatre in Chicago, Il.

CAST

Fonsia Dorsey	Jessica Tandy
Weller Martin	Hume Cronyn

A comedy in two acts and four scenes. The action takes place at the present time in a home for the elderly.

Martha Swope Photo

Hume Cronyn, Jessica Tandy

GREASE

Book, Music and Lyrics, Jim Jacobs, Warren Casey; Director, Tom Moore; Musical Numbers and Dances Staged by Patricia Birch; Scenery, Douglas W. Schmidt; Costumes, Carrie F. Robbins; Associate Director, Michael Martorella; Assistant Choreographer, Kathi Moss; Musical Direction, Elizabeth Myers; Orchestrations, Michael Leonard; Vocal and Dance Arrangements, Louis St. Louis; General Management, Theatre Now, Inc.; Presented by Kenneth Waissman and Maxine Fox; Opened Oct. 10, 1976 at the Shubert Theatre in Boston, Ma., and still touring May 31, 1979; For original New York production, see THEATRE WORLD, Vol. 28

CAST

Miss Lynch	Dorothy Leon
Patty Simcox	Ann-Ngaire Martin
Eugene Florczyk	Tom Harris
Jan	Patricia Douglas
Marty	Linda Lyons
Betty Rizzo	Lisa Orberg
Doody	Al Flannagan
Roger	Randy Stumpf
Kenickie	Terry Michos
Sonny LaTierri	Jim Shankman
Frenchy	Laurie Graff
Sandy Dumbrowski	Mary Murray
Danny Zuko	Rex Smith
Vince Fontaine	Steve Groff
Johnny Casino/Teen Angel	Joe Rifici
Cha-Cha DiGregorio	Sherry Berman

UNDERSTUDIES: Lesley Berry, Jane Portela, Robert Reynolds, Paul Greeno

For musical numbers, see Broadway Calendar, page 63.

**Eddie Bracken, Carol Channing
in "Hello, Dolly!"**

HELLO, DOLLY!

Book, Michael Stewart; Music and Lyrics, Jerry Herman; Based on play by Thorton Wilder, "The Matchmaker"; Director, Lucia Victor; Choreographer, Ron Crofoot; Conductor, Jack Everly; Settings, Oliver Smith; Lighting, Martin Aronstein; Musical Director, John L. DeMain; Production Supervisor, Jerry Herman; Stage Managers, Pat Tolson, T. L. Boston; General Management, Jack Schlissel/Jay Kingwill; Press, Solters & Roskin, Milly Schoenbaum; Presented by James Nederlander in conjunction with Charles Lowe Productions; Opened Wednesday, April 4, 1979 at the Opera House Theatre in Reno, Nevada, and closed there June 3, 1979.

CAST

Dolly Gallagher Levi	Carol Channing
Horace Vandergelder	Eddie Bracken
Cornelius Hackl	Lee Roy Reams
Mrs. Molloy	Florence Lacy
Barnaby Tucker	Leonard John Crofoot
Minnie Fay	K. T. Baumann
Ermengarde	Ruth Berber
Rudolph	Robert L. Hultman
Ambrose	Bill Bateman
Ernestina	P. J. Nelson

MUSICAL NUMBERS: I Put My Hand In, It Takes a Woman, Put on Your Sunday Clothes, Ribbons Down My Back, Motherhood, Dancing, Before the Parade Passes By, Elegance, The Waiters' Gallop, Hello Dolly!, Polka Contest, It Only Takes a Moment, So Long Dearie, Finale

A musical comedy in 2 acts and 13 scenes. The action takes places in Yonkers and Manhattan in the past.

For original production, see THEATRE WORLD, Vol. 20.

MAN OF LA MANCHA

By Dale Wasserman; Music, Mitch Leigh; Lyrics, Joe Darion; Production and Musical Staging, Albert Marre; Setting and Lighting, Howard Bay; Costumes, Howard Bay, Patton Campbell; Musical Director, Lawrence Brown; General Manager, Charles A. Eisler; Stage Managers, Kay Vance, Michael Sinclair, Laura deBuys; Wardrobe, Joan Eaton; Hairstylist, J. Alexander Scafa; Tour Management, Manny Kladitis; Presented by Eugene V. Wolsk; Press, John A. Prescott. Opened Thursday, Aug. 3, 1978, at the Music Hall in Boston, Ma., and still touring May 31, 1979. For original NY production, see THEATRE WORLD, Vol. 22.

CAST

Don Quixote (Cervantes)	Richard Kiley
Sancho	Tony Martinez
The Horse/Tenorio a Muleteer	Ben Vargas
The Mule/Jose a Muleteer	Hector Mercado
The Innkeeper	Bob Wright
Maria, the innkeeper's wife	Carolyn Friday
Pedro Head Muleteer	Dan Hannafin
Anselmo, a Muleteer/Barber	Ted Forlow
Juan a Muleteer	Mark Holliday
Paco a Muleteer	Anthony DeVecchi
Aldonza	Susan Waldman
Fermina/Moorish Dancer	Jane Seaman
Guitarist	Robert Ferry
Jorge a Muleteer	Edmond Varrato
Fernando a Muleteer/Guard	Sal Provenza
Antonia	Frances Roth
Housekeeper	Marceline Decker
Padre	David Wasson
Dr. Carrasco	Ian Sullivan
Captain	Renato Cibelli
Guard	Michael St. Paul

MUSICAL NUMBERS: Man of La Mancha, It's All the Same, Dulcinea, I'm Only Thinking of Him, I Really Like Him, What Does He Want of Me, Little Bird, Barber's Song, Golden Helmet of Mambrino, To Each His Dulcinea, The Quest, The Combat, The Dubbing, The Abduction, Moorish Dance, Aldonza, The Knight of the Mirrors, A Little Gossip, The Psalm.

A play performed without intermission; suggested by the life and works of Miguel de Cervantes y Saavedra.

Richard Kiley, Tony Martinez in "Man of La Mancha"

KC Kizziah, Susanne Egli in "Hamlet" Right Center: Mary Agen Cox, Ted Holland in "A Midsummer Night's Dream"

NATIONAL SHAKESPEARE COMPANY
Sixteenth Year

Artistic Director-Producer, Philip Meister; General Manager, Deborah Teller; Tour Director, Michael Hirsch; Scenic and Lighting Design, Terry Bennett; Scenic Artist, Sarah Oliphant; Costumes, Linda Carpenter, Carol Daly; Technical Director, Christopher Wells; Fencing Master, J. Eiche; Company Manager, KC Kizziah; Stage Managers, KC Kizziah, Rodney W. Clark; Music Director, Marc Falcone. Opened Oct. 3. 1978 in Machia, Me., and closed May 13, 1979 in Amherst, Ma.

COMPANY

Julian Bailey, Rodney W. Clark, Mary Agen Cox, Susanne Egli, J. Eiche, Charles Fontana, Ted Holland, KC Kizziah, Carole McGee, Jerry Peters, Harpo Root, Christopher Wells

PRODUCTIONS: "Hamlet" directed by Mario Siletti, and "A Midsummer Night's Dream" directed by Philip Meister

SUGAR BABIES

Conceived by Ralph G. Allen and Harry Rigby; Sketches by Ralph G. Allen based on traditional material; Music, Jimmy McHugh; Lyrics, Dorothy Fields, Harold Adamson, Al Dubin; Additional Music and Lyrics, Arthur Malvin; Presented by Terry Allen Kramer and Harry Rigby in association with Columbia Pictures; Associate Producer, Jack Schlissel; Staged and Choreographed by Ernest Flatt, Sketches Directed by Rudy Tronto; Entire Production Supervised by Ernest Flatt, Scenery and Costumes, Raoul Pene DuBois; Lighting, Gilbert V. Hemsley, Jr.; Vocal Arrangements, Arthur Malvin; Musical Director, Glen Roven; Orchestrations, Dick Hyman; Dance Music Arrangements, Arnold Gross; Associate Producers, Thomas Walton Associates, Frank Montalvo; Hairstylist, Joseph Dal Corso; General Management, Jack Schlissel/Jay Kingwill; Company Manager, Alan Wasser; Stage Managers, Christopher Kelly, Bob Burland, Jay B. Jacobson, David Campbell; Wardrobe, Peta E. Ullmann, Irene Ferrari; Press, Henry Luhrman, Bill Miller, Terry M. Lilly, Kevin P. McAnarney. Opened Tuesday, May 8, 1979 at Curran Theatre in San Francisco, and still touring May 31, 1979.

CAST

Mickey Rooney, Ann Miller, Scot Stewart, Ann Jillian, Tom Boyd, Peter Leeds, Jack Fletcher, Jimmy Mathews, Sis Stone, Bob Williams, Chris Elia, Laura Booth, Barbara Hanks, Robin Manus, Barbara Mandra, Diane Duncan, Rose Scudder, Christine Busini, Debbie Gornay, Jeri Kansas, Linda Ravinsky, Michele Rogers, Patti Watson, Faye Fujisaki Mar, Jonathan Aronson, Eddie Pruett, Jeff Veazey, Michael Radigan.

UNDERSTUDIES: Tom Boyd (Mickey Rooney), Rose Scudder (Ann Miller), Diane Duncan (Ann Jillian), Michael Radigan (Scot Stewart), Hank Brunjes (Tom Boyd), Tom Boyd (Leed/Fletcher/Mathews/Stone), Swing Dancers: Hank Brunjes, Laurie Sloan

A burlesque musical in 2 acts and 30 scenes.

Mickey Rooney, Ann Miller
(also above and top)

Top: Ann Jillian, Mickey Rooney

154

TIMBUKTU!

Music and Lyrics, Robert Wright, George Forrest; From the themes of Alexander Borodin and African Folk Music; Book, Luther Davis; Based on musical "Kismet" by Charles Lederer and Luther Davis, and the play by Edward Knoblock; Directed, Choreographed and Costumed by Geoffrey Holder; Musical Direction, Supervision, Arrangements and Incidental Music, Charles H. Coleman; Scenery, Tony Straiges; Lighting, Ian Calderon; Sound, Abe Jacob; Additional Orchestrations, Bill Brohn; Produced in association with Sarnoff International Enterprises, William D. Cunningham, and JFK Center for Performing Arts; Presented by James M. Nederlander, David Smerling and Julian Colby in association with Luther Davis; General Management, Gatchell & Neufeld; Associate Producer, Alan Eichler; Company Manager, Drew Murphy; Stage Managers, Peter Lawrence, James Woolley; Hairstylist and Makeup, Michael Smith; Sound, Larry Spurgeon; Assistant Musical Director, John Cartwright; Technical Director, Arthur Siccardi; Wardrobe, Frank Green, Judith Giles; Press, Solters & Roskin, Joshua Ellis, Lisa Kasteler, Jasper Vance, Sophronia McBride-Pope, David LeShay. Opened Wednesday, Sept. 20. 1978 at the Fisher Theatre in Detroit, Mi., and closed Feb. 4, 1979 at the Pantages Theatre in Los Angeles, Ca.

CAST

The Chakaba (Stiltwalker)/Witchdoctor/Orange Merchant/Antelope	Luther Fontaine
Beggar/Woman in Garden	Elaine Beener
Beggar	Donald H. Coleman
Hadji	Gregg Baker
Marsinah, daughter of Hadhi	Vanessa Shaw
Child	Deborah Waller
M'Ballah of the River	Daniel Barton
Najua/Bird of Paradise	Dyane Harvey
The Wazir	George Bell
Chief Policeman	Ronald A. Richardson
Strongman	Tony Carroll
Sahleem-La-Lume, Wazir's wife of wives	Eartha Kitt
Princesses of Baguezane	Deborah K. Brown, Lynda Karen, Patricia Lumpkin
Munshi, servant to the Mansa	Homer Bryant
The Mansa of Mali	Bruce A. Hubbard
Antelope	William McPherson
Zubbediya	Priscilla Baskerville

CITIZENS OF TIMBUKTU: Daniel Barton, Priscilla Baskerville, Elaine Beener, Deborah K. Brown, Tony Carroll, Donald H. Coleman, Cheryl Cummings, Christopher Dean, Luther Fontaine, Michael F. Harrison, Jan Hazell, Lynda Karen, Patricia Lumpkin, Joe Lynn, William McPherson, Gwen Moten, Tony Ndogo, Autris Paige, Ray Pollard, Martial Roumain, Gayle P. Samuels, Deborah Waller, Chet Washington, Swing Couple: Leah Bass, Charles E. Grant

MUSICAL NUMBERS: Rhymes Have I, Fate, In the Beginning Woman, Baubles Bangles and Beads, Stranger in Paradise, Gesticulate, Night of My Nights, My Magic Lamp, Rahadlakum, and This Is My Beloved, Golden Land Golden Life, Zubbediya, Sands of Time.

A musical in two acts and twelve scenes. The action takes place during the year 1361 (of Islam 752) in Timbuktu, in the ancient Empire of Mali, West Africa.
For original Broadway production, see THEATRE WORLD, Vol. 34.

Bruce A. Hubbard, George Bell, Gregg Baker, Vanessa Shaw Top Right: Shaw, Baker, Eartha Kitt

Tony Carroll, Eartha Kitt Above: Bruce A. Hubbard, Vanessa Shaw

Garry Q. Lewis (Scarecrow), Bobby Hill (Lion), Deborah Malone, Jai Oscar St. John (Tinman)

THE WIZ

Book, William F. Brown; Music and Lyrics, Charlie Smalls; Suggested by "The Wonderful Wizard of Oz" by L. Frank Baum; Director, Geoffrey Holder; Choreography, and Musical Numbers, George Faison; Settings. Peter Wolf, Costumes, Geoffrey Holder; Lighting, Tharon Musser; Orchestrations, Harold Wheeler; Vocal Arrangements, Charles H. Coleman; Dance Arrangements, Timothy Graphenreed; Musical Direction Joel Alan Levine; Presented by Tom Mallow in association with James Janek; Production Associates, Jerry R. Moore, Richard Martini; Company Manager, Sheila R. Phillips; Stage Manager, J. S. McKie, Jr., Luis Montero, Randy Flood; Wardrobe, Linda Berry, Frederick Lloyd; Props, Arthur Evans; Sound, Kit Bond; Assistant Director, Donald Christy; Production Assistant, David Kerley; Press, Barbara Glenn, Opened June 23, 1978 in Wilmington, Del. and closed July 1, 1979 in Portland, Or. For original NY production, see THEATRE WORLD, Vol 31.

CAST

Aunt Em	Juanita Fleming
Toto	Toto
Dorothy	Deborah Malone†
Uncle Henry	Randy Flood
Tornado	Leah Randolph
Munchkins	Stanley Ramsey, Harold Johnson, Venida Evans, Sharon K. Brooks, Tenita L. Jordan
Addaperle	John-Ann Washington
Yellow Brick Road	Germaine Edwards, David Robertson, Ron Blanco, Eddie Jordan
Scarecrow	Garry Q. Lewis
Crows	Sheri Moore, Carla Earle, Allison Renee Manson
Tinman	Jai Oscar St. John
Lion	Bobby Hill
Stranger	Randy Flood
Kalidahs	Carla Earle, Sheri Moore, Stanley Ramsey, Harold Johnson, Michael Sampson, Keith Simmons
Poppies	Allison Renee Manson, Sharon K. Brooks, Joy Goodson, Leah Randolph
Field Mice	Venida Evans, Tenita L. Jordan, Eartha D. Robinson
Royal Gatekeeper	Randy Flood
The Wiz	Charles Douglass
Evillene	Gwendolyn J. Shepherd
Lord High Underling	Randy Flood
Soldier Messenger	Harold Johnson
Winged Monkey	Germaine Edwards
Glinda	Juanita Fleming

Emerald City Citizens: Michael Sampson, Ron Blanco, Germaine Edwards, David Robertson, Eddie Jordan, Keith Simmons, Allison Renee Manson, Joy Goodson, Sharon K. Brooks, Carla Earle, Sheri Moore, Leah Randolph, Tenita L. Jordan

MUSICAL NUMBERS: The Feeling We Once Had, Tornado Ballet, He's the Wizard, Soon as I Get Home, I Was Born on the Day before Yesterday, Ease on Down the Road, Slide Some Oil to Me, Mean Ole Lion, Kalidah Battle, Be a Lion, Lion's Dream, Emerald City Ballet, So You Wanted to Meet the Wizard, What Would I Do If I Could Feel, No Bad News, Funky Monkeys, Everybody Rejoice, Who Do You Think You Are, If You Believe, Y'All Got It!, A Rested Body Is a Rested Mind, Home.

A musical comedy in 2 acts and 16 scenes.

† Succeeded by Lillias D. White

**Top Left: Eric Sawyer
Below: Deborah Malone (C)**

YOUR ARMS TOO SHORT TO BOX WITH GOD

Conceived from the Book of St. Matthew by Vinnette Carroll; Music and Lyrics, Alex Bradford; Additional Music and Lyrics, Micki Grant; Director, Vinette Carroll; Sets and Costumes, William Schroder; Lighting, Richard Winkler; Set Supervisor, Michael J. Hotopp; Orchestrations and Dance Music, H. B. Barnum; Musical Direction, Grenoldo Frazier; Choral Arrangements, Chapman Roberts; Choreography, Talley Beatty; General Manager, James Janek; Production Coordinators, Jerry R. Moore, Richard Martini; Press, Sandra Manley/Merlin Group; Company Manager, Ken Krezel; Stage Managers, Carleton Scott Alsop, Bardell Conner, Gregory Nicholas; Wardrobe, Donna Peck; Sound, Dave Hunt, Christopher Bond; Presented by Tom Mallow in association with James Janek /American Theatre Productions. Opened Friday, January 19, 1979 and still touring May 31, 1979. For original Broadway production, see THEATRE WORLD, Vol. 33.

CAST

Ida M. Broughton, Julius Richard Brown, Bardell Conner, Ralph Farrington, Gwendolyn Nelson Fleming, Thomas J. Fouse, Jr., Jamil K. Garland, Elijah Gill, L. Michael Gray, William-Keebler Hardy, Jr., Robert Earl Helms, Jennifer-Yvette Holliday, Jeannine Otis, Dwayne Phelps, Leonard Piggee, Leslie Hardesty Sisson, Allysia C. Sneed, Quincella Swyningan, Faruma S. Williams, Linda E. Young

MUSICAL NUMBERS

Beatitudes, We're Gonna Have a Good Time, There's a Stranger in Town, Do You Know Jesus/He's a Wonder, Just a Little Bit of Jesus Goes a Long Way, We Are the Priests and Elders, Something Is Wrong in Jerusalem, It Was Alone/I Know I Have to Leave Here, Be Careful Whom You Kiss, Trial, It's Too Late, Judas Dance, Your Arms Too Short to Box with God, Give Us Barrabas, See How They Done My Lord, Come on Down, Can't No Grave Hold My Body Down, Didn't I Tell You, When the Power Comes, Everbody Has His Own Way, Down by the Riverside, I Love You So Much Jesus, The Band

Martha Swope Photos

Elijah Gill, Quincella Swyningan, Gwendolyn Nelson Fleming Top: William-Keebler Hardy, Jr.

Top: Jennifer-Yvette Holliday

BACK COUNTRY

Book and Lyrics, Jaques Levy: Music, Stanley Walden; Based on J. M. Synge's "The Playboy of the Western World"; Director, Jacques Levy; Choreography, Margo Sappington; Scenery, Peter Larkin; Costumes, Pearl Somner; Lighting, Neil Peter Jampolis; Hairstylist, Patrik D. Moreton; Sound, Robert Kerzman; Orchestrations, Dance and Vocal Arrangements, Stanley Walden; Musical Director, Susan Romann; General Manager, Robert S. Fishko; Press, Elizabeth Rodman, Harriett Trachtenberg, Hal Lubin; Assistant Manager, Louise Bayer; Production Coordinator, Robert Chambers; Wardrobe, William B. Campbell; Assistant to Mr. Levy, Marge Pfleiderer; Company Manager, Gintare Sileika; Stage Managers. Richard Scanga, Cheryl Raab. Presented by Eugene V. Wolsk in association with Harvey Granat. Opened at the Wilbur Theatre in Boston on Friday, Sept. 8, 1978 and closed there Sept. 23, 1978.

CAST

Philly Cullen	Stuart Germain
Michael James	Rex Everhart
Pegeen Mike	Suzanne Lederer
Floyd Beavis	Harry Groener
Christy Mahon	Ken Marshall
Evalina	Terri Treas
Bitsy	Pamela Pilkenton
Sister	Nancy Holcombe
Lucy Jane DuRambeau Finletter	Barbara Andres
Passerby	John G. Kellogg

STANDBYS; Harry Groener (Christy), Terri Treas (Pegeen), B. J. Hardin (Floyd), George Riddle (Michael/Philly/Passerby), Malita Barron (Lucy), Patti Canuso (Evalina/Bitsy/Sister).

MUSICAL NUMBERS: Mother of Spring, Little Girl Again, Child of the Devil, Mr. Moon and Lady Fire, Heaven on My Mind, Hay Pitchin', The Western Slope, All the Men in My Life, Diamond Jim Brady, The Fiddler's Tune, As a Boy, Too Much Pain, As a Girl, Old Man, Through the Shadows

A musical in 2 acts and 5 scenes. The action takes place during early spring of 1884 in a rustic tavern in an out-of-the-way rural area in West Kansas.

Ken Howard Photos

Rex Everhart, Stuart Germain

Barbara Andres, Ken Marshall Left Center: Harry Groener, Ken Marshall

BROADWAY, BROADWAY

By Terrence McNally; Director, Robert Drivas; Scenery, Peter Larkin; Costumes, Florence Klotz; Lighting, Ian Calderon; Sound, Gary Harris; Director's Assistants, Tony DeSantis, Martin Jackman; Assistant to Producer, Patti Hassler; Hairstylist, Michael of New York; Producer, Edgar Bronfman, Jr.; General Manager, James Walsh; Stage Managers, Larry Forde, Arlene Grayson; Press, Alpert/LeVine, Randi Cone, Marcia Gever; Opened Monday, September 4, 1978 at the Forrest Theatre in Philadelphia, and closed there Sept. 16, 1978.

CAST

James Wicker .... James Coco
Gus Washington .... Frankie Faison
Virginia Noyes............................. Jean DeBaer
Frank Finger .... Peter Friedman
Julia Budder .... Geraldine Page
Peter Austen .... Richard Backus
Ira Drew .... Bill Moor

STANDBYS AND UNDERSTUDIES: Rose Arrick (Julia), Norman Snow (Peter/Frank/Ira), Arlene Grayson (Virginia)

A comedy in two acts. The action takes place at the present time in Julia Budder's townhouse.

Top: James Coco, Geraldine Page

James Coco

HOME AGAIN, HOME AGAIN

Music, Cy Coleman; Book, Russell Baker; Lyrics, Barbara Fried; Director, Gene Saks; Dances and Musical Staging, Onna White; Scenery, Peter Larkin; Costumes, Jane Greenwood; Lighting, Neil Peter Jampolis; Hairstylist and Makeup, Steve Atha; Musical Direction, Stanley Lebowsky; Dance Arrangements, Cy Coleman; Orchestrations, Jim Tyler; Vocal Arrangements, Cy Coleman, Stanley Lebowsky; Dance Music Coordinator, Dorothea Freitag; Associate Choreographer, Martin Allen; Associate Producer, Joseph Harris; Produced by Irwin Meyer, Stephen R. Friedman in association with Kenneth D. Laub and Warner Plays, Inc.; General Managers, Joseph Harris, Ira Bernstein; Company Manager, Sam Pagliaro; Stage Managers, Ed Aldridge, Craig Jacobs, James Lockhart, Victoria Merrill; Wardrobe, William Campbell; Assistant Conductor, Arthur Wagner; Assistant to Director, Lu Webster; Wigs, Bob Kelly; Press, Betty Lee Hunt, Maria Cristina Pucci, Fred Hoot. Opened Monday, March 12, 1979 at American Shakespeare Theatre, Stratford, Ct., and closed April 14, 1979 at the Royal Alexandra in Toronto. Canada.

CAST

Voice/Winckelmann/Watchman	James Lockhart
TJ	Ronny Cox
Hamilton Witherspoon/Editor/Reverend/ Governor/Banker/Sgt./Boss	Dick Shawn
Grandmother	Lisa Ann Cunningham
Hugo	Mike Kellin
Riley	Rex Everhart
Young TJ	William Morrison
Ramsey/Corveen	Mordecai Lawner
Copy Boy/Lieutenant	Dale Christopher
Chicken/Harris	Bob Freschi
Cop/Edmund	David Horwitz
Helen	Teri Ralston
Lila	Anita Morris
Andrea	Lisa Kirk
Robert	Robert Polenz
Linda	Jeannine Taylor
Kenneth	Tim Waldrip
Unborn Woman	Susan Cella

STANDBYS AND UNDERSTUDIES: David Horwitz (TJ), Rex Everhart (Hugo/Witherspoon), Susan Cella (Helen/Andrea), Deborah Moldow (Linda), James Lockhart (Riley/Corveen/Hugo), Philomena Nowlin (Lila), D. Michael Heath (Robert/Kenneth), Gian-Carlo Vellutino (Young TJ)

SINGERS: Susan Cella, Dale Christopher, Ned Coulter, Lisa Ann Cunningham, Bob Freschi, D. Michael Heath, David Horwitz, Terry Iten, Deborah Moldow

DANCERS: Lisa Guignard, Ken Henley, Dirk Lumbard, Bill Nabel, Caroline Nova, Philomena Nowlin, Don Swanson, Karen Tamburrelli, Alternates: Maggy Gorill, Ron Schwinn

MUSICAL NUMBERS: America Is Bathed in Sunlight, Thomas Jefferson Witherspoon, When the Going Gets Tough, I'm Your Guy, All for Love, When It Comes to Loving, Wedding Song, That Happy American, Home Again, Superland, What'll It Take, Big People, I Gotta, French, Tell It to Me Dad, Traveling Together, Winter Rain, America Don't Know How Any More, The Way I See It, Finale

A musical in two acts. The action takes place in the United States from 1925 to the present.

Roger Greenawalt Photos

Tim Waldrip, Ronny Cox

**Lisa Kirk Above: William Morrison, Dick Shawn
Top: Mike Kellin, Dick Shawn, Rex Everhart**

JOLEY

Book and Lyrics, Herbert Hartig; Music, Milton DeLugg; Director, Jay Harnick; Choreography and Musical Staging, George Bunt; Scenery, David Chapman; Costumes, Carol H. Beule; Lighting, Marc B. Weiss; Musical Direction, Liza Redfield; Orchestrations, Walt Levinsky; Dance and Vocal Arrangements, Donald Jonston; Hairstylist, Patrick D. Moreton; Assistant Choreographer, Bob Heath; Production Coordinator, David Kissell; Presented by Bob Funking and Bill Stutler by special arrangement with Jeff Britton; Press, M. J. Boyer; Stage Manager, Robert H. Barth. Opened Friday, March 2, 1979 at Northstage Theatre, Glen Cove, NY, and closed there April 22, 1979.

CAST

Harry Akst/Ren Shields/Camembert/	
Ray Henderson	Mitchell Greenberg
Louis Epstein/Printer/Dumond	Clement Fowler
Al Jolson	Larry Kert
George Jessel/Lee Shubert/Buddy DeSylva/Doctor	Gibby Brand
Hersch Yoelson	Randy Brenner
Asa Yoelson/Georgie Yoelson	Jeff Yonis
Rabbi Moses Yoelson	Jerry Jarrett
Harry Jolson	Merwin Goldsmith
Naomi Yoelson/Lulu	Gloria Hodes
Rose/Suzette/Ruby	Suzanne Walker
Etta/First Nurse	Ilene Frazer
Hessi	Laura Ackermann
Aggie Beeler	Diana Broderick
Agent/Jake Shubert/Impressario/Joe Schenck	Mitchell Jason
Joe Palmer/Patapouf/H. M. Warner/	
Harry Cohn	Kurt Knudson
Mitzi	Dana Moore
Josie/Second Nurse	Eileen Casey
Henrietta Keller/Nun/Erle	Joleen Fodor
Ethel Delmar/Texas Guinan	Lisby Larson
Jimmy	Albert Stephenson
Louella Parsons	Dorothy Stanley

ENSEMBLE: Laura Ackermann, Diana Broderick, Eileen Casey, Ilene Frazer, Bob Heath, Timothy R. Kratoville, Dana Moore, Stephen Moore, Danny Robins, Randy Skinner, Dorothy Stanley, Albert Stephenson

MUSICAL NUMBERS: I'm Just Wild About Harry, Here We Are Again, Song of the Immigrant Mothers, Melons, You Ain't Seen Nuthin' Yet, Henrietta, Darktown Strutters Ball, Shubert Serenade, Robert E. Lee Cakewalk, Swanee, Rockabye Your Baby, Mrs. Ulysses, A Graceful Exit, Dullest Couple in Scarsdale, Toot-Toot Tootsie, Alabamy Bound, 'Ello Hengland 'Ello, Mama, Sonny Boy, Ruby, This Time, Pardon Me Porter, Pettin' on the Old Porch Swing, The Kissing Rock, Times Square, I Gotta Perform, World War Two Medley, Oh! You Beautiful Doll, Finale

A musical in two acts about the life and times of Al Jolson from 1894 to 1950.

Frank Parlatore Photos

Right Center: Larry Kert

OH, KAY!

Book, Guy Bolton, P. G. Wodehouse; New Version, Thomas Meehan; Music, George Gershwin; Lyrics, Ira Gershwin; Direction and Choreography, Donald Saddler; Associate Choreographer, Mercedes Ellington; Producer, Cyma Rubin; Associate Producers, Raoul Pene du Bois, Nathan J. Miller, Keith Davies; Produced in association with The Kennedy Center for Performing Arts; Production Design, Raoul Pene du Bois; Lighting, Beverly Emmons; Sound, Richard Fitzgerald; Dance Arranger and Musical Director, Wally Harper; Orchestrations, Bill Byers; Vocal Arranger, William Elliott; General Manager, C. Edwin Knill; Press, Merle Debuskey, Robert Larkin; Company Manager, Manuel L. Levine; Stage Managers, Nicholas Russiyan, James Bernardi, Robert O'Rourke; Wardrobe, Elonzo Dann, Mary Eno; Hairstylists, Joseph J. Dal Corso, Robert V. Spezzacatena; Production Assistant, Steven Kennedy. Opened Thursday, July 20, 1978 at the Royal Alexandra Theatre in Toronto, Canada, and closed at Kennedy Center Opera House in Washington, D.C.

CAST

Shorty McGee	Jack Weston
Lady Kay Wellington	Jane Summerhays
Jimmy Winter	David-James Carroll†1
Tommy Potter/Freddy LaRue	Gene Castle
Constance Washburn	Marie Cheatham
Agent Baldwin	David Cromwell†2
Oliver Wellington, Duke of Argyle	Reno Roop
Velma Delmar	Alexandra Korey
Senator Albert G. Washbrook	Thomas Ruisinger
Polly	Janet Arters
Molly	Louise Arters
Minister/M. C./Al Fresco	Joe Palmieri
Lefty	Bob Morrisey
Cigarette Girl	Annette Michelle
Thugs	Jameson Foss, Peter Heuchling
Bootleggers	Jon Engstrom, Michael Lichefeld, Bob Morrisey, J. Thomas Smith

ENSEMBLE: Barbara Hanks, Holly Jones, Jean McLaughlin, Annette Michelle, Diana Lee Mirras, Dana J. Moore, Terry Reiser, Yveline Semeria, Dorothy Stanley, Roxanna White, Linda Kinnaman (Swing), Stephen Bray, Jon Engstrom, Jameson Foss, Tom Garrett, Peter Heuchling, Timothy R. Kratoville, Michael Lichtefeld, Dirk Lumbard, Bob Morrisey, Danny Robbins, J. Thomas Smith, Thomas J. Stanton, Bob Heath (Swing)

UNDERSTUDIES: Eddie Lawrence (Shorty), Annette Michelle (Velma), Bob Morrisey (LaRue), Joe Palmieri (Washbrook)

A musical in 2 acts and 4 scenes with a prologue, The action takes place in 1933 in Southampton L. I., N.Y.

† Succeeded by: 1. Jim Weston, 2. Eddie Lawrence

Richard Braaten Photos

Top Left: Jack Weston and chorus
Below: Jane Summerhays and chorus

Jane Summerhays, Jim Weston

SEMMELWEISS

By Howard Sackler; Director, Edwin Sherin; Scenery, John Wulp; Costumes, Ann Roth; Lighting, Marc Weiss; Sound, Charles Gross; Scenery Supervision, Lynn Pectal; Producer, Robert Whitehead; Associate Producer, Claus Von Bulow; General Manager, Oscar E. Olesen; Assistant to Director, Emilie Fanchon Condon; Production Assistants, Bill Becker, Henry Moore, Leslie Rollins, Leslie Spohn; Assistant to Producer, Doris Blum; Stage Managers, William Dodds, Jay Adler, William Radka, Patricia Fay; Press, Seymour Krawitz. Opened Monday, Oct. 9, 1978 at the Eisenhower Theater, Kennedy Center, Washington, D.C., and closed there on Nov. 4, 1978.

CAST

Colin Blakely, Lee Richardson, Stefan Gierasch, Patricia Routledge, with William Roerick, Barton Heyman, David Schramm, Maureen Silliman, Sam Gray, Lizabeth Pritchett, Mell Cobb, Harriet Hall, Gregory Abels, Sally Bagot, Peter Blaxill, Chet Carlin, Kathleen Gray, Kenneth Gray, Curt Karibalis, Pamela Rose Kilburn, Robert Lanchester, R. Bruce MacDonald, Priscilla Manning, Michelle Maulucci, William Newman, Jill Ober, J. Gilpin, John Spencer, Madelon Thomas, John C. Vennema, Stephan Mark Weyte, Christin Whittington

A drama in 3 acts and 19 scenes.

Richard Braaten Photos

David Schramm, William Roerick, Lee Richardson, Colin Blakely, Sam Gray, John C. Vennema Top Left: Colin Blakely Below: Patricia Routledge, David Schramm Right Center: Colin Blakely

ACT: A CONTEMPORARY THEATRE

Seattle, Washington
June 1, 1978–May 31, 1979
Fourteenth Season
Artistic Director, Gregory A. Falls; Musical Director, Stan Keen; General Manager, Andrew M. Witt; Technical Director/Lighting Design, Phil Schermer; Costume Designer, Mac Perkins; Press, Louise Campion Cummings; Stage Managers, Eileen MacRae Murphy; Company Managers, Jody Harris, Sandy Cruse; President, Mrs. E. L. Pierce Milholland

PRODUCTIONS AND CASTS

HENRY IV, PART I by William Shakespeare with Denis Arndt, Shaun Austin-Olsen, Edward Baran, Jack Bittner, Catherine Butterfield, Ted D'Arms, Richard Hawkins, John Michael Hosking, Richard Knisely, Allan Lurie, Marie Mathay, James W. Monitor, Barry Mulholland, Steven Nabors, Elaine Nalee, Merritt Olsen, Si Osborne, Jeffrey L. Prather, Brian Thompson, Robert John Zenk, Gregory A. Falls (Director)

THE SHADOW BOX by Michael Cristofer with Denis Arndt, Dorothy Chace, Ted D'Arms, Sylvia Gassell, Richard Hawkins, Zoaunne LeRoy, Si Osborne, Eve Roberts, Robert John Zenk, Robert Loper (Director)

BALLYMURPHY by Michael Neville with Denis Arndt, Shaun Austin-Olsen, Edward Baran, Kelly Fitzpatrick, Bernard Frawley, Richard Hawkins, David Jones, Tanny McDonald, Michael McKee, James W. Monitor, Pat McNamara, Si Osborne, John Shuman, Kelly Walters, Gregory A. Falls (Director)

THE SEA HORSE by Edward J. Moore with David Canary and Janice Fuller, M. Burke Walker (Director)

MAKASSAR REEF by Alexander Ruzo with Denis Arndt, Erik Fredricksen, John Kauffman, Laurie Lapinski, Tanny McDonald, Armin Shimerman, Ruben Sierra, Barbara Tarbuck, Bill Ludel (Director)

ANYTHING GOES with book by Guy Bolton, P. G. Wodehouse, Howard Lindsay and Russel Crouse; Music and Lyrics, Cole Porter. CAST: Adrienne Angel, Ken Branch, Dale Christopher, Elizabeth Cole, Adrienne Dussault, Douglas Easley, Robert Loper, Diane Maggion, Terri McRay, Nancy Miller, James W. Monitor, Jeffrey L. Prather, Janine Sawyer, Leo Schmidt, Kura D. Shepard, Thomas Spickard, Kelly Walters, Judith Haskell (Director-Choreographer)

A CHRISTMAS CAROL by Charles Dickens and adapted by Gregory A. Falls, with Lyle Bicknell, David Colacci, Alex Denisof, Richard Farrell, John Gilbert, Brenda Hubbard, Marie Mathay, James W. Monitor, William Moreing, Si Osborne, Jim Royce, Mark Sather, Lisa Sisley, Jean Smart, Robert John Zenk, Gregory A. Falls (Director)

Chris Bennion Photos

Right: Denis Arndt, Tanny McDonald in "Makassar Reef" Above: Dorothy Chace, Zoaunne LeRoy in "Shadow Box" Top: David Canary, Janice Fuller in "Sea Horse"

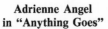

**Adrienne Angel
in "Anything Goes"**

"Ballymurphy"

CENTER THEATRE GROUP
AHMANSON THEATRE

Los Angeles, California
September 29, 1978–June 2, 1979
Twelfth Season

Robert Fryer, Managing Director; Manager, Charles Mooney, Assistant Manager, Barbara Houck; Production Associate, Robert Linden; Production Coordinator, Michael Grossman; Production Administrator, Ralph Beaumont; Press, Rupert Allan, James H. Hansen, Ann Wareham, Michelle McGrath; Administrative Coordinator, Joyce Zaccaro; Co-Chairmen, Armand S. Deutsch, Charlton Heston; President, Walter Mirisch

PRODUCTIONS AND CASTS

DRACULA by Hamilton Deane, John L. Balderston from Bram Stoker's novel; Director, Dennis Rosa; Scenery and Costumes, Edward Gorey; Lighting, Roger Morgan; Company Manager, Robert P. Bron; Stage Managers, Michael Maurer, John Weeks, Chaz Denny, Mary Dierson; Special Effects, Chic Silber; Assistant Director, Steven Deshler; Press, Solters & Roskin, Joshua Ellis, Milly Schoenbaum, Stan Brody. CAST: Margaret Whitton (Lucy), Victoria Page (Maid), Nick Stannard (Jonathan), Dalton Dearborn (Dr. Seward), David Hurst (Van Helsing), John Long (Renfield), Fritz Sperberg (Butterworth), Jeremy Britt (Dracula)

WORLD PREMIERE (Friday, Dec. 1, 1978) of THEY'RE PLAING OUR SONG by Neil Simon; Music, Marvin Hamlisch; Lyrics, Carole Bayer Sager; Director, Robert Moore; Musical Numbers, Patricia Birch; Orchestrations, Ralph Burns, Richard Hazard, Gene Page; Music Direction, Larry Blank; Scenery and Projections, Douglass W. Schmidt; Costumes, Ann Roth; Lighting, Tharon Musser; Presented by Emanuel Azenberg; General Manager, Jose Vega; Company Manager, Susan Bell; Stage Managers, Robert D. Currie, Philip Cusack, Lani Sundsten; Associate Conductor, Fran Liebergall; Press, Bill Evans, Judi Davidson, Dick Kitzrow, Claudia McAllister. CAST: Robert Klein (Vernon), Lucie Arnaz (Sonia), Wayne Mattson, Andy Roth, Greg Zadikov, Helen Castillo, Celia Celnik Matthau, Debbie Shapiro, Max Stone, Lani Sundsten. See Broadway Calendar, page 28.

A MAN FOR ALL SEASONS by Robert Bolt; Director, Jack O'Brien; Setting, Sam Kirkpatrick; Costumes, Robert Morgan; Lighting, Gilbert V. Hemsley, Jr.; Music, Conrad Susa; Production Associate, Robert Linden; Technical Supervisor, Robert Routolo; Assistant to Director, Stephen Willems; Sound, Roger Gans; Wardrobe, Eddie Dodds; Hairstylist, Jean Rapollo; Production Assistant, Marc Seaton. CAST: Charlton Heston (Sir Thomas More), J. Kenneth Campbell (Wm. Roper), John Glover (Richard Rich), Jack Gwillim (Duke of Norfolk), Gerald Hiken (Common Man), Patrick Hines (Cardinal Wolsey), Stephen Macht (Henry VIII), Katherine McGrath (Lady Margaret More), Ken Ruta (Thomas Cromwell), Inga Swenson (Lady Alice More), G. Wood (Signor Chapuys), Earl Boen (Archbishop of Canterbury), Tom Henschel (Chapuys' attendant), Kres Mersky (Catherine of Aragon), Terrence O'Connor (Anne Boleyn), Attendants: Gregory Bell, Don Bilotti, Bill Furnell, Ken Letner, J. Stuart West

PYGMALION by George Bernard Shaw; Director, John Dexter; Sets and Costumes, Jocelyn Herbert, Andrew Sanders; Lighting, Andy Phillips; Associate Director, Riggs O'Hara; Production Associate, Robert Linden; Production Supervised by Peter J. Hall; Stage Managers, George Boyd, Patrick Watkins. CAST: Robert Stephens (Higgins), Roberta Maxwell (Eliza), Maureen O'Sullivan (Mrs. Higgins), Milo O'Shea (Doolittle), William Roerick (Col. Pickering), Neva Patterson (Mrs. Eynsford Hill), Margaret Hilton (Mrs. Pearce), Dale Hodges (Clara), James David Cromar (Freddy), Rosemary Lord (Parlour Maid), Philip Carroll (Bystander), Peter MacPherson (1st Bystander), Martin Azarow (Bystander), Sandra Caron (Bystander), Olive Dunbar (Bystander), Porter (Bystander), Joel Triemstra (Bystander), Patrick Watkins (Bystander), Jill Wilde (Bystander), Alan Mixon (Standby for Prof. Higgins)

Kenn Duncan, Jay Thompson, Lydia Heston, Steve Smith Photos

Right Center: Roberta Maxwell, Robert Stephens in "Pygmalion" Above: Katherine McGrath, J. Kenneth Campbell, Inga Swenson, Charlton Heston in "A Man for All Seasons" Top: Nick Stannard, Jeremy Brett, Dalton Dearborn in "Dracula"

William Roerick, Maureen O'Sullivan, Robert Stephens in "Pygmalion"

CENTER THEATRE GROUP
MARK TAPER FORUM

Los Angeles, California
July 7, 1978–July 1, 1979
Twelfth Season

Artistic Director, Gordon Davidson; General Manager, William P. Wingate; Associate Artistic Director, Edward Parone; Director Improvisational Theatre Project, John Dennis; Director for New Programs, Kenneth Brecher; Director of New Theatre for Now Festival, Gwen Arner; Director Forum Laboratory, David Schweizer; Press, Nancy Hereford, Anthony Sherwood, Gail Browne; Staff Designers, Tharon Musser, Peter J. Hall; Stage Managers, Mark Wright, Milt Commons, Earl L. Frounfelter, Jonathan Barlow Lee, James T. McDermott, Mary Michele Miner

PRODUCTIONS AND CASTS

ZOOT SUIT written and directed by Luis Valdez (*World Premiere*) with Edward James Olmos, Daniel Valdez, Abel Franco, Lupe Ontiveros, Evelina Fernandez, Tony Plana, Charles Aidman, Karen Hensel, Rose Portillo, Enrique Castillo, Mike Gomez, Paul Mace, Angela Moya, Rachel Levario, Roberta Delgado Esparza, Greg Rosatti, Sheryl Cooper, Miguel Delgado, Tom Demenkoff, Ronald Linares, Vikie Shecketer, Rose Aragon, Vincent Duke Milana, Frank McCarthy, Arthur Hammer, Ronald Linares, Tom Demendoff. See Broadway Calendar, page 36.

DUSA, FISH, STAS AND VI by Pam Gems (*American Premiere*); Director, Edward Parone: with Marybeth Hurt, Dianne Wiest, Jennifer Warren, Fran Brill

TERRA NOVA by Ted Tally; Director, Gordon Davidson; with Donald Moffat, James Cromwell, Laura Esterman, Ian Trigger, Scott Hylands, William Glover, Guy Boyd

THE TEMPEST by William Shakespeare; Director, John Hirsch; with Anthony Hopkins, James Phipps, Rod Loomis, Neil Flanagan, Kenneth Marshall, Patrick Hines, David Mitchell, Howard Brunner, Stephen Schnetzer, Stephanie Zimbalist, Brent Carver, Michael Bond, Joseph R. Sicari, Richard B. Shull, Jonathan Gries, Elise Caitlin, Paul Haber, Paul Bowman, Wendy Zaro, Priscilla Baskerville, Candace Rogers

A CHRISTMAS CAROL by Charles Dickens, adapted by Doris Baizley; Director, John Dennis; with Barry Cutler, Andy Rivas, Paul Zegler, George Ceres, Donna Lynn Leavy, Michael McNeilly, Carlo Allen, Deborah Tilton, David McKnight, Arrow Brown IV, Dan Gerrity, Nancy Lane-Sheehy, Bruce French, Donna Fuller

THE HOSHO SCHOOL OF NOH THEATRE performing "Tsunemasa" and "Hagoromo"

Jay Thompson, Steve Smith Photos

Left: Stephanie Zimbalist, Brent Carver, Anthony Hopkins, Michael Bond (below) Top: Sal Lopez, Andy Tennant, Becky Gonzalez in "Zoot Suit"

Donald Moffat, James Cromwell in "Terra Nova"

Dianne Wiest, Jennifer Warren, Fran Brill, Marybeth Hurt in "Dusa, Fish, Stas & Vi"

Cherry Davis, Jack Manning in "Maud Gonne Says No to the Poet" Right: David Birney in "The Biko Inquest"

MARK TAPER FORUM
LABORATORY PRODUCTIONS

THE FAR OTHER SIDE OF A VERY THIN LINE by James Shepard and Philip Baker Hall; Directors, Philip Baker Hall, Andrea Frye; with Marion Akbar, Theodore Majied, Rachel Bard, Hal Bokar, George Brooks, J. B. Brown, Tommy Busch, Michael Anthony Favorito, Richie Freeman, Sonny Gibson, Rodni Hardison, Lyvingston Holms, Larry, Gary Manolian, Paul H. Nicholas, Al Robertson, Herman Smith, W. Burton Tardy, Leary Tracy

JAZZ SET by Ron Milner (*World Premiere*) with Myrna White, Anthony Gourdine, Le Tari, Earl Billings, Lonny Stevens, Fred Pinkard

THE LOST ONES adapted from a work by Lee Breuer and Samuel Beckett, with the Mabou Mines: Jo Anne Akalaitis, Lee Breuer, Ruth Maleczech, Fred Neumann, Terry O'Reilly, Bill Raymond, David Warrilow

KID TWIST by Len Jenkin with Raymond Singer, Craig Richard Nelson, Jenny O'Hara, Herb Voland, Tony Abatemarco, Martin Azarow, Todd Susman, Jeffrey Chandler, Michael Tucci, Vincent Schiavelli, John A. Neris, Regie Baff, Momo Yashima

THE TAKING AWAY OF LITTLE WILLIE by Tom Griffin (*World Premiere*) with Cooper Neal, Dana Ivey, Robin Gammell, Timothy Wead, Alan Oppenheimer, Jo de Winter, Talia Balsam

IN CAMERA by Robert Pinger (*World Premiere*) with Lurene Tuttle, Howard Brunner, Ellen Fitzhugh, David Rupprecht, Leon Ames, Cindie Haynie

A LIFE IN A DAY: LUCKY LINDY by Dick D. Zigun with Noreen Hennessy, Archie Hahn

MAUD GONNE SAYS NO TO THE POET by Susan Rivers with Cherry Davis, Nicole Hamilton, Jack Manning

THE TROUBLE WITH EUROPE by Paul D'Andrea (*World Premiere*) with Mark Herrier, Benjamin Jurant, Kathleen Doyle, Hamilton Camp, Bruce French, Jonathan Frakes

THE IDOL MAKERS by Stephen Davis Parks (*World Premiere*) with Janette Lane Bradbury, Mitch Carter, Sean Michael Rice, Zachary Lewis, Jonathan Banks, Alley Mills

THE BIKO INQUEST by Norman Fenton and Jon Blair with David Birney, Roger Bowen, Burke Byrnes, Paul Carr, Brian Greene, Philip Baker Hall, Jack Hogan, Ryan MacDonald, James Nolan, Martin Shakar, Matthew Tobin

THE VIENNA NOTES by Richard Nelson with Nelson Welch, Ronnie Claire Edwards, Beverly Sanders, Tom Rosqui, Paul Brancato

ORMER LOCKLEAR by Marc Norman (*World Premiere*) with William Katt, Jeff Greenberg, Maggie King, Marian Tucker, Susan Krebs, Richard Kline, Julie Payne, Anthony Greco, Joe Romano, Carl Stoner

IMPROVISATIONAL THEATRE PROJECT

John Dennis (Director), Jef Labes (Composer/Musician), Linda Alper, Roberto Covarrubias, Paul Dillon, Donna Fuller, Doug Griffin, Paul Gustie, Mark Herrier, Michael McNeilly, Barry Moore, Tony Papenfuss

Steve Smith, Jay Thompson Photos

Right Center: William Katt, Julie Payne in "Ormer Locklear"

Lurene Tuttle, Ellen Fitzhugh in "In Camera"

Paul Ukena, Patrick Tovatt, Cass Morgan in "Gold Dust" Left: William McNulty, Sherry Steiner in "The Runner Stumbles" Top: Leo Burmester, Patrick Tovatt in "Lone Star"

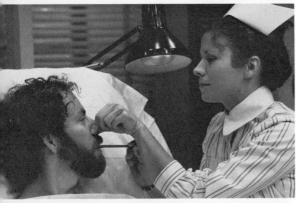

ACTORS THEATRE OF LOUISVILLE

Louisville, Kentucky
October 12, 1978–May 20, 1979
Eleventh Season

Producing Director, Jon Jory; Administrative Director, Alexander Speer; Associate Director, Trish Pugh; Press, Ronette McNulty, Gary Yawn; Directors, Peter Bennett, Larry Deckel, Ray Fry, Michael Hankins, Patrick Henry, Jon Jory, Charles Kerr, Richard Russell Ramos, Daniel Sullivan, R. Stuart White; Musical Directors, Peter Ekstrom, Jim Wann; Choreographer, Margaret Castleman Schwartz; Sets, David B. Hager, Paul Owen, Joe Varga, Richard Kent Wilcox; Costumes, Kurt Wilhelm; Lighting, Jeff Hill, Paul Owen; Props, Sam Garst, Sandra Strawn; Technical Directors, Tom Conley, Joseph Ragey, Tom Rupp; Costumiere, Mary Lou Owen; Stage Managers, Bob Burrus, James A. Gelarden, Benita Hofstetter, Bob Hornung, Frazier Marsh, Susana Meyer, Cass Morgan

COMPANY

Neville Aurelius, Jim Baker, Peter Bartlett, Kathy Bates, Susan Berger, Richard Bowne, Suzy Brabeau, Kent Broadhurst, Elaine Bromka, Leo Burmester, Bob Burrus, Douglas Clark, Lynn Cohen, Barry Corbin, Peggy Cowles, Gloria Dorson, Lee Ann Fahey, Ray Fry, Reedy Gibbs, Lisa Goodman, Michael Hankins, Benita Hofstetter, Robert Jackson, Leona Johnson, Victor Jory, Michael Kevin, J. Jeffrey Kilgore, Susan Kingsley, Meredith Ludwig, Deborah May, Vaughn McBride, William McNulty, Cass Morgan, William Myers, Adale O'Brien, Moultrie Patten, John Pielmeier, Anne Pitoniak, Trip Plymale, Nicola Sheara, Howard Lee Sherman, Sherry Steiner, James Sutorius, Diane Tarleton, Patrick Tovatt, Paul Ukena, Jr., Susan Willis, Daniel Ziskie

PRODUCTIONS

"The Play's the Thing," "The Runner Stumbles," "A Christmas Carol," "What Every Woman Knows," "The Gin Game," "Room Service," "The Shadow Box"

Premiere Productions: "Whose Life Is It Anyway?," "The Splits," "Holidays," "Matrimonium" with music and lyrics by Peter Ekstrom, "Find Me," "Crimes of the Heart," "Circus Valentine," "Lone Star," "Pvt. Wars," "The Home Fires," "Roman Games," "Gold Dust" with music and lyrics by Jim Wann, "Early Times"

Lee Anne Fahey, Susan Kingsley, Kathy Bates in "Crimes of the Heart"

Left Center: James Sutorius, Reedy Gibbs in "Whose Life Is It Anyway?"

ALASKA REPERTORY THEATRE

Anchorage/Fairbanks, Alaska
October 3, 1978–April 29, 1979
Third Season

Artistic Director, Robert J. Farley; Producing Director, Paul V. Brown; Production Manager, Gary D. Anderson; Sets, Jamie Greenleaf; Lighting, James Sale; Technical Director, Hugh Hall; Costumes, Nanrose Buchman; Business Manager, Mark Somers; Press, Jack Lloyd, Bonnie Harris, Susan Scott; Stage Managers, Dan Sedgwick, Emil Holloway, David Locey; President, Pamela Towill; Directors, Robert J. Farley, Martin L. Platt, Gary D. Anderson

PRODUCTIONS AND CASTS

THE FOURPOSTER by Jan de Hartog; Director, Clayton Corzatte; Stage Manager, Nikos Kafkalis. CAST: Mitchell Edmonds, Tanny McDonald

A CHRISTMAS CAROL by Charles Dickens; Adapted by Martin L. Platt; Director, Robert J. Farley. CAST: Betty Arnett, Marty Decker, Dana Dittman, Danielle Dittman, Mitchell Edmonds, Harry Frazier, Stephen Haraden, John Heginbotham, Tom Jacobs, Georgianna Lane, Cynthia Lee, John Lenz, Miller Lide, Anne Lilly, Marsha Lilly, Kenneth McClendon, Doug McConnell, Joe Meek, Susan Mendel, Scott Merrick, Emily Merrill, James Morrison, Philip Pleasants, Luan Schooler, Earl Stirling, Susan Uchitel, Joan Ulmer, Mary Pat Plymale, Cristeta Mathias

TERRA NOVA by Ted Tally; Director, Robert J. Farley. CAST: Marshall Borden, Miller Lide, Joe Meek, Philip Pleasants, James Secrest, Jean Smart, Eric Uhler

THE TAMING OF THE SHREW by William Shakespeare; Director, Martin L. Platt. CAST: Charles Antalosky, William Arnold, Dennis Bateman, Nicholas Cosco, Marty Decker, Shannon Eubanks, Harry Frazier, Stephen Haraden, Peter Jack, John-Fredrick Jones, Georgianna Lane, Deborah LaVine, Kenneth McClendon, Gannon McHale, Susan Mendel, Scott Merrick, James Morrison, Philip Pleasants, William Preston, Luan Schooler, Mark Varian

SLOW DANCE ON THE KILLING GROUND by William Hanley; Director, Gary D. Anderson. CAST: Kim Delgado, Mary Gallagher, Stefan Schnabel

DEATHTRAP by Ira Levin; Director, Robert J. Farley. CAST: John Abajian, Clayton Corzatte, Miller Lide, Susan Ludlow, Etain O'Malley

Jim Lavrakas Photos

Right: Philip Pleasants, Jean Smart in "Terra Nova" Top: Mary Gallagher, Stefan Schnabel, Kim Delgado in "Slow Dance on the Killing Ground"

Eric Uhler, Joe Meek, Miller Lide, James Secrest in "Terra Nova"

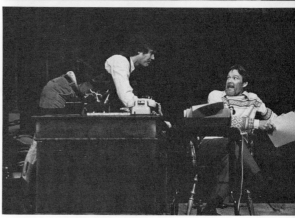

John Abajian, Clayton Corzatte in "Deathtrap"

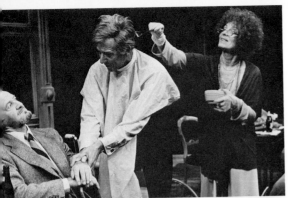

ALLEY THEATRE

Houston, Texas
October 14, 1978–June 3, 1979
Executive Director, Nina Vance; Executive Producer, Herschell Wilkenfeld; Managing Director, Iris Siff; Business Manager; Bill Halbert; Press, Bob Feingold; Directors, Beth Sanford, Arthur Laurents, Leslie Yeo; Production/Company Manager, Bettye Fitzpatrick; Stage Managers, Rutherford Cravens, Trent Jenkins, Hal Meng, Raymond Benson; Production Assistant, John Vreeke; Designers, Jonathan Duff, Matt Grant, Ellen Ryba; Technical Director, William Lindstrom; Props, Tandova Jade Ecenia, Wade Petty; Philip A. Sayles, President

PRODUCTIONS AND CASTS

SCREAM (*World Premiere*) by Arthur Laurents; Directed by the author, assisted by Beth Sanford; Setting, William and Jean Eckart; Costumes, Ellen Ryba; Lighting, Jonathan Duff. CAST: Richard Dow (Sonny), Viveca Lindfors (Nessa), David Opatoshu (Itzhak), Robyn Goodman (Rochelle), Albert Paulsen (Julius). A play in 2 acts and 3 scenes. The action takes place at the present time in a living room on the second floor of a house in Kew Gardens, Queens, New York.

ALICE IN WONDERLAND by Lewis Carroll; Adapted by Eva LeGallienne and Florida Friebus; Music, Raymond Benson; Director, Beth Sanford. CAST: Patti Slover, Kathryn Paul, J. Shane McClure, Valerie Noyes, Chip Pankey, James Kelly, Tom Lent, Gale Childs, Steven Ortego, Gram Smith, Pamela Anson, Jess Tomlinson, Vernon Grote, Valerie Noyes, J. Shane McClure, Robin Moseley, Steven Ortego, Margaret Humphreys, Monique Morgan

THE HAPPY TIME by Samuel Taylor; Director, Leslie Yeo. CAST: Craig Schaeffer, Maurice Good, Irena Mayeska, Eric House, Anthony Manionis, Joel Kenyon, Lillian Evans, Monique Morgan, Kathy Jo Witt, Harold Suggs, David Hudson, Trent Jenkins

ARTICHOKE by Joanna M. Glass; Director, Beth Sanford. CAST: Jack Van Evera, David Wurst, Michael Donaghue, Linda Thorson, Patti Slover, Robert Symonds, Anthony Manionis

DON JUAN IN HELL by George Bernard Shaw; Director, John Vreeke. CAST: Michael Allinson, Pat Galloway, Roderick Cook, Robert Symonds

SIDE BY SIDE BY SONDHEIM with music and lyrics by Stephen Sondheim; Director, Beth Sanford; Musical Director, Sterling Tinsley; Pianists, Sterling Tinsley, Don Looser. CAST: Cathy Brewer-Moore, David Christmas, Judy Rice, Robert Symonds

Carl Davis, Dome City Photos

Left: Robert Symonds, Michael Allinson, Pat Galloway, Roderick Cook in "Don Juan in Hell" Above: Craig Schaefer, Irena Mayeska, Maurice Good in "The Happy Time" Top: David Opatoshu, Albert Paulsen, Viveca Lindfors in "Scream"

Linda Thorson, Anthony Manionis in "Artichoke"

Cathy Brewer-Moore, David Christmas, Judy Rice, in "Side by Side by Sondheim"

ALLIANCE THEATRE COMPANY
Atlanta, Georgia
November 2, 1978–May 20, 1979
Managing Director, Bernard Havard; Artistic Director, Fred Chappell; Associate Director, Wallace Chappell; Press, Sandra Johnson, Sandra Holden, Betty Blondeau; Production Manager, Gully Sanford; Stage Managers, D. Wayne Hughes, Allen Wright; President of the Board, Alfred D. Kennedy, Jr.; Scenic Artist, Juanita Kaylor; Wardrobe, Lorraine Crane; Props, Barbara Hall; Production Assistant, Carolyn Zachery; Business Manager, Edith Love; Costumes, Thom Coates; Lighting, Michael Stauffer, Roger Foster, Carol Graebner; Sets, W. Joseph Stell, Virginia Dancy, Elmon Webb, Roger Foster, Thom Coates, Michael Stauffer, Jonathan Arkin

PRODUCTIONS AND CASTS

THE SHADOW BOX by Michael Cristofer; Director, Fred Chappell. CAST: Terry Beaver, Ray Aranha, Harry Nixon, Venida Evans, Alan Mixon, Kurt Johnson, Elizabeth Fleming, Anne Lynn, Elizabeth Council, Jacques Wilson

PETER PAN by J. M. Barrie; Director, John Going. CAST: Penny Fuller, Laurence Hugo, Ludi Claire, Ron Nakahara, Stuart McDaniel, Tim Rutland, Valerie Charles, Burke Allison, Travis Fine, Barbara Hancock, Tim Webber, David Broshar, Chris Neiman, David Charles, Brian Charles, Tyronne Kinnlaw, Gary Goodson, David Cioffi, William Colquitt, Skip Foster, Tom Key, Donald G. Moore, Morris Brown, Al Hamacher, Jeff Mitchell, Mark Newkirk, Keith Carmichael, James Watson, Kelley Cole, Leon Cofer, Chris Kayser, Jamese Carey, Jennifer Cole, Vanessa Flanders, Alexis Kelley, Alexandra Stynchcombe

THE LITTLE FOXES by Lillian Hellman; Director, Fred Chappell. CAST: Bernardine Mitchell, Tyronne Kinnlaw, Linda Wilson Stephens, Robert Bloodworth, James Donadio, Dana Ivey, Anthony Savon, Donald C. Moore, Valerie Charles, Alan Mixon

ABSURD PERSON SINGULAR by Alan Ayckbourn; Director, Donald Ewer. CAST: Barbara Berge, Tony Tanner, Donald Ewer, Betty Leighton, Marion Lines, Fred Thompson

THE ROBBER BRIDEGROOM adapted from the novella by Eudora Welty; Book and Lyrics, Alfred Uhry; Music, Robert Waldman; Director, Fred Chappell; Musical Director, Michael Fauss; Choreographer, Haila Strauss. CAST: Lara Teeter, Donalyn Petrucci, Mary Leigh Stahl, Floyd King, Steven McCloskey, Ernie Sabella, Kent Stephens, Anne Gartlan, Judith Sullivan, Nancy Jane Clay, Barry Thomas, David McCann, Jeffery Brocklin, Nancy Farrar, Elia English, Glenn Turner

OTHELLO by William Shakespeare; Director, Wallace Chappell. CAST: Richard Dreyfuss, Dorothy Fielding, Paul Winfield, James Donadio, Edward Lee, John Hadden, Stuart Culpepper, Terry Beaver, Ron Nakahara, Steven McCloskey, Skip Foster, Kristin Linklater, Ken Raskin, Valerie Charles, Jeffery Brocklin, Michael Cowell, Ron Culbreth, Kerry Graham, Al Hamacher, Charlie Hensley, David McCann, Malik Purley, Kent Stephens, Linda Wilson Stephens

Children's Theatre productions of "The Halloween Tree," "Rumpelstiltskin and Other Tales from the Brothers Grimm," "Umbrella Players"

Charles Rafshoon Photos

Top: Penny Fuller, Laurence Hugo in "Peter Pan"
Right: Paul Winfield, Dorothy Fielding, Richard Dreyfuss (rear) in "Othello" Below: Dana Ivey, Donald C. Moore in "The Little Foxes"

Venida Evans, Ray Aranha, Harry Nixon in "The Shadow Box"

AMERICAN CONSERVATORY THEATRE

San Francisco, California
October 14, 1978–June 2, 1979
Thirteenth Season

General Director, William Ball; Executive Director, Edward Hastings; Executive Producer, James B. McKenzie; Conservatory Director, Allen Fletcher; Production Director, Benjamin Moore; Production Supervisor, Kendall Tieck; Production Coordinator, Mary Garrett; Scenery and Costumes, Robert Blackman, Martha Burke, Cathy Edwards, Robert Fletcher, Ralph Funicello, Henry May, Michael Miller, Robert Morgan, Richard Segar, Walter Watson; Lighting, F. Mitchell Dana, Richard Devin, Dirk Epperson; Music, Larry Delinger, Lee Hoiby, Jon Olson, Conrad Susa; Stage Managers, James Haire, James L. Burke, Raymond Stephen Gin, Suzanne Fry, Cornelia Twitchell; Props, Glenn Lloyd, Chuck Olsen; General Manager, Stewart Slater; Press, Jim Kerber, Richard D. Carreon; Directors, William Ball, Allen Fletcher, Edward Hastings, Nagle Jackson, Tom Moore, Laird Williamson

COMPANY

Candace Barrett, Joseph Bird, Raye Birk, Libby Boone, Joy Carlin, Penelope Court, Kathryn Crosby, Peter Davies, Daniel Davis, Heidi Helen Davis, Richard Denison, Barbara Dirickson, Peter Donat, Sabin Epstein, Kate Fitzmaurice, Bennet Guillory, Janice Garcia, Lawrence Hecht, Leslie Hicks, Elizabeth Huddle, Daniel Kern, Gerald Lancaster, Anne Lawder, Michael X. Martin, William McKereghan, DeAnn Mears, Delores Y. Mitchell, Mark Murphey, Thomas M. Nahrwold, Thomas Oglesby, Michael Oglesby, Michael O'Guinne, Frank Ottiwell, William Paterson, Susan E. Pellegrino, Ray Reinhardt, Cynthia Sikes, Randall Smith, Robertson Smith, Bonnie Tarwater, Sydney Walker, Marrian Walters, Isiah Whitlock, Jr., Bruce Williams, Michael Winters

PRODUCTIONS

"The Winter's Tale" by William Shakespeare, "A Month in the Country" by Ivan Turgenev, "Ah, Wilderness!" by Eugene O'Neill, "The Circle" by W. Somerset Maugham, "A Christmas Carol" by Charles Dickens, "Heartbreak House" by George Bernard Shaw, "5th of July" by Lansford Wilson, "The Visit" by Friedrich Duerrenmatt, "Hay Fever" by Noel Coward, "Hotel Paradiso" by Georges Feydeau and Maurice Desvallieres

William Ganslen Photos

Right: William Paterson, Barbara Dirickson in "The Circle" Above: Mark Murphey, Isiah Whitlock, Jr. in "5th of July" Top: Elizabeth Huddle, Raye Birk in "Hotel Paradiso"

Elizabeth Huddle, Peter Donat in "A Month in the Country"

Kathryn Crosby, Thomas M. Nahrwold, Gerald Lancaster in "Ah, Wilderness!"

ARENA STAGE

Washington, D. C.
October 13, 1978–June 24, 1979

Producing Director, Zelda Fichandler; Associate Producing Director/Producer 1978-79-80 Seasons, David Chambers; Executive Director, Thomas C. Fichandler; Production Coordinator, Nancy Quinn; Press, Thomas O'Connor; Directors, David Chambers, Liviu Ciulei, Edward J. Cornell, Walton Jones, Sheldon Larry, Gary Pearle, Richard Russell Ramos, Alan Schneider, Horacena J. Taylor; Sets, Douglas C. Wager; Sets, Zack Brown, Karl Eigsti, David Lloyd Gropman, Ming Cho Lee, Hugh Lester, William Ritman, Tony Straiges, Wynn Thomas, Robert Yodice; Costumes, Jess Goldstein, William Ivey Long, Alvin Perry, Dunya Ramicova, Marjorie Slaiman; Lighting, Hugh Lester, Roger Milliken, William Mintzer, Shirley Prendergast; Composers, Tim Eyermann, Mel Marvin, John McKinney; Choreographers, Virginia Freeman, Mary Kyte, Thommie Walsh; Technical Director, Henry R. Gorfein; Stage Managers, Art Bundey, Clinton Turner Davis, Stephen J. McCorkle, John J. Mulligan, Susan Proctor

COMPANY

Ernest Abuba, Stanley Anderson, Lowell Arwood, Ethel Ayler, Doug Baker, Bruce Baldwin, Robin Bartlett, Christopher Bauer, Elizabeth Bauer, Richard Bauer, Reed Birney, James Beard, Jane Bloom, Charles Brown, Graham Brown, Leslie Cass, Jordan Charney, Alma Cuervo, Terrence Currier, Arthur Dawkins, Terry Detweiler, Nedra Dixon, John Doolittle, Franchelle Stewart Dorn, Kathryn Dowling, Donna Drake, Kimberly Farr, Sarah Felcher, Kevin Fisher, Kitty Fitzgibbon, Frances Foster, Richard Frank, Arthur French, Michael Gates, Carlos Juan Gonzalez, Joe Grifasi, Georgine Hall, Jack Hallett, Mark Hammer, Roxanne Hart, Lois Hathaway, Ken Hedberg, Carol Hexner, Dick Hosemann, Joanne Hrkach, Charles Hunter, Stephen James, Annalee Jefferies, James Jenner, Timothy Jerome, Gerry Kasarda, Jeff Keller, Kevin Kline, Marilyn Kray, Mary Kyte, Carlos Laguana, David Lipman, Sherman Lloyd, Jodi Long, Larkin Malloy, Christopher McHale, Iliff McMahan, Stephen Mendillo, Carolyn Mignini, Barbara Montgomery, Christina Moore, Frank Muller, Jessica Norton, Joe Palmieri, Bernie Papure, Nancy Paris, Joseph Pinckney, Robert Prosky, Richard Russell Ramos, Mike Redford, William Converse Roberts, Lillie Robertson, William Russ, Jay O. Sanders, Paul Schierhorn, Ned Schmidtke, James Selby, Henry Sgrecci, Barbara Sohmers, Edmonde Sorenson, Cary Anne Spear, Rebecca Street, Glenn Taylor, David Toney, Celia Weston, Jack Eric Williams, Samm-Art Williams, Crissy Wilzak, Halo Wines, Mary Catherine Wright, John Wylie, Jerry Zaks, Irwin Ziff

PRODUCTIONS

"Tales from the Vienna Woods" by Odon von Horvath, "The 1940's Radio Hour" by Walton Jones, "Ah, Wilderness!" by Eugene O'Neill, "Curse of the Starving Class" by Sam Shepard, "Don Juan" by Moliere, "Nevis Mountain Dew" by steve carter, "Idiot's Delight" by Robert Sherwood, "The Past" by Anthony Giardina, "Disabilities" by Ron Melville Whyte, "Casualities" by Karolyn Nelke

WORLD PREMIERES: "Loose Ends" by Michael Weller, "Tintypes: A Ragtime Revue" by Kyte, Marvin and Pearle.

Joe B. Mann Photos

Donna Drake, Crissy Wilzak, Stephen James in "The 1940's Radio Hour" Top: "Tales from the Vienna Woods"

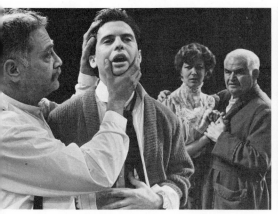

Mark Hammer, James Jenner, Barbara Sohmers, Robert Prosky in "Ah, Wilderness!"

Kathryn Dowling, Stanley Anderson in "Don Juan"

AMERICAN THEATRE ARTS

Los Angeles, California
June 1, 1978–May 31, 1979
Artistic Director, Donald Eitner; Production Director, Joseph Ruskin; Administrator, Nancy Jeris; Managing Director, James N. Bennett; Conservatory Director, Gary Brockette; Art Director, James J. Agazzi; Lighting Vance Sorrels; Press, Lillian Laserson

COMPANY

Craig Abernethy, Howard Adler, John Terry Bell, Hal Bokar, Carla Borelli, Gary Brockette, Richard Bull, Lisa Carole, Barbara Collentine, Joanne Dalsass, Earlene Davis, Rob Donohoe, Jeffrey Druce, Rolly Fanton, Gary Farr, Betty Ferber, Bill Ferber, Louise Fitch, Frobert Garrison, Lou Genevrino, Tanya George, David Gilliam, Harvey Gold, Daniel Grace, Nick Holt, Nancy Jeris, Carol Locatell, Justin Lord, Maureen McIlroy, Maurice Manson, Greg Michaels, Nora Morgan, Kip Niven, Joseph Ruskin, Patricia Ruskin, Robert Sampson, Sara Shearer, Maggie Sullivan, Jayne Taini, Rebecca Westberg

PRODUCTIONS

"Here Come the Clowns" by Philip Barry, "Misalliance" by George Bernard Shaw, "Time Remembered" by Jean Anouilh, and *World Premiere* of "Joggers" by Maureen McIlroy

Dean Larson Photos

Barbara Collentine, Richard Bull in "Joggers"
Top: Daniel Grace, Hal Bokar, Jayne Taini
in "Here Come the Clowns"

ARIZONA THEATRE COMPANY

Tucson, Arizona
November 7, 1978–April 29, 1979
Artistic Director, Sandy Rosenthal; Managing Director, David Hawkanson; Directors, Peter Wexler, Clarke Gordon, Sandy Rosenthal, Israel Hicks, Mark Lamos, Patrick Adiarte; Sets, Reagan Cook, J. Michael Gillette, Peggy Kellner, Peter Wexler, Dan Dryden, Bil Mikulewicz; Costumes, Carolie Jean Tarble, Peggy Kellner, Bobbi Culbert, Robin R. Willoughby; Lighting, Dan T. Willoughby; Stage Managers, Susanne Faull, Michael Brunner, Craig Weindling; Press, Barbara Rowedder, Laurie Beene, Barbara R. Levy

RESIDENT COMPANY: Robert Claiborne, Jeffrey Combs, Tony DeBruno, Robert Ellenstein, Dee Maaske, John McMurtry, Penny Metropulos, Kate Michelle, Benjamin Stewart, Roberta Streicher

GUEST ARTISTS: John Anderson, William Burns, Carol Calkins, Marilyn Coleman, Ron Doering, James Gooden, Robert Jackson, Henry M. Kendrick, Robert Kya-Hill, Dan Leach, Robert F. LuPone, David Marsh, Mary Mendoza, Lois Parker, Richard Peterson, Ruth Snelgrove, Stephen Spinella, John Wilson, Bill Wine

PRODUCTIONS

"Starting Here, Starting Now" by Richard Maltby, Jr. and David Shire, "Cold Storage" by Ronald Ribman, "A Christmas Carol" by Charles Dickens and adapted by Keith Fowler, "Tartuffe" by Moliere in a translation by Richard Wilbur, "The Royal Hunt of the Sun" by Peter Shaffer, "Boesman and Lena" by Athol Fugard, "The Show-Off" by George Kelly

Timothy Woodbridge Fuller Photos

Robert LuPone, Robert Ellenstein in "Cold Storage" Above: Marilyn Coleman in "Boesman"

Top Left: John Anderson, Bill Wine
in "The Royal Hunt of the Sun"

ASOLO STATE THEATRE

Sarasota, Florida
June 1, 1978–May 31, 1979

Executive Director, Richard G. Fallon; Artistic Director, Robert Strane; Managing Director, Howard J. Millman; Assistant Artistic Director, Thomas Edward West; Press, Edith N. Anson; Sets, Holmes Easley, Robert C. Barnes, John Scheffler, Rick Pike, Bennet Averyt, Howard Bay, David Emmons; Costumes, Catherine King, Flozanne John, Diane Berg, Sally A. Kos; Lighting, Martin Petlock; Technical Director, Victor Meyrich; Stage Managers, Marian Wallace, Stephanie Moss

COMPANY

1978: Robert Beseda, George Brengel, Hal Carter, Deanna Dunagan, Brit Erickson, Elizabeth Horowitz, David S. Howard, Max Howard, Bette Oliver, William Pitts, Eberle Thomas, Isa Thomas, Stephen Van Benschoten, Bradford Wallace, Neal Kenyon, Robert Strane, Kathleen Archer, Maryann Barulich, Howard A. Branch, Jr., Ritch Brinkley, Lou Ann Csaszar, John Green, Arthur Hanket, Angela L. Lloyd, Jean McDaniel, Kim Ivan Motter, Joseph Reed, Robert Walker, Porter Anderson, Carolyn Blackinton, Raye Blakemore, Dov Fahrer, Marilyn Foote, Bruce Howe, Christine Joelson, Jeff King, Michael L. Locklair, Carolyn Ann Meeley, Ann Stafford, Janet Nawrocki, Evan S. Parry, James St. Clair

1979: Douglas H. Baker, Robert Beseda, Bill Blackwood, Pam Guest, David S. Howard, Max Howard, Monique Morgan, Robert Murch, Patricia Oetken, Bette Oliver, Chuck Patterson, William Pitts, Barbara Sohmers, Isa Thomas, Bradford Wallace, Porter Anderson, Carolyn Blackinton, Dov Fahrer, Marilyn Foote, Christine Joelson, Jeff King, Michael L. Locklair, Carolyn Ann Meeley, Janet Nawrocki, Evan Parry, Ann Stafford, Susannah Berryman, Gregory Bowman, Tara Buckley, Marnie Carmichael, James Clarke, James Daniels, Paula Dewey, Helen Halsey, Terence R. Harris, Dan Haughey, Judith Heck, Mark Hirschfield, Alan Kimberly Clardy Malugen, Paul Singleton

GUEST ARTISTS: Paul Barry, John Ulmer, Sandra C. Hastie, Thomas Grunewald

PRODUCTIONS

She Stoops to Conquer, The School for Wives, Travesties, Richard III, The Man Who Came to Dinner, The Inspector General, Catsplay, Design for Living, The Shadow Box, Volpone, Let's Get a Divorce, Long Day's Journey into Night, A History of the American Film, and *World Premiere* of "archy and friends" conceived and staged by Jim Hoskins with music and lyrics by John Franceschina

Gary W. Sweetman Photos

Right: "A History of the American Film"
Above: Robert Beseda, Barbara Sohmers,
Robert Murch in "Design for Living"
Top: Isa Thomas, Bette Oliver
in "Catsplay"

Pam Guest, David Howard, Robert
Beseda in "Let's Get a Divorce"

Stephen Van Benchoten, Max Howard
in "Travesties"

175

BARTER THEATRE

Abingdon, Virginia
April 17, to November 5, 1978
Forty-sixth Season

Artistic Director/Producer, Rex Partington, Business Manager, Pearl Hayter; Press, Becky Rose; Stage Directors, Dorothy Marie, Ada Brown Mather, John W. Morrow, Jr., Rex Partington, Owen Phillips, Kenneth Robbins, John-Olon Scrymgeour, Edward Stern; Musical Director, Byron Grant; Sets, Bennet Averyt, Gregory Buch, F. Leonard Darby, Parmalee Welles; Costumes, Carr Garnett, Sigrid Insull; Lighting, Cindy Limauro, Sara Ross Morgan, Tony Partington; Stage Managers, Laura Burroughs, Tyson Stephenson, Steven Woolf; Technical Director, F. Leonard Darby

PRODUCTIONS AND CASTS

BORN YESTERDAY with Katherine Carlson, Terry Hinz, Ralph Redpath, John W. Morrow, Jr., Rec Partington, Cleo Holladay, Tyson Stephenson, William Turner, Ellen Donkin, Michael O'Brien, James Scott Hager, Dennis Moser, Carol Chittum

THE CORN IS GREEN with William Turner, Beverly Jensen, Fillmore McPherson IV, Ellen Donkin, Dennis Moser, John W. Morrow, Jr., Pamela Danser, Kristen Lowman, Cleo Holladay, Ralph Redpath, Sam Blackwell, Michael O'Brien, Dennis Moser, Owen Phillips, Carol Chittum, Catherine Rhea, Joan Varium

TARTUFFE with Pamela Danser, Terry Hinz, Beverly Jensen, Sam Blackwell, Kristen Lowman, Ralph Redpath, William Turner, John W. Morrow, Jr., Katherine Carlson, Rex Partington, Tyson Stephenson, Catherine Rhea

I DO! I DO! with Gary Daniel, Sandy Laufer, Adrienne Doucette

THE OWL AND THE PUSSYCAT with John Schak, Sandy Laufer

OH, COWARD! with Adrienne Doucette, Roger Kozol, Nicholas Wyman

VANITIES with Kristen Lowman, Beverly Jensen, Ellen Donkin

THE APPLE TREE with Nicholas Wyman, Sandy Laufer, Roger Kozol, Sam Blackwell, Carol Chittum, Adrienne Doucette, Larry Hansen, Terry Hinz, Kelli Kahn, Jolly King, John W. Morrow, Jr., Michael O'Brien, Capi Rhea, Tyson Stephenson, Joan Varnum

THE SECOND MAN with Cleo Holladay, John W. Morrow Jr., Sam Blackwell, Beverly Jensen, Thomas Brittingham

HOW THE OTHER HALF LOVES with Cleo Holladay, Ara Watson, Rex Partington, John W. Morrow, Jr., Sam Blackwell, Beverly Jensen

HAY FEVER with Mary Anne Dempsey, Samuel Blackwell, Jane Ridley, Cleo Holladay, Michael Graves, Con Roche, Mary Neufled, Henry Gardner, Beverly Jensen

THE WONDERFUL ONES! with Beverly Jensen, Samuel Blackwell, Tyson Stephenson, Anne Varley

Left: Adrienne Doucette, Roger Kozol, Nicholas Wyman in "Oh, Coward!" Top: Kristen Lowman, Ralph Redpath in "Tartuffe"

Terry Hinz, Katherine Carlson in "Born Yesterday"

John Morrow, Jr., Cleo Holladay, Sam Blackwell in "The Corn Is Green"

John W. Morrow, Jr., John H. Fields, David Shepherd, Marina Posvar in "The Play's the Thing" Right: John H. Fields, Maury Cooper, Patricia Boyette in "Twelfth Night"

CALIFORNIA ACTORS THEATRE

Los Gatos, California
October 12, 1978 - May 20, 1979
Executive Director, Sheldon Kleinman; General Manager, Francine E. Gordon; Artistic Director, Charles Maryan; Managing Director, Ken Barton; Press, Eileen Barnes; Stage Managers, Siobhan Phelan, John DeChant; Administrative Staff, Elizabeth Alfs, Kathleen Kurz, Karl Schuck

PRODUCTIONS AND CASTS

FARCES BY CHEKOV with Jack R. Marks, Joel Parks, Marina Posvar, Peggy Cowles, Kurtwood Smith, Maury Cooper

BUS STOP with Judith Ann Miller, Patricia Boyette, Jack R. Marks, Elizabeth Kemp, John W. Morrow, Jr., Tom Ramirez, Maury Cooper, David Shepherd

PLAYING WITH FIRE with Jack R. Marks, Patricia Boyette, Joel Parks, Elizabeth Kemp, David Shepherd, Judith Ann Miller

THE COLLECTION with John W. Morrow, Jr., David Shepherd, Duane Sidden, Marina Posvar

HOLIDAY with Marina Posvar, Al Blair, Doreen Remo, Joel Parks, Elizabeth Kemp, David Shepherd, John H. Fields, John W. Morrow, Jr., Judith Ann Miller, Duane Sidden, Patricia Boyette

THE PLAY'S THE THING with Maury Cooper, John H. Fields, David Shepherd, Marina Posvar, John W. Morrow, Jr., Duane Sidden, Al Mellinkoff, Kevin Coffey

TWELFTH NIGHT with Frank Savino, Randall King, Ken Barton, Elizabeth Kemp, Gregory L. Mortensen, John H. Fields, Patricia Boyette, Maury Cooper, Marina Posvar, John W. Morrow, Jr., Thomas S. Oleniacz, David Shepherd, Duane Sidden, Gregory L. Mortensen, John Davies, Kim Foscato, DeLynn Howes, Beth Meyer

CRIMES OF THE HEART with Marina Posvar, Patricia Boyette, David Shepherd, Joyce Harris, Melissa Weber, Maury Cooper, Joel Parks

World Premiere of PLYMOUTH ROCK by William Hamilton, with Joel Parks (Harry Stockton), Marina Posvar (Gwen Stockton), Peggy Cowles (Phoebe Henshaw), Kurtwood Smith (Ward Henshaw), Peter Brandon (Robert Morgan), Patricia Boyette (Sara Morgan)

Peggy Cowles
in "Plymouth Rock"

CENTER STAGE

Baltimore, Maryland
September 29, 1978–May 27, 1979
Artistic Director, Stan Wojewodski, Jr.; Managing Director, Peter W. Culman; Press, Sally Livingston; Stage Managers, Rene J. Mainguy, Amanda Mengden

PRODUCTIONS AND CASTS

THE SHADOW BOX by Michael Cristofer; Direcor, Stan Wojewodski, Jr.; Set, Andrew Jackness; Costumes, Bob Wojewodski; Lighting, Judy Rasmuson. CAST: Daniel Szelag, Joseph Costa, Richard L. Malone, Susan Peretz, Steven Gilborn, Terry O'Quinn, Holly Barron, Tana Hicken, Sudie Bond

BORN YESTERDAY by Garson Kanin; Director, Steven Robman; Set, Charles Cosler; Costumes, Dona Granata; Lighting, Spencer Mosse. CAST: Verna Day, Rudolph Willrich, Richard L. Malone, Alan Silver, Norman Smith, Daniel Szelag, Christine Baranski, Robert Pastene, Joseph R. Snair, Laura J. Castro, Perry Alexander, Jr., David O. Petersen, Vivienne Shub

A CHRISTMAS CAROL: SCROOGE AND MARLEY (*World Premiere*) Israel Horovitz's adaptation of Charles Dickens' novel; Director, Robert Allan Ackerman; Set, Hugh Landwehr; Costumes, Bob Wojewodski; Lighting, Arden Fingerhut; Sound, David Campbell; Movement, Jeff Duncan. CAST: Nicholas Kepros, Robert Pastene, Terry O'Quinn, Theodore May, Daniel Szelag, Gregory T. Daniels, David O. Petersen, Richard L. Malone, Charlotte Harvey, Albert Cauffman, Alan Silver, Vivienne Shub, Brenda Thomas, Christine Baranski, Denise Koch, Richard Dix, Tana Hicken, Carter Michel, Michael Schondel, Jeremy Craig Kasten, William Salisbury, John LaFarge

G. R. POINT by David Berry; Director, William Devane; Set, Peter Larkin; Lighting, Neil Peter Jampolis, Jane Reisman; Costumes, Laura H. Castro; Sound, Kirk Nurock. CAST: Lazaro Perez, Howard E. Rollins, Jr., Michael Jeter, Michael Moriarty, Mark Jenkins, Paul Espel, Mansoor Najee-ullah, Herb Rice, Lori Tan Chinn

YOU CAN'T TAKE IT WITH YOU by Kaufman and Hart; Director, Stan Wojewodski, Jr., Set, John Kasarda; Costumes, Hilary Sherred; Lighting, Bonnie A. Brown. CAST: Mary Hara, Cynthia Crumlish, Sharita Hunt, Richard Dix, Zeke Zaccaro, Daniel Szelag, Earl Arremis Johnson, Jr., Robert Donley, Michael Gross, Michael McCarty, Vivienne Shub, Bob Horen, Roberta Lund, Richard L. Malone, John W. Russell, Jr.

MEASURE FOR MEASURE by William Shakespeare; Director, Stan Wojewodski, Jr.; Set, Hugh Landwehr; Costumes, Dona Granata; Lighting, Arden Fingerhut. CAST: Robert Burr, Terry O'Quinn, Bob Horen, Philip Kraus, Michael Gross, Daniel Szelag, Richard L. Malone, G. Brock Johnson, Richard Dix, Zeke Zaccaro, Michael McCarty, John W. Russell, Jr., Vivienne Shub, Julia Augenstein, Tana Hicken, Laura J. Castro, Denise Koch, Peter Van Norden

BONJOUR LA BONJOUR by Michel Tremblay; Director, Stan Wojewodski, Jr.; Set, Hugh Landwehr; Costumes, Bob Wojewodski; Lighting, Spencer Mosse. CAST: Robert Donley, Georgine Hall, Vivienne Shub, Kenneth Meseroll, Megan Cole, Nancy Donahue, June Squibb, Pat Karpen

Richard Anderson Photos

Right: Richard L. Malone, Joseph Costa, Susan Peretz in "The Shadow Box"

Michael Gross, Daniel Szelag, Richard L. Malone, Philip Kraus in "Measure for Measure" Top: Herb Rice, Lori Tan Chinn, Michael Moriarty, Michael Jeter, Howard E. Rollins, Jr. in "G. R. Point"

"You Can't Take It with You"

Robert Pastene, Nicholas Kepros in "A Christmas Carol"

CENTER STAGE, INC.

Austin, Texas
July 28, 1978–July 8, 1979
Artistic Director, Jimmy Costello; Business Manager, Bil Pfuderer; Press, Cristine Wallis; Program Coordinators, Mac Williams, Jeanette Brown; Sets, Jimmy Costello, Bil Pfuderer, Lee Duran, Michael Peshka; Costumes, Joe York, Sarah Byrne; Assistant to Director, Julie K. White

PRODUCTIONS AND CASTS

THE CLUB by Eve Merriam with R. Laven, J. White, V. J. Pelfreyman, J. K. Jones, J. Tobias, L. Weekins, M. DeMore

DANCE ON A COUNTRY GRAVE by Kelly Hamilton with Paul Beutel, Melanie Renee Guilbeault, Ray Weikel, Julee McClelland, Jessie K. Jones, Julia Tobias, Wanda Pierce, Bill Johnson, Julie White, Tony Bove, Nick Wilkinson, Byron Mathews, Deborah Ann Mussett, Dan Lewis, Mark Welch

A LIFE IN THE THEATRE by David Mamet with Mike McKay, Mac Williams, David Bottrell

CATCH 22 by Joseph Heller with Greg Barrios, John Brown, Denise Brouillette, Jose Cruz, Dan Lewis, Wade Bingham, Debora Duckett, Herb Eagan, Dave Ellis, Charles Gruber, Steve Haire, Oliver Handley, Sharon Handley, Joe Korbel, Dan Lewis, Peter Madison, Mike Malone, Julee McClelland, Jace Minor, Ron Pinkard, David McRee, Erol Stone, John Susskind, Steve Swanson, Mark Welch, Susanne Wells, Manuel Zarate

THE BELLE OF AMHERST by William Luce with Cristine Wallis

AMERICAN BUFFALO by David Mamet with Eric Henshaw, John M. Jackson, Nick Sweet

LADIES AT THE ALAMO by Paul Zindel with Daryl Cates, Ella Rankin, Julee C. McClelland, Kathryn Wilson, B. J. Strode

COMPANY by Stephen Sondheim, George Furth with Barry Eisenberg, Judy Dillen, Ray Weikel, Ann Threlkeld, Paul Beutel, Sharon Davis, Scottie Wilkison, Peter F. Madison, Deborah Ann Mussett, Rene Gerard Chapa, Karen Kuykendahl, Richard Gartner, Laura White, Shelly Graham, Susan Kwant, Ann D. Armstrong, Mary E. Marin, Lauralynn Makaj, Julia Tobias, Michelle Alexander, Leslie Perry, Julie White

PORGY AND BESS IN CONCERT with Thomas Carey, Naomi George, Robert Merritt, Shirley Baines, Carol Brice, Glover Parham, Betty Harris, Julian V. C. Reed

BLEACHER BUMS with Johnny Lopez, John M. Jackson, Joe York, Diane Kellerman, Marty Ossefort, B. J. Strode, Stephen Schwartz, Duane Skoog

POE by Stephen Most and the Organic Theatre with Eric Henshaw, Doug Sivad, Ginger Gillman, Jan Jones, Polly Coffin, Mike McKay, Johnny Lopez, David Bottrell, Sarah Byrne, Gary Coll, Joy Poth, Hal D. Shelton, B. J. Strode

WHO'S ON FIRST with Sharon Wood and Jack Hensley

THE GOLDEN FLEECE with Liz Quinn, J. Charlie McKinney

and *World Premieres* of A FRIEND OF THE FAMILY by Nick Wilkinson with Jane Herrick, Hal Shelton, Bunch Brittain, Byron Mathews, Gwen Rodgers, Jessie K. Jones, Robin Laven, Ann Williamson, Daniel Lewis, and DIAGILEV by Mary Martin with Bernard Siben

Debbe Sharpe, John H. Mason III Photos

Cast of "Company" Top: Manuel Zarate, Denise Brouillette in "Catch 22"

**Cristine Wallis
in "The Belle of Amherst"**

**Eric Henshaw in "American Buffalo"
Above: Daryl Cates in "Ladies at the Alamo"**

CINCINNATI PLAYHOUSE
Cincinnati, Ohio
October 10, 1978–June 17, 1979
Producing Director, Michael Murray; Managing Director, Robert W. Tolan; Associate Director, John Valente; Stage Directors, Michael Murray, Edward Berkeley, John Going; Musical Director, Carmon DeLeone; Choreographer, Dennis Grimaldi; Fights, Marshall Shnider; Sets, Paul Shortt, Duke H. Durfee, Karl Eigsti, Marjorie Kellogg, Neil Peter Jampolis; Costumes, Jennifer von Mayrhauser, Ann Firestone, Caley Summers, Annie Peacock Warner; Lighting, Neil Peter Jampolis, Duke H. Durfee, Hugh Lester, Pat Collins, Duane Schuler; Sound, Kim Zimmerman; Production Manager, Duke H. Durfee; Stage Managers, Ed Oster, Vicky West Zimmerman, Claudia Burk, J. David Lancaster; Press, Avis J. Yuni, Daniel Schay; Business Manager, Mary Beth Gardner; Company Manager, J. Dewey Hawthorne, Props, Nancy Gilmore

PRODUCTIONS AND CASTS

ROMEO AND JULIET with Andy Backer, William Converse-Roberts, Diane Danzi, Edwin Dundon, Michael Govan, Richard Hoyt, J. Jeffrey Kilgore, J. David Lancaster, Terry Layman, Elizabeth Moore, Tania Myren, Don Plumley, Gregory J. Procaccino, Verner Rieck, Jim Semmelman, Marshall Shnider, Adrian Sparks, David Upson, Susan Ball, Darnell Davis, James A. Howard, Christopher Klein, Paul Krakovsky, Christine Parks, Donald Volpenhein, Patricia Camp Wilson, Joseph Zimmerman

OTHERWISE ENGAGED with Richard Council, Edmond Genest, Jim Oyster, Ann C. Twomey, Eric Uhler, J. T. Walsh, Meg Wynn-Owen

ROOM SERVICE with George Brengel, Dan Diggles, Edwin Dundon, J. R. Horne, Keith Mackey, Jerry McGee, Moultrie Patten, Timothy S. Perrino, Keith Perry, Patricia Richardson, Lynn Ritchie, William G. Schilling, Robert Silver, Rudolph Willrich

HEDDA GABLER with John Aylward, Kurt Beattie, Mary Diveny, Jonathan Farwell, Cordis Heard, Giulia Pagano, Marian Primont

THE BUDDY SYSTEM (World Premiere) by Jonathan Marc Feldman, with Victor Bevine, James DeMarse, Patrick Scott Downey, Ron Fassler, David Garrison, Jody Gelb, Douglas Warhit, David Wohl

MAN OF LA MANCHA with Alex Bernardo, David Canary, Doug Carfrae, Andrew Charles, Stephanie Cotsirilos, Henry D'Alessandris, John Ferrante, Marshall Hagins, Gene Harris, Donald Mark, Michael McCarty, Gary McGurk, Taylor Reed, Mary Rocco, Richard Sabellico, Sonja Stuart, Kevin Brooks Winkler, Susan Ball, Timothy S. Perrino, Rick Schafer, Mary Lee Stallsmith, Timothy deZarn, Kenneth Durnbaugh, Thomas W. Hafner, Katie Higgins, Mike Kalthoff, Cathy Lesser, Scott Moening, Mary Shaw, Joseph Zimmerman

Sandy Underwood Photos

Taylor Reed, David Canary, Stephanie Cotsirilos in "Man of La Mancha" Above: Giulia Pagano, Kurt Beattie in "Hedda Gabler"

Marshall Shnider, Adrian Sparks in "Romeo and Juliet" Top Left: Patrick Scott Downey, David Garrison in "The Buddy System"

James Richards, Richard Oberlin, Kelly Lawrence,
Teresa Wright in "Threads" Top Right: Sharon
Bicknell, June Gibbons, Joe D. Lauck in "Something's
Afoot"

CLEVELAND PLAY HOUSE

Cleveland, Ohio
October 11, 1978–April 29, 1979
Sixty-third Season

Director, Richard Oberlin; Associate Director, Larry Tarrant; Business Manager, Nelson Isekeit; Press, Edwin P Rapport, Jane Floriano, Rita Buchanan, Gary Stross; Stage Directors, Paul Lee, Evie McElroy, Richard Halverson, Richard Oberlin, Larry Tarrant; Sets, Richard Gould; Props, David Smith; Costumes, Diane Dalton; Estelle Painter; Sound/Lighting, Stephen Bellamy; Stage Managers, Varney Knapp, Richard Oberlin, Stanley R. Suchecki, Larry Tarrant; Company Manager, Stanley R. Suchecki

COMPANY

Kenneth Albers, Sharon Bicknell, Sydney Erskine, Jo Farwell, Jonathan Farwell, Paul Floriano, June Gibbons, Richard Halverson, James P. Kisicki, Joe D. Lauck, Allen Leatherman, Paul Lee, Harper Jane McAdoo, Evie McElroy, Richard Oberlin, William Rhys, James Richards, Carol Schultz, Wayne Turney

GUEST ARTISTS: Directors: Kenneth Albers, Jonathan Bolt, Judith Haskell; Designer, Paul Rodgers; Actors, Mary Adams-Smith, Jo Anna Collins, Julia Curry, James Finney, David O. Frazier, Margaret Hamilton, Providence Hollander, Kelly Lawrence, Alec McCowen, Leonard Nimoy, Carolyn Reed, Robert Rhys, Gary Smith, Dudley Swetland, Christina Whitmore, William Windom, Teresa Wright

PRODUCTIONS

"Night Must Fall," "The Shadow Box," "The Importance of Being Earnest," "Gemini," "Equus," "The Odyssey," "Something's Afoot," "Thurber I & II," "St. Mark's Gospel," "Vincent," "A Christmas Carol"

World Premieres; "Threads" by Jonathan Bolt, "The Last of the Marx Brothers' Writers" by Louis Phillips

Mike Edwards Photos

Margaret Hamilton, James Richards
in "Night Must Fall"

CITY THEATRE COMPANY

Pittsburgh, Pennsylvania
March 23, - August 26, 1979
Artistic Director/Producer, Mark Lione; Press, Jim Wilhelm; Scenic and Costume Designer, Virginia E. Hildreth; Lighting, Victor McPoland, John Gilles, David Groupe; Sound, Mark Firley; Stage Manager, Jim Wilhelm; Technical Directors, David Groupe, John Gilles

COMPANY

Jim Frederick, Randell Haynes, Jennifer Johanos, Katie Karlovitz, J. Christopher O'Connor, Lee Phifer, Joseph Pilato, J. Neil Prell, Nathaniel Ritch, Helena Ruoti GUEST ARTISTS: Shevra Tait, Geoffrey Hitch, Katie Karlovitz

PRODUCTIONS

"Table Manners" by Alan Ayckbourn, "Postcards" by James Prideaux, "Hopscotch" by Israel Horovitz, "The Misanthrope" by Moliere, "A Chinaman's Whisper" (*World Premiere*) by C. V. Peters, "The Pantomime Man" by Dan Kamin

Right: Joseph Pilato, Helena Ruoti in "Table Manners" Top: Helena Ruoti, Randell Haynes in "Hopscotch"

CRICKET THEATRE

Minneapolis, Minnesota
October 19, 1978–June 9, 1979
Artistic Director, Lou Salerni; Producing Director, Bill Semans; Business Manager, Marcy Dowse; Press, Betsy Husting, Penny Pray; Technical Director, Phillip Billey; Stage Manager, Kimberly Francis Kearsley; Sets, Thom Roberts, Phillip Billey, Dick Leerhoff, Jerry Williams; Lighting, Phillip Billey, Michael Vennerstrom; Costumes, Christopher Beesley; Props, Robert Davis; Guest Directors, Pat Patton, Peter Thompson, Howard Dallin

PRODUCTIONS AND CASTS

MOURNING PICTURES by Honor Moore with Camille Gifford, Chris Forth, Michael Galloway, Carole Kastigar, Peter Moore, Wayne Ballantyne, Dolores Noah

A BREEZE FROM THE GULF by Mart Crowley with Carol Thibeau, Peter Moore, Clive Rosengren

5th OF JULY by Lanford Wilson with Lindsey Ginter, Carol Thibeau, Nancy Bagshaw, Joe Horvath, Jan Haflich, Peter Moore, Amy Buchwald, David Morgan

A LIFE IN THE THEATRE by David Mamet with Bill Schoppert, Allen Hamilton

ALEOLA by Gaetan Charlebois (*U. S. Premiere*) with Carmen Tremblay, Andre Saint Denis

World Premieres of SORT OF A LOVE SONG by Glenn Allen Smith with Clive Rosengren, Emily Grinspan, Wayne Ballantyne, Robert Mailand, Gwen Jackson, James Craven, C. Michael Leopard, Merle McDill, Peter Moore, Kathleen Perkins, Richard Costigan, Amy Buchwald, Gordon Cronce, Paul Sorenson, Sarah Moser-Riley

THE D. B. COOPER PROJECT by John Orlock with Don Amendolia, Fred Thompson, Clive Rosengren, Camille Gifford, Jane Murray, Dolores Noah

Craig Litherland Photos

Emily Grinspan, Clive Rosengren, Gwen Jackson in "Sort of a Love Song"

Top Left: Bill Schoppert, Allen Hamilton in "A Life in the Theatre"

DALLAS THEATRE CENTER

Dallas, Texas
October 10, 1978–August 4, 1979
Managing Director, Paul Baker; Associate Director, Mary Sue Jones; Stage Directors, Paul Baker, Ryland Merkey, Ken Latimer, John Logan, Randolph Tallman; Sets, Peter Wolf, Mary Sue Jones, Virgil Beavers, Yoichi Aoki, Peter Lynch, John Henson; Costumes, John Henson, Kathleen Latimer, Cheryl Denson, Susan Sleeper; Lighting, Allen Hibbard, Linda Blase, Robert Duffy Randy Moore; Stage Managers, Andrew Gaupp, Michael Scudday, James Eddy, Suzanne Chiles, Michael Kreuger, Ronni Lopez, Dennis Vincent, Wayne Lambert; Press, Lynn Trammell

COMPANY

Yoichi Aoki, Virgil Beavers, Linda Blase, Judith Davis, Cheryl Denson, John Figlmiller, Robyn Flatt, Martha Goodman, Tim Green, C. P. Hendrie, John Henson, Allen Hibbard, Mary Sue Jones, Preston Jones, Kathleen Latimer, Ken Latimer, Sallie Laurie, John Logan, Rebecca Logan, Steven Mackenroth, Ryland Merkey, Norma Moore, Randy Moore, Sally Netzel, Mona Pursley, Bryant J. Reynolds, Synthia Rogers, Mary Rohde, Glenn Allen Smith, Louise Mosley Smith, Robert A. Smith, John R. Stevens, Randolph Tallman, Jacque Thomas, Lynn Trammell, Lee Wheatley, Ronald Wilcox

PRODUCTIONS

"The Royal Family" (Kaufman-Ferber), "A Midsummer Night's Dream" (Musical by Randolph Tallman and Steven Mackenroth), "A Texas Trilogy" (Preston Jones), "The Devil's General" (Zuckmayer), "As You Like It" (Shakespeare), and *World Premiere* of "Blood Money" with book and lyrics by M. G. Johnston and music by Jim Abbott.

Linda Blase Photos

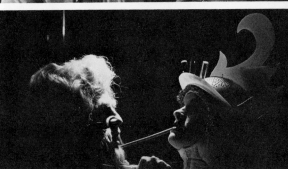

Robert A. Smith, Candy Buckley in "Blood Money"
Top: Preston Jones, Randy Moore in
"A Texas Trilogy"

Sharon Douglas, George Wilson, Paula Davis in "The Offering" Above: Dee Andrus, Barbara Busby in "The Doorbell"

DETROIT REPERTORY THEATRE

Detroit, Michigan
November 2, 1978–June 24, 1979
Artistic Director, Bruce E. Millan; Executive Director, Robert Williams; Production Coordinator, Marylynn Kacie; Program and Planning Coordinator, Judith Goode Moran; Lighting, Dick Smith; Sets, Marshall Kotzin, Sal Lupo, Joseph Zubrick; Costumes, Barbara Busby; Scenic Artist, John Knox; Stage Managers, Valarie Hawkind, Marge Miller, Dee Andrus, Deborah Patrick, Sharon Douglas; Sound, Lissa Bisario

PRODUCTIONS AND CASTS

THE OFFERING by Gus Edwards; Director, Robert Williams. Cast: George Wilson, Sharon Douglas, Michael Jay, Paula Davis

BOTH YOUR HOUSES by Maxwell Anderson; Director, Bruce E. Millan. CAST: Dee Andrus, Pat Ansuini, William Boswell, Louise Bradford, Sharon Douglas, Darius L. Dudley, Jesse Harris, Sandra Hines, Willie Hodge, Sam Kirkland, Jesse Newton, Richard W. Villaire, Keith Wallace, Robert Williams, John T. Young

EVE by Larr Fineberg; Director, Dee Andrus (*U. S. Premiere*) CAST: Barbara Busby, William Boswell, Sam Kirkland, George Wilson, Council Cargle, Pat Ansuini

THE DOORBELL by Paul Simpson; Director, Bruce E. Millan (*World Premiere*). CAST: Dee Andrus, Barbara Busby, Robert Williams

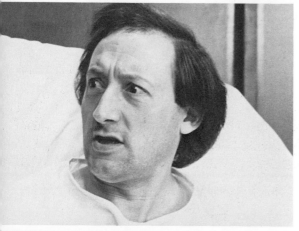

Michael Tolaydo, Glynis Bell, Leonardo Cimino, David Cromwell in "Richard II" Left: John Neville-Andrews in "Whose Life Is It Anyway?" Top: Glynis Bell, Helen Carey in "Merry Wives of Windsor"

FOLGER THEATRE GROUP
Washington, D. C.
October 11, 1978–July 15, 1979
Producer, Louis W. Scheeder; Associate Producer, Michael Sheehan; Production Manager, T. C. Behrens; Business Manager, Mary Ann deBarbieri; Company Manager. Thomas Madden; Technical Director, Michael Foley; Sound, Jim Bloch; Stage Managers, Tom DeMauro, Shannon J. Sumpter; Press, Paula Bond

PRODUCTIONS AND CASTS

THE MERRY WIVES OF WINDSOR by William Shakespeare; Director, Mikel Lamber; Music, William Penn; Set, Hugh Lester; Costumes, Jess Goldstein; Lighting, Paul Gallo. CAST: Leonardo Cimino, David Cromwell, Ralph Cosham, Terry Hinz, Thomas Carson, Michael Tolaydo, David Hodge, John Neville-Andrews, Karen Wadman, Glynis Bell, Helen Carey, Marc Lee Adams, Carlos Juan Gonzales, Daniel Lewin, Marion Lines, Shepard Sobel, Albert Corbin, Eric Zwemer, Peter Vogt, George Dunlap, Nick Mathwick, Peter Suddeth

THE TRADEDY OF KING RICHARD THE SECOND by William Shakespeare; Director, Louis W. Scheeder; Music, William Penn; Set, Scott Johnson; Lighting, Hugh Lester; Costumes, Nancy Thun. CAST: Michael Tolaydo, Leonardo Cimino, Terry Hinz, John Neville-Andrews, June Hansen, Jim Beard, David Bromwell, George Dunlap, Carlos Juan Gonzales, Howard Levy, Shepard Sobel, Albert Corbin, Glynis Bell, Peter Vogt, Marc Lee Adams, David Hodge, Richard Cochrane, Thomas Carson, Eric Zwemer, Nick Mathwick, David Hornstein, Ralph Cosham, Karen Wadman, Karen Bayly, Mikel Lambert

BENEFIT OF A DOUBT by Edward Clinton; Director, Barnet Kellman; Set, Philipp Jung; Lighting, Randy Becker; Costumes, Tom McAlister. CAST: Carol Kane, Elizabeth Council, Stephen Mendillo, Mikel Lambert, Geraldine Court, Ray Aranha

AS YOU LIKE IT by William Shakespeare; Director, Louis W. Scheeder; Music, William Penn; Set and Lighting, Hugh Lester; Costumes, Hilary A Sherred; Choreography, Virginia Freeman. CAST: Leonardo Cimino, Richard Dix, Howard Levy, Ralph Cosham, Wesley Grant, Stuart Lerch, Michael Tolaydo, Marc Lee Adams, Eric Uhler, William Preston, Kevin Murray, David Cromwell, Shepard Sobel, Ray Aranha, Eric Zwemer, Brian Corrigan, Helen Carey, Glynis Bell, Cynthia Crumlish, Franchelle Stewart Dorn, Karen Bayly, Jim Beard, Richard Cochrane, Nick Mathwick, Josh Billings

U. S. Premiere of WHOSE LIFE IS IT ANYWAY? by Brian Clark; Director, Louis W. Scheeder; Set and Lighting, Hugh Lester; Costumes, Jess Goldstein. CAST: John Neville-Andrews, Mary Hara, Judith Ivey, Alvin Hippolyte, Marion Lines, Ralph Cosham, Mikel Lambert, Peter Vogt, David Cromwell, Terry Hinz, Shepard Sobel, Marc Barrett, Albert Corbin, Eric Zwemer

Joan Marcus Photos

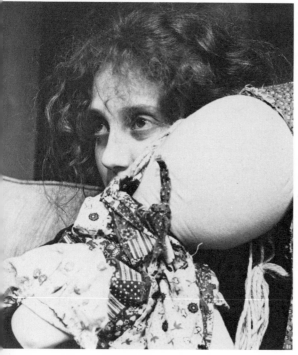

**Carol Kane
in "Benefit of a Doubt"**

GEORGE STREET PLAYHOUSE

New Brunswick, N. J.
October 20, 1978–May 26, 1979
Producing Director, Eric Krebs; Managing Director, John Herochik; Press, Sandy Berger; Technical Directors, Gary Kechly, Jeff Berzon; Lighting, Daniel Stratman; Sets, Daniel M. Proett; Costumes, Sandra Wallace; Stage Managers, Holly DeYong, Cheri Bogdan; Sound, Fran Covais

PRODUCTIONS AND CASTS

SCHOOL FOR WIVES by Moliere; Director, Eric Loeb; Costumes, Jeanette Oleksa; Set, Bob Phillips. CAST: P. J. Barry, Nancy Mette, John B. Jellison, Alice Travis, John Pielmeier, Harry Carlson, Dylan Ross, Woody Beam

LONG DAY'S JOURNEY INTO NIGHT by Eugene O'Neill; Director, Paul Austin. CAST: Frank Lattimore, Dolores Kenan, Robertson Carricart, Bill Cwikowski, Katherine Cortez

SIZWE BANSI IS DEAD by Athol Fugard, Winston Ntshona, John Kani, and STATEMENTS AFTER AN ARREST UNDER THE IMMORALITY ACT by Athol Fugard; Set, Christopher Nowak; Director, Harold Scott. CAST: Lou Ferguson, Joe Seneca, Jan Granger, Phil Kraus

TWELFTH NIGHT by William Shakespeare; Director, Bob Hall; Set and Costumes, Bob Hall, Sandra Wallace. CAST: Joseph Culliton, Samuel Maupin, Roy Doliner, Lisa McMillan, Dave Anderson, David Richmond, Maggie Hawthorne, K. C. Wilson, Beth Dixon, Michael Burg, Donavon Diez, Allan Carlsen, David Swatling

World Premieres of PETTYCOAT LANE by Judd Woldin; Based on tales "The King Of Schnorrers" by Israel Zangwill; Director, Eric Krebs; Choreography and Musical Staging, Nora Peterson; Costumes, Vickie McLaughlin; Musical Director, Bruce Kirle. CAST: Gene Lindsey, Sandra Lavalle, Ralph Bruneau, Virginia Ness, Fred Sanders, Jack Sevier, Steve Liebman, Donna Monroe, Katharine Buffaloe, Richard Ryder, Robert Blumenfeld
DANCE FOR ME SIMEON by Joseph Maher; Director, Isaac Schambelan. CAST: Joseph Warren, Fred Sanders, Myra Carter

Suzanne Karp Krebs Photos

**Nancy Mette, John Jellison in "School for Wives"
Top: Richard Ryder, Jack Sevier in
"Pettycoat Lane"**

GEVA THEATRE

Rochester, N. Y.
September 29, 1978–:March 18, 1979
Managing Director, Jessica L. Andrews; Artistic Director, Gideon Y. Schein; Costumes, Linda J. Vigdor; Lighting, Lee DeLorme; Business Manager, Timothy C. Norland; Stage Manager, Marcy Gamzon; Press, Jayne McLean, James Guido; Props, Sandy Struth; Technical Director, Ian O'Connor

PRODUCTIONS AND CASTS

A STREETCAR NAMED DESIRE by Tennessee Williams with Caril Powell, Nora Chester, Dennis Predovic, Carolyn Hurlburt, Tony Pasqualini, Michael Hartman, Pania Brown, Beth Dixon, David Chandler, Michael Hawke, Lois Hoskin, Richard Wilkins

DIAMOND STUDS by Jim Wann with Tricia Austin, Susan J. Baum, David Chandler, Mark Hardwick, Michael Hartman, Peter Kairo, Gina McMather, Cass Morgan, Matthew Oppenheimer, Trip Plymale, S. Jay Rankin, Joel Robertson, Bruce E. Rodgers, Jim Wann, Richard Wilkins

SIZWE BANSI IS DEAD by Athol Fugard, John Kani, Winston Ntshona with Brent Jennings, Basil Wallace

RUE DE L'AMOUR by Georges Feydeau, adapted by Mawby Green and Ed Feilbert. CAST: Peggy Fleche, Wayne DeCesar, Edward Kaye-Martin, Charles Maggiore, Kendall March, Davis Hall, Alan Zampese, Brooks Morton, Kevin O'Leary, Lance Taubold

A MOON FOR THE MISBEGOTTEN by Eugene O'Neill with Anita Birchnall, Brian Benben, Paul Anderson, Edmond Genest, Tony Pasqualini

THE HOSTAGE by Brendan Behan with Rebecca Schull, William R. Riker, Stephan Mark Weyte, Kim Sullivan, Susan Lichtman, Tony Pasqualini, Sharon Harrison, Alan Zampese, Peter J. Saputo, Lois Hoskin, Linda Swenson, Peggy Fleche, Michael Hartman, Eddy McDonald, Lance Davis

**Lance Davis, Lois Hoskin, Michael Hartman
in "The Hostage" Above: Anita Birchnall,
Edmond Genest in "Moon for the Misbegotten"**

Jerome Kilty, Leonard Frey in "Two-Part Inventions" Left: Meeshach Taylor in "Native Son"

GOODMAN THEATRE

Chicago, Illinois
October 12, 1978–June 24, 1979
Artistic Director, Gregory Mosher; Managing Director, Janet Wade; General Manager, Roche Schulfer; Associate Artistic Director/Playwright-in-residence, David Mamet; Press, Liz Skrodzki; Business Manager, Barbara Janowitz; Production Manager, Philip Eickhoff; Stage Managers, Joseph Drummond, Chuck Henry; Props, James Swank; Scenic Artist, Mary Rauscher; Directors, Tony Mockus, Michael Feingold, Mel Shapiro, Tony Tanner, Gregory Mosher; Sets, Joseph Nieminski, David Lloyd Gropman, John Wulp, Lynn Pecktal, John Lee Beatty; Costumes, Christa Scholtz, James Edmund Brady, Willa Kim, Clifford Capone; Lighting, Pat Collins, Robert Christen, Jennifer Tipton; Choreography, Gus Giordano

PRODUCTIONS AND CASTS

NATIVE SON with Melva Williams, Meshach Taylor, Faye Ternipsede-Bradbury, Derrick Maurice Evans, Barry Reneau, Fernand Larrieu, Jr., Eric Stratton, Howard Stratton, Sonja Lanzener, Ralph Foody, Pat Terry, Dawn Davis, Keith Szarabajka, Celestine Heard, Mike Genovese, Paul Butler, Mike Nussbaum, Colin Stinton, Ron Dean, David Stettler, David E. Chadderdon, Michael Gorman, Bill Hollis, Tom McKeon, David Mink

A CHRISTMAS CAROL with Val Bettin, Susan Dafoe, Mark Christopher Maranto, Michael C. Pabis, Judy Barbosa, Blaine Lesnik, Frank Howard, Ralph Foody, William J. Norris, Robert Scogin, Tim Halligan, John Ostrander, Laurence Russo, Kerry Stephen O'-Connor, J. Pat Miller, Honor Finnegan, Will Fenno, Annabel Armour, William C. Fitzsimmons, Michael Dunn, Lawrence McCauley, Mary Pat Byrne, Jodean Culbert, Philip Hoffman, Jeanine Morick, Fred Thomas, Del Close

CURSE OF THE STARVING CLASS with John Malkovich, Jane Alderman, Glenne Headley, Jack Wallace, Richard Baird, Bradley Mott, Dennis Vero, Timothy Jenkins, Vinny Guastaferro

U. S. PREMIERES:
EMIGRES by Slawomir Mrozek with J. Pat Miller and Ray Rayner
THE ISLAND by Athol Fugard with Meshach Taylor, Lionel Smith

WORLD PREMIERES:
TWO-PART INVENTIONS by Richard Howard with Avril Gentles, Leonard Frey, Kathleen Hart, Jerome Kilty
BOSOMS AND NEGLECT by John Guare with Kate Reid, Paul Rudd, Marian Mercer
LONE CANOE by David Mamet; Music and Lyrics by Alaric Jans; with Susan Dafoe, Norman Snow, Colin Stinton, Sam Tsoutsouvas
SCENES AND REVELATIONS by Elan Garonzik with David Chadderdon, Susan Dafoe, Tim Halligan, Janice St. John, Sonja Lanzener, Nan Wade

Thomas England Photos

Norman Snow, Sam Tsoutsouvas, Susan Dafoe in "Lone Canoe"

Left Center: Sonja Lanzener, Nan Wade, Susan Dafoe, Janice St. John in "Scenes and Revelations"

THE GUTHRIE THEATER

Minneapolis, Minnesota
June 1, 1978–February 24, 1979

Artistic Director, Alvin Epstein; Managing Director, Donald Schoenbaum; Production Manager, Jon Cranney; Associate Director, Stephen Kanee; Resident Director, Emily Mann; Music Director, Dick Whitbeck; Lighting, Ronald M. Bundt; Costumes, Jack Edwards; Technical Director, Neil McLeod; Props, Michael Berry; Press, Melissa R. Cohen; Stage Managers, Bob Bye, Diane DeVita, Sharon Ewald, Michael Facius, Mary Hunter; Sound, Tom Bolstad; Guest Artists, Dunya Ramicova, David L. Gropman, Desmond Heeley, Zack Brown, Marjorie Kellogg, Jennifer Von Mayrhauser, Jack Barkla, Carrie Robbins, Tony Straiges, Peter Mark Schifter, Steven Robman, Carmen de Lavallade, William Bolcom

COMPANY

Barbara Bryne, Donald Buka, David Canary, David Cecsarini, Oliver Cliff, Michael Damon, Jake Dengel, Cara Duff-MacCormick, Ron Faber, Don R. Fallbeck, Patricia Fraser, Peter Michael Goetz, James Hartman, Rosemary Hartup, Tom Hegg, Susan Isenberg, Randall Duk Kim, Stephen Lang, Tara Loewenstern, Heather MacDonough, Peter MacNicol, W. H. Macy, Nancy Marvy, Jack McLaughlin, Joan Morris, Amy Nissen, Gordon Oas-Heim, Guy Paul, Joseph Regalbuto, Barbara Reid, Maura Shaffer, Margaret Silk, Roy K. Stevens

PRODUCTIONS

"Boy Meets Girl" by Bela and Samuel Spewack, "Hamlet" by William Shakespeare, "A Christmas Carol" by Charles Dickens adapted by Barbara Field, "The Beggar's Opera" by John Gay, *U. S. Premiere* of "Bonjour La Bonjour" by Michel Tremblay, *American Premiere* of "The Pretenders" by Henrik Ibsen, and *World Premiere* of "Teibele and Her Demon" by Isaac Bashevis Singer and Eve Friedman

Boyd Hagen Photos

Right: Peter Michael Goetz, Alvin Epstein in "Marriage" Top: Joseph Regalbuto, Robert Pastene in "Bonjour La Bonjour"

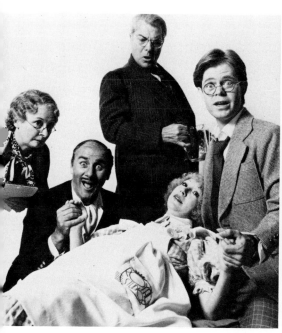

Barbara Bryne, Peter Michael Goetz, Donald Buka, ...ra Duff-MacCormick, W. H. Macy in "Boy Meets Girl"

F. Murray Abraham, Laura Esterman in "Teibele and Her Demon"

HARTFORD STAGE COMPANY
Hartford, Connecticut
October 6, 1978 - June 17, 1979
Producing Director, Paul Weidner; Managing Director, William Stewart; Press, Averill Kaufman; Business Manager, Alan Toman; Technical Director, Randy Engels; Stage Manager, Fred Hoskins

PRODUCTIONS AND CASTS

CATCHPENNY TWIST by Stewart Parker (*American Premiere*); Director Irene Lewis; Music, Shaun Davey; Lyrics, Stewart Parker; Set, Hugh Landwehr; Costumes, Linda Fisher; Lighting, Arden Fingerhut; Musical Director-Arranger, Richard DeRosa. CAST: Jarlath Conroy, Paddy Croft, Cynthia Crumlish, Bernard Frawley, John Horn, Pat Karpen, Patti LuPone

BOY MEETS GIRL by Bella and Samuel Spewack; Director, Bill Ludel; Set, John Falabella; Costumes, Lowell Detweiler. CAST: Jeff Brooks, George Bowe, Donna Donnelly, Terry Fox, Peter Jolly, William Leach, Lowry Miller, Robert Moberly, Neil Napolitan, Ann Pie, Joel Polis, Roberta Sterne, Maggie Thatcher, Paul C. Thomas, Edgar Wilcock

WEDDING BAND by Alice Childress; Director, Paul Weidner; Set, Lowell Detweiler; Costumes, Claire Ferraris; Lighting, Steve Woodring. CAST: Verona Barnes, Trazana Beverley, Rosanna Carter, Deloris Gaskins, Elizabeth Goldberg, Elizabeth Hartman, Richard Kavanaugh, Hubert Kelly, Jr., William Leach, Ruth Maynard, Cheryl Sharpe

GALILEO by Bertolt Brecht, translated by Charles Laughton; Director, Paul Weidner; Setting and Costumes, John Conklin; Lighting, Peter Hunt; Music, Richard Peaslee. CAST: John Basinger, Ron Bertrand, Dennis Boutsikaris, George Bowe, Wilhelmina Cox, Bernard Erhard, Rick Ferro, Eric Foster, Bernard Frawley, Anthony Grano, Ted Guhl, Anthony Heald, William Leach, James Lyons, Richard Mathews, Carla Meyer, Paul Milikin, Roberta Mills, John Newton, Marilynn Scott, Alexander Scourby, Erik Shack, David Shaw, Stephen L. Slossberg, Theodore Sorel, Henry Thomas, Paul C. Thomas, Margaret Thomson, Thomas C. White, Edgar Wilcock

THE MATCHMAKER by Thornton Wilder; Director, Daniel Sullivan; Set, John Falabella; Costumes, Elizabeth Covey; Lighting, Judy Rasmuson, CAST: Wilhelmina Cox, Dawn Didadick, Donna Donnelly, Bernard Frawley, Anthony Heald, Michael Craig, Macon McCalman, Paul Milikin, Roberta Mills, Jerry Reid, Theodore Sorel, Kate McGregor-Stewart, Stephen Stout, Paul C. Thomas, Sada Thompson, Victoria Zussin

BONJOUR LA BONJOUR by Michel Tremblay, translated by John Van Burek and Bill Glassco; Director, Paul Weidner; Setting, David Lloyd Gropman; Costumes, Linda Fisher; Lighting, Paul Gallo. CAST: Barbara Caruso, Anthony Heald, Anne Lynn, Sharon Madden, Frederikke Meister, Ann Shropshire, William Swetland, Margaret Thomson

Lanny Nagler Photos

Left: Paul C. Thomas, Sada Thompson in "The Matchmaker" Above: Deloris Gaskins, Richard Kavanaugh in "Wedding Band" Top: Patti LuPone in "Catchpenny Twist"

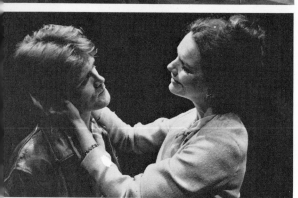

Anthony Heald, Barbara Caruso in "Bonjour La Bonjour"

Bernard Frawley, Richard Mathews, David Shaw, Alexander Scourby, Paul C. Thomas in "Galileo"

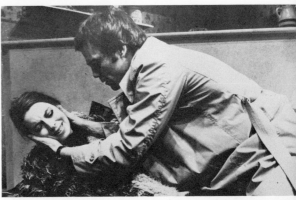

John Straub, Margot Tenney Top: Ludi
Claire, Kathleen Kelly in "The Little
Foxes" Right: Stephen Temperley, Aida
Berlin in "Absurd Person Singular"

HARTMAN THEATRE COMPANY

Stamford, Connecticut
November 1, 1978–April 8, 1979
Fourth Season

Producing Directors, Margot and Del Tenney; Managing Director, Roger L. Meeker; Press, Deborah Weiner; General Manager, Jacqueline Frankel; Production Manager, J. D. Ferrara; Stage Managers, David N. Feight, J. Thomas Fifian; Directors, Tony Giordano, Gene Frankel, Del Tenney, Joey Patton; Designers, J. D. Ferrara, Rachel Kurland, John Falabella, John Gisondi, Jeff Davis, John Wright Stevens, Sarah Nash Gates, Daniel J. Farley, James Tilton, Rick Butler, Hugh Landwehr, David Murin, John McLain, Kathleen Egan, Roger Meeker

PRODUCTIONS AND CASTS

TWO FOR THE SEESAW with Jill O'Hara and Ben Masters

THE DIARY OF ANNE FRANK with Carl Low, Jacqueline Coslow, Saylor Creswell, Lori Putnam, Sally Mercer, Margot Tenney, Hy Anzell, Joan de Marrais, Gilbert Cole, Eugene Troobnick

ABSURD PERSON SINGULAR with Jacqueline Coslow, Saylor Creswell, Aida Berlyn, Stephen Temperley, Margot Tenney, Ron Randell

THE LITTLE FOXES with Laurence Hugo, Dominic Chianese, Ludi Claire, Margot Tenney, Kathleen Kelly, J. Gilpin, Deloris Gaskins, Hand Frazier, Ernest Graves, John Straub

THE FANTASTICKS with Nancy Nichols, Cameron Smith, David Canary, Douglas Fisher, Stephen Daley, Warren Kelley, Don Moran, Laurence Hugo

THE AUCTION TOMORROW by Jerry L. Crawford (*World Premiere*, Jan. 24, 1979); Director, Del Tenney; CAST: Stephen Joyce, Carol Mayo Jenkins, Charles Bateman, Patricia Englund

Gerry Goodstein Photos

**Top Right: Jill O'Hara, Ben Masters
in "Two for the Seesaw"**

**Stephen Joyce, Carol Mayo Jenkins in "Auction
Tomorrow" Above: Lori Putnam, Gilbert Cole
in "Diary of Anne Frank"**

**Edith Owen, David O. Peterson
in "Ten Little Indians" Left: Bernard
Kates, Patricia Wheel in "A Delicate
Balance"**

INDIANA REPERTORY THEATRE

Indianapolis, Indiana
October 20, 1978–March 31, 1979
Seventh Season

Producing Director, Benjamin Mordecai; Artistic Director, Edward Stern; Business Manager, Kathy Ramsey; Press, Edward Cimbala, Jimmy Seacat; Production Manager, Chris Armen; Stage Managers, Joel Grynheim, James K. Tinsley; Technical Director, David L. Ramsey; Directors, John Going, Thomas Gruenewald, Woodie King, Jr., Sanford Robbins, Edward Stern, Daniel Sullivan; Settings, Robert Barnett, Ursula Belden, John Doepp, Eric Head, James Leonard Joy, David Potts, William Schroder; Costumes, Michael J. Cesario, Elizabeth Covey, Jess Goldstein, William Schroder, Kenneth M. Yount; Lighting, Geoffrey T. Cunningham, Jeff Davis, Paul Gallo

PRODUCTIONS AND CASTS

DEAR LIAR by Jerome Kilty with Katharine Houghton, Ken Jenkins

13 RUE DE L'AMOUR by Georges Feydeau with Eugene Anthony, Avril Gentles, Michael Hendricks, Katharine Houghton, Ken Jenkins, Donald Johnson, Bernard Kates, Meredith Ludwig, Peter Thoemke, Patrick Tovatt

SIZWE BANSI IS DEAD by Athol Fugard, John Kani and Winston Ntshona with Lou Ferguson and William Jay

A DELICATE BALANCE by Edward Albee with Roger DeKoven, Allison Giglio, Mary Hara, Bernard Kates, Edith Owen, Patricia Wheel

THE IMPORTANCE OF BEING EARNEST by Oscar Wilde with Eric Booth, Le Clanche du Rand, Katherine Ferrand, June Gibbons, Donald Johnson, Bernard Kates, John Milligan, Edith Owen, Adrian Sparks

TEN LITTLE INDIANS by Agatha Christie with George Axler, Sheila Coonan, Donald Johnson, Bernard Kates, Priscilla Lindsay, John Milligan, Edith Owen, David O. Petersen, Gerald Richards, Ron Siebert, Peter Thoemke

THE GOODBYE PEOPLE by Herb Gardner with Linda Atkinson, George Axler, Mark Fleischman, Donald Johnson, Bernard Kates, Phillip Piro

THE SCAMP! by Moliere; (Adapted by Sanford Robbins) with Jessica DuBord, Melanie Hague, Jeffrey Horowitz, Donald Johnson, Anderson Matthews, Theodore May, Reid Nelson, Alan Silver, Andrew Traines

**Patrick Tovatt, Katharine Houghton, Ken Jenkins
in " 13 Rue de L'Amour"**

**Left Center: William Jay, Lou Ferguson
in "Sizwe Bansi Is Dead"**

INNER CITY CULTURAL CENTER

Los Angeles, California
July 1, 1978–June 30, 1979
Artistic Director, C. Bernard Jackson; Administrative Director, Elaine Kashiki; Production Coordinator, Virginia Wing; Press, Suzanne Shelton; Technical Director, Dennis Wilkerson

PRODUCTIONS AND CASTS

SUMMER SUNS/TALES OF NIGHT directed by George C. Wolfe; Music, Darrell Hutcherson; Costumes, Lori Cloud; Stage Manager, Lawrence Jackson. CAST: Willard T. Chandler, Denise Cloud, Paula Dickson, Robert Ferrari, Ric Gallego, Otee Jones, Deborah Kennedy, Ann E. Lewis, John Wayne Love, Robert Lozano, Lelia Meza, Demetri Mina, Robert Rivera, Anthony Scott, Penni Thomas, Darrell Hutcherson, Isaias Santiago

INNER CITY by Eva Merriam; Director, Sandi Sheffey; Music, Roger Neal; Set, Dennis Wilkerson; Stage Manager, John Ortiz; Choreography, Cheryl Tyre-Smith. CAST: Graham Benskin, Melodie Cochran, Mary Davis, Madelyn Looney, Quentiz Lee, Renita Robinson, Khalilah Shahid, Leon Stewart, Jesse Sotomayer, Regan Talley, Chanse Taylor, Joseph G. Williams, Gregg Wooden, Rashik Shakoor, Keith Washington

FLY BLACKBIRD by C. B. Jackson, James V. Hatch; Director, Larry White; Choreography, Chester Whitmore, Xavier Chatman; Set, Estela Scarlata; Lighting, William Collins; Costumes, Devonne Davis. CAST: Andre Bennett, Robin Carter, Eula Cooper, Loretta Gilstrap, Martha Gooden, Eve Holloway, Judy Momii Hoy, Anna Johnson, Doug Johnson, Keith Jones, Herb Mendelsohn, Jeff Stayton, Chester Whitmore, Lance Smith, Delaney Vaughn, Tracy Nelson, Penny Reagan, Dennis Reese, Tracy Roberson, Marta Rodriguez, Karen Shelby, Kevin Stone, James Bigbee, Victor Hall, Roger Neal, Cliff Wright

MOJO and THE STRING by Alice Childress; Director, Floyd Gaffney; Set, Dennis Wilkerson; Lighting, Terry Smith. CAST: "Mojo" with Peggy Hutcherson, Ken Snell, "The String" with Jim Mapp, Helen Martin, Dorothy Butts, Amalie Collier, Elma Jackson, Gloria Parker, Tom S. Pitts, Marlo Sturdivant, Larry White

Cast of "Beautiful Senoritas"

LA CELESTINA adapted and directed by Alvaro Custodio in cooperation with the Bilingual Foundation of the Arts; Producer, Carmen Zapata; Set, Estela Scarlata; Lights, Jose Lopez; Costumes, Frances Acosta; Music, Mark Elson; Stage Manager, Ed Lucero. CAST: Lillian Adams, Denise Carpitano, Don Cervantes, Ivonne Coll, Carlos Petrel, Alfredo Rodriguez, Irene De Bari, Haydee Du Barry, Robert Dunlap, David Estuardo, Rose Ramos, James Victor, Irma Garcia, Frank Hill, Julio Medina, Ilka Tanya Payan, Victoria Richart

LULU by Frank Wedekind; Director, Martin Magner; Translated and Adapted by Carl R. Mueller; Set, Dennis Wilkerson; Lights, Terry Smith; Costumes, Carl Garrison; Stage Manager, Christina Brnabic. CAST: Mercedes Alberti, Tom Ceurvorst, Harald O. Dyrenforth, Carmen Filpi, Dale Harriman, Rhonda Jackson, Morrell P. Morton, Valorie Niccore, Michael Nissman, Philip Persons, Bob Pone, Michael Pritchard, Soreanna Sano, Mark Shahn, Cheryl Turner, Havre Von Lambach

THE NUTCRACKER TRILOGY by C. B. Jackson who directed; Set, Dennis Wilkerson; Lights, D. C. Staging; Costumes, Terence Tam Soon; Music Director, Roger Neal; Stage Manager, Antoine James. CAST: Chris Calloway, Jesse Dizon, Erika Hawkins, Charles Henderson, Judy Momii Hoy, June Kim, Keny Long, Paunita Nichols, Marta Rodriguez, James Terry Smith, Les Blevins Tuckcho, Cheryl Tyre-Smith, Hatsuo Uda

BACKALLEY TALES written and directed by George C. Wolfe; Music, Paul Balfour; Producer, Virginia Wing; Set, David Flaten; Lights, Michael Birney; Costumes, Terence Tam Soon. CAST: Bill Cobbs, Sharon Cox, Greta Craddolph, Loretta Gilstrap, Lill Greenwood, Lance Hardy, Diane Harris, Mitchell Lee Horn, Carnetta Jones, Richard Jones, James King, Leonard Lightfeather, John Love, Rose Mallett, Barbara Sherrill, Reginald Montgomery, Iona Morris, Joe Peer, Penny Reagan, Wesley Thompson, Cheryl Turner, Larry White

JESSE AND THE BANDIT QUEEN by David Freeman; Director, Nicholas Lewis; Producer, Wally Taylor; Set, Dennis Wilkerson; Light, G. Naeemah Perry; Stage Manager, Tony Allen; with Gamy L. Taylor, Wally Taylor

BEAUTIFUL SENORITAS by Dolores Prida; Directors, Eduardo Machado, Ilka Tanya Payan; Choreography, Joanne Figueros; Musical Director, Bob Zeigler; Set, Nora Chavooshian; Light, Alec Watt; Costumes, Harriette Machado. CAST: Roseanna Campos, Gabrielle Gazon, Ron Godines, Peggy Hutcherson, Jeannie Linero, Rosamaria Marquez, Ilka Tanya Payan

IAGO written and directed by C. B. Jackson, adapted from the works of Giraldo Cinthio and William Shakespeare. CAST: Beah Richards, Sab Shimano, Cheryl Tyre-Smith

Carnetta Jones, Reginald Montgomery in "Backalley Tales"

LONG WHARF THEATRE

New Haven, Connecticut
October 19, 1978–June 24, 1979
Fourteenth Season

Artistic Director, Arvin Brown; Executive Director, M. Edgar Rosenblum; Press, Rosalind Heinz, Patrick Lombard; Directors, Peter Bennett, Arvin Brown, Allen Fletcher, William Francisco, Kenneth Frankel, Edward Gilbert; Sets, John Conklin, David Jenkins, John Hensen, Marjorie Kellogg, Steven Rubin; Costumes, Linda Fisher, Carol Oditz, Mary Strieff, Bill Walker; Lighting, Jamie Gallagher, Judy Rasmuson, Ronald Wallace; Stage Managers, James Harker, Anne Keefe, Kate Pollock

PRODUCTIONS AND CASTS

JOURNEY'S END by R. C. Sherriff with Emery Battis, Harry Groener, Edward Herrmann, John McMartin, Stephen Mendillo, Roger Newman, William Sadler, Joel Stedman, Douglas Stender, Nicholas Woodeson

I SENT A LETTER TO MY LOVE by Bernice Rubens (*World Premiere*) with Emery Battis, Joyce Ebert, Geraldine Fitzgerald, Kate Reid, William Swetland

SUMMERFOLK by Maxim Gorky with Emery Battis, David Butler, Mary Carney, Veronica Castang, Megan Cole, Joyce Ebert, Mark Graham, George Hearn, Thomas Hulce, Dorrie Kavanaugh, Kurt Knudson, Pamela Payton-Wright, Sarah Peterson, Rex Robbins, Josef Sommer, Joel Stedman, William Swetland

BIOGRAPHY by S. N. Behrman with Andra Akers, Eunice Anderson, John Braden, Richard Dow, Richard Kuss, Johanna Leister, James Sutorius, Eugene Troobnick

ROSMERSHOLM by Henrik Ibsen with Emery Battis, Joyce Ebert, Richard Kavanaugh, Frank Latimore, Paul Shenar, Kate Wilkinson

HILLBILLY WOMEN by Elizabeth Stearns; Music and Lyrics, Clint Ballard, Jr. (*World Premiere*) with Sharon Goldman, Robin Howard, Jacqueline Knapp, Susan Peretz, Lois Smith, Katherine Squire, Janet Ward

PRIVATES ON PARADE by Peter Nichols; Music, Dennis King (*American Premiere*) with Emery Battis, Jim Dale, Joe Grifasi, Robert Joy, Alvin K. U. Lum, Tom Matsusaka, Gavin Reed, James Seymour, Joel Stedman, Douglas Stender, Suzanne Stone

William L. Smith Photos

Right Top: Paul Shenar, Joyce Ebert in "Rosmersholm" Below: Edward Herrmann, John McMartin in "Journey's End"

**Jim Dale
in "Privates on Parade"**

**Geraldine Fitzgerald, William Swetland
in "I Sent a Letter to My Love"**

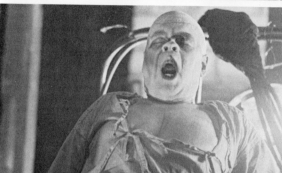

Pamela Lewis in "The Three Sisters"
Right: Keith Jochim in "Frankenstein"
Top: Wil Love, Keith Jochim in "A
Penny for a Song"

LORETTO-HILTON REPERTORY THEATRE

St. Louis, Missouri
October 13, 1978–April 8, 1979
Producing Director, David Frank; Consulting Director, Davey Mar-lin-Jones; Administrative Director, Thomas K. Warner; Press, Sarah Jones, Kathy Salomon; Associate Producer, Michael P. Pitek III; Production Manager, Vic Gialanella; Technical Director/Pro-duction Coordinator, Jack Conant; Assistant to Producers/Com-pany Manager, Joyce Volker; Stage Managers, Glenn Dunn, Margaret Stuart-Ramsey, Marnie Powers; Production Assistants, Patricia Ann Brennan, Jay MacNamee; Sets, Paul Wonsek, Tim Jozwick, James Walker; Props, John Roslevich, Jr.; Costumes, John Carver Sullivan, Catherine B. Reich; Lighting, Peter E. Sargent.

RESIDENT COMPANY

Eric Brooks, Brendan Burke, Alan Clarey, Jonathan Gillard, Robert Darnell, Stephen McKinley Henderson, Keith Jochim, Jo-neal Joplin, Wil Love, Robert Spencer, Susan Maloy Wall, Addie Walsh, Bari K. Willerford.

PRODUCTIONS AND GUEST ARTISTS

THE ICEMAN COMETH by Eugene O'Neill with Bob Ari, Bob Breuler, Duane Jones, Peter Miner, Karen Connolly (set), Carr Garnett (Costumes)

PENNY FOR A SONG by John Whiting with Charlotte Booker, Edward Eyerman, Joey Gottlieb, Timothy Meyers

FATHER'S DAY by Oliver Hailey with Sharon Ernster, Lynn Ann Leveridge, Anne Murray, Leonard Peters (Director)

THE THREE SISTERS by Anton Chekhov with Regina David, Julia Duffy, Pamela Lewis, Frederikke Meister, Dana Mills, Etain O'Malley, Geoffrey Sherman (Director), Stephen Ross (Lighting)

FRANKENSTEIN by Victor Gialanella with Charlotte Booker, Edward Eyerman, Mary Ellen Falk, Gian Cavallini, James Harper, Grady Larkins (Set)

CURSE OF THE STARVING CLASS by Sam Shepard with Mary Fogarty, James McDonnell, Julia Duffy, Eddie Jones, William Metzo, Bert Hinchman, Sheldon Larry (Director), Paul Steinberg (Set)

OLD TIMES by Harold Pinter with Kurt Garfield, Margery Shaw, Margaret Winn, Suzanne Session Larkins (Costumes)

BY GRAND CENTRAL STATION I SAT DOWN AND WEPT by Geoffrey Sherman and Adrienne Burgess, adapted from the novel by Elizabeth Smart (*World Premiere*) with Linda Cook, Lenka Pe-terson, Michael Thompson, Geoffrey Sherman (Director)

Michael Eastman Photos

Margery Shaw, Margaret Winn
in "Old Times"

Gordon Thompson, Fiona Reid, Deborah Kipp in "A Bee in Her Bonnet" Right: John Christopher Jones, Thomas Hill, Stephen Markle in "Death of a Salesman"

MANITOBA THEATRE CENTRE
Winnipeg, Canada
October 13, 1978–May 19, 1979

Artistic Director, Arif Hasnain; Managing Director, Gregory Poggi; Press, Max Tapper; Production Manager, Dwight Griffin; Technical Director, Ron Kresky; Stage Directors, Arif Hasnain, Gregory Tuck, Stephen Katz, Richard Digby-Day, Lewis Baumander, Kurt Reis, Michael Nawson, Richard Cottrell; Sets and Costumes, Peter Wingate, Kari Hagness, Brian H. Jackson, Maxine Graham, Neil Peter Jampolis; Lighting, Michael Whitfield, Monty Schneider, Robert C. Reinholdt, Edsel Hilchie, Ron Kresky, Neil Peter Jampolis; Stage Managers, Ihor Sychylo, Christina Trunn, Donna McLaurin

PRODUCTIONS AND CASTS

FOREVER YOURS, MARIE-LOU by Michel Tremblay with Alexe Duncan, Elan Ross Gibson, Peter Rogan, Theresa Tova

A DOLL'S HOUSE by Henrik Ibsen (new translation by John Lingard) with Anna Friedman, Lisa Griffin, Dana Ivey, Deborah Kipp, Ami Kotler, Stephen Markle, George Morfogen, Suzanne Mott, Wayne Robson, Ian Watson

THE ADVENTURES OF ROBIN HOOD by Clive Endersby with William Davidson, William Dunlop, Peter Elliott, Marvin Karon, Jim Mezon, Suzanne Mott, Fred Penner, Peter Pawlyshyn, Wayne Robson, Paula Achappert, Howard Storey, Kate Trotter

THEATRE BEYOND WORDS with Paulette Hallich, Terry Judd, Larry Lefebvre, Harro Maskow, Robin Patterson

THE DAY JAKE MADE 'ER RUN by W. O. Mitchell with Jay Brazeau, Alexe Duncan, David Gillies, Cynthia Tymchuk, Ian Watson

HOW THE OTHER HALF LOVES by Alan Ayckbourn with Marcia Bennett, John Cutts, Peter Dvorsky, Ann Firbank, Basil Hoskins, Ruth Priwer

DEATH OF A SALESMAN by Arthur Miller with Gordon Clapp, Walter Flanagan, Judy Greenberg, Thomas Hill, Helen Hughes, John Christopher Jones, Marvin Karon, Stephen Markle, Fred Penner, Maida Rogerson, Guy Sanvido, Patrusha Sarakula, Rebecca Toolan, Ted Wynne

THE ZOO STORY by Edward Albee and SEXUAL PERVERSITY IN CHICAGO by David Mamet with Elan Ross Gibson, Peter Haworth, Richard Hilger, Lora Staley

VERONICA'S ROOM by Ira Levin with John-Peter Linton, Milton Selzer, Anne Shropshire, Lora Staley

SIZWE BANSI IS DEAD by Athol Fugard with Charles Grant-Greene, Sam Singleton

A BEE IN HER BONNET by Georges Feydeau (new translation by Brian Blakey) with Karen Barker, John Bayliss, James Blendick, Shirley Douglas, Alexe Duncan, William Dunlop, Peter Elliott, Judy Greenberg, Edward Greenhalgh, Roland Hewgill, Richard Hilger, Deborah Kipp, Alison MacLeod, Peter Millard, Fiona Reid, Gordon Thomson, Ian Watson

Daniel Teichman Photos

Basil Hoskins, Ann Firbank in "How the Other Half Loves"

Left Center: Milton Selzer, Lora Staley in "Veronica's Room"

MARRIOTT'S LINCOLNSHIRE THEATRE

Lincolnshire, Illinois
June 7, 1978–May 27, 1979
Producer, Richard S. Kordos; Sets, Jeffrey Harris; Stage Manager, Joseph Sturniolo; Technical Director, Pat Nesladek; Props, Terry Jenkins; Costumes, Susan Clare; Press, Harshe, Rotman & Druck

PRODUCTIONS AND CASTS

THE MOST MARVELOUS NEWS with Eve Arden, Brooks West, Lillian Garrett-Bonner

FINISHING TOUCHES with Barbara Rush, Tony Mockus, Ron Parady, Barbara Robertson, Jay Footlik, John Shepherd, Michael Hendricks, Lynn Mansbach

GUYS AND DOLLS with Ken Berry, Brenda Thomson, Vivian Watson, Mark Hutter, Augie Amato, Michael Rosen, Jim Brett, Nathan Davis, Scott Wilson, Barbara Moroz, Louie Lanciloti, Tom Harmon, Ted Raymond, Sherry Narens, Howard Fishlove, Pam Cecil, Janet Louer, Krista Neumann, Judith Smith, Jim Brett, John Paizis, Bruce Senesac, Brian van den Broucke

THE RAINMAKER with John Gavin, Kathleen Melvin, Chuck Stransky, George Womack, Chelcie Ross, Greg Vinkler, Gerald Walling, S. J.

HARVEY with David Doyle, Val Bettin, George Brengel, Jane MacIver, Kenned MacIver, Mary Best, Annabel Armour, David Whitaker, Chuck Stransky, Roslyn Alexander, Lou DeCrescenzo

Joseph Jedd Photos

Right Top: Brooks West, Eve Arden in "The Most Marvelous News"

Below: Tony Mockus, Barbara Rush in "Finishing Touches"

George Womack, Greg Vinkler, Chuck Stransky, John Gavin, Kathleen Melvin in "Rainmaker"

Ken Berry, Vivian Watson in "Guys and Dolls"

McCARTER THEATRE COMPANY

Princeton, New Jersey
October 5, 1978–April 22, 1979
Producing Director, Michael Kahn; Managing Director, Edward A. Martenson, Production Manager, Mark S. Krause; Press, Kirby F. Smith; Administrative Director, George Parides; Technical Director, Rafe Scheinblum; Directors, Michael Kahn, Frith Banbury, Gerald Gutierrez, Sheldon Epps, Vivian Matalon; Sets, Michael H. Yeargan, Lawrence King, Ed Wittstein, John Lee Beatty, John Shaffner, William Ritman; Costumes, Jane Greenwood, Andrew B. Marly, John Lee Beatty, Jeanette Oleksa; Lighting, John McLain, Richard Nelson

PRODUCTIONS AND CASTS

A MONTH IN THE COUNTRY by Ivan Turgenev with Tammy Grimes, Paul Hecht, Jack Bittner, Bette Henritze, Jane Cronin, Jason Scott, Mark Lamos, Lawrence Holofcener, Louis Zorich, Amanda Michael Plummer, Robert Symonds, Bara-Cristin Hansen, Charles White

THE ASPEN PAPERS adapted by Sir Michael Redgrave with Antonia Rey, Laurinda Barrett, Barry Boys, Kathleen Maguire, Ruth Ford, Peter DeMaio

NO TIME FOR COMEDY by S. N. Behrman with Sarallen, Patricia Elliott, Richard Clarke, Peter Coffield, Carrie Nye, Oliver Dixon, Larry Pine

PUT THEM ALL TOGETHER by Anne Commire (*World Premiere*) with Mariette Hartley, Rosemary DeAngelis, Charlie Fields, Evelyn Hibbler, Cathy Coray, Parker McCormick, Barry Jenner, Maggie Tucker, Hansford Rowe

BLUES IN THE NIGHT by Sheldon Epps with David Brunetti, Jean Dushon, Suzanne M. Henry, Mary Louise

HEARTBREAK HOUSE by George Bernard Shaw with Jeanne Ruskin, Bette Henritze, Frank Hamilton, Charlotte Moore, Rachel Gurney, John Wardwell, Jack Ryland, Robert Nichols, Robert Stattel, Tom McDermott

Cliff Moore Photos

Left: Patricia Elliott, Larry Pine in "No Time for Comedy" Top: Ruth Ford, Antonia Rey in "The Aspern Papers"

Mariette Hartley, Charlie Fields in "Put Them All Together"

Amanda Plummer, Tammy Grimes in "A Month in the Country"

Michael Tylo, Polly Rowles, Patricia Reilly "Ring Round the Moon" Right: Edmund Lyndeck, Carolyn Lagerfelt, Tom Spackman, Michael Allinson in "The Devil's Disciple"

MEADOW BROOK THEATRE

Rochester, Michigan
October 12, 1978–May 27 1979
Artistic & General Director, Terence Kilburn; Assistant to Director, Frank Bollinger; Directors, Terence Kilburn, Charles Nolte, John Ulmer; Sets, Peter-William Hicks, Douglas Wright, Donald Beckman; Lighting, Frederick Fonner, Scott Brown, Richard Henson, Jean Montgomery, Benjamin Levenberg; Stage Managers, Alice Galloway, Michael Shann, Thomas Spence; Technical Director, Douglas A. Wright; Costumes, Mary L. Bonnell; Wardrobe, Mary Ellen Bacon; Props, Carolyn Hull, Robert Herrle

PRODUCTIONS AND CASTS

THE DEVIL'S DISCIPLE with Michael Allinson, Curtis J. Armstrong, Dan C. Bar, Michel Cullen, Harry Ellerbe, James R. Hartman, Carolyn Lagerfelt, Ray Lonergan, Edmund Lyndeck, Patricia Reilly, Tom Spackman, Joan White

THAT CHAMPIONSHIP SEASON with Frederick Ainsworth, Richard Jamieson, Eric Tavaris, Paul Vincent, Joseph Warren

RING ROUND THE MOON with Mary Benson, Leigh Burch, Harry Ellerbe, Martha Gaylord, Cheryl Giannini, Richard Jamieson, Jerry Jarrett, Patricia Reilly, Polly Rowles, Eric Tavaris, Michael Tylo

THE CAINE MUTINY COURT-MARTIAL with Curtis J. Armstrong, Booth Colman, Michel Cullen, J. L. Dahlmann, Peter Galman, Ken Graham, Richard Jamieson, Peter McRobbie, Charles Nolte, Michael Rothhaar, Daniel Buchen, Wade Kelley, Robert Herrle, Jack Prokop, Ronald S. Merkin, Donald W. Dailey, Robert LaPratt

BLITHE SPIRIT with Michael Allinson, Jeanne Arnold, Mary Benson, Valerie French, Cheryl Giannini, Ken Graham, Louise Martin

THE DEADLY GAME with Michel Cullen, Humphrey Davis, Harry Ellerbe, Cheryl Giannini, Richard Jamieson, Donald C. Moore, Albert M. Ottenheimer, Judith Tillman

THE ROMANCE OF SHAKESPEARE with Jonathan Alper, Michel Cullen, Deborah Eckols, Patricia Reilly

BERLIN TO BROADWAY WITH KURT WEILL with Jenny Brown, Richard Marshall, Andy McAvin, Ty McConnell, Henrietta Valor, Ted Kociolek

Dick Hunt Photos

Right Center: Andy McAvin, Richard Marshall, Jenny Brown, Henrietta Valor, Ty McConnell in "Berlin to Broadway with Kurt Weill"

Jeanne Arnold, Valerie French, Michael Allinson, Cheryl Giannini in "Blithe Spirit"

MILWAUKEE REPERTORY THEATRE

Milwaukee, Wisconsin
September 15, 1978–May 20, 1979
Artistic Director, John Dillon; Managing Director, Sara O'Connor; Costumes, Susan Tsu, Nanzi Adzima, Pat McGourty, Maura Smolover; Lighting, Arden Fingerhut, Scott Johnson, Spencer Mosse; Sets, John Lee Beatty, David Emmons, David Jenkins, Scott Johnson, Marjorie Kellogg, Maura Smolover; Choreographers, Martha Myers, Allan Sobek; Fights, Michael Tezla; Stage Manager, Rod Pilloud; Production Manager, Bennett Taber; Press, Richard Bryant, Susan Medak

COMPANY

Tom Blair, Nesbitt Blaisdell, Pamela Blake, Lisa Brailoff, Ritch Brinkley, Jenny Burton, Greg Cesario, Roy Cooper, Joan Croydon, Earle Edgerton, Peter Francis-James, Ronald Frazier, Beulah Garrick, Mike Genovese, Cynthia Green, Diane Heles, Thomas Hulce, Peter Jolly, Richard Loder, Don Lowe, Jack McLaughlin-Gray, Valerie Mahaffey, Stephen Markle, Anderson Matthews, W. Chad Mitchell, Daniel Mooney, Heather Moore, Susanne Peters, James Pickering, Rose Pickering, Richard Pilcher, Janet Reed, Penelope Reed, Petie Seale, Ruth Schudson, Mary Shelley, Larry Shue, Gary Smiley, Bruce Somerville, Henry Strozier, Michael Tezla, Maggie Thatcher, Jaison Walker

PRODUCTIONS

"Romeo and Juliet" by William Shakespeare, "Merton of the Movies" by George S. Kaufman and Marc Connelly, "The Taming of the Shrew" by William Shakespeare, and *World Premieres* of "The Freeway" by Peter Nichols, "Island" by Peter Link, and "Fighting Bob" by Tom Cole

Mark Avery Photos

Ronald Frazier in "Fighting Bob"
Above: "The Freeway" Top: "Island"

Top: "The Taming of the Shrew"
Below: "Romeo and Juliet"

MISSOURI REPERTORY THEATRE
Kansas City, Missouri
July 1, 1978–March 4, 1979
Producing Director, Patricia McIlrath; Directors, Michael Langham, Francis Cullinan, James Assad, Boris Tumarin, Andrew Tsubaki, Vincent Dowling, John Reich; Production Manager, Raymond Bonnard; Press, Charlotte Legg, Beth Winter; Stage Managers, Joseph DePauw, Joyce McBroom, Ron Durbian, Cristine Michael; Sets, James Leonard Joy, Jack Montgomery, Daniel Thomas Field, Barry Bengsten, John Ezell, Carolyn Leslie Ross; Lighting, Joseph Appelt, Delbert Unruh, Michael Scott; Costumes, Vincent Scasselatti, Baker S. Smith, Judith Dolan; Sound, Michael Schweppe, Susan Selvey, Les Appelt; Choreographer, Eden Lee Murray; Technical Directors, Frederick G. Roberts, Douglas C. Taylor

COMPANY
Walter Atamaniuk, Peter Aylward, Charlotte Booker, Richard C. Brown, Liza Cole, John Cothran, Jr., Ellen Crawford, Robert Elliott, James Robert Daniels, Art Ellison, Nina Furst, Robin Humphrey, Stephen Keener, John Maddison, Merle Moores, Holmes Osborne, Alan Nichols, Juliet Randall, Nancy Reardon, Ronetta Wallman, Beatrice Winde, Ronald Wendschuh, James M. Armstrong, Daniel Barnett, Madylon Brandstetter, Cheri Buie, Suzanne Curry, Steve Doolittle, Ross A. Freese, Buckner Gibbs, Mark S. Gilman, Martha Hamblin, Eric Hendricks, Carole Hughes, Christopher L. Jones, Kathy Kennedy, Stephen Lee, Dennis C. Martin, Peter Massey, Martin Merritt, Jennifer Moudy, Jack Morgan, Jess Lynn, Elizabeth Savage, Susan Selvey, Steve Smith, Douglass Stewart, David Weamer

PRODUCTIONS
"Julius Caesar," "Light Up the Sky," "The Shadow Box," "The Sea Gull," "Rashomon," "The Happy Hunter," "Bus Stop," "The Little Foxes"

Right: Walter Atamaniuk, Peter Massey, Robin Humphrey, Richard Brown in "The Little Foxes"
Top: Charlotte Booker, Stephen Keener in "The Happy Hunter"

Mike Genovese, Ellen Crawford in "Horse Latitudes/The Pokey"

NORTH LIGHT REPERTORY
Evanston, Illinois
October 14, 1978–April 14, 1979
Producing Director, Gregory Kandel; General Manager, Rock Kershaw; Assistant to Director, Janet Wilson; Business Manager, Susan Flahaven; Press, William Prenevost, Kristin Overn; Sets, Maher Ahmad; Costumes, Marsha Kowal, Christa Scholtz; Resident Playwright, Grace McKeaney; Stage Manager, John P. Kenny; Technical Director, J. Douglas Flahaven

PRODUCTIONS AND CASTS
THAT CHAMPIONSHIP SEASON by Jason Miller with B. J. Jones, David Whitaker, Ronald Parady, Charles Stransky, Tony Mockus

COMING OF AGE by Frank Cucci with Roslyn Alexander, Ellen Crawford, Norman Tobin, B. J. Jones

HORSE LATITUDES/THE POKEY by Stephen Black with Ellen Crawford, Mike Genovese, Connie McGrail, Bobby Ackerman

THE CLUB by Eve Merriam with Tracy Friedman, Julienne Marshall, Mary Cobb, Jill Shellabarger, Iris Lieberman, June Shellene, Adjora McMillan

Lisa Ebright Photos

PAPER MILL PLAYHOUSE
Millburn, N. J.
September 6, 1978–July 1, 1979
Executive Producer, Angelo Del Rossi; General Manager, Wade Miller; Press, Albertina Reilly; Stage Managers, Gregory Nicholas, Suzanne Hayden, Candace Baer, Victor A. Gelb, Barbara Schneider; Sets, Helen Pond, Herbert Senn, Gibbs Murray, Billy Puzo, Associate Theatrical Design; Lighting, Helen Pond, Herbert Senn, Richard Dorfman

PRODUCTIONS AND CASTS

COUNT DRACULA by Ted Tiller with Farley Granger, Peter Marklin, David Sabin, Stratton Walling, Louise Kirtland, Roger Baron, Caryn West, Howard Renensland, James Van Treuren

JOLSON (*World Premiere*, Nov. 8, 1978) Music and Lyrics, Irwin Levine, L. Russell Brown; Book, Leslie Eberhard, David Levy; Direction and Choreography, Bill Guske, with Clive Baldwin, Sherry Rooney, Joseph Leon, Nina Dova, Reuben Schafer, George Bamford, Maureen Brennan, Humphrey Davis, Renee Roy, Scott Stevensen, Kaylyn Dillehay, Ron Schwinn, Hal Shane, Bob Heath, Ken Mitchell, Michael Lichtefeld, Suzanne Walker, Dennis Batutis, Barbara Hanks, Paula Lynn, Barbara Mandra, Roxanna White

SAME TIME, NEXT YEAR by Bernard Slade; Director, Warren Crane, with Betsy Palmer, Nicholas Hormann

NO SEX PLEASE, WE'RE BRITISH by Anthony Marriott and Alistair Foot; Director, Vivan Matalon, with Rachel Gurney, Francis Bethencourt, Alexander Reed, Susan Sharkey, David Snell, John Wardwell, Elaine Hausman, Joan Inwood, Stephen Temperley

THE MIRACLE WORKER by William Gibson; Director, Ted Weiant, with Cristine Rose, Kathy Bernard, Jack Axelrod, Holly Clark, John Henry Cox, Paul Craggs, Gussie Harris, Rod Houts, Edith Larkin, Amy Nathan, JoLynn Sciarro, Laurie Thorp, Joan Wooters, Gabrielle Fish

SHENANDOAH with Music by Gary Geld; Lyrics, Peter Udell; Book, James Lee Barrett, Peter Udell, Philip Rose; Based on Screenplay by James Lee Barrett; Direction and Choreography, Robert Johanson; Musical Director, Jonathan Anderson. CAST: John Raitt, Melody Meitrott, Tricia Witham, Scott Bakula, Robert Browning, Mark Jacoby, Gary Todd, Joey Young, Kelly Walters, Randy Hugill, Gary J. Munch, Earl McCarroll, Gary Barker, Leslie Feagan, Robert Johanson, George Kmeck, Dan McGeachy, Ed Sala, Robert Stoekle, William A. Wright

THE SOUND OF MUSIC with Music by Richard Rodgers; Lyrics, Oscar Hammerstein 2nd; Book, Howard Lindsay, Russel Crouse; Direction and Choreography, Robert Johanson. CAST: Barbara Meister, Jean-Pierre Aumont, Lizabeth Pritchett, Woody Romoff, Sheila Smith, Melody Meitrott, Robert Johanson, Lois Holmes, Richard Kinter, Earl McCarroll, Ronald Highley, Rebecca Hoodwin, Joanne Highley, Lauren Lipson, Roddy Kinter, Alys Clemmitt, Jason Scott, Jean Marie, Wendy St. Clair, Lisa Carol Greaves, Carol Conway, Alyson Bristol, Melanie Helton, Mimi Sherwin

THE STUDENT PRINCE with Music by Sigmund Romberg; Original Book and Lyrics, Dorothy Donnelly; Book Revision, Jerome Chodorov; Lyric Revision and Additional Lyrics, Forman Brown; New Musical Adaptation, Harper MacKay; Direction and Choreography, Robert Johanson. CAST: Allan Jones, Harry Danner, Judith McCauley, Rogert Weil, Grace Keagy, Earl McCarroll, Carol Conway, William J. Coppola, Billy Beckham, Kevin Lane Dearinger, Kenneth Kantor, Robert Stoeckle, Martin Van Treuren, Patti Allison, Rod Houts, Cheryl Moore, Linda Posner, Kenneth F. Bell, Stephen Berger, Michael Feeley, Larr D. French, Karl Heist, Dennis J. Maher, Gene Masoner, Edward Prostak, Craig Stuart, J. Thomas Wierney

Terence Gili Photos

Left Center: Melody Meitrott, John Raitt, Tricia Witham in "Shenandoah" Above: Clive Baldwin in "Jolson" Top: Caryn West, Farley Granger in "Count Dracula"

Cristine Rose, Kathy Bernard in "The Miracle Worker"

PAF PLAYHOUSE

Huntington Station, N. Y.
January 4, 1979–June 30, 1979
The Performing Arts Foundation of Long Island: Producer, Jay Broad; General Manager, Joel Warren; Business Manager, James Savage; Press, George Nichols, Susan Wallach; Production Manager, Eugene Blythe; Technical Director, Steven Greer; Stage Managers, Jim Thesing, Jody Boese, Doug Laidlaw, Patricia Ann Speelman; Sets, Ursula Belden, David Potts, Suzanne Benton, Philipp Jung, David Lloyd Gropman, David Chapman; Costumes, A. Christina Giannini, Judy Dearing, Joe Eula, William Ivey Long, Patricia McGourty; Lighting, Victor En Yu Tan, Dennis Parichy, Beverly Emmons, Larry Crimmins, David F. Segal, Judy Rasmuson

PRODUCTIONS AND CASTS

AN ANGEL COMES TO BABYLON by Friedrich Durrenmatt; (*American Premiere*) Director, Jay Broad, with C. K. Alexander, Karan Baer, James Cahill, Don Casey, John Clarkson, Mitchell Jason, Kender Jones, Gary Krawford, Heather Lupton, Shaine Marinson, Earl McCarroll, Carl Northgard, Nellie O'Brien, William Pardue, Kerry Prep, Ken Sears, Ben Siegler, Michael Strobel, Steven Villano, Paul Walker, Kelly Walters, James Zitlow

SLUGGER by Shelby Buford, Jr.; (*World Premiere*) Director, Marshall W. Mason, with Robert E. Barnes, Jr., Jeff Daniels, Alan Feinstein, Lois Foraker, Sabra Jones, Steve Spiegel, John Strasberg, Deborah Taylor

I AM A WOMAN conceived by Viveca Lindfors and Paul Austin; Director, Paul Austin; Performed by Viveca Lindfors

GOSSIP by George F. Walker; Director, Peter Mark Schifter, with Gerry Bamman, Robert Blumenfeld, Roy Brocksmith, Dan Desmond, Christine Ebersole, Anne Francine, Anna Levine, Douglas Stender, Jack Wrangler

GOODNIGHT GRANDPA by Walter Landau; (*World Premiere*) Director, Jay Broad, with Jack Aaron, Jean Barker, Ellen Fiske, Beryl Garner, Martin Haber, Robert Earl Jones, Sam Levene, Albert M. Ottenheimer, Stefan Schnabel, Ruth Vool

LOVED by Olwen Wymark; Director, Arthur Storch, with Richard Abernethy, Le Clanche du Rand, Tom Keena, Dina Merrill, Nancy Mette, Jeffrey Ware

Gerry Goodstein Photos

Jack Wrangler, Anne Francine, Dan Desmond, Gerry Bamman in "Gossip" Top: Alan Feinstein, Sabra Jones, John Strasberg in "Slugger"

PENNSYLVANIA STAGE COMPANY

Allentown, Pennsylvania
October 18, 1978–March 18, 1979
Second Season
Producing Director, Gregory S. Hurst; Managing Director, Jeff Gordon; Directors, Robert Nigro, David E. Rodale, Paul Austin, Charles Gray, Eric Loeb; Sets, Jonathan Arkin, Jim Chesnutt, Jack McGroder, Peter Dean Beck; Costumes, Molly Maginnis, Jim Chesnutt, Jack McGroder, Sandra Wallace, David E. Rodale; Lighting, John Gage, Gregory Chabay, Sean Murphy, Carol Waaser; Business Manager, Linda Y. Goldstein; Production Manager, Jerry Litwin; Press, Connie Hansell

PRODUCTIONS AND CASTS

KNOCK KNOCK with James Hilbrandt, Jesse Caldwell, Bill Tatum, Valerie Beaman

SAME TIME, NEXT YEAR with Valerie Beaman, Bill Tatum

GIFT OF THE MAGI with Bernadette LaBorne, Pamela Myers, Michael Hirsch, Richard Kevlin-Bell

LONG DAY'S JOURNEY INTO NIGHT with Frank Latimore, Dolores Kenan, Robertson Carricart, Bill Cwikowski, Katherine Cortez

ANGEL STREET with Jennifer Sternberg, Michael Lipton, Maureen Torsney, Yvonne Molloy, W. B. Brydon

THE GOOD DOCTOR with Eric Loeb, John Jellison, Alice Travis, Sami Behar, Katherine von Funk

Laurence Barkan Photos

Jennifer Sternberg, Michael Lipton in "Angel Street"
Above: Bill Tatum, Valerie Beaman
in "Same Time, Next Year"

PHILADELPHIA DRAMA GUILD

Philadelphia, Pennsylvanis
October 20, 1978–April 8, 1979
Artistic Director, Douglas Seale; Managing Director, David A. Hale; Press, Roy A. Snyder, Janis Freeman Nelson; Artistic and Administrative Coordinator, Lillian Steinberg; Sets, John Kasarda; Costumes, David Murin, Liz Bass, Kristina Watson; Lighting, Spencer Mosse; Production Supervisor, Gerald Nobles; Directors, Douglas Seale, Tony van Bridge, Thomas Bullard

PRODUCTIONS AND CASTS

THE AU PAIR MAN by Hugh Leonard, with Moya Fenwick and David Rounds

ARMS AND THE MAN by Bernard Shaw, with Valerie von Volz, Betty Leighton, Susan Greenhill, David Rounds, Douglas Wing, James Maxwell, Robert Gerringer, Leonard Frey

PRIVATE LIVES by Noel Coward, with Susan Greenhill, David Rounds, Douglas Wing, Louise Troy, Marilynn Meyrick

THE BLOOD KNOT by Athol Fugard, with Basil Wallace and Thomas Kopache

THE NIGHT OF THE IGUANA by Tennessee Williams, with Joseph Canuso, Louise Troy, Jim Pomilo, Steven Gilborn, Tom McBride, Jona Huber, Richard Marr, Margaret Leary, Douglas Wing, Catherine Byers, Valerie von Volz, Susan Greenhill, Douglas Seale, Mark McGovern

Peter Lester Photos

Right Center: David Rounds, Moya Fenwick in "The Au Pair Man" Below: Thomas Kopache, Basil Wallace in "Blood Knot" Top: Douglas Seale, Louise Troy, Steven Gilborn, Valerie von Volz in "Night of the Iguana"

**Kate Young, James Prescott in "Private Lives"
Above: Patricia Cena in "The Boy Friend"**

PLAYHOUSE THEATRE COMPANY

Pittsburgh, Pennsylvania
September 15, 1978–June 3, 1979
General Director, Mark Lewis; Producer, James O. Prescott; Directors, Roderick Carter, William Leech, James O. Prescott, Donald Wadsworth; Sets, Boyd Ostroff, Al Kirschman; Costumes, Mary Turner, Shima Orans, Don Di Fonso; Lighting, Jennifer Ford, Alan Forino; Production Manager, Mary Turner; Technical Director, Alan Forino; Assistant to Director, Carol Berger; Press, Thomas Hischak

COMPANY

Nancy Chesney, James O. Prescott, Hugh Rose, Kate Young, George Eisenhauer, Larry Heller, Katie Karlovitz, Richard Rauh, Helene Ruoti, and students from Point Park College

PRODUCTIONS

Private Lives by Noel Coward, La Ronde by Arthur Schnitzler, The Boy Friend by Sandy Wilson, The Last of the Red Hot Lovers by Neil Simon, Romeo and Juliet by William Shakespeare, Our Town by Thornton Wilder, The Frog Princess and the Witch, The Ghost of Mr. Penny, Beauty and the Beast, Hansel and Gretel

Douglas Andrews, Michael Frielander Photos

PITTSBURGH PUBLIC THEATER

Pittsburgh, Pennsylvania
September 27, 1978–May 6, 1979
General Director, Ben Shaktman; Press, Jane Frank, Audrey Reichblum, Marie Nugent-Head; Administrative Manager, Mark Rosenthal; Technical Director, Bruce Miller; Directors, Ben Shaktman, Terry Schreiber, Micah Lewensohn, Regge Life; Sets, Bruce Miller, Ben Shaktman, John Jensen, Cletus Anderson, Hal Tine; Costumes, Laura Crow, David Toser; Lighting, Bennet Averyt; Stage Managers, Roy Backes, Doug Bergman, Mimi Jordan Sherin; Dialect Coach, Nora Dunfee

PRODUCTIONS AND CASTS

THE BLOOD KNOT by Athol Fugard, with David Little and Damien Leake

OF MICE AND MEN by John Steinbeck, with Pope Brock, David Clarke, David Connell, Russell Gold, Owen Hollander, Trent Jones, David Little, Beth McDonald, Douglas R. Nielsen, Nicholas Wyman

THE IMPORTANCE OF BEING EARNEST by Oscar Wilde, with Beth Dixon, Russell Gold, Caroline Lagerfelt, Samuel Maupin, Hugh A. Rose, John Scanlan, Michele Seyler, Douglas Stender, Carol Teitel

ASHES by David Rudkin, with Beth Dixon, Berkeley Harris, Gloria Maddox, John C. Vennema

VANITIES by John Heifner, with Elaine Bromka, Sally Dunn, Suzanne Toren

FOR COLORED GIRLS WHO HAVE CONSIDERED SUICIDE/WHEN THE RAINBOW IS ENUF by Ntozake Shange, with Judyie Brandt, Celestine DeSaussure, Gail Grate, Crystal Lilly, Carol E. Pennyfeather, Pamela Poitier, Freda Scott

KRAPP'S LAST TAPE/COME AND GO/ACT WITHOUT WORDS II three one-act plays by Samuel Beckett, with Roy Poole, Elaine Bromka, Suzanne Toren, Sally Dunn, Berkeley Harris, John C. Vennema

PREMIERE of FACES OF LOVE created and performed by Carol Teitel

Jack Weinhold, Nancy Adam Photos

Nicholas Wyman, Beth McDonald, David Little in "Of Mice and Men" Top: John C. Vennema, Berkeley Harris, Beth Dixon, Gloria Maddox in "Ashes"

PLAYMAKERS REPERTORY COMPANY

Chapel Hill, North Carolina
October 11, 1978–April 8, 1979
Third Season
Executive Director, Arthur L. Housman; Artistic Director, Tom Haas; Managing Director, Edgar Marston; Business Manager, Suellen Herstine; Administrative Assistant, Anne Denise Ford; Technical Director, David M. Glenn; Lighting, Howell Binkley, Linwood Taylor; Props, Stephen Studnicka; Costumes, Bobbi Owen; Costumes, Judy Adamson; Stage Manager, Errol Selsby; Press, Priscilla Bratcher

PRODUCTIONS AND CASTS

DRACULA: THE VAMPIRE KING by Tom Haas, with Frank Raiter, Teresa Westbrook, John Daggan, David Adamson, Cristine Rose, Dan Westbrook, Dan Desmond, Michael Lipton

THREADS by Jonathan Bolt; (*World Premiere,* Nov. 8, 1978) Director, Amy Saltz, with Allan Carlsen, Dan Westbrook, John Daggan, Lenka Peterson, Frank Raiter, Suzanne Gilbert, Brian McNally, Teresa Westbrook, Belinda M. Mitchell, Carl Solem

COLD STORAGE by Ronald Ribman, with Michael Lipton, Teresa Westbrook, Andy Backer

LONG DAY'S JOURNEY INTO NIGHT by Eugene O'Neill, with Frank Raiter, Ann Shepherd, Robert Burke, John Daggan, Catherine Taylor

MACBETH by William Shakespeare, with Frank Raiter, John Daggan, Tom Sasser, Matthew B. Clayton, Donald N. Capparella, David Schramm, Cigdem Onat, Gregg Almquist, Campbell Haas, David Adamson, William Perley, Teresa Westbrook, Kristy Orringer, James Hollingsworth, Jamie Orringer, Charlie Finks, Steve Plescia, Dan Westbrook, Brian McNally, Jack Couch, Jim Burleson, Fairley Grimes, Ken Strong, Catherine Taylor, Anne Liske, Marcia Wiesenfeld

YOU CAN'T TAKE IT WITH YOU by George S. Kaufman and Moss Hart, with Gloria Dorson, Teresa Westbrook, Catherine Taylor, Wayne Maxwell, Gerald Unks, Dan Westbrook, John Daggan, Frank Raiter, Sarah Albertson, James Burleson, Brian McNally, Russell Graves, Gillian Plescia, Russell Gold, Ann Shepherd, Anne Liske, Marcia Wiesenfeld, Jack Couch

Michael Bigelow Dixon Photos

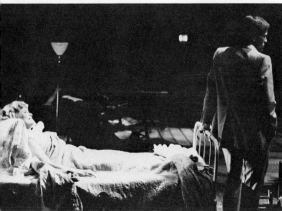

Lenka Peterson, Allan Carlsen in "Threads"
Above: "You Can't Take It with You"

THE REPERTORY COMPANY

Philadelphia, Pennsylvania
September 21, 1978–May 26, 1979
Artistic Directors, Daniel Oreskes, Barry Sattels; Administrative
Director, Robin Dechert

COMPANY

Daniel Oreskes, Barry Sattels, Wallace Schultz, Ben Sweetwood,
Trace Moe, Chris Essler, Marian Mazza, Frank Lyons, P. J. Lyons,
Sarah Labov, Bayard Walder, Delia Mirarchi, Lin Kennedy, Pat
Generalis, Jackie Fisher, MaryAnne DeProphetis, Justin Douglas,
Patrice Carey, Phyllis Holtzman

PRODUCTIONS

A Flea in Her Ear by Georges Feydeau, Rosencrantz and Guildenst-
ern Are Dead by Tom Stoppard, The King Stag by Carlo Gozzi,
American Buffalo by David Mamet, The Second Shepherd's Play
(Anonymous), Spoon River by Edgar Lee Masters, Bedtime Story by
Sean O'Casey

**Right Top: Daniel Oreskes
in "American Buffalo"**

ST. NICHOLAS THEATRE COMPANY

Chicago, Illinois
September 1978–June 1979
Artistic Director, Steven Schachter; Managing Director, Peter
Schneider; Business Manager, Nancy Cook; Press, Tom Thompson

PRODUCTIONS

(Cast list not submitted)
"Little Eyolf," "Fifth of July," and *Premieres* of "Funeral March for
a One-Man Band," "The Curse of an Aching Heart," and "All
Honorable Men"

**Right Center: Michelle Callahan, John Reeger,
Michael Dunn in "Funeral March for
a One-Man Band"**

SOUTH COAST REPERTORY THEATRE

Costa Mesa, California
November 9, 1978–July 27, 1979
Fourteenth Season
Artistic Directors, David Emmes, Martin Benson; Directors,
Martin Benson, David Emmes, John-David Keller, Daniel Sullivan;
Designers, Dawn Chiang, Cliff Faulkner, Louise Hayter, Dwight
Richard Odle, Michael Devine, Thomas Ruzika, Susan Tuohy; Vo-
cal Director, James Wilson

COMPANY

George Archambeault, Pamela Benson, Ronald Boussom, Wynne
Ellen Broms, Steve DeNaut, Diane dePriest, James E. dePriest,
Richard Doyle, John Ellington, Wayne Grace, Arye Gross, Leslie
Jones, Kathryn Johnson, John-David Keller, Scotty King, Art
Koustik, Hal Landon, Jr., Charles Lanyer, Anni Long, Martha
McFarland, Rosemary Mallett, Ron Michaelson, John Napierala,
Cherie Patch, Steve Patterson, Lee Shallat, Howard Shangra, Jo
Sidoli, Ann Siena-Schwartz, Caroline Smith, Don Tuche, and
GUEST ARTISTS: Derek Murcott, Pauline Hague, Alison Evans,
Sandy McCallum, DeAnn Mears, Anne Swift, E. D. Harris, Jerome
Kilty, Jody Horowitz, Charles Marowitz, Robert Benedetti

PRODUCTIONS

"The Time of Your Life" by William Saroyan, "The Contractor" by
David Storey, "The Sorrows of Frederick" by Romulus Linney,
"The Learned Ladies" by Moliere (new Wilbur Translation), "Peg
O' My Heart" by J. Hartley Manners

Barry Slobin, Don Hamilton Photos

**DeAnn Mears, Irene Roseen, John-David Keller
in "The Learned Ladies"**

SEATTLE REPERTORY THEATRE

Seattle, Washington
October 25, 1978–May 20, 1979
Artistic Director, Duncan Ross; Producing Director, Peter Donnelly; Costumes, Lewis D. Rampino; Technical Director, Robert Scales; Stage Manager, Marc Rush; Press, Shirley Dennis; Business Manager, Marene Wilkinson

PRODUCTIONS AND CASTS

A PENNY FOR A SONG by John Whiting, with Christopher Hewett, James Cahill, Dale Reynolds, Mark E. Sather, Gil Rogers, Roxanne Hart, Jacob Brooke, Brooks Morton, Richard Mathews, Richard E. Arnold, Harry Helm, Scott Honeywell, Margaret Hall, Denise Pollock, Peter Lohnes

THE MASTER BUILDER by Henrik Ibsen, translated by Sam Engelstad and Jane Alexander; Director, Vivian Matalon. CAST: Harris Laskawy, Rachel Gurney, Clayton Corzatte, John Eames, Mark Herrier, Joan Inwood, Catherine Burns, Denise Pollock, April Moody, Frances Haertel, Sally Kniest, Laurel Watt, Mara Scott-Wood, Anne Cooper, Peter Lohnes

SIDE BY SIDE BY SONDHEIM by Stephen Sondheim, with Martha Danielle, Jess Richards, Jana Robbins, Paul Shyre

THE GLASS MENAGERIE by Tennessee Williams, with Eve Roberts, Suzanne Collins, David Ossian, Gary Dontzig

CATSPLAY by Istvan Orkeny, translated by Clara Gyorgyey, with Anne Gerety, Emma Trekman, Pauline Flanagan, Marjorie Nelson, Jean Smart, Michael Santo, Robert Gerringer, Molly Dodd, Deems Urquhart

FALLEN ANGELS by Noel Coward, with Millie Slavin, William Glover, Liza Cole, Michael Santo, Jean Smart, Jean-Paul Vignon

Greg Gilbert Photos

**Right: Denise Pollock, Gil Rogers, Mark E. Sather, Margaret Hall in "A Penny for a Song"
Above: Jana Robbins, Martha Danielle, Jeff Richards, Paul Shyre in "Side by Side by Sondheim" Top: Harris Laskaway, Rachel Gurney, Clayton Corzatte, Catherine Burns in "The Master Builder"**

**Eve Roberts, David Ossian
in "The Glass Menagerie"**

**Robert Gerringer, Anne Gerety
in "Catsplay"**

205

STAGE WEST

West Springfield, Massachusetts
November 16, 1978–April 29, 1979
Producing Director, Stephen E. Hayes; General Manager, Robert A. Rosenbaum; Stage Managers, Steven Woolf, Rachael Lindhart; Press, Michele Boudreau, Mary Bensel; Technical Director, Paul J. Horton; Directors, Edward Stern, Cash Baxter, Harold Scott, Timothy Near, Marc B. Weiss, Davey Marlin-Jones; Costumes, Sigrid Insull, Karen Kinsella, Christina Weppner; Sets, Tom Cariello, Joe Long, Jerry Rojo, Marc B. Weiss, Bernard J. Vyzga; Lighting, Leslie Spohn, Robby Monk, John Gisondi, Paul J. Horton

PRODUCTIONS AND CASTS

A RAISIN IN THE SUN by Lorraine Hansberry, with Janet League, Greg Dyson, Hannibal Penney, Jr., Roxanne Reese, Leila Danette, Carlos Carrasco, Rick Khan, Hugh Karraker, Charles Holmond, Tim Blake, Eric Moreland

A CHRISTMAS CAROL by Charles Dickens; adapted by Rae Allen and Timothy Near with Stephen E. Hays, Ronald Bishop, Charles O. Lynch, Judson Earney, Douglas Fisher, David Silber, Hugh Karraker, David Pursley, Laurel Near, Ray Lyons, Amelia Hays, Margaret Lunsford, Judy Jurgaitis, Mary Irey, Valery Daemke, Josie Lawrence, Roman Alis, Eric Moreland, Scott Myers, Michael Moynihan

MOUSETRAP by Agatha Christie, with Judy Jergaitis, Hugh Karraker, Charles O. Lynch, Charlotte Jones, Douglas Fisher, Susanne Peters, David Pursley, Judson Earney

GOOD EVENING by Peter Cook and Dudley Moore, with Alan Kass and J. T. Walsh

A VIEW FROM THE BRIDGE by Arthur Miller with Bob Dio, Patrick Desmond, Don Perkins, Victor Arnold, Dottie Dee, Margaret Winn, John Tormey Vasili Bogazianos, Roger Patnode, Daniel Damelin, Jo-D Ayres, Maurice Dashevsky, Russ Decker

HOW THE OTHER HALF LOVES by Alan Ayckbourn, with Margaret Winn, Timothy Near, Don Perkins, John Tormey, Patrick Desmond, Dottie Dee

Alan Epstein Photos

Left: Don Perkins, Timothy Near, John Tormey in "How the Other Half Loves" Top: Alan Kass, J. T. Walsh in "Good Evening"

Janet League, Hannibal Penney, Jr. in "A Raisin in the Sun"

Victor Arnold, Vasili Bogazianos, Dottie Dee, Margaret Winn, John Tormey in "A View from the Bridge"

206

**Trazana Beverley (C) in "For Colored Girls . . ."
Right: Court Miller, Nancy Donohue, Peter Evans
in "The Runner Stumbles" Below: James C. Burge,
Gwyllum Evans, Betsy Palmer in "Countess Dracula"**

STUDIO ARENA THEATRE

Buffalo, New York
October 6, 1978–May 5, 1979
Fourteenth Season
Executive Producer, Neal DuBrock; General Manager, Stanley D. Silver; Associate to the Producer, Michael T. Healy; Press, Blossom Cohan; Company Manager, Steven J. Caffery; Stage Manager, Beverly J. Andreozzi; Technical Director, John T. Baun; Props, Marion Mooney, Laura Heller; Costumes, A. Holly Olsen, Mary-Camille Schwindler; Sound, Walter Bakos; Production Assistant, William L. McMullen

PRODUCTIONS AND CASTS

FUNNY FACE with Music by George Gershwin; Lyrics, Ira Gershwin; Book, Fred Thompson, Paul Gerard Smith, with revised book by Neal Du Brock. CAST: James Brennan, Bette Glenn, Ellen Greene, April Shawhan, Denny Shearer, Ronald Young, John Remme, Linda Ravinsky, Karen St. George, David Monzione, Eddie Pruett, Bobby Longbottom, Sally O'Donnell, Carol Wade, Brad Witsger

FOR COLORED GIRLS WHO HAVE CONSIDERED SUICIDE WHEN THE RAINBOW IS ENUF by Ntozake Shange; Director, Oz Scott, with Trazana Beverley, Joyce Hanley, Denise Marcia, Diann McCannon, Kaaren Ragland, Veronica Terrell, Linda Thomas Wright

A CHRISTMAS CAROL by Charles Dickens, adapted by Rae Allen and Timothy Near; Director, Warren Enters. CAST: Steven Sutherland, Frank Borgman, Patricia Cosgrove, Judith Dowd, Christina Gillespie, Jean Hebborn, Roger Kozol, Cynthia Milstead, Bill Nunnery, Carroll W. Rue, Stan Sayer, Tom Spackman, Dee Victor, Bruce Wall, Frederic Warriner, Douglas Crane, William Lennon, Adam Martin, Lisa Seyfert

COUNTESS DRACULA! written and directed by Neal DuBrock (*World Premiere,* Jan. 5, 1979) with Betsy Palmer, James C. Burge, Gwyllum Evans, Richard Fitzpatrick, Judith Dowd, Jay Lowman, Patricia Cosgrove

THE RUNNER STUMBLES by Milan Stitt; Director, Warren Enters; with Peter Evans, Nancy Donohue, Court Miller, Rachel Taylor, Allan Frank, Mary Lou Rosato, Bruce Probst, Steve Carroll, Sally Anne Tackus

CATSPLAY by Istvan Orkeny in a translation by Clara Gyorgyey; Director, Stephen Porter. CAST: Charlotte Jones, Esther Benson, Lois Markle, Patricia Wheel, David Pursley, Tandy Cronyn, William Ferriter, Joan Croydon, Charles Mayer

THE MADWOMAN OF CENTRAL PARK WEST by Phyllis Newman and Arthur Laurents; Director, Arthur Laurents; Performed by Phyllis Newman

Phototech Studio Photos

**Denny Shearer, April Shawhan
in "Funny Face"**

207

Floyd King, Ann Mitchell, Ann McDonough
in "She Stoops to Conquer" Left: Entire
company of "The Butterfingers Angel ..." Top:
Basil Wallace, Thomas Kopache in "Blood Knot"

SYRACUSE STAGE

Syracuse, New York
October 20, 1978–May 20, 1979
Producing Director, Arthur Storch; Managing Director, James A.
Clark; Business Manager, Linda L. Southam; Press, Charlaine Mar-
tin; Stage Managers, David Semonin, Patricia Ann Speelman,
Donna K. Seigfreid; Sets, William Schroder, John Arnone, John
Kasarda, Elmon Webb, Virginia Dancy, Jack Doepp; Costumes,
James Berton Harris, Nanzi Adzima, Patricia McGourty, Liz Bass,
William Schroder; Lighting, Barry Arnold, Geoffrey T. Cunning-
ham, Judy Rasmuson, James E. Stephens, Spencer Mosse

PRODUCTIONS AND CASTS

SHE STOOPS TO CONQUER by Oliver Goldsmith; Director, John
Going; with Robert Blackburn, Ann Mitchell, Floyd King, Giulia
Pagano, Ann McDonough, Ivar Brogger, Michael Guido, Peter Col-
ford, Carlton Colyer, B. J. Slack, John Ahlin, Gary Arvedon, Eric
Weiss, Joe Davis, Keith Taylor, Kevin M. Shumway, Leslie A Wells,
Fred Lopez, Gerard Moses

THE WORLD OF SHOLOM ALEICHEM by Arnold Perl; Direc-
tor, Steven Kaplan; with Max Gulack, Christopher Coddington,
Ellen Fiske, Bernie Passeltiner, Ruth Fenster, Randy Paradise,
Floyd King

THE BLOOD KNOT by Athol Fugard; Director, Thomas Bullard;
with Basil Wallace, Thomas Kopache

OTHERWISE ENGAGED by Simon Gray; Director, Harold
Stone; with Munson Hicks, Patrick Turner, Peter C. Johnson, Curt
Karibalis, Jeanne Cullen, Lowry Miller, Wanda Bimson

THE GLASS MENAGERIE by Tennessee Williams; Director,
Harold Scott; with Victoria Boothby, William Carden, Jeanne Cullen, Michael Martin

LOVED by Olwen Wymark; (*American Premiere*) Director, Arthur
Storch; with Dina Merrill, Richard Abernethy, Le Clanche du
Rand, Jeffrey Ware, Tom Kenna, Nancy Mette

THE BUTTERFINGERS ANGEL, MARY AND JOSEPH,
HEROD THE NUT, AND THE SLAUGHTER OF 12 HIT
CAROLS IN A PEAR TREE by William Gibson; Director, Arthur
Storch; with Mike Kellin, Lisa Pelikan, Tom Villard, Munson Hicks,
David Wohl, Virgil Rogerson, Tazewell Thompson, Katherine
Knowles, Sally Moffet, Marianne Tatum, Rachel Ticotin, George H.
Johnson, Ellen Theresa McCarthy, Pat Page, Jaymie Meyer, Dee
Fetters, Peter Colford, Robert E. Krigbaum, Mark Gallagher, John
Vona, Jay B. Stone, Eileen Strempel, Rachel Potash, Mike
McCurdy, Meredith Mancini, Sarah Pickett, Thomas Walter White
III

Robert Lorenz/Main Street Photos

Dina Merrill, Tom Keena
in "Loved"

THEATRE BY THE SEA

Portsmouth, New Hampshire
July 1, 1978 - May 27, 1979
Producing Director, Jon Kimbell; Managing Director, Drew Souerwine; Press, Sandi Bianco; Administrative Assistants, Jean Caldwell, Connie Barron, Marie Cartier; Stage Managers, William Michael Maher, Glenn Medas; Costumes, Kathie Iannicelli; Lighting and Sound, James Trudeau; Technical Director, Roger Rutledge; Props, Carol Walker; Wardrobe, Dolly D'tremont, Joan Voss

PRODUCTIONS AND CASTS

RELATIVELY SPEAKING by Alan Ackbourn; Director, Richard Magavero; Set, Bob Phillips. CAST: Tom Celli, Lois Diane Hicks, Michael LaGue, Ginny Russell

THE RUNNER STUMBLES by Milan Stitt; Director, Thomas R. Bloom. CAST: Euan Bagshawe, John Becker, Tom Celli, Herbert DuVal, Mary Fogarty, Michael LaGue, Ginny Russell, Stephanie Voss, Bonnie Wilbur

MURDER AT THE VICARAGE by Agatha Christie, dramatized by Moie Charles and Barbara Toy; Director, Russell Treyz. CAST: Euan Bagshawe, Gary Brubach, Tom Celli, Herbert DuVal, Nancy Walton Fenn, Mary Fogarty, Mark Guerette, Michael LaGue, Ginny Russell, Stephanie Voss, Carol Walker, Bonnie Wilbur

UNCLE VANYA by Anton Chekhov; New translation by John Murrell; Director, Jon Kimbell. CAST: Euan Bagshawe, Tom Celli, Herbert DuVal, Nancy Walton Fenn, Mary Fogarty, Ginny Russell, Stephanie Voss, Dexter Witherell

THE SEA HORSE by Edward Moore; Director, Tom Celli; with Michael Beirne and Janice Fuller

STARTING HERE, STARTING NOW by David Shire and Richard Maltby, Jr.; Director, John Montgomery; Musical Director, Bob McNamee; Set, Larry Fulton. CAST: Judith Bliss, Connie Coit, Daniel Fortus

OKLAHOMA! by Rodgers and Hammerstein, and ONCE UPON A MATTRESS by Jay Thompson, Marshall Barer, Dean Fuller; Music, Mary Rodgers; Lyrics, Marshall Barer; Director, Russell Treyz; Choreography, John Montgomery; Musical Director, John Clifton. CAST: Roger Adams, Martha Arnold, Gary Brubach, Tamara Burkhead, Darlene Butler, Tom Celli, Marie Clark, Sue Anne Gershenson, Mark Guerette, Michael Guerette, Claire LaTessa, John Maher, Annette Miller, David Penhald, Anne Richardson, Ginny Russell, James Sears, Jeff Starbird, Elyse Thierry, Scott Weintraub, Michael Ford Welch, Doris Yeager

Thomas R. Bloom Photos

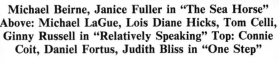

**Michael Beirne, Janice Fuller in "The Sea Horse"
Above: Michael LaGue, Lois Diane Hicks, Tom Celli,
Ginny Russell in "Relatively Speaking" Top: Connie
Coit, Daniel Fortus, Judith Bliss in "One Step"**

THEATRE THREE

Dallas, Texas
October 1978–August 1979
Founder, Norma Young; Producer-Director, Jac Alder; Associate Director, Charles Howard; Assistant to Producer, Nancy Akers; Press, Terri Taylor; Costumes, Patty Greer McGarity; Musical Director, John Humphrey

PRODUCTIONS

(Cast list not submitted)
"The Shadow Box" by Michael Cristofer, "Happy End" by Bertolt Brecht and Kurt Weill, "The Runner Stumbles" by Milan Stitt, "Small Craft Warnings" by Tennessee Williams, "Starting Here, Starting Now" by David Shire and Richard Maltby, Jr., "Jumpers" by Tom Stoppard, "Side by Side by Sondheim" with music by Stephen Sondheim

Andy Hanson Photo

**Larry O'Dwyer, Cecilia Flores
in "The Miser"**

209

Barbara Meek, Ed Hall, Jeffrey Duarte in "The Shadow Box" Top: Cast of "Jack the Ripper"

Howard London, Norman Smith, Barbara Orson, Richard Jenkins in "Awake and Sing!" Top: Ricardo Pitts Wiley, David Kennett in "Uncle Tom's Cabin"

TRINITY SQUARE REPERTORY COMPANY

Providence, Rhode Island
September 28, 1978–June 3, 1979

Director, Adrian Hall; Administrator, G. David Black; Press, Marion Simon, Scotti DeDonato; General Manager, E. Timothy Langan; Musical Director, Richard Cumming; Sets, Robert D. Soule, Matthew Jacobs; Lighting, John F. Custer, Eugene Lee; Costumes, Mary Aiello Bruce, Annette Rossi, Vittorio Capecce, Ann Morrell; Choreography, Sharon Jenkins; Technical Director, David Ward; Props, Sandra Nathanson, Tom Walden, Cheryl Ottaviano; Stage Managers, Maureen Gibson, Dennis Blackledge; Directors, Adrian Hall, Larry Arrick, Ron Pember, Timothy Crowe, Peter Gerety

COMPANY

Rob Anderson, Robert Black, Bonnie Sacks Black, Dan Butler, Robert J. Colonna, Timothy Crowe, Carmen deLavallade, Timothy Donoghue, Monique Fowler, Peter Gerety, Ed Hall, Richard Jenkins, David C. Jones, Melanie Jones, David Kennett, Richard Kneeland, Howard London, Mina Manente, Lois Markle, Linda Martin, Derek Meader, Barbara Meek, Elizabeth Moore, Barbara Orson, Ford Rainey, Margo Skinner, Neva Small, Norman B. Smith, Amy Van Nostrand, Daniel Von Bargen, Rose Weaver, Ricardo Pitts Wiley

PRODUCTIONS

"A Life in the Theatre," "A Christmas Carol," "Father's Day," "The Shadow Box," "Awake and Sing," "Death of a Salesman," "Who's Afraid of Virginia Woolf," *American Premiere* of "Jack the Ripper" by Denis DeMarne and Ron Pember, and *World Premiere* of "Uncle Tom's Cabin; A History" by Adrian Hall and Richard Cumming

Robert Emerson, Jack Spratt Photos

Left Center: Robert Black, Richard Kneeland in "A Life in the Theatre"

Bonnie Sacks Black, Margo Skinner, Mina Manente in "Father's Day"

VIRGINIA MUSEUM THEATRE

Richmond, Virginia
September 29, 1978–March 24, 1979
Twenty-fourth Season
Artistic Director, Tom Markus; Administrative Director, Baylor Landrum; General Manager, Loraine Slade; Press, David Griffith, Don Dale; Production Manager/Apprentice Coordinator, Terry Burgler; Technical Director, Thomas Knapp

PRODUCTIONS AND CASTS

VOLPONE by Ben Jonson, adapted by Robert A. Potter and Tom Markus; Director, Tom Markus; Scenery, Joseph A. Varga; Costumes, Lana Fritz; Lighting, Patricia A. Connors; Stage Manager, Doug Flinchum; Choreography, Warren Kelley; Sound, Tom Wynkoop. CAST: Jack Axelrod, Maury Erickson, John H. Fields, Robert Foley, Robert Gerringer, Warren Kelley, Ernie Meier, Margery Murray, Edward Stevlingson, Sam Tsoutsouvas, Jan van der Swaagh, Fiddle Viracola.

THE FANTASTICKS by Tom Jones and Harvey Schmidt; Director, Joey Patton; Musical Director, Dougee Zeno. CAST: Jack Axelrod, Maury Erickson, John H. Fields, Robert Foley, Lowell Harris, Warren Kelley, Margery Murray, Nancy Nichols

DEAR LIAR by Jerome Kilty; Director, Tom Markus; with Patricia Falkenhain, Robert Gerringer

PRIVATE LIVES by Noel Coward; Director, Tom Markus; Lighting, Curt Senie. CAST: Stephanie Braxton, Maury Erickson, Dan Hamilton, Barre Hunt, Margery Murray

Dennis McWaters, Katherine Wetzel Photos

Right: Maury Erickson, Stephanie Braxton, Dan Hamilton, Margery Murray in "Private Lives" Top: Robert Foley, Sam Tsoutsouvas, Robert Gerringer, Margery Murray, Warren Kelley in "Volpone"

Louis Zorich, Olympia Dukakis, Jessica Allen, W. T. Martin in "Who's Afraid of Virginia Woolf?" Above: Louis Zorich in "The Homecoming"

THE WHOLE THEATRE COMPANY

Montclair, New Jersey
October 17, 1978–June 17, 1979
Producing Director, Arnold Mittelman; Artistic Director, Olympia Dukakis; General Manager, Sylvia S. Traeger; Press, Gerald R. Fierst; Directors, Apollo Dukakis, Olympia Dukakis, Arnold Mittelman; Sets, Paul Dorphley, Ray Recht, Anthony Krivitski; Costumes, Sigrid Insull; Lighting, Marshall Spiller; Stage Manager, Charles R. Traeger

COMPANY

Maggie Abeckerly, Jessica Allen, Jason Bosseau, Remi Barclay, Tom Brennan, Judith Delgado, Apollo Dukakis, Olympia Dukakis, Gerald Fierst, Marjorie Fierst, W. T. Martin, Lynn Clifton Martin, Arnold Mittelman, Stefan Peters, Glenna Peters, Louis Zorich
GUEST ACTORS: Georgia Hester, Jordan Myers, Alan Ansara, P. L. Carling, John Canary, James Nesbet Clark, Frank Dwyer, Ronald Durling, Yusef Bulof, Owen Rachleff, Steven Ryan

PRODUCTIONS

The Trojan Women, The Imaginary Invalid, The Homecoming, Arms and the Man, Who's Afraid of Virginia Woolf?

Above: Olympia Dukakis in "The Trojan Women"

211

YALE REPERTORY THEATRE

New Haven, Connecticut
September 29, 1978–May 21, 1979

Director, Robert Brustein; Managing Director, Robert J. Orchard; Business Manager, Abigail P. Fearon; Press, Jan Geidt; Designers, Michael Yeargan, Dunya Ramicova; Lighting, William B. Warfel; Production Supervisor, John Robert Hood; Technical Directors, Bronislaw Sammler, Theodore G. Ohl; Assistant Production Supervisor, Jonathan Seth Miller; Stage Managers, Frank S. Torok, H. Lloyd Carbaugh, Julie Haber; Costumer, Elizabeth Bauer; Props, Hunter Nesbitt Spence; Assistant Managing Directors, Brian Mann, Suzanne Sato, Richard Ostracher; Sets, Tony Straiges, Adrianne Lobel, Andrew Jackness, Michael Yeargan, Thomas Lynch; Costumes, Dunya Ramicova, Marjorie Graf, Nan Cibula, Adrianne Lobel, Susan Hilferty; Lighting, Thomas Skelton, Robert Jared, William M. Armstrong, William B. Warfel

PRODUCTIONS AND CASTS

TALES FROM THE VIENNA WOODS (*American Premiere*) by Odon von Horvath; Director, Keith Hack; with Norma Brustein, Robert Burr, David Clennon, Katherine Clarke, Eric Elice, Clarence Felder, Elizabeth Franz, Jeremy Geidt, John Glover, Richard Grusin, Carol Kane, Nancy Mayans, H. S. Murphy, Elizabeth Norment, Rebecca Nelson, Mary Van Dyke

MISTAKEN IDENTITIES: Two new American plays: "Identity Crisis" by Christopher Durang; Director, Frank Torok, with Katherine Clarke, Mark Linn-Baker, Nancy Mayans, David K. Miller, Darcy Pulliam; "Guess Work" (*World Premiere*) by Robert Auletta; Director, Robert Gainer; with David Clennon

MAHAGONNY, A Chamber of The Rise and Fall of the City of Mahagonny; Director, Keith Hack; Musical Director, Gary Fagin; with Ellen Barber, Robert Burr, Katherine Clarke, Eric Elice, June Gable, Jeremy Geidt, John Glover, David Alan Grier, Michael Gross, Jonathan Marks, Nancy Mayans, Fred Melamed, David K. Miller, Darcy Pulliam, John Seitz

BURIED CHILD by Sam Shepard; Director, Adrian Hall, with Joseph Costa, Polly Draper, Clarence Felder, Elizabeth Franz, Jeremy Geidt, Ford Rainey, John Seitz, Tony Shalhoub

THE BUNDLE (*American Premiere*) by Edward Bond; Director, John Madden; with Joseph Costa, Peter Crombie, Alice Drummond, R. N. Foerster, Jeremy Geidt, Richard Grusin, Nicholas Kepros, Tom Klunis, Warren Manzi, Rebecca Nelson, Elizabeth Norment, Marianne Owen, Geoffrey M. Pierson, Ford Rainey, Alan Rosenberg, John Gould Rubin, Tony Shalhoub, Mary Van Dyke, William McGlinn

THE SEA GULL by Anton Chekhov, translated by Jean-Claude van Itallie; Director, Robert Brustein, with Norma Brustein, Katherine Clarke, Caris Corfman, Robert Dean, Joseph Costa, Eric Elice, Elizabeth Franz, Clarence Felder, Jeremy Geidt, Addison Powell, Michael Wager, Rosa Vega

AS YOU LIKE IT by William Shakespeare; Director, Andrei Belgrader, with William Converse-Roberts, Peter Crombie, Thomas Derrah, Polly Draper, Eric Elice, Jeremy Geidt, Richard Grusin, Moses Gunn, Mark Linn-Baker, William McGlinn, Nancy Mayans, Fred Melamed, David K. Miller, H. S. Murphy, Elizabeth Norment, Marianne Owen, Ann Sachs, Tony Sherer, Jeff Ginsberg, David Prittie, Bernard Sundstedt, Katherine Borowitz, Jenny Davis, Barbara Jones, Isy Monk, Hillary Nelson

Eugene Cook Photos

Carol Kane in "Tales from the Vienna Woods"
Above: Ann Sachs in "As You Like It"

Top: "Mahagonny" Left: "The Sea Gull"
Below: "Buried Child"

ANNUAL SHAKESPEARE FESTIVALS

ALABAMA SHAKESPEARE FESTIVAL

Anniston, Alabama
July 14–August 19, 1978
Seventh Season

Artistic Director, Martin L. Platt; Managing Director, Anne F. Zimmerman; Assistant Manager, Glenda E. Knight, Stage Managers, Arlene Ritz, Charles Otte, Patricia Cochran; Guest Director, Fred Chappell; Conservatory Director, Sydney Hibbert; Fencing Master, James Donadio; Choreographer, Joseph King; Speech and Dialects, James Eckhouse; Assistant to Mr. Platt, James Rugino; Set and Lighting, Michael Stauffer; Technical Director, Roger Foster; Props, Allison Biggers, Amelia Dyer; Costumes, Lynne Emmert; Wardrobe Mistress, Lorraine Crane; Josephine E. Ayers, President; William J. Davis, Chairman of the Board

COMPANY

Charles Antalosky, Terry Beaver, Donald Bednarz, Robert Bloodworth, Gayle Brownlee, Patricia Caffey, James Donadio, James Eckhouse, Matthew Faison, Lynn Fitzpatric, Sydney Hibbert, George Holmes, Henry House, Peter Jack, Ridge Johnson, Wendy Kaufman, Joseph King, Deborah LaVine, David McCann, William McHale, Judith Marx, Jane Moore, Joseph Naftel, Philip Pleasants, James Rugino, Mark Varian, William Verderber

PRODUCTIONS

"Othello," "The Merchant of Venice," "Private Lives," "Measure for Measure," "A Lover's Complaint," "Clarence Darrow," "The Taming of the Shrew"

Jerry Harris Photos

**Right: Judith Marx, James Donadio
in "Taming of the Shrew"**

"The Merchant of Venice" Above: Judith Marx, Philip Pleasants in "Measure for Measure"

Philip Pleasants, Sydney Hibbert in "Othello" Above: Philip Pleasants as Clarence Darrow 213

AMERICAN SHAKESPEARE THEATRE

Stratford, Connecticut
July 5–August 6, 1978
Artistic Director, Gerald Freedman; William W. Goodman, Chairman of the Board; Konrad Matthaei, President; Richard Bader, Executive Director; Press: Kathryn Romanik, Richard Pheneger, Tom Holehan

TWELFTH NIGHT
or What You Will

By William Shakespeare; Director, Gerald Freedman; Set, Ming Cho Lee; Costumes, Jeanne Button; Lighting, David Segal; Incidental Music and Songs, John Morris; Choreography, Graciela Daniele; Production Supervisor, Mary Porter Hall; Assistant to Director, Kathy Barber; Props, Susan Stassick; Production Assistant, Jamie Clark; Stage Manager, John Beven

CAST

Orsino, Duke of Illyria	Laurence Guittard
Curio	Stephen Temperley
Valentine	Brooks Baldwin
Viola	Lynn Redgrave
Sea Captain, friend to Viola	Theodore Sorel
Sailor	David Challenger
Sir Toby Belch, Olivia's uncle	Joseph Bova
Maria, Olivia's woman	Mary Louise Wilson
Sir Andrew Aguecheek	Stephen Vinovich
Feste, a clown	Mark Lamos
Olivia, a countess	Penny Fuller
Malvolio, steward to Olivia	Bob Dishy
Sebastian, Viola's brother	Philip Kraus
Antonio, sea captain, friend to Sebastian	Robert Stattel
Officers/Lords	David Challenger, Bill Roberts
Priest	Theodore Sorel
Olivia'a Ladies	Jacqueline Coslow, Patricia Hodges
Singers	Christine Radman, Gene Sager, Joel Sager, Winifred Sager

UNDERSTUDIES: Patricia Hodges (Viola), Jacqueline Coslow (Olivia/Maria), Christine Radman, Winifred Sager (Olivia's Ladies), Theodore Sorel (Antonio), David Challenger (Orsino/Priest/Captain), Robert Stattel (Malvolio), Stephen Temperley (Andrew/Sebastian/Valentine), Brooks Baldwin (Sir Toby), Bill Roberts (Feste, Curio)

Phyllis Crowley Photos

**Lynn Redgrave, Penny Fuller
in "Twelfth Night"**

**Julia Brothers, Time Winters, Nancy Siddons-
Daniels, Ted Levine in "Twelfth Night"**

CHAMPLAIN SHAKESPEARE FESTIVAL

Burlington, Vermont
July 6, - August 12, 1978
Twentieth Season
Producer-Director, Edward J. Feidner; Stage Designer, Robert Little; Costumes, Mary Brownlow; Music Director, Liz McGlinchey; Technical Director, Daniel C Beopple; Vocal Coach, Robert Barker; Lighting, Andrew Mack; Props, Eugenie B. Seidenberg; Stage Manager, Robert Lovell; Business Manager, Alice Cook; Press, Heidi Racht

COMPANY

Ray Aranha, Bob Barker, Tom Blachly, Julia A. Brothers, Josh Conescu, Stacey Gladstone, Kip Kinnard, Ted Velive, Leon Maetell, Cort Millar, Andrew Hill Newman, Greg Patnaude, Ric Priem, Robert B. Putnam, Neave Rake, Vince Rossano, Nancy Siddons-Daniels, Matthew Skeele, Duncan Stephens, Rick Whitmore, Tom Winslow, Time Winters, Carol Czina, Kristin Davis, Ginny West

PRODUCTIONS: "Twelfth Night" and "Othello"

Charles Trottier Photos

**Above: Ray Aranha, Nancy Siddons-Daniels
in "Othello"**

COLORADO SHAKESPEARE FESTIVAL

Boulder, Colorado
July 2–August 18, 1978
Twenty-first Season

Executive Director, Daniel S. P. Yang; Press, Beverly Shaw, Nora Donovan; Administrative Assistant, Lou Crnkovich; Musical Director, Bruce Howard White; Directors, Robert L. Benedetti, Martin Cobin, Audrey Stanley; Designers, Dan Cryden, Norvid Jenkins Roos, Jim Doyle, Richard Riddell, Rondi Hillstrom Davis, Maribeth Kwass, Lynn Ellen McLeod; Coordinators, David A. Busse, Audrey V. Wilson, Jane Page, Toni Diemont; Technical Staff, J. Andrew Burgreen, Jean Conley, Edward E. Ellert, Peter Gottlieb, Ron Keller, Dan Kotlowitz, John Lawrence Rothrock

COMPANY

Sharon Ammen, C. V. Bennett, Gigi Benson, Jeffrey Brownson, David Bryant, Shirley Carnahan, J. H. Crouch, William Davis, Leonardo DeFilippis, James Finnegan, Larry Friedlander, Peter D. Giffin, Brad Gordon, Susannah Halston, Carol Hansche, Robin Hodge, William Johnson, Margaret Kasahara, Jan Krelle, Don Laventhall, Barbara Lehmann, Kjeld Erik Lyth, Richard Marcus, Richard Maynard, Rod Mays, Cole McMartin, Rainard Rachelle, Lawrence Resse, Edward Lloyd Rogers, Dan Sanders, Cathy Schaeffer, Margie Shaw, Philip C. Sneed, Alan Tilson, Allan Trautman, David M. Wells, Steve West, Charles Wilcox, Robert Willson, Jay R. Wisecarver

PRODUCTIONS

"Twelfth Night," "Othello," "Henry IV, Part I"

Seth Perlman Photos

**Top Right: Colorado Shakespeare
Festival Theatre
(No production photos submitted)**

GLOBE OF THE GREAT SOUTHWEST

Odessa, Texas
June 24,–August 13, 1978
Tenth Season

Producer-Director, Charles David McCally; Directors, Charles David McCally, Regina Walker McCally; Costumes, Walter Robin Findlay; Technical Director, Jeff McKay; Press, Wanda Snodgrass; Chairman of the Board, Ted Lorenz, Jr.

COMPANY

J. David Weddington, Susan Melissa Hatfield, Jack Coleman, Stephen Riggs, Jessica Phelps, Frederic Chrislip, David Minton, Gail Felt, Raynor Nicholson, Joseph Blankenship, Rhonda Clark, Jerry Dickey, James Bottom, Jeff McKay, Walter Robin Findlay, Terry Lister, Craig Campbell, Jorge Marie Skelton, Ardis Kathryn Beggs, Bryan Burrows, James Cunningham, Brett Elise McCally, Courtney Lynn Skelton, Ruth Aldridge, Jimmila Hogan, Lindy Nichols, Betsy Blair

PRODUCTIONS

"Othello" staged and directed by Charles David McCally, "Love's Labour's Lost" staged and directed by Regina Wallace, "The House of Saul" by Agnes Sanford, staged and directed by Charles David McCally

**Joseph Blankenship, Jillian Raye in "Othello"
Right Center: Globe Theatre**

215

GLOBE PLAYHOUSE

Los Angeles, California
June 1, 1978–May 26, 1979
Executive Producer-Founder-Artistic Director, R. Thad Taylor; Art Director, Jean Blanchette; Business Manager, Susan P. Marrone; Production Coordinator, James Malbrough; Costumes, Phyliss Adams; General Manager, Edward E. Milder; Press, Harriet Held; Lighting, Michael M. Bergfeld; Presented by the Shakespeare Society of America; Recipient of 1978 Los Angeles Drama Critics Circle Award

PRODUCTIONS AND CASTS

THE TRAGEDIE OF ANTHONIE AND CLEOPATRA with Robert J. Arcuri, Douglas Blair, Arnold Bankston, Allen C. Barker, Mark Bringelson, Isabel Cooley, Joe Lee Corey, Don Eaton, Carmen Fortino, Jeffrey G. Forward, Joyce Hanley, Gordon Haight, Paul Harvey, Robin James, Larry Ketchum, Ben Michael Lamb, Tom Lancaster, Cherie Lynne, Dane Madsen, James Malbrough, Stephen Mancini, Michael Matthews, Margo C. Ormes, Randy Parker, Susan Peters, Sheril Sakai, Vance Valencia, Ollie West, Doug Whitt, Eugenia Wright, Craig Wyckoff

PERICLES PRINCE OF TYRE with Robert J. Arcuri, Douglas Blair, Sharon Borek, Eugene Brezany, Randall Cohen, David Cooper, James Loren, James Malbrough, Stephen Mancini, Michael Matthews, Marcia Mohr, Lawrence Parks, Mariana Rence, P. A. Rollins, Suzanna Peters, Lee Stevens, Concetta Tomei, Steve Ventin, Craig Wyckoff

THE TRAGICALL HISTORIE OF HAMLET, PRINCE OF DENMARK with James-Scott Bell, Mark Bringelson, Ann Bronston, Douglas Broyles, Timothy Callaghan, Evan Cole, Jo de Winter, Richard Epcar, Donald Forney, Barbara Foster, Abraham Gordon, Richard Hale, Barbara Halperin, Ed Harris, Paul Jenkins, Heather Lowe, Steve Mancini, Michael Matthews, Samuel Mathews, Barbara Newborn, Joanie Orazco, Michael Richards, Neil Smith, Ken Strong, Steve Stuart, Delbert Spain, Raymond Thompson, Jeff Woodward, Eugene Zilberman

ROMEO AND JULIET by Charles Gounod, and THE MERRY WIVES OF WINDSOR by Otto Nicolai were sung in English by Arnet Amos, Frank Avalos, Jeannie Baldwin, Jennifer Burke, Eugene Brezany, James Canning, Camillo Coogan, Darrel Couturier, Thomas F. Ferraro, Tina E. Ferraro, Carolyn Ferritto, Catherine Fiasca, Judith M. Gagnon, Mary Gavagan, Jeffrey Gerstein, Terrence Slavin, Sam Sorrow, Susan Stewart, Dan Turiel, Herb Ware, Jerome Weitzman, Mona Williams, Abel Verdier

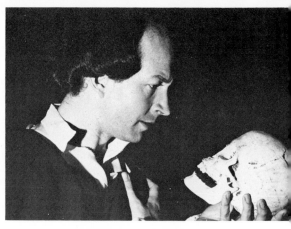

Douglas Broyles as Hamlet

TWELFTH NIGHT OR WHAT YOU WILL with Jack Manning, Noreen Hennessy, Terry Gordon, Ron Morhous, Marilyn Doddsfrank, Sandra MacGregor, Charles Hyman, John Salazar, Susan Tanner, Henry McCreath-Kaiser, Ronald Salley, Herb Mendelsohn, Jorga Ursin

THE LIFE OF TYMON OF ATHENS with Lawrence Parks, Nocona Aranda, Eugene Brezany, Barry Burke, Walter Cass, Barbara Downs, Stephen Duke, William Angus Erwin, Joseph Grace, James King, John LeGrande, James Malbreaux, Stephen Mancini, Peter Martyniuk, Phillip Ray Newsome, Suzanna Peters, Michael Richards, Patti Richards, Ed Stone, Ellen Suits, Minnie Wallace

SHAKESPEARE'S MANUSCRIPTS? by William Shakespeare and R. Thad Taylor; *World Premiere* with R. Thad Taylor as narrator, and Evan Cole, Marcus Garrett, Casey Kramer, Lynne McQuaker, Dane Madsen, Stephen Mancini, James Malbreaux, Charles Matheny, Ron Morhous, Cynthia Morris, Nancy Sue Morris, Judy Pies, Angela Slater, Kay Worthington

THE TRAGEDIE OF MACBETH with Paul Aron, Jon M. Benson, Richard Blue, Kathleen Buchanan, Randall Cohen, Jeffrey G. Forward, Martin Gish, Doug Kerr, Jerry King, Karl F. Kirgis, Dan McNally, David Raymond Maier, Dina Marie, Norma Chalfin Melone, Jennifer Newbery, Phillip Ray Newsome, Gloria Parker, Razak Rahim, Daniel Ruark, Leo E. Sauer, Catherine-Lynne Shannon, Dale Swann, Fred Fate

THE SECOND PART OF HENRY THE SIXTH with Kevin Scott Allen, Stephen Rory Brown, Mary Burkin, Joanne Casey, Ross Clark, Michael Coon, Roger Jones, Frank Lenart, Gina Marria Makris, Charles Matheny, Steven J. Paull, Tony Perrotta, Michael Richards, Steve Rogers, Christopher Sands, Margaret Silbar, Patrick Skelton, Ed Thomas

THE THIRD PART OF HENRY THE SIXTH with same cast as preceding play

CORIOLANUS with Lee Cohn, Stephen Hinkey, Henry Hoffman, Richard Holden, Charles Hyman, Sandra MacGregor, Nicholas Maultsby-Jones, Sara Maultsby, Maria Mayenzet, Herb Mendelsohn, Maryann Nagel, Ronald Salley, Walter Scholtz, Miranda Smith

A MIDSOMMER NIGHTS DREAME with Cathy Allyn, David Allyn, Hank Barrows, Guy Bongiovanni, A'leshia Brevard, Ann Bronston, Beaumont Bruestle, Vincent Caristi, Stephen D'Ambrose, James Howard Davis, Shannon Eubanks, J. D. Hall, Charles Hutchins, Barbara Kingsley, Sheila Marcus, Mary Michele, Michelle Mindlin, Mary Monaghan, Mark Palko, Michael Ross-Oddo, Stephen E. Stuart, Stephen Jon Stuart, Teaka, Larry Vigus

MEASURE FOR MEASURE with Peter Beckman, Richard Blood, Jane Carpenter, Kathleen Conklin, Sharon Crabtree, Michael J. Cutt, Timothy Cutt, Roger Harkenrider, Christine Kirsch, Frank Lenart, Daniel Mahar, Maria Mayenzet, Paul McEvoy, Maryann Nagel, Walter Scholz, David Hunt Stafford, Stephanie Stern, Bonnie Snyder, Kevin Stock, Al Strobel, John Tallman, Paul Teschke, Allan Trautman

Sealy the Photographer Photos

Cast of "Shakespeare's Manuscripts" with author R. Thad Taylor (C)

Left Center: Norma Chalfin Melone, Doug Kerr in "Macbeth"

GREAT LAKES SHAKESPEARE FESTIVAL

Lakewood, Ohio
July 6,–September 30, 1978
Seventeenth Season

Artistic Director, Vincent Dowling; Administrative Director, Bruce Halverson; Press, Ksenia Roshchakovsky, Bill Rudman; Directors, Roger Hendricks Simon, Daniel Sullivan; Sets, John Ezell; Costumes, Kurt Wilhelm; Lighting, Richard Coumbs; Musical Director, Stuart W. Raleigh; Stage Managers, Olwen O'Herlihy, Christine Michael; Technical Director, Richard Archer

COMPANY

Jon Peter Benson, Norman Berman, Tom Blair, Richard Dix, Bairbre Dowling, V. G. Dowling, Donna Emmanuel, Tom Hanks, Bernard Kates, Dennis Lipscomb, George Maguire, MichaelJohn McGann, Frederic-Winslow Oram, Holmes Osborne, Edith Owen, Steve Ryan, Sara Woods

PRODUCTIONS

"Two Gentlemen of Verona" and "In the Troublesome Reign of King John" by William Shakespeare, "Polly" by John Gay, "What Every Woman Knows" by J. M. Barrie, "Wild Oats" by John O'-Keeffe, "The Nine Days Wonder of Will Kemp" compiled by Chris Harris and John David

Marianne Pojman Photos

Right: Edith Owen, Bairbre Dowling in "What Every Woman Knows" Top: Sara Woods, Charles Brown, Richard Dix in "King John"

Dennis Lipscomb in "Two Gentlemen of Verona"

Lora Staley, Tom Hanks in "Two Gentlemen of Verona"

217

NATIONAL SHAKESPEARE FESTIVAL

San Diego, California
June 16, through September 17, 1978
Twenty-ninth Season

Producing Director, Craig Noel; General Manager, Robert McGlade; Art Director, Peggy Kellner; Press, William B. Eaton; Technical Director, Steve Lavino; Stage Managers, Thomas Hall, Anne Salazar, Crystal Van Horn; Costumes, Peggy Kellner, Robert Morgan, Robert Blackman; Lighting, Sean Murphy; Composer, Conrad Susa; Dramaturge, Diana Maddox; Sound, Dan Dugan, Martha Gish, Roger Gans; Combat Staging, Mark Kincaid

COMPANY

DeVeren Bookwalter, C. Wayland Capwell, Kelsey Grammer, Eric Christmas, Nathan Haas, Neil Hunt, Barry Kraft, Ronald Long, Sandy McCallum, Katherine McGrath, John McMurtry, Dakin Matthews, John H. Napierala, Jean-Pierre Stewart, Deborah Taylor, Ellen Tobie, G. Wood, Bonnie Johnston, Valeda Turner, Richard Bradshaw, Mark Brey, James K. Fagerle, Jeffrey Combs, Craig Fisch, Stephen Godwin, Michael Hill, Jody Horowitz, Jerry Jones, Mark Kincaid, Scott William Kinney, Sally Klein, Allen Loebs, Maria Mayenzet, Kathleen O'Sullivan, Jonathan Perpich, Henri Halpern, Maile Klein, Matthew Redding, Brian Salmon, Jenny Parsons, Roger Smith, Mark Kuker, Frank Adams, Ken Hendrickson, Helen Rimland, James Hansen, Stan Glickman, Kandis Chappell, Clara Rodriguez, Lindell Nisbet, Douglas Sheehan, David Pursley, Don Sparks, Coye Arnold

PRODUCTIONS

"A Midsummer Night's Dream" directed by Jack O'Brien, "King Henry V" directed by Craig Noel and Eric Christmas, "The Winter's Tale" directed by Peter Donat, "How the Other Half Loves" directed by Wayne Bryan

Bill Reid Photos

Left: "The Winter's Tale" Top: DeVeren Bookwalter, Ellen Tobie, Jean-Pierre Stewart in "The Winter's Tale"

**DeVeren Bookwalter (C) as Henry V
Above: "How the Other Half Loves"**

Jean-Pierre Stewart, Katherine McGrath in "A Midsummer Night's Dream"

Eric Tavaris, Eric Booth, Davis Hall, Bob Ari in "Hamlet"

Ellen Barry, Geddeth Smith, Catherine Byers, Terence Marinan in "Arms and the Man"

NEW JERSEY SHAKESPEARE FESTIVAL

Madison, New Jersey
June 27 through November 5, 1978
Fourteenth Season
Artistic Director, Paul Barry; Associate Director/Press, Ellen Barry; Stage Managers, James J. Thesing, Gary C. Porto; Lighting, Gary C. Porto; Scenery, Don A. Coleman; Costumes, Jeffrey L. Ullman, Alice S. Hughes; Assistant Producer, Susan Socolowski; Administrative Assistant, Helen Marsh Rybka; Props, Debra Waxman; Costumes, Carla Froeberg; Musical Director, Brian Lynner; Mime, Judy Noble

COMPANY

Bob Ari, Ellen Barry, Paul Barry, Catherine Byers, Eric Booth, Brendan Burke, Davis Hall, J. C. Hoyt, Robin Leary, Brian Lynner, Terence Marinan, Susanne Marley, Charles Noel, Nicola Sheara, Geddeth Smith, Eric Tavaris, Ian Thomson, Yvonne A. G. Albrecht, Maetin Amada, Joseph J. Bachalis, Alice M. Barrett, Claudia Black, Paul Carlin, Greg Cesear, Bob Collins, Richard W. Corso, David Crespy, Gerard J. Cullity, Janice Davis-Lane, Julie DeLaurier, Melinda C. Finberg, Dana Graham, Jan Granger, Paul Michael Heffler, Margi Heiple, Jennifer Hiers, Ted Holland, Bob Hull, Ann B. Kuelling, LuAnne Lange, Melisse Lewis, Laura Livingston, Michael Lopez, Megan MacPherson, Dianna Paradis Maddocks, James D. McDowell, Philip McKinley, Catherine Joan McQueen, Mary Pat Millea, Robin L. Nagy, John Nichols, Courtney Noel-Hardy, John Riker O'Hara, Jr., Eduardo Patino, Bernadette Quigley, Ann H. Rawlinson, Andrea Richman, Raymond Sammak, Marion Sanders, Cynthia A. Smith, Peter F. Smith, Natalie Sokoloff, Ellen Spier, Amy Stoller, Dennis Tekula, Timothy Toney, Thomas Tresser, Stewart W. Turner, Nela Wagman, Jim Walker, Forrest Lee Wallace, Kathryn Willis

Blair Holley Photos

**Center: Eric Tavaris, Davis Hall, Bob Ari in "Rosencrantz & Guildenstern Are Dead"
Right: Paul Barry, Nicola Sheara in "The Country Girl"**

Brian Lynner (front), Eric Booth, J. C. Hoyt, Joseph Bachalis in "Love's Labour's Lost"

NEW YORK SHAKESPEARE FESTIVAL

Delacorte Theater/Central Park, NYC
July 5, through September 3, 1978
Twenty-second Season

Producer, Joseph Papp; Associate Producer, Bernard Gersten; Direction and Sets, Wilford Leach; Costumes, Carol Oditz; Lighting, Jennifer Tipton; Music and Musical Direction, Richard Weinstock; General Manager, Robert Kamlot; Production Supervisor, Jason Steven Cohen; Production Manager, Andrew Mihok; Technical Director, Mervyn Haines, Jr.: Produced in cooperation with the City of New York; Press, Merle Debuskey, Bob Ullman, Richard Kornberg

ALL'S WELL THAT ENDS WELL

Mark Linn Baker (Bertram), Frances Conroy (Diana), John Ferraro (Lavatch), George Guidall (Lafew), Larry Pine (Parolles), Remak Ramsay (King of France), Pamela Reed (Helena), Barbara Williams (Widow), Elizabeth Wilson (Countess), and Michael Arian, Donald Arrington, Dennis Boutsikaris, Joel Brooks, Tom Costello, Richard Green, Stephen Hanan, Michael Haynes, Nancy Heikin, James Lally, Ted May, Deborah Rush, Michael Strows, Otis Stuart, Richard Zobel

THE TAMING OF THE SHREW

John Bottoms (Gremio), Joel Brooks (Grumio), Tom Costello (Christopher Sly), John Ferraro (Tranio), Stanley Flood (Servant-/Officer), Kathryn Grody (Hostess/Widow), George Guidall (Vincentio), Max Gulack (Baptista Minola), Stephen Hanan (Priest/Tailor), Anthony Holland (Lord/Pedant), Jim Jansen (Curtis/Player), Raul Julia (Petruchio), James Lally (Lucentio), Larry Pine (Hortensio), Edborah Rush (Bianca), Meryl Streep (Kate), Nicholas Woodeson (Huntsman/Biondello), Richard Zobel (Bartholomew/Servant)

George E. Joseph Photos

Susan Cook, Sy Friedman, George Joseph Photos

Top Right: Remak Ramsay, Mark Linn Baker, Pamela Reed, and Below: Pamela Reed, Larry Pine in "All's Well That Ends Well"

Deborah Rush, Meryl Streep in "The Taming of the Shrew"

Meryl Streep, Raul Julia (also above) in "The Taming of the Shrew"

OREGON SHAKESPEAREAN FESTIVAL

Ashland, Oregon
February 3,–September 24, 1978
Forty-third Season

President, Robert C. Bernard; Founder/Consultant, Angus L. Bowmer; General Manager, William W. Patton; Producing Director, Jerry Turner; Directors, Michael Addison, Sabin Epstein, William Glover, Elizabeth Huddle, Judd Parkin, Pat Patton, Jerry Turner; Costumes, Robert Blackman, Phyllis A. Corcoran, Jeannie Davidson, Merrily Ann Murray; Sets, William Bloodgood, Richard L. Hay; Lighting, Dirk Epperson, Robert Peterson; Choreographer, Judith Kennedy; Fight Direction, David L. Boushey; Production Manager, Pat Patton; Props, Paul James Martin; Stage Managers, Dennis Bigelow, Kent Conrad, Jeffrey Hirsch, Michael B. Paul, Melinda E. Pittman; Technical Director, R. Duncan MacKenzie; Press, Margaret Rubin

COMPANY

Bruce Paul Abbott, Rex E. Allen, Jeffrey Allin, Anthony Amendoal, Larry R. Ballard, Jahnna Beecham, Marc Berman, Francine L. Borovkoff, Jack Wellington Cantwell, Mimi Carr, Richard Denison, Patrick DeSantis, Cameron Dokey, Stuart Duckworth, Richard Farrell, William Ferriter, Danny Frishman, Bruce T. Gooch, Keith Grant, Rick Hamilton, Terry Hays, Malcolm Hillgartner, Michael Kevin, Ruth Elodie King, Dan Kremer, Robert MacDougall, Kenned MacIver, Thomas S. Oleniacz, Brigit Olson, Eric Olson, Fredi Olster, HoAnn JoAnn Johnson Patton, Pat Patton, Shirley Patton, Rex Rabold, Richard Rossi, Margaret Rubin, Michael Santo, Randy Schaub, John Shepard, Gary Sloan, Bo Smith, Mark Smith, Clista Towne Strother, Mary Turner, Lachlan Wilkerson, Ronald Edmundson Woods, Grover Zucker, Tracy Andersen, Robert E. Baird, Barb Boswell, John Clover, Matthew Grady, Cooper A. Lewis, Todd Maddox, Pat Patton III, and dancers: Ronald Boardman, Susan Bull, David Eakle, George Gourley, Jim Hejna, Ray Houle, Alana Hunter, Judith Kennedy, Mary Molodovsky, Clydine Scales, Thomas A. Scales, Leslie Velton

PRODUCTIONS

The Taming of the Shrew, The Tempest, The Tragedy of King Richard III, and Timon of Athens by William Shakespeare, Tartuffe by Moliere, Mother Courage and Her Children by Bertolt Brecht, The Effect of Gamma Rays on Man-in-the-moon Marigolds by Paul Zindel, Night of the Tribades by Per Olov Enquist, Miss Julie by August Strindberg, Private Lives by Noel Coward

Hank Kranzler Photos

Right: "The Taming of the Shrew" Above: Fredi Olster, Rick Hamilton in "Taming of the Shrew" Top: Kenned MacIver, Michael Santo in "Richard III"

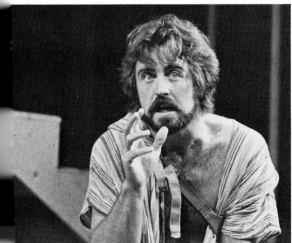

**Michael Kevin
in "Timon of Athens"**

**Rex Rabold, Terry Hays
in "Tartuffe"**

**Ted Follows, Brian Bedford, Margot Dionne
in "The Winter's Tale"**

STRATFORD FESTIVAL OF CANADA

Stratford, Ontario
June 5, through October 14, 1978
Twenty-sixth Season

Artistic Director, Robin Phillips; Director Festival Stage, William Hutt; Executive Producer, John Hayes; Director Third Stage, Peter Moss; Design, Daphne Dare; Production Manager, Peter Roberts; Technical Director, Kent McKay; Press, Ann Selby, Douglas Allan; Music Director, Berthold Carriere; Music Administrator, Arthur Lang; Stage Managers, Nora Polley, Vincent Berns, Martin Bragg, Colleen Stephenson, Michael Benoit, Laurie Freeman, Marcia Muldoon; Company Manager, Barry MacGregor; Directors, Robin Phillips, Keith Batten, Brian Bedford, Ted Follows, Pamela Hawthorn, Urjo Kareda, Brian Macdonald, Lotfi Mansouri, Peter Moss, John Palmer, Alan Scarfe, Eric Steiner, John Wood; Designers, Daphne Dare, Susan Benson, Desmond Heeley, Mary Kerr, Shawn Kerwin, Michael Maher, Robin Fraser Paye, John Pennoyer, Phillip Silver; Lighting, Harry Frehner, Gil Wechsler, Michael J. Whitfield

COMPANY

Stewart Arnott, Karen Austin, Theodore Baerg, Bob Baker, Rodger Barton, Keith Batten, Paul Batten, Stephen Beamish, Rod Beattie, Brian Bedford, Robert Benson, Christopher Blake, Mervyn Blake, Domini Blythe, Paul Bowman, Christopher Britton, Barbara Budd, Graeme Campbell, Helen Carscallen, Richard Curnock, Jennifer Dale, Margot Dionne, Peter Donaldson, Eric Donkin, Wilfrid Dube, David Dunbar, Mary Durkan, Edward Evanko, Michael Fletcher, Ted Follows, Edda Gaborek, Maurice Good, Lewis Gordon, Dawn Greenhalgh, Susan Gudgeon, Jeffrey Guyton, Richard Hardacre, Dean Hawes, Max Helpmann, Martha Henry, Bernard Hopkins, Donald Hunkin, Stephen Hunter, Peter Hutt, William Hutt, Patricia Idlette, Gerald Isaac, Alicia Jeffery, Richardo Keens-Douglas, Lorne Kennedy, Joel Kenyon, Francois-Regis Klanfer, Barry Kozak, John Lambert, Anne Linden, Pamela Macdonald, Anna MacKay-Smith, C. R. MacPherson, Barbara Maczka, Frank Maraden, Marti Maraden, Andrea Martin, Roberta Maxwell, F. Braun McAsh, James McGee, Dion McHugh, Richard McMillan, Jim McQueen, Richard Monette, Marylu Moyer, William Needles, Nicholas Pennell, Jennifer Phipps, John Pollard, Douglas Rain, Maida Rogerson, Stephen Russell, Robert Ruttan, Mary Savidge, Alan Scarfe, Robert Selkirk, Maggie Smith, Rex Southgate, Barbara Stephen, Barbara Stewart, Winston Sutton, Caralyn Tomlin, Michael Totzke, Robert Vigood, Colleen Wagner, Cathy Wallace, Gregory Wanless, Peggy Watson, Jack Wetherall, Richard Whelan, Ian White, John Wojda, Barrie Wood, Tom Wood, Elias Zarou, Carole Zorro

PRODUCTIONS

"As You Like It," "The Merry Wives Of Windsor," "Macbeth," "The Winter's Tale," "Julius Caesar," "Titus Andronicus" by William Shakespeare, "Candide" by Voltaire, adapted by Hugh Wheeler with lyrics by Richard Wilbur and additional lyrics by Stephen Sondheim and John Latouche, "Uncle Vanya" by Anton Chekhov, translated by John Murrell, "The Devils" by John Whiting, "Judgement" by Barry Collins, "Heloise and Abelard" from poems by Ronald Duncan, "Private Lives" by Noel Coward, "Ned and Jack" by Sheldon Rosen, "Medea: A Fable" by Larry Fineberg, "Four Plays by Samuel Beckett," "Stargazing" by Tom Cone

**Top: Domini Blythe, Bernard Hopkins, Bob Baker,
Maggie Smith in "As You Like It" Left: Alan
Scarfe, Patricia Idlette, William Hutt
in "The Merry Wives of Windsor"**

**Barbara Stephen, Nicholas Pennell
in "Julius Caesar"**

THEATER AT MONMOUTH

Monmouth, Maine
June 28,–September 3, 1978
Artistic Director, Tom Markus; Costumes, Lana Fritz; Director, Jonathan Alper; Production Manager and Lighting Designer, Curt Senie; Scenery, Joseph A. Varga; Stage Manager, Jody Boese; Technical Director, Stephen A. Woody; Press, Faye Melton; Managing Director, Glen Cooper; Wardrobe, Linda Rice

COMPANY

Jack Axelrod, Glenn Beatty, Geoff Becker, Barbara Bratt, Lynn Cohen, Peter Colford, Timothy Craig, Richard de Faut, Ray Dooley, Beth Dunlap, Warren Kelley, James E. Maxwell, Richard Pilcher, Bronson Alcott Pinchot, William Preston, Nick Savian, Sam Tsoutsouvas, Jan Kirk van der Swaagh, Valerie von Volz, Robert Walsh

PRODUCTIONS

"Hamlet," "Rosencrantz and Guildenstern Are Dead," "As You Like It," "Volpone," "Old King Cole"
(No photos submitted)

Below: Theater at Monmouth

Douglas Rain as Macbeth Top: William
Hutt, Martha Henry in "Uncle Vanya" (Stratford)

THEATRE VENTURE '79

Beverly, Massachusetts
April 30–May 19, 1979
Seventeenth Season
Executive Vice President, Stephan Slane; Manager, Theda Taylor; Assistant Managers, Brian Donnell, Laurie Hughes; Press, Peter Downs; Stage Manager, Dan Richard Preston; Props, Tracy Doyle; Wardrobe, Beverley Gordon; Sound, William Schapiro; Production Staff, Faith Baum, James Cooley, Lisa Kadra, Christian Kuhlthau, Jay McDaniel, Tom Schanley; Set, Eve Lyon; Costumes, Jeffrey Ullman; Director, Robert Dufy

HAMLET

John Strobaeus (Bernardo), Jason Howard (Francisco), Gregory Brown (Horatio), Pirie MacDonald (Claudius), Kelsey Grammer (Laertes), John A. Coe (Polonius), DeVeren Bookwalter (Hamlet), Annette Hunt (Gertrude), Lynn Watson (Ophelia), Joseph D. Giardina (Ghost of Hamlet's father), Quinn Halford (Rosencrantz), Michael Ostrowski (Guildenstern), Gary Garth (Player King/Gravedigger), Mara Clark (Duenna), Tom Schanley (Attendant) digger), Mara Clark (Duenna), Tom Schanley (Attendant)

Peter Downs Photos

DeVeren Bookwalter as Hamlet
with Pirie MacDonald, Kelsey Grammer

PULITZER PRIZE PRODUCTIONS

1918–Why Marry?, 1919– No award, 1920–Beyond the Horizon, 1921–Miss Lulu Bett, 1922–Anna Christie, 1923–Icebound, 1924–Hell-Bent fer Heaven, 1925–They Knew What They Wanted, 1926–Craig's Wife, 1927–In Abraham's Bosom, 1928–Strange Interlude, 1929–Street Scene, 1930–The Green Pastures, 1931–Alison's House, 1932–Of Thee I Sing, 1933–Both Your Houses, 1934–Men in White, 1935–The Old Maid, 1936–Idiot's Delight, 1937–You Can't Take It with You, 1938–Our Town, 1939–Abe Lincoln in Illinois, 1940–The Time of Your Life, 1941–There Shall Be No Night, 1942–No award, 1943–The Skin of Our Teeth, 1944–No award, 1945–Harvey, 1946–State of the Union, 1947–No award, 1948–A Streetcar Named Desire, 1949–Death of a Salesman, 1950–South Pacific, 1951–No award, 1952–The Shrike, 1953–Picnic, 1954–The Teahouse of the August Moon, 1955–Cat on a Hot Tin Roof, 1956–The Diary of Anne Frank, 1957–Long Day's Journey into Night, 1958–Look Homeward, Angel, 1959–J. B., 1960–Fiorello!, 1961–All the Way Home, 1962–How to Succeed in Business without Really Trying, 1963–No award, 1964–No award, 1965–The Subject Was Roses, 1966–No award, 1967–A Delicate Balance, 1968–No award, 1969–The Great White Hope, 1970–No Place to Be Somebody, 1971–The Effect of Gamma Rays on Man-in-the-Moon Marigolds, 1972–No award, 1973–That Championship Season, 1974–No award, 1975–Seascape, 1976–A Chorus Line, 1977–The Shadow Box, 1978–The Gin Game, 1979–Buried Child

NEW YORK DRAMA CRITICS CIRCLE AWARDS

1936–Winterset, 1937–High Tor, 1938–Of Mice and Men, Shadow and Substance, 1939–The White Steed, 1940–The Time of Your Life, 1941–Watch on the Rhine, The Corn is Green, 1942–Blithe Spirit, 1943–The Patriots, 1944–Jacobowsky and the Colonel, 1945–The Glass Menagerie, 1946–Carousel, 1947–All My Sons, No Exit, Brigadoon, 1948–A Streetcar Named Desire, The Winslow Boy, 1949–Death of a Salesman, The Madwoman of Chaillot, South Pacific, 1950–The Member of the Wedding, The Cocktail Party, The Consul, 1951–Darkness at Noon, The Lady's Not for Burning, Guys and Dolls, 1952–I Am a Camera, Venus Observed, Pal Joey, 1953–Picnic, The Love of Four Colonels, Wonderful Town, 1954–Teahouse of the August Moon, Ondine, The Golden Apple, 1955–Cat on a Hot Tin Roof, Witness for the Prosecution, The Saint of Bleecker Street, 1956–The Diary of Anne Frank, Tiger at the Gates, My Fair Lady, 1957–Long Day's Journey into Night, The Waltz of the Toreadors, The Most Happy Fella, 1958–Look Homeward Angel, Look Back in Anger, The Music Man, 1959–A Raisin in the Sun, The Visit, La Plume de Ma Tante, 1960–Toys in the Attic, Five Finger Exercise, Fiorello!, 1961–All the Way Home, A Taste of Honey, Carnival, 1962–Night of the Iguana, A Man for All Seasons, How to Succeed in Business without Really Trying, 1963–Who's Afraid of Virginia Woolf?, 1964–Luther, Hello, Dolly!, 1965–The Subject Was Roses, Fiddler on the Roof, 1966–The Persecution and Assassination of Marat as Performed by the Inmates of the Asylum of Charenton under the Direction of the Marquis de Sade, Man of La Mancha, 1967–The Homecoming, Cabaret, 1968–Rosencrantz and Guildenstern Are Dead, Your Own Thing, 1969–The Great White Hope, 1776, 1970–The Effect of Gamma Rays on Man-in-the-Moon Marigolds, Borstal Boy, Company, 1971–Home, Follies, The House of Blue Leaves, 1972–That Championship Season, Two Gentlemen of Verona, 1973–The Hot l Baltimore, The Changing Room, A Little Night Music, 1974–The Contractor, Short Eyes, Candide, 1975–Equus, The Taking of Miss Janie, A Chorus Line, 1976–Travesties, Streamers, Pacific Overtures, 1977–Otherwise Engaged, American Buffalo, Annie, 1978–Da, Ain't Misbehavin', 1979–The Elephant Man, Sweeney Todd

AMERICAN THEATRE WING
ANTOINETTE PERRY (TONY) AWARD PRODUCTIONS

1948–Mister Roberts, 1949–Death of a Salesman, Kiss Me, Kate, 1950–The Cocktail Party, South Pacific, 1951–The Rose Tattoo, Guys and Dolls, 1952–The Fourposter, The King and I, 1953–The Crucible, Wonderful Town, 1954–The Teahouse of the August Moon, Kismet, 1955–The Desperate Hours, The Pajama Game, 1956–The Diary of Anne Frank, Damn Yankees, 1957–Long Day's Journey into Night, My Fair Lady, 1958–Sunrise at Campobello, The Music Man, 1959–J. B., Redhead, 1960–The Miracle Worker, Fiorello! tied with The Sound of Music, 1961–Becket, Bye Bye Birdie, 1962–A Man for All Seasons, How to Succeed in Business without Really Trying, 1963–Who's Afraid of Virginia Woolf?, A Funny Thing Happened on the Way to the Forum, 1964–Luther, Hello, Dolly!, 1965–The Subject Was Roses, Fiddler on the Roof, 1966–The Persecution and Assassination of Marat as Performed by the Inmates of the Asylum of Charenton under the Direction of the Marquis de Sade, Man of La Mancha, 1967–The Homecoming, Cabaret, 1968–Rosencrantz and Guildenstern Are Dead, Hallelujah Baby!, 1969–The Great White Hope, 1776, 1970–Borstal Boy, Applause, 1971–Sleuth, Company, 1972–Sticks and Bones, Two Gentlemen of Verona, 1973–That Championship Season, A Little Night Music, 1974–The River Niger, Raisin, 1975–Equus, The Wiz, 1976–Travesties, A Chorus Line, 1977–The Shadow Box, Annie, 1978–Da, Ain't Misbehavin', Dracula, 1979–The Elephant Man, Sweeney Todd

1979 THEATRE WORLD AWARD WINNERS

PHILIP ANGLIM
of "The Elephant Man"

LUCIE ARNAZ
of "They're Playing Our Song"

LAURIE KENNEDY
of "Man and Superman"

GREGORY HINES
of "Eubie!"

KEN JENNINGS
of "Sweeney Todd"

SUSAN KINGSLEY
of "Getting Out"

CHRISTINE LAHTI
of "The Woods"

MICHAEL JETER
of "G. R. Point"

EDWARD JAMES OLMOS
of "Zoot Suit"

KATHLEEN QUINLAN
of "Taken in Marriage"

SARAH RICE
of "Sweeney Todd"

MAX WRIGHT
of "Once in a Lifetime"

THEATRE WORLD AWARDS PARTY: Thursday, May 24, 1979: Top: Anne Reinking, Charles Repole, Dorothy Loudon, George Grizzard, Eileen Heckart, Eli Wallach; Gregory Hines, Jane Alexander, Len Cariou, Nell Carter, Ken Page, Victor Garber, Tammy Grimes Below: Edward James Olmos, Ken Page; Marshall W. Mason, Maureen Stapleton; Carol Lynley (for Kathleen Quinlan), Ann Reinking; Second Row from Bottom: Christine Lahti; Victor Garber, Margaret Phillips, Radie Harris, Anne Jackson; Ken Jennings, Len Cariou; Bottom: Lucie Arnaz, Charles Repole, Tammy Grimes, Thom Christopher, D'Jamin Bartlett, Laurie Kennedy, George Grizzard

Van Williams Photos

Top: Michael Jeter, Eileen Heckart; Susan Kingsley, Dorothy Loudon; Max Wright, Tammy Grimes; Below: Armelia McQueen, Nell Carter, Barnard Hughes; Joan Bennett Wilde, David Wilde; Melba Moore, Juliette Koka; Second Row from Bottom: Sarah Rice, Victor Garber; Ann Reinking, Eli Wallach; Philip Anglim, Jane Alexander; Bottom Row: Lucie Arnaz, Len Cariou; Dorothy Loudon, Eli Wallach, Anne Jackson, George Grizzard; Gregory Hines, Nell Carter

Van Williams Photos

Richard Burton   **Elizabeth Ashley**   **James Earl Jones**   **Rosemary Harris**   **John Raitt**

PREVIOUS THEATRE WORLD AWARD WINNERS

1944–45: Betty Comden, Richard Davis, Richard Hart, Judy Holliday, Charles Lang, Bambi Linn, John Lund, Donald Murphy, Nancy Noland, Margaret Phillips, John Raitt

1945–46: Barbara Bel Geddes, Marlon Brando, Bill Callahan, Wendell Corey, Paul Douglas, Mary James, Burt Lancaster, Patricia Marshall, Beatrice Pearson

1946–47: Keith Andes, Marion Bell, Peter Cookson, Ann Crowley, Ellen Hanley, John Jordan, George Keane, Dorothea MacFarland, James Mitchell, Patricia Neal, David Wayne

1947–48: Valerie Bettis, Edward Bryce, Whitfield Connor, Mark Dawson, June Lockhart, Estelle Loring, Peggy Maley, Ralph Meeker, Meg Mundy, Douglass Watson, James Whitmore, Patrice Wymore

1948–49: Tod Andrews, Doe Avedon, Jean Carson, Carol Channing, Richard Derr, Julie Harris, Mary McCarty, Allyn Ann McLerie, Cameron Mitchell, Gene Nelson, Byron Palmer, Bob Scheerer

1949–50: Nancy Andrews, Phil Arthur, Barbara Brady, Lydia Clarke, Priscilla Gillette, Don Hanmer, Marcia Henderson, Charlton Heston, Rick Jason, Grace Kelly, Charles Nolte, Roger Price

1950–51: Barbara Ashley, Isabel Bigley, Martin Brooks, Richard Burton, James Daly, Cloris Leachman, Russell Nype, Jack Palance, William Smothers, Maureen Stapleton, Marcia Van Dyke, Eli Wallach

1951–52: Tony Bavaar, Patricia Benoit, Peter Conlow, Virginia de Luce, Ronny Graham, Audrey Hepburn, Diana Herbert, Conrad Janis, Dick Kallman, Charles Proctor, Eric Sinclair, Kim Stanley, Marian Winters, Helen Wood

1952–53: Edie Adams, Rosemary Harris, Eileen Heckart, Peter Kelley, John Kerr, Richard Kiley, Gloria Marlowe, Penelope Munday, Paul Newman, Sheree North, Geraldine Page, John Stewart, Ray Stricklyn, Gwen Verdon

1953–54: Orson Bean, Harry Belafonte, James Dean, Joan Diener, Ben Gazzara, Carol Haney, Jonathan Lucas, Kay Medford, Scott Merrill, Elizabeth Montgomery, Leo Penn, Eva Marie Saint

1954–55: Julie Andrews, Jacqueline Brookes, Shirl Conway, Barbara Cook, David Daniels, Mary Fickett, Page Johnson, Loretta Leversee, Jack Lord, Dennis Patrick, Anthony Perkins, Christopher Plummer

1955–56: Diane Cilento, Dick Davalos, Anthony Franciosa, Andy Griffith, Laurence Harvey, David Hedison, Earle Hyman, Susan Johnson, John Michael King, Jayne Mansfield, Sarah Marshall, Gaby Rodgers, Susan Strasberg, Fritz Weaver

1956–57: Peggy Cass, Sydney Chaplin, Sylvia Daneel, Bradford Dillman, Peter Donat, George Grizzard, Carol Lynley, Peter Palmer, Jason Robards, Cliff Robertson, Pippa Scott, Inga Swenson

1957–58: Anne Bancroft, Warren Berlinger, Colleen Dewhurst, Richard Easton, Tim Everett, Eddie Hodges, Joan Hovis, Carol Lawrence, Jacqueline McKeever, Wynne Miller, Robert Morse, George C. Scott

1958–59: Lou Antonio, Ina Balin, Richard Cross, Tammy Grimes, Larry Hagman, Dolores Hart, Roger Mollien, France Nuyen, Susan Oliver, Ben Piazza, Paul Roebling, William Shatner, Pat Suzuki, Rip Torn

1959–60: Warren Beatty, Eileen Brennan, Carol Burnett, Patty Duke, Jane Fonda, Anita Gillette, Elisa Loti, Donald Madden, George Maharis, John McMartin, Lauri Peters, Dick Van Dyke

1960–61: Joyce Bulifant, Dennis Cooney, Sandy Dennis, Nancy Dussault, Robert Goulet, Joan Hackett, June Harding, Ron Husmann, James MacArthur, Bruce Yarnell

1961–62: Elizabeth Ashley, Keith Baxter, Peter Fonda, Don Galloway, Sean Garrison, Barbara Harris, James Earl Jones, Janet Margolin, Karen Morrow, Robert Redford, John Stride, Brenda Vaccaro

1962–63: Alan Arkin, Stuart Damon, Melinda Dillon, Robert Drivas, Bob Gentry, Dorothy Loudon, Brandon Maggart, Julienne Marie, Liza Minnelli, Estelle Parsons, Diana Sands, Swen Swenson

1963–64: Alan Alda, Gloria Bleezarde, Imelda De Martin, Claude Giraud, Ketty Lester, Barbara Loden, Lawrence Pressman, Gilbert Price, Philip Proctor, John Tracy, Jennifer West

1964–65: Carolyn Coates, Joyce Jillson, Linda Lavin, Luba Lisa, Michael O'Sullivan, Joanna Pettet, Beah Richards, Jaime Sanchez, Victor Spinetti, Nicolas Surovy, Robert Walker, Clarence Williams III

1965–66: Zoe Caldwell, David Carradine, John Cullum, John Davidson, Faye Dunaway, Gloria Foster, Robert Hooks, Jerry Lanning, Richard Mulligan, April Shawhan, Sandra Smith, Lesley Ann Warren

1966–67: Bonnie Bedelia, Richard Benjamin, Dustin Hoffman, Terry Kiser, Reva Rose, Robert Salvio, Sheila Smith, Connie Stevens, Pamela Tiffin, Leslie Uggams, Jon Voight, Christopher Walken

1967–68: David Birney, Pamela Burrell, Jordan Christopher, Jack Crowder (Thalmus Rasulala), Sandy Duncan, Julie Gregg, Stephen Joyce, Bernadette Peters, Alice Playten, Michael Rupert, Brenda Smiley, Russ Thacker

1968–69: Jane Alexander, David Cryer, Blythe Danner, Ed Evanko, Ken Howard, Lauren Jones, Ron Leibman, Marian Mercer, Jill O'Hara, Ron O'Neal, Al Pacino, Marlene Warfield

1969–70: Susan Browning, Donny Burks, Catherine Burns, Len Cariou, Bonnie Franklin, David Holliday, Katharine Houghton, Melba Moore, David Rounds, Lewis J. Stadlen, Kristoffer Tabori, Fredricka Weber

1970–71: Clifton Davis, Michael Douglas, Julie Garfield, Martha Henry, James Naughton, Tricia O'Neil, Kipp Osborne, Roger Rathburn, Ayn Ruymen, Jennifer Salt, Joan Van Ark, Walter Willison

1971–72: Jonelle Allen, Maureen Anderman, William Atherton, Richard Backus, Adrienne Barbeau, Cara Duff-MacCormick, Robert Foxworth, Elaine Joyce, Jess Richards, Ben Vereen, Beatrice Winde, James Woods

1972–73: D'Jamin Bartlett, Patricia Elliott, James Farentino, Brian Farrell, Victor Garber, Kelly Garrett, Mari Gorman, Laurence Guittard, Trish Hawkins, Monte Markham, John Rubinstein, Jennifer Warren, Alexander H. Cohen (Special Award)

1973–74: Mark Baker, Maureen Brennan, Ralph Carter, Thom Christopher, John Driver, Conchata Ferrell, Ernestine Jackson, Michael Moriarty, Joe Morton, Ann Reinking, Janie Sell, Mary Woronov, Sammy Cahn (Special Award)

1974–75: Peter Burnell, Zan Charisse, Lola Falana, Peter Firth, Dorian Harewood, Joel Higgins, Marcia McClain, Linda Miller, Marti Rolph, John Sheridan, Scott Stevensen, Donna Theodore, Equity Library Theatre (Special Award)

1975–76: Danny Aiello, Christine Andreas, Dixie Carter, Tovah Feldshuh, Chip Garnett, Richard Kelton, Vivian Reed, Charles Repole, Virginia Seidel, Daniel Seltzer, John V. Shea, Meryl Streep, A Chorus Line (Special Award)

1976–77: Trazana Beverley, Michael Cristofer, Joe Fields, Joanna Gleason, Cecilia Hart, John Heard, Gloria Hodes, Juliette Koka, Andrea McArdle, Ken Page, Jonathan Pryce, Chick Vennera, Eva LeGallienne (Special Award)

1977–78: Vasili Bogazianos, Nell Carter, Carlin Glynn, Christopher Goutman, William Hurt, Judy Kaye, Florence Lacy, Armelia McQueen, Gordana Rashovich, Bo Rucker, Richard Seer, Colin Stinton, Joseph Papp (Special Award)

1978–79: Philip Anglim, Lucie Arnaz, Gregory Hines, Ken Jennings, Michael Jeter, Laurie Kennedy, Susan Kingsley, Christine Lahti, Edward James Olmos, Kathleen Quinlan, Sarah Rice, Max Wright, Marshall W. Mason (Special)

| Betty Aberlin | Eric Aaron | Mary Alice | Donald Ainsworth | Mary Ellen Ashley |

BIOGRAPHIES OF THIS SEASON'S CAST

AARON, ERIC. Born Oct. 27, 1954 in Eugene, OR. Attended UOr., Portland State U. Debut OB 1978 in "Can-Can."

AARON, JACK. Born May 1, 1933 in NYC. Attended Hunter Col, Actors Workshop. OB in "Swim Low Little Goldfish," "Journey of the Fifth Horse," "The Nest," "One Flew over the Cuckoo's Nest," "The Birds," "The Pornographer's Daughter," "Love Death Plays," "Unlikely Heroes."

ABELS, GREGORY. Born Nov. 6, 1941 in Jersey City, NJ. Studied with Stella Adler. Debut 1970 OB in "War of the Roses," followed by "Macbeth," "Phoebus," "Oedipus at Colonus," "I Love Thee Freely," "Veil of Infamy," "The Boss," "The Violano Virtuoso."

ABERLIN, BETTY. Born Dec. 30, 1942 in NYC. Graduate Bennington College. Debut OB 1954 in "Sandhog," followed by "Upstairs at the Downstairs," "I'm Getting My Act Together," Bdwy 1964 in "Cafe Crown."

ABRAHAM, F. MURRAY Born Oct. 24, 1939 in Pittsburgh, Pa. Attended UTex. OB bow 1967 in "The Fantasticks," followed by "An Opening in the Trees," "Fourteenth Dictator," "Young Abe Lincoln," "Tonight in Living Color," "Adaptation," "Survival of St. Joan," "The Dog Ran Away," "Fables," "Richard III," "Little Murders," "Scuba Duba," "Where Has Tommy Flowers Gone?," "Miracle Play," "Blessing," "Sexual Perversity in Chicago," "Landscape of the Body," "The Master and Margarita," Bdwy in "The Man in the Glass Booth" (1968), "6 Rms Riv Vu," "Bad Habits," "The Ritz," "Legend,"

ABRAMS, ALAN. Born Mar. 16, 1950 in Boston, Ma. Graduate Boston U. Debut 1975 OB in "Tenderloin," Bdwy 1979 in "Sarava."

ADAMS, MOLLY. Born in Portchester, NY. Graduate Smith Col. Debut OB 1973 in "Older People," followed by "Hot 1 Baltimore," "The Unicorn in Captivity," Bdwy 1979 in "Bedroom Farce."

ADLER, CHARLIE M. Born Oct. 2, 1956 in Patterson, NJ. Debut OB 1978 in "Family Business."

AIDMAN, CHARLES. Born Jan. 31, 1930 in Indianapolis, In. Graduate Ind. U., Neighborhood Playhouse. Debut OB 1957 in "Career," Bdwy 1963 in "Spoon River Anthology," followed by "Zoot Suit."

AIELLO, DANNY. Born June 20, 1935 in NYC. Debut OB 1975 in "Lamppost Reunion" for which he received a Theatre World Award, followed by "Wheelbarrow Closers," "Gemini," "Knockout."

AINSWORTH, DONALD. Borm June 27, 1953 in Washington, DC. Graduate Oberlin Col, Drama Studio. Debut 1979 OB in "La Ronde."

ALANN, LLOYD. Born Aug. 15, 1952 in The Bronx, NY. Attended Lehman Col. Bdwy debut 1975 in "Grease."

ALDERFER, ERIC. Born Nov. 14, 1954 in Springfield, Oh. Attended Wheaton Col., UCin. Debut 1979 OB in ELT's "Mary."

ALEXANDER, JANE. Born Oct. 28, 1939 in Boston, Ma. Attended Sarah Lawrence Col., UEdinburgh. Bdwy debut 1968 in "The Great White Hope" for which she received a Theatre World Award, followed by "6 Rms Riv Vu," "Find Your Way Home," LC's "Hamlet," "The Heiress," "First Monday in October," OB in "Losing Time."

ALDREDGE, TOM. Born Feb. 28, 1928 in Dayton, O. Attended Dayton U., Goodman Theatre. Bdwy bow 1959 in "The Nervous Set," followed by "UTBU," "Slapstick Tragedy," "Everything in the Garden," "Indians," "Engagement Baby," "How the Other Half Loves," "Sticks and Bones," "Where's Charley?," "Leaf People," "Rex," "Vieux Carre," "St. Joan," "Stages," "On Green Pond," OB in "The Tempest," "Between Two Thieves," "Henry V," "The Premise," "Love's Labour's Lost," "Troilus and Cressida," "Butter and Egg Man," "Ergo," "Boys in the Band," "Twelfth Night," "Colette," "Hamlet," "The Orphan," "King Lear," "Iceman Cometh."

ALEXANDER, TERRY. Born Mar. 23, 1947 in Detroit, MI. Wayne State U. graduate. Bdwy debut 1971 in "No Place to be Somebody" OB in "Rashomon," "Glass Menagerie," "Breakout," "Naomi Court," "Streamers," "Julius Caesar," "Nongogo."

ALICE, MARY. Born Dec. 3, 1941 in Indianola, MS. Debut OB 1967 in "Trials of Brother Jero," followed by "The Strong Breed," "Duplex," "Thoughts," "Miss Julie," "House Party," "Terraces," "Heaven and Hell's Agreement," "In the Deepest Part of Sleep," "Cockfight," "Julius Caesar," "Nongogo," "Second Thoughts," "Spell #7." Bdwy 1971 in " No Place to Be Somebody."

ALLEN, DEBBIE (a.k.a. Deborah) Born Jan. 16, 1950 in Houston, Tx. Graduate Howard U. Debut OB 1972 in "Ti-Jean and His Brothers," followed by "Anna Lucasta," Bdwy in "Raisin" (1973), "Ain't Misbehavin'."

ALLEN, JAYNE MEADOWS. Born Sept. 27, 1923 in WuChang, China. Attended St. Margaret's Sch. Bdwy debut 1941 in "Spring Again," followed by "Another Love Story," "The Odds on Mrs. Oakley," "Many Happy Returns," "Kiss Them for Me," "Once in a Lifetime."

ALLEN, SCOTT. Born Aug. 29, 1948 in Morristown, NJ. Attended Union Col., AMDA. Bdwy debut 1973 in "A Chorus Line," followed by "King of Hearts."

ALLMON, CLINTON. Born June 13, 1941 in Monahans, TX. Graduate Okla. State U. Bdwy debut 1969 in "Indians," followed by "The Best Little Whorehouse in Texas," OB in "The Bluebird," "Khaki Blue," "One Sunday Afternoon."

ANDERSON, THOMAS. Born Nov. 28, 1906 in Pasadena, Ca. Attended Pasadena Jr. Col., AmThWing. Bdwy debut 1934 in "4 Saints in 3 Acts," followed by "Roll Sweet Chariot," "Cabin in the Sky," "Native Son," "Set My People Free," "How Long Till Summer," "A Hole in the Head," "The Great White Hope," "70, Girls, 70," OB in "Conquering Thursday," "The Peddler," "The Dodo Bird," "Don't Play Us Cheap," "Anna Lucasta."

ANDRES, BARBARA. Born Feb. 11, 1939 in NYC. Catholic U. graduate. Bdwy debut 1969 in "Jimmy," followed by "The Boy Friend," "Rodgers and Hart," "Rex," "On Golden Pond."

ANDREWS, GEORGE LEE. Born Oct. 13, 1942 in Milwaukee, Wi. Debut OB 1970 in "Jacques Brel Is Alive," followed by "Starting Here Starting Now," Bdwy in "A Little Night Music" (1973), "On the 20th Century."

ANDROS, DOUGLAS. Born Nov. 27 in NYC. Attended NYU. Debut 1958 OB in "The Good Woman of Setzuan," followed by "Last of the Red Hot Lovers," "Smoking Pistols," "This Side of Paradise," "Most Happy Fella," "Piaf—A Remembrance."

ANGELA, JUNE. Born Aug. 18, 1959 in NYC. Bdwy debut 1970 in "Lovely Ladies, Kind Gentlemen," "The King and I" (1977).

ANGLIM, PHILIP. Born Feb. 11, 1953 in San Francisco, Ca. Yale graduate. Debut OB and Bdwy 1979 in "The Elephant Man" for which he received a Theatre World Award.

ARBEIT, HERMAN. Born Apr. 19, 1925 in Brooklyn, NY. Attended CCNY, HB Studio, Neighborhood Playhouse. Debut 1939 OB in "The Golem," followed by "Awake and Sing," "A Delicate Balance," "Yentl the Yeshiva Boy," Bdwy 1975 in "Yentl."

ARI, BOB. Born July 1, 1949 in NYC. Graduate Carnegie-Mellon U. Debut OB in "Boys from Syracuse" (1976), followed by "Gay Divorce," "Devour the Snow."

ARNAZ, LUCIE. Born July 17, 1951 in Los Angeles, Ca. Bdwy debut 1979 in "They're Playing Our Song" for which she received a Theatre World Award.

ARONIN, MICHAEL J. Born Nov. 5, 1944 in NYC. Bdwy debut 1979 in "Knockout."

ARONSON, JONATHAN. Born June 17, 1953 in Miami, Fl. Attended Dade Col. AMDA. Bdwy debut 1979 in "Whoopee!" followed OB by "Tip-Toes."

ASHLEY, MARY ELLEN. Born June 11, 1938 in Long Island City, NY. Graduate Queens Col. Bdwy debut 1943 in "Innocent Voyage," followed by "By Appointment Only," "Annie Get Your Gun," "Yentl," OB in "Carousel," "Yentl the Yeshiva Boy," "Polly," "Panama Hattie," "Soft Touch," "Suddenly the Music Starts."

ASTREDO, HUMBERT ALLEN. Born in San Francisco, Ca. Attended SFU. Debut 1967 OB in "Arms and the Man," followed by "Fragments," "Murderous Angels," "Beach Children," "End of Summer," "Knuckle," "Grand Magic," "Big and Little," Bdwy in "Les Blancs," "An Evening with Richard Nixon. . . ."

AUBERJONOIS, RENE. Born June 1, 1940 in NYC. Graduate Carnegie Inst. With LCRep in "A Cry of Players," "King Lear," and "Twelfth Night," Bdwy in "Fire," "Coco," "Tricks," "The Good Doctor," "Break A Leg," BAM Co. in "The New York Idea," "Three Sisters," "The Play's the Thing," and "Julius Caesar."

Dennis Bailey **Cynthia Belgrave** **David Francis Barker** **Margery Beddow** **David Berman**

AUSTIN, BETH. Born May 23, 1952 in Philadelphia, PA. Graduate Point Park Col., Pittsburgh Playhouse. Debut OB 1977 in "Wonderful Town" (ELT), Bdwy 1977 in "Sly Fox," followed by "Whoopee!"

AYR, MICHAEL. Born Sept. 8, 1953 in Great Falls, MT. Graduate SMU. Debut 1976 OB in "Mrs. Murray's Farm," followed by "The Farm," "Ulysses in Traction," "Lulu" "Cabin 12," "Stargazing," "The Deserter."

BABATUNDE, OBBA. Born in Jamaica, NY. Attended Brooklyn Col. Debut OB 1970 in "The Secret Place," followed by "Guys and Dolls," "On Toby Time," "The Breakout," "Scottsbourough Boys," "Showdown Time," "Dream on Monkey Mt.," "Sheba," Bdwy 1978 in "Timbuktu."

BACKUS, RICHARD. Born Mar. 28, 1945 in Goffstown, NH. Harvard graduate. Bdwy debut 1971 in "Butterflies Are Free," followed by "Promenade, All" for which he received a Theatre World Award, "Ah, Wilderness!," OB in "Studs Edsel," "Gimme Shelter."

BAILEY, DENNIS. Born Apr. 12, 1953 in Grosse Pointe Woods, MI. UDetroit graduate. Debut 1977 OB in "House of Blue Leaves," Bdwy 1978 in "Gemini."

BALABAN, ROBERT. Born Aug. 16, 1945 in Chicago, IL. Attended Colgate, NYU. Debut 1967 OB in "You're a Good Man, Charlie Brown," followed by "Up Eden," "White House Murder Case," "Basic Training of Pavlo Hummel," "The Children," Bdwy in "Plaza Suite" (1968), "Some of My Best Friends," "The Inspector General."

BARANSKI, CHRISTINE. Born May 2, 1952 in Buffalo, NY. Graduate Juilliard Sch. Debut OB 1978 in "One Crack Out," followed by "Says I Says He."

BARBOUR, ELEANOR. Born Jan. 23, 1945 in NYC. Graduate Hofstra U. Debut 1976 OB in "Follies," followed by "Manhattan Breakdown."

BARBOUR, THOMAS. Born July 25, 1921 in NYC. Princeton, Harvard graduate. Bdwy in "Portrait of a Queen," "Great White Hope," "Scratch," "The Lincoln Mask," OB in "Twelfth Night," "Merchant of Venice," "Admirable Bashville," "River Line," "The Lady's Not for Burning," "The Enchanted," "Antony and Cleopatra," "The Saintliness of Margery Kemp," "Dr. Willy Nilly," "Under the Sycamore Tree," "Epitaph for George Dillon," "Thracian Horse," "Old Glory," "Sjt. Musgrave's Dance," "Veil of Infamy," "Nestless Birds," "The Seagull," "Wayside Motor Inn," "Arthur," "The Grinding Machine," "The Terrorists."

BARKER, DAVID FRANCIS Born Sept. 5, 1955 in Phildaelphia, Pa. Graduate Duquesne U. Debut OB 1978 in "Are You Now...."

BARNES, SCOTT. Born May 30, 1954 in Pittsburgh, Pa. Graduate Cincinnati Consv. Bdwy debut 1978 in "King of Hearts."

BARNEY, JAY. Born Mar. 14, 1918 in Chicago, Il. Attended Chicago U., Theatre Wing, Actors Studio. Bdwy debut 1948 in "Hope's the Thing with Feathers" and "The Respectful Prostitute," followed by "Detective Story," "The Number," "The Grass Harp," "Richard III," "Stockade," "The Immoralist," "The Trial," "Young and Beautiful," "Eugenia," "Fig Leaves Are Falling," "All the Girls Came Out to Play," OB in "A Certain Young Man," "Beyond Desire," "Goa," "The David Show," "Man with a Flower in His Mouth," "Mary."

BARON, EVALYN. Born Apr. 21, 1948 in Atlanta, Ga. Graduate Northwestern, UMinn. Debut OB 1979 in "Scrambled Feet."

BARRETT, LESLIE. Born Oct. 30, 1919 in NYC. Bdwy debut 1936 in "But for the Grace of God," followed by "Enemy of the People," "Dead End," "Sundown," "There's Always a Breeze," "Primrose Path," "Stroke of 8," "Horse Fever," "Good Neighbor," "All in Favor," "Counsellor-at-law," "Deadfall," "Rhinoceros," "The Investigation," "Slapstick Tragedy," "What Did We Do Wrong," OB in "Hamp," "The Contractor," "Play Me, Zoltan," "Savages," "The Dragon," "Trial of Dmitri Karamatzov," "Purple Dust," "My Old Friends."

BARRIE, BARBARA. Born May 23, 1931 in Chicago, IL. Graduate UTex. Bdwy debut 1955 in "The Wooden Dish," followed by "Happily Never After," "Company," "Selling of the President," "Prisoner of Second Avenue," "California Suite," OB in "The Crucible," "Beaux Stratagem," "Taming of the Shrew," "Twelfth Night," "All's Well That Ends Well," "Horseman, Pass By," "Killdeer," "Big and Little."

BARROWS, DIANA. Born Jan. 23, 1966 in NYC. Bdwy debut 1975 in "Cat on a Hot Tin Roof," followed by "Panama Hattie" (ELT), "Annie."

BARTON, DANIEL. Born Jan. 23, 1949 in Buffalo, NY. Attended Buffalo State, Albany State. Bdwy debut 1976 in "The Poison Tree," followed by "Timbuktu."

BATES, KATHY. Born June 28, 1948 in Memphis, TN. Graduate Southern Methodist U. Debut OB 1976 in "Vanities."

BATTEN, TOM. Born in Oklahoma City. OK. Graduate USC. Bdwy debut 1961 in "How to Succeed in Business ...," followed by "Mame," "Gantry," "Mack and Mabel," "She Loves Me," "On the 20th Century."

BAXLEY, BARBARA. Born Jan. 1, 1925 in Porterville, Ca. Attended Pacific Col., Neighborhood Playhouse. Bdwy debut 1948 in "Private Lives," followed by "Out West of Eighth," "Peter Pan," "I Am a Camera," "Bus Stop," "Camino Real," "Frogs of Spring," "Oh, Men! Oh, Women!," "Flowering Peach," "Period of Adjustment," "She Loves Me," "Three Sisters," "Plaza Suite," "Me Jack, You Jill," "Best Friend," OB in "Brecht on Brecht," "Measure for Measure," "To Be Young, Gifted and Black," "Oh, Pioneers," "Are You Now or Have you Ever...."

BAXTER, KEITH. Born Apr. 29, 1935 in Newport, Wales. Graduate RADA. Bdwy debut 1961 in "A Man for All Seasons" for which he received a Theatre World Award, followed by "The Affair," "Avanti," "Sleuth," "A Meeting by the River."

BEAL, JERRY. Born Nov. 11, 1946 in NYC. Graduate Brandeis U. AADA. Debut 1974 OB in "Ionescopade," followed by "A Foot in the Door."

BEARD, BETSY. Born Nov. 9, 1949 in Tulsa, Ok. Graduate Tulsa U. Bdwy debut 1975 in "Shenandoah," followed by "Equus," OB in "Polly," "Antigone," "Mary."

BECKHAM, WILLARD. Born Nov. 6, 1948 in Hominy, Ok. Graduate Cleaveland Inst. of Music. Debut OB 1972 in "Crazy Now," followed by "Camp Meeting," Bdwy in "Lorelei," "Something's Afoot," "The Utter Glory of Morrissey Hall."

BEDDOW, MARGERY. Born Dec. 13, 1937 in Grosse Pointe, MI. Studied with Herbert Berghoff. Bdwy debut 1959 in "Redhead," followed by "Fiorello!," "Showboat," "The Conquering Hero," "We Take the Town," "Take Me Along," "Little Me," "Here's Love," "Ulysses in Nighttown," OB in "Sing Melancholy baby."

BELGRAVE, CYNTHIA. Born in NYC. Graduate Boston U. Bdwy debut 1959 in "Raisin in the Sun," followed by "The Amen Corner," OB in "Take a Giant Step," "The Blacks," "Funny-house of a Negro," "Trials of Brother Jero," "Citizen Bezique," "Emma," "Making Peace," "Remembrance."

BELL, BRIAN. Born Apr. 18, 1945 in NYC. Graduate UDenver. Debut 1977 OB in "The Passion of Dracula."

BELLOMO, JOE. Born Apr. 12, 1938 in NYC. Attended Manhattan Sch. of Music. Bdwy bow 1960 in "New Girl in Town," followed by CC's "South Pacific" and "Guys and Dolls," OB in "Cindy," "Fantasticks."

BENDO, MARK. Born Jan. 28, 1964 in NYC. Studied with Lee Strasberg. Debut 1977 OB in "The Dream Watcher," followed by "All the Way Home," Bdwy 1979 in "On Golden Pond."

BEREZIN, TANYA. Born Mar. 25, 1941 in Philadelphia, Pa. Attended Boston U. Debut 1967 OB in "The Sandcastle," followed by "Three Sisters," "Great Nebula in Orion," "him," "Amazing Activity of Charlie Contrare," "Battle of Angels," "Mound Builders," "Serenading Louie," "My Life," "Brontosaurus," "Glorious Morning."

BERGSTROM, JOHN. Born July 23, 1941 in Kewanee, IL. Graduate InU. Debut 1975 OB in "And So to Bed," Bdwy 1977 in "Caesar and Cleopatra."

BERLINGER, WARREN. Born Aug. 31, 1937 in Brooklyn, NY. Bdwy credits include "Annie Get Your Gun," "Happy Time," "Bernardine," "Take a Giant Step," "Anniversary Waltz," "A Roomful of Roses," "Blue Denim" for which he received a Theatre World Award, "Come Blow Your Horn," "A Broadway Musical."

BERMAN, DAVID. Born Oct. 26, 1950 in Cleveland, Oh. Debut 1976 OB in "Marco Polo," followed by "Auto-Destruct," "Pins and Needles," "Chinchilla," "Getting Out," Bdwy 1978 in "Man and Superman."

BERNARD, KATHY. Born July 27, 1964 in Holyoke, Ma. Debut 1979 OB in "The Miracle Worker."

Trazana Beverley   **Gary Berner**   **Sydney Blake**   **Vasili Bogazianos**   **Cathy Brewer-Moore**

BERNARDI, HERSCHEL. Born in NYC in 1923. Began career at age of 3. Credits include "The World of Sholom Aleichem," "Fiddler on the Roof," "Bajour," "Zorba," "The Goodbye People."

BERNER, GARY. Born in Mt. Kisco, NY. Attended Hampshire Col., Brandeis U. Debut 1979 OB in "Minnesota Moon" followed by "The Runner Stumbles."

BEVERLEY, TRAZANA. Born Aug. 9, 1945 in Baltimore, MD. Graduate NYU. Debut 1969 OB in "Rules for Running Trains," followed by "Les Femmes Noires," "Geronimo," Bdwy in "My Sister, My Sister," "For Colored Girls Who Have Considered Suicide When the Rainbow Is Enuf" for which she received a Theatre World Award.

BIKEL, THEODORE. Born May 2, 1924 in Vienna, Aust. Attended RADA. Bdwy bow 1955 in "Tonight in Samarkand," followed by "The Lark," "Rope Dancers," "The Sound of Music," "Pousse-Cafe," "The Inspector General."

BINDIGER, EMILY. Born May 10, 1955 in Brooklyn, NY. Graduate HS Performing Arts. Debut 1973 OB in "Sisters of Mercy," followed by "Songs from The City Streets," Bdwy 1977 in "Shenandoah."

BIRNEY, REED. Born Sept. 11, 1954 in Alexandria, Va. Attended Boston U. Bdwy debut 1977 in "Gemini," OB in "The Master and Margarita."

BISHOP, KELLY (formerly Carole). Born Feb. 28, 1944 in Colorado Springs, CO. Bdwy debut 1967 in "Golden Rainbow," followed by "Promises, Promises," "On The Town," "Rachel Lily Rosenbloom," "A Chorus Line," OB in "Piano Bar."

BISHOP, RONALD. Born Mar. 28, 1923 in New Haven, Ct. Ithaca Col. graduate. Bdwy bow 1943 in "Othello," followed by "Julius Caesar," "The Visit," "A Meeting by the River," OB in "Galileo," "St. Joan," "Survival of St. Joan," "Total Eclipse."

BLAIR, PAMELA. Born Dec. 5, 1949 in Arlington, VT. Attended Ntl. Acad. of Ballet. Made Bdwy debut in 1972 in "Promises, Promises," followed by "Sugar," "Seesaw," "Of Mice and Men," "Wild and Wonderful," "A Chorus Line," OB in "Ballad of Boris K," "The Best Little Whorehouse in Texas," "King of Hearts."

BLAISDELL, BRAD. Born Mar. 15, 1949 in Baltimore, Md. Debut 1975 OB in "Tenderloin," Bdwy 1976 in "Going Up," followed by "I Love My Wife."

BLAKE, SYDNEY. Born Feb. 4, 1951 in Rome, Italy. Smith Col. graduate. Debut 1971 OB in "One Flew over the Cuckoo's Nest," followed by "El Grande de Coca Cola," "Fashion," "So Long 174th ST.," "Super Spy," Bdwy in "Once in a Lifetime."

BLOCH, SCOTTY. Born Jan. 28 in New Rochelle, NY. Attended AADA. Debut 1945 OB in "Craig's Wife," followed by "Lemon Sky," "Battering Ram," "Richard III," "In Celebration," "An Act of Kindness," "The Price."

BLUM, MARK. Born May 14, 1950 in Newark, NJ. Graduate UPa., UMinn. Debut 1976 OB in "The Cherry Orchard," followed by "Green Julia," "Say Goodnight, Gracie."

BLUMENFELD, ROBERT. Born Feb. 26, 1943 in NYC. Graduated Rutgers, Columbia U. Bdwy debut 1970 in "Othello," OB in American Savoyards productions, "The Fall and Redemption of Man," "Tempest," "The Dybbuk," "Count Dracula," "Nature and Purpose of the Universe."

BODIN, DUANE. Born Dec. 31, 1932 in Duluth, Mn. Bdwy debut 1961 in "Bye Bye Birdie," followed by "La Plume de Ma Tante," "Here's Love," "Fiddler on the Roof," "1776," "Sweeney Todd."

BOGAZIANOS, VASILI. Born Feb. 1, 1949 in NYC. Graduated San Francisco State Col. Debut 1978 OB in "P. S. Your Cat Is Dead" for which he received a Theatre World Award.

BOND, SUDIE. Born July 13, 1928 in Louisville, Ky. Attended Rollins Col. OB in "Summer and Smoke," "Tovarich," "American Dream," "Sandbox," "Endgame," "Theatre of the Absurd," "Home Movies," "Softly Consider the Nearness," "Memorandum," "Local Stigmatic," "Billy," "New York! New York!," "Cherry Orchard," " Albee Directs Albee," Bdwy in "Waltz of the Toreadors," "Auntie Mame," "The Egg," "Harold," "My Mother, My Father and Me," "The Impossible Years," "Keep It in the Family," "Quotations from Chrmn. Mao Tse-Tung," "American Dream," "Forty Carats," "Hay Fever," "Grease."

BORDO, ED. Born Mar. 3, 1931 in Cleveland, OH. Graduate Allegheny Col. LAMDA. Bdwy bow 1964 in "The Last Analysis," followed by "Inquest," "Zalmen or the Madness of God," "Annie," OB in "The Dragon," "Waiting for Godot," "Saved."

BORRELLI, JIM. Born Apr. 10, 1948 in Lawrence, MA. Graduate Boston Col. NY Debut OB 1971 in "Subject to Fits," followed by "Grease."

BOSCO, PHILIP. Born Sept. 26, 1930 in Jersey City, NJ. Graduate Catholic U. Credits: "Auntie Mame," "Rape of the Belt," "Ticket of Leave Man" (OB), "Donnybrook," "Man for All Seasons," "Mrs. Warren's Profession," with LCRep in "The Alchemist," "East Wind," "Galileo," "St. Joan," "Tiger at the Gate," "Cyrano," "King Lear," "A Great Career," "In the Matter of J. Robert Oppenheimer," "The Miser," "The Time of Your Life," "Camino Real," "Operation Sidewinder," "Amphitryon," "Enemy of the People," "Playboy of the Western World," "Good Woman of Setzuan," "Antigone," "Mary Stuart," "Narrow Road to the Deep North," "The Crucible," "Twelfth Night," "Enemies," "Plough and the Stars," "Merchant of Venice," and "A Streetcar Named Desire," "Henry V," "Threepenny Opera," "Streamers," "Stages," "St. Joan," "The Biko Inquest," "Man and Superman," "Whose Life Is It Anyway."

BOUTSIKARIS, DENNIS. Born Dec. 21, 1952 in Newark, NJ. Graduate Hampshire Col. Debut 1975 OB in "Another Language," followed by "Funeral March for a One-Man Band," "All's Well that Ends Well."

BOYDEN, PETER. Born July 19, 1945 in Leominster, Ma. Graduate St. Anselm's Col., Smith Col. Debut OB in "One Flew over the Cuckoo's Nest," followed by "Nice Girls," "Claw," "Berkeley Square," "Pericles," "Pig!," Bdwy in 'Whoopee!" (1979).

BRASINGTON, ALAN. Born in Monticello, NY. Attended RADA. Bdwy debut 1968 in "Pantagleize," followed by "The Misanthrope," "Cock-a-Doodle Dandy" and "Hamlet" with APA, "A Patriot for Me," "Sterling Silver" (OB).

BRENNAN, TOM. Born Apr. 16, 1926 in Cleveland, Oh. Graduate Oberlin, Western Reserve. Debut 1958 OB in "Synge Trilogy," followed by "Between Two Thieves," "Easter," "All in Love," "Under Milkwood," "An Evening with James Purdy," "Golden Six," "Pullman Car Hiawatha," "Are You Now or Have You . . .," "Diary of Anne Frank."

BREWER-MOORE, CATHY. Born Jan. 9, 1948 in Brunswick, Ga. Attended New School, AADA. Bdwy debut 1973 in "Seesaw," followed by OB in "Wonderful Town," "Mary."

BRISEBOIS, DANIELLE. Born June 28, 1969 in Brooklyn, NY. Bdwy debut 1977 in "Annie."

BROCKSMITH, ROY. Born Sept. 15, 1945 in Quincy, IL. Debut OB 1971 in "Whip Lady," followed by "The Workout," "Beggar's Opera," "Polly," "Threepenny Opera," "The Master and Margarita," Bdwy in "The Leaf People" (1975), "Stages," "Tartuffe."

BRODERICK, DIANA. Born July 15, in NYC. Attended NYU. Bdwy debut 1979 in "The Best Little Whorehouse in Texas."

BROOKES, JACQUELINE. Born July 24, 1930 in Montclair, NJ. Graduate UIowa, RADA. Bdwy debut 1955 in "Tiger at the Gates," followed by "Watercolor," "Abelard and Heloise," OB in "The Cretan Woman" for which she received a Theatre World Award, "The Clandestine Marriage," "Measure for Measure," "Duchess of Malfi," "Ivanov," "Six Characters in Search of an Author," "An Evening's Frost," "Come Slowly, Eden," "The Increased Difficulty of Concentration," "The Persians," "Sunday Dinner," "House of Blue Leaves," "A Meeting by the River," "Owners," "Hallelujah," "Dream of a Blacklisted Actor," "Knuckle," "Mama Sang the Blues," "Buried Child," "On Mt. Chimorazo."

BROOKS, JEFF. Born Apr. 7, 1950 in Vancouver, Can. Attended Portland State U. Debut 1976 OB in "Titanic," followed by "Fat Chances," "The Nature and Purpose of the Universe," Bdwy in "A History of the American Film" (1978).

BROOKS, JOEL. Born Dec. 17, 1949 in NYC. Graduated Hunter Col., UMin., AADA. Debut 1974 OB in "Auto Destruct," followed by "Fog and Mismanagement," "Museum," "All's Well That Ends Well," "Taming of the Shrew."

BROOKS, RANDALL ANNE. Born Feb. 16, 1969 in Panama Canal Zone. Bdwy debut 1978 in "Annie."

BROWN, GEORGIA. Born Oct. 21, 1933 in London. NY debut 1957 OB in "Threepenny Opera," Bdwy 1962 in "Oliver!," followed by "Side by Side by Sondheim," "Carmelina."

BROWN, GRAHAM. Born Oct. 24 in NYC. Graduate Howard U. OB in "Widower's Houses," "The Emperor's Clothes," "Time of Storm," "Major Barbara," "Land Beyond the River," "The Blacks," "Firebugs," "God Is a (Guess What?)," "An Evening of One Acts," "Man Better Man," "Behold! Cometh the Vanderkellans," "Ride a Black Horse," "Great MacDaddy," "Eden," "Nevis Mountain Dew," "Season Unravel," Bdwy in "Weekend," "Man in the Glass Booth," "River Niger," "Pericles," "Black Picture Show," "Kings."

Loren Brown   **Marcus B. F. Brown**   **Jan Buttram**   **John C. Capudice**   **Barbara Caruso**

BROWN, LOREN. Born Dec. 15, 1952 in Kansas City, Mo. Graduate Stanford U, AADA. Debut 1978 OB in "The Grinding Machine."

BROWN, MARCUS B. F. Born July 17, 1952 in Philadelphia, Pa. LaSalle Col. graduate. Bdwy debut 1978 in "Stop the World, I Want to Get Off."

BRUCE, SHELLEY. Born May 5, 1965 in Passaic, NJ. Debut OB 1973 in "The Children's Mass," Bdwy 1977 in "Annie."

BRUNEAU, RALPH. Born Sept. 22, 1952 in Phoenix, Az. Graduate UNotre Dame. Debut 1974 OB in "The Fantasticks," followed by "Saints," "Suddenly the Music Starts," "On a Clear Day You Can See Forever."

BRYNNER, YUL. Born June 15, 1915 in Sakhalin Island, Japan. Bdwy debut 1946 in "Lute Song," followed by "The King and I," (also 1977 revival), "Home Sweet Homer."

BUCHAN, MARK. Born Sept. 28, 1950 in Regina, Sas., Can. Graduate USaskatchewan, UWash. Debut 1979 OB in "I'm Getting My Act Together and Taking It on the Road."

BUCHTRUP, BJARNE. Born Aug. 11, 1942 in Copenhagen, Den. Bdwy debut 1966 in "Annie Get Your Gun," followed by "Finian's Rainbow," "Oklahoma!," "Come Summer," "Minnie's Boys," "Ari," "No, No, Nanette," "Gigi," "The Grand Tour."

BULOFF, JOSEPH. Born Dec. 6, 1907 in Wilno, Lith. Bdwy debut 1936 in "Don't Look Now," followed by "Call Me Ziggy," "To Quito and Back," "The Man from Cairo," "Morning Star," "Spring Again," "My Sister Eileen," "Oklahoma!," "The Whole World Over," "Once More with Feeling," "Fifth Season," "Moonbirds," "The Wall," OB in "Yoshke Musikant," "The Price."

BURKHARDT, GERRY. Born June 14, 1946 in Houston, TX. Attended Lon Morris Col. Bdwy debut 1968 in "Her First Roman," followed by "The Best Little Whorehouse in Texas."

BURKE, GERARD A. Born Feb. 20, 1925 in Dublin, Ire. Studied at Abbey Theatre in Dublin. Debut OB 1960 in "Shadow and Substance," followed by "Delightful Season," "Sherlock Holmes," "The Importance of Being Earnest."

BURNS, EILEEN. Born in Hartsdale, NY. Has appeared in "Native Son," "Christopher Blake," "Small Hours," "American Way," "The Women," (1936), "Merrily We Roll Along," "Daughters of Atreus," "First Lady," "Mourning Becomes Electra," OB in "Albee Directs Albee."

BURRELL, PAMELA. Born Aug. 4, 1945 in Tacoma, Wa. Bdwy debut 1966 in "Funny Girl," followed by "Where's Charley?," OB in "Arms and the Man" for which she received a Theatre World Award, "Berkeley Square," "The Boss," "Biography: A Game," "Strider: Story of a Horse."

BURRUS, BOB. Born Sept. 14, 1938 in Holdenville, Ok. Attended UChicago, Oklahoma City U. Debut 1979 OB in "Getting Out."

BURSKY, JAY. Born Mar. 27, 1954 in Cleveland, OH. Graduated Indiana U. OB and Bdwy debut 1978 in "The Best Little Whorehouse in Texas."

BUTTRAM, JAN. Born June 19, 1946 in Clarkesville, TX. Graduate NTex-State. Debut 1974 OB in "Fashion," Bdwy 1978 in "The Best Little Whorehouse in Texas."

CAHILL, JAMES. Born May 31, 1940 in Brooklyn, NY. Bdwy debut 1967 in "Marat/deSade," followed by "Break a Leg," OB in "The Hostage," "The Alchemist," "Johnny Johnson," "Peer Gynt," "Timon of Athens," "An Evening for Merlin Finch," "The Disintegration of James Cherry," "Crimes of Passion," "Rain," "Screens," "Total Eclipse," "Entertaining Mr. Sloane," "Hamlet."

CALDER, JUDITH. Born Oct. 7 in New Haven, Ct. Graduate Hofstra U., RADA. Debut OB 1977 in "A Flea in Her Ear," followed by "Warlock," "Gimme Shelter."

CALDWELL, GISELA. Born April 3 in Enid, OK. Graduate Geo. Washington U. Debut 1972 OB in "The Effect of Gamma Rays . . . ," followed by "Cappella," Bdwy in "Three Sisters " (1973), "Beggars Opera," "Measure for Measure."

CALKINS, MICHAEL. Born Apr. 27, 1948 in Chicago, IL. Graduate Webster Col. Debut 1973 OB in "Sisters of Mercy," followed by "Love! Love! Love!", "Lifesongs."

CALL, ANTHONY D. Born Aug. 31, 1940 in Los Angeles, CA. Attended UPa. Debut 1969 OB in "The David Show," followed by "Frequency," Bdwy in "Crown Matrimonial," "The Trip Back Down."

CAMPISI, TONY. Born May 8 in Cleveland, Oh. Attended USanta Clara. Debut 1977 OB in "K," followed by "The Caseworker," "Music Hall Sidelights," "Pvt. Wars."

CAPODICE, JOHN C. Born Dec. 25, 1941 in Chicago, Il. Attended Goodman School, London's Webber-Douglas Academy. Debut 1978 OB in "A Prayer for My Daughter," followed by "Henry V"(CP), "Getting Out."

CARA, IRENE. Born Mar. 18, 1958 in NYC. Bdwy debut 1968 in "Maggie Flynn," followed by "The Me Nobody Knows," "Via Galactica," "Got Tu Go Disco," OB in "Lotta," "Ain't Misbehavin."

CARBERRY, JOSEPH. Born May 5, 1948 in NYC. Attended Lawrence U, Brandeis U. Debut 1974 OB in "Short Eyes," followed by "Leaving Home," "Nesting."

CARIOU, LEN. Born Sept. 30, 1939 in Winnipeg, Can. Bdwy debut 1968 in "House of Atreus," followed by "Henry V" and "Applause" for which he received a Theatre World Award, "Night Watch," "A Little Night Music," "Cold Storage," "Sweeney Todd," OB in "A Sorrow Beyond Dreams."

CARLIN, THOMAS. Born Dec. 10, 1928 in Chicago, Il. Attended Loyola U., Catholic U. Credits include "Time Limit!," "Holiday for Lovers," "Man in the Dog Suit," "A Cook for Mr. General," "Great Day in the Morning," "A Thousand Clowns," "The Deputy," "Players," OB in "Thieves Carnival."

CARLO, JOHANN. Born May 21, 1957 in Buffalo, NY. Attended London's Webber-Douglass Academy. Debut 1978 OB in "Grand Magic," followed by "Artichoke," "Don Juan Comes Back from the War."

CARMEN, JULIE. Born Apr. 4, 1954 in Mt. Vernon, NY. Graduate SUNY, Neighborhood Playhouse. Debut OB 1973 in "Blood Wedding," followed by "St. Joan," "Block Party," "Cold Storage."

CARNEY, GRACE. Born Sept. 15, 1911 in Hartford, CT. Attended Columbia U, CCNY. Debut OB 1959 in "A Family Portrait," followed by "Billygoat Eddie," "Whitsuntide," "My Old Friends," Bdwy in "Donnybrook," "Eccentricities of a Nightingale," "Vieux Carre," "Angel."

CARNEY, MARY. Born Jan. 26, 1950 in Syracuse, NY. Graduate SONY Albany. Debut 1978 OB in "Othello." followed by "Just a Little Bit Less Than Normal."

CARPENTER, CARLETON. Born July 10, 1926 in Bennington, Vt. Attended Northwestern. Bdwy bow 1944 in "Bright Boy," followed by "Career Angel," "Three to Make Ready," "Magic Touch," "John Murray Anderson's Almanac," "Hotel Paradiso," "A Box of Watercolors," "Hello, Dolly!," OB in "A Stage Affair," "Boys in the Band," "Dylan," "Greatest Fairy Story Ever Told," "Good Old Fashioned Revue," "Miss Stanwyck Is Still in Hiding."

CARROLL, DANNY. Born May 30, 1940 in Maspeth, NY. Bdwy bow 1957 in "Music Man," followed by "Flora the Red Menace," "Funny Girl," "George M!," "Billy," "Ballroom," OB in "Boys from Syracuse," "Babes in the Wood."

CARROLL, DAVID-JAMES. Born July 30, 1950 in Rockville Centre, NY. Graduate Dartmouth Col. Debut 1975 in "A Matter of Time," followed by "Joseph and the Amazing Technicolor Dreamcoat," Bdwy "Rodgers and Hart" (1975), "Where's Charley?"

CARRUTHERS, JAMES. Born May 26, 1931 in Morristown, NJ. Attended Lafayette Col., HB Studio. Debut 1959 OB in "Our Town," followed by "Under the Sycamore Tree," "Misalliance," "The Hostage," "Telemachus Clay," "Shadow of a Gunman," "Masks," "Biography: A Game," "Lulu," Bdwy in "Poor Murderer."

CARTER, DIXIE. Born May 25, 1939 in McLemoresville, Tn. Graduate Memphis State U. Debut 1963 OB in "The Winter's Tale," followed by "Carousel." "The Merry Widow," "The King and I," at LC, "Sextet," "Jesse and the Bandit Queen" for which she received a Theatre World Award, "Fathers and Sons," "Taken in Marriage," Bdwy in "Pal Joey" (1976).

CARTER, NELL. Born Sept. 13 in Birmingham, AL. Bdwy debut 1971 in "Soon," followed by "Jesus Christ Superstar," "Dude," "Don't Bother Me, I Can't Cope," "Ain't Misbehavin' " for which she received a Theatre World Award, OB in "Iphigenia in Taurus," "Bury the Dead," "Fire in the Mindhouse," "The Dirtiest Show in Town."

CARUSO, BARBARA. Born in East Orange, NJ. Graduate Douglass Col., RADA. Debut 1969 OB in "The Millionairess," followed by "Picture of Dorian Gray," "Wars of the Roses," "Chez Nous," "Ride a Cock Horse," Bdwy 1976 in "Night of the Iguana."

CASHIN, TOM. Born Oct. 9, 1953 in Brooklyn, NY. Attended Hunter Col. Debut OB and Bdwy 1978 in "The Best Little Whorehouse in Texas."

Tim Cassidy　　**Helen Castillo**　　**Lee Chew**　　**Lori Chinn**　　**Rene Clemente**

CASPER, RICHARD. Born Jan. 21, 1949 in Springfield, Il. Graduate Northwestern U. Bdwy debut 1971 in "Much Ado about Nothing," OB in "Pins and Needles."

CASS, PEGGY. Born May 21, 1926 in Boston, Ma. Attended Wyndham Sch. Credits include "Touch and Go," "Live Wire," "Bernardine," "Othello," "Henry V," "Auntie Mame" for which she received a Theatre World Award, "A Thurber Carnival," "Children from Their Games," "Don't Drink the Water," "Front Page"(69), "Plaza Suite," OB in "Phoenix '55," "Are You Now or Have You Ever Been."

CASSIDY, TIM. Born Mar. 22, 1952 in Alliance, OH. Attended UCincinnati. Bdwy debut 1974 in "Good News," followed by "A Chorus Line."

CASTANG, VERONICA. Born Apr. 22, 1938 in London, Eng. Attended Sorbonne. Bdwy debut 1966 in "How's the World Treating You?," followed by "The National Health," "Whose Life Is It Anyway?," OB in "The Trigon," "Sjt. Musgrave's Dance," "Saved," "Water Hens," "Self-Accusation," "Kaspar," "Ionescapade," "Statements after and Arrest under the Immorality Act," "Ride a Cock Horse."

CASTILLO, HELEN. Born Feb. 5, 1955 in Santurce, PR. Graduate UPR, Juilliard. Bdwy debut 1979 in "They're Playing Our Song."

CATLIN, FAITH. Born Sept. 19, 1949 in Troy, NY. Graduate Boston U. Debut 1969 OB in "Pequod," followed by "Approaching Simone," "Summer Brave," "Hot 1 Baltimore," "American Glands," "The Catch," "Augusta," Bdwy in "Da."

CHAMBERLAIN, RICHARD. Born Mar. 31, 1935 in Beverly Hills, Ca. Attended Pomona Col. Bdwy debut 1976 in "Night of the Iguana," OB in "Fathers and Sons."

CHANNING, CAROL. Born Jan. 31, 1921 in Seattle, Wash. Attended Bennington Col. Bdwy debut 1941 in "No for an Answer," followed by "Let's Face It," "Proof Through the Night," "Lend an Ear" for which she received a Theatre World Award, "Gentlemen Prefer Blonds," "Wonderful Town," "The Vamp," "Show Girl," "Hello Dolly!" (also 1978 revival), "Four on a Garden," "Lorelei."

CHARLES, PAUL. Born July 29, 1947 in NYC. Attended Quintano Sch. Has appeared in "Best Foot Forward" (OB), "Kelly," "Royal Hunt of the Sun," "A Joyful Noise," "La Strada," "A Chorus Line."

CHARLES, WALTER. Born Apr. 4, 1945 in East Stroudsburg, Pa. Graduate Boston U. Bdwy debut 1973 in "Grease," followed by "1600 Pennsylvania Avenue," "Knickerbocker Holiday," "Sweeney Todd."

CHAYKIN, MAURY. Born July 27, 1949 in Brooklyn, NY. Graduate UBuffalo. Debut 1978 OB in "Gimme Shelter."

CHEN, KITTY. Born in Shanghai, China. Graduate Brown U. Debut 1972 OB in "A Maid's Tragedy," followed by "The King and I," "Rashomon," "And the Soul Shall Dance."

CHEW, LEE. Born Feb. 8, 1949 in Roanoke, Va. Graduate VaU. Debut 1978 OB in "Can-Can."

CHIANESE, DOMINIC. Born Feb. 24, 1932 in NYC. Graduate Brooklyn Col. Debut 1952 OB with American Savoyards, followed by "Winterset," "Jacques Brel Is Alive . . . ," "Ballad for a Firing Squad," "City Scene," "End of the War," Bdwy in "Oliver!," "Scratch," "The Water Engine."

CHINN, LORI. Born July 7 in Seattle, Wa. Bdwy debut 1970 in "Lovely Ladies, Kind Gentlemen," OB in "Coffins for Butterflies," "Hough in Blazes," "Peer Gynt," "King and I," "Children," "Secret Life of Walter Mitty," "Bayou Legend," "Primary English Class," "G. R. Point."

CHOI, HYE-YOUNG. Born Oct. 22, 1946 in Seoul, Korea. Graduate Manhattan Sch. of Music. Bdwy debut 1977 in "The King and I."

CHRISTIAN, ROBERT. Born Dec. 27, 1939 in Los Angeles. Attended UCLA. OB in "The Happening," "Hornblend," "Fortune and Men's Eyes," "Boys in the Band," "Behold! Cometh the Vanderkellans," "Mary Stuart," "Narrow Road to the Deep North," "Twelfth Night," "The Past Is the Past," "Going through Changes," "Black Sunlight," "Terraces," "Blood Knot," "Boesman and Lena," "Statements after and Arrest under the Immorality Act," "Julius Caesar," "Coriolanus," Bdwy in "We Bombed in New Haven," "Does a Tiger Wear a Necktie?," "An Evening with Richard Nixon," "All God's Chillun."

CHRISTOPHER, PAULA. Born Jan. 22, 1953 in Washington, Pa. Graduate UPittsburgh. Debut 1978 OB in "Taxi Tales."

CHRISTOPHER, RICHARD. Born Nov. 1, 1948 in Ft. Knox, Ky. Graduate SWLaU. Bdwy debut 1973 in "Seesaw," followed by "King of Hearts," OB in "Three Musketeers."

CIFALA, JO-ANN. Born Dec. 31 in Washington, DC. Attended Butler U. Bdwy debut 1976 in "Very Good Eddie," followed by "Going Up," "Whoopee!"

CILENTO, WAYNE. Born Aug. 25, 1949, in The Bronx, NY. Graduate State U. Brockport. Bdwy in "Irene," "Rachel Lily Rosenbloom," "Seesaw," "A Chorus Line," "The Act," "Dancin'."

CISSEL, CHUCK. Born Oct. 3, 1948, in Tulsa, OK. Graduate UOkla. Bdwy debut 1971 in "Purlie," followed by "Lost in the Stars," "Via Galactica," "Don't Bother Me, I Can't Cope," "A Chorus Line."

CLANTON, RALPH. Born Sept. 11, 1914 in Fresno, CA. Attended Pasadena Playhouse. On Bdwy in "Victory Belles," "Macbeth," "Richard III," "Othello," "Lute Song," "Cyrano," "Antony and Cleopatra," "Design for a Stained Glass Window," "Taming of the Shrew," "Burning Glass," "Vivat! Vivat Regina!," "The Last of Mrs. Lincoln," OB in "Ceremony of Innocence," "Endecott and the Red Cross," "The Philanderer," BAM Co.'s "New York Idea," and "Three Sisters," "You Never Can Tell," "Candida."

CLARK, BRYAN E. Born Apr. 5, 1929 in Louisville, KY. Graduate Fordham U. Bdwy debut 1978 in "A History of the American Film,"OB in "Winning Isn't Everything."

CLARK, CHERYL. Born Dec. 7, 1950 in Boston, MA. Attended Ind. U., NYU. Bdwy debut 1972 in "Pippin," followed by "Chicago," "A Chorus Line."

CLARK, JOSH. Born Aug. 16, 1955 in Bethesda, MD. Attended NC Sch. of Arts. Debut 1976 OB in "The Old Glory," followed by "Molly," "Just a Little Bit Less Than Normal," "Rear Column."

CLARKE, RICHARD. Born Jan. 31, 1933 in England. Graduate U Reading. With LCRep in "St. Joan," "Tiger at the Gates," "Cyrano de Bergerac," followed by Bdwy in "Conduct Unbecoming," 'Elephant Man,' OB in "Old Glory."

CLARKSON, JOHN. Born Jan. 19, 1932 in London, Eng. Graduate Oxford U. Debut OB 1971 in "Murderous Angels," followed by "An Evening with Ma Bell," "Staircase," "Just a Little Bit Less Than Normal," Bdwy in "No Sex Please, We're British," "My Fair Lady."

CLEMENT, ALAN. Born July 13, 1927 in Buffalo, NY. Graduate UBuffalo. Debut 1971 OB in "The Price," followed by "Joe Egg," "Inadmissible Evidence," "Antigone," "Love from a Stranger," "La Ronde."

CLEMENT, CLARIS. Born July 11, 1950 in Philadelphia, PA. Graduate Rollins Col. Debut 1976 OB in "Noel and Cole," Bdwy 1978 in "On the 20th Century."

CLEMENTE, RENE. Born July 2, 1950 in El Paso, TX. Graduate West Tex. State U. Bdwy debut 1977 in "A Chorus Line."

CLIFFORD, CLINT. Born Sept. 6, 1952 in NYC. Graduate Colgate U. Debut 1979 OB in "Annie Get Your Gun," followed by "On a Clear Day You Can See Forever."

CLOSE, GLENN. Born May 19, 1947 in Greenwich, CT. Graduate William & Mary Col. Bdwy debut 1974 with Phoenix Co. in "Love for Love," "Member of the Wedding," and "Rules of the Game," followed by "Rex," "Crucifer of Blood," OB in "The Crazy Locomotive," "Uncommon Women and Others."

COCA, IMOGENE. Born Nov. 18, 1908 in Philadelphia, PA. Bdwy debut 1925 in "When You Smile," followed by "Garrick Gaieties," "Flying Colors," "New Faces," "Fools Rush In," "Who's Who," "Folies Bergere," "Straw Hat Revue," "All in Fun," "Concert Varieties," "Janus," "Girls in 509," "On the 20th Century."

COFFIN, FREDERICK. Born Jan. 16, 1943 in Detroit, MI. Graduate UMich. Debut 1971 OB in "Basic Training of Pavlo Hummel," followed by "Much Ado about Nothing," "King Lear," "As You Like It," "Boom Boom Room," "Merry Wives of Windsor," "Secret Service," "Boy Meets Girl," "Hot Grog," Bdwy in "We Interrupt This Program" (1975).

COGGIN, BARBARA. Born Feb. 27 in Chattanooga, TN. Attended Peabody Col. Bdwy debut 1970 in "Lovely Ladies, Kind Gentlemen," followed by "Poor Murderer," OB in "The Drunkard," "One for the Money, etc.," "Judy: A Garland of Songs," "Rag Doll," "Museum," "Tune the Grand Up."

COLBERT, CLAUDETTE. Born Sept. 13, 1903 in Paris, Fr. Bdwy debut 1925 in "Wild Westcotts," followed by "Ghost Train," 'Kiss in a Taxi," "The Barker," "Mulberry Bush," "La Gringa," "Tin Pan Alley," "Dynamo," "See Naples and Die," "Janus," "The Marriage-Go-Round," "Jake, Julia and Uncle Joe," "Irregular Verb to Love," "The Kingfisher."

Kay Cole   **Austin Colyer**   **Miriam Colon**   **Leonard John Crofoot**   **Jane Cronin**

COLBY, CHRISTINE, Born Feb. 27 in Cincinnati, Oh. Attended UCincinnati. Bdwy debut 1978 in "Dancin'."

COLE, KAY. Born Jan. 13, 1948 in Miami, Fl. Bdwy debut 1961 in "Bye Bye Birdie," followed by "Stop the World I Want to Get Off," "Roar of the Greasepaint . . .," "Hair," "Jesus Christ Superstar," "Words and Music," "Chorus Line," OB in "The Cradle Will Rock," "Two if by Sea," "Rainbow," "White Nights," "Sgt. Pepper's Lonely Hearts Club Band."

COLE, NORA. Born Sept. 10, 1953 in Louisville, Ky. Attended Beloit Col., Goodman Sch. Debut 1977 OB in "Movie Buff," followed by "Cartoons for a Lunch Hour."

COLES, ZAIDA. Born Sept. 10, 1933 in Lynchburg, Va. Credits include OB "The Father," "Pins and Needles," "Life and Times of J. Walter Smintheus," "The Cherry Orchard," "Bayou Legend," "Divine Comedy," "Second Thoughts," Bdwy in "Weekend," "Zelda."

COLLINS, PAUL. Born July 25, 1937 in London, Eng. Attended Los Angeles City & State Col. OB in "Say Nothing," "Cambridge Circus," "The Devils," "Rear Column," Bdwy in "Royal Hunt of the Sun," "A Minor Adjustment," "A Meeting by the River."

COLON, MIRIAM. Born in 1945 in Ponce, PR. Attended UPR., Actors Studio. Bdwy debut 1953 in "In the Summer House," OB in "Me, Candido," "The Ox Cart," "Passion of Antigona Perez," "Julius Caesar."

COLTON, CHEVI. Born Dec. 21 in NYC. Attended Hunter Col. OB in "Time of Storm," "Insect Comedy," "The Adding Machine," "O Marry Me," "Penny Change," "The Mad Show," "Jacques Brel is Alive . . .," "Bits and Pieces," "Spelling Bee," Bdwy in "Cabaret," "Grand Tour."

COLYER, AUSTIN. Born Oct. 29, 1935 in Brooklyn, NY. Attended SMU. Credits include "Darwin's Theories," "Let It Ride," "Maggie Flynn," CC's "Brigadoon," "Music Man" and "How to Succeed in Business . . .," "Jimmy," "Desert Song," "Pal Joey"(76), "I Remember Mama," OB in "Show Me Where the Good Times Are."

COMBS, DAVID. Born June 10, 1949 in Reno, NV. Graduate UNev., Wayne State U. Bdwy debut 1975 in "Equus," OB in "The Passion of Dracula."

CONNER, BYRON. Born Dec. 5, 1953 in Gadsden, AL. Graduate Ithaca Col. Debut 1978 OB in "The Taming of the Shrew," followed by "On a Clear Day You Can See Forever."

CONROY, JARLATH. Born Sept. 30, 1944 in Galway, Ir. Attended RADA. Bdwy debut 1976 in "Comedians," followed by "The Elephant Man."

CONTI, TOM. Born in Glasgow, Scot. Attended UGlasgow. Bdwy debut 1979 in "Whose Life Is It Anyway?"

CONWAY, KEVIN. Born May 29, 1942 in NYC. Debut 1968 OB in "Muzeeka," followed by "Saved," "The Plough and the Stars," "One Flew over the Cuckoo's Nest," "When You Comin' Back, Red Ryder?," "Long Day's Journey into Night," Bdwy in "Indians," "Moonchildren," "Of Mice and Men," "The Elephant Man."

COOK, JILL. Born Feb. 25, 1954 in Plainfield, NJ. Bdwy debut 1971 in "On the Town," followed by "So Long, 174th Street," "Dancin'," "Best Little Whorehouse in Texas," OB in "Carnival."

COONAN, SHEILA. Born June 28, 1922 in Montreal, Can. Attended McGill U. Appeared in "Red Roses for Me," "A Taste of Honey," "The Hostage," "The Great White Hope," OB in "Hogan's Goat," "Macbeth," "A Song for the First of May," "Happy Hunter," "Just the Immediate Family."

COOPER, MARILYN. Born Dec. 14, 1936 in NYC. Attended NYU. Appeared in "Mr. Wonderful," "West Side Story," "Brigadoon," "Gypsy," "I Can Get It for You Wholesale," "Hallelujah, Baby!," "Golden Rainbow," "Mame," "A Teaspoon Every 4 Hours," "Two by Two," "On the Town," "Ballroom," OB in "The Mad Show," "Look Me Up."

COOPER, PEGGY. Born Mar. 31, 1931 in Huntington, WVa. Graduate Baldwin-Wallace Cons. Bdwy debut 1968 in "Zorba," followed by "La Strada," "The Rothschilds," "Goodtime Charley," "On the 20th Century."

COOTE, ROBERT. Born Feb. 4, 1909 in London, Eng. Bdwy debut 1953 in "The Love of Four Colonels," followed by "Dear Charles," "My Fair Lady" (1956 & '76), "Jockey Club Stakes," "Bedroom Farce."

COPELAND, MAURICE. Born June 13, 1911 in Rector, Ar. Pasadena Playhouse graduate. Bdwy debut 1974 in "The Freedom of the City," followed by "The First Monday in October," OB in "Henry V."

CORBIN, BARRY. Born Oct. 16, 1940 in LaMesa, Tx. Attended Texas Tech. Bdwy debut 1969 in ASF's "Othello," followed OB in "Masquerade," "Crystal and Fox," "Holy Ghosts," "Getting Out."

CORDES, KATHRYN. Born Oct. 2 in Paterson, NJ. Juilliard graduate. Debut 1977 OB in "Wonderful Lives," followed by "Saints," "Oklahoma!"

COREY, JILL. Born Sept. 30 in Avonmore, Pa. Attended Bergen Com. Col., AADA. Debut 1979 OB in "Telecast."

COSTIGAN, KEN. Born Apr. 1, 1934 in NYC. Graduate Fordham U., Yale U. Debut 1960 OB in "Borak," followed by "King of the Dark Chamber," "The Hostage," "Next Time I'll Sing to You," "Curley McDimple," "The Runner Stumbles," "Peg o' My Heart," "The Show-Off," "Midsummer Night's Dream," "Diary of Anne Frank," Bdwy 1962 in "Gideon."

COWAN, EDIE. Born Apr. 14 in NYC. Graduate Butler U. Bdwy debut 1964 in "Funny Girl," followed by "Sherry," "Annie."

COWLES, MATTHEW. Born Sept. 28, 1944 in NYC. Attended Neighborhood Playhouse. Bdwy bow 1966 in "Malcolm," followed by "Sweet Bird of Youth," OB in "King John," "The Indian Wants the Bronx," "Triple Play," "Stop, You're Killing Me!," "The Time of Your Life," "Foursome," "Kid Champion," "End of the War."

COX, CATHERINE. Born Dec. 13, 1950 in Toledo, Oh. Wittenberg U. graduate. Bdwy debut 1976 in "Music Is," followed by "Whoopee!," OB in "By Strouse."

COX, RICHARD. Born May 6, 1948 in NYC. Yale graduate. Debut 1970 OB in "Saved," followed by "Fuga," "Moonchildren," Bdwy in "The Sign in Sidney Brustein's Window," "Platinum."

CRABTREE, DON. Born Aug. 21, 1928 in Borger, TX. Attended Actors Studio. Bdwy bow 1959 in "Destry Rides Again," followed by "Happiest Girl in the World," "Family Affair," "Unsinkable Molly Brown," "Sophie," "110 in the Shade," "Golden Boy," "Pousse Cafe," "Mahagonny" (OB), "The Best Little Whorehouse in Texas."

CRAIG, DONALD. Born Aug. 14, 1941 in Abilene, TX. Graduate Hardin-Simmons Col., UTex. Debut 1975 OB in "Do I Hear a Waltz?" (ELT). Bdwy 1977 in "Annie."

CRISP, QUENTIN. Born Dec. 25, 1908 in Carshalton, Eng. NY debut 1978 OB in "An Evening with Quentin Crisp."

CRISTOFER, MICHAEL. Born Jan. 22, 1945 in Trenton, NJ. Attended Catholic U. Made debut 1977 OB in "The Cherry Orchard" for which he received a Theatre World Award, followed by "Conjuring an Event," "Chinchilla."

CROFOOT, LEONARD JOHN. Born Sept. 20, 1948 in Utica, NY. Bdwy debut 1968 in "The Happy Time," followed by "Come Summer," "Gigi," OB in "Circus," "Joseph and the Amazing Technicolor Dreamcoat."

CRONIN, JANE. Born Apr. 4, 1936 in Boston, MA. Attended Boston U. Bdwy debut 1965 in "Postmark Zero," OB in "Bald Soprano," "One Flew over the Cuckoo's Nest," "Hot 1 Baltimore," "The Gathering," "Catsplay," "The Violano Virtuoso," "Afternoons in Vegas," "The Frequency."

CRONYN, HUME. Born July 18, 1911 in London, Can. Attended McGill U., AADA. Bdwy debut 1934 in "Hipper's Holiday," followed by "Boy Meets Girl," "High Tor," "Room Service," "There's Always a Breeze," "Escape This Night," "Off to Buffalo," "Three Sisters," "Weak Link," "Retreat to Pleasure," "Mr. Big," "Survivors," "Four-poster," "Madam, Will You Walk" (OB), "The Honeys," "A Day by the Sea," "Man in the Dog Suit," "Triple Play," "Big Fish, Little Fish," "Hamlet," "The Physicists," "A Delicate Balance," "Hadrian VII," "Promenade All," "Noel Coward in Two Keys," "Krapp's Last Tape," "Happy Days," "Act without Words," "The Gin Game."

CROUCH, KENSYN. Born Oct. 27, 1932 in Ilford, Eng. Attended RADA. NY debut 1978 OB in "Gimme Shelter."

CROUSE, LINDSAY ANN. Born May 12, 1948 in NYC. Radcliffe graduate. Bdwy debut 1972 in "Much Ado about Nothing," followed by OB in "The Foursome," "Fishing," "Long Day's Journey into Night," "Total Recall," "Father's Day."

CRYER, GRETCHEN. Born Oct. 17, 1935 in Indianapolis, In. Graduate DePauw U. Bdwy in "Little Me," "110 in the Shade," OB in "Now Is the Time for All Good Men," "Gallery," "Circle of Sound," "I'm Getting My Act Together . . ."

CUERVO, ALMA. Born Aug. 13, in Tampa, Fl. Graduated Tulane U., Yale U. Debut 1977 OB in "Uncommon Women and Others," followed by "A Foot in the Door," Bdwy in "Once in a Lifetime," "Bedroom Farce."

| John Cunningham | Randy Danson | Joseph d'Angerio | Jane Dentinger | Bob DeFrank |

CULLUM, JOHN. Born Mar. 2, 1930 in Knoxville, TN. Graduate U. Tenn. Bdwy bow 1960 in "Camelot," followed by "Infidel Caesar," "The Rehearsal," "Hamlet," "On a Clear Day You Can See Forever" for which he received a Theatre World Award, "Man of LaMancha," "1776," "Vivat! Vivat Regina!," "Shenandoah," "Kings," "The Trip Back Down," "On the 20 Century," OB in "Three Hand Reel," "The Elizabethans," "Carousel," "In the Voodoo Parlor of Marie Leveau," "The King and I" (JB).

CUMMINGS, CONSTANCE. Born May 15, 1910 in Seattle, Wa. Bdwy debut 1928 in "Treasure Girl," followed by "The Little Show," "This Man's Town," "June Moon," "Accent on Youth," "Young Madame Conti," "Madame Bovary," "If I Were You," "One-Man Show," "The Rape of the Belt," "Hamlet" ('69), "Wings."

CUNNINGHAM, JOHN. Born June 22, 1932 in Auburn, NY. Graduate of Yale and Dartmouth. OB in "Love Me Little," "Pimpernel," "The Fantasticks," "Love and Let Love," "The Bone Room," "Dancing in the Dark," Bdwy in "Hot Spot," "Zorba," "Company," "1776."

CURRY, CHRISTOPHER. Born Oct. 22, 1948, in Grand Rapids, MI. Graduated UMich. Debut 1974 OB in "When You Comin' Back, Red Ryder?" followed by "The Cherry Orchard," "Spelling Bee," "Ballymurphy," "Isadora Duncan Sleeps with the Russian Navy," "The Promise," Bdwy in "The Crucifer of Blood."

CURTIS, KEENE. Born Feb. 15, 1925 in Salt Lake City, UT. Graduate UUtah. Bdwy bow 1949 in "Shop at Sly Corner," with APA in "School for Scandal," "The Tavern," "Anatole," "Scapin," "Right You Are," "Importance of Being Earnest," "Twelfth Night," "King Lear," "Seagull," "Lower Depths," "Man and Superman," "Judith," "War and Peace," "You Can't Take It with You," "Pantagleize," "Cherry Orchard," "Misanthrope," "Cocktail Party," "Cock-a-Doodle Dandy" and "Hamlet," "A Patriot for Me," "The Rothchilds," "Night Watch," "Via Galactica," "Annie," OB in "Colette," "Ride across Lake Constance."

CUSACK, PHILIP. Born May 10, 1934 in Boston, Ma. Attended Emerson Col. Bdwy bow 1966 in "3 Bags Full," followed by "God's Favorite," "The Good Doctor," "The Gingerbread Lady," "Children, Children," "Let Me Hear You Smile," "California Suite," "They're Playing Our Song," OB in "Boys in the Band."

DABDOUB, JACK. Born Feb. 5 in New Orleans, La. Graduate Tulane U. OB in "What's Up," "Time for the Gentle People," "The Peddler," "The Dodo Bird," "Annie Get Your Gun," Bdwy in "Paint Your Wagon," "My Darlin' Aida," "Happy Hunting," "Hot Spot," "Camelot," "Baker Street," "Anya," 'Annie Get Your Gun" (LC), "Her First Roman," "Coco," "Man of La Mancha."

d'ANGERIO, JOSEPH. Born Feb. 10, 1949 in Newark, NJ. Graduate URI. Bdwy debut 1979 in "Carmelina."

DABDOUB, JACK. Born Feb. 5 in New Orleans, La. Graduate Tulane U. OB in "What's Up," "Time for the Gentle People," "The Peddler," "The Dodo Bird," "Annie Get Your Gun," Bdwy in "Paint Your Wagon," "My Darlin' Aida," "Happy Hunting," "Hot Spot," "Camelot," "Baker Street," "Anya," "Annie Get Your Gun" (LC), "Her First Roman," "Coco," "Man of La Mancha."

d'ANGERIO, JOSEPH. Born Feb. 10, 1949 in Newark, NJ. Graduate URI. Bdwy debut 1979 in "Carmelina."

DANIELLE, SUSAN. Born Jan. 30, 1949 in Englewood, NJ. Graduate Wm. Paterson Col. Debut 1979 OB in "Tip-Toes."

DANNER, DOROTHY FRANK. Formerly Dorothy Frank. Born July 8, 1941 in St. Louis, Mo. Bdwy debut 1959 in "Once Upon a Mattress," followed by "Sail Away," "Tenderloin," "No Strings," "New Faces of 1968," "Different Times," "Begger on Horseback"(LC), "Irene," "Ballroom," OB in "Boys from Syracuse."

DANSON, RANDY. Born Apr. 30, 1950 in Plainfield, NJ. Graduate Carnegie-Mellon. Debut 1978 OB in "Gimme Shelter," followed by "Big and Little."

DAVIDSON, JACK. Born July 17, 1936 in Worcester, MA. Graduate Boston U. Debut 1968 OB in "Moon for the Misbegotten," followed by "Battle of Angels," "Midsummer Night's Dream," "Hot l Baltimore," "A Tribute to Lili Lamont," "Ulysses in Traction," "Lulu," "Hey, Rube." "In the Recovery Lounge," "The Runner Stumbles," "Winter Signs," Bdwy in "Capt. Brassbound's Conversion" (1972), "Anna Christie."

DAVIS, ANDREW. Born Aug. 9, 1950 in San Antonio, Tx. Graduate UNew Orleans, Yale. Bdwy debut 1978 in "Crucifer of Blood," OB in "Word of Mouth," "Says I Says He."

DAVIS, BRUCE ANTHONY. Born Mar. 4, 1959 in Dayton, Oh. Attended Juilliard. Bdwy debut 1979 in "Dancin'."

DAVIS, CLAYTON. Born May 18, 1948 in Pensacola, Fl. Graduate Princeton U., FlaStateU. Debut 1978 OB in "Oklahoma!"

DAVIS, OSSIE. Born Dec. 18, 1917 in Cogdell, Ga. Attended Howard U. Bdwy bow 1946 in "Jeb," followed by "Anna Lucasta," "Leading Lady," "Smile of the World," "Wisteria Trees," "Royal Family"(CC), "Green Pastures," "Remains to Be Seen," "Touchstone," "No Time for Sergeants," "Jamaica," "Raisin in the Sun," "Purlie Victorious," "The Zulu and the Zayda," "Ain't Supposed to Die a Natural Death," OB in "Ballad of Bimshire," "Take It from the Top."

DAVIS, SAMMY, JR. Born Dec. 8, 1925 in NYC. Bdwy bow 1956 in "Mr. Wonderful," followed by "Golden Boy," "Stop the World, I Want to Get Off."

DAVIS, SYLVIA. Born Apr. 10, 1910 in Philadelphia, Pa. Attended Temple U., AmTheatreWing. Debut 1949 OB in "Blood Wedding," followed by "Tobacco Road," "Orpheus Descending," "Autumn Garden," "Madwoman of Chaillot," "House of Bernarda Alba," "My Old Friends," Bdwy in "Nathan Weinstein, Mystic, Conn." (1966), "Xmas in Las Vegas."

DEARDORFF, DAVIS. Born Apr. 28, 1947 in Bremen, In. Graduate Manchester Col. Debut 1974 OB in "Oh, Lady! Lady!," followed by "P.S. Your Cat is Dead."

de BANZIE, LOIS. Born May 4 in Glasgow, Scot. Bdwy debut 1966 in "Elizabeth the Queen," followed by "Da," OB in "Little Murders," "Mary Stuart," "People Are Living There," "Ride Across Lake Constance," "The Divorce of Judy and Jane," "What the Butler Saw," "Man and Superman," "The Judas Applause."

DEE, RUBY. Born Oct. 27, 1923 in Cleveland, Oh. Hunter Col. graduate. Bdwy debut 1946 in "Jeb," followed by "Anna Lucasta," "Smile of the World," "Long Way Home," "Raisin in the Sun," "Purlie Victorious," OB in "World of Sholom Aleichem," "Boesman and Lena," "Wedding Band," "Hamlet," "Take It from the Top."

DeFABEES, RICHARD. Born Apr. 4, 1947 in Englewood, NJ. Graduate Georgetown U. Debut 1973 OB in "Creeps," followed by "Monsters (Sideshow)," Bdwy in "The Skin of Our Teeth," "Whose Life Is It Anyway?"

DeFRANK, ROBERT. Born Nov. 29, 1945 in Baltimore, Md. Graduate Towson State, Essex Community Col. Debut 1977 OB in "The Crazy Locomotive," followed by "The Taming of the Shrew," "The Madman and the Nun."

DeGHELDER, STEPHAN. Born Oct. 6, 1945 in Independence, Mo. Attended UMo. Debut 1959 OB in "Once upon a Mattress," followed by "It's a Mod Mod World," "Sancocho," Bdwy in "Hello, Dolly!" (1967), "Celebration."

DeKOVEN, ROGER. Born Oct. 22, 1907 in Chicago, Il. Attended UChicago, Northwestern, Columbia. Bdwy bow 1926 in "Juarez and Maximilian," followed by "Mystery Man," "Once in a Lifetime," "Counselor-at-Law," "Murder in the Cathedral," "Eternal Road," "Brooklyn U.S.A.," "The Assassin," "Joan of Lorraine," "Abie's Irish Rose," "The Lark," "Hidden River," "Compulsion," "Miracle Worker," "Fighting Cock," "Herzl," OB in "Deadly Game," "Steal the Old Man's Bundle," "St. Joan," "Tiger at the Gates," "Walking to Waldheim," "Cyrano de Bergerac," "An Enemy of the People," "Ice Age," "Prince of Homburg," "Biography: A Game," "Strider."

DE LAPPE, GEMZE. Born Feb. 28, 1925 in Portsmouth, VA. Attended Hunter Col. Credits include "Oklahoma!," "The King and I," "Paint Your Wagon," "Juno," "Brigadoon," OB in "Gorey Stories."

DEMPSEY, JEROME. Born Mar. 1, 1929 in St. Paul, MN. Toledo U graduate. Bdwy bow 1959 in "West Side Story," followed by "The Deputy," "Spofford," "Room Service," "Love Suicide at Schofield Barracks," "Dracula," OB in "Cry of Players," "Year Boston Won the Pennant," "The Crucible," "Justice Box," "Trelawny of the Wells," "The Old Glory," "Six Characters in Search of an Author," "Threepenny Opera."

DENTINGER, JANE. Born Sept. 9, 1951 in Rochester, NY. Ithaca Col. graduate. Debut 1974 OB in "All My Sons," followed by "Pericles," "Vanities."

DEROSKI, BONNIE. Born June 8, 1961 in Neptune, NJ. Debut 1977 OB in "Landscape of the Body," followed by "A New England Legend."

DERN, BRUCE. Born June 4, 1936 in Chicago, Il. Attended UPa. Bdwy debut 1958 in "The Shadow of a Gunman," followed by "Strangers."

| Jay Devlin | Mary Donnet | Dean Dittman | M'El Dowd | Lucien Douglas |

DeSALVO, ANNE. Born Apr. 3 in Philadelphia, PA. OB in "Iphigenia in Aulis," "Lovers and Other Strangers," "The First Warning," "Warringham Roof," "God Bless You, Mr. Rosewater," Bdwy 1977 in "Gemini."

DeSHIELDS, ANDRE. Born Jan. 12, 1946 in Baltimore, MD. Graduate U Wisc. Bdwy debut 1973 in "Warp," followed by "Rachel Lily Rosenbloom," "The Wiz," "Ain't Misbehavin'." OB in "2008½."

DEVLIN, JAY. Born May 8, 1929 in Ft. Dodge, Ia. OB in "The Mad Show," "Little Murders," "Unfair to Goliath," "Ballymurphy," Bdwy 1978 in "King of Hearts."

DeVRIES, JON. Born Mar. 26, 1947 in NYC. Graduate Bennington Col., Pasadena Playhouse. Debut 1977 OB in "The Cherry Orchard," followed by "Agamemnon," Bdwy in "The Inspector General."

DEWHURST, COLLEEN. Born June 3, 1926 in Montreal, Can. Attended Downer Col., AADA. Bdwy debut 1952 in "Desire under the Elms," followed by "Tamburlaine the Great," "Country Wife," "Caligula," "All the Way Home," "Great Day in the Morning," "Ballad of the Sad Cafe," "More Stately Mansions," "All Over," "Mourning Becomes Electra," "Moon for the Misbegotten," "Who's Afraid of Virginia Woolf?," "An Almost Perfect Person," OB in "Taming of the Shrew," "The Eagle Has Two Heads," "Camille," "Macbeth," "Children of Darkness" for which she received a Theatre World Award, "Antony and Cleopatra" (CP), "Hello and Goodbye," "Good Woman of Setzuan" (LC), "Hamlet" (NYSF), "Are You Now or Have You Ever Been," "Taken in Marriage."

DILLON, MIA. Born July 9, 1955 in Colorado Springs, CO. Graduate Penn State U. Bdwy debut 1977 in "Equus," followed by "Da," OB in "The Crucible."

DISHY, BOB. Born in Brooklyn, NY. Graduate Syracuse U. Bdwy debut 1955 in "Damn Yankees," followed by "Can-Can" (CC'62), "Flora the Red Menace," "Something Different," "The Goodbye People," "A Way of Life," "The Creation of the World and Other Business," "American Millionaire," "Sly Fox," "Murder at the Howard Johnson's," OB in "Chic," "When the Owl Screams," "Wrecking Ball," "By Jupiter," "Unknown Soldier and His Wife."

DITTMAN, DEAN. Born Sept. 12, 1932 in Frontenac, KS. Attended Kan. State Col., Sorbonne. Bdwy debut 1958 in "Most Happy Fella," followed by Music Man," "Sunday Man," "On the 20th Century," OB in "The Cradle Will Rock."

DIXON, MacINTYRE. Born Dec. 22, 1931 in Everett, MA. Emerson Col. graduate. OB in "Quare Fellow," "Plays for Bleecker Street," "Stewed Prunes," "Cat's Pajamas," "Three Sisters," "3 X 3," "Second City," "Mad Show," "Meow!," "Lotta," "Rubbers," "Conjuring an Event," Bdwy in "Xmas in Las Vegas," "Cop-Out," "Story Theatre," "Metamorphoses," "Twigs," "Over Here!," "Once in a Lifetime."

DON, CARL. Born Dec. 15, 1916 in Vitebsk, Russia. Attended Western Reserve U. Bdwy debut 1954 in "Anastasia," followed by "Romanoff and Juliet," "Dear Me, the Sky Is Falling," "The Relapse," "The Tenth Man," "Zalmen," "Wings," OB in "Richard III," "Twelfth Night," "Winterset," "Arms and the Man," "Between Two Thieves," "He Who Gets Slapped," "Jacobowsky and the Colonel," "Carnival."

DONHOWE, GWYDA. Born Oct. 20, 1933 in Oak Park, IL. Attended Drake U., Goodman Th. Bdwy debut 1957 in "Separate Tables," followed by "Half a Sixpence," "The Flip Side," "Paris Is Out," "Applause," with APA in "The Show-Off," "War and Peace," "Right You are," and "You Can't Take It with You," "Shadow Box," "A Broadway Musical," OB in "Philosophy in the Boudoir," "Rondelay," "How Far Is It to Babylon?"

DONNELLY, DONAL. Born July 6, 1931 in Bradford, Eng. Bdwy debut 1966 in "Philadelphia, Here I Come!," followed by "A Day in the Death of Joe Egg," "Sleuth," "The Faith Healer," Bdwy OB in "My Astonishing Self."

DONNET, MARY. Born July 18, 1953 in Englewood, NJ. Graduate Sarah Lawrence Col. Debut OB in "La Ronde."

DORRIN, JOHN. Born July 17, 1920 in Omaha, NE. Attended Los Angeles City Col. Bdwy debut 1944 in "Song of Norway," followed by "Silk Stockings," "Most Happy Fella," "Best Man," "My Fair Lady," "What Makes Sammy Run?," "Fade Out, Fade In," "Carousel," "Annie Get Your Gun," "Finian's Rainbow," "St. Joan," "I'm Solomon," "Oklahoma" (JB), "New Girl in Town" (ELT), "Gigi," "Show Boat" (JB), "Knickerbocker Holiday," "Finian's Rainbow" (JB), "I Remember Mama."

DOUGLAS, LUCIEN. (Formerly Lucien Zabielski) Born Aug. 5, 1949 in Torrington, Ct. Graduate UConn., RADA. Debut OB 1972 in "Hope Is the Thing with Feathers," followed by "Naked," "Under Milk Wood," "The Tempest," "Candida."

DOVA, NINA. Born Jan. 15, 1926 in London, Eng. Attended Neighborhood Playhouse. Debut 1954 OB in "I Feel Wonderful," followed by "A Delicate Balance," "Naked," "Strider," Bdwy in "Zorba," "The Rothschilds," "Saturday Sunday Monday."

DOWD, M'EL. Born Feb. 2 in Chicago, Il. Attended Goodman Theatre. OB in "Macbeth," "A Midsummer Night's Dream," "Romeo and Juliet," "Julius Caesar," "Royal Gambit," "The Emperor," "Invitation to a Beheading," "Mercy Street," "Gun Play," "Songs from the City Streets," Bdwy debut 1958 in "Methuselah," followed by "A Case of Libel," "Sweet Bird of Youth," "Camelot," "The Right Honourable Gentleman," "Sound of Music" (CC), LCRep's "Unknown Soldier and His Wife" and "Tiger at the Gates," "Everything in the Garden," "Dear World," "Not Now, Darling," "Ambassador."

DOYLE, LEE H. Born Apr. 20, 1928 in Cleveland, Oh. Attended Tokyo U. Debut 1965 OB in "By Jupiter," followed by "Threepenny Opera," "Here Come the Clowns," "Woyzeck," "Miss Stanwyck Is Still in Hiding," Bdwy 1976 in "Going Up."

DRIVER, JOHN. Born Jan. 16, 1947 in Erie, Pa. Graduate Smith Col., Northwestern U. Debut OB 1972 in "One Flew over the Cuckoo's Nest," followed by "Scrambled Feet," Bdwy in "Grease" (1973), "Over Here" for which he received a Theatre World Award.

DRUM, LEONARD. Born Feb. 21 in Pittsfield, MA. Graduate UNMex., Columbia. Bdwy debut in "Kaleidoscope," "The Golden Six," "On the Town," "O Marry Me!," "The Giants' Dance," "Gay Divorce," Bdwy 1967 in "Marat/deSade." (1967), "Whoopee!"

DUELL, WILLIAM. Born Aug. 30, in Corinth, NY. Attended Ill. Wesleyan, Yale. OB in "Portrait of the Artist . . . ," "Barroom Monks," "Midsummer Night's Dream," "Henry IV," "Taming of the Shrew," "The Memorandum," "Threepenny Opera," Bdwy in "A Cook for Mr. General," "Ballad of the Sad Cafe," "Ilya, Darling," "1776," "Kings," "Stages," "The Inspector General."

DUFFY, JULIA. Born June 27, 1951 in St. Paul, Mn. Graduate AADA. Bdwy debut 1978 in "Once in a Lifetime."

DUKES, DAVID. Born June 6, 1945 in San Francisco, Ca. Attended Mann Col. Bdwy debut 1971 in "School for Wives," followed by "Don Juan," "The Play's the Thing," "The Visit," "Chemin de Fer," "Holiday," "Rules of the Game," "Love for Love," "Travesties," "Dracula," OB in "Rebel Women."

DUNAGAN, DEANNA. Born May 25 in Monahans, Tx. Graduate UTx, Trinity U. Bdwy debut 1979 in "Man and Superman."

EASTERBROOK, LESLIE. Born July 29, 1949 in Los Angeles, CA. Stephens Col. graduate. Bdwy debut 1976 in "California Suite," followed by "On the 20th Century."

eda-YOUNG, BARBARA. Born Jan. 30, 1945 in Detroit, Mi. Bdwy debut 1968 in "Lovers and Other Strangers," OB in "The Hawk," LCRep's "The Time of Your Life," "Camino Real," "Operation Sidewinder," "Kool Aid" and "A Streetcar Named Desire," "The Gathering," "The Terrorists," "Drinks before Dinner."

EDMEAD, WENDY. Born July 6, 1956 in NYC. Graduate NYCU. Bdwy debut 1974 in "The Wiz," followed by "Stop the World . . ."

EDWARDS, BRANDT. Born Mar. 22, 1947 in Holly Springs, MS. Graduate UMiss. NY debut off and on Bdwy 1975 in "A Chorus Line."

ELKIN, PAUL M. Born Jan. 8, 1953 in New Haven, Ct. Graduate Boston Cons., Southern Ct. State Col. Bdwy debut 1979 in "Whoopee!"

ELLIOTT, PATRICIA. Born July 21, 1942 in Gunnison, CO. Graduate U. Colo., London Academy. Debut with LCRep 1968 in "King Lear," and "A Cry of Players," followed OB in "Henry V," "The Persians," "A Doll's House," "Hedda Gabler," "In Case of Accident," "Water Hen," "Polly," "But Not for Me," "By Bernstein," "Prince of Homburg," "Artichokes," Bdwy bow 1973 in "A Little Night Music" for which she received a Theatre World Award, followed by "The Shadow Box," "Tartuffe," "13 Rue de L'Amour."

ENGSTROM, JON. Born in Fresno, Ca. Bdwy debut 1971 in "No, No, Nanette," followed by "The Pajama Game," "Very Good Eddie," OB in "Tip-Toes."

ENO, TERRY. Born June 5, 1946 in Miami, FL. Attended Miami U., HB Studio. Bdwy debut in "Irene," followed by "Good News," OB in "Buy Bonds Buster," "Joseph and the Amazing Technicolor Dreamcoat," "Sing Melancholy Baby."

ENSSLEN, DICK. Born Dec. 19, 1926 in Reading PA. Attended Musical Theatre Academy. Bdwy debut 1964 in "Anyone Can Whistle," followed by "Bajour," "Education of Hyman Kaplan," "Canterbury Tales," "Desert Song," "Annie," "I Remember Mama."

EPSTEIN, DIANE. Born Jan. 26, 1951 in Brooklyn, NY. Graduate Bronx Com. Col. Bdwy debut in "Whoopee!"

EPSTEIN, PIERRE. Born July 27, 1930 in Toulouse, France. Graduate UParis, Columbia. Bdwy bow 1962 in "A Shot in the Dark," followed by "Enter Laughing," "Bajour," "Black Comedy," "Thieves," "Fun City," OB in "Incident at Vichy," "Threepenny Opera," "Too Much Johnson," "Second City," "People vs. Ranchman," "Promenade," "Cakes with Wine," "Little Black Sheep," "Comedy of Errors," "A Memory of Two Mondays," "They Knew What They Wanted," "Museum," "The Bright and Golden Land," "Manny."

ERIC, DAVID. Born Feb. 28, 1949 in Boston, MA. Graduate Neighborhood Playhouse. Debut OB 1971 in "Ballad of Johnny Pot," followed by "Love Me, Love My Children," "Oklahoma!," Bdwy in "Yentl" (1975), "Shenandoah."

ERNEST, PATRICA. Born Dec. 26, 1951 in Far Rockaway, NY. Graduate Manhattan Sch. of Music. Debut 1978 OB in "Mlle. Modiste," followed by "Martha," "The Grand Duke," "The Merry Widow."

ERWIN, BARBARA. Born June 30, 1937 in Boston, MA. Debut 1973 OB in "The Secret Life of Walter Mitty," followed by "Broadway," Bdwy 1977 in "Annie," followed by "Ballroom."

ESAU, KEITH. Born Sept. 1, 1958 in Brooklyn, NY. Attended Juilliard. Debut 1979 OB in "Julius Caesar," followed by "Coriolanus."

ESPEL, PAUL. Born Aug. 17, 1947 in Clarksburg, WVa. Graduate Villanova U., Neighborhood Playhouse. Bdwy debut 1975 in "The Ritz," OB in "G. R. Point."

ESTERMAN, LAURA. Born Apr. 12, in NYC. Attended Radcliffe, LAMDA. Debut 1969 OB in "The Time of Your Life" (LCR), followed by "Pig Pen," "The Carpenters," "Ghosts," "Waltz of the Toreadors," "Macbeth" (LC), "The Seagull," "Rubbers," "Yanks 3, Detroit 0," "Golden Boy," "Out of Our Father's House," "The Master and Margarita," "Chinchilla," Bdwy 1974 "God's Favorite."

ESTES, MICHAEL P. Born July 10, 1955 in St. Louis, Mo. Attended Butler U. Debut 1978 OB in "Can-Can," followed by "Mary."

EVANS, PETER. Born May 22, 1950 in Englewood, NJ. Graduate Yale, London Central School of Speech. Debut OB 1975 in "Life Class," followed by "Streamers," "A Life in the Theatre," "Don Juan Comes Back from the War."

EVERETT, TOM. Born Oct. 21, 1948 in Oregon. Graduate NYU, LAMDA. Debut 1972 OB in "Elizabeth I," followed by "Boccaccio," "Hosanna," "A Midsummer Night's Dream," "A Life in the Theatre," "Winning Isn't Everything," "Rockaway Boulevard," Bdwy in "Habeas Corpus."

FABER, RON. Born Feb. 16, 1933 in Milwaukee, Wi. Graduate Marquette U. Debut OB 1959 in "An Enemy of the People," followed by "The Exception and the Rule," "America, Hurrah," "Ubu Cocu," "Terminal," "They Put Handcuffs on Flowers," "Sr. Selavy's Magic Theatre," "Troilus and Cressida," "The Beauty Part," "Woyzeck," "St. Joan of the Stockyards," Bdwy in "Medea" (1973), "First Monday in October."

FABIANI, JOEL. Born Sept. 28, 1936 in Watsonville, Ca. Attended LaSierra, Actors Workshop. Debut 1963 OB in "Dark Corners," followed by "Ashes," "I'm Getting My Act Together . . .," Bdwy in "Love for Love," "Beyond the Fringe," "Rules of the Game."

FALKENHAIN, PATRICA. Born Dec. 3, 1926 in Atlanta, Ga. Graduate Carnegie-Mellon, NYU. Debut 1946 OB in "Juno and the Paycock," followed by "Hamlet," "She Stoops to Conquer," "Peer Gynt," "Henry IV," "The Plough and the Stars," "Lysistrata," "Beaux Stratagem," "The Power and the Glory," Bdwy in "Waltz of the Toreadors," "The Utter Glory of Morrissey Hall."

FALZONE, PAUL. Born May 18, 1947 in St. Louis, Mo. Attended AADA. Debut 1978 OB in "The International Stud."

FAYE, JOEY. Born July 12, 1910 in NYC. Bdwy bow 1938 in "Sing Out the News," followed by "Room Service," "Meet the People," "The Man Who Came to Dinner," "Milky Way," "Boy Meets Girl," "Streets of Paris," "Allah Be Praised," "The Duchess Misbehaves," "Tidbits of 1948," "High Button Shoes," "Top Banana," "Tender Trap," "Man of LaMancha," "70 Girls 70," OB in "Lyle," "Naomi Court," "Awake and Sing," "Coolest Cat in Town."

FEAGAN, LESLIE. Born Jan. 9, 1951 in Hinckley, Oh. Graduate Ohio U. Debut 1978 OB in "Can-Can."

FELDSHUH, TOVAH. Born Dec. 27. Graduate Sarah Lawrence Col. Bdwy debut 1973 in "Cyrano," followed by "Dreyfus in Rehearsal," "Rodgers and Hart," "Yentl" for which she received a Theatre World Award, "Sarava," OB in "Yentl the Yeshiva Boy," "Straws in the Wind," "Three Sisters."

FERGUSON, LOU. Born Aug. 8, 1944 in Trinidad, WI. Debut OB 1970 in "A Season in the Congo," followed by "Night World," "La Gente," "Shoe Shine Parlor," "The Defense," "Rum an' Coca Cola," "Remembrance."

Diane Epstein **Daniel S. Fortus**

FERRER, JOSE. Born Jan. 8, 1912 in Santurce, PR. Princeton graduate. Bdwy debut 1935 in "A Slight Case of Murder," followed by "Spring Dance," "Brother Rat," "In Clover," "How to Get Tough about It," "Missouri Legend," "Mamba's Daughters," "Key Largo," "Charley's Aunt," "Vickie," "Let's Face It," "Othello," "Cyrano de Bergerac," "Volpone," "Angel Street," "Four One-Act Comedies," "The Alchemist," "The Long Voyage Home," "Insect Comedy," "Silver Whistle," "20th Century," "The Shrike," "Richard III," "Edwin Booth," "The Girl Who Came to Supper," "Man of La Mancha," OB in "A Life in the Theatre," "White Pelicans."

FISHER, DOUGLAS. Born July 9, 1934 in Brooklyn, NY. Attended St. John's U, AADA. Debut 1963 OB in "Best Food Forward," followed by "Frere Jacques," "Devil's Disciple," "Accent on Youth," "Lost in the Stars," "Say, Darling," "Shoestring Revue," "Penthouse Legend," "Call Me Madam," "Marjorie Daw," "God Bless You, Mr. Rosewater."

FISKE, ELLEN. Born May 1 in Paterson, NJ. Graduate Wilmington Col., Ohio U. Debut 1974 OB in "Arms and the Man," followed by "La Ronde," Bdwy in "The Royal Family."

FITZGERALD, FERN. Born Jan. 7, 1947 in Valley Stream, NY. Bdwy debut 1976 in "Chicago," followed by "A Chorus Line."

FITZGERALD, GERALDINE. Born Nov. 24, 1914 in Dublin, Ire. Bdwy debut 1938 in "Heartbreak House," followed by "Sons and Soldiers," "Doctor's Dilemma," "King Lear," "Hide and Seek," "Ah, Wilderness," "The Shadow Box," "A Touch of the Poet," OB in "Cave Dwellers," "Pigeons," "Long Day's Journey into Night," "Everyman and Roach," "Streetsongs."

FLAGG, TOM. Born Mar. 30, 1949 in Canton, Oh. Attended Kent State U., AADA. Debut 1975 OB in "The Fantasticks," followed by "Give Me Liberty," Bdwy in "Legend," "Shenandoah," "Players."

FLANAGAN, PAULINE. Born June 29, 1925 in Sligo, Ir. Debut 1958 OB in "Ulysses in Nighttown," followed by "Pictures in the Hallway," "LCRep's "Antigone," "The Crucible," and "The Plough and the Stars," "Later," Bdwy in "God and Kate Murphy," "The Living Room," "The Innocents."

FOGT, JULIE ANN. Born Apr. 4, 1953 in Galion, Oh. Attended UCincinnati. Debut 1979 OB in "On a Clear Day You can See Forever."

FONDA, HENRY. Born May 16, 1905 in Grand Island, Ne. Attended UMinn. Bdwy debut 1929 in "Game of Love and Death," followed by "I Loved You Wednesday," "Forsaking All Others," "New Faces of 1934," "The Farmer Takes a Wife," "Mr. Roberts," "Point of No Return," "Caine Mutiny Court Martial," "Two for the Seesaw," "Silent Night, Lonely Night," "Critics Choice," "A Gift of Time," "Generation," "Our Town," "Clarence Darrow," "First Monday in October."

FORD, CLEBERT. Born Jan. 29, 1932 in Brooklyn, NY. Graduate CCNY, Boston U. Bdwy debut 1960 in "The Cool World," followed by "Les Blancs," "Ain't Supposed to Die a Natural Death," "Via Galactica," "Bubbling Brown Sugar," "The Last Minstrel Show," OB in "Romeo and Juliet," "Antony and Cleopatra," "Ti-Jean and His Brothers," "The Blacks," "Ballad for Bimshire," "Daddy," "Gilbeau," "Coriolanus."

FORSYTHE, HENDERSON. Born Sept. 11, 1917 in Macon, MO. Attended UIowa. OB in "The Iceman Cometh," "The Collection," "The Room," "A Slight Ache," "Happiness Cage," "Waiting for Godot," "In Case of Accident," "Not I" (LC), "An Evening with the Poet-Senator," "Museum," "How Far Is It to Babylon?," Bdwy in "The Cellar and the Well," "Miss Lonelyhearts," "Who's Afraid of Virginia Woolf?," "Malcolm," "Right Honourable Gentleman," "Delicate Balance," "Birthday Party," "Harvey," "Engagement Baby," "Freedom of the City," "Texas Trilogy," "The Best Little Whorehouse in Texas."

FORTUS, DANIEL. Born Jan. 6, 1953 in Brooklyn, NY. Bdwy debut 1963 in "Oliver," followed by "Minnie's Boys," "Molly," OB in "Friends and Enemies," "A Day in the Life of just about Everyone," "2 by 5," "Pins and Needles."

FOSTER, FRANCES. Born June 11 in Yonkers, NY. Bdwy debut 1955 in "The Western Trees," followed by "Nobody Loves an Albatross," "Raisin in the Sun," "The River Niger," "First Breeze of Summer," OB in "Take a Giant Step," "Edge of the City," "Tammy and the Doctor," "The Crucible," "Happy Ending," "Day of Absence," "An Evening of One Acts," "Man Better Man," "Brotherhood," "Akokawe," "Rosalee Pritchett," "Sty of the Blind Pig," "Ballet Behind the Bridge," "Good Woman of Setzuan" (LC), "Behold! Cometh the Vanderkellans," "Orrin," "Boesman and Lena," "Do Lord Remember Me," "Nevis Mountain Dew," "Daughters of the Mock."

FOSTER, GLORIA. Born Nov. 15, 1936 in Chicago, IL. Attended IllStateU, Goodman Th. Debut 1963 OB in "In White America," followed by "Medea" for which she received a Theatre World Award, "Yerma," "A Hand Is on the Gate," "Black Visions," "The Cherry Orchard," "Agamemnon," "Coriolanus."

FOX, BERNARD M. Born May 11, 1927 in Port Talbot, S. Wales. Bdwy debut 1978 in "13 Rue de L'Amour."

FRANCINE, ANNE. Born Aug. 8, 1917 in Philadelphia, Pa. Bdwy debut 1945 in "Marriage is for Single People," followed by "By the Beautiful Sea," "Great Sebastians," "Tenderloin," "Mame," "A Broadway Musical," OB in "Guitar," "Valmouth," "Asylum," "Are You Now or Have You . . ."

FRANCIS-JAMES, PETER. Born Sept. 16, 1956 in Chicago, Il. Attended Hampshire Col., graduate RADA. Debut 1979 OB in "Julius Caesar."

FRANKLIN, NANCY. Born in NYC. Debut 1959 OB in "Buffalo Skinner," followed by "Power of Darkness," "Oh, Dad, Poor Dad . . . ," "Theatre of Peretz," "Seven Days of Mourning," "Here Be Dragons," "Beach Children," "Safe Place," "Innocent Pleasures," Bdwy in "Never Live over a Pretzel Factory," "Happily Never After," "The White House."

FRANKS, LAURIE. Born Aug. 14, 1929 in Lucasville, Or. Bdwy debut 1956 in "Bells Are Ringing," followed by "Copper and Brass," "Pleasures and Palaces," "Something More," "Anya," "Mame," "The Utter Glory of Morrissey Hall," OB in "Leave It to Jane."

FRANZ, ELIZABETH. Born June 18, 1941 in Akron, OH. Attended AADA. Debut 1965 in "In White America," followed by "One Night Stands of a Noisy Passenger," "The Real Inspector Hound," "Augusta," Bdwy in "Rosencrantz and Guildenstern Are Dead," "The Cherry Orchard."

FREEMAN, AL, JR. Born Mar. 21, 1934 in San Antonio, TX. Attended CCLA. Bdwy in "The Long Dream," "Tiger, Tiger Burning Bright," "Living Premise," "Blues for Mr. Charlie," "Dozens," "Look to the Lilies," OB in "Slave," "Dutchman," "Trumpets of the Lord," "Medea," "The Great MacDaddy," "One Crack Out."

FREEMAN, ANN. Born in Portsmouth, Eng. Bdwy debut 1967 in "Life with Father," followed by OB's "Present Laughter," "The Home," "The Crucible."

FREEMAN, ARNY. Born Aug. 28, 1908 in Chicago, IL. Bdwy bow 1949 in "A Streetcar Named Desire," followed by "The Great Sebastians," "Tall Story," "Hot Spot," "What Makes Sammy Run?," "Cactus Flower," "Minnie's Boys," "Much Ado about Nothing," "Sunshine Boys," "Working," OB in "Gay Divorce," "Dream Girl," "The Shrike," "Gun Play."

FREEMAN, JONATHAN. Born Feb. 5, 1950 in Bay Village, Oh. Graduate Ohio U. Debut 1974 OB in "The Miser," followed by Bill Baird Marionette Theatre, "Babes in Arms," Bdwy in "Sherlock Holmes," "Platinum."

FREEMAN, MORGAN. Born June 1, 1937 in Memphis, TN. Attended LACC. Bdwy bow 1967 in "Hello, Dolly!," followed by "The Mighty Gents," OB in "Ostrich Feathers," "Niggerlovers," "Exhibition," "Black Visions," "Cockfight," "White Pelicans," "Julius Caesar," "Coriolanus."

FRENCH, ARTHUR. Born in NYC. Attended Brooklyn Col. Debut 1962 OB in "Raisin' Hell in the Sun," followed by "Ballad of Bimshire," "Day of Absence," "Happy Ending," "Jonah," "Black Girl," "Ceremonies in Dark Old Men," "An Evening of One Acts," "Man Better Man," "Brotherhood," "Perry's Mission," "Rosalee Pritchett," "Moonlight Arms," "Dark Tower," "Brownsville Raid," "Nevis Mt. Dew," "Julius Caesar," Bdwy in "Ain't Supposed to Die a Natural Death," "The Iceman Cometh," "All God's Chillun Got Wings."

FRIEDMAN, PETER. Born Apr. 24, 1949 in NYC. Graduate Hofstra U. Debut 1971 OB in "James Joyce Memorial Liquid Theatre," followed by "Big and Little," Bdwy in "The Visit," "Chemin de Fer," "Love for Love," "Rules of the Game."

FULLER, JANICE. Born June 4 in Oakland, Ca. Attended RADA. Debut OB 1975 in "Ice Age," followed by "A Night at the Black Pig," "Grand Magic."

FURRY, DALE. Born Nov. 25, 1952. Graduate E. Ill. U. Debut 1979 OB in "On a Clear Day You Can See Forever."

GABLE, JUNE. Born June 5, 1945 in NYC. Carnegie Tech graduate. OB in "Macbird," "Jacques Brel Is Alive and Well . . .," "A Day in the Life of Just about Everyone," "Mod Donna." "Wanted," "Lady Audley's Secret," "Comedy of Errors," "Chinchilla," Bdwy in "Candide" (1974).

GAFFIGAN, CATHERINE. Born Dec. 25 in NYC: graduate Catholic U. Debut 1966 OB in "Journey of the Fifth Horse," followed by Bdwy 1979 in "Whose Life Is It Anyway?"

GALIANO, JOSEPH. Born Mar. 26, 1944 in Beaumont, TX. Graduate SMU. Debut 1976 OB in "The Fantasticks."

GALLAGHER, HELEN. Born in 1926 in Brooklyn, NY. Bdwy debut 1947 in "Seven Lively Arts," followed by "Mr. Strauss Goes to Boston," "Billion Dollar Baby," "Brigadoon," "High Button Shoes," "Touch and Go," "Make a Wish," "Pal Joey," "Guys and Dolls," "Finian's Rainbow," "Oklahoma!," "Pajama Game," "Bus Stop," "Portofino," "Sweet Charity," "Mame," "Cry for Us All," "No, No, Nanette," "A Broadway Musical," OB in "Hothouse," "Tickles by Tucholsky," "The Misanthrope."

GARBER, VICTOR. Born Mar. 16, 1949 in London, Can. Debut 1973 OB in "Ghosts" for which he received a Theatre World Award, followed by "Joe's Opera," "Cracks," Bdwy in "Tartuffe," "Deathtrap," "Sweeney Todd."

GARDENIA, VINCENT. Born Jan. 7, 1923 in Naples, Italy. Debut 1955 OB in "In April Once," followed by "Man with the Golden Arm," "Volpone," "Brothers Karamazov," "Power of Darkness," "Machinal," "Gallows Humor," "Theatre of the Absurd," "The Lunatic View," "Little Murders," "Pass-

ing Through from Exotic Places," "The Carpenters," Bdwy in "The Visit" (1958), "Rashomon," "The Cold Wind and the Warm," "Only in America," "The Wall," "Daughter of Silence," "Seidman & Son," "Dr. Fish," "Prisoner of Second Avenue," "God's Favorite," "California Suite," "Ballroom."

GARDNER, BRENDA Born Nov. 1, 1944 in Lynn, Ma. Graduate Boston U. Debut OB 1967 with American Savoyards, followed by "Wings," "My Old Friends," Bdwy in "Shenandoah," "Grease."

GARDNER, JEANNETTE. Born in Kinston, NC. Graduate Greensboro Col. Debut 1974 OB in "I'll Die if I Can't Live Forever," followed by "Carnival," "Musical Brittania."

GARFIELD, DAVID. Born Feb. 6, 1941 in Brooklyn, NY. Graduate Columbia, Cornell U. OB in "Hang Down Your Head and Die," "Government Inspector," "Old Ones," "Family Business," Bdwy in "Fiddler on the Roof," "The Rothschilds."

GARRETT, BOB. Born Mar. 2, 1947 in NYC. Graduate Adelphi U. Debut OB 1971 in "Godspell," Bdwy in "Grease."

GARY, HAROLD. Born May 7, 1910 in NYC. Bdwy bow 1928 in "Diamond Lil," followed by "Crazy with the Heat," "A Flag Is Born," "Guys and Dolls," "Oklahoma!," "Arsenic and Old Lace," "Billion Dollar Baby," "Fiesta," "The World We Make," "Born Yesterday," "Will Success Spoil Rock Hunter?," "Let It Ride," "Counting House," "Arturo Ui," "A Thousand Clowns," "Enter Laughing," "Illya, Darling," "The Price," "The Sunshine Boys," "Pal Joey."

GATES, LARRY. Born Sept. 24, 1915 in St. Paul, Mn. Attended UMinn. Bdwy bow 1939 in "Speak of the Devil," followed by "Twelfth Night," "Bell, Book and Candle," "Taming of the Shrew," "Love of Four Colonels," "Teahouse of the August Moon," "Sing Me No Lullaby," "Carefree Tree," "Poor Murderer," "First Monday in October," OB in "A Case of Libel," "Carving a Statue," "Hamlet."

GAVON, IGORS. Born Nov. 14, 1937 in Latvia. Bdwy bow 1961 in "Carnival," followed by "Hello, Dolly!" "Marat/deSade," "Billy," "Sugar," "Mack and Mabel," "Musical Jubilee," OB in "Your Own Thing," "Promenade," "Exchange," "Nevertheless They Laugh," "Polly," "The Boss," "Biography: A Game," "Strider."

GEFFNER, DEBORAH. Born Aug. 26, 1952 in Pittsburgh, PA. Attended Juilliard, HB Studio. Debut 1978 OB in "Tenderloin," Bdwy in "Pal Joey," "A Chorus Line."

GELFER, STEVEN. Born Feb. 21, 1949 in Brooklyn, NY. Graduate NYU, Ind.U. Debut 1968 OB in "West Side Story," followed by "Beggar's Opera," "Do I Hear a Waltz?," "American Dance Machine," Bdwy in "Gypsy" (1974), "Whoopee!"

GELKE, BECKY. Born Feb. 17, 1953 in Ft. Knox, KY. Graduate Western Ky.U. Debut 1978 OB and Bdwy in "The Best Little Whorehouse in Texas."

GENEST, EDMOND. Born Oct. 27, 1943 in Boston, Ma. Attended Suffolk U. Debut 1972 OB in "The Real Inspector Hound," Bdwy in "Dirty Linen/New-Found Land," "Whose Life Is It Anyway?"

GHOSTLEY, ALICE. Born Aug. 14, 1926 in Eve, Mo. Attended UOkla. Bdwy debut in "New Faces of 1952," followed by "Sandhog," "Livin' the Life," "Trouble in Tahiti," "Shangri-La," "Maybe Tuesday," "Thurber Carnival," "The Beauty Part," "The Sign in Sidney Brustein's Window," "Love Is a Ball," "Annie."

GIBSON, KAREN. (formerly Karen Zenker). Born Jan. 9 in Columbus, Oh. Attended Ohio State U. Debut 1975 OB in "The Three Musketeers," followed by Bdwy in "My Fair Lady" (1976), "On the 20th Century," "The Utter Glory of Morrisey Hall."

GIERASCH, STEFAN. Born Feb. 5, 1926 in NYC. On Bdwy in "Kiss and Tell," "Snafu," "Billion Dollar Baby," "Montserrat," "Night Music," "Hatful of Rain," "Compulsion," "Shadow of a Gunman," "War and Peace," "Of Mice and Men," "Tartuffe," OB in "7 Days of Mourning," "AC/DC," "Owners," "Nellie Toole & Co." "The Iceman Cometh," "Man with a Flower in His Mouth," "Old Tune."

GILDIN, KENNETH. Born Feb. 2, 1955 in NYC. Graduate Tufts U. Debut 1978 OB in "Oklahoma!" followed by "On a Clear Day You Can See Forever."

GILLETTE, ANITA. Born Aug. 16, 1938 in Baltimore, MD. Debut 1960 OB in "Russell Patterson's Sketchbook" for which she received a Theatre World Award, followed by Bdwy's "Carnival," "All American," "Mr. President," "Guys and Dulls" (CC), "Don't Drink the Water," "Cabaret," "Jimmy," "Rich and Famous" (OB), "Chapter Two."

GINGOLD, HERMIONE. Born Dec. 9, 1897 in London, Eng. Bdwy debut 1953 in "John Murray Anderson's Almanac," followed by "Sleeping Prince," "First Impressions," "From A to Z," "Milk and Honey," "Oh, Dad, Poor Dad, Mama's Hung You . . . ," "A Little Night Music," "Side by Side by Sondheim."

GIOMBETTI, KAREN. Born May 24, 1955 in Scranton, Pa. Graduate NYU. Debut 1978 in "Stop the World. I want to Get Off."

GIOVANNI, PAUL. Born Oct 25, 1940 in Atlantic City, NJ. Graduate St. Joseph Col., Catholic U. Bdwy debut 1978 in "Crucifer of Blood."

GLANVILLE, MAXWELL. Born Feb. 11, 1918 in Antigua, BWI. Attended New School. Bdwy debut 1946 in "Walk Hard," followed by "Anna Lucasta," "How Long Till Summer," "Freight," "Autumn Garden," "Take a Giant Step," "Cat on a Hot Tin Roof," "Simply Heavenly," "Interlock," "Cool World," "The Strike," "Golden Boy," "We Bombed in New Haven," "Zelda," OB in over 250 plays including "The Blacks," "Nat Turner," "Simple," "Lady Day," "Penance," "Anna Lucasta."

GLEASON, PAUL. Born May 4, 1941 in Miami, FL. Graduate Fla. State U.

Debut 1973 OB in "One Flew Over the Cuckoo's Nest," followed by "Economic Necessity," "Niagra Falls," "Alfred th Great," "The Violano Virtuoso."

GLYNN, CARLIN. Born Feb. 19, 1940 in Cleveland, OH. Attended Sophie Newcomb Col., Actors Studio. Debut 1959 OB in "Waltz of the Toreadors," Bdwy debut 1978 in "The Best Little Whorehouse in Texas" for which she received a Theatre World Award.

GODFREY, LYNNIE. Born Sept. 11, 1952 in NYC. Hunter Col. graduate. Debut 1976 OB in "I Paid My Dues," Bdwy 1978 in "Eubie!"

GODREAU, MIGUEL. Born Oct. 17, 1946 in Puerto Rico. Appeared with Alvin Ailey Dance Co., Harkness Ballet, Bdwy in "Dear World," "Timbuktu."

GOLDBLUM, JEFF. Born Oct. 22, 1952 in Pittsburgh, Pa. Attended Neighborhood Playhouse. Debut 1971 on Bdwy in "Two Gentlemen of Verona," OB in "El Grande de Coca Cola," "Our Late Night," "City Sugar."

GOLDSMITH, MERWIN. Born Aug. 7, 1937 in Detroit, Mi. Graduate UCLA, Old Vic. Bdwy debut 1970 in "Minnie's Boys," followed by "The Visit," "Chemin de Fer," "Rex," "Dirty Linen," OB in "Hamlet as a Happening," "Chickencoop Chinaman," "Wanted," "Comedy," "Rubbers," "Yankees 3, Detroit 0," "Trelawny of the Wells," "Chinchilla."

GOODMAN, JOHN. Born June 20, 1952 in St. Louis, Mo. Graduate Southwest Mo. State U. Debut OB 1978 in "A Midsummer Night's Dream."

GORDON, KEITH. Born Feb. 3, 1961 in NYC. Debut 1976 OB in "Secrets of the Rich," followed by "A Traveling Companion," "Suckers," "Gimme Shelter."

GORMAN CLIFF. Born Oct. 13, 1936 in NYC. Attended UCLA. OB in "Hogan's Goat," "Boys in the Band," "Ergo," Bdwy in "Lenny," "Chapter Two."

GOUGH, MICHAEL. Born Nov. 23, 1917 in Malaya. Attended Old Vic School. Bdwy debut 1937 in "Love of Women," followed by "The Fighting Cock," "Bedroom Farce."

GOULD, GORDON. Born May 4, 1930 in Chicago, Il. Yale graduate. With APA in "Man and Superman," "War and Peace," "Judith," "Lower Depths," "Right You Are," "Scapin," "Impromptu at Versailles," "You Can't Take It with You," "The Hostage," "The Tavern," "A Midsummer Night's Dream," "Merchant of Venice," "Richard II," "Much Ado about Nothing," "Wild Duck," "The Show-Off," and "Pantagleize," OB in "Strider," Bdwy in "Freedom of the City."

GOULD, HAROLD. Born Dec. 10, 1923 in Schenectady, NY. Graduate SUNY, Cornell. NY bow in LC's "The Increased Difficulty of Concentration" and "Amphitryon," followed by OB in "House of Blue Leaves," "Touching Bottom."

GOUTMAN, CHRISTOPHER. Born Dec. 19, 1952 in Bryn Mawr, PA. Graduate Haverford Col., Carnegie-Mellon U. Debut 1978 OB in "The Promise" for which he received a Theatre World Award, followed by "Grand Magic."

GRACIE, SALLY. Born in Little Rock, Ar. Attended Neighborhood Playhouse. Bdwy debut 1942 in "Vickie," followed by "At War with the Army," "Dinosaur Wharf," "Goodbye Again," "Major Barbara," "Fair Game," "But Seriously," OB in "Naomi Court," "Dream Come True."

GRAFF, ILENE. Born Feb. 28 in NYC. Graduate Ithaca Col. Bdwy debut 1968 in "Promises, Promises," followed by "Grease," "I Love My Wife."

GRAFF, RANDY. Born May 23, 1955 in Brooklyn, NY. Graduate Wagner Col. Debut 1978 OB in "Pins and Needless," Bdwy in "Sarava," "Grease."

GRAHAM, DONNA. Born Sept. 28, 1964 in Philadelphia, PA. Bdwy debut 1977 in "Annie."

GRAMMIS, ADAM. Born Dec. 8, 1947 in Allentown, PA. Graduate Kutztown State Col. Bdwy debut 1971 in "Wild and Wonderful," followed by "Shirley MacLaine Show," "A Chorus Line," OB in "Dance Continuum," "Joseph and the Amazing Technicolor Dreamcoat."

GRANGER, JAN. Born Jan. 21, 1953 in Pasadena, Ca. Attended USCal., HB Studio. Debut 1978 OB in "A Midsummer Night's Dream."

GRAY, BRUCE. Born Sept. 7, 1936 in San Juan, PR. Graduate UToronto. Debut 1976 OB in "Who Killed Richard Cory?," followed by "Richard II," "Total Recall," "Winter Signs."

GREAN, ROBIN. Born Oct. 2, 1949 in NYC. Attended Ithaca Col., Marymount Col. Bdwy debut 1971 in "Jesus Christ Superstar," followed by "Bette Midler at the Palace," "Uzis on the ½ Shell," "Platinum."

GREEN, MARY-PAT. Born Sept. 24, 1951 in Kansas City, Mo. Attended UKan. Bdwy debut 1974 in "Candide," followed by "Sweeney Todd."

GREENE, ELLEN. Born Feb. 22 in NYC. Attended Ryder Col. Debut 1973 in "Rachel Lily Rosenbloom," followed OB by "In the Boom Boom Room," "Threepenny Opera," "The Nature and Purpose of the Universe."

GREENE, JAMES. Born Dec. 1, 1926 in Lawrence, MA. Graduate Emerson Col. OB In "The Iceman Cometh," "American Gothic," "The King and the Duke," "The Hostage," "Plays for Bleecker Street," "Moon in the Yellow River," "Misalliance," "Government Inspector," "Baba Goya," LCRep 2 years, "You Can't Take It with You," "School for Scandal," "Wild Duck," "Right You Are," "The Show-Off," "Pantagleize," "Festival of Short Plays," "Nourish the Beast," "One Crack Out," "Artichoke," Bdwy in "Romeo and Juliet," "Girl on the Via Flaminia," "Compulsion," "Inherit the Wind," "Shadow of a Gunman," "Andersonville Trial," "Night Life," "School for Wives," "Ring Round the Bathtub," "Great God Brown," "Don Juan."

GREENE, RICHARD. Born Jan. 8, 1946 in Miami, Fl. Graduate Fla. Atlantic U. Debut 1971 with LCRep in "Macbeth," followed by "Play Strindberg,"

"Mary Stuart," "Narrow Road to the Deep North," "Twelfth Night," and "The Crucible," "Family Business," Bdwy 1977 in "Romeo and Juliet."

GREGORIO, ROSE. Born in Chicago, Il. Graduate Northwestern, Yale. Debut 1962 OB in "The Days and Nights of Beebee Fenstermaker," followed by "Kiss Mama," "The Balcony," "Bivouac at Lucca," "Journey to the Day," "Diary of Anne Frank," Bdwy in "The Owl and the Pussycat," "Daphne in Cottage D," "Jimmy Shine," "The Cuban Thing," "The Shadow Box."

GREY, JOEL. Born Apr. 11, 1932 in Cleveland, Oh. Attended Cleveland Play House. Bdwy debut 1951 in "Borscht Capades," followed by "Come Blow Your Horn," "Stop the World—I Want to Get Off," "Half a Sixpence," "Cabaret," "George M!," "Goodtime Charley," "Grand Tour," OB in "The Littlest Revue," "Harry, Noon and Night," "Marco Polo Sings a Solo."

GRIMES, TAMMY. Born Jan. 30, 1934 in Lynn, MA. Attended Stephens Col., Neighborhood Playhouse. Debut 1956 OB in "The Littlest Revue," followed by "Clerambard," "Molly." "Trick," "Are You Now or Have You Ever Been," Bdwy in "Look after Lulu" (1959) for which she received a Theatre World Award, "The Unsinkable Molly Brown," "Rattle of a Simple Man," "High Spirits," "The Only Game in Town," "Private Lives," "Musical Jubilee," "California Suite," "Tartuffe."

GRIZZARD, GEORGE. Born Apr. 1, 1928 in Roanoke Rapids, VA. Graduate UNC. Bdwy bow 1954 in "All Summer Long," followed by "The Desperate Hours," "Happiest Millionaire" for which he received a Theatre World Award, "Disenchanted," "Big Fish, Little Fish," with APA 1961–62, "Who's Afraid of Virginia Woolf?," "Glass Menagerie," "You Know I Can't Hear You . . .," "Noel Coward's Sweet Potato," "Gingham Dog," "Inquest," "Country Girl," "Creation of the World and Other Business," "Crown Matrimonial," "The Royal Family," "California Suite", "Man and Superman."

GROH, DAVID. Born May 21, 1939 in NYC. Graduate Brown U., LAMDA. Debut 1963 OB in "The Importance of Being Eranest," followed by "Elizabeth the Queen"(CC), "The Hot 1 Baltimore," Bdwy in "Chapter Two."

GROLLMAN, ELAINE. Born Oct. 22, 1928 in The Bronx, NY. Debut 1974 OB in "Yentl the Yeshiva Boy," followed by "Kaddish," "The Water Hen," "Millions of Miles," "Come Back, Little Sheba," "Biography: A Game," Bdwy in "Yentl."

GROSS, MICHAEL. Born in 1947 in Chicago, Ill. UILL and Yale graduate. Debut 1978 OB in "Sganarelle."

GROSSMAN, HENRY. Born Oct. 11, 1938 in NYC. Studied at Actors Studio. Debut 1961 OB in "The Magistrate," followed by "Galileo."

GUERRASIO, JOHN. Born Feb. 18, 1950 in Brooklyn, NY. Attended Bklyn Col, Boston U. Debut 1971 OB in "Hamlet," followed by "And They Put Handcuffs on Flowers," "Eros and Psyche," "The Marriage Proposal," "Macbeth," "K," "Sunday Promenade," "Family Business."

GUEST, NICHOLAS. Born May 5, 1951 in NYC. Graduate New School. Debut 1974 OB in "Once in a Lifetime," followed by "Last Days of the Wichita Kid," "Out to Brunch," "A Midsummer Night's Dream."

GUIDA, MARIA. Born May 1, 1953 in Jackson Heights, NY. Graduate NYU. Debut 1972 OB in "Bread and Roses," followed by "Fallen Angeles," "Impromptu," "Dutchman," Bdwy in "King of Hearts."

GUIDALL, GEORGE. Born June 7, 1938 in Plainfield, NJ. Attended UBuffalo, AADA. Bdwy debut 1969 in "Wrong Way Light Bulb," followed by "Cold Storage," OB in "Counsellor-at-Law." "Taming of the Shrew," "All's Well That Ends Well."

GUITTARD, LAWRENCE. Born July 16, 1939 in San Francisco, Ca. Stanford U. graduate. Bdwy debut 1965 in "Baker Street," followed by "Anya," "Man of La Mancha," "A Little Night Music" for which he received a Theatre World Award, "Rodgers and Hart," "She Loves Me," OB in "Umbrellas of Cherbourg."

GULACK, MAX. Born May 19, 1928 in NYC. Graduate CCNY, Columbia U. Debut OB 1952 in "Bonds of Interest," followed by "Warrior's Husband," "Worm in the Horseradish," "Marcus in the High Grass," "Country Scandal," "Song for the First of May," "Threepenny Opera," "Taming of the Shrew."

GUNTON, BOB. Born Nov. 15, 1945 in Santa Monica, CA. Attended UCal. Debut 1971 OB in "Who Am I?," followed by "The Kid," "Desperate Hours," "Tip-Toes," Bdwy in "Happy End" (1977), "Working," "King of Hearts."

GUSKIN, PAUL. Born Sept. 12, 1939 in Brooklyn, NY. Attended Pratt Inst., HB Studio. Debut 1979 OB in "Manny."

GWYNNE, FRED. Born July 10, 1926 in NYC. Harvard graduate. Bdwy debut 1952 in "Mrs. McThing," followed by "Love's Labour's Lost," "Frogs of Spring," "Irma La Douce," "Here's Love," "The Lincoln Mask," "Cat on a Hot Tin Roof," "A Texas Trilogy," "Angel," "Players," OB in "More Than You Deserve," "Fair Game," "Grand Magic."

HADARY, JONATHAN. Born Oct. 11, 1948 in Chicago, Il. Attended Tufts U. Debut 1974 OB in "White Nights," followed by "El Grande de Coca-Cola," "Songs from Pins and Needles," "God Bless You, Mr. Rosewater," "Pushing 30," Bdwy 1977 in "Gemini" (also OB).

HADDOW, JEFFREY. Born Oct. 8, 1947 in NYC. Northwestern U. graduate. Debut 1979 OB in "Scrambled Feet."

HAINES, A. LARRY. Born Aug. 3, 1917 in Mt. Vernon, NY. Attended CCNY. Bdwy bow 1962 in "A Thousand Clowns," followed by "Generation," "Promises, Promises," "Last of the Red Hot Lovers," "Twigs," "No Hard Feelings," "Tribute."

HALEY, JIM. Born June 8, 1950 in NYC. Graduate Fordham, Rutgers U. Debut 1978 OB in "Are You Now or Have You Ever Been."

HALL, GEORGE. Born Nov. 19, 1916 in Toronto, Can. Attended Neighborhood Playhouse. Bdwy bow 1946 in "Call Me Mister," followed by "Lend an Ear," "Touch and Go," "Live Wire," "The Boy Friend," "There's a Girl in My Soup," "An Evening with Richard Nixon . . .," "We Interrupt This Program," "Man and Superman," OB in "The Balcony," "Ernest in Love," "A Round with Ring," "Family Pieces," "Carousel," "The Case against Roberta Guardino," "Marry Me! Marry Me!," "Arms and the Man," "The Old Glory," "Dancing for the Kaiser."

HALLER, TOBIAS. Born Sept. 30, 1951 in Baltimore, Md. Towson State Col. graduate. Debut 1971 OB in "Now There's Just the Three of Us," followed by "The Screens," "Gorey Stories," "The Madman and the Nun," Bdwy in "The Last of Mrs. Lincoln," "Gorey Stories."

HALLEY, BEN, JR. Born Aug. 6, 1951 in Harlen, NY. Graduate CCNY, Yale. Bdwy debut 1978 in "A History of the American Film.," OB in "Julius Caesar," "Coriolanus."

HALLOW, JOHN. Born Nov. 28, 1924 in NYC. Attended Neighborhood Playhouse. Bdwy bow 1954 in "Anastasia," followed by "Ross," "Visit to a Small Planet," "Foxy," "Oh, Dad, Poor Dad . . .," "Ben Franklin in Paris," "3 Bags Full," "Don't Drink the Water," "Hadrian VII," "Tough to Get Help," "Ballroom," "A New York Summer," OB in "Hamlet," "Do I Hear a Waltz?"

HAMMER, ARTHUR. Born Apr. 17, 1932 in Cleveland, Oh. Attended Antioch Col., AADA. Debut 1955 OB in "Lysistrata," followed by "Rocket to the Moon," Bdwy in "Zoot Suit."

HAMMIL, JOHN. Born May 9, 1948 in NYC. Attended UCLA. Bdwy debut 1972 in "Purlie," followed by "Oh! Calcutta!," "Platinum," OB in "El Grande de Coca-Cola," "Songs from the City Streets."

HANNING, GERALDINE. Born in Cleveland, Oh., Graduate Ct. Col. Western Reserve U. Debut 1954 OB in "Praise of Folly," followed by "In Good King Charles' Golden Days," "Philanderer," "Lysistrata," "Alcestis Comes Back," "Under the Gaslight," "One for the Money," "The Constant Wife."

HANNUM, KRISTIE. Born June 12, 1955 in Memphis, Tn. Graduate Principia Col., Young Vic. Debut 1979 OB in "On a Clear Day You Can See Forever."

HANSEN, LARRY. Born Mar. 11, 1952 in Anacortes, Wa. Graduate Western Wash. U. Debut 1978 OB in "Can-Can."

HARRINGTON, DELPHI. Born Aug. 26 in Chicago, Il. Northwestern U. graduate. Debut 1960 OB in "Country Scandal," followed by "Moon for the Misbegotten," "Baker's Dozen," "The Zykovs," Bdwy in "Thieves," "Everything in the Garden," "Romeo and Juliet," "Chapter 2."

HARRIS, BAXTER. Born Nov. 18, 1940 in Columbus, KS. Attended U Kan. Debut 1967 OB in "America Hurrah," followed by "The Reckoning," "Wicked Women Revue," "More Than You Deserve," "Pericles," "him," "Battle of Angels," "Down by the River. . . .," Bdwy in "A Texas Trilogy" (1976), "Dracula."

HARRIS, CHARLENE. Born Mar. 16, 1925 in Chicago, Il. Bdwy debut 1950 in "Bless You All," OB in "Divine Comedy," "Cartoons for the Lunch Hour."

HARRIS, JULIE. Born Dec. 2, 1925 in Grosse Point, Mi. Attended Yale U. Bdwy debut 1945 in "It's a Gift," followed by "Henry V," "Oedipus," "Playboy of the Western World," "Alice in Wonderland," "Macbeth," "Sundown Beach" for which she received a Theatre World Award, "The Young and the Fair," "Magnolia Alley," "Montserrat," "The Member of the Wedding," "I Am a Camera," "Mlle. Colombe," "The Lark," "Country Wife," "Warm Peninsula," "Little Moon of Alban," "A Shot in the Dark," "Marathon '33," "Ready When You Are, C.B.," "Hamlet" (CP), "Skyscraper," "40 Carats," "And Miss Reardon Drinks a Little," "Voices," "The Last of Mrs. Lincoln," "The Au Pair Man" (LC), "In Praise of Love," "Belle of Amherst," "Break a Leg!"

HARRISON, REX. Born Mar. 5, 1908 in Huyten, Eng. Attended Liverpool Col. Bdwy debut 1936 in "Sweet Aloes," followed by "Anne of a Thousand Days," "Bell, Book and Candle," "Venus Observed," "Love of Four Colonels," "My Fair Lady," "Fighting Cock," "Emperor Henry IV," "In Praise of Love," "Caesar and Cleopatra," "The Kingfisher."

HART, ROXANNE. Born in 1952 in Trenton, NJ. Attended Skidmore and Princeton U. Bdwy debut 1977 in "Equus," followed by "Loose Ends."

HARTMAN, ELEK. Born Apr. 26, 1922 in Canton, OH. Graduate Carnegie Tech, OB in "Where People Gather," "Goa," "Loyalties," Bdwy in "We Bombed in New Haven" (1968), "Angel."

HAWKINS, TRISH. Born Oct. 30, 1945 in Hartford, CT. Attended Radcliffe, Neighborhood Playhouse. Debut OB 1970 in "Oh! Calcutta!" followed by "Iphigenia," "The Hot l Baltimore" for which she received a Theatre World Award, "him," "Come Back, Little Sheba," "Battle of Angels," "Mound Builders," "The Farm," "Ulysses in Traction," "Lulu," "Hogan's Folly," Bdwy 1979 in "Some of My Best Friends."

HAYNES, TIGER. Born Dec. 13, 1907 in St. Crox, VI. Bdwy bow 1956 in "New Faces," followed by "Finian's Rainbow," "Fade Out—Fade In," "The Pajama Game," "The Wiz," "A Broadway Musical."

HAYS, REX DAVID. Born June 17, 1946 in Hollywood, CA. Graduate San Jose State U., Brandeis U. Bdwy debut 1975 in "Dance with Me," followed by "Angel.", "King of Hearts."

HEARD, CORDIS. Born July 27, 1944 in Washington, DC. Graduate Chatham Col. Bdwy debut 1973 in "Warp," followed by "The Elephant Man," OB in "Vanities."

HEARN, GEORGE. Born June 18, 1934 in St. Louis, MO. Graduate Southwestern Col. OB in "Macbeth," "Antony and Cleopatra," "As You Like It,"

"Richard III," "Merry Wives of Windsor," "Midsummer Night's Dream," "Hamlet," "Horseman, Pass By." Bdwy in "A Time for Singing," "The Changing Room." "An Almost Perfect Person." "I Remember Mama."

HEATH, SIGRID. Born Jan, 29, 1947 in St. Lucia, BWI. Attended UNC. Debut 1976 OB in "Lovesong," followed by "Identity and Other Crises.", Bdwy 1979 in "I Remember Mama."

HELLMAN, BONNIE. Born Jan. 10, 1950 in San Francisco, Ca. Graduate Cal. State U. Bdwy debut 1979 in "The Utter Glory of Morrissey Hall."

HEMSLEY, WINSTON DeWITT. Born May 21, 1947 in Brooklyn, NY. Bdwy debut 1965 in "Golden Boy," followed by "A Joyful Noise," "Hallelujah, Baby," "Hello, Dolly!," "Rockabye Hamlet," "A Chorus Line," OB in "Buy Bonds Buster."

HENDERSON, JO. Born in Buffalo, NY. Attended WMiU. OB in "Camille," "Little Foxes," "An Evening with Merlin Finch," "20th Century Tar," "A Scent of Flowers," "Revival," "Dandelion Wine," "My Life," "Ladyhouse Blues."

HENDRICKSON, REILY. Born Apr. 30, 1930 in Chicago, IL. Graduate AADA. Debut 1962 OB in "The Country Girl," followed by "Exiles," "The Seagull," "Blithe Spirit," "The Hostage," "Ring Round the Moon," "Hotel Paradiso," "The Happy Hunter," "The Suicide."

HENRITZE, BETTE. Born May 3 in Betsy Layne, KY. Graduate UTenn. OB in "Lion in Love," "Abe Lincoln in Illinois," "Othello," "Baal," "Long Christmas Dinner," "Queens of France," "Rimers of Eldritch," "Displaced Person," "Acquisition," "Crime of Passion," "Happiness Cage," "Henry VI," "Richard III," "Older People," "Lotta," "Catsplay," Bdwy in "Jenny Kissed Me" (1948), "Pictures in the Hallway," "Giants, Sons of Giants," "Ballad of the Sad Cafe," "The White House," "Dr. Cook's Garden," "Here's Where I Belong," "Much Ado about Nothing," "Over Here," "Angel Street," "Man and Superman."

HERLIHY, ED. Born in Boston, Ma. Bdwy debut 1968 in "Mame," OB in "Born Yesterday," "Rubbers," "Yankees 3, Detroit O," "God Bless You, Mr. Rosewater."

HEWETT, CHRISTOPHER, Born Apr. 5 in England, attended Beaumont Col. Bdwy debut 1957 in "My Fair Lady," followed by "First Impressions," "Unsinkable Molly Brown," "Kean," "The Affair," "Hadrian VII," "Music Is," OB in "Tobias and the Angel," "Trelawny of the Wells," "Finian's Rainbow" (JB)., "New Jerusalem."

HICKS, LOIS DIANE. Born Sept. 3, 1940 in Brooklyn, NY. Graduate NYCCC, AADA. Debut 1979 OB in "On a Clear Day You Can See Forever."

HIGGINS, JAMES. Born June 1, 1932 in Worksop, Eng. Graduate Cambridge U., Yale. Debut 1963 OB in "The Magistrate," followed by "Stevie," Bdwy in "The Zulu and the Zayda," "Whose Life Is It Anyway?"

HIGGINS, MICHAEL. Born Jan. 20, 1926 in Bklyn. Attended Theatre Wing. Bdwy bow 1946 in "Antigone," followed by "Our Lan'," "Romeo and Juliet," "The Crucible," "The Lark," "Equus," "Whose Life Is It Anyway?," OB IN "White Devil," "Carefree Tree,""Easter,""The Queen and the Rebels," "Sally, George and Martha," "L'Ete," "Uncle Vanya," "The Iceman Cometh," "Molly.," "Artichoke."

HIKEN, GERALD. Born May 23, 1927 in Milwaukee, WI. Attended UWis. OB in "Cherry Orchard," "Seagull," "Good Woman of Setzuan," "The Misanthrope," "The Iceman Cometh," "The New Theatre," "Strider," Bdwy in "Lovers," "Cave Dwellers," "Nervous Set," "Fighting Cock," "49th Cousin," "Gideon," "Foxy," "Three Sisters," "Golda."

HILLIARD, KEN. Born June 9, 1946 in Pittsburgh, Pa. Graduate Ind. U. Bdwy debut 1978 in "On the 20th Century."

HILLMAN, GEORGE. Born Sept. 21, 1906 in NYC. Attended Lincoln U. After 35 years with Hillman Brothers dance team, made debut OB in "Curley McDimple," followed by "Suddenly the Music Starts."

HINES, GREGORY. Born Feb. 14, 1946 in NYC. Bdwy debut 1954 in "The Girl in Pink Tights," followed by "Eubie!" for which he received a Theatre World Award.

HIRSCH, JUDD. Born Mar. 15, 1935 in NYC. Attended AADA. Bdwy debut 1966 in "Barefoot in the Park," followed by "Chapter Two," OB in "On the Necessity of Being Polygamous," "Scuba Duba," "Mystery Play," "Hot L Baltimore," "Prodigal," "Knock Knock.", "Life and/or Death," "Talley's Folly."

HIRSCH, MICHAEL. Born Jan. 1, 1947 in Brooklyn, NY. Graduate Ithaca Col. Debut 1978 OB in "Company," followed by "Tip-Toes."

HLIBOK, BRUCE, Born July 31, 1960 in NYC. Debut OB and Bdwy 1978 in "Runaways." OB in "Wonderland in Concert."

HOFF, ROBIN. Born Jan. 4, 1952 in Washington, DC. Studied at Harkness House. Debut 1974 OB in "Carousel," followed by "Fiddler on the Roof," "Pins and Needles."

HOFFMAN, JANE. Born July 24, in Seattle, Wa. Graduate UCal. Bdwy debut 1940 in " 'Tis of Thee," followed by "Crazy with the Heat," "Something for the Boys," "One Touch of Venus," "Calico Wedding," "Mermaids Singing," "Temporary Island," "Story for Strangers," "Two Blind Mice," "Rose Tattoo," "The Crucible," "Witness for the Prosecution," "Third Best Sport," "Rhinoceros," "Mother Courage and Her Children," "Fair Game for Lovers," "A Murderer among Us," "Murder among Friends," OB in "American Dream," "Sandbox," "Picnic on the Battlefield," "Theatre of the Absurd," "Child Buyer," "A Corner of the Bed," "Someone's Comin' Hungry," "Increased Difficulty of Concentration," "American Hamburger League," "Slow Memories," "Last Analysis," "Dear Oscar," "Hocus-Pocus," "Lessons."

HOFMAIER, MARK. Born July 4, 1950 in Philadelphia, Pa. Graduate UAz. Debut 1978 OB in "A Midsummer Night's Dream."

HOGAN, JONATHAN. Born June 13, 1951 in Chicago, IL. Graduate Goodman Theatre. Debut OB 1972 in "The Hot 1 Baltimore," followed by "Mound Builders," "Harry Outside," "Cabin 12," "5th of July." "Glorious Morning," Bdwy in "Comedians" (1976). "Otherwise Engaged."

HOLBROOK, RUBY. Born Aug. 28, 1930 in St. John's, Nfld. Attended Denison U. Debut 1963 OB in "Abe Lincoln in Illinois," followed by "Hamlet," "James Joyce's Dubliners," "Measure for Measure," "The Farm," Bdwy 1979 in "Da."

HOLGATE, RONALD. Born May 26, 1937 in Aberdeen, SD. Attended Northwestern U., New Eng. Cons. Debut 1961 OB in "Hobo," followed by "Hooray, It's a Glorious Day," Bdwy in "A Funny Thing Happened on the Way . . .," "Milk and Honey," "1776," "Saturday Sunday Monday," "The Grand Tour."

HOLLAND, ANTHONY. Born Oct. 17, 1933 in Brooklyn, NY. Graduate UChicago. OB in "Venice Preserved," "Second City," "Victim of Duty," "New Tenant," "Dynamite Tonight," "Quare Fellow," "White House Murder Case," "Waiting for Godot," "Tales of the Hasidim," "Taming of the Shrew," "Diary of Anne Frank," Bdwy in "My Mother, My Father and Me," "We Bombed in New Haven," "Dreyfus in Rehearsal," "Leaf People."

HOLM, CELESTE. Born Apr. 29, 1919 in NYC. Attended UCLA, UChicago. Bdwy debut 1938 in "Gloriana," followed by "The Time of Your Life," "Another Sun," "Return of the Vagabond," "8 O'Clock Tuesday," "My Fair Ladies," "Papa Is All," "All the Comforts of Home," "Damask Cheek," "Oklahoma!," "Bloomer Girl," "She Stoops to Conquer," "Affairs of State," "Anna Christie," "The King and I," "His and Hers," "Interlock," "Third Best Sport," "Invitation to a March," "A Month in the Country" (OB), "Mame," "Candida," "Habeas Corpus," "The Utter Glory of Morrissey Hall."

HORGAN, PATRICK. Born May 26, 1929 in Nottingham, Eng. Attended Stoneyhurst Col. Bdwy debut 1958 in "Redhead," followed by "Heartbreak House," "The Devil's Advocate," "The Aspern Papers," "The Complaisant Lover," "Beyond the Fringe," "Baker Street," "Crown Matrimonial," "Deathtrap," OB in "The Importance of Being Earnest."

HORMANN, NICHOLAS. Born Dec. 22, 1944 in Honolulu, HI. Graduate Oberlin, Yale. Bdwy debut 1973 in "The Visit," followed by "Chemin de Fer." "Holiday," "Love for Love," "Rules of the Game," "Member of the Wedding," "St. Joan," OB in "Ice Age," "Marco Polo.", "Artichoke."

HORNER, CARRIE. Born July 18, 1965 in Portchester, NY. Debut 1978 OB in "Drinks Before Dinner," Bdwy 1979 in "I Remember Mama."

HORVATH, JAMES. Born Aug. 14, 1954 in Chicago, Il. Graduate Triton Col., Butler U. Debut 1978 OB in "Can-Can."

HOSBEIN, JAMES. Born Sept. 24, 1946 in Benton Harbor, MI. Graduate UMich. Debut 1972 OB in "Dear Oscar," followed by "Darrel and Carol and Kenny and Jenny," Bdwy 1977 in "Annie."

HOTY, TONY. Born Sept. 29, 1949 in Lakewood, OH. Attended Ithaca Col., WVaU. Debut 1974 OB in "Godspell" (also Bdwy 1976), followed by "Joseph and the Amazing Technicolor Dreamcoat."

HOUTS, ROD. Born Dec. 15, 1906 in Warrensburg, Mo. Graduate MoU, NYU, Goodman Theatre. Bdwy debut 1932 in "Lucrece," OB in "Gallery Gods," "The Miracle Worker," "Early Dark," "The Dybbuk," "A Far Country," "Three Sisters."

HOYT, J. C. Born Mar. 6, 1944 in Mankato, Mn. UMinn. graduate. Debut 1975 OB in "Heathen Piper," followed by "la Ronde."

HUBBARD, ELIZABETH. Born Dec. 22 in NYC. Graduate Radcliffe Col., RADA. Bdwy debut 1960 in "The Affair," followed by "The Passion of Josef D," "The Physicists," "A Time for Singing," "A Day in the Death of Joe Egg," "Children, Children," "I Remember Mama" (1979), OB in "The Threepenny Opera," "Boys from Syracuse."

HUDSON, TRAVIS. Born Feb. 2 in Amarillo, Tx. UTx graduate. Bdwy debut in "New Faces of 1962," followed by "Pousse Cafe," "Very Good Eddie," "The Grand Tour," OB in "Triad," "Tattooed Countess," "Young Abe Lincoln," "Get Thee to Canterbury," "The Golden Apple," "Annie Get Your Gun" (JB).

HUGHES, BARNARD. Born July 16, 1915 in Bedford Hills, N.Y. Attended Manhattan Col. OB in "Rosmersholm," "A Doll's House," "Hogan's Goat," "Lime," "Older People," "Hamlet" "Merry Wives of Windsor," "Pericles," BAM Co.'s "Three Sisters." Bdwy in "The Ivy Green," "Dinosaur Wharf," "Teahouse of the August Moon" (CC), "A Majority of One," "Advise and Consent," "The Advocate," "Hamlet," "I Was Dancing," "Generation," "How Now, Dow Jones?," "Wrong Way Light Bulb," "Sheep On The Runway," "Abelard and Heloise," "Much Ado About Nothing," "Uncle Vanya," "The Good Doctor," "All Over Town." "Da."

HUGHES, TRESA. Born Sept. 17, 1929 in Washington, DC. Attended Wayne U. OB in "Electra," "The Crucible," "Hogan's Goat," "Party on Greenwich Avenue," "Fragments," "Passing through from Exotic Places," "Beggar on Horseback" (LC), "Early Morning," "The Old Ones," Bdwy in "Miracle Worker," "The Devil's Advocate," "Dear Me, the Sky Is Falling," "Last Analysis," "Spofford," "Man in the Glass Booth," "Prisoner of Second Avenue," "Tribute."

HUNT, ANNETTE. Born Jan. 31, 1938 in Hampton, Va. Graduate Va. Intermont Col. Debut 1957 OB in "Nine by Six," followed by "The Taming of the Shrew," "Medea," "The Anatomist," "The Misanthrope," "The Cherry Orchard," "Electra," "Last Resort," "The Seducers," "A Sound of Silence," Bdwy 1972 in "All the Girls Came Out to Play."

HUNT, W. M. Born Oct. 9 in St. Petersburg, Fl. Graduate UMich. Debut OB 1973 in "The Proposition," followed by "The Glorious Age," "Mary."

HURT, WILLIAM. Born Mar. 20, 1950 in Washington, DC. Graduate Tufts U., Juilliard. Debut 1976 OB in "Henry V," followed by "My Life," "Ulysses in Traction," "Lulu," "5th of July," "The Runner Stumbles," He received a 1978 Theatre World Award for his performances with Circle Repertory Theatre.

HUTTON, C. A. Born May 19, 1950 in West Grove, Pa. Graduate Wash. Col. Bdwy debut 1978 in "Gorey Stories," OB in "Telecast."

HYMAN, EARLE. Born Oct. 11, 1926 in Rocky Mount, NC. Attended New School, Theatre Wing. Bdwy debut 1943 in "Run, Little Chillun," followed by "Anna Lucasta," "Climate of Eden," "Merchant of Venice," "Othello," "Julius Caesar," "The Tempest," "No Time for Sergeants," "Mr. Johnson" for which he received a Theatre World Award, "St. Joan," "Hamlet," "Waiting for Godot," "Duchess of Malfi." "Les Blancs," OB in "The White Rose and the Red," "Worlds of Shakespeare," "Jonah," "Life and Times of J. Walter Smintheus," "Orrin," "Cherry Orchard," "House Party," "Carnival Dreams," "Agamemnon," "Othello.", "Julius Caesar," "Coriolanus," "Remembrance."

INNERARITY, MEMRIE. Born Feb 11, 1945 in Columbus, MS. Attended USMiss. Debut 1976 OB in "The Club." followed by "The Heebie Jeebies."

IRVING, GEORGE S. Born Nov. 1, 1922 in Springfield, Ma. Attended Leland Power Sch. Bdwy bow 1943 in "Oklahoma!," followed by "Call Me Mister," "Along Fifth Avenue," "Two's Company." "Me and Juliet," "Can-Can," "Shinbone Alley," "Belles Are Ringing," "The Good Soup," "Tovarich," "A Murderer among Us," "Alfie," "Anya," "Galileo," "Up Eden" (OB), "4 on a Garden," "An Evening with Richard Nixon . . .," "Irene," "Who's Who in Hell," "All over Town," "So Long 174th St." "Once in a Lifetime," "I Remember Mama" (1979).

JABLONS, KAREN. Born July 19, 1951 in Trenton, NJ. Juilliard graduate. Debut 1969 OB in "The Student Prince," followed by "Sound of Music," "Funny Girl," "Boys from Syracuse," "Sterling Silver," "People In Show Business Make Long Goodbyes." Bdwy in "Ari," "Two Gentlemen of Verona," "Lorelei," "Where's Charley?," "A Chorus Line."

JACKSON, ANNE. Born Sept. 3, 1926 in Allegheny, Pa. Attended Neighborhood Playhouse. Bdwy debut 1945 in "Signature," followed by "Yellow Jack," "John Gabriel Borkman," "The Last Dance," "Summer and Smoke," "Magnolia Alley," "Love Me Long," "Lady from the Sea," "Never Say Never." "Oh, Men! Oh, Women!," "Rhinoceros," "Luv," "The Exercise," "Inquest," "Promenade All!," "Waltz of the Toreadors," OB in "The Tiger," "The Typist," "Marco Polo Sings a Solo," "Diary of Anne Frank."

JAFFE, SAM. Born Mar. 8, 1898 in NYC. Debut 1915 in "The Clod," followed by "Samson and Delilah," "The Main Line," "The Jazz Singer," "Grand Hotel," "The Eternal Road," "A Doll's House," "The Gentle People," "This Time Tomorrow," "An Enemy of the People," "Mlle. Colombe," "The Sea Gull" (1954), "A Meeting by the River."

JAMES, JESSICA. Born Oct. 31, 1933 in Los Angeles, CA. Attended USC. Bdwy debut 1970 in "Company," followed by "Gemini," OB in "Nourish the Beast." "Hothouse," "Loss of Innocence," "Rebirth Celebration of the Human Race," "Silver Bee," "Gemini."

JAMROG, JOSEPH. Born Dec. 21, 1932 in Flushing, NY. Graduate CCNY. Debut 1970 OB in "Nobody Hears a Broken Drum," followed by "Tango," "And Whose Little Boy Are You?," "When You Comin' Back, Red Ryder?," "Drums at Yale," "The Boy Friend," "Love Death Plays," "Too Much Johnson."

JANSEN, JIM. Born July 27, 1945 in Salt Lake City. UT. Graduate U Utah. NYU. Debut OB 1973 in "Moonchildren," followed by "Marco Polo Sings a Solo," "Chez Nous," "Taming of the Shrew," "God Bless You, Mr. Rosewater," Bdwy 1974 in "All over Town."

JARKOWSKY, ANDREW. Born in NYC. Graduate CCNY. Debut OB 1974 in "Festival of Short Plays," followed by "Cakes with Wine," "The Boss," "The Grinding Machine," Bdwy in "The Trip Back Down."

JARRETT, BELLA. Born Feb. 9, 1931 in Adairsville, Ga. Graduate Wesleyan Col. Debut 1958 OB in "Waltz of the Toreadors," followed by "Hedda Gabler," "The Browning Version," "Cicero," "Pequod," "Welcome to Andromeda," Bdwy 1978 in "Once in a Lifetime."

JASPER, ZINA. Born Jan. 29, 1939 in The Bronx, NY. Attended CCNY. Bdwy debut 1967 in "Something Different." followed by "Paris Is Out," OB in "Saturday's Children," "Moondreamers," "A Dream out of Time," "Quail Southwest," "On Green Pond," "Artichoke."

JAY, MARY. Born Dec. 23, 1939 in Brooklyn, NY. Graduate UMaine, AmTh-Wing. Debut 1962 OB in "Little Mary Sunshine," followed by "Toys in the Attic," "Telecast," Bdwy in "The Student Gypsy."

JAY, WILLIAM. Born May 15, 1935 in Baxter Springs, Ks. Attended Omaha U. Debut 1963 OB in "Utopia," followed by "The Blacks," "Loop the Loop," "Happy Ending," "Day of Absence," "Hamlet" and "Othello" (CP), "Song of the Lusitanian Bogey," "Ceremonies in Dark Old Men," "Man Better Man," "The Harangues," "Brotherhood," "Perry's Mission," "Rosalee Pritchett," "Sister Sadie," "Coriolanus," "Getting Out."

JENKINS, CAROL MAYO. Born Nov. 24 in Knoxville, TN. Attended Vanderbilt U., UTn., London Central Sch. of Speech. Bdwy debut 1969 in "The Three Sisters," followed by "There's One in Every Marriage," "Kings," "First Monday in October," OB in "Zinnia."

JENKINS, MARK. Born May 8, 1943 in Butte, Mt. Attended UWyoming,

Actors Studio. Debut OB 1966 in "Macbeth," followed by "King John," "Carricknabauna," "G. R. Point."

JENNINGS, KEN. Born Oct. 10, 1947 in Jersey City, NJ. Graduate St. Peter's Col. Bdwy Debut 1975 in "All God's Chillun Got Wings," followed by "Sweeney Todd" for which he received a Theatre World Award.

JETER, MICHAEL. Born Aug. 26, 1952 in Lawrenceburg, Tn. Graduate Memphis State U. Bdwy debut 1978 in "Once in a Lifetime," OB in "The Master and Margarita," "G. R. Point" for which he received a Theatre World Award.

JOHANN, DALLAS. Born June 15, 1944 in Madison, Wi. Bdwy bow 1968 in "The Happy Time," followed by "Maggie Flynn," OB in "Sing Melancholy Baby."

JOHANSON, DON. Born Oct. 19, 1952 in Rock Hill, SC. Graduate USC. Bdwy debut 1976 in "Rex," OB in "The American Dance Machine."

JOHNSON, KURT. Born Oct. 5, 1952 in Pasadena, CA. Attended LACC, Occidental Col. Debut 1976 OB in "Follies," followed by "Walking Papers," "A Touch of Marble," Bdwy in "Rockaby Hamlet," "A Chorus Line."

JOHNSON, LORNA. Born Oct. 19, 1943 in Pa. Graduate West Chester State Col. Debut 1979 OB in "The Last Days at the Dixie Girl Cafe."

JOHNSON, MARLA. Born Mar. 21. 1956 in NYC. Graduate Georgian Court Col. Debut 1979 OB in "The Miracle Worker."

JOHNSON, MEL, JR. Born Apr. 16, 1949 in NYC. Graduate Hofstra U. Debut 1972 OB in "Hamlet," followed by "Love! Love! Love!," Bdwy in "On the 20th Century," "Eubie!"

JOHNSON, ONNI. Born Mar. 16, 1949 in NYC. Graduate Brandeis U. Debut 1964 in "Unfinished Business," followed by "She Stoops to Conquer," "22 Years," "The Master and Margarita," Bdwy in "Oh, Calcutta!"

JOHNSON, PAGE. Born Aug. 25, 1930 in Welch, WV. Graduate Ithaca Col. Bdwy bow 1951 in "Romeo and Juliet," followed by "Electra," "Oedipus," "Camino Real," "In April Once" for which he received a Theatre World Award, "Red Roses for Me," "The Lovers," "Equus," OB in "The Enchanted," "Guitar," "4 in 1," "Journey of the Fifth Horse," APA's "School for Scandal," "The Tavern" and "The Seagull," "Odd Couple," "Boys In The Band," "Medea."

JOHNSON, TINA. Born Oct. 27, 1951 in Wharton, Tx. Graduate North Tx. State U. Debut 1979 OB in "Festival."

JONES, EDDIE. Born in Washington, PA. Debut 1960 OB in "Dead End," followed by "Curse of the Starving Class," "The Ruffian on the Stair," Bdwy 1974 in "That Championship Season."

JOSEPH, STEPHEN. Born Aug. 27, 1952 in Shaker Heights, Oh. Graduate Carnegie-Mellon, Fla. State U. Debut 1978 OB in "Oklahoma!"

JOSLYN, BETSY. Born Apr. 19, 1954 in Staten Island, NY. Graduate Wagner Col. Debut 1976 OB in "The Fantasticks," Bdwy 1979 in "Sweeney Todd."

JOY, ROBERT. Born Aug. 17, 1951 in Montreal, Can. Graduate Nfld. Memorial U., Oxford U. Debut 1978 OB in "The Diary of Anne Frank."

JULIA, RAUL. Born Mar. 9, 1940 in San Juan, PR. Graduate UPR. OB in "Macbeth," "Titus Andronicus" (CP), "Theatre in the Streets," "Life Is a Dream," "Blood Wedding," "Ox Cart," "No Exit," "Memorandum," "Frank Gagliano's City Scene," "Your Own Thing," "Persians," "Castro Complex," "Pinkville," "Hamlet," "King Lear," "As You Like It," "Emperor of Late Night Radio," "Threepenny Opera," "The Cherry Orchard," "Taming of the Shrew," Bdwy bow 1968 in "The Cuban Thing," followed by "Indians," "Two Gentlemen of Verona," "Via Galactia," "Where's Charley?," "Dracula."

KAGAN, DIANE. Born in Maplewood, NJ. Graduate Fla. State U. Debut 1963 OB in "Asylum," followed by "Days and Nights of Beebee Fenstermaker," "Death of the Well-Loved Boy," "Madam de Sade," "Blue Boys," "Alive and Well in Argentina," "Little Black Sheep," "The Family," "Ladyhouse Blues," Bdwy in "Chinese Prime Minister," "Never Too Late," "Any Wednesday," "Venus Is," "Tiger at the Gates" (LC), "Vieux Carre."

KAGEN, DAVID. Born Sept. 27, 1948 in Somers Point, NJ. Graduate Carnegie Tech. Debut 1978 OB in "Family Business."

KAMEL, STANLEY. Born Jan. 1, 1947 in New Brunswick, NJ. Graduate Boston U. Bdwy debut 1978 in "Platinum."

KANTOR, KENNETH. Born Apr. 6, 1949 in The Bronx, NY. Graduate SUNY, Boston U. Debut 1974 OB in "Zorba," followed by "Kiss Me Kate," Bdwy in "The Grand Tour."

KARR, PATTI Born July 10 in St. Paul, MN. Attended TCU. Bdwy debut 1953 in "Maggie," followed by "Carnival in Flanders," "Pipe Dream," "Bells Are Ringing," "New Girl in Town," "Body Beautiful," "Bye Bye Birdie," "New Faces of 1962," "Come on Strong," "Look to the Lilies," "Different Times," "Lysistrata," "Seesaw," "Irene," "Pippin," "A Broadway Musical," OB in "A Month of Sundays," "Up Eden."

KAVA, CAROLINE. Born in Chicago, IL. Attended Neighborhood Playhouse. Debut 1975 OB in "Gorky," followed by "Threepenny Opera," "The Nature and Purpose of the Universe," Bdwy 1978 in "Stages."

KAVANAUGH, RICHARD. Born in 1943 in NYC. Bdwy debut 1977 in "Dracula."

KAYE, ANNE. Born Sept. 6 in New Haven, Ct. Attended Emerson Col., AMDA. Debut 1967 OB in "Now Is the Time for All Good Men," followed by "Have I Got One For You," "The Fantasticks," "Mahagonny," "Val, Christie and the Others," Bdwy in "Good News" (1974), "The Utter Glory of Morrissey Hall."

KAYE, JUDY. Born Oct. 11, 1948 in Phoenix, AZ. Attended UCLA, Ariz. State U. Bdwy debut 1977 in "Grease," followed by "On the 20th Century" for which she received a Theatre World Award.

KEACH, STACY. Born June 2, 1941 in Savannah, Ga. Graduate UCal., Yale, LAMDA. Debut 1967 OB in "Macbird," followed by "Niggerlovers," "Henry IV," "Country Wife," "Hamlet," Bdwy in "Indians," "Deathtrap."

KEAGY, GRACE. Born Dec. 16 in Youngstown, Oh. Attended New Eng. Consv. Debut 1974 OB in "Call Me Madam," Bdwy in "Goodtime Charley," "The Grand Tour," "Carmelina."

KEARNEY, LYNN. Born Apr. 9, 1951 in Chicago, Il. Graduate NYU. Bdwy debut 1978 in "Annie."

KELL, MICHAEL. Born Jan. 18, 1944 in Jersey City, NJ. Attended HB Studio. Debut 1972 OB in "One Flew Over The Cuckoo's Nest," followed by "Boom Boom Room," "Golden Boy," "Streamers," "Awake and Sing," "Mr. Shandy," Bdwy 1979 in "Loose Ends."

KELLIN, MIKE. Born Apr. 26, 1922 in Hartford, Ct. Attended Trinity Col, Yale. Bdwy bow 1949 in "At War with the Army," followed by "Bird Cage," "Stalag 17," "The Emperor's Clothes," "The Time of Your Life," "Pipe Dream," "Who Was That Lady?," "God and Kate Murphy," "Ankles Aweigh," "Rhinoceros," "Odd Couple," "Mother Courage," OB in "Taming of the Shrew," "Diary of a Scoundrel," "Purple Dust," "Tevya and His Daughters," "Winkelberg," "Winterset," "Joan of Loraine," "Bread," "American Buffalo," "Duck Variations," "Are You Now or Have You Ever Been."

KELLY, K. C. Born Nov. 12, 1952 in Baraboo, WI. Attended UWisc. Debut 1976 OB in "The Chicken Ranch," followed by Bdwy in "Romeo and Juliet" (1977), "The Best Little Whorehouse in Texas."

KELTON, GENE. Born Oct 21, 1938 in Flagstaff, Az. Bdwy in "Once upon a Mattress," "Destry Rides Again," "Subways Are for Sleeping," "Here's Love," "Fade Out-Fade In," "Skyscraper," "Mame," "Dear World," "Applause," "Juno," "Ballroom," OB in "Contrast."

KENDALL, RICHARD. Born Jan. 6, 1945 in Ottawa, Can. Bdwy debut 1970 with National Theatre of the Deaf, OB in "The Suicide."

KENNEDY, LAURIE. Born Feb. 14, 1948 in Hollywood, Ca. Graduate Sarah Lawrence Col. Debut 1974 OB in "End of Summer," followed by "A Day in the Death of Joe Egg," Bdwy in "Man and Superman" (1978) for which she received a Theatre World Award.

KENNEDY, TARA. Born Aug. 8, 1971 in Yonkers, NY. Bdwy debut 1979 in "I Remember Mama."

KERMOYAN, MICHAEL. Born Nov. 29, 1925 in Fresno, Ca. Attended Stanford U., USC. Bdwy bow 1954 in "The Girl in Pink Tights," followed by "Whoop-Up," "Happy Town," "Camelot," "Happiest Girl in the World," "Fly Blackbird," "Ross," "Tovarich," "Anya," "The Guide," "Desert Song," "The King and I," OB in "Carousel," "Sandhog," "Angels of Anadarko."

KERNER, NORBERTO. Born July 19, 1929 in Valparaiso, Chile. Attended Piscator Workshop, Goodman Theatre. Debut 1971 OB in "Yerma," followed by "I Took Panama," "The F. M. Safe," "My Old Friends."

KESTLY, JONATHAN. Born Jan. 18, 1947 in Milwaukee, Wi. Graduate UWisc., Neighborhood Playhouse. Debut 1978 OB in "Can-Can."

KEYES, DANIEL. Born May 6, 1914 in Concord, MA. Attended Harvard. Bdwy debut 1954 in "The Remarkable Mr. Pennypacker," followed by "Bus Stop," "Only in America," "Christine," "First Love," "Take Her, She's Mine," "Baker Street," "Dinner at 8," "I Never Sang for My Father," "Wrong Way Light Bulb," "A Place for Polly," "Scratch," "Rainbow Jones," "Angel," OB in "Our Town," "Epitaph for George Dillon," "Plays for Bleecker St.," "Hooray! It's a Glorious Day!," "Six Characters in Search of an Author," "Sjt. Musgrave's Dance," "Arms and the Man," "Mourning Becomes Electra," "Salty Dog Saga," "Hot l Baltimore." "Artichoke."

KHOUTIEFF, JEANNINE. Born Nov. 6, 1956 in Michigan. Graduate SUNY. Debut 1979 OB in "Biography: A Game," followed by "Strider."

KILEY, RICHARD. Born Mar. 31, 1922 in Chicago, IL. Attended Loyola U. Bdwy debut 1953 in "Misalliance" for which he received a Theatre World Award, followed by "Kismet," "Sing Me No Lullaby," "Time Limit!" "Redhead," "Advise and Consent," "No Strings," "Here's Love," "I Had a Ball," "Man of La Mancha" (also LC and 1977 revival), "Her First Roman," "The Incomparable Max," "Voices," "Absurd Person Singular," "The Heiress," "Knickerbocker Holiday."

KILLMER, NANCY. Born Dec. 16, 1936 in Homewood, IL. Graduate Northwestern U. Bdwy debut 1969 in "Coco," followed by "Goodtime Charley," "So Long, 174th Street," OB in "Exiles." "A Little Night Music," "Sweeney Todd," OB in "Exiles," "Mrs. Murray's Farm."

KIMBROUGH, CHARLES. Born May 23, 1936 in St. Paul, MN. Graduate Ind. U., Yale. Bdwy bow 1969 in "Cop-Out," followed by "Company," "Love for Love," "Rules of the Game," "Candide," "Mr. Happiness," "Same Time, Next Year," OB in "All in Love," "Struts and Frets," "Troilus and Cressida," "Secret Service," "Boy Meets Girl," "Drinks before Dinner."

KIMMINS, KENNETH. Born Sept. 4, 1941 in Brooklyn, NY. Graduate Catholic U. Debut 1966 OB in "The Fantasticks," followed by "All My Sons," "Nasty Rumors and Final Remarks," Bdwy in "Fig Leaves Are Falling," "Gingerbread Lady," "Company," "Status Quo Vadis," "Magic Show."

KING, JOHN MICHAEL. Born May 13, 1926 in NYC. Attended AADA. Bdwy debut 1951 in "Courtin' Time," followed by "Music in the Air," "Of Thee

I Sing," "Buttrio Square," "Me and Juliet," "Ankles Aweigh," "Hit the Trail," "Fanny," "My Fair Lady" for which he received a Theatre World Award, "Anya," "On a Clear Day You Can See Forever," "The King and I," "Carmelina," OB in "Have I Got One for You," "Sound of Music."

KINGLEY, LESLEY. See Lesley Rein.

KINGSLEY, SUSAN. Born Mar. 1, 1946 in Middlesboro, Ky. Graduate UKy, FlaStateU, LAMDA. Debut 1978 OB in "Getting Out" for which she received a Theatre World Award.

KIRSCH, CAROLYN. Born May 24, 1942 in Shreveport, LA. Bdwy debut 1963 in "How to Succeed . . . ," followed by "Folies Bergere," "La Grosse Valise," "Skyscraper," "Breakfast at Tiffany's," "Sweet Charity," "Hallelujah, Baby!," "Dear World," "Promises, Promises," "Coco," "Ulysses in Nighttown," "A Chorus Line," OB in "Silk Stockings," Telecast.

KITT, EARTHA. Born Jan. 26, 1928 in North, SC. Appeared with Katherine Dunham and in clubs before Bdwy debut in "New Faces of 1952," followed by "Mrs. Patterson," "Shinbone Alley," "Timbuktu."

KLEIN, ROBERT. Born Feb. 8, 1942 in NYC. Graduate Alfred U., Yale. OB in "Six Characters in Search of an Author," "Second City Returns," "Upstairs at the Downstairs," Bdwy in "The Apple Tree," "New Faces of 1968," "Morning, Noon and Night," "They're Playing Our Song."

KLINE, KEVIN. Born Oct. 24, 1947 in St. Louis, MO. Graduate Ind. U., Juilliard. Debut 1970 OB in "Wars of Roses," followed by "School for Scandal," "Lower Depths," "The Hostage," "Women Beware Women," "Robber Bridegroom," "Edward II," "The Time of Your Life," "Beware the Jubjub Bird," "Dance on a Country Grave," Bdwy in "Three Sisters," "Measure for Measure," "Beggar's Opera," "Scapin," "On the 20th Century," "Loose Ends."

KLUNIS, TOM. Bdwy debut 1961 in "Gideon," followed by "The Devils," "Henry V," "Romeo and Juliet," "St. Joan," OB in "The Immoralist," "Hamlet," "Arms and the Man," "Potting Shed," "Measure for Measure," "Romeo and Juliet," "The Balcony," "Our Town," "Man Who Never Died," "God is My Ram," "Rise, Marlowe," "Iphigenia in Aulis," "Still Life," "The Master and Margarita."

KNIGHT, SHIRLEY. Born July 5 in Goessel, KS. Attended Phillips U., Wichita U. Bdwy debut 1964 in "The Three Sisters," followed by "We Have Always Lived in a Castle," "The Watering Place," "Kennedy's Children," OB in "Journey to the Day," "Rooms," "Happy End," "Landscape of the Body," "A Lovely Sunday for Creve Coeur," "Losing Time."

KNIGHT, WAYNE. Born Aug. 7, 1955 in NYC. Graduate UGa. Bdwy debut 1979 in "Gemini."

KOBS, DOROTHY. Born Oct. 16, 1930 in Windsor, Wi. Attended Sol Ross State Col., UWisc. Debut 1979 OB in "The Importance of Being Earnest."

KOPYC, FRANK. Born Aug. 6, 1948 in Troy, NY. Graduate Yankton Col. Debut 1973 OB in "Pop," followed by "Fiorello!," Bdwy in "Sweeney Todd."

KOREN, JEANNE. Born Aug. 12, 1955 in Buffalo, NY. Attended Buffalo State, HB Studio. Debut 1979 OB in "Biography: A Game."

KOTTKE, DAVID. Born Nov. 8, 1952 in Detroit, Mi. Attended Butler U., NYSU Fredonia. Debut 1976 OB in "Don't Step on My Olive Branch," followed by Bdwy in "Sarava."

KRESSIN, LIANNE. Born Jan. 5, 1952 in Rochester, Pa. Graduate UTenn. Debut 1977 OB in "The Present Tense," followed by "Grand Magic."

KURNITZ, JULIE. Born Sept. 8, 1942 in Mt. Vernon, NY. Attended UWisc., NYU. Debut 1968 OB in "In Circles," followed by "Peace," "Joan," "The Faggot," "Not Back with the Elephants," Bdwy in "Minnie's Boys," "Gorey Stories."

KUSS, RICHARD. Born July 17, 1927 in Astoria, NY. Atrended Ithaca Col. Debut 1951 OB in "Mother Said No," followed by "A Maid's Tragedy," "Winning Isn't Everything," Bdwy in "J.B.," "Wait until Dark," "Solitaire/Double Solitaire," "Golda."

LACEY, FLORENCE. Born July 22, 1948 in McKeesport, PA. Graduate Pittsburgh Playhouse. Bdwy debut 1978 in "Hello, Dolly!" for which she received a Theatre World Award, followed by "The Grand Tour."

LACHOW, STAN. Born Dec. 20, 1931 in Brooklyn, NY. Graduate Roger Williams U. Debut 1977 OB in "Come Back, Little Sheba," followed by "Diary of Anne Frank," Bdwy in "On Golden Pond."

LAGERWALL, BERIT. Born May 8, 1945 in Sweden. Debut 1977 OB in "A Servant of Two Masters," followed by "Old Man Joseph and His Family," "Moliere in spite of Himself," "Devour the Snow."

LAHTI, CHRISTINE. Born Apr. 4, 1950 in Detroit, Mi. Graduate UMich., HB Studio. Debut 1979 OB in "The Woods" for which she received a Theatre World Award.

LAMOS, MARK. Born March 10, 1946 in Chicago, IL. Attended Northwestern U. Bdwy debut 1972 in "The Love Suicide at Schofield Barracks," followed by "The Creation of the World and Other Business," "Cyrano," "Man and Superman," OB in "City Sugar."

LAMPERT, ZOHRA. Born May 13, 1936 in NYC. Attended Chicago U. Bdwy debut 1956 in "Major Barbara," followed by "Maybe Tuesday," "Look, We've Come Through," "First Love," "Mother Courage," "Nathan Weinstein, Mystic, Conn." "Lovers and Other Strangers," "The Sign in Sidney Brustein's Window," "Unexpected Guests," OB in "Venus Observed," "Diary of a Scoundrel," LCRep's "After the Fall" and "Marco Millions," "Drinks before Dinner."

LANCHESTER, ROBERT. Born Aug. 2, 1941 in Boston, Ma. Graduate MIT,

UCBerkeley. Bdwy bow 1969 in "A Flea in Her Ear," followed by "Three Sisters," "The Utter Glory of Morrissey Hall," OB in "Greenwillow," "Johnny Belinda," "The Perfect Mollusc," "King Lear."

LANDERS, MATT. Born Oct. 21, 1952 in Mohawk Valley, NY. Attended Boston Cons. Debut OB 1974 in "Godspell," followed by "Mama's Little Angels," "Telecast," Bdwy in "Grease" (1975), "Working."

LANE, NATHAN. Born Feb. 3, 1956 in Jersey City, NJ. Debut 1978 OB in "A Midsummer Night's Dream."

LANG, CHARLEY. Born Oct. 24, 1955 in Passaic, NJ. Graduate Catholic U. Bdwy debut 1978 in "Da."

LANGELLA, FRANK. Born Jan. 1, 1940 in Bayonne, NJ. Graduate Syracuse U. Debut 1963 OB in "The Immoralist," followed by "The Old Glory," "Good Day," "White Devil," "Yerma," "Iphigenia in Aulis," "A Cry of Players," "Prince of Homburg," Bdwy in "Seascape," "Dracula."

LANSBURY, ANGELA. Born Oct. 16, 1925 in London, Eng. Bdwy debut 1957 in "Hotel Paradiso," followed by "A Taste of Honey," "Anyone Can Whistle," "Mame," "Dear World," "Gypsy," "The King and I" (1978), "Sweeney Todd."

LARKIN, EDITH. Born Jan. 31, 1921 in NYC. Attended Vassar. Bdwy debut 1940 in "The Male Animal," OB in "Plaza Suite," "5th of July," "The Miracle Worker," "Let's Get a Divorce."

LaROSA, JULIUS. Born Jan. 2, 1930 in Brooklyn, NY. Bdwy bow 1962 in "Come Blow Your Horn," followed by OB in "Kiss Mama," "A Broadway Musical."

LASSER, LOUISE. Born in NYC. Attended Brandeis U. Bdwy debut 1962 in "I Can Get It for You Wholesale," followed by "Henry, Sweet Henry," "The Chinese and Dr. Fish," "Thieves," OB in "The Third Ear," "Are You Now or Have You Ever Been."

LAURIA, DAN. Born Apr. 12, 1947 in Brooklyn, NY. Graduate SConnState, UConn. Debut 1978 OB in "Game Plan."

LAWSON, ROGER. Born Oct. 11, 1942 in Tarrytown, NY. Attended Fredonia Col. Bdwy debut 1967 in "Hello, Dolly!," OB in "Pins and Needles," "Billy Noname," "Dinner at the Ambassador's," "One Free Smile," "Nongogo," "Dispatches."

LEARY, DAVID. Born Aug. 8, 1939 in Brooklyn, NY. Attended CCNY. Debut 1969 OB in "Shoot Anything That Moves," followed by "Macbeth," "The Plough and the Stars," Bdwy in "The National Health," "Da."

LeBLANC, DIANA-JEANNE. Born May 22, 1948 in Phoenix, Az. Attended UCal. Debut 1979 OB in "On a Clear Day You Can See Forever."

LeCLERC, JEAN. Born July 7, 1945 in Montreal, Can. Graduate Quebec U. Bdwy debut 1979 in "Dracula."

LEE, IRVING. Born Nov. 21, 1948 in NYC. Boston U. graduate. Debut 1969 OB in "Kiss Now," followed by "Ride the Winds," "A Visit with Death," Bdwy in "Pippin" (1973), "Rockabye Hamlet," "A Broadway Musical."

LeFEVER, KIT. Born Dec. 18, 1953 in Elizabeth, NJ. Graduate AADA. Debut 1978 OB in "The Show-Off."

LeMASSENA, WILLIAM. Born May 23, 1916 in Glen Ridge, NJ. Attended NYU. Bdwy bow 1940 In "Taming of the Shrew," followed by "There Shall Be No Night," "The Pirate," "Hamlet," "Call Me Mister," "Inside U.S.A.," "I Know, My Love," "Dream Girl," "Nina," "Ondine," "Fallen Angels," "Redhead," "Conquering Hero," "Beauty Part," "Come Summer," "Grin and Bare it," "All over Town," "A Texas Trilogy," "Deathtrap," OB in "The Coop," "Brigadoon," "Life with Father," "F. Jasmine Addams," "The Dodge Boys."

LEMMON, JACK. Born Feb. 8, 1925 in Boston, Ma. Harvard graduate. Bdwy debut 1953 in "Room Service," followed by "Face of a Hero," "Tribute."

LEON, JOSEPH. Born June 8, 1923 in NYC. Attended NYU, UCLA. Bdwy debut 1950 in "Bell, Book and Candle," followed by "Seven Year Itch," "Pipe Dream," "Fair Game," "Gazebo," "Julia, Jake and Uncle Joe," "Beauty Part," "Merry Widow," "Henry, Sweet Henry," "Jimmy Shine," "All over Town," "California Suite," "The Merchant," "Break a Leg," OB in "Come Share My House," "Dark Corners," "Interrogation of Havana," "Are You Now or Have You Ever Been."

LEONARDOS, URYLEE, Born May 14, in Charleston, SC. Attended Manhattan Sch. of Music. Bdwy debut 1943 in "Carmen Jones," followed by "Shangri-La," "Bells Are Ringing," "Wildcat," "Sophie," "Milk and Honey," "110 in the Shade," "Bajour," "Ilya, Darling," "Dear World," "Desert Song," "1600 Pennsylvania Ave.," "The Royal Family," OB in "Billy Noname," "Fixed."

LESTER, BARBARA. Born Dec. 27, 1928 in London, Eng. Graduate Columbia U. Bdwy debut 1956 in "Protective Custody," followed by "Legend of Lizzie," "Luther," "Inadmissible Evidence," "Johnny No-Trump," "Grin and Bare It," "Butley," "Man and Superman," OB in "Electra," "Queen after Death," "Summer of the 17th Doll," "Richard II," "Much Ado about Nothing," "One Way Pendulum," "Abelard and Heloise," "There's One in Every Marriage."

LEVINE, RICHARD S. Born July 16, 1954 in Boston, Ma. Graduate Juilliard. Debut 1978 OB in "Family Business," followed by Bdwy in "Dracula."

LEWIS, GILBERT. Born Apr. 6, 1941 in Philadelphia, Pa. Attended Morgan State Col. Bdwy bow 1969 in "The Great White Hope," OB in "Who's Got His Own," "Transfers," "Ballet behind the Bridge," "Coriolanus."

LEWIS, JENIFER. Born Jan. 25, 1957 in St. Louis, Mo. Graduate Webster College. Bdwy debut 1979 in "Eubie."

LINDIG, JILLIAN. Born Mar. 19, 1944 in Johnson City, TX. Debut 1969 OB in "Brownstone Urge," followed by "AC/DC," "The Constant Wife," Bdwy in "Equus."

LINK, TERESA. Born Sept. 20, 1951 in South Bend, In. Graduate Boston Cons. IllStateU. Debut 1978 OB in "The Passion of Dracula."

LIPPIN, RENEE. Born July 26, 1946 in NYC. Graduate Adelphi U. Debut 1970 OB in "The Way It Is," Bdwy in "Fun City," "The Inspector General."

LIPTON, MICHAEL. Born Apr. 27, 1925 in NYC. Attended Queens Col. Credits include "Caesar and Cleopatra," "The Moon Is Blue," "Sing Me No Lullaby," "Wake Up, Darling," "Tenth Man," "Separate Tables," "Inquest," "Loose Ends," OB in "Lover," "Trigon," "Long Christmas Dinner," "Hamp," "Boys in the Band," "Justice Box," "Cold Storage."

LISTER, DOROTHY DANIELS. Born Feb. 28, 1934 in Pensacola, FL. Attended NYU, Hunter Col. Bdwy bow 1968 in "Here's Where I Belong," followed by "Ballroom," OB in "Of Thee I Sing," "Hark."

LITHGOW, JOHN. Born Oct. 19, 1945 in Rochester, NY. Graduate Harvard U. Bdwy debut 1973 in "The Changing Room," followed by "My Fat Friend," "Comedians," "Anna Christie," "Once in a Lifetime," "Spokesong," "Bedroom Farce," OB in "Hamlet," "Trelawny of the Wells," "A Memory of Two Mondays," "Secret Service," "Boy Meets Girl."

LITTLE, DAVID. Born Mar. 21, 1937 in Wadesboro, NC. Graduate Wm. & Mary Col., Catholic U. Debut 1967 OB in "MacBird," followed by "Iphigenia in Aulis," "Antony and Cleopatra," "Antigone," "An Enemy of the People," "Three Sons," "God Bless You, Mr. Rosewater," Bdwy in "Thieves," "Zalmen, or the Madness of God."

LITTLER, SUSAN. Born Dec. 31, 1948 in Lancashire, Eng. Attended Webber-Douglas Academy. Bdwy debut 1979 in "Bedroom Farce."

LO, RANDON. Born June 12, 1949 in Oakland, Ca. Graduate UCalBerkeley. Debut 1978 in "Stop the World, I Want to Get Off."

LOCANTE, SAM. Born Sept. 12, 1918 in Kenosha, Wi. Graduate UWis., Goodman Sch. Bdwy bow 1955 in "Anniversary Waltz," followed by "Hidden Stranger," "Moonbirds," OB in "The Beaver Coat," "The Soldier," "Virgin Producers," "Game Plan," "The Time of Your Life," "Stone Killers," "Happy Anniversary," "Middle of the Night," "The Wrong Man."

LOGAN, ELE. Born Feb. 3, 1922 in Great Falls, Mt. Graduate Northwestern, Humbolt State U. Debut 1958 OB in "Ladies in Retirement," followed by "A Flea in Her Ear," "Reflections," "Simple Gifts," "On a Clear Day You Can See Forever."

LOUDON, DOROTHY. Born Sept. 17, 1933 in Boston, MA. Attended Emerson Col., Syracuse U. Debut 1961 OB in "World of Jules Feiffer," Bdwy 1963 in "Nowhere to Go but Up" for which she received a Theatre World Award, followed by "Noel Coward's Sweet Potato," "Fig Leaves Are Falling," "Three Men on a Horse," "The Women," "Annie," "Ballroom."

LOUISE, MARY. Born July 10, in Baltimore, MD. Attended American Theatre Wing. Debut 1962 OB in "Fly Blackbird," followed by "Unsung Cole," "Suddenly the Music Starts," Bdwy in "Funny Girl."

LOVE, EDWARD. Born June 29, 1952 in Toledo, OH. Graduate Ohio U, NYU. Debut 1972 OB in "Ti-Jean and His Brothers," followed by "Spell #7," Bdwy in "Raisin," "A Chorus Line," "Dancin'."

LOWE, GWEN HILLIER. Born Mar. 26 in Queens, NY. Attended HB Studio. Bdwy debut 1969 in "Hello, Dolly!," followed by "No, No, Nanette," OB in "Curly McDimple," "Tip-Toes."

LOWERY, MARCELLA. Born Apr. 27, 1945 in Jamaica, NY. Hunter Col. graduate. Debut 1967 OB in "Day of Absence," followed by "American Pastoral," "Ballet Behind the Bridge," "Jamimma," "A Recent Killing," "Miracle Play," "Welcome to Black River," "Anna Lucasta," Bdwy in "A Member of The Wedding" (1975).

LOWNDS, PETER. Born Aug. 5, 1944 in NYC. Yale graduate. Debut 1976 OB in "Benito Cereno," followed by "The Hostage," "Isadora Duncan Sleeps with The Russian Navy," "Unlikely Heroes," "Loyalties."

LUCAS, J. FRANK. Born in Houston, TX. Graduate TCU. Debut 1943 OB in "A Man's House," followed by "Coriolanus," "Edward II," "Long Gallery," "Trip to Bountiful," "Orpheus Descending," "Guitar," "Marcus in the High Grass," "Chocolates," "To Bury a Cousin," "One World at a Time," Bdwy in "Bad Habits," "The Best Little Whorehouse in Texas."

LUCKINBILL, LAURENCE. Born Nov. 21, 1938 in Ft. Smith, AR. Graduate UArk., Catholic U. Bdwy debut in "A Man for All Seasons," followed by "Beekman Place," "Poor Murderers," "The Shadow Box," "Chapter 2," OB in "Oedipus Rex," "There's a Play Tonight," "Fantasticks," "Tartuffe," "Boys in the Band," "Horseman, Pass By," "Memory Bank," "What the Butler Saw," "A Meeting by the River," "Alpha Beta," "A Prayer for My Daughter," "Life of Galileo."

LUDWIG, KAREN. Born Oct. 9, 1942 in San Francisco, CA. Bdwy debut 1964 in "The Deputy," followed by "The Devils," OB in "Trojan Women," "Red Cross," "Muzeeka," "Huui, Huui," "Our Late Night," "The Seagull," "Museum," "Nasty Rumors."

LUGENBEAL, CAROL. Born July 14, 1952 in Detroit, MI. Graduate U.S. International U. Bdwy debut 1974 in "Where's Charley?," followed by "On the 20th Century."

LUNA, BARBARA. Born Mar. 2 in NYC. Bdwy debut 1951 in "The King and I," followed by "West Side Story" (LC), "A Chorus Line."

LUZ, FRANK C. Born Dec. 22 in Cambridge, Ma. Attended NMxStateU. Debut 1974 OB in "The Rivals," followed by "Fiorello!," Bdwy 1979 in "Whoopee!"

LYMAN, DOROTHY. Born Apr. 18, 1947 in Minneapolis, MN. Attended Sarah Lawrence Col. Debut OB in "America Hurrah," followed by "Pequod,"

"American Hamburger League," "Action," "Fefu and Her Friends," "Later."

LYMAN, WILLIAM. Born May 20, 1948 in Stowe, Vt. Boston U. graduate. Debut 1978 OB in "The Passion of Dracula," followed by "The Grinding Machine."

LYNDECK, EDMUND. Born Oct. 4, 1925 in Baton Rouge, La. Graduate Montclair State Col., Fordham U. Bdwy debut 1969 in "1776," followed by "Sweeney Todd," OB in "The King and I" (JB), "Mandragola," "A Safe Place," "Amoureuse," "Piaf: A Remembrance."

MacDONALD, PIRIE. Born Mar. 24, 1932 in NYC. Graduate Harvard U. Debut 1957 OB in "Under Milk Wood," followed by "Zoo Story," "Innocent Pleasure," "Romance," Bdwy in "Shadow and Substance," "Golden Fleecing," "Big Fish, Little Fish," "Death of a Salesman," "But Not for Me."

MacHALE, DEBORAH B. Born Aug. 21, 1951 in Gulfport, Ms. Graduate UTx. Debut 1977 OB in "Dance on a Country Grave," followed by "Bread and Roses," "La Ronde."

MacINTOSH, JOAN E. Born Nov. 25, 1945 in NJ. Graduate Beaver Col., NYU. Debut OB 1969 in "Dionysus in '69," followed by "Makbeth," "The Beard," "Tooth of Crime," "Mother Courage," "Marilyn Project," "Seneca's Oedipus," "St. Joan of the Stockyards," "Wonderland in Concert," "Dispatches."

MacKENZIE, WENNDY LEIGH. Born Oct. 19, 1955 in Los Angeles, Ca. Attended LACC, UCLA. Debut OB 1965 in "Oliver," Bdwy 1978 in "Platinum."

MADDEN, DONALD. Born Nov. 5, 1933 in NYC. Attended CCNY. Bdwy debut 1958 in "Look Back in Anger," followed by "First Impressions," "Step on a Crack," "One by One," "White Lies," "Black Comedy," OB in "Julius Caesar" for which he received a Theatre World Award, "Lysistrata," "Pictures in a Hallway," "Henry IV," "She Stoops to Conquer," "Octoroon," "Hamlet," "Ceremony of Innocence," "Henry VI," "Richard III," "A Doll's House," "Hedda Gabler," "The Philanderer," "Scribes," "Trick."

MADDEN, SHARON. Born July 8, 1947 in St. Louis, MO. Debut 1975 OB in "Battle of Angels," followed by "The Hot l Baltimore," "Who Killed Richard Cory?," "Mrs. Murray's Farm," "The Passing of Corky Brewster," "Brontosaurus," "Ulysses in Traction," "Lulu," "In the Recovery Lounge."

MADURGA, GONZALO. Born Jan. 21, 1932 in Havana, Cuba. Graduate LIU. Debut 1961 OB in "King of the Dark Camber," followed by "The Fantasticks," "Macbeth," "Romeo and Juliet," Bdwy 1979 in "Carmelina."

MAGGART, BRANDON. Born Dec. 12, 1933 in Carthage, Tn. Graduate UTn. OB in "Sing Muse!," "Like Other People," "Put It in Writing" for which he received a Theatre World Award, "Wedding Band," "But Not For Me," "Romance," Bdwy in "Kelly," "New Faces of 1968," "Applause," "Lorelei," "We Interrupt This Program."

MAGNUSEN, MICHAEL. Born Jan. 18, 1951 in Oshkosh, Wi. Graduate Lawrence U. Debut 1979 OB in "Festival."

MAHAFFEY, VALERIE. Born June 16, 1953 in Sumatra, Indonesia. Graduate UTx. Debut 1975 OB in "Father Uxbridge Wants to Marry," followed by "Bus Stop," "Black Tuesday," Bdwy in "Rex," "Dracula."

MAHER, JOSEPH. Born Dec. 29, 1933 in Westport, Ire. Bdwy bow 1964 in "The Chinese Prime Minister," followed by "The Prime of Miss Jean Brodie," "Henry V," "There's One in Every Marriage," "Who's Who in Hell," "Days in the Trees," "Spokesong," OB in "The Hostage," "Live Like Pigs," "Importance of Being Earnest," "Eh?," "Local Stigmatic," "Mary Stuart," "The Contractor," "Savages."

MANLEY, MARK. Born July 10, 1954 in Newark, NJ. Attended Jersey City State. Debut 1979 OB in "Mary."

MANN, P. J. Born Apr. 9, 1953 in Pasadena, Ca. Bdwy debut 1976 in "Home Sweet Homer," followed by "A Chorus Line," "Dancin'."

MANSOUR, GEORGE, P., JR. Born Apr. 16, 1949 in Youngstown, Oh. Attended Juilliard. Bdwy debut 1972 in "Jesus Christ Superstar," OB in "Adventures of Scaramouche."

MARCH, ELLEN. Born Aug. 18, 1948 in Brooklyn, NY. Graduate AMDA. Debut 1967 OB in "Pins and Needles," Bdwy in "Grease," "Once in a Lifetime."

MARCH, KENDALL. Born in Boston, Ma. Graduate Sarah Lawrence Col. Bdwy debut 1969 in "The Front Page," OB in "Ballad of John Ogilvie," "The Autograph Hound," "A Midsummer Night's Dream."

MARCHAND, NANCY. Born June 19, 1928 in Buffalo, NY. Carnegie Tech graduate. Debut 1951 in "Taming of the Shrew" (CC), followed by "Merchant of Venice," "Much Ado about Nothing," "Three Bags Full," "After the Rain," LCRep's "The Alchemist," "Yerma," "Cyrano de Bergerac," "Mary Stuart," "Enemies" and "The Plough and the Stars," "40 Carats," "And Miss Reardon Drinks a Little," "Veronica's Room," OB in "The Balcony," "Children," "Taken in Marriage."

MARCUM, KEVIN. Born Nov. 7, 1955 in Danville, Il. Attended UIll. Bdwy debut 1976 in "My Fair Lady," followed by "I Remember Mama."

MARDIROSIAN, TOM. Born Dec. 14, 1947 in Buffalo, NY. Graduate UBuffalo. Debut 1976 OB in "Gemini," followed by "Grand Magic," "Losing Time," Bdwy in "Happy End," "Magic Show."

MARGULIES, DAVID. Born Feb. 19, 1937 in NYC. Graduate CCNY. Debut 1958 OB in "Golden Six," followed by "Six Characters in Search of an Author," "Tragical Historie of Dr. Faustus," "Tango," "Little Murders," "Seven Days of Mourning," "Last Analysis," "An Evening with the Poet Senator," "Kid Champion," "The Man with the Flower in His Mouth," "The Old Tune," Bdwy in "The Iceman Cometh" (1973), "Zalmen, or the Madness of God," "Comedians," "Break a Leg."

MARIANO, PATTI. Born June 12, 1945 in Philadelphia, Pa. Bdwy debut 1957 in "Music Man," followed by "Bye Bye Birdie," "Sail Away," "I Had a Ball," "George M!," OB in "Country Girl," "Me and Juliet," "Godspell," "American Dance Machine."

MARIE, JULIENNE. Born in 1943 in Toledo, Oh. Attended Juilliard. Has appeared in "The King and I," "Whoop-Up!," "Gypsy," "Foxy," "Do I Hear a Waltz?," "Ballroom," OB in "The Boys from Syracuse" for which she received a Theatre World Award, "Othello," "Comedy of Errors," "The Trojan Women."

MARK, MICHAEL. Born Mar. 14, 1950 in NYC. Northwestern U. graduate. Bdwy debut 1977 in "I Love My Wife."

MARSHALL, LARRY. Born Apr. 3, 1944 in Spartanburg, SC. Attended Fordham U., New Eng. Cons. Bdwy debut in "Hair," followed by "Two Gentlemen of Verona," "A Midsummer Night's Dream," "Rockabye Hamlet," "Porgy and Bess," "A Broadway Musical."

MARTIN, MILLICENT. Born June 8, 1934 in Romford, Eng. Attended Italia Conti Sch. Bdwy debut 1954 in "The Boy Friend," followed by "Side by Side by Sondheim," "King of Hearts."

MARTIN, VIRGINIA. Born Dec. 2, 1932 in Chattanooga, TN. Attended Theatre Wing. Appeared in "South Pacific," "Pajama Game," "Ankles Aweigh," "New Faces of 1956," "How to Succeed in Business . . . ," "Little Me," "Carmelina," OB in "Buy Bonds Buster," "Joseph and the Amazing Technicolor Dreamcoat," "Sing Melancholy Baby."

MARTIN, W. T. Born Jan. 17, 1947 in Providence, RI. Attended Lafayette Col. Debut 1972 OB in "The Basic Training of Pavlo Hummel," followed by "Ghosts," "The Caretaker," "Are You Now or Have You Ever Been."

MASIELL, JOE. Born Oct. 27, 1939 in Brooklyn, NY. Attended HB Studio. Debut 1964 in "Cindy," followed by "Jacques Brel Is Alive and . . . ," "Sensations," "Leaves of Grass," "How to Get Rid of It," "A Matter of Time," "Tickles by Tucholsky," "Not at the Palace," Bdwy in "Dear World," "Different Times," "Jacques Brel Is . . . ," "Got Tu Go Disco."

MASON, CRAIG. Born July 1, 1950 in Rochester, MN. Graduate Yale U. Debut 1978 OB in "Allegro," followed by "On a Clear Day You Can See Forever."

MASON, JAMES. Born May 15, 1909 in Huddersfield, Eng. Attended Cambridge, Gate Theatre, Old Vic. Bdwy debut 1947 in "Bathsheba," followed by "The Faith Healer."

MASTERSON, DEBORA. Born July 9, 1950 in Burbank, Ca. Attended UUtah, Catholic Inst. (Paris). Bdwy debut 1978 in "Stop the World, I Want to Get Off."

MATTHEWS, DONNA. Born June 4, 1959 in Paterson, NJ. Debut OB 1979 in "Shindig."

MATTSON, WAYNE. Born July 13, 1952 in Rochester, Mn. Attended Allan Hancock Col., Pacific Cons. Bdwy debut 1974 in "Lorelei," followed by "Music Is," "They're Playing Our Song."

MAUPIN, SAMUEL. Born Dec. 27, 1947 in Portsmouth, VA. Graduate Va. Commonwealth U. Debut 1977 OB in "The Passion of Dracula."

MAY, BEVERLY. Born Aug. 11, 1927 in East Wellington, BD, Can. Graduate Yale U. Debut 1976 OB in "Female Transport," Bdwy 1977 in "Equus," followed by "Once in a Lifetime," "Whose Life Is It Anyway?"

MAY, DEBORAH S. Born Sept. 28, 1948 in Lafayette In. Attended IndU., Am. Consv. Theatre. Bdwy debut 1978 in "Once in a Lifetime."

MAYRON, MELANIE JOY. Born Oct. 20, 1952 in Philadelphia, Pa. Graduate AADA. Bdwy debut 1979 in "The Goodbye People."

McCALL, JANET. Born June 26, 1935 in Washington, DC. Graduate PennState. Debut 1960 OB in "The Golden Apple," followed by "Life Is a Dream," "Tattooed Countess," "The Bacchantes," "Jacques Brel Is Alive . . . ," "How to Get Rid of It," "Cockeyed Tiger," Bdwy in "Camelot," "1776," "2 by 2," "Jacques Brel Is . . . ," "She Loves Me," "I Remember Mama."

McCALL, NANCY. Born Jan. 12, 1948 in Atlanta, Ga. Northwestern U. graduate. Debut 1975 OB in "Godspell," followed by "The Heebie Jeebies."

McCANN, CHRISTOPHER. Born Sept. 29, 1952 in NYC. Graduate NYU. Debut 1975 OB in "The Measures Taken," followed by "Ghosts," "Woyzzeck," "St. Joan of the Stockyards," "Buried Child."

McCARTY, MICHAEL. Born Sept. 7, 1946 in Evansville, In. Graduate IndU, Mich. State U. Debut 1976 OB in "Fiorello!," Bdwy in "Dirty Linen," "King of Hearts."

McCONNELL, TY. Born Jan. 13, 1940 in Coldwater, Mi. Graduate UMich. Debut 1962 OB in "The Fantasticks," followed by "Promenade," "Contrast," "Fashion," "The Dubliners," "Lovesong," "Super Spy," Bdwy in "Lion in Winter," "Dear World."

McCOWEN, ALEC. Born May 26, 1925 in Tunbridge Wells, Eng. Attended RADA. Bdwy debut 1951 in "Antony and Cleopatra," followed by "Caesar and Cleopatra," "King Lear," "Comedy of Errors," "After the Rain," "Hadrian VII," "The Philanthropist," "The Misanthrope," "Equus," OB in "St. Mark's Gospel."

McDERMOTT, KEITH. Born in Houston, Tx. Attended LAMDA. Bdwy debut 1976 in "Equus," followed by "A Meeting by the River."

McDONALD, TANNY. Born Feb. 13, 1939 in Princeton, In. Graduate Vassar Col. Debut OB with Am. Savoyards, followed by "All in Love," "To Broadway

with Love," "Carricknabauna," "Beggar's Opera," "Brand," "Goodbye, Dan Bailey," "Total Eclipse," "Gorky," "Don Juan Comes Back from the War," Bdwy in "Fiddler on the Roof," "Come Summer," "The Lincoln Mask."

McDONNELL, MARY. Born in 1952 in Ithaca, NY. Graduate SUNY Fredonia. Debut OB 1978 in "Buried Child."

McDONOUGH, ANN. Born in Portland, Me. Graduate Towson State. Debut 1975 OB in "Trelawny of the Wells," followed by "Secret Service," "Boy Meets Girl," "Scribes," "Uncommon Women," "City Sugar."

McFARLAND, ROBERT. Born May 7, 1931 in Omaha, NE. Graduate UMich, Columbia U. Debut 1978 OB in "The Taming of the Shrew."

McGILL, EVERETT. Born Oct. 21, 1945 in Miami Beach, FL. Graduate UMo., RADA. Debut OB 1971 in "Brothers," followed by "The Father," "Enemies," Bdwy in "Equus" (1974), "A Texas Trilogy," "The Merchant," "Dracula."

McGREEVEY, ANNIE. Born in Brooklyn, NY. Graduate AADA. Bdwy debut 1971 in "Company," followed by "The Magic Show," "Annie," OB in "Booth Is Back in Town."

McGREGOR-STEWART, KATE. Born Oct. 4, 1944 in Buffalo, NY. Graduate Beaver Col., Yale U. Bdwy debut 1975 in "Travesties" followed by "A History of the American Film," OB in "Titanic," "Vienna Notes."

McINERNEY, BERNIE. Born Dec. 4, 1936 in Wilmington, DE. Graduate UDel., Catholic U. Bdwy debut 1972 in "That Championship Season," followed by OB in "Life of Galileo," "Losing Time."

McINTYRE, BILL. Born Sept. 2, 1935 in Rochester, NY. Debut OB 1970 in "The Fantasticks," Bdwy in "Secret Affairs of Mildred Wild," "Legend," "The Inspector General."

McKENNA, SIOBHAN. Born May 24, 1922 in Belfast, Ire. UDublin graduate. Bdwy debut 1955 in "Chalk Garden," followed by "St. Joan," "Rope Dancers," "Hamlet" (OB title role), "Here Are Ladies," "A Meeting by the River."

McKITTERICK, TOM. Born Jan. 23 in Cleveland, Oh. Amherst graduate. Debut 1978 OB in "Fathers and Sons," followed by "Say Goodnight, Gracie."

McLERIE, ALLYN ANN. Born Dec. 1, 1926 in Grand Mere, Can. Bdwy debut 1943 in "One Touch of Venus," followed by "Where's Charley?" for which she received a Theatre World Award, "Miss Liberty," "Time Limit," "West Side Story," "South Pacific" (CC), "The Beast in Me," "Show Boat" (LC), OB in "Dynamite Tonite," "Dancing in the Dark."

McLERNON, PAMELA. Born March 1 in Lynn, Ma. Lowell State Col. graduate. Debut 1975 OB in "Tenderloin," Bdwy in "Sweeney Todd."

McMAHON, JIM. Born Nov. 1, 1939 in Wilkes-Barre, Pa. Graduate Villanova U. Debut 1968 OB in "Madwoman of Chaillot," followed by "Piano Bar."

McNAMARA, MAUREEN. Born Mar. 17, 1957 in NYC. Studied at HB Studio. Debut 1978 OB in "Company," followed by "Festival."

McNAMARA, ROSEMARY. Born Jan. 7, 1943 in Summit, NJ. Attended Newark Col. OB in "The Master Builder," "Carricknabauna," "Rocket to the Moon," "The Most Happy Fella" (CC), Bdwy in "The Student Gypsy."

McQUEEN, ARMELIA. Born Jan. 6, 1952 in North Carolina. Attended HB Studio, Bklyn. Consv. Bdwy debut 1978 in "Ain't Misbehavin" for which she received a Theatre World Award.

McROBBIE, PETER. Born Jan. 31, 1943 in Hawick, Scot. Yale graduate. Debut 1976 OB in "The Wobblies," Bdwy 1979 in "Whose Life Is It Anyway?"

McSPADDEN, BECKY. Born Dec. 14, 1949 in Norfolk, VA. Graduate UNeb. Bdwy debut 1974 in "Candide," followed by "The Utter Glory of Morrissey Hall," OB in "Company."

MEACHAM, PAUL. Born Aug. 5, 1939 in Memphis, Tn. Graduate UTn, MichStateU. Debut 1973 OB in "Twelfth Night," followed by "The Homecoming," "The Tempest," "Moby Dick," "The Crucible," "The Passion of Dracula."

MEADOWS, NANCY. Born July 11, 1953 in Glen Rock, NJ. Debut 1979 OB in "Mary."

MERCADO, HECTOR. Born in NYC in 1949. Graduate H. S. Performing Arts. Attended Harkness Ballet Sch., HB Studio. Bdwy debut 1960 in "West Side Story," followed by "Man of LaMancha" (and 1977 revival), "Mass," "Dr. Jazz," "1600 Pennsylvania Ave.," "Your Arms Too Short to Box with God," OB in "Sancocho," "People in Show Business Make Long Goodbyes."

MERCER, MARIAN. Born Nov. 26, 1935 in Akron, Oh. UMich. graduate. Bdwy debut 1960 in "Greenwillow," followed by "Fiorello!," "Promises, Promises" for which she received a Theatre World Award, "A Place for Polly," "Hay Fever," "Stop the World, I Want to Get Off," "Bosoms and Neglect," OB in "Little Mary Sunshine," "Hotel Passionato," "Your Own Thing."

MERCER, SALLY. Born Jan. 19, 1952 in Rochester, NY. Ithaca Col. graduate. Debut 1979 OB in "The Importance of Being Earnest."

MEREDITH, LEE. Born Oct. 22, 1947 in River Edge, NJ. Graduate AADA. Bdwy debut 1969 in "A Teaspoon Every Four Hours," followed by "The Sunshine Boys," "Once in a Lifetime."

MERLIN, JOANNA. Born in Chicago, Il. Attended UCLA. Debut 1958 OB in "The Breaking Wall," followed by "Six Characters in Search of an Author," "Rules of the Game," "Thistle in My Bed," "Canadian Gothic/American Modern," Bdwy in "Becket," "A Far Country," "Fiddler on the Roof," "Shelter," "Uncle Vanya."

MERRILL, DINA. Born Dec. 29, 1925 in NYC. Attended AADA, AMDA, Geo. Washington U. Bdwy debut 1975 in "Angel Street," OB in "Are You Now or Have You Ever Been."

MERRYMAN, MONICA. Born June 2, 1950 in Sao Paulo, Brazil. Graduate EMichU. Debut 1975 OB in "East Lynne," followed by "A Night at the Black Pig," "Vanities," "The Voice of the Turtle."

MERSON, SUSAN. Born Apr. 25, 1950 in Detroit, MI. Graduate Boston U. Bdwy debut 1974 in "Saturday Sunday Monday," followed by OB "Vanities."

MERYL, CYNTHIA. Born Sept. 25, 1950 in NYC. Graduate Ind. U. Bdwy debut 1976 in "My Fair Lady," OB in "Before Sundown." "The Canticle," "The Pirate," "Dames at Sea," "Gay Divorce," "Sterling Silver."

METZO, WILLIAM. Born June 21, 1937 in Wilkes-Barre, Pa. King's Col. graduate. Debut 1963 in "The Bald Soprano," followed by "Papers," "A Moon for the Misbegotten," "Arsenic and Old Lace," "Super Spy," Bdwy in "Cyrano" (1973).

MICHALSKI, JOHN. Born June 7, 1948 in Hammond, In. Juilliard graduate. Bdwy debut 1973 in "Beggar's Opera," followed by "Measure for Measure," "Herzl," "Gorey Stories," OB in "Hamlet," "Much Ado about Nothing."

MILANA, VINCENT DUKE. Born. Apr. 11, 1939 in Newark, NJ. Graduate Carroll U., Neighborhood Playhouse. With APA, and OB in "Abe Lincoln in Illinois," "Taming of the Shrew," "Color of Darkness," "Cannibals," "Now Is the Time," "The Birds," "12 Angry Men," "The Rapists," Bdwy in "Zoot Suit."

MILES, ROSS. Born in Poughkeepsie, NY. Bdwy debut 1962 in "Little Me," followed by "Baker Street," "Pickwick," "Darling of the Day," "Mame," "Jumpers," "Goodtime Charley," "Chicago," "Dancin'."

MILGRIM, LYNN. Born Mar. 17, 1944 in Philadelphia, PA. Graduate Swarthmore Col., Harvard U. Debut 1969 OB in "Frank Gagliano's City Scene," followed by "Crimes of Passion," "Macbeth," "Charley's Aunt," "The Real Inspector Hound," "Rib Cage," "Museum," Bdwy in "Otherwise Engaged," "Bedroom Farce."

MILLER, MARTHA. Born Aug. 30, 1929 in New Bedford, Ma. Graduate Carnegie-Mellon U. Debut OB 1956 in "House of Connolly," followed by "A Place without Morning," "Julius Caesar," "Major Barbara," "In the Summer House," "Merry Wives of Windsor," "Rimers of Eldritch," "Heartbreak House," "The Importance of Being Earnest."

MILLER, PATRICIA. Born Dec. 1, 1950 in Seattle, Wa. Graduate UGa. Debut 1978 OB in "Vanities."

MILLER, VALERIE-JEAN. Born Aug. 22, 1950 in Miami Beach, Fl. Bdwy debut 1978 in "Dancin'."

MILLIGAN, TUCK (a.k.a. Jacob) Born Mar. 25, 1949 in Kansas City, Mo. Graduate UKC. Bdwy debut 1976 in "Equus," followed by "Crucifer of Blood," OB in "Beowulf."

MINER, JAN. Born Oct. 15, 1917 in Boston, Ma. Debut 1958 OB in "Obligato," followed by "Decameron," "Dumbbell People," "Autograph Hound," "A Lovely Sunday for Creve Coeur," Bdwy in "Viva Madison Avenue," "Lady of the Camelias," "Freaking Out of Stephanie Blake," "Othello," "The Milk Train Doesn't Stop Here Anymore," "Butterflies Are Free," "The Women," "Pajama Game," "Saturday Sunday Monday," "The Heiress," "Romeo and Juliet."

MINNELLI, LIZA. Born Mar. 12, 1946 in Los Angeles, CA. Attended UParis, HB Studio. Debut 1963 OB in "Best Foot Forward" for which she received a Theatre World Award, followed by "Are You Now or Have You Ever Been," Bdwy in "Flora, the Red Menace," "Liza," "Chicago," "The Act."

MISTRETTA, SAL. Born Jan. 9, 1945 in Brooklyn, NY. Ithaca Col. graduate. Bdwy debut 1976 in "Something's Afoot," followed by "On the 20th Century."

MITZMAN, MARCIA. Born Feb. 28, 1959 in NYC. Attended SUNY Purchase, Neighborhood Playhouse. Debut 1978 OB in "Promises, Promises," followed by "Taming of the Shrew," Bdwy 1979 in "Grease."

MIYAMOTO ANNE. Born in Honolulu, HI. Graduate UHaw., NYU. Debut 1962 OB in "Yanks Are Coming," "And the Soul Shall Dance," Bdwy 1977 in "Basic Training of Pavlo Hummel."

MIZELLE, VANCE. Born Aug. 6, 1934 in Atlanta, Ga. Graduate Davidson Col, UGa. Debut 1975 OB in "Hamlet," followed by "On a Clear Day You Can See Forever."

MONTEITH, JOHN. Born Nov. 1, 1948 in Philadelphia, Pa. Graduate Boston U. Debut OB 1973 in "The Proposition," followed by "See America First," Bdwy 1979 "Monteith and Rand."

MOONEY, DEBRA. Born in Aberdeen, SD. Graduate Auburn, UMinn. Debut 1975 OB in "Battle of Angels," followed by "The Farm," "Summer and Smoke," "Stargazing," Bdwy 1978 in "Chapter 2."

MOOR, BILL. Born July 13, 1931 in Toledo, OH. Attended Northwestern U., Dennison U. Bdwy debut 1964 in "Blues for Mr. Charlie," followed by "Great God Brown," "Don Juan," "The Visit," "Chemin de Fer," "Holiday," "P.S. Your Cat Is Dead," "Night of the Tribades," "The Water Engine," OB in "Dandy Dick," "Love Nest," "Days and Nights of Beebee Fenstermaker," "The Collection," "The Owl Answers," "Long Christmas Dinner," "Fortune and Men's Eyes," "King Lear," "Cry of Players," "Boys in the Band," "Alive and Well in Argentina," "Rosmersholm," "The Biko Inquest."

MOORE, CHARLOTTE. Born July 7, 1939 in Herrin, IL. Attended Smith Col., Washington, U. Bdwy debut 1972 in "The Great God Brown," followed by "Don Juan," "The Visit," "Chemin de Fer," "Holiday," "Love for Love," "Member of the Wedding," OB in "Out of Our Father's House," "A Lovely Sunday for Creve Couer."

MORENZIE, LEON. Born in Trinidad, WI. Graduate Sir George William U. Debut 1972 OB in "Ti-Jean and His Brothers," followed by "The Cherry Orchard," "Cockeyed Tiger," "Twilight Dinner," "Rum and Coca Cola," "Old Phantoms," "Season Unravel," Bdwy in "The Leaf People."

MORFOGEN, GEORGE. Born Mar. 30, 1933 in NYC. Graduate Brown U, Yale. Debut 1957 OB in "Trial of D. Karamazov," followed by "Christmas Oratorio," "Othello," "Good Soldier Schweik," "Cave Dwellers," "Once in a Lifetime," "Total Eclipse," "Ice Age," "Prince of Homburg," "Biography: A Game," Bdwy in "The Fun Couple."

MORGAN, GARY. Born Jan. 2, 1950 in Passaic, NJ. Attended Fairleigh Dickinson U. Debut 1958 OB in "Comic Strip," Bdwy in "All the Way Home," "A Gift of Time," "King of Hearts."

MORIARTY, MICHAEL. Born Apr. 5, 1941 in Detroit, MI. Graduate Dartmouth, LAMBDA. Debut OB 1963 in "Antony and Cleopatra," followed by "Peanut Butter and Jelly," "Long Day's Journey into Night," "Henry V," "Alfred the Great," "Our Father's Failing," "G. R. Point," Bdwy in "Trial of the Catonsville 9," "Find Your Way Home" for which he received a Theater World Award, "Richard III" (LC).

MORIN, MICHAEL. Born Aug. 4, 1950 in Vineland, NJ. Graduate Villanova U. Debut 1976 OB in "Rio Grande," followed by "La Ronde."

MORRISEY, BOB. Born Aug. 15, 1946 in Somerville, MA. Attended UWis. Debut 1974 OB in "Ionescapade," followed by "Company," "Lifesongs," Bdwy in "The Grand Tour."

MORSELL, FRED. Born Aug. 3, 1940 in NYC. Debut 1971 OB in "Any Resemblance to Person Living or Dead," followed by "Merchant of Venice," "Enclave," "Rubbers," "Yankees 3, Detroit 0," "My Old Friends."

MOTLEY, KEVIN. Born Oct. 28, 1958 in Philadelphia, Pa. Attended Rutgers U. Debut 1978 OB in "Are You Now or Have You Ever Been."

MURPHY, ROSEMARY. Born Jan. 13, 1927 in Munich, Ger. Attended Neighborhood Playhouse, Actors Studio. Bdwy debut 1950 in "Tower beyond Tragedy," followed by "Look Homeward, Angel," "Period of Adjustment," "Any Wednesday," "Delicate Balance," "Weekend," "Death of Bessie Smith," "Butterflies Are Free," "Ladies at the Alamo," "Cheaters," OB in "Are You Now or Have You Ever Been."

MURRAY, BRIAN. Born Oct. 9, 1939 in Johannesburg, S.A. Debut 1964 OB in "The Knack," followed by "King Lear," "Ashes," Bdwy in "All in Good Time," "Rosencrantz and Guildenstern Are Dead," "Sleuth," "Da."

MURRAY, MARC. Born Jan. 25, 1955 in NYC. Attended Ithaca Col., HB Studio. Debut 1978 OB in "Godsong," followed by "Fall of Masada," "The Importance of Being Earnest," "A Marriage Proposal."

MURRAY, PEG. Born in Denver, CO. Attended Western Reserve U. OB in "Children of Darkness," followed by "A Midsummer Night's Dream," "Oh, Dad, Poor Dad . . .," "Small Craft Warnings," "Enclave," "Landscape of the Body," "A Lovely Sunday for Creve Couer," Bdwy in "The Great Sebastians" (1956), "Gypsy," "Blood, Sweat and Stanley Poole," "She Loves Me," "Anyone Can Whistle," "The Subject Was Roses," "Something More," "Cabaret," "Fiddler on the Roof," "Royal Family."

MUSANTE, TONY. Born June 30, 1936 in Bridgeport, Ct. Graduate Oberlin Col. Debut 1960 OB in "Borak," followed by "The Balcony," "Theatre of the Absurd," "Half-Past Wednesday," "The Collection," "Tender Heel," "Kiss Mama," "Mme. Mouse," "Zoo Story," "Match-Play," "Night of the Dunce," "Gun Play," "A Memory of Two Mondays," "27 Wagons Full of Cotton," "Grand Magic," Bdwy 1975 in "P.S. Your Cat Is Dead."

MUSNICK, STEPHANIE. Born Apr. 12, 1950 in Philadelphia. PA. Graduate Villanova U. Bdwy debut 1977 in "Gemini."

NATHAN, AMY. Born in Va. Graduate Radcliffe Col., Neighborhood Playhouse. Debut 1979 OB in "The Miracle Worker," followed by "Quail Southwest," "October Wedding," "The Ride Across Lake Constance."

NATWICK, MILDRED. Born June 19, 1908 in Baltimore, Md. Bdwy debut 1932 in "Carrie Nation," followed by "The Wind and the Rain," "Distaff Side," "End of Summer," "Love from a Stranger," "Candida," "Star Wagon," "Missouri Legend," "Blithe Spirit," "Playboy of the Western World," "Grass Harp," "Coriolanus," "Waltz of the Toreadors," "Day the Money Stopped," "The Firstborn," "Critic's Choice," "Barefoot in the Park," "Our Town," "Landscapes"(LC), "70 Girls 70," "Bedroom Farce."

NAUGHTON, JAMES. Born Dec. 6, 1945 in Middletown, CT. Graduate Brown, Yale U. Debut 1971 OB in "Long Day's Journey Into Night" for which he received a Theatre World Award, followed by "Drinks Before Dinner," "Losing Time," Bdwy 1977 in "I Love My Wife."

NEAL, ALBERT. Born Nov. 8, 1953 in South Orange, NJ. Graduate Boston U. Debut 1978 OB in "Family Business."

NEAR, TIMOTHY. Born Feb. 23, 1945 in Los Angeles, Ca. Graduate San Francisco State Col., LAMBDA. Debut 1978 OB in "The Immediate Family."

NEGRO, MARY-JOAN. Born Nov. 9, 1948 in Brooklyn, NY. Debut 1972 OB in "The Hostage," followed by "Lower Depths," "Women Beware Women," "Ladyhouse Blues," "The Promise," Bdwy in "Three Sisters," "Measure for Measure," "Beggar's Opera," "Wings."

NELSON, P. J. Born Nov. 17, 1952 in NYC. Attended Manhattan Sch. of Music. Bdwy debut 1978 in "Hello, Dolly!"

NERSESIAN, ROBERT. Born July 31, 1950 in Englewood, NJ. Graduate UVa, Yale. Debut 1977 OB in "Counsellor-at-Law," followed by "Oklahoma!," "The Dybbuk."

NETTLETON, LOIS. Born in Oak Park, Il. Attended Goodman Theatre, Actors Studio. Bdwy Debut 1949 in "The Biggest Thief in Town," followed by "Darkness at Noon," "Cat on a Hot Tin Roof," "God and Kate Murphy,"

248

"Silent Night, Lonely Night," "A Streetcar Named Desire"(LC), "Strangers," OB in "They Knew What They Wanted."

NEVILLE-ANDREWS, JOHN. Born Aug. 23, 1948 in Woking Surrey, Eng. Attended Westminster Tech. Col. Debut 1973 OB in "El Grande de Coca-Cola," followed by "Bullshot Drummond," Bdwy in "The Elephant Man."

NEWMAN, ELLEN. Born Sept. 5, 1950 in NYC. Attended San Diego State U., Central Sch. London. Debut 1972 OB in "Right You Are," followed by LCRep's "Merchant of Venice" and "Streetcar Named Desire," "The Importance of Being Earnest," "A Midsummer Night's Dream."

NEWMAN, WILLIAM. Born June 15, 1934 in Chicago, Il. Graduate UWash., Columbia. Debut 1972 OB in "The Beggar's Opera," followed by "Are You Now or Have You Ever Been," "Conflict of Interest," "Mr. Runaway," "Uncle Vanya," Bdwy in "Over Here," "Rocky Horror Show," "Strangers."

NEWTON, JOHN. Born Nov. 2, 1925 in Grand Junction, Co. UWash. graduate. Debut 1951 OB in "Othello," followed by "As You Like It," "Candida," "Candaules Commissioner," "Sextet," "LCRep's," "The Crucible," and "A Streetcar Named Desire," "The Rivals," Bdwy in "Weekend," "First Monday in October."

NEWTON-DAVIS, BILLY. Born Apr. 26 in Cleveland, Oh. Graduate Ohio U. Debut 1975 OB in "Bayou Legend," Bdwy in "Bubbling Brown Sugar," "Stop the World, I Want to Get Off."

NICHOLS, JOSEPHINE. Born Nov. 11. 1913 in Lawrenceville, IL. Graduate UOkla., Columbia U. Debut 1960 OB in "The Prodigal," followed by "Roots," "The Golden Six," "The Adding Machine," "The Storm," "Uncommon Women and Others," "The Grinding Machine," Bdwy in "On an Open Roof." "The Skin of Our Teeth."

NICHOLS, ROBERT. Born July 20, 1924 in Oakland, Ca. Attended Coll. of Pacific, RADA. Debut 1978 OB in "Are You Now or Have You Ever Been," Bdwy in "Man and Superman."

NILES, MARY ANN. Born May 2, 1933 in NYC. Attended Miss Finchley's Ballet Acad. Bdwy debut in "Girl from Nantucket," followed by "Dance Me a Song," "Call Me Mister," "Make Mine Manhattan," "La Plume de Ma Tante," "Carnival," "Flora the Red Menace," "Sweet Charity," "George M!," "No, No, Nanette," "Irene," "Ballroom," OB in "The Boys from Syracuse," CC's "Wonderful Town" and "Carnival."

NOLEN, JOYCE. Born Oct. 5, 1950 in Philadelphia, Pa. Debut 1967 OB in "Curley McDimple," Bdwy in "Different Times," "A Matter of Time," "Stop the World, I Want to Get Off."

NOONAN, TOM. Born Apr. 12, 1951 in Greenwich, Ct. Yale graduate. Debut 1978 OB in "Buried Child."

NORTH, ALAN. Born Dec. 23, 1927 in NYC. Attended Columbia U. Bdwy bow 1955 in "Plain and Fancy," followed by "South Pacific," "Summer of the 17th Doll," "Requiem for a Nun," "Never Live over a Pretzel Factory," "Dylan," "Spofford," "Finian's Rainbow" (JB), "Music Man" (JB).

NOVA, CAROLINE. Born Jan. 15, 1950 in Flushing, NY. Debut 1978 OB in "Oklahoma!"

NOVY, NITA. Born June 13, 1950 in Wilkes-Barre, Pa. Duke U. graduate. Bdwy debut 1960 in "Gypsy," followed by "Sound of Music," OB in "How to Succeed . . .," "Maggie Flynn," "Too Much Johnson."

NUNNERY, BILL. Born Nov. 23, 1942 in Sanford, NC. Attended Lees-McRae Col., UNC. Bdwy debut 1978 in "The Inspector General."

NUTE, DON. Born Mar. 13, in Connellsville, Pa. Attended Denver U. Debut OB 1965 in "The Trojan Women," followed by "Boys in the Band," "Mad Theatre for Madmen," "The Eleventh Dynasty," "About Time," "The Urban Crisis," "Christmas Rappings," "The Life of a Man," "A Look at the Fifties."

O'BRIEN, SYLVIA. Born May 4, 1924 in Dublin, Ire. Debut OB 1961 in "O Marry Me," followed by "Red Roses for Me," "Every Other Evil," "3 by O'Casey," "Essence of Woman." "Dear Oscar," Bdwy in "Passion of Josef D.," "Right Honourable Gentleman," "Loves of Cass McGuire," "Hadrian VII," "Conduct Unbecoming," "My Fair Lady," "Da."

O'CONNELL, PATRICIA. Born May 17 in NYC. Attended AMThWing. Debut 1958 in "The Saintliness of Margery Kemp," followed by "Time Limit," "An Evening's Frost," "Mrs. Snow," "Electric Ice," "Survival of St. Joan," "Rain," "The Rapists," "Who Killed Richard Cory?," Bdwy in "Criss-Crossing," "Summer Brave," "Break a Leg."

O'CONNOR, KEVIN. Born May 7 in Honolulu, Hi. Attended UHi., Neighborhood Playhouse. Debut 1964 OB in "Up to Thursday," followed by "Six from LaMama," "Rimers of Eldritch," "Tom Paine," "Boy on the Straightback Chair," "Dear Janet Rosenberg," "Eyes of Chalk," "Alive and Well in Argentina," "Duet," "Trio," "The Contractor," "Kool Aid," "The Frequency," Bdwy in "Gloria and Esperanza," "The Morning after Optimism," "Figures in the Sand."

O'DELL, K. LYPE. Born Feb. 2, 1939 in Claremore, OK. Graduate Los Angeles State Col. Debut 1972 OB in "Sunset," followed by "Our Father," "Ice Age," "Prince of Homburg," "Passion of Dracula."

OEHLER, GRETCHEN. Born in Chicago, IL. Attended Goodman Theatre Sch. Debut 1971 OB in "The Homecoming," Bdwy 1977 in "Dracula."

OFFT, TOM. Born Oct. 6, 1950 in Wallington, NJ. Attended Paterson Col., HB Studio. Debut 1974 in "Music! Music!" (CC), followed by "A Musical Jubilee," OB in "Pins and Needles."

O'HARE, MICHAEL. Born May 6, 1952 in Chicago, Il. Debut 1978 OB in "Galileo," Bdwy in "Players," followed by "Man and Superman."

OKARSKI, DAVE. Born June 21, 1950 in NYC. Graduate Beloit Col. Debut

1977 OB in "Come Back, Little Sheba," followed by "A New England Legend."

OLIN, KEN. Born July 30, 1954 in Chicago, Il. Graduate UPa. Debut 1978 OB in "Taxi Tales."

OLIVA, RALPH. Born June 29, 1926 in Brooklyn, NY. Studied with Stellar Adler, Philip Burton, Gene Frankel. Debut 1978 OB in "Game Plan."

OLMOS, EDWARD JAMES. Born Feb. 24, 1947 in Los Angeles, Ca. Graduate CSLA. Bdwy debut 1979 in "Zoot Suit" for which he received a Theatre World Award.

O'NEILL, GENE. Born Apr. 7, 1951 in Philadelphia, Pa. Graduate Loyola U. Bdwy debut 1976 in "Poison Tree," followed by "Best Little Worehouse in Texas," OB in "Afternoons in Vegas."

ORMAN, ROSCOE. Born June 11, 1944 in NYC. Debut 1962 OB in "If We Grow Up," followed by "Electronic Nigger," "The Great McDaddy," "The Sirens," "Every Night When the Sun Goes Down," "Last Street Play," "Julius Caesar," "Coriolanus."

OUSLEY, ROBERT. Born July 21, 1946 in Waco, Tx. Graduate Baylor U. Debut 1975 OB in "Give Me Liberty," followed by Bdwy 1979 in "Sweeney Todd."

OWENS, ELIZABETH. Born Feb. 26, 1938 in NYC. Attended New School, Neighborhood Playhouse. Debut 1955 OB in "Dr. Faustus Lights the Lights," followed by "Chit Chat on a Rat," "The Miser," "The Father," "Importance of Being Earnest," "Candida," "Trumpets and Drums." "Oedipus," "Macbeth," "Uncle Vanya," "Misalliance," "Master Builder," "American Gothics," "The Play's the Thing" "The Rivals," "Death Story," "The Rehearsal," "Dance on a Country Grave" "Othello," "Candida," Bdwy in "The Lovers," "Not Now Darling," "The Play's the Thing."

OWENS, JILL. Born May 26, 1948 in Illinois. Attended State UIowa. Bdwy debut 1971 in "No, No Nanette," followed by "Pippin," OB in "Tip-Toes."

PACINO, AL. Born Apr. 25, 1940 in NYC. Attended Actors Studio. Bdwy bow 1969 in "Does a Tiger Wear a Necktie?" for which he received a Theatre World Award followed by "The Basic Training of Pavlo Hummel," "Richard III." OB in "Why Is a Crooked Letter?," "Peace Creeps," "The Indian Wants the Bronx," "Local Stigmatic," "Camino Real" (LC).

PAGANO, GIULIA. Born July 8, 1948 in NYC. Attended AADA. Debut 1977 OB in "The Passion of Dracula."

PAGE, KEN. Born Jan. 20, 1954 in St. Louis, MO. Attended Fontbonne Col. Bdwy debut 1976 in "Guys and Dolls" for which he received a Theatre World Award followed by "The Wiz," "Ain't Misbehavin."

PALMIERI, JOSEPH. Born Aug. 1, 1939 in Brooklyn, NY. Attended Catholic U. OB in NYSF 1965, "Cyrano de Bergerac," "Butter and Egg Man," "Boys in the Band," "Beggar's Opera," "The Family," "The Crazy Locomotive," "Umbrellas of Cherbourg," Bdwy in "Lysistrata," "Candide."

PANKIN, STUART. Born Apr. 8, 1946 in Philadelphia, PA. Graduate Dickinson Col., Columbia U. Debut OB 1968 in "Wars of the Roses," followed by "Richard III," "Timon of Athens," "Cymbeline," "Mary Stuart," "Narrow Road to the Deep North," "Twelfth Night," "The Crucible," "Wings," "A Glorious Age," "Joseph and the Amazing Technicolor Dreamcoat," BAM's "Three Sisters."

PAOLUCCI, ROBERT. Born in Quincy, MA. Graduate Fordham U. Debut 1974 OB in "Inherit the Wind," followed by "The Taming of the Shrew."

PAPE, JOAN. Born Jan. 23, in Detroit MI. Graduate Purdue U., Yale. Debut 1972 OB in "Suggs," followed by "Bloomers," "Museum," "Funeral Games," "Getting Out," Bdwy in "The Secret Affairs of Mildred Wild," "Cat on a Hot Tin Roof," "A History of the American Film."

PARDON, AURELIO. Born Aug. 4, 1951 in Cuba. Debut 1973 OB in "Smith," followed by "Antony and Cleopatra."

PARKER, ELLEN. Born Sept. 30, 1949 in Paris, Fr. Graduate Bard Col. Debut 1971 OB in "James Joyce Liquid Memorial Theatre," followed by "Uncommon Women and Others," Bdwy in "Equus," "Strangers."

PARKER, HOWARD. Born Aug. 3, 1933 in Tampa, Fl. Attended Pasadena Playhouse, HB Studio. Debut 1959 OB in "Once upon a Mattress," Bdwy in "Juno," "Ballroom."

PARKER, ROXANN. Born Apr. 24, 1948 in Los Angeles, Ca. Graduate USCal. Debut 1979 OB in "Festival."

PARRY, WILLIAM. Born Oct. 7, 1947 in Steubenville, OH. Graduate Mt. Union Col. Bdwy debut 1971 in "Jesus Christ Superstar," followed by "Rockabye Hamlet," "The Leaf People," OB in "Sgt. Pepper's Lonely Hearts Club Band," "The Conjuror," "Noah," "The Misanthrope," "Joseph and the Amazing Technicolor Dreamcoat," "Agamemnon.", "The Coolest Cat in Town," "Dispatches."

PEARL, IRWIN. Born Oct. 14, 1945 in Brooklyn, NY. Graduate Hofstra U. Bdwy bow 1970 in "Minnie's Boys," followed by "Fiddler on the Roof" (1976), OB in "Big Hotel," "Ergo," "Invitation to a Beheading," "Babes in Arms," "The Taming of the Shrew."

PEARTHREE, PIPPA. Born Sept. 23, 1956 in Baltimore, Md. Attended NYU. Bdwy debut 1977 in "Grease," followed by "Whose Life Is It Anyway?"

PELUSO, CLAUDIA. Born Mar. 1, 1952 in Brooklyn, NY. Graduate Penn State. OB in "Cartoons," "The New American," "The Brinks Job," "Grand Magic."

PELZER, BETTY. Born in Berkeley, Ca. Graduate Stanford U. Bdwy debut 1979 in "Wings."

PEN, POLLY. Born Mar. 11, 1954 in Chicago, Il. Ithaca Col. graduate. Debut 1978 OB in "The Taming of the Shrew," followed by "The Gilded Cage," Bdwy in "The Utter Glory of Morrissey Hall."

PENDLETON, WYMAN. Born Apr. 18, 1916 in Providence, RI. Graduate Brown U. Bdwy in "Tiny Alice," "Malcolm," "Quotations from Chairman Mao Tse-Tung," "Happy Days," "Henry V," "Othello," "There's One in Every Marriage," "Cat on a Hot Tin Roof," OB in "Gallows Humor," "American Dream," "Zoo Story," "Corruption in the Palace of Justice," "Giant's Dance," "Child Buyer," "Happy Days," "Butter and Egg Man," "Othello," "Albee Directs Albee."

PENN, EDWARD. Born in Washington, DC. Studied at HB studio. Debut 1965 OB in "The Queen and the Rebels," followed by "My Wife and I," "Invitation to a March," "Of Thee I Sing," "Fantasticks," "Greenwillow," "One for the Money," "Dear Oscar," "Speed Gets the Poppys," "Man with a Load of Mischief," "Company," "The Constant Wife," "Tune the Grand Up!," Bdwy bow 1975 in "Shenandoah."

PERETZ, SUSAN. Born in NYC; graduate UBuffalo. Debut 1972 OB in "American Gothic," followed by "42 Seconds from Broadway," "Comedy of Errors," "Hillbilly Women," Bdwy 1977 in "Ladies at the Alamo."

PEREZ, LAZARO. Born Dec. 17, 1945 in Havana, Cuba. Bdwy debut 1969 in "Does a Tiger Wear a Neck-tie?," OB in "Romeo and Juliet," "12 Angry Men," "Wonderful Years," "Alive," "G. R. Point."

PERRY, KEITH. Born Oct. 29, 1931 in Des Moines, Ia. Graduate Rice U. Fletcher Sch. Bdwy debut 1965 in "Pickwick," followed by "I'm Solomon," OB in "Epicene, the Silent Woman."

PESSAGNO, RICK. Born June 27, 1957 in Philadelphia, Pa. Bdwy debut 1979 in "Whoopee!," OB in "Tip-Toes."

PETERSEN, ERIKA. Born Mar. 24, 1949 in NYC. Attended NYU. Debut 1963 OB in "One Is a Lonely Number," followed by "I Dream I Dwelt in Bloomingdale's," "F. Jasmine Addams," "The Dubliners," "P.S. Your Cat Is Dead."

PETRICOFF, ELAINE. Born in Cincinnati, OH. Graduate Syracuse U. Bdwy debut 1971 in "The Me Nobody Knows," followed by "Grease," OB in "Hark!," "Ride the Winds," "Cole Porter," "Pins and Needles."

PETTY, ROSS. Born Aug. 29, 1946 in Winnipeg, Can Graduate U Manitoba Debut 1975 OB in "Happy Time," followed by "Maggie Flynn," "Carnival.", Bdwy in "Wings."

PHELPS, ELEANOR. Born in Baltimore, MD. Vassar graduate. Bdwy debut 1928 in "Merchant of Venice," followed by "Richard II," "Criminal Code," "Trick for Trick," "Seen But Not Heartd," "Flight to the West," "Queen Bee," "We the People," "Six Characters in Search of an Author," "Mr. Big," "Naughty-Naught," "The Disenchanted," "Picnic," "My Fair Lady" (1956 & 76). "40 Carats," "Crown Matrimonial," "Royal Family," OB in "Garden District," "Color of Darkness," "Catsplay," "Don Juan Comes Back from the War."

PHILLIPS, PETER. Born Dec. 7, 1949 in Darby, Pa. Graduate Dartmouth Col., RADA. Debut 1976 OB in "Henry V," followed by "The Cherry Orchard," "Total Eclipse," "Catsplay," "Warriors from a Long Childhood," Bdwy in "Equus" (1977)

PICARDO, ROBERT. Born Oct. 27, 1953 in Philadelphia, PA. Graduate Yale U. Debut 1975 OB in "Sexual Perversity in Chicago," followed by "Visions of Kerouac," "The Primary English Class," "Gemini" (also Bdwy '77).

PIETRI, FRANK. Born July 6, 1934 in Ponce, PR. Attended Georgetown U., AADA. Debut 1956 OB in "Out of This World," followed by "Ah! Wilderness," Bdwy in "Destry Rides Again," "Wildcat," "Nowhere to Go but Up," "What Makes Sammy Run?," "Golden Rainbow," "Promises, Promises," "Seesaw," "Ballroom."

PINCUS, WARREN. Born Apr. 13, 1938 in Brooklyn, NY. Attended CCNY. OB in "Miss Nefertiti Regrets," "Circus," "Magician," "Boxcars," "Demented World," "In the Time of Harry Harrass," "Yoshe Kolb," Bdwy in "Zalmen, or the Madness of God," "Gemini.", "The Inspector General."

PIRO, PHILLIP. Born Jan. 10, 1943 in Detroit, Mi. Attended Wayne State U. Debut 1969 OB in "Stop, You're Killing Me!", followed by "American Hamburger League," "Grand Magic."

PITCHFORD, DEAN. Born July 29, 1951 in Honolulu, Hi. Yale U. graduate. Debut 1971 OB in "Godspell," followed by "Saints," "Umbrellas of Cherbourg," Bdwy in "Pippin."

PLANA, TONY. Born Apr. 19, 1953 in Havana, Cuba. Attended Loyola U., RADA. Bdwy debut 1979 in "Zoot Suit."

PLUMMER, AMANDA MICHAEL. Born Mar. 23, 1957 in NYC. Attended Middlebury Col., Neighborhood Playhouse. Debut 1979 OB in "Artichoke."

PLUMMER, CHRISTOPHER. Born Dec. 13, 1929 in Toronto, Can. Bdwy debut 1954 in "Starcross Story," followed by "Home Is the Hero," "The Dark Is Light Enough" for which he received a Theatre World Award," "Medea," "The Lark," "Night of the Auk," "J. B.," "Arturo Ui," "Royal Hunt of the Sun," "Cyrano," "The Good Doctor," OB in "Drinks before Dinner."

POLIS, JOEL. Born Oct. 3, 1951 in Philadelphia, PA. Graduate USC, Yale. Debut 1976 OB in "Marco Polo," followed by "Family Business."

POMERANTZ, JEFFREY DAVID. Born July 2, 1945 in NYC. Attended Northwestern U., RADA. Bdwy debut (as Jeffrey David-Owen) 1975 in "The Leaf People," followed by "The Ritz," "Equus," OB in "John Gabriel Borkman," "Museum," "5th of July."

POSER, LINDA. Born Mar. 10 in Los Angeles, Ca. Graduate San Francisco State U. Debut 1973 OB in "Call Me Madam," followed by "The Boy Friend," Bdwy in "On the 20th Century," "The Grand Tour."

POTTER, CAROL. Born May 21, 1948 in NYC. Graduate Radcliffe Col. Debut 1974 OB in "The Last Days of British Honduras," followed by "Gemini" (1977 OB & Bdwy).

POTTER, DON. Born Aug. 15, 1932 in Philadelphia, Pa. Debut 1961 OB in "What a Killing," followed by "Sunset," "You're a Good Man, Charlie Brown," "One Cent Plain," "Annie Get Your Gun" (JB), Bdwy 1974 in "Gypsy."

PRADO, FRANCISCO. Born Nov. 3, 1941 in San Juan, PR. Graduate UPR. Debut 1977 OB in "G. R. Point," followed by "Julius Caesar," "Coriolanus," "Antony and Cleopatra."

PRESNELL, HARVE. Born Sept 14, 1933 in Modesto, Ca. Attended USCal. Bdwy bow 1960 in "The Unsinkable Molly Brown," followed by "Carousel," "Annie Get Your Gun" (JB).

PRITCHETT, LIZABETH. Born Mar. 12, 1920 in Dallas, Tx. Attended SMU. Bdwy debut 1959 in "Happy Town," followed by "Sound of Music," "Maria Golovin," "The Yearling," "A Funny Thing Happened on the Way . . .," OB in "Cindy," "The Real Inspector Hound," "The Karl Marx Play," "Show Boat" (JB), "Umbrellas of Cherbourg."

PROFANATO, GENE. Born Dec. 9, 1964 in NYC. Bdwy debut 1970 in "Lovely Ladies, Kind Gentlemen," followed by "The King and I" (1977).

PUGLIESE, JOSEPH. Born in Toa Alta, PR on July 27, 1952. Attended Juilliard. Bdwy debut 1975 in "The Lieutenant," followed by "Rockabye Hamlet," "American Dance Machine," OB in "Chinchilla."

PULLIAM, ZELDA. Born Oct. 18 in Chicago, Il. Attended Roosevelt U. Bdwy debut 1969 in "Hello, Dolly!," followed by "Purlie," "Raisin," "Pippin," "Dancin'," OB in "Croesus and the Witch."

QUINLAN, KATHLEEN. Born Nov. 19, 1954 in Pasadena, Ca. Attended Marin Col. Debut OB 1978 in "Taken in Marriage" for which she received a Theatre World Award.

QUINN, TOM. Born Oct. 6, 1934 in NYC. Attended IndU., CCNY. Debut 1974 OB in "Moonchildren," followed by "Boom Boom Room," "Oklahoma!"

RAMIREZ, RAMIRO (RAY). Born Feb. 1, 1939 in NYC. Attended CCNY. OB in "Down in the Valley," "Shakespeare in Harlem," "Harold Arlen Songbook," "Sancocho."

RAMSAY, REMAK. Born Feb. 2, 1937 in Baltimore, MD. Graduate Princeton U. Debut 1964 OB in "Hang Down Your Head and Die," followed by "The Real Inspector Hound," "Landscape of the Body," "All's Well That Ends Well" (CP), "Rear Column," Bdwy in "Half a Sixpence," "Sheep on the Runway," "Lovely Ladies, Kind Gentlemen," "On the Town," "Jumpers," "Private Lives," "Dirty Linen."

RAMSEL, GENA. Born Feb. 19, 1950 in El Reno, OK. Graduate SMU. Bdwy debut 1974 in "Lorelei," followed by "The Best Little Whorehouse in Texas," OB in "Joe Masiell Not at the Palace."

RAMSEY, MARION. Born May 10, 1947 in Philadelphia, Pa. Bdwy bow 1969 in "Hello, Dolly!," followed by "The Me Nobody Knows," "Rachel Lily Rosenbloom," "Eubie!," OB in "Soon," "Do It Again," "Wedding of Iphigenia," "20081/2."

RAND, SUZANNE. Born Sept. 8, 1949 in Chicago, Il. Graduate Stephens Coll. Debut OB 1973 in "The Proposition," Bdwy 1979 in "Monteith and Rand."

RANDELL, RON. Born Oct. 8, 1920 in Sydney, Aust. Attended St. Mary's Col. Bdwy debut 1949 in "The Browning Version," followed by "A Harlequinade," "Candida," "World of Suzie Wong," "Sherlock Holmes," "Mrs. Warren's Profession" (LC), "Measure for Measure" (CP), OB in "The Grinding Machine."

RANDOLPH, BILL. Born Oct. 11, 1953 in Detroit, Mi. Attended Allen Hancock Col., SUNY Purchase. Bdwy debut 1978 in "Gemini."

RAPHAEL, GERRIANNE. Born Feb. 23, 1935 in NYC. Attended New Sch., Columbia. Bdwy in "Solitaire," "A Guest in the House," "Violet," "Good-bye, My Fancy," "Seventh Heaven," "Li'l Abner," "Saratoga," "Man of LaMancha," "King of Hearts," OB in "Threepenny Opera," "The Boy Friend," "Ernest in Love," "Say When," "The Prime of Miss Jean Brodie."

RASCHE, DAVID. Born Aug. 7, 1944 in St. Louis, MO. Graduate Elmhurst Col., U Chicago. Debut 1976 OB in "John," followed by "Snow White," "Isadora Duncan Sleeps with the Russian Navy," "End of the War," Bdwy in "Shadow Box" (1977).

RAWLINS, LESTER. Born Sept. 24, 1924 in Farrell, PA. Attended Carnegie Tech. Bdwy in "Othello," "King Lear," "The Lovers," "A Man for All Seasons," "Herzl," "Romeo and Juliet," "Da," OB in "Endgame," "Quare Fellow," "Camino Real," "Hedda Gabler," "Old Glory," "Child Buyer," "Winterset," "In the Bar of a Tokyo Hotel," "The Reckoning," "Nightride."

RAWLS, EUGENIA. Born Sept. 11, 1916 in Macon, Ga. Attended UNC. Bdwy debut 1934 in "The Children's Hour," followed by "To Quito and Back," "Journeyman," "Little Foxes," "Guest in the House," "Man Who Had All the Luck," "Strange Fruit," "The Shrike," "The Great Sebastians," "First Love," "Case of Libel," "Sweet Bird of Youth," OB in "Poker Session," "Just the Immediate Family," "Tallulah, A Memory."

REAMS, LEE ROY. Born Aug. 23, 1942 in Covington, KY. Graduate U. Cinn. Cons. Bdwy debut 1966 in "Sweet Charity," followed by "Oklahoma!" (LC). "Applause," "Lorelei," "Show Boat" (JB), "Hello Dolly!" (1978)., OB in "Sterling Silver."

REDFIELD, MARILYN. Born May 2, 1940 in Chicago, Il. Graduate Vassar, Harvard, HB Studio. Debut 1973 OB in "The Rainmaker," followed by "Monologia," "Mod Madonna," "King of the U.S.," "Too Much Johnson."

REED, ALAINA. Born Nov. 10, 1946 in Springfield, OH. Attended Kent State U. Bdwy debut in "Hair" (original and 1977), followed by "Eubie!," OB in "Sgt. Pepper's Lonely Hearts Club Band."

REED, ALEXANDER. Born June 9, 1916 in Clearfield, Pa. Graduate Columbia U. Debut 1956 OB in "Lady from the Sea," followed by "All the King's Men," "Death of Satan," "The Balcony," "Call Me by My Rightful Name," "Studs Edsel," "The Coroner's Plot," Bdwy in "Witness," "Lost in the Stars," "The Skin of Our Teeth," "First Monday in October."

REED, PAMELA. Born Apr. 2, 1949 in Tacoma, WA. Graduate U Wash. Bdwy debut 1978 in "The November People," OB in "The Curse of the Starving Class.," "All's Well That Ends Well" (CP), "Seduced," "Getting Out."

REEHLING, JOYCE. Born Mar. 5, 1949 in Baltimore, MD. Graduate NC Sch. of Arts. Debut 1976 OB in "Hot l Baltimore," followed by "Who Killed Richard Cory?," "Lulu," "5th of July.," "The Runner Stumbles," "Life and/or Death"

REESE, ROXANNE. Born June 6, 1952 in Washington, DC. Graduate Howard U. Debut l974 OB in "Freedom Train," followed by "Feeling Good," "No Place to Be Somebody," "Spell #7" Bdwy 1976 in "For Colored Girls Who Have Considered Suicide . . ."

REID, KATE. Born Nov. 4, 1930 in London, Eng. Attended Toronto U. Bdwy debut 1962 in "Who's Afraid of Virginia Woolf?," followed by "Dylan," "Slapstick Tragedy," "The Price," "Freedom of the City," "Cat on a Hot Tin Roof," "Bosoms and Neglect."

REIN, LESLEY. Born Jan. 8, 1952 in Chiswick, Eng. Debut 1978 OB in "Can-Can."

REINAS, GINNY. Born Nov. 23, 1953 in Philadelphia, Pa. Graduate Vassar Col. Debut 1978 OB in "Oklahoma!," followed by "On a Clear Day You Can See Forever."

REINHOLT, GEORGE. Born Aug. 22, 1940 in Philadelphia, Pa. OB in "Misalliance," "The Bald Soprano," "Colombe," Bdwy in "Cabaret," "The Grand Tour."

REINKING, ANN. Born Nov. 10, 1949 in Seattle, WA. Attended Joffrey Sch., HB Studio. Bdwy debut 1969 in "Cabaret," followed by "Coco," "Pippin," "Over Here" for which she received a Theatre World Award, "Goodtime Charley," "A Chorus Line," "Chicago," "Dancin'."

REISNER, CHRIS. Born Aug. 31, 1951 in NYC. Attended HB Studio. Debut 1978 OB in "Can-Can," after four years with Nikolais Dance Theatre.

RENENSLAND, HOWARD. Born Apr. 4, 1948 in Leavenworth, KS. Graduate Washburn U, Trinity U. Debut 1977 OB in "Nest of Vipers." followed by "Happy Hunter." "The Suicide."

REPOLE, CHARLES. Born May 24, 1945 in Brooklyn, NY. Graduate Hofstra U. Bdwy debut 1975 in "Very Good Eddie" for which he received a Theatre World Award, followed by "Finian's Rainbow (JB)., "Whoopee!"

REY, ANTONIA. Born Oct. 12, 1927 in Havana, Cuba. Graduate Havana U. Bdwy debut 1964 in "Bajour," followed by "Mike Downstairs," "Engagement Baby," "The Ritz," OB in "Yerma." "Fiesta in Madrid," "Camino Real" (LC), "Back Bog Beast Bait," "Rain," "42 Seconds from Broadway," "A Streetcar Named Desire" (LC), "Simpson Street."

RHOMBERG, VINCE. Born Sept. 15, 1954 in St. Louis, Mo. Webster Col. graduate. Debut 1979 OB in "Mary."

RHYS, ROBERT C. Born Jan. 23, 1951 in Lexington, MA. Attended Ntl. Th. Inst. Bdwy debut 1972 in "Jumpers." followed by "The Rocky Horror Show," OB in "YMCA," "Joseph and the Amazing Technicolor Dreamcoat."

RICE, SARAH. Born Mar. 5, 1955 in Okinawa, attended Ariz State U. Debut 1974 OB in "The Fantasticks," Bdwy 1979 in "Sweeney Todd" for which she received a Theatre World Award.

RICHARDS, PAUL-DAVID. Born Aug. 31, 1935 in Bedford, In. Graduate IndU. Bdwy debut 1959 in "Once upon a Mattress," followed by "Camelot," "It's Superman!," A Joyful Noise," "1776," OB in "Black Picture Show," "Devour the Snow."

RICHARDSON, PATRICIA. Born Feb 23 in Bethesda, Md. Graduate Southern Methodist U. Bdwy debut 1974 in "Gypsy," followed by "Loose Ends," OB in "Coroner's Plot," "Vanities," "Hooters," "The Frequency."

RIDLEY, GARY H. Born Feb. 5, 1948 in Tulsa, Ok. Attended NE Okla State U. Debut 1975 OB in "The Vagabond King," followed by repertoire of Light Opera of Manhattan.

RIFKIN, RON. Born Oct. 31, 1939 in NYC. NYU graduate. Bdwy debut 1960 in "Come Blow Your Horn." followed by "The Goodbye People." OB in "Rosebloom."

RILEY, LARRY. Born June 21, 1952 in Memphis, Tn. Graduate Memphis State U. Bdwy debut 1978 in "A Broadway Musical," followed by "I Love My Wife," OB in "Street Songs." "Amerika." "Plane Down."

RINEHART, ELAINE. Born Aug. 16, 1952 in San Santonio, TX. Graduate NC Sch of Arts. Debut 1975 OB in "Tenderloin," Bdwy in "The Best Little Whorehouse in Texas."

RIZZO, RICHARD W. Born Mar. 9, 1944 in Quincy, Ma. Graduate Northeastern U. Debut 1979 OB in "The Miracle Worker."

ROBBINS, JANA. Born Apr. 18, 1947 in Johnstown, Pa. Graduate Stephens Col. Bdwy debut 1974 in "Good News." followed by "I Love My Wife," OB in "Tickles by Tucholsky," "Tip-Toes."

ROBBINS, REX. Born in Pierre, SD. Bdwy debut 1964 in "One Flew Over the Cuckoo's Nest," followed by "Scratch," "The Changing Room," "Gypsy,"

"Comedians," "An Almost Perfect Person," "Players," OB in "Servant of Two Masters," "The Alchemist," "Arms and the Man," "Boys in the Band," "A Memory of Two Mondays," "They Knew What They Wanted," "Secret Service," "Boy Meets Girl," BAM Co.'s "Three Sisters," "The Play's the Thing" and "Julius Caesar," "Artichoke."

ROBERTS, TONY. Born Oct. 22, 1939 in NYC. Graduate Northwestern U. Bdwy bow 1962 in "Something about a Soldier," followed by "Take Her, She's Mine," "Last Analysis," "The Cradle Will Rock" (OB), "Never Too Late," "Barefoot in the Park," "Don't Drink the Water," "How Now, Dow Jones," "Play It Again, Sam," "Promises, Promises," "Sugar," "Absurd Person Singular," "Murder at the Howard Johnson's."

ROBERTSON, WILLIAM. Born Oct. 9, 1908 in Portsmouth, VA. Graduate Pomona Col. Bdwy debut 1936 in "Tapestry in Grey." followed by "Cup of Trembling," "Liliom," "Our Town." "Caesar and Cleopatra," OB in "Uncle Harry," "Shining Hour." "Kibosh," "Sun-Up," "The Last Pad," "Hamlet." "Girls Most Likely to Succeed," "The Petrified Forest," "The Minister's Black Veil," "Santa Anita," "Babylon," "Midsummer Night's Dream," "A Touch of the Poet." "The Zykovs," "Rimers of Eldrich," "The Crucible." "Lulu," "Fathers and Sons," "Chinchilla."

ROCCO, MARY. Born Sept. 12, 1933 in Brooklyn, NY. Graduate Queens Col., CCNY. Debut 1976 OB in "Fiorello!," followed by "The Constant Wife."

ROCKAFELLOW, MARILYN. Born Jan. 22, 1943 in New Monmouth, NH. Graduate Rutgers U. Bdwy debut 1979 OB in "La Ronde."

ROGERS, GIL. Born Feb. 4, 1934 in Lexington. KY. Attended Harvard. OB in "The Ivory Branch," "Vanity of Nothing," "Warrior's Husband," "Hell Bent fer Heaven," "Gods of Lightning." "Pictures in the Hallway," "Rose," "Memory Bank," "A Recent Killing," "Birth," "Come Back, Little Sheba," "Life of Galileo." "Remembrance," Bdwy in "The Great White Hope," "The Best Little Whorehouse in Texas."

ROMAGUERA, JOAQUIN. (a.k.a. Fidel Romann) Born Sept. 5, 1932 in Key West, Fl. Graduate Fla. Southern Col. Debut 1961 OB in "All in Love," followed by "Sweeney Todd."

ROSE, CRISTINE. Born Jan. 31, 1951 in Lynwood, Ca. Graduate Stanford U. Debut 1979 OB in "The Miracle Worker," followed by "Don Juan Comes Back from the War."

ROSE, GEORGE. Born Feb. 19, 1920 in Bicester, Eng. Bdwy debut with Old Vic 1946 in "Henry IV," followed by "Much Ado about Nothing," "A Man for All Seasons," "Hamlet," "Royal Hunt of the Sun," "Walking Happy." "Loot," "My Fair Lady," (CC '68), "Canterbury Tales," "Coco." "Wise Child," "Sleuth," "My Fat Friend." "My Fair Lady," "She Loves Me," BAM's "The Play's the Thing," "The Devil's Disciple," and "Julius Caesar.," "The Kingfisher."

ROSE, JOHN. Born Aug. 24, 1939 in Ottawa, KS. Attended City Col. San Francisco, USC. Bdwy debut 1976 in "The Night of the Iguana," followed by "St. Joan."

ROSE, MARGOT. Born July 17, 1951 in Pittsburgh, Pa. Attended Yale. NC School of Arts. Debut 1978 OB in "I'm Getting My Act Together and Taking It on the Road."

ROSE, NORMAN. Born June 23, 1917 in Philadelphia, Pa. Graduate George Washington U. Bdwy in "Cafe Crown," "St. Joan," "Land of Fame," "Richard III." "Fifth Season," OB in "Career," "Hemingway Hero," "Wicked Cooks." "Empire Builders," "The Old Ones," "The Wait."

ROSENBAUM, DAVID. Born in NYC. Debut OB 1968 in "America Hurrah," "The Cavedwellers," "Evenings with Chekhov," "Out of the Death Cart." "After Miriam," "The Indian Wants the Bronx." "Allergy," "Family Business," Bdwy in "Oh! Calcutta!"

ROSS, HOWARD. Born Aug. 21, 1934 in NYC. Attended Juilliard, NYU. Bdwy debut 1965 in "Oliver," followed by "1600 Pennsylvania Avenue," "Carmelina," OB in "Jacques Brel Is Alive," "Beggar's Opera," "Philemon." "Isadora Duncan Sleeps with the Russian Navy."

ROSS, JUSTIN. Born Dec. 15, 1954 in Brooklyn, NY. Debut 1974 OB in "More Than you Deserve," Bdwy 1975 in "Pippin," followed by "A Chorus Line."

ROTH, ANDY. Born Jan. 5, 1952 in NYC. Graduate Brown U.. Juilliard. Bdwy debut 1979 in "They're Playing Our Song."

ROWE, HANSFORD. Born May 12, 1924 in Richmond, Va. Graduate URichmond. Bdwy debut 1968 in "We Bombed in New Haven," followed by "Porgy and Bess," OB in "Curley McDimple," "The Fantasticks," "Last Analysis," "God Says There Is No Peter Ott." "Mourning Becomes Electra," "Bus Stop," "Secret Service," "Boy Meets Girl," "Getting Out."

RUANE, JANINE. Born Dec. 17, 1963 in Philadelphia, PA. Bdwy debut 1977 in "Annie."

RUBIO, YOLANDA. Born Nov. 10, 1954 in Los Angeles, Ca. Attended UCLA. Debut 1979 OB in "On a Clear Day You Can See Forever."

RUCKER, BO. Born Aug. 17, 1948 in Tampa, FL. Studied with Stella Adler, Lee Strasburg. Debut 1978 OB in "Native Son" for which he received a Theatre World Award, followed by "Blues for Mr. Charlie."

RUDD, PAUL. Born May 15, 1940 in Boston, MA. OB in "Henry IV," followed by "King Lear," "A Cry of Players," "Midsummer Night's Dream," "An Evening with Merlin Finch," "In the Matter of J. Robert Oppenheimer," "Elagabalus," "Streamers" (LC). "Henry V" (CP), "Boys in the Band," "Da," "The Show-Off." Bdwy in "The Changing Room," "The National Health," "The Glass Menagerie," "Ah, Wilderness!." "Romeo and Juliet." "Bosoms and Neglect."

RULE, CHARLES. Born Aug. 4, 1928 in Springfield, MO. Bdwy bow 1951 in "Courtin' Time," followed by "Happy Hunting." "Oh. Captain!." "Conquering Hero," "Donnybrook," "Bye, Bye Birdie," "Fiddler on the Roof." "Henry, Sweet Henry," "Maggie Flynn," "1776," "Cry for Us All," "Gypsy." "Goodtime Charley," "On the 20th Century."

RUPERT, MICHAEL. Born Oct. 23, 1951 in Denver. CO. Attended Pasadena Playhouse. Bdwy debut 1968 in "The Happy Time" for which he received a Theatre World Award, followed by "Pippin.," OB in "Festival."

RUSHING, SHIRLEY. Born Jan. 12 in Savannah, Ga. Attended Juilliard, Brooklyn Col. Debut 1977 OB in "The Web," followed by "A Season to Unravel."

RUSKIN, JEANNE. Born Nov. 6 in Saginaw. MI. Graduate NYU. Bdwy debut 1975 in "Equus." followed by "Says I Says He" (OB).

RUTHERFORD, MARY MICHELE. Born Sept. 1, 1950 in NYC. Attended the Sorbonne in Paris. Bdwy debut 1979 in "Wings."

RYAN, CHARLES. Born Aug. 26, 1950 in NYC. Adelphi U. graduate. Debut 1974 OB in "Zorba," followed by "The Mikado," "Words-Fourplay," "Montpelier Pazazz," "Trouble in Tahiti," "Telecast."

RYAN, MICHAEL. Born Mar. 19, 1929 in Wichita, Ks. Attended St. Benedict's Col., Georgetown U. Bdwy debut 1960 in "Advise and Consent." followed by "The Complaisant Lover," OB in "Richard III," "King Lear," "Hedda Gabler," "The Barroom Monks," "Portrait of the Artist as a Young Man," "Autumn Garden," "Naomi Court," "The Terrorists."

RYAN, STEVEN. Born June 19. 1947 in NYC. Graduate Boston U., UMinn. Debut 1978 OB in "Winning Isn't Everything."

RYDER, RICHARD. Born Aug. 20, 1942 in Rochester, NY. Attended Colgate U., Pratt Inst. Bdwy debut 1972 in "Oh, Calcutta!," followed by "Via Galactica," OB in "Rain," "Oh, Pshaw!," "The Dog beneath the Skin," "Polly," "Lovers," "Green Pond," "Piano Bar."

SABELLICO, RICHARD. Born June 29, 1951 in NYC. Attended C.W.Post Col. Bdwy debut 1974 in "Gypsy," OB in "Gay Divorce," "La Ronde," "Manhattan Breakdown."

SABIN, DAVID. Born Apr. 24, 1937 in Washington, DC. Graduate Catholic U. Debut 1965 OB in "The Fantasticks," followed by "Now Is the Time for All Good Men." "Threepenny Opera" (LC). "You Never Can tell," "The Master and Margarita," Bdwy in "The Yearling," "Slapstick Tragedy," "Jimmy Shine," "Gantry," "Ambassador," "Celebration," "Music Is." "The Water Engine."

SABO, JUDY. Born July 2, 1940 in Arlington, NJ. Attended Stafford Hall, Brookdale Col. Bdwy debut 1979 in "Carmelina."

SACHS, ANN. Born Jan. 23, 1948 in Boston, MA. Carnegie Tech graduate. Bdwy debut 1970 in "Wilson in the Promise Land," followed by "Dracula." "Man and Superman," OB in "Tug of War," "Sweetshoppe Miriam," "Festival of American Plays."

SANCHEZ, JAIME. Born Dec. 19, 1938 in Rincon, PR. Attended Actors Studio. Bdwy bow 1957 in "West Side Story," followed by "Oh, Dad, Poor Dad . . .," "A Midsummer Night's Dream," OB in "The Toilet," "Conerico Was Here to Stay" for which he received a Theatre World Award, "Ox Cart," "The Tempest," "Merry Wives of Windsor," "Julius Caesar." "Coriolanus."

SANDERS, JAY O. Born Apr. 16, 1953 in Austin, Tx. Graduate SUNY Purchase. Debut 1976 OB in "Henry V," followed by "Measure for Measure," "Scooping," "Buried Child." Bdwy 1979 in "Loose Ends."

SANTELL, MARIE. Born July 8 in Brooklyn, NY. Bdwy debut 1957 in "Music Man," followed by "A Funny Thing Happened on the Way . . .," "Flora the Red Menace," "Pajama Game," "Mack and Mabel." OB in "Hi, Paisano!," "Boys from Syracuse," "Peace," "Promenade," "The Drunkard," "Sensations," "The Castaways," "Fathers and Sons."

SAPUTO, PETER J. Born Feb. 2, 1939 in Detroit, Mi. Graduate Eastern Mich. U., Purdue U. Debut 1977 OB in "King Oedipus," followed by "Twelfth Night." "Bon Voyage," "The Happy Haven," "Sleepwalkers," "Humulus the Mute," Bdwy in "Once in a Lifetime."

SARANDAN, CHRIS. Born July 24, 1942 in Beckley, WVa. Graduate UWVa., Catholic U. Bdwy debut 1970 in "The Rothschilds," followed by "Two Gentlemen of Verona," OB in "Marco Polo Sings a Solo," "The Devil's Disciple," "The Woods."

SARNO, JANET. Born Nov. 18, 1933 in Bridgeport, Ct. Graduate SCTC, Yale U. Bdwy debut 1963 in "Dylan." followed by "Equus," "Knockout," OB in "6 Characters in Search of an Author," "Who's Happy Now." "Closing Green," "Fisher," "Survival of St. Joan," "The Orphan," "Mamma's Little Angels."

SAUNDERS, MARY. Born Dec. 14. 1945 in Morristown, NJ. Graduate Mt. Holyoke. Middlebury. Debut 1975 OB in "The Gift of the Magi," Bdwy 1979 in "The Utter Glory of Morrissey Hall."

SAUNDERS, NICHOLAS. Born June 2, 1914 in Kiev, Russia. Bdwy debut 1942 in "Lady in the Dark" followed by "A New Life," "Highland Fling," "Happily Ever After," "The Magnificent Yankee," "Anastasia," "Take Her, She's Mine," "A Call on Kuprin," "Passion of Josef D.," OB in "An Enemy of the People," "End of All Things Natural," "The Unicorn in Captivity."

SCARDINO, DON. Born in Feb. 1949 in NYC. Attended CCNY. On Bdwy in "Loves of Cass McGuire," "Johnny No-Trump," "My Daughter, Your Son," "Godspell," "Angel," "King of Hearts," OB in "Shout from the Rooftops," "Rimers of Eldrich," "The Unknown Soldier and His Wife," "Godspell," "Moonchildren," "Kid Champion," "Comedy of Errors," "Secret Service," "Boy Meets Girl," "Scribes," "I'm Getting My Act Together . . ."

SCHACT, SAM. Born Apr. 19, 1936 in The Bronx, NY. Graduate CCNY. OB in "Fortune and Men's Eyes." "Cannibals," "I Met a Man," "The Increased Difficulty of Concentration" (LCR), "One Night Stands of a Noisy Passenger," "Owners," "Jack Gelber's New Play," "The Master and Margarita," Bdwy in "The Magic Show," "Golda."

SCHAEFER, CRAIG. Born Aug. 24, 1953 in San Gabriel, CA. Attended UCLA. Debut 1975 OB in "Tenderloin." followed by "Joseph and the Amazing Technicolor Dreamcoat."

SCHECHTER, DAVID. Born Apr. 12. 1956 in NYC. Bard Col. Neighborhood Playhouse graduate. Debut 1976 OB in "Nightclub Cantata," followed by "Dispatches," Bdwy in "Runaways" (1978).

SCHENKKAN, ROBERT. Born Mar. 19, 1953. Graduate Cornell U., UTex. Debut 1978 OB in "The Taming of the Shrew.," followed by "Last Day at the Dixie Girl Cafe," "The Passion of Dracula."

SCHILKE, MICHAEL. Born Dec. 10, 1953 in Sulphur, Ok. Graduate Dennison U.. UCincinnati. Debut 1978 OB in "Tribute to Women," followed by "On a Clear Day You Can See Forever."

SCHNABEL, STEFAN. Born Feb. 2, 1912 in Berlin, Ger. Attended UBonn, Old Vic. Bdwy bow 1937 in "Julius Caesar," followed by "Shoemaker's Holiday," "Glamour Preferred," "Land of Fame," "Cherry Orchard," "Around the World in 80 Days," "Now I Lay Me Down to Sleep," "Idiot's Delight," "Love of Four Colonels," "Plain and Fancy," "Small War on Murray Hill," "A Very Rich Woman," "A Patriot for Me," OB in "Tango," "In the Matter of J. Robert Oppenheimer," "Older People," "Enemies," "Little Black Sheep," "Rosmersholm," "Passion of Dracula."

SCHNEIDER, JANA. Born Oct. 24, 1951 in McFarland, Wi. Graduate UWisc. Debut 1976 OB in "Women Behind Bars," followed by "Telecast," Bdwy in "The Robber Bridegroom."

SCHNEIDER, JAY. Born May 8, 1951 in Brooklyn, NY. Graduate Brandeis U. Debut 1979 OB in "On a Clear Day You Can See Forever," followed by Light Opera of Manhattan.

SCHRAMM, DAVID. Born Aug. 14, 1946 in Louisville, KY. Attended Western Ky. U., Juilliard. Debut 1972 OB in "School for Scandal," followed by "Lower Depths," "Women Beware Women," "Mother Courage," "King Lear," "Duck Variations," Bdwy in "Three Sisters," "Next Time I'll Sing to You," "Edward II," "Measure for Measure," "The Robber Bridegroom." "Bedroom Farce."

SCHULL, REBECCA. Born Feb. 22 in NYC. Graduate NYU. Bdwy debut 1976 in "Herzl," followed by "Golda." OB in "Mother's Day," "Fefu and Her Friends.," "On Mt. Chimborazo."

SCIARRO, JO LYNN. Born Sept. 4, 1954 in Baltimore, Md. Temple U. graduate. Debut 1979 OB in "The Miracle Worker."

SCOLLAY, FRED J. Born March 19 in Roxbury, Ma. Attended Bishop-Lee Sch. of Drama. Debut OB in the 1950's at Blackfriars Theatre, followed by many other plays, including "Game Plan," Bdwy 1961 in "The Devil's Advocate."

SCOTT, MICHAEL. Born Jan. 24, 1954 in Santa Monica, CA. Attended Cal. State U. Debut 1978 OB and Bdwy in "The Best Little Whorehouse in Texas."

SEACAT, SANDRA. Born Oct. 2 in Greensburg, Ks. Attended Northwestern U., Actors Studio. Bdwy debut 1964 in "Three Sisters," Followed by "A Streetcar Named Desire," "Sly Fox," OB in "The Wilder Plays," "Laughwind." "Natural Affection," "A View from the Bridge," "The Lesson."

SEAMON, EDWARD. Born Apr. 15, 1937 in San Diego, CA. Attended San Diego State Col. Debut 1971 OB in "The Life and Times of J. Walter Sminthous," followed by "The Contractor." "The Family," "Fishing," "Feedlot," "Cabin 12," "Rear Column." "Devour the Snow," Bdwy in "The Trip Back Down.."

SEER, RICHARD. Born Oct. 13. 1949 in Anchorage, AK, Graduate Cal. State U. Debut 1972 OB in "Hey Day," followed by "Joseph and the Amazing Technicolor Dreamcoat," Bdwy in "Da" for which he received a 1978 Theatre World Award.

SELDES, MARIAN. Born Aug. 23, 1928 in NYC. Attended Neighborhood Playhouse. Bdwy debut 1947 in "Medea," followed by "Crime and Punishment," "That Lady," "Tower Beyond Tragedy," "Ondine," "On High Ground." "Come of Age," "Chalk Garden," "The Milk Train Doesn't Stop Here Anymore," "The Wall," "A Gift of Time," "A Delicate Balance," "Before You Go," "Father's Day," "Equus," "The Merchant," "Deathtrap," OB in "Different," "Ginger Man," "Mercy Street," "Candle in the Wind," "Isadora Duncan Sleeps with the Russian Navy."

SELL, JANIE. Born Oct. 1, 1941 in Detroit, MI. Attended UDetroit. Debut 1966 OB in "Mixed Doubles," followed by "Dark Horses," "Dames at Sea," "By Bernstein." Bdwy in "George M!," "Irene," "Over Here" for which she received a Theatre World Award, "Pal Joey," "Happy End.," "I Love My Wife."

SELMAN, LINDA. Born Sept. 14 in NYC. Graduate NYCU. Bdwy debut 1968 in "You Know I Can't Hear You . . .," followed by "Night Watch," "Herzl," "Richard III," OB in "The Criminals," "Wake and Sing," "Drinks Before Dinner."

SERRA, RAYMOND. Born Aug. 13, 1937 in NYC. Attended Rutgers U., Wagner Col. Debut 1975 OB in "The Shark," followed by "Mamma's Little Angels," "Manny," Bdwy in "The Wheelbarrow Closers."

SERRECCHIA, MICHAEL. Born Mar. 26. 1951 in Brooklyn. NY. Attended Brockport State U. Teachers Col. Bdwy debut 1972 in "The Selling of the President," followed by "Heathen!," "Seesaw." "A Chorus Line," OB in "Lady Audley's Secret."

SETRAKIAN, ED. Born Oct. 1, 1928 in Jenkintown. WVa. Graduate Concord Col., NYU. Debut 1966 OB in "Drums in the Night," followed by "Othello," "Coriolanus," "Macbeth," "Hamlet," "Baal." "Old Glory," "Futz," "Hey Rube," "Seduced," Bdwy in "Days in the Trees," "St.Joan," "The Best Little Whorehouse in Texas."

SHAPIRO, DEBBIE. Born Sept. 29. i954 in Los Angeles, Ca. Graduate LACC. Bdwy debut 1979 in "They're Playing Our Song."

SHARMA, BARBARA. Born Sept. 14, 1942. OB credits include "The Boy Friend," "Italian Straw Hat," "Cole Porter Revisited," Bdwy in "Fiorello!," "Little Me," "Sweet Charity," "Hallelujah, Baby!," "Her First Roman." "Come Summer," "Last of the Red Hot Lovers," "I Love My Wife."

SHEA, JOHN V. Born Apr. 14 in North Conway, NH. Graduate Bates Col., Yale. Debut OB 1974 in "Yentl, the Yeshiva Boy," followed by "Gorky," "Battering Ram," "Safe House," "The Master and Margarita." Bdwy in "Yentl" (1975) for which he received a Theatre World Award, "Romeo and Juliet."

SHEARER, DENNY. Born July 30, 1941 in Canton, Oh. Attended HB Studio. Debut 1968 OB in "Up Eden," followed by "American Dance Machine," Bdwy in "No, No Nanette," "Music Is," "Bubbling Brown Sugar."

SHELLEY, CAROLE. Born Aug. 16, 1939 in London, Eng. Bdwy debut 1965 in "The Odd Couple," followed by "Astrakhan Coat," "Loot," "Noel Coward's Sweet Potato." "Hay Fever," "Absurd Person Singular," "The Norman Conquests." "The Elephant Man," OB in "Little Murders," "The Devil's Disciple," "The Play's the Thing."

SHELLEY, JULIA. Born in Belfast, Ire. Attended RADA. Bdwy debut 1978 in "King of Hearts."

SHELTON, REID. Born Oct. 7, 1924 in Salem, OR. Graduate U. Mich. Bdwy bow 1952 in "Wish You Were Here," followed by "Wonderful Town," "By the Beautiful Sea," "Saint of Bleecker Street." "My Fair Lady," "Oh! What a Lovely War!," "Carousel" (CC), "Canterbury Tales." "Rothschilds," "1600 Pennsylvania Avenue." "Annie," OB in "Phedre," "Butterfly Dream," "Man with a Load of Mischief," "Beggars Opera," "The Contractor," "Cast Aways."

SHIMERMAN, ARMIN. Born Nov. 5, 1949 in Lakewood, NJ. Graduate UCLA. Debut 1976 in "Threepenny Opera" (LC), followed by "Silk Stockings" (ELT), Bdwy in " St. Joan." (1977). "I Remember Mama." (1979)

SHORT, SYLVIA. Born Oct. 22, 1927 in Concord, Ma. Attended Smith Col., Old Vic. Debut 1954 OB in "The Clandestine Marriage," followed by "Golden Apple," "Passion of Gross," "Desire Caught by the Tail." "City Love Story," "Family Reunion," "Beaux Stratagem," "Just a Little Bit Less Than Normal." "Nasty Rumors," "Says I, Says. He," Bdwy in "King Lear" (1956).

SHULTZ, TONY. Born Aug. 8. 1947 in Los Angeles, Ca. Graduate UCal. Berkeley. Bdwy debut 1974 in "Grease," followed by "Platinum."

SIDNEY, P. JAY. Bdwy debut 1934 in "Dance with Your Gods," followed by "20th Century," "Carmen Jones," "Green Pastures," "Run, Little Chillun," "Jeb." "The Cool World," "The Octoroon" (OB), "The Winner," "The Playroom," "First Monday in October."

SIEPI, CESARE. Born Feb. 10, 1923 in Milan, Italy. After a career with Metropolitan Opera, made Bdwy debut 1962 in "Bravo, Giovanni," followed by "Carmelina."

SILLIMAN, MAUREEN. Born Dec 3 in NYC. Attended Hofstra U. Bdwy debut 1975 in "Shenandoah," followed by "I Remember Mama," OB in "Umbrellas of Cherbourg."

SILVA, GENO. Born Jan. 20, 1948 in Albuquerque, NMX. Attended UNMx. Bdwy debut 1979 in "Zoot Suit."

SIMMONDS, STANLEY. Born July 13 in Brooklyn, NY. Attended Roosevelt Col. Bdwy debut 1927 in "My Maryland," followed by "Castles in the Air," "Simple Simon," "If the Shoe Fits." "Brigadoon," "Call Me Madam," "Silk Stockings." "Li'l Abner," "Fiorello." "Let It Ride," "I Can Get It for You Wholesale," "How Now, Dow Jones," "Maggie Flynn," "Jimmy," "Mack and Mabel," "On the 20th Century."

SIMPSON, MARY KEY. Born May 4, 1953 in Key West, Fl. Graduate UCincinnati, AADA. Debut 1978 OB in "A Midsummer Night's Dream."

SIMPSON, STEVE. Born Sept. 3, 1947 in Perryton, Tx. Graduate UOk., Wake Forest U. Debut 1973 OB in "The Soldier," followed by "Thieves Carnival," "Birdland."

SINGLETON, SAM. Born Feb. 11, 1940 in Charleston, SC. Attended Dramatic Workshop. OB in "Aria Da Capo," "The Dumb Waiter," "Beautiful Dreamer," "Great Goodness of Life," "Life and Times," "Jazznite," "Anna Lucasta."

SISTI, MICHAELAN. Born May 27, 1949 in San Juan, PR. Graduate UBuffalo. Debut 1978 OB in "A Midsummer Night's Dream."

SMITH, ALEXIS. Born June 8, 1921 in Penticton, Can. Attended LACC. Bdwy debut 1971 in "Follies." followed by "The Women," "Summer Brave," "Platinum."

SMITH, EBBE ROE. Born June 25, 1949 in San Diego, CA. Graduate San Francisco State U. Debut 1978 OB in "Curse of the Starving Class.," "New Jerusalem."

SMITH, LOIS. Born Nov. 3. 1930 in Topeka, KS. Attended UWash. Bdwy debut 1952 in "Time Out for Ginger." followed by "The Young and Beautiful," "Wisteria Tress," "Glass Menagerie," "Orpheus Descending," "Stages," OB in "Sunday Dinner." "Present Tense." "The Iceman Cometh," "Harry Outside," "Hillbilly Women," "Touching Bottom."

SMITH, NICK. Born Jan. 13, 1932 in Philadelphia, Pa. Attended Boston U. Debut 1963 OB in "The Blacks," followed by "Man Is Man," "The Connec-

tion," "Blood Knot," "No Place to Be Somebody," "Androcles and the Lion," "So Nice They Named It Twice," "In the Recovery Lounge."

SMITH, RUFUS. Born July 11, 1917 in Smithfield, VA. Attended UVa. Bdwy bow 1938 in "Knickerbocker Holiday," followed by "Queen of Spades," "Park Avenue." "Street Scene," "Allegro," "Mr. Roberts," "Paint Your Wagon." "Pipe Dream," "Goldilocks," "Fiorella." "A Gift of Time," "Come on Strong," "The Advocate," "3 Bags Full," "Annie Get Your Gun," "Halfway Up the Tree," "The Education of Hyman Kaplan," "On the 20th Century."

SMITH, SHEILA. Born Apr. 3, 1933 in Conneaut, Oh. Attended Kent State U., Cleveland Play House. Bdwy debut 1963 in "Hot Spot," followed by "Mame" for which she received a Theatre World Award, "Follies," "Company," "Sugar," OB in "Taboo Revue," "Anthing Goes," "Best Foot Forward," "Sweet Miani." "Fiorello!" (CC)

SMOTHERS, DICK. Born in 1935 in NYC. Attended San Jose State Col. Bdwy debut 1978 in "I Love My Wife."

SMOTHERS, TOM. Born Feb. 2, 1937 in NYC. Attended San Jose State Col. Bdwy debut 1979 in "I Love My Wife."

SMYTHE, MARCUS. Born Mar. 26, 1950 in Berea, Oh. Graduate Otterbein Col., Ohio U. Debut 1975 OB in "Tenderloin," followed by "The Suicide."

SNYDER, NANCY E. Born Dec. 2, 1949 in Kankakee, IL. Graduate Webster Col., Neighborhood Playhouse, Bdwy debut 1976 in "Knock, Knock," OB in "The Farm," "My Life," "Lulu," "Cabin 12," "5th of July," "My Cup Ranneth Over," "Glorious Morning," "Stargazing."

SOBOLOFF, ARNOLD. Born Nov. 11, 1930 in NYC. Attended Cooper Union. OB in "Threepenny Opera," "Career," "Brothers Karamazov," "Vincent," "Bananas," "Papp," "Camino Real," "Are You Now or Have You Ever Been?." "Music! Music!." "The Sea," Bdwy in "Mandingo," "The Egg," "Beauty Part," "One Flew over the Cuckoo's Nest," "Anyone Can Whistle." "Bravo Giovanni." "Sweet Charity," "Mike Downstairs," "Cyrano," "The Act." "The Inspector General."

SOCKWELL, SALLY. Born June 14 in Little Rock, AR. Debut 1976 OB in "Vanities."

SOMMER, JOSEF. Born June 26, 1934 in Greifswald, Ger. Carnegie-Tech graduate. Bdwy bow 1970 in "Othello," followed by "Children, Children," "Trial of the Catonsville 9," "Full Circle," "Who's Who in Hell," "The Shadow Box," "Sopkesong," OB in "Enemies," "Merchant of Venice," "The Dog Ran Away." "Drinks Before Dinner."

SPEROS, JO. Born June 24, 1956 in Chicago, Il. Bdwy debut 1974 in "Mack and Mabel." followed by "The Lieutenant," "Rex," "Pippin," "A Chorus Line," "The Grand Tour."

SPINDELL, AHVI. Born June 26, 1954 in Boston, Ma. Attended Ithaca Col, UNH, Juilliard. Bdwy debut 1977 in "Something Old, Something New," OB in "Antony and Cleopatra."

SQUIBB, JUNE. Born Nov. 6 in Vandalia, IL. Attended Cleveland Play House, HB Studio. Debut 1956 OB in "Sable Brush," followed by "Boy Friend," "Lend an Ear," "Another Language," "Castaways," "Funeral March for a One-Man Band," "Gorey Stories," Bdwy in "Gypsy" (1960), "The Happy Time.," "Gorey Stories."

SQUIRE, KATHERINE. Born Mar. 9, 1903 in Defiance, OH. Attended Ohio Wesleyan, Cleveland Playhouse. Bdwy debut 1932 in "Black Tower," followed by "Goodbye Again," "High Tor," "Hipper's Holiday," "What a Life," "Liberty Jones," "The Family," "Shadow of a Gunman," "Traveling Lady," OB in "Roots," "This Here Nice Place," "Boy on a Straight-Back Chair," "Catsplay.," "Hillbilly Women."

ST. JOHN, MARCO. Born May 7, 1939 in New Orleans, La. Fordham U. graduate. Bdwy bow 1964 in "Poor Bitos," followed by "And Things That Go Bump in the Night," "The Unknown Soldier and His Wife," "Weekend," "40 Carats," APA's "We Comrades Three" and "War and Peace," OB in "Angels of Anadarko," "Man of Destiny," "Timon of Athens," "Richard III," "Awake and Sing."

STANLEY, GORDON. Born Dec. 20, 1951 in Boston, MA. Graduate Brown U.. Temple U. Debut 1977 OB in "Lyrical and Satirical," followed by "Allegro."

STAPLETON, MAUREEN. Born June 21, 1925 in Troy, NY. Attended HB Studio. Bdwy debut 1946 in "Playboy of the Western World," followed by "Antony and Cleopatra," "Detective Story," "Bird Cage," "The Rose Tattoo" for which she received a Theatre World Award. "The Emperor's Clothes," "The Crucible," "Richard III," "The Seagull," "27 Wagons Full of Cotton," "Orpheus Descending," "The Cold Wind and the Warm," "Toys in the Attic," "Glass Menagerie" (1965 & '75), "Plaza Suite," "Norman, Is That You?," "Gingerbread Lady," "Country Girl," "Secret Affairs of Mildred Wild," "Gin Game."

STEINBERG, ROY. Born Mar. 24, 1951 in NYC. Graduate Tufts U., Yale. Debut 1974 OB in "A Midsummer Night's Dream," followed by "Firebugs," "The Doctor in spite of Himself," "Romeo and Juliet," Bdwy in "Wings."

STENBORG, HELEN. Born Jan. 24, 1925 in Minneapolis, MN. Attended Hunter Col. OB in "A Doll's House," "A Month in the Country," "Say Nothing," "Rosmersholm," "Rimers of Eldrich," "Trial of the Catonsville 9," "Hot L Baltimore," "Pericles," "Elephant in the House," "A Tribute to Lili Lamont." "Museum," "5th of July," "In the Recovery Lounge," Bdwy in "Sheep on the Runway." "Da."

STEPHENSON, ALBERT. Born Aug. 23, 1947 in Miami, FL. Attended Boston Consv. Bdwy debut 1973 in "Irene," followed by "Debbie Reynolds Show." "The Act," "A Broadway Musical."

STERNGAGEN, FRANCES. Born Jan. 13, 1932 in Washington DC. Vassar graduate, OB in "Admirable Bashful," "Thieves' Carnival," "Country Wife," "Ulysses in Nighttown." "Saintliness of Margery Kemp," "The Room," "A Slight Ache," "Displaced Person," "Playboy of the Western World" (LC), Bdwy in "Great Day in the Morning," "Right Honourable Gentleman," with APA in "Cocktail Party," and "Cock-a-doodle Dandy," "The Sign in Sidney Brustein's Window," "Enemies" (LC), "The Good Doctor," "Equus," "Angel.," "On Golden Pond."

STEVENS, SUSAN. Born in 1942 in Louisville, Ky. Attended Jackson Col., AMDA. Debut 1978 OB in "The Price of Genius!"

STEVENS, WESLEY. Born Apr. 6, 1948 in Evansville, IN. Graduate UVa Ohio State U. Debut 1978 OB in "Othello.," followed by "The Importance of Being Earnest."

STEVENSEN, SCOTT. Born May 4. 1951 in Salt Lake City, Ut. Attended USCal. Bdwy debut 1974 in "Good News" for which he received a Theatre World Award, followed by OB in "2 by 5," "Bea's Place,"

STEWART, JEAN-PIERRE. Born May 4, 1946 in NYC. Graduate CCNY. OB in "Henry IV," "King Lear," "Cry of Players," "In the Matter of J. Robert Oppenheimer," "The Miser." "Long Day's Journey into Night." "American Night Cry," "The Old Ones" "Dancing for the Kaiser." "Primary English Class," "Mamma Sang the Blues," "Museum.," "Strangers."

STEWART, JOHN. Born May 21, 1934 in Brooklyn, NY. Bdwy debut 1947 in "High Button Shoes." followed by "Love Life," "Happy Time." "The King and I," "Grass Harp," "Bernardine" for which he received a Theatre World Award, "Sleeping Prince," "Waltz of the Toreadors," "Generation," "First Monday in October," OB in "Tattooed Countess," JB in "The King and I" and "Carousel."

STONE, MAX. Born Oct. 23, 1954 in Greenville, Tx. Attended Tx Christian U., SMU. Bdwy debut 1979 in "They're Playing Our Song."

STONE, ROBIN. Born Sept. 22. 1951 in Buffalo, NY. Graduate USIU. Debut 1979 OB in "Mary."

STORM·JAMES. Born Aug. 12, 1943 in Chicago, Il. Debut 1962 OB in "On Borrowed Time," Bdwy in "You Can't Take It with You," "Man and Superman."

STOVALL, COUNT. Born Jan. 15, 1946 in Los Angeles, CA. Graduate UCal. Debut 1973 OB in "He's Got a Jones," followed by "In White America." "Rashomon," "Sidnee Poet Heroical." "A Photo.," "Julius Caesar," "Coriolanus," "Spell #7."

STRASSER, ROBIN. Born May 7, 1945 in NYC. Bdwy debut 1963 in "The Irregular Verb to Love," followed by "The Country Girl" (CC)," "A Meeting by the River" (OB), "Chapter 2."

STRATTON, JOHN. Born Apr. 15 in San Francisco, Ca. Attended HB Studio. Debut 1955 OB in "The Chair," followed by "Leave It to Jane," "Two if by Sea," "Sing Melancholy Baby," Bdwy in "Sweet Charity."

STRAW, JACK. Born Feb. 19, 1925 in Manchester, NH. Attended AADA. Bdwy debut 1978 in "Once in a Lifetime."

STREEP, MERYL. Born Sept. 22 in Summit, NJ. Graduate Vassar, Yale, Debut 1975 OB in "Trelawny of the Wells." followed by "27 Wagons Full of Cotton" for which she received a Theatre World Award, "A Memory of Two Mondays," "Secret Service," "Henry V," "Measure for Measure" (CP), "The Cherry Orchard," (LC), "Taming of the Shrew," "Taken in Marriage," Bdwy in "Happy End" (1977).

STRONG, MICHAEL. Born Feb. 8, 1923 in NYC. Graduate Brooklyn Col., Neighborhood Playhouse. Bdwy debut 1941 in "Spring Again," followed by "Russian People," "Counter-Attack," "Eve of St. Mark," "Men to the Sea," "Whole World Over," "Detective Story," "Anastasia," "Firstborn," "Gypsy," "A Far Country," "Rhinoceros," "Emperor's Clothes," "Enemy of the People," LCRep's "After the Fall," "Incident at Vichy," "But for Whom Charlie," and "Marco Millions," OB in "A Month in the Country," "Dance of Death," "The Sponsor.," "Taxi Tales."

STROUD, MICHAEL. Born Dec. 21, 1934 in Exeter, Devonshire, Eng. Bdwy debut 1979 in "Bedroom Farce.

STUART, JAY. Born in Brooklyn, NY. Bdwy debut 1970 in "Cry for Us All," followed by "Applause," "Pajama Game," "The Grand Tour."

STUART, LYNNE. Born Sept. 30 in Lakeland, Fl. Attended Tampa U., NYCol. of Music. Bdwy debut 1953 in "Kismet," followed by "New Girl in Town," "Bells Are Ringing," "High Spirits," "The Women," OB in "Turn the Grand Up!"

STUBBS, JIM. Born Mar. 19, 1949 in Charlotte, NC. Graduate NCSchool of Arts. Bdwy debut 1975 in "Dance with Me," OB in "The Passion of Dracula."

STUCKMANN, EUGENE. Born. Nov. 16, 1917 in NYC. Bdwy bow 1943 in "Richard III," followed by "Counsellor-at-Law," "Othello," "The Tempest," "Foxhole in the Parlor," "Henry VIII," "Androcles and the Lion," "Yellow Jack," "Skipper Next to God," "A Patriot for Me." "First Monday in October," OB in "The Web and the Rock."

SULLIVAN, JEREMIAH. Born Sept. 22, 1937 in NYC. Harvard graduate. Bdwy debut 1957 in "Compulsion," followed by "The Astrakhan Coat," "Philadelphia, Here I Come!." "A Lion in Winter," "Hamlet," OB in "Ardele," "A Scent of Flowers," "House of Blue Leaves," "Gogol," "The Master and Margarita."

SUNDSTEN, LANI. Born Feb. 27, 1949 in NYC. Attended Am. Col. in Paris. Bdwy debut 1970 in "The Rothschilds," followed by "Tricks," "California Suite," "Scapino," "They're Playing Our Song," OB in "Carousel," "In the Boom Boom Room."

SUROVY, NICOLAS. Born June 30, 1944 in Los Angeles, CA. Attended Northwestern U., Neighborhood Playhouse. Debut 1964 OB in "Helen" for which he received a Theatre World Award, followed by "Sisters of Mercy," Bdwy in "Merchant.," "Crucifer of Blood."

SWANN, ELAINE. Born May 9 in Baltimore, Md. Attended UNC. Bdwy debut 1957 in "The Music Man," followed by "Greenwillow," "A Thurber Carnival," "My Mother, My Father and Me," "Jennie," OB in "Miss Stanwyck Is Still in Hiding."

SWARBRICK, CAROL. Born Mar. 20, 1948 in Inglewood, CA. Graduate UCLA, NYU. Debut 1971 OB in "Drat!," followed by "The Glorious Age," Bdwy in "Side-by-Side by Sondheim.", "Whoopee!"

SWIFT, ALLEN. Born Jan. 16, 1924 in NYC. Debut 1961 OB in "Portrait of the Artist," followed by "Month of Sundays," "Where Memories Are Magic," "My Old Friends," Bdwy in "Student Gypsy" (1963), "Checking Out."

TANANIS, ROBERT. Born Mar. 22, 1939 in Pittsburgh, Pa. Graduate St. Vincent's Col. Bdwy debut 1967 in "Spofford," OB in "Damn Yankees," "Gay Company," "Telecast."

TANDY, JESSICA. Born June 7, 1909 in London, Eng. Attended Greet Acad. Bdwy debut 1930 in "The Matriarch," followed by "Last Enemy" "Time and the Conways," "White Steed," "Geneva," "Jupiter Laughs," "Anne of England," "Yesterday's Magic," "A Streetcar Named Desire," "Hilda Crane," "Fourposter," "The Honey's," "A Day by the Sea," "Man in the Dog Suit," "Triple Play," "Five Finger Exercise," "The Physicists," "A Delicate Balance," "Home," "All Over," LCRep's "Camino Real," "Not I" and "Happy Days," "Noel Coward in Two Keys," "The Gin Game."

TARLETON, DIANE. Born in Baltimore, MD. Graduate UMd. Bdwy debut 1965 in "Anya," followed by "a Joyful Noise," "Elmer Gantry," "Yentl," OB in "A Time for the Gentle People," "Spoon River Anthology," "International Stud," "Too Much Johnson."

TASK, MAGGIE. Born July 4 in Marion, Oh. Attended Wright Col. Bdwy debut 1960 in "Greenwillow," followed by "a Family Affair," "Tovarich," CC's "Most Happy Fella" and "Carousel," "Funny Girl," "Kelly," "Anya," "A Time for Singing," "Darling of the Day," "Education of Hyman Kaplan," "Sound of Music," "CoCo," "Sweeney Todd," OB in "Sing Melancholy Baby."

TAYLOR, GEORGE. Born Sept. 18, 1930 in London, Eng. Attended AADA. Debut 1972 OB in "Hamlet," followed by "Enemies" (LC), "The Contractor," "Scribes," "Says I, Says He," Bdwy in "Emperor Henry IV," "The National Health."

TAYLOR, JEANNINE. Born June 2, 1954 in Hartford, Ct. Graduate New Eng. Consv. Debut 1979 OB in "Umbrellas of Cherbourg."

TAYLOR, ROBIN. Born May 28 in Tacoma, Wa. Graduate UCLA. Debut 1979 OB in "Festival."

TAYLOR-DUNN, CORLISS. Born Dec. 1, 1945 in Cleveland, Oh. Graduate Central State U., UMich. Bdwy debut 1977 in "Bubbling Brown Sugar," OB in "Pins and Needles" (1978).

TAYLOR-MORRIS, MAXINE. Born June 16 in NYC. Graduate NYU. Debut 1977 OB in "Counsellor-at-Law," followed by "Manny."

TEITEL, CAROL. Born Aug. 1, 1929 in NYC. Attended AmTh Wing. Bdwy debut 1957 in "The Country Wife," followed by "The Entertainer," "Hamlet," "Marat/deSade," "A Flea in Her Ear," "Crown Matrimonial," "All Over Town," in "Way of the World," "Juana La Loca," "An Evening with Ring Lardner," "Misanthrope," "Shaw Festival," "Country Scandal," "The Bench," "Colombe," "Under Milk Wood," "7 Days of Mourning," "Long Day's Journey into Night," "The Old Ones," "Figures in the Sand," "World of Sholom Aleichem," "Big and Little," "Duet," "Trio."

TENNEY, CARYL. (a.k.a. Carol Jeanne) Born July 11 in Thatcher, Az. Bdwy debut 1968 in "I'm Solomon," followed by "Two by Two," "Desert Song," "Carmelina."

THACKER, RUSS. Born June 23, 1946 in Washington, DC. Attended Montgomery Col. Debut 1967 in "Life with Father" (CC), followed by OB in "Your Own Thing" for which he received a Theatre World Award, "Dear Oscar," "Once I Saw a Boy Laughing," "Music! Music!" (CC), "Tip-Toes," Bdwy in "Grass Harp," "Heathen," "Home Sweet Homer," "Me Jack You Jill."

THOME, DAVID. Born July 24, 1951 in Salt Lake City, UT. Bdwy debut 1971 in "No, No, Nanette," followed by "Different Times," "Good News," "Rodgers and Hart," "A Chorus Line."

THOMPSON, JEFFREY V. Born March 21, 1952 in Cleveland, Oh. Graduate Ohio U. Debut 1976 OB in "Homeboy," followed by "Macbeth," "Season's Reasons," "Helen," Bdwy 1978 in "Eubie!"

THORNE, RAYMOND. Born Nov. 27, 1934 in Lackawanna, NY. Graduate UConn. Debut 1966 OB in "Man with a Load of Mischief," followed by "Rose," "Dames at Sea," "Love Course," "Blue Boys" Bdwy 1977 in "Annie."

THORNTON-SHERWOOD, MADELEINE (formerly Madeleine Sherwood). Born Nov. 13, 1926 in Montreal, Can. Attended Yale U. OB in "Brecht on Brecht," "Medea," "Hey You, Light Man," "Friends and Relations," "Older People," "Oh Glorious Tintinnabulation," "Getting Out," Bdwy in "The Chase," "The Crucible," "Cat on a Hot Tin Roof," "Invitation to a March," "Camelot," "Arturo Ui," "Do I Hear a Waltz?," "Inadmissible Evidence," "All Over!"

TONER, THOMAS. Born May 25, 1928 in Homestead, Pa. Graduate UCLA. Bdwy debut 1973 in "Tricks," followed by "The Good Doctor," "All over Town," "A Texas Trilogy," "The Inspector General," OB in "Pericles,"

"Merry Wives of Windsor," "A Midsummer Night's Dream," "Richard III."

TORGERSEN, ELIZABETH. Born Oct. 24 in St. Paul, Mn. Graduate UMinn, Berghof Studio. Debut 1978 OB in "Just the Immediate Family."

TORN, RIP. Born Feb. 6, 1931 in Temple, TX. Graduate UTx. Bdwy bow 1956 in "Cat on a Hot Tin Roof," followed by "Sweet Bird of Youth," for which he received a Theatre World Award, "Daughter of Silence," "Strange Interlude," "Blues for Mr. Charlie," "Country Girl" (CC), "Glass Menagerie," OB in "Chapparal," "The Cuban Thing," "The Kitchen," "Deer Park," "Dream of a Blacklisted Actor," "Dance of Death," "Macbeth," "Barbary Shore," "Creditors," "Seduced."

TORRES, ANDY. Born Aug. 10, 1945 in Ponce, PR. Attended AMDA. Bdwy debut 1969 in "Indians," followed by "Purlie," "Don't Bother Me, I Can't Cope," "The Wiz," "Guys and Dolls," OB in "Billy Noname," "Suddenly the Music Starts."

TOVATT, ELLEN. Born in NYC. Attended Antioch Col., LAMDA. Debut 1962 OB in "Taming of the Shrew," followed by "The Show-Off," "Don Juan Comes Back from the War," Bdwy in "The Great God Brown," "The Visit," "Chemin de Fer," "Holiday," "Love for Love," "Rules of the Game," "Herzl."

TOWERS, CONSTANCE. Born May 20, 1933 in Whitefish, MT. Attended Juilliard, AADA. Bdwy debut 1965 in "Anya," followed by "Show Boat," (LC), "Carousel" (CC), "Sound of Music," (CC'67, JB '70 & '71), "Engagement Baby," "The King and I" (CC'68, JB '72, Bdwy '77).

TOWERS, IAN MICHAEL. Born Aug. 21, 1951 in Rockville Centre, NY. Appeared with NYC Opera before Bdwy debut 1979 in "Carmelina."

TOWNSEND, JUDITH. Born Nov. 16, 1951 in Chesapeake, VA. Graduate E. Carolina U., Fla. State U. Debut 1978 OB in "The Taming of the Shrew."

TRONTO, RUDY. Born July 14, 1928 in Peekskill, NY. Bdwy debut 1960 in "Irma La Douce," followed by "Carnival," "Man of La Mancha," "Ballroom," OB in "Boys from Syracuse," "Secret Life of Walter Mitty," "Smile, Smile, Smile."

TROOBNICK, GENE. Born Aug. 23, 1926 in Boston, MA. Attended Ithaca Col., Columbia U. Bdwy bow 1960 in "Second City," followed by "The Odd Couple," "Before You Go," "The Time of Your Life," OB in "Dynamite Tonight," "A Gun Play," "Tales of the Hasidim," "Wings," "Sganarelle."

TROY, HECTOR. Born May 25, 1941 in NYC. OB in "Waiting for Lefty," "The Miser," "Winterset," "Summertree," "The Unicorn in Captivity," Bdwy in "Does a Tiger Wear a Necktie?"

TSOUTSOUVAS, SAM. Born Aug. 20, 1948 in Santa Barbara, Ca. Attended UCal, Juilliard. Debut 1969 in NYSF's "Peer Gynt," followed by "Twelfth Night," "Timon of Athens," and "Cymbeline," OB in "School for Scandal," "The Hostage," "Women Beware Women," "Lower Depths," Bdwy in "Three Sisters," "Measure for Measure," "Beggar's Opera," "Scapin," "Dracula."

TUCCI, MICHAEL. Born Apr. 15, 1946 in NYC. Graduate C.W. Post Col. Debut 1974 OB in "Godspell," followed by "Jules Feiffer's Hold Me!," "Drinks Before Dinner," Bdwy in "Grease" (1975), "Spokessong."

TURCO, TONY. Born Jan. 17, 1917 in NYC. Debut 1979 OB in "Telecast."

TURNER, KATHLEEN. Born June 19, 1954 in Springfield, Mo. Graduate Southwest Mo. State. Bdwy debut 1978 in "Gemini."

TURQUE, MIMI. Born Sept. 30, 1939 in Brooklyn, NY. Graduate Brooklyn Col. Bdwy bow 1945 in "Carousel," followed by "Seeds in the Wind," "The Enchanted," "Cry of the Peacock," "Anniversary Waltz," "Carnival," "Man of La Mancha," OB in "Johnny Summit," "The Dybbuk," "Romeo and Juliet," "The Happy Journey," "God Bless You, Mr. Rosewater."

TYNES, BILL. Born Nov. 9, 1956 in Placentia, Ca. Attended AzState U, Cal-State U. Debut 1977 OB in "The Three Sisters," followed by "Can-Can," "Strider."

UHLER, ERIC. Born Feb. 25, 1949 in Youngstown, Oh. Graduate Ohio U. Bdwy debut 1978 in "Once in a Lifetime."

ULLMANN, LIV. Born Dec. 16, 1938 in Touro, Japan. Debut 1975 in "A Doll's House" (LC), Bdwy in "Anna Christie," "I Remember Mama" (1979).

URMSTON, KENNETH. Born Aug. 6, 1929 in Cicinnati, OH. Attended Xavier U. Bdwy debut 1950 in "Make A Wish," followed by "Top Banana," "Guys and Dolls," "John Murray Anderson's Almanac," "Can-Can," "Silk Stockings," "Oh Captain!," "Bells Are Ringing," "Redhead," "Madison Avenue," "Tenderloin," "We Take the Town," "Lovely Ladies, Kind Gentlemen," "Follies," "Pippin," "Ballroom."

VAN AKEN, GRETCHEN. Born Nov. 15, 1940 in Ridgeway, Pa. Graduate Emerson Col., London Central School. Bdwy debut 1964 in "Oliver!" followed by "Walking Happy," OB in "Digging for Apples," "Wanted," "The Making of Americans," "Oklahoma!"

VAN DEVERE, TRISH. Born Mar. 9, 1945 in Englewood, NJ. Graduate Ohio Wesleyan U. Debut 1967 OB in "Kicking Down the Castle," "The Violano Virtuoso," Bdwy 1975 in "All God's Chillun Got Wings," followed by "Sly Fox."

VAN NORDEN, PETER. Born Dec. 16, 1950 in NYC. Graduate Colgate U., Neighborhood Playhouse. Debut 1975 OB in "Hamlet," followed by "Henry V," "Measure for Measure," "A Country Scandal," "Hound of the Baskervilles," "Tartuffe," "Antigone," "Bingo," "Taming of the Shrew," "The Balcony," Bdwy in "Romeo and Juliet" (1977), "St. Joan," "Inspector General."

VANNUYS, ED. Born Dec. 28, 1930 in Lebanon, IN. Attended Ind. U. Debut 1969 OB in "No Place to Be Somebody," followed by "Conflict of Interest," "The Taming of the Shrew," "God Bless You, Mr. Rosewater," Bdwy in "Black Terror."

VAN PATTEN, JOYCE. Born Mar. 9, 1934 in Kew Gardens, NY. Bdwy bow 1941 in "Popsy," followed by "This Rock," "Tomorrow the World," "The Perfect Marriage," "The Wind is 90," "Desk Set," "A Hole in the Head," "Murder at the Howard Johnson's," OB in "Between Two Thieves," "Spoon River Anthology."

VAN TREUREN, MARTIN. Born Dec. 6, 1952 in Hawthorne, NJ. Graduate Montclair State Col. Debut 1978 OB in "Oklahoma!"

VARRONE, GENE. Born Oct. 30, 1929 in Brooklyn, NY. Graduate LIU. Bdwy in "Damn Yankees," "Take Me Along," "Ziegfeld Follies," "Goldilocks," "Wildcat," "Tovarich," "Subways Are for Sleeping," "Bravo Giovanni," "Drat! The Cat," "Fade Out-Fade In," "Don't Drink the Water," "Dear World," "Coco," "A Little Night Music," "So Long 174th St.," "Knickerbocker Holiday," "The Grand Tour," OB in "Promenade."

VESTOFF, VIRGINIA. Born Dec. 9, 1940 in NYC. Bdwy debut 1960 in "From A to Z," followed by "Irma La Douce," "Baker Street," "1776," "Via Galactica," "Nash at 9," "Boccacio," "Spokesong," OB in "The Boy Friend," "Crystal Heart," "Fall Out," "New Cole Porter Revue," "Man with a Load of Mischief," "Love and Let Love," "Short-Changed Review," "The Misanthrope," "Drinks Before Dinner," "I'm Getting My Act Together . . . "

VIDNOVIC, MARTIN. Born Jan. 4, 1948 in Falls Church, VA. Attended Cincinnati Consv. of Music. Debut 1972 OB in "The Fantasticks," followed by Bdwy in "Home Sweet Homer" (1976), "The King and I" (1977).

VIGARD, KRISTEN. Born May 15, 1963 in St. Paul, Mn. Debut 1970 OB in "A Cheap Trick," followed by " 100 Miles from Nowhere," "Wedding Band," Bdwy in "Annie," "Hair" (1978), "I Remember Mama."

VILEEN, ELLIOTT. Born Dec. 14, 1950 in Pittsburgh, PA. Graduate RI Sch. of Design, Temple U. Debut 1977 OB in "The Passion of Dracula."

VILLAIRE, HOLLY. Born Apr. 11, 1944 in Yonkers, NY. Graduate UDetroit, UMich. Debut 1971 OB in "Arms and the Man," followed by "Purity," "Eyes of Chalk," "Anna-Luse," "Village Wooing," "The Fall and Redemption of Man," BAM Co.'s "New York Idea," "Three Sisters," "Devil's Disciple," " The Play's the Thing," and "Julius Caesar," "God Bless You, Mr. Rosewater," Bdwy in "Scapino" (1974), "Habeas Corpus."

VINOVICH, STEVE. Born Jan. 22, 1945 in Peoria, IL. Graduate UIll., UCLA, Juilliard. Debut 1972 OB in "The Robber Bridegroom," followed by "King John," "Father Uxbridge Wants to Marry," Bdwy in "Robber Bridegroom" (1976), "The Magic Show," "The Grand Tour," "Loose Ends."

VITA, MICHAEL. Born in 1941 in NYC. Studied at HB Studio. Bdwy debut 1967 in "Sweet Charity," followed by "Golden Rainbow," "Promises, Promises," "Chicago," "Ballroom," OB in "Sensations," "That's Entertainment," "Rocket to the Moon."

VITELLA, SEL. Born July 7, 1934 in Boston, MA. Graduate San Francisco Inst. of Music. Debut 1975 OB in "The Merchant of Venice," followed by "Gorey Stories," Bdwy in "Something's Afoot" (1976), "Gorey Stories."

VOGEL, DAVID. Born Oct. 19, 1922 in Canton, OH. Attended UPa, Bdwy debut 1948 in "Ballet Ballads," followed by "Gentlemen Prefer Blondes," "Make a Wish," "The Desert Song," OB in "How to Get Rid of It," "The Fantasticks," "Miss Stanwyck Is Still in Hiding."

VON SCHERLER, SASHA. Born Dec. 12, in NYC. Bdwy debut 1959 in "Look after Lulu," followed by "Rape of the Belt," "The Good Soup," "Great God Brown," "First Love," "Alfie," "Harold," "Bad Habits," OB in "Admirable Bashville," "The Comedian," "Conversation Piece," "Good King Charles' Golden Days," "Under Milk Wood," "Plays for Bleecker Street," "Ludlow Fair," "Twelfth Night," "Sondra," "Cyrano de Bergerac," "Crimes of Passion," "Henry VI," "Trelawny of the Wells," "Screens," "Soon Jack November," "Pericles," "Kid Champion," "Henry V," "Comanche Cafe," "Museum," "Grand Magic."

VOSKOVEC, GEORGE. Born June 19, 1905 in Sazava, Czech. Graduate Dijon U. Bdwy debut 1945 in "The Tempest," followed by "Love of 4 Colonels," "His and Hers," "The Seagull," "Festival," "Uncle Vanya," "A Call on Kuprin," "Tenth Man," "Big Fish, Little Fish," "Do You Know the Milky Way?," "Hamlet," "Cabaret," "Penny Wars," "All Over," BO in "The Alchemist," "East Wind," "Galileo," "Oh Say Can You See L. A.?," "Room Service," "Brecht on Brecht," "All Is Bright," "The Cherry Orchard," "Agamemnon," "Happy Days."

WALDRON, MICHAEL. Born Nov. 19, 1949 in West Orange, NJ. Graduate Columbia U. Debut 1979 OB in "Mary."

WALDROP, MARK. Born July 30, 1954 in Washington, DC. Graduate Cincinnati Consv. Debut 1977 OB in "Movie Buff," Bdwy in "The Grand Tour."

WALKER, PETER. Born July 24, 1927 in Mineola, NY. Bdwy debut 1955 in "Little Glass Clock," followed by "Dear World," "Follies," "Where's Charley?" OB in "Dancing for the Kaiser," "My Old Friends."

WALKER, RANDOLPH. Born Feb. 8. 1929 in London, Eng. Rollins Col. graduate. Debut 1975 OB in "Don Juan in Hell," followed by "The Heretic," "Chalk Garden," "Royal Family," "Lion in Winter," Bdwy 1977 in "The King and I."

WALLACE, TIMOTHY. Born July 24, 1947 in Racine, Wi. Graduate UWisc., PennState U. Debut 1976 OB in "The Rimers of Eldritch," followed by "Dance on a Country Grave," Bdwy in "King of Hearts."

WALLACH, ELI. Born Dec. 7, 1915 in Brooklyn, NY. Graduate UTx, CCNY. Bdwy bow 1945 in "Skydrift," followed by "Henry VIII," "Androcles and the Lion," "Alice in Wonderland," "Yellow Jack," "What Every Woman Knows," "Antony and Cleopatra," "Mr. Roberts," "Lady from the Sea," "The Rose

Sel Vitella	**Katherine Wallach**	**James Ray Weeks**	**Nancy Weems**	**Ralph David Westfa**

Tatoo" for which he received a Theatre World Award, "Mlle. Colombe," "Teahouse of the August Moon," "Major Barbara," "The Cold Wind and the Warm," "Rhinoceros," "Luv," "Staircase," "Promenade, All!," "Waltz of the Toreadors," "Saturday, Sunday Monday," OB in "The Diary of Anne Frank."

WALLACH, KATHERINE. Born July 13, 1938 in NYC. Attended Sarah Lawrence Col., Neighborhood Playhouse. Debut 1978 OB in "The Diary of Anne Frank."

WALLACH, ROBERTA. Born Aug. 2, 1955 in NYC. Attended Bennington Col., Columbia U., Neighborhood Playhouse. Debut 1978 OB in "The Diary of Anne Frank."

WALLER, KEN. Born Apr. 12, 1945 in Atlanta, Ga. Graduate Piedmont Col. Debut 1976 OB in "The Boys from Syracuse," Bdwy 1979 in "Sarava."

WALTERS, FREDERICK. Born July 19, 1930 in Schenectady, NY. Graduate Centenary Col., Rutgers U. Debut 1979 in "Biography: A Game."

WARD, CHARLES. Born Oct. 24, 1952 in Los Angeles, CA. Soloist with American Ballet Theatre before 1978 Bdwy debut in "Dancin'."

WARD, DOUGLAS TURNER. Born May 5, 1930 in Burnside, LA. Attended UMich. Bdwy bow 1959 in "A Raisin in the Sun," followed by "One Flew Over the Cuckoo's Nest," "Last Breeze of Summer," OB in "The Iceman Cometh," "The Blacks," "Pullman Car Hiawatha," "Bloodknot," "Happy Ending," "Day of Absence," "Kongi's Harvest," "Ceremonies in Dark Old Men," "The Harangues," "The Reckoning," "Frederick Douglass through His Own Words," "River Niger," "The Brownsville Raid," "The Offering," "Old Phantoms."

WARD, JANET. Born Feb. 19 in NYC. Attended Actors Studio. Bdwy debut 1945 in "Dream Girl," followed by "Anne of a Thousand Days," "Detective Story," "King of Friday's Men," "Middle of the Night," "Miss Lonelyhearts," "J.B.," "Cheri," "The Egg," "Impossible Years," "Of Love Remembered," OB in "Chapparal," "The Typists," "The Tiger," "Summertree," "Dream of a Blacklisted Actor," "Cruising Speed 600 MPH," "One Flew over the Cuckoo's Nest," "Love Gotta Come by Saturday Night," "Home Is the Hero," "Love Death Plays," "Olympic Park," "Hillbilly Women."

WARDWELL, JOHN. Born in Rockland, Me. Graduate UMe., Oxford. Bdwy debut 1967 in "90 Day Mistress," followed by "Nathan Weinstein, Mystic, Conn.," "Fire!," "First Monday in October," "Utter Glory of Morrissey Hall," OB in "Single Man at a Party" "In White America," "All the King's Men," "Fireworks," "We Bombed in New Haven," "The Contractor," "The Dog Ran Away," "Richard III."

WATSON, DOUGLASS. Born Feb. 24, 1921 in Jackson, Ga. Graduate UNC. Bdwy bow 1947 in "The Iceman Cometh," followed by "Antony and Cleopatra" for which he received a Theatre World Award, "Leading Lady," "Richard III," "The Happiest Years," "That Lady," "Wisteria Trees," "Romeo and Juliet," "Desire under the Elms," "Sunday Breakfast," "Cyrano de Bergerac," "Confidential Clerk," "Portrait of a Lady," "The Miser," "The Young and Beautiful," "Little Glass Clock," "Country Wife," "Man for All Seasons," "Chinese Prime Minister," "Marat/deSade," "Prime of Miss Jean Brodie," "Pirates of Penzance," "Over Here," OB in NYSF's "Much Ado about Nothing," "King Lear" and "As you Like It," "The Hunger," "Dancing for the Kaiser," "Money," "My Life," "Sightlines," "Glorious Morning."

WEAVER, FRITZ. Born Jan. 19, 1926 in Pittsburgh, PA. Graduate UChicago. Bdwy debut 1955 in "Chalk Garden" for which he received a Theatre World Award, followed by "Protective Custody," "Miss Lonelyhearts," "All American," "Lorenzo," "The White House," "Baker Street," "Child's Play," "Absurd Person Singular," OB in "The Way of the World," "White Devil," "Doctor's Dilemma," "Family Reunion," "The Power and the Glory," "Great God Brown," "Peer Gynt," "Henry IV," "My Fair Lady" (CC), "Lincoln," "The Biko Inquest," "The Price."

WEDGEWORTH, ANN. Born Jan. 21 in Abilene, Tx. Attended UTex. Bdwy debut 1958 in "Make a Million," Followed by "Blues for Mr. Charlie," "Last Analysis," "Thieves," "Chapter Two," OB in "Chapparal," "The Crucible" "Days and Nights of Beebee Fenstermaker," "Ludlow Fair," "Line."

WEEKS, JAMES RAY. Born Mar. 21, 1942 in Seattle. WA. Graduate UOre., AADA. Debut 1972 in LCR's "Enemies," "Merchant of Venice" and "A Streetcar Named Desire," followed by OB's "49 West 87th," "Feedlot," "The Runner Stumbles," "Glorious Morning." "Just the Immediate Family," "The Deserter," "Life and/or Death," "Devour the Snow," Bdwy in "My Fat Friend," "We Interrupt This Program."

WEEMS, NANCY. Born Dec. 30, 1948 in Glendale, Ca. Attended Stephens Col. Debut 1972 OB in "Servant of Two Masters," followed by "The Lounge Player," "Antony and Cleopatra."

WEIL, ROBERT E. Born Nov. 18, 1914 in NYC. Attended NYU. Bdwy bow in "New Faces of 1941," followed by "Burlesque," "Becket," "Once upon a Mattress," "Blood, Sweat and Stanley Poole," "Night Life," "Arturo Ui," "Beggar on Horseback" (LC), "Lenny," "Happy End," OB in "Love Your Crooked Neighbor," "Felix," "My Old Friends."

WEISS, GORDON J. Born June 16, 1949 in Bismarck, ND. Attended Moorhead State Col. Bdwy debut 1974 in "Jumpers," followed by "Goodtime Charley," "King of Hearts."

WELLES, JOAN. Born Nov. 30, 1943 in NYC. Graduate CUNY, Yale. Debut 1978 OB in "P.S. Your Cat Is Dead," followed by "Antony and Cleopatra."

WESTFALL, RALPH DAVID. Born July 2, 1934 in North Lewisburg, Oh. Graduate Ohio Wesleyan U., SUNY New Paltz. Debut 1977 OB in "Richard III," followed by "The Importance of Being Earnest."

WESTON, JACK. Born Aug. 21, 1924 in Cleveland, OH. Attended Cleveland Playhouse, AmThWing. Bdwy debut 1950 in "Season in the Sun." followed by "South Pacific," "Bells Are Ringing," "California Suite," "The Ritz," "Cheaters," "Break a Leg."

WHITE, ALICE. Born Jan. 6, 1945 in Washington, DC. Oberlin Col. graduate. Debut 1977 OB in "The Passion of Dracula."

WHITEHEAD, PAXTON. Born in Kent, Eng. Attended Webber-Douglas Acad. Bdwy debut 1962 in "The Affair," followed by "Beyond the Fringe," "Candida," "Habeas Corpus," "Crucifer of Blood," OB in "Gallows Humour," "One Way Pendulum" "A Doll's House," "Rondelay."

WHITENER, WILLIAM. Born Aug. 17, 1951 in Seattle, WA. With Joffrey Ballet before Bdwy debut 1978 in "Dancin'."

WHITTON, MARGARET. (formerly Peggy). Born Nov. 30 in Philadelphia, Pa. Debut 1973 OB in "Baba Goya," followed by "Arthur," "The Wager," "Nourish the Beast," "Another Language," "Chinchilla."

WILKINSON, KATE. Born Oct. 25 in San Francisco, CA. Attended San Jose State Col. Bdwy debut 1967 in "Little Murders," followed by "Johnny No-Trump," "Watercolor," "Postcards," "Ring Round the Bathtub," "The Last of Mrs. Lincoln," "Man and Superman," OB in "La Madre," "Earnest in Love," "Story of Mary Surratt," "Bring Me a Warm Body," "Child Buyer," "Rimers of Eldritch," "A Doll's House," "Hedda Gabler," "Real Inspector Hound," "The Contractor," "When the Old Man Died."

WILLIAMS, BARBARA. Born May 24 in Milwaukee, Wi. Attended Northwestern U. Bdwy in "Damn Yankees," "Music Man," "Different Times," OB in "Streets of NY," "Horse Opera," "All's Well That Ends Well."

WILLIAMS, JACK ERIC. Born Mar. 28, 1944 in Odessa, Tx. Attended Tx. Tech. U. Debut 1975 OB in "The Homecoming," followed by "Threepenny Opera," "Where's the Beer, Fritz?" "The Tempest," Bdwy 1979 in "Sweeney Todd."

Margaret Whitton   **Jack Eric Williams**   **Amy Wright**   **Peter Yoshida**   **Peg Zitko**

WILSON, ELIZABETH. Born Apr. 4, 1925 in Grand Rapids, MI. Attended Neighborhood Playhouse. Bdwy debut 1953 in "Picnic," followed by "Desk Set," "Tunnel of Love," "Big Fish, Little Fish," "Sheep on the Runway," "Sticks and Bones," "Secret Affairs of Mildred Wild," "The Importance of Being Earnest," OB in "Plaza 9," "Eh?," "Little Murders," "Good Woman of Setzuan," "Uncle Vanya," "Threepenny Opera," "All's Well That Ends Well," "Taken in Marriage."

WILSON, K. C. Born Aug. 10, 1945 in Miami, FL. Attended AADA. Debut 1973 OB in "Little Mahogonny," followed by "The Tempest," "Richard III," "Macbeth," "Threepenny Opera," "The Passion of Dracula."

WILSON, KEVIN. Born May 26, 1950 in Indianapolis, In. Graduate UMd., HB Studio. Bdwy debut 1977 in "Shenandoah," followed by "Carmelina."

WILSON, MARY LOUISE. Born Nov. 12, 1936 in New Haven, CT. Graduate Northwestern U. OB in "Our Town," "Upstairs at the Downstairs," "Threepenny Opera," "A Great Career," "Whispers on the Wind," "Beggar's Opera," "Buried Child," Bdwy in "Hot Spot," "Flora, the Red Menace," "Criss-Crossing," "Promises, Promises," "The Women," "Gypsy," "The Royal Family," "The Importance of Being Earnest."

WINDSOR, JOHN. Born Dec.10, 1952 in Evanston, Il. Graduate AzState U. Bdwy debut in "Pippin," OB in "Don't Step on My Olive Branch," "Festival."

WINKLER, KEVIN BROOKS. Born Feb. 9, 1954 in Nowata, Ok. Graduate San Diego State U. Debut 1978 OB in "A Midsummer Night's Dream."

WINSTON, HATTIE. Born Mar. 3, 1945 in Greenville, MS. Attended Howard U. OB in "Prodigal Son," "Day of Absence," "Pins and Needles," "Weary Blues," "Man Better Man," "Billy Noname," "Sambo," "The Great Mac-Daddy," "A Photo," "Oklahoma!," Bdwy in "The Me Nobody Knows," "Two Gentlemen of Verona," "I Love My Wife."

WINSTON, LEE. Born Mar. 14, 1941 in Great Bend, KS. Graduate UKan. Debut 1966 OB in "The Drunkard," followed by "Show Boat"(LC), "Little Mahogonny," "Good Soldier Schweik," Bdwy in "1600 Pensylvania Avenue," "Carmelina."

WISE, WILLIAM. Born May 11, 1940 in Chicago, Il. Attended Bradley U., Northern Ill. U. Bdwy debut 1970 OB in "Adaptation/Next," followed by "The Hot 1 Baltimore," "Just the Immediate Family."

WISEMAN, JOSEPH. Born May 15, 1919 in Montreal, Can. Attended CCNY. Bdwy in "Journey to Jerusalem," "Abe Lincoln in Illinois," "Candle in the Wind," "Three Sisters," "Storm Operation," "Joan of Lorraine," "Antony and Cleopatra," "Detective Story," "That Lady," "King Lear," "Golden Boy," "The Lark," "Zalmen, or the Madness of God," OB in "Marco Millions," "Incident at Vichy," "In the Matter of J. Robert Oppenheimer," "Enemies," "Duchess of Malfi," "Last Analysis," "The Lesson."

WONG, JANET. Born Aug. 30, 1951 in Berkeley, CA. Attended UCal. Bdwy debut 1977 in "A Chorus Line."

WOOD, JOHN. Born in 1931 in Derbyshire, Eng. Attended Oxford U. Bdwy debut 1967 in "Rosencrantz and Guildenstern Are Dead," followed by "Sherlock Holmes," "Travesties," "Tartuffe," "Deathtrap."

WOODARD, CHARLAINE. Born Dec. 29 in Albany, NY. Graduate Goodman Sch. of Drama., SUNY. Debut 1975 OB in "Don't Bother Me, I Can't Cope," Bdwy in "Hair" (1977), "Ain't Misbehavin'."

WOODS, RICHARD. Born May 9, 1921 in Buffalo, NY. Graduate Ithaca Col. Bdwy in "Beg Borrow or Steal," "Capt. Brassbound's Conversion," "Sail Away," "Coco," "Last of Mrs. Lincoln," "Gigi," "Sherlock Holmes," "Murder among Friends," "The Royal Family," "Deathtrap," "Man and Superman," OB in "The Crucible," "Summer and Smoke," "American Gothic," "Four-in-one," "My Heart's in the Highlands," "Eastward in Eden," "The Long

Gallery," "The Year Boston Won the Pennant," "In the Matter of J. Robert Oppenheimer" (LC), with APA in "You Can't Take It with You," "War and Peace," "School for Scandal," "Right You Are," "The Wild Duck," "Pantagleize," "Exit the King," "The Cherry Orchard," "Cock-a-doodle Dandy," and "Hamlet."

WOODSON, SALLY. Born Aug. 28, 1951 in St. Louis, Mo. Graduate KanU. Debut 1978 OB in "Oklahoma!"

WORTH, IRENE. Born June 23, 1916 in Nebraska. Graduate UCLA. Bdwy debut 1943 in "The Two Mrs. Carrolls," followed by "The Cocktail Party," "Mary Stuart," "Toys in the Attic," "King Lear," "Tiny Alice," "Sweet Bird of Youth," "The Cherry Orchard" (LC), OB in "Happy Days."

WORTH, PENNY. Born Mar. 2, 1950 in London, Eng. Attended Sorbonne, Paris. Bdwy debut 1970 in "Coco," followed by "Irene," "Annie."

WRIGHT, AMY. Born Apr. 15, 1950 in Chicago, Il. Graduate Beloit Col. Debut 1977 OB in "The Stronger," followed by "Nightshift," "Hamlet," "Miss Julie."

WRIGHT, MAX. Born Aug. 2, 1943 in Detroit, Mi. Attended Wayne State U. Bdwy debut 1968 in "The Great White Hope," followed by "The Cherry Orchard," "Basic Training of Pavlo Hummel," "Stages," "Once in a Lifetime" for which he received a Theatre World Award, "The Inspector General," "Richard III."

WRIGHT, WILLIAM. Born Jan. 21, 1943 in Los Angeles, CA. Graduate UUtah, Bristol Old Vic. Debut 1973 OB in "Merchant of Venice" (LC), "The Way of the World," "The Constant Wife," Bdwy 1976 in "Equus."

WYNKOOP, CHRISTOPHER. Born Dec. 7, 1943 in Long Branch, NJ. Graduate AADA. Debut 1970 OB in "Under the Gaslight," followed by "And So to Bed," "Cartoons for a Lunch Hour."

YODER, JERRY. Born in Columbus, Oh. Graduate Ohio State U. Bdwy debut 1973 in "Seesaw," followed by "Goodtime Charley," "Chicago," "Best Little Whorehouse in Texas," OB in "Boys from Syracuse."

YOSHIDA, PETER. Born May 28, 1945 in Chicago, Il. Graduate UIll., Princeton U., AADA. Debut 1965 OB in "Coriolanus," followed by "Troilus and Cressida," "Santa Anita '42." "Pursuit of Happiness," "Servant of Two Masters."

ZAKS, JERRY. Born Sept. 7, 1946 in Germany. Graduate Dartmouth, Smith Col. Bdwy debut 1973 in "Grease," followed by "Once in a Lifetime," OB in "Death Story," "Dream of a Blacklisted Actor," "Kid Champion," "Golden Boy," "Marco Polo," "One Crack Out."

ZALKIND, DEBRA. Born Mar. 30, 1953 in NYC. Graduate Juilliard. Appeared with several dance companies before Bdwy debut 1978 in "The Best Little Whorehouse in Texas."

ZANG, EDWARD. Born Aug. 19, 1934 in NYC. Graduate Boston U. OB in "Good Soldier Schweik," "St. Joan," "Boys in the Band," "The Reliquary of Mr. and Mrs. Potterfield," "Last Analysis," "As You Like It," "More than You Deserve," "Polly," "Threepenny Opera," BAM Co.'s "New York Idea," "The Misanthrope," Bdwy in "Crucifer of Blood."

ZAVAGLIA, RICHARD. Born Mar. 25, 1937 in Newark, NJ. Attended HB Studio, AADA. OB in "Skater," "As You Like It," "Life of Galileo," Bdwy 1979 in "Chapter 2."

ZIERING, IAN. Born Mar. 30, 1964 in Newark, NJ. Bdwy debut 1979 in "I Remember Mama."

ZIMMERMAN, MARK. Born Apr. 19, 1952 in Harrisburg, Pa. Graduate UPa. Debut 1976 OB in "Fiorello!," followed by "Silk Stockings," "On a Clear Day You Can See Forever."

ZITKO, PEG. Born Aug. 9, 1950 in St. Louis, Mo. Graduated Southern Ill. U. Debut 1979 OB in "Mary."

OBITUARIES

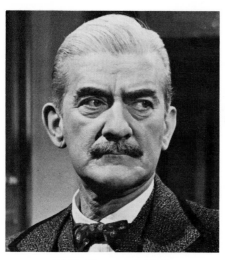

Celia Adler (1954)

Philip Bourneuf (1966)

Staats Cotsworth (1973)

CELIA ADLER, 89, actress on Yiddish and Bdwy stages, died Jan. 31, 1979 in NYC after suffering a stroke. She began her theatrical career at six months in the arms of her mother, and ultimately became known as "first lady of the Yiddish theatre." In 1918 she helped open the first Yiddish Art Theatre in NY, and subsequently appeared in almost every European and South American country. Her credits include "The Eternal Wanderer," "Mrs. Warren's Profession," "Othello," "The Cherry Orchard," "Green Fields," "The Mute," "The Dybbuk," "Tenth Commandment," "God, Man and Devil," "Major Noah," "Millions," "Once upon a Time," "Laugh Night," "Round the Family Table," "Life Marches On," "A Flag Is Born," "Sands of the Negev," "A Devil's Game," "A Worm in Horseradish." She was married three times. Surviving are a son, two half sisters and two half brothers, including actors Luther and Stella Adler.

JAY ADLER, 82, actor-member of the noted theatrical family, died Sept. 23, 1978 after a long illness in Woodland Hills, Ca. He appeared in both Yiddish and English language productions including "Man Bites Dog," "Blind Alley," "Prelude," "Bury the Dead," "Blind Alley," "Cafe Crown." A daughter survives, as well as his brother and sister, actors Luther and Stella Adler.

RALPH ALSWANG, 62, Chicago-born designer of sets and innovative theatres, died of a heart attack Feb. 15, 1979 in NYC. After designing for the Army Air Corp production of "Winged Victory," his credits include over 100 stage sets, including "Home of the Brave," "A Young Man's Fancy," "Story for Strangers," "Peter Pan" (1950), "Two's Company," "The Rainmaker," "Time Limit!," "Affair of Honor," "Sunrise at Campobello," "A Raisin in the Sun," "Come Blow Your Horn." He also designed costumes and lighting. He is survived by two daughters and a son.

BUFORD ARMITAGE, 80, Tennessee-born actor and stage manager, died Nov. 3, 1978 after a long illness in Mt. Kisco, NY. Among his credits are "The Mud Turtle," "Move On," "Undertow," "School for Virtue," "John Brown," "Kill That Story," "Fourposter," "The Wisteria Trees," "Say Darling," "The Shrike," "The Young and the Beautiful." He also served as general manager for City Center productions. His wife, actress Claire Waring, survives.

ROBERT ALAN AURTHUR, 56, NY-born dramatist and producer, died Nov. 20, 1978 of lung cancer in NYC. In addition to his work for stage, screen and television, he wrote magazine articles, short stories, and was a columnist for Esquire Magazine. He received several awards for his tv dramas. His stage plays include "A Very Special Baby," "Kwamina," and "Carry Me Back to Morningside Heights." Surviving are his second wife and a daughter, and two sons and a daughter by his first wife, actress Beatrice Arthur.

IVAN BLACK, 75, NJ-born press agent for theatres and clubs for more than 40 years, died in NYC Mar. 25, 1979 of a respiratory failure from emphysema. He was a charter member of the Association of Theatrical Press Agents and Managers. He is survived by his wife, three sons and a daughter.

PHILIP BOURNEUF, 71, versatile Massachusetts-born actor on stage, screen and tv, was found dead Mar. 23, 1979 in his apartment in Santa Monica, Ca. After his Bdwy debut in "The Night Remembers" in 1934, his credits include "Beggarman, Thief," "Dead End," "Ten Million Ghosts," "One for the Money," "Taming of the Shrew," "Native Son," "The Rivals," "The Moon Vine," "Richard III," "Winged Victory," "Flamingo Road," "Henry VIII," "Androcles and the Lion," "The Last Dance," "A Temporary Island," "Miss Liberty," "What Every Woman Knows," "The Doctor's Dilemma," "Lute Song," "Caligula," "A Touch of the Poet," and "A Case of Libel." He was divorced from actress Frances Reid.

ANGUS L. BOWMER, 74, teacher, actor and founder of the Oregon Shakespeare Festival, died May 26, 1979 in Ashland, Or. He was born in Bellingham, Wa., and graduated from University of Washington. In 1935 he opened the Festival in Ashland and was its producing director until 1971. His wife survives.

NORMA BRUSTEIN, 50, stage and tv actress, and teacher, died Apr. 9, 1979 of a massive cardiac arrest in New Haven, Ct. She was the wife of Robert Brustein, director and dean of the Yale Drama School, where she was on the faculty. In NYC she had appeared in "The Iceman Cometh," "The Big Knife," "The Warm Peninsula," "Career," "Threepenny Opera," "Talk to Me Like the Rain," and "Sganarelle." Surviving in addition to her second husband are two sons.

HAROLD P. (HAL) BURDICK, 84, actor and writer, died June 12, 1978 in NYC. On stage his credits include "Ivory Branch," "Apple Cart," "Auntie Mame," "Anniversary Waltz," "Solid Gold Cadillac," "Death of a Salesman," "Calculated Risk," "The Last Love of Don Juan," "Friends and Lovers," "Billygoat Eddie." He created the radio and tv series "Night Editor," and was Judge Grant on tv's "Edge of Night" series. A son survives.

DONALD BURR, (nee Edgar Lush) 71, Cincinnati-born singer, actor, director, died Feb. 27, 1979 in Lyons, NJ. After his debut in 1935 in "Walk a Little Faster," his credits include "Twelfth Night," "The Rivals," "The Would-Be Gentleman," "Annie Get Your Gun," "Skyscraper," and "Sherry!" Surviving are his wife, actress Billie Worth, a son and a daughter.

ELIZABETH CALDWELL, 52, production stage manager of the Los Angeles company of "Annie," was killed Oct. 19, 1978 when she was hit by a car in L.A. Her Broadway credits include "Canterbury Tales," "Butterflies Are Free," "Sherlock Holmes," "Treemonisha," "Find Your Way Home," and "Flower Drum Song." She had also been a coordinator for Equity Library Theatre. Her father survives.

FLORA CAMPBELL, 67, retired Oklahoma-born actress, died Nov. 6, 1978 of cancer in Stamford, Ct. Her Broadway debut in 1934 in "Whatever Possessed Her," was followed by "Laughing Woman," "The Country Wife," "Excursions," "Many Mansions," "Glamour Preferred," "The Land Is Bright," "All for All," "Foxhole in the Parlor," "Curious Savage," "Only in America," "Angels of Anadarko," and "Journey to the Day." She had also appeared in several daytime radio and tv series, including "Valiant Lady," "Love of Life," "Edge of Night" and "Secret Storm." No reported survivors.

JOAN CHANDLER, 55, stage and screen actress, died May 11, 1979 in NYC. After her Broadway debut in 1944 in "The Late George Apley," she subsequently appeared in "Where's Charley?," "The Lady from the Sea," "My 3 Angels," "The Tempest," "The Disenchanted." She had been married and divorced twice. A daughter survives.

FRED COE, 64, Mississippi-born producer and director for Broadway and television, died of a heart attack Apr. 29, 1979 in Los Angeles, Ca. For tv he produced over 500 presentations. On Broadway he presented "The Trip to Bountiful," "Two for the Seesaw," "The Miracle Worker," "All the Way Home," "Gideon," "A Thousand Clowns," "Xmas in Las Vegas," "Wait until Dark," and "Georgy." His second wife, a son and daughter survive, as do a son and daughter by his first marriage.

FAY COMPTON, 84, British stage and screen actress, died Dec. 12, 1978 in London. She was Sir James M. Barrie's favorite actress and he wrote "Mary Rose" for her. She debuted in his "Peter Pan," and subsequently in five other plays written by him. She appeared twice on Broadway, in "Olympia," and "God and Kate Murphy." She was married four times, and is survived by a son, director Anthony Pelissier.

STAATS COTSWORTH, 71, Illinois-born stage, radio, tv and screen actor, died Apr. 9, 1979 in his NYC apartment. He was also a recognized painter. He had appeared in over 40 plays on Broadway, including "Alice in Wonderland," "Romeo and Juliet," "Murder at the Vanities," "Macbeth," "She Stoops to Conquer," "Advise and Consent," "Hamlet," "Right Honourable Gentleman," "A Patriot for Me." He was married twice to actresses, the late Muriel Kirkland, and Josephine Hutchinson who survives.

PAUL CRABTREE, 60, actor, writer, producer and director for theatre and television, died Mar. 21, 1979 of a heart attack while directing in Hershey, Pa. In NY he was seen in "Oklahoma!," followed by "Kiss and Tell," "The Streets Are Guarded," "Men to the Sea," "Skydrift," "The Iceman Cometh," "Story for a Sunday Evening," "Lo and Behold!." He directed "This Time Tomorrow," "The Silver Whistle," "Texas Li'l Darlin'," "Midsummer," "A Stage Affair." He also founded two regional theatres where he wrote, produced and directed. Surviving are his widow, actress-director Mary Evelyn Ducey, and seven children.

EDITH CRAIG, 71, stage and screen actress, died in Tenafly, NJ Mar. 2, 1979 after a long illness. Her career began in 1926 in "George White's Scandals," followed by "Ziegfeld Follies," "Earl Carroll's Vanities," "Separate Rooms," "Life with Father." She appeared in over 40 films. A sister survives.

ALAN CROFOOT, 49, Canadian-born opera singer, jumped to his death March 5, 1979 in Dayton, Oh. In addition to appearing with the NYC and Metropolitan Operas, he appeared on Broadway in "Oliver!" and London's "Man of LaMancha." His marriage ended in divorce.

DAN DAILEY, 62, NY-born stage, screen and tv actor, died of anemia Oct. 16, 1978 in Los Angeles, Ca. He began his song and dance routine in vaudeville at the age of 6. His Bdwy debut was in 1936 in "Babes in Arms," followed by "Stars in Your Eyes," "I Married an Angel," and "Catch Me If You Can." His three marriages ended in divorce. Surviving are a brother and two sisters, one, actress Irene Dailey.

JAMES DALY, 59, Wisconsin-born stage, screen and tv actor, died of a heart attack July 3, 1978 in Nyack, NY where he was preparing to appear in a stage production of "Equus." On Bdwy he had appeared in "Born Yesterday," "Man and Superman," "The Devil's Disciple," "Billy Budd," "Mary Rose," "Major Barbara" for which he received a Theatre World Award, "St. Joan," "Dark Legend," "Merchant of Venice," "Glass Menagerie," "Handful of Fire," "J.B.," "The Advocate," "The White House," "Period of Adjustment," and "Trial of the Catonsville 9." He is survived by a son and three daughters, including actress Tyne Daly.

CLAUDE DAUPHIN, 75, nee Legrand in Corbeil, France, died in Paris Nov. 16, 1978 of an intestinal occlusion. He began his career as a scenic and costume designer, but became a versatile stage and film actor in both French and English. He appeared on Broadway in "No Exit," "The Happy Time," "Janus," "Clerambard," and Off Bdwy in "The Deadly Game," and "Giants, Sons of Giants." He made over 80 films. His three marriages ended in divorce. Three children survive.

THAYER DAVID, 51, nee David Thayer Hersey in Medford, Ma., stage, tv and film actor, died of a heart attack July 17, 1978 in NYC. He had appeared on Bdwy in "The Relapse," "King Lear," "Mr. Johnson," "Protective Custody," "A Man for All Seasons," "Andorra," "The Seagull," "The Crucible," "Royal Hunt of the Sun," "Those That Play the Clowns," "Jockey Club Stakes," OB in "Carefree Tree," "White Devil," "Oscar Wilde," "The Bench," "Uncle Vanya," "The Minister's Black Veil." He was divorced from actress Valerie French.

BILL DOLL, 68, West Virginia-born press agent, died of cancer March 2, 1979 in Englewood, NJ. He retired in 1976 after suffering a stroke. He had publicized over 200 Broadway productions, including Mike Todd productions for 30 years. Two sons survive.

WILLIAM EDMONSON, 76, stage, film and television actor, died of a heart attack May 28, 1979 in his Los Angeles, Ca., home. His Broadway credits include "Marco Millions," "Deep Harlem," "Two for Fun," "The Iceman Cometh," "The Rope Dancers," and "Handful of Fire." Two sons survive.

RUTH ETTING, 80, Nebraska-born singer-actress, died after a long illness Sept. 24, 1978 in Colorado Springs, Co. She began her career singing in nightclubs before being starred on Broadway in "Ziegfeld Follies," followed by "Whoopee!," "9:15 Revue," "Simple Simon," "Transatlantic Rhythm." She also appeared in films, and popularized many songs by regular appearances on radio shows, and by recordings. A movie of her life was made in 1955: "Love Me or Leave Me." She was the widow of pianist Myrl Alderman. A step-son survives.

DEREK FAIRMAN, 73, NY-born former actor, died May 19, 1979 after a prolonged illness in San Francisco, Ca. On Broadway he had appeared in "Cinderelative," "Twelfth Night," "In the Best of Families," "The Man Who Changed His Name," "The Best People," "Fresh Fields," "Springtime for Henry," "Susan and God," "Sea Legs," "The Lady Has a Heart," "Save Me the Waltz," "The Circle," and "This Is the Army." After WW2 he turned to interior decorating. No reported survivors.

James Daly (1964)

Claude Dauphin (1971)

Thayer David (1973)

Gene Galvin (1972)

Lou Gilbert (1970)

Kate Harrington (1956)

LOU FRIZZELL, 59, stage, screen and tv actor, died June 17, 1979 after a lengthy illness in his home in Los Angeles, Ca. His credits on Broadway include "Oklahoma!," "The Balcony," "Desire under the Elms," "Great Day in the Morning," "Red Roses for Me," "Quare Fellow," "The Andersonville Trial," OB in "Pullman Car Hiawatha," "After the Fall" and "Marco Millions." On tv he had recurring roles in "Bonanza," "Mary Hartman," "Owen Marshall." His father survives.

EDWARD (EDDIE) FULLER, 67, Missouri-born actor for 45 years, died instantly Jan. 22, 1979 when hit by a truck in NYC. He had appeared in "Whatever Possessed Her," "Sing for Your Supper," "The Cradle Will Rock," "Good as Gold," "The American Way," and the 1959 revival of "Guys and Dolls." No reported survivors.

GENE GALVIN, 63, Seattle-born retired actor, died March 24, 1979 in Los Angeles, Ca., after a long illness. He had appeared in "Lute Song," "A Streetcar Named Desire," "Born Yesterday," "Leonard's Folly," "Flight from Fear," "A Temporary Island," "Burlesque," "Curley McDimple," "White Steed," and "Othello." For 15 years he had been associated with the Shady Lane Playhouse, in Marengo, Il. No reported survivors.

WILLIAM GARGAN, 73, Brooklyn-born actor on stage and screen, died of a heart attack Feb. 17, 1979 aboard a plane from NYC to San Diego, Ca. He appeared in "Aloma of the South Seas," "War Song," "Headquarters," "Out of a Blue Sky," "Roar China!," "She Lived Next to the Firehouse," "He," "The Animal Kingdom," "The Best Man." He starred in many films and tv roles as a detective, especially "Martin Kane, Private Eye." In 1960 he lost his larynx to cancer and dedicated himself to teaching others who were similarly afflicted, to speak, and to traveling for the American Cancer Society. His widow and two sons survive.

HERBERT V. GELLENDRE, 77, London-born actor, teacher, director and producer, died Nov. 30, 1978 in NYC after a long illness. He came to NY as a youth, and subsequently as an actor appeared in "The Scarlet Letter," "The Trumpet Shall Sound," "Granite," "Much Ado about Nothing," "At the Gate of the Kingdom," "Doctor Knock," and "Martine." He taught at the Neighborhood Playhouse, AmThWing, and AADA. His third wife survives.

LOU GILBERT, 69, Illinois-born stage and screen character actor, died of a heart attack on Nov. 6, 1978 in Riseda, Ca. His credits include "Common Ground," "Beggars Are Coming to Town," "Truckline Cafe," "Hope Is the Thing with Feathers," "Sundown Beach," "Detective Story," "Dream Girl," "The Whole World Over," "Anna Christie," "His and Hers," "Abie's Irish Rose," "A Streetcar Named Desire," "Diary of Anne Frank," "The Egg," "The Great White Hope," "Creation of the World and Other Business," OB in "A Month in the Country," "Dynamite Tonite," "Baba Goya," "As You Like It," "Nourish the Beast," "Old Man Joseph and His Family." His widow, a son and a daughter survive.

SHMULIK GOLDSTEIN, 70, comedian of Yiddish stage, died of a heart attack on Nov. 23, 1978 in NYC. He began his career in his native Poland, and subsequently performed in the Soviet Union and Paris before moving to the U.S. in 1953. In NYC he had been seen in "The World Is a Stage," "Don't Worry Brother!," "Let's Sing Yiddish," "Sing Israel Sing," "From Israel with Laughter," "To Be or Not To Be—What Kind of Question Is That?," "Yoshe Kolb," "It's Hard to Be a Jew," "The Big Winner," "The Fifth Season," and "The Inheritors." He leaves two sons; one is actor Harry Gold.

KATE HARRINGTON, 74, Idaho-born actress on stage, screen and tv, died after a stroke Nov. 23, 1978 in NYC. Her credits include "Slightly Married," "Buy Me Blue Ribbons," "The Happiest Millionaire," OB in "Morning's at 7," "Days and Nights of Beebee Fenstermaker," "Not a Way of Life," "Michigan South," "Stephen D." She is survived by her husband, a son and a daughter.

DAN HOGAN, 54, Administrative Aide to AEA's Executive Secretary, and former actor, died June 22, 1978 in NYC. He had appeared in "Madam Will You Walk," "Don Juan in the Russian Manner," "Hadrian VII," "Joe Egg," OB in "A Scent of Flowers" and "Salome." No reported survivors.

EDWARD HOLMES, 66, Canadian-born stage, film and tv actor, died July 12, 1977 in NYC. His theatre credits include "Richard III," "Measure for Measure," "Taming of the Shrew," "Merchant of Venice," "Henry VIII," "Gideon," "Dinner at 8," "Freedom of the City." A son survives.

ANNE IVES, 92, stage, film and tv actress, died May 15, 1979 in NYC. Born in Providence, RI, she made her debut in stock before Broadway in 1906 in "The Chorus Lady." Later credits include "Point of No Return," "Sister Oakes," "The Crucible," "Masquerade," "Her Master's Voice," "Hedda Gabler," "Uncle Vanya," "Unexpected Guests," "Effect of Gamma Rays on. . .," "Good Woman of Setzuan," "The Contractor," "Ice Age." No reported survivors.

IRVING JACOBSON, 80, Cincinnati-born star of Yiddish theatre for more than 20 years, died Dec. 17, 1978 in NYC. He had appeared in over 50 Yiddish productions, and on Broadway in "Enter Laughing," "So Long 174th Street" and "Man of La Mancha" for over 7 years. A son survives.

WILLARD KEEFE, 80, retired theatrical publicist, died July 2, 1978 in Englewood, NJ. Born in Minnesota, he had been a newspaper reporter, drama critic, screenwriter and playwright before turning to theatre publicity. He was a charter member of The Association of Theatrical Press Agents and Managers. His daughter survives.

RICHARD KELTON, 35, stage and tv actor, died from carbon monoxide poisoning Jan. 11, 1979 while filming on location in Colorado. He was in the "Centennial" tv series and his dressing room had not been properly ventilated to dispose of the fumes from a generator under his trailer-mounted room where he was studying his lines. He was born in North Dakota, and made his Bdwy debut in 1976 in "Who's Afraid of Virginia Woolf?" for which he received a Theatre World Award. Among his many tv parts he was the co-starring role in the series "Quark." Surviving are his widow and a son.

VICTOR KILIAN, 88, NJ-born character actor on stage, screen and tv, was found beaten to death Mar. 11, 1979 in his Hollywood apartment. He made his Bdwy debut in 1924 in "Desire under the Elms," and subsequently in "Beyond the Horizon," "Nightstick," "Hobo,"

"Adam's Wife," "Man Bites Dog," "Heat Lightning," "Peace on Earth," "Valley Forge," "Solitaire," "Miracle in the Mountains," "Look Homeward, Angel," "The Gang's All Here," and "Gideon." He is probably best known for his role of Mary Hartman's flashing grandfather in the tv series "Mary Hartman, Mary Hartman." He is survived by a son.

MORT MARSHALL, 60, nee Mortimer Haig Lichtenstein, died of a coronary arrest Feb. 1, 1979 in his native NYC. He was a character actor on stage, film and tv. His Bdwy credits include "Crime and Punishment," "Gentlemen Prefer Blondes," "Of Thee I Sing," "Best House in Naples," "Men of Distinction," "Ziegfeld Follies," "All American," "Little Me," "Gypsy," "The Music Man," "Minnie's Boys," "A Funny Thing Happened on the Way to the Forum." Surviving are his widow and two daughters.

OLIVER MESSEL, 74, British costume and scenic designer, died July 13, 1978 in his home in Barbados. Among the many Broadway productions for which he was designer are "The Country Wife," "The Play's the Thing," "Tough at the Top," "Romeo and Juliet," "The Little Hut," "House of Flowers," "The Dark Is Light Enough," "Rashomon," "Traveller without Luggage," "Gigi." He was the uncle of Lord Snowdon who survives.

FELICIA MONTEALEGRE, 56, stage and tv actress, died of cancer June 16, 1978 in East Hampton, NY. Born in Costa Rica, she made her acting debut in Chile before coming to NYC in 1944. Her credits include "If Five Years Pass," "Swan Song," "Merchant of Venice," "International Set," "Henry V," "Pelleas and Melisande," "The Little Foxes," "Les Troyens," "Poor Murderers." She is survived by her husband, composer-conductor Leonard Bernstein, two daughters and a son.

ODETTE MYRTIL, 80, French-born stage and film singer-actress, died of a stroke Nov. 18, 1978 in Doylestown, Pa. She had appeared in "Vogues of 1924," "The Love Song," "Countess Maritza," "White Lilacs," "Broadway Nights," "Tattle Tales," "The Cat and the Fiddle," "The Red Mill," "Maggie" and "Saratoga Trunk." After she retired she operated her own restaurant Chez Odette in New Hope, Pa. A son survives.

Anne Ives (1973)

ERIN O'BRIEN-MOORE, 77, stage, screen, radio and tv actress, died May 3, 1979 in her native Los Angeles, Ca. Her career was hampered in 1939 when she was burned in a restaurant fire, however she had extensive plastic surgery and returned to the stage. Her credits include "The Makropulis Secret," "My Country," "Street Scene," "Riddle Me This," "Men Must Fight," "Tortilla Flat," "Apology," "State of the Union," and "A Streetcar Named Desire." She was a co-star of the tv series "Ruggles." Her marriage to critic Mark Barron ended in divorce.

DENIS O'DEA, 75, Irish stage and screen actor, died Nov. 5, 1978 at his home in Dublin. A prominent member of the Abbey Theatre, he made his Broadway debut with the company in 1932 in "The Far-Off Hills," "The White-Headed Boy," "The New Gossoon," "The Rising of the Moon" and "Oedipus Rex." He later appeared in "The Righteous Are Bold." He is survived by his wife, actress Siobhan McKenna."

ALEXANDER ORFALY, 43, Brooklyn-born actor on stage and film, was killed Jan. 22, 1979 in an auto accident in Hollywood, Fl., while on tour with "Oklahoma!" He had appeared on Broadway in "South Pacific," "How Now, Dow Jones," "Ari," "Sugar," "Cyrano," "Fiddler on the Roof," and Off Bdwy in "The End of All Things Natural," "Mahagonny," "Johnny Johnson," "Ride the Winds" and "Polly." His parents, a brother and two sisters survive.

MINERVA PIOUS, 75, Russian-born stage, radio, film and tv actress, died Mar. 16, 1979 in NYC. Her stage credits include "The Ziegfeld Follies" (she succeeded Fanny Brice), "The World of Sholom Aleichem," "Dear Me, the Sky Is Falling," "The Last Analysis." She was best known for her Mrs. Nussbaum on the Fred Allen show. No reported survivors.

ETHEL REMEY, age unreported, NY-born stage and tv actress, died Feb. 28, 1979 in Neptune, NJ. After her Broadway debut in 1922 in "Rose Briar," she appeared in "Connie Goes Home," "Such Is Life," "Virtue's Bed," "Take My Tip," "Forsaking All Others," "I'll Take the High Road," "Our Town," "Chicken Every Sunday," "Tenting Tonight," "Family Portrait," "The Women," and "Clerambard." She is probably best known as the mother of Lisa in the tv series "As the World Turns" in which she had been performing since 1961. Illness forced her to retire in 1978. A sister survives.

Richard Kelton (1976)

WELLS RICHARDSON, 81, retired actor, died Feb. 22, 1979 in New Rochelle, NY. After his debut in 1928 in "Fast Life," his credits include "His Majesty's Car," "Park Avenue Ltd.," "Between Two Worlds," "The Hook-Up," "The Duke in Darkness," "Buy Me Blue Ribbons," "The Bad Seed," "Donogoo," and "The Cherry Orchard." No reported survivors.

SAUL RICHMAN, 62, theatrical press agent for over 40 years, died of cancer Jan. 14, 1979 in San Diego, Ca. His many clients included Guy Lombardo's Royal Canadians and the Jones Beach Theatre for over 20 years. He is survived by his widow.

GENE RUPERT, 47, actor-singer died of a heart attack May 14, 1979 in NYC. His credits include "A Midsummer Night's Dream," "Romeo and Juliet," "Arms and the Man," "Twelfth Night," "Time to Go," "Valmouth," "Square in the Eye," "A Time for Singing," "Hogan's Goat," "Barefoot in the Park," "Promises, Promises," "The Trip Back Down," "Finishing Touches," "An Evening with Richard Nixon. . ." and "Players." He also appeared in the tv series "All My Children," "The Guiding Light," "As the World Turns" and "Ryan's Hope." Surviving are his widow and two sons.

DANNY RUVOLO, 22, NY-born actor-dancer, was killed Nov. 17, 1978 in an auto crash on Long Island, NY. He began dancing at five, and had appeared in such productions as "Ulysses in Nighttown," "Rex," "Lorelei," "Pippin," and "A Chorus Line." No reported survivors.

HENRIETTE SCHNITZER, 84, Yiddish actress, died May 4, 1979 in Miami Beach, Fl. She began her career at 8 in her native Rumania. After coming to the U.S. she appeared in such productions as "Naomi," "One Life for Another," "Alexander Pushkin," "Mazal Dorf Men," "Awake and Sing," "Green Fields," "The Bronx Express," "Gabriel and His Women," "Potash and Perlmutter." For 15 years she appeared on the radio show "The Goldbergs." A daughter survives.

Robert Shaw (1973)

ROBERT SHAW, 51, English-born stage and screen actor, playwright and novelist, died of a heart attack near his home in County Mayo, Ire. After his Broadway debut in 1961 in "The Caretaker," he later appeared in "The Physicists," "Gantry," "Old Times," and "Dance of Death." His greatest popularity was as a film actor, but he preferred to be known for his literary efforts. He is survived by his third wife and ten children by previous wives.

ANN SHOEMAKER, 87, stage, screen, radio and tv actress, died of cancer Sept. 18, 1978 in Los Angeles, Ca. After her Bdwy debut in 1910 in "Nobody's Widow," her credits include "The Great God Brown," "The Noose," "We All Do," "Speakeasy," "Whispering Friends," "Tonight at 12," "Button, Button," "The Novice and the Duke," "Silent Witness," "Black Sheep," "Ah, Wilderness!," "Proof through the Night," "Rich Full Life," "Woman Bites Dog," "Dream Girl," "Twilight Walk," "The Living Room," "Separate Tables," "Importance of Being Earnest," "Half a Sixpence," "The Bad Seed," and "Separate Tables." She was the widow of British actor Henry Stephenson. A daughter survives.

QUEENIE SMITH, 80, musical comedy star, film and tv actress, died of cancer Aug. 5, 1978 in Burbank, Ca. Her career began as a child in California before reaching stardom on Broadway in several musical comedies. Her credits include "Just Because," "Orange Blossoms," "Cinders," "Helen of Troy," "Sitting Pretty," "Be Yourself!," "Tip-Toes," "Judy," "The Street Singer," "Little Racketeer," "The Blue Widow," "Uncle Tom's Cabin," "Every Thursday," "Marie Antoinette in Pennsylvania," "Hit the Deck." After 1935, she appeared in many films, and on tv. She was divorced from the late Robert Garland, drama critic. No reported survivors.

JOHN SWOPE, 70, photographer and producer, died May 11, 1979 in Santa Monica, Ca. He was married to actress Dorothy McGuire who survives, as do a son and daughter.

SOINTU SYRJALA, 74, Canadian-born innovative scenic designer, was found dead of natural causes in his apartment in NYC on Apr. 10, 1979. After designing his first play "Precedent" in 1931, his credits include "Stevedore," "The Milky Way," "Blind Alley," "Remember the Day," "Swing Your Lady," "Pins and Needles," "We Will Never Die," and "The Fourposter." From 1951 until his retirement in 1972 because of failing eyesight, he devoted his talent to tv. His widow and a son survive.

MABEL TALIAFERRO, 91, stage and screen actress, died Jan. 24, 1979 in Honolulu, Ha., where she had moved several years previous. She was one of the first stars of the silent screen, and a veteran of more than 100 plays, having begun her career at the age of two. Her stage credits include "Children of the Ghetto," "Land of Heart's Desire," "Polly of the Circus," "Mrs. Wiggs of the Cabbage Patch," "The Piper," "Alice in Wonderland," "Ann Adams, Spinster," "Back Fire," "The Man Who Came to Dinner," "George Washington Slept Here," "Claudia," "Victory Belles," "Bloomer Girl," and "Springtime Folly." She was married twice, but left no reported survivors.

OLIVE TEMPLETON, 96, stage, film and tv actress, died May 29, 1979 in her NYC apartment. After her debut in 1899 in "Peer Gynt," her credits include "The Philadelphia Story," "The Swan," "Happy Hunting," "Uncle Vanya." She was a regular on the tv series "Mr. Peepers." She retired in 1919 when she married John L. Flannery, but returned after his death in 1937. A brother survives.

MAY THOMPSON, 88, retired star of musical comedies, died Nov. 18, 1978 in Devon, Pa. English-born, she came to the U.S. at 16 to dance in "The Half Moon," subsequently appearing in "You're in Love," "Fancy Free," "Oui, Madame," "Angel Face," "Katinka," "Century Revue." She was married twice, and leaves a grandson.

IVY TROUTMAN, 96, NJ-born actress, died Jan. 12, 1979 in her home in Tinton Falls, NJ. After her debut in 1902 in "The Last Appeal," her credits include "If I Were King," "Pretty Peggy," "College Widow," "The Other Girl," "The Witching Hour," "Return from Jerusalem," "Baby Mine," "A Pair of Sixes," "The Road Together," "De Luxe," "A Room in Red and White," "Tell Me Pretty Maiden," "Dear Octopus," "Kind Lady," "A Kiss for Cinderella," and "The Late George Apley." She was divorced from artist Waldo Peirce.

BORIS TUMARIN, 68, Latvia-born character actor, director, and a founding teacher of Juilliard's Theatre Center, died Jan. 28, 1979 in NYC. After his NYC debut in 1941 in "The Emperor's New Clothes," he appeared in "Winter Soldiers," "The Family," "The Victors," "Prescott Proposals," "Anastasia," "The Innkeepers," "Three Sisters," "The Devil's Advocate," "Garden of Sweets," "Merchant of Venice," "Venus at Large," "Whisper into My Good Ear," "Firebugs," "Traveller without Luggage," "The Giants' Dance," "Tenth Man," "Man in the Glass Booth," and "The Merchant." A stepson survives.

MAURICE WELLS, 76, Nebraska-born actor, died of cancer June 26, 1978 in Pasadena, Ca. His credits include "Major Barbara," "We the People," "Between Two Worlds," "Creeping Fire," "Woman of the Soil," "Hallowe'en," "Pygmalion," "Elizabeth the Queen," "Spring Thaw," "Escape This Night," "Glorious Morning," "Only the Heart." For a number of years he operated a summer theatre in Nantucket, Ma. He is survived by two stepchildren.

MARIAN WINTERS, 54, NYC-born stage and tv actress, and writer, died of cancer Nov. 3, 1978 in NYC. After her debut in 1948 in "E=MC2," her credits include "Hippolytus," "King John," "Dream Girl," "I Am a Camera" for which she received a Theatre World Award, "The Dark Is Light Enough," "Sing Me No Lullaby," "Cherry Orchard," "Auntie Mame," "Tall Story," "49th Cousin," "Nobody Loves an Albatross," "Mating Dance," "Deathtrap." Surviving is her husband.

GIG YOUNG, 64, nee Byron Barr, stage, screen and tv actor, shot and killed his wife of three weeks and himself on Oct. 19, 1978 in his NYC apartment. On Broadway he had appeared in "Oh, Men! Oh, Women!," "Teahouse of the August Moon," "Under the Yum-Yum Tree," "There's a Girl in My Soup." He had parts in over 50 films, and received an Academy Award for "They Shoot Horses, Don't They?" He was married five times. A daughter survives.

Mabel Taliaferro (1907)

Marian Winters (1978)

Gig Young (1968)

INDEX

267

271

274